UNDERSTANDING AND APPLYING NEW YORK CORRECTION LAW ARTICLE 23-A

UNDERSTANDING AND APPLYING NEW YORK CORRECTION LAW ARTICLE 23-A

A Historical Look at Conviction Record Discrimination through United States Supreme Court Decisions, New York Courts, The New York Division of Human Rights and Ban The Box Initiatives.

Richie F. Levine

Master of Science in Legal Studies
Bachelor of Science in Paralegal Studies
Associate in Business Administration
Advanced Certified Paralegal (N.A.L.A)

UNDERSTANDING AND APPLYING NEW YORK CORRECTION LAW ARTICLE 23-A

ISBN:

Printed in the United States of America

Cover design and Layout
Judith A. Moose & Sarah B. Dancer

FOREWORD

The arrival of Richie F. Levine's authoritative treatise dealing with the law, procedures and policies governing New York State's efforts to regulate discrimination against ex-offenders could not be more timely. We are presently engaged in a national conversation over how to address the failures of a criminal justice system that has proven dysfunctional across the spectrum of its concerns, from policing to bail conditions to plea bargaining through to the reliability of convictions, sentencing, probation and parole. Calls for reform of mass incarceration and overly punitive sentencing policies, such as use of mandatory minimums, have come from officials in both political parties.

While major changes in policy have yet to take place, it's obvious that most of the nearly two million men and women serving time in prison will eventually be released, raising the critical question of whether society will take significant action to reduce the risk of their return to custody. Similar challenges apply to the several million more Americans who are currently subject to various forms of criminal process supervision such as probation, parole and conditioned court orders. It has always been clear that employment is our best defense against recidivism, yet rarely have lawmakers shined in marking out a path for ex-offenders to seize occupational opportunity. On the contrary, both state and federal laws have, until recently, been more likely to raise barriers to both public and private employment and licensure for those with criminal records, often supporting overbroad occupational bans rather than encouraging evaluation of individual change, growth and qualification.

In 1976, under the farsighted leadership of Republican State Senator John Dunne, New York attempted through the legislation signed into law by Democratic governor Hugh Carey to take a different approach. The law in question is the subject of this treatise. It sought to balance fears that ex-offenders would continue anti social behavior in the workplace with recognition of an overriding need to support rehabilitation efforts through ending discrimination in employment[1]. Since its passage the legal framework best known as Article 23-A of the Correction Law has been both narrowed and broadened by amendment, interpretation and significant litigation resulting in decisions by administrative agencies and virtually every court in the state, as well as in some instances federal courts applying state law principles. As a result, what may have seemed at the outset as a relatively simple set of propositions—to sustain a refusal of public or private employment or licensure an offense must be rationally related to the job or activity sought, save in the existence of some overriding risk—now requires a specialist lawyer approach. Article 23A has given birth to a complicated set of rules, procedures, options and deadlines that require guidance by learned analysis of the sort one would want in dealing with any set of thorny legal issues.

Understanding and Applying New York Correction Law Article 23-A is that resource. A stunning achievement, this book provides ex-offender, activist and attorney with a comprehensive background up to the present in the history, policy development and court decisions applying Article 23A. Just as important the treatise serves as a road map (including forms) to follow to initiate corrective action where discrimination is alleged. I cannot imagine undertaking efforts to enforce the New York law or in understanding its policy implications without consulting this treatise.

As society comes closer to realization that the consequences of unregulated punitive impulses and runaway fears of criminal behavior, though natural occurrences in a complex modern society, must be carefully evaluated in light of their practical economic and social impact, we can expect greater public support for genuine efforts to help offenders move into constructive ways of life. With his scholarship, Mr. Levine has made a signal contribution to a future where social reintegration can become a reality for many Americans who have previously felt hopeless and frustrated in their efforts to change for the better.

Michael Meltsner
Matthews Distinguished University Professor of Law
Northeastern University School of Law
July, 2015 Rockport Massachusetts

---

[1] As set forth in the text, infra, in 1973 along with two socially committed and brilliant Columbia Law students, Marc Kaplan and William Lane, I published a model act to aid in the rehabilitation of offenders in the Syracuse Law Review. We chose the upstate Review strategically, with a long odds hope to attract state legislators who might otherwise consider our proposal one forthcoming from elitist liberals from far off Manhattan. Months after publication, I received a phone call from Senator Dunne who to our amazement had not only read the article but decided he would try to make it law. As Chair of the Codes Committee he had great influence with his colleagues and after making certain changes (his staff is responsible for the "risk" provisions of the statute) Article 23A became law effective January 1, 1977. It was the first law of its kind enacted by any American state.

"Automatic prohibitions and reflexive limitations pertaining to the employment of ex-offenders are arbitrary, irrational and dysfunctional. Such a process which effectively imposes a strong presumption against the employment of ex-offenders regardless of the job cannot be shown to advance any legitimate state interest."

1976 Legislative Memorandum #11 written by the N.Y.C.L.U.

CONTENTS

When I first began researching and assembling this book in 2010 in an effort to assist re-entrants and educate employers, I never imagined that there was so little guidance and case law for what can be defined as the most successful employment reintegration statute developed in the country. While arrest and conviction record in New York State are protected classes since January 1, 1977, the cases that establish precedent make up a very small percentage of guidance in the last 40 years either through the New York State Division of Human Rights, City Commission on Human Rights or the New York courts (Supreme Court, Appellate Division and Court of Appeals for private and public employers). The ultimate burden of the Complainant, to prove discrimination, is not always an easy one to meet. The culprit of agency and court dismissals can often be non-factual pleadings, lack of direct or indirect evidence (the *"prima facie burden"*) and ignorance of the statute of limitations. Often crucial documents are not properly annexed as exhibits, theories not expounded upon correctly and causes of action not easily identified.

To put it in perspective, in over 40 years since it went into effect, only 8 cases have made it to the Court of Appeals, New York's highest court since January 1, 1977 on the basis of conviction record. All but one have been public agency cases. Such cases provide the highest definitive guidance for the statute and are binding on state agencies. This further demonstrates that interpretation of *New York Correction Law Article 23-A* and its provisions happens to be a niche area of law where there are a small percentage of cases that establish solid precedent and there is lots of space to fill in the blanks with agency or lower court interpretations. This book is guidance for a niche area of law.

The uniqueness of the New York Human Rights Law concerning re-entrants and their rights deserves more credence then it has gotten since 1977. While I must commend the New York legislature for removing the unfair discrimination against applicants who have arrest and conviction records versus those with no arrest or criminal records, it has left several loopholes that private companies (and a few public state agencies) have exploited in order to avoid having to adhere to the law and encourage the hire of re-entrants. One of those glaring holes is print advertisements that often utilize *"clean criminal background"* or *"no criminal record"* to convey their message to applicants. I applaud the New York City Human Rights Commission for enforcing the toughest Ban the Box law of any city to combat this prevalent evil. Now only if the rest of New York State banned the box through legislature initiatives.

Back in 1977 the use of private company background checks through third parties was not only limited to federal and some state jobs it was virtually non-existent. At that time it was not cost effective to run a background check en mass and it was impossible for third party companies to maintain a prolific database as they do in the 21st century. There was no quick mechanism for instant results in place in 1977 that would easily confirm in seconds you were dealing with someone who had a conviction record. Over time public records have become easily accessible so much so that even expunged arrest records can be found. The mark on the ex-offender never truly disappears because the penalty for criminal convictions remain forever intertwined with society's establishment of collateral consequences.

The reality is that the dynamics of someone with a conviction record being able to obtain a job to support themselves was a clear problem the legislature felt obliged to address because it is a problem that cannot be eradicated without the state's help. The lack of hiring of ex-offenders due to background checks only grew worse after September 11, 2001 and the terrorist attacks on the United States. Next to asking the conviction record question and checking "yes" on an application, passing a background check became the new norm of easy denial of employment of public and private employers. If the check box is the symbol of failure and doom, the background check is where employment hopes and dreams go to die. The effect of asking someone to "pass" a background check might have worked when such a "pass" was not viewed as an immediate denial back 30 years ago but in 2019 it has come to eliminate over 70 million applicants all at once.

The single most frequent problem in obtaining employment in the United States for an ex-offender is passing a background check after an offer of employment has been extended. It is much more common that an ex-offender "fails" the background check and the employment offer is withdrawn then the ex-offender manages to be employed or the license is granted and the "pass" is obtained. After all you hardly see anyone outside the conviction record class who has a clean criminal background have difficulty passing a criminal background check, do you?

So what do most companies ask themselves when they are presented with an ex-offender to hire with a conviction record and bar them from employment? Telling over 70 million people in our country they can't work because they have a conviction record by imposing senseless bars to employment only exasperates the problem and serves no business necessity. Why teach a person, who is incarcerated for years a trade, or studies to become a lawyer, doctor or licensed professional a way to make a living and waste our tax payer money and then because of their felony tell them they cannot get licensed or employed in that very profession? Such reflexive limitations are senseless and run counter to the state's expressed goal of rehabilitation and to promote the hire and licensure of ex-offenders in New York.

What you read before you has been crafted to increase knowledge and discussion and availability to all, not just New Yorkers. Included in this book are the latest case law research, forms, ideas and the ban the box efforts, to counter a world that discriminates against felons and those with misdemeanors every day. Here is to opening up your eyes to the limitless possibilities before you. Carpe Diem.

Yours Truly,

Richie F. Levine
M.S. Legal Studies, Advanced Cert. Paralegal N.A.L.A.February, 2019 Albany, New York

PART I

HISTORY AND ORIGINS OF NEW YORK CORRECTION LAW
ARTICLE 23-A

With all the advancement made in civil rights during the 1960's when Congress legislated Title VII to promote equal rights and established the Equal Employment Opportunity Commission to enforce those rights, a person with a criminal conviction still remains a second class citizen. Felons are disenfranchised and specifically targeted under federal and state law, which impose automatic statutory barriers to employment. Upon criminal pleas, the individual accumulates civil sanctions that often prohibit the person convicted from obtaining licensures upon release from prison back into society. This severely hinders their rehabilitation due to the licensing barriers erected by the state and federal governments that require high moral character, which a person with a conviction cannot demonstrate. These civil consequences are known as "collateral consequences" of a conviction and are rarely mentioned when one is sentenced in court to a crime. They have profound effects upon the communities the newly released ex- offender now enters as a job seeker because it encourages high unemployment and without a job no taxes are being paid. The search for financial employment remains an issue that is all around us, but few states and even the government want to address it.

Other than New York, Wisconsin and Hawaii passing pro-ex offender statutes for employment that address the evil, the silence of 47 other states and the federal government to make ex-offenders a protected class in employment with certain exceptions has resulted in continued prejudice and discrimination. There is no dispute that the facts support that the United States of America continues to hold the highest incarceration rate per capita of adult offenders worldwide and has failed to offer restoration of rights to its millions of incarcerated as a means of reentering and securing employment. New York remains the only state to give civil rights restoration to any conviction record through Certificate of Relief of Civil Disabilities.

The United States Supreme Court in <u>Smith v. Texas, 233 U.S. 630 (1914)</u> has even recognized the right to work "*In so far as a man is deprived of the right to labor his liberty is restricted, his capacity to earn wages and acquire property is lessened, and he is denied the protection which the law affords those who are permitted to work. Liberty means more than freedom from servitude and the constitutional guarantee is an assurance that the citizen shall be protected in the right to use his powers of mind and body in any lawful calling.*" The court concluded all men are entitled to the equal protection of the law in their right to work for the support of themselves and families.

One of the major reasons that Title VII does not directly protect ex-offenders is because our society views a criminal record as a result of a person's individual choice to break the law, reflecting incompetence and immorality.[1] In comparison to gender, race and age which are immutable characteristics that are protected by the federal government, the perception is that conviction record is a result of poorly thought out decisions by an individual and that employers are making sensible hiring decisions based on past criminal activity and the nature of their business. Across the country it is an accepted "rational" practice to show felons the door even if there is no direct relationship to the job duties or the criminality is extremely distant in time of occurrence. While minorities can file a claim with the EEOC, whites are unprotected.

Throughout the United States, other than in New York, the ability to restore civil and licensing rights is lost upon a felony conviction. The ability to be licensed in numerous occupations remains the invisible unspoken punishment once an individual chooses to plea or is found guilty of a criminal offense by a judge or jury. Judges never mention the collateral consequences before sentencing and lawyers who are supposed to represent you never discuss it before you take your plea. Other than a pardon, which is rarely granted, a felon endures being stripped of the ability to be licensed, even in a field that has nothing to do with their felony conviction. Often, employers place a premium on the trustworthiness of employees, especially when the ability to monitor employee performance is imperfect and no system is in place for proper supervision. This argument often takes the shape of ex-offenders (re-entrants) not having the "good moral character" required for the license they seek and there is no direct relationship to their crime. The ability to get a license is compromised entirely because of a felony or misdemeanor conviction without any look into the individual's crime, unique circumstances, rehabilitative efforts or time that has passed. In fact, even the best Ban the Box laws just move the denial of employment from the first interview to the end of the process.

---

[1] Thomas M. Hruz, The Unwisdom of the Wisconsin Fair Employment Act's Ban of Employment Discrimination on the Basis of a Conviction Records, 85 MARQ. L. REV. 779 (2002)

A - Felons Are Not A Suspect Class- U.S. Supreme Court Overview

Are people with criminal records part of a suspect class? A suspect class is one that has historically been subject to discrimination and protected by the federal government such as national origin and race. The United States Supreme Court does not view conviction record as a suspect class but has determined there must be a rational basis to impose a bar to employment.[2] To understand how we got to this point we have to look at how the United States Supreme Court, the nation's highest court, has dealt with allowing states to deny licensure and continue to deem felons unfit for most jobs. The Supreme Court has charted a somewhat erratic course in evaluating record-based restrictions in the last 117 years, with New York being at the center of many of those important decisions.

In the case of Hawker v. People of New York, 170 U.S. 189 (1898) the Court upheld a law criminalizing the practice of medicine by persons with felony convictions. The defendant, Dr. Hawker, was convicted in 1878 of performing an illegal abortion. He served his time, and then resumed the practice of medicine. In 1893 and 1895, the legislature of New York passed public health laws making it illegal for convicted felons to practice medicine. Dr. Hawker argued that depriving him of his right to practice medicine was additional punishment that violated the ex post facto clause. The Court, however, concluded that persons with felony records are *"excluded from obtaining [a medical] license, not as an additional punishment, but because the conviction of a felony is evidence of the unfitness of such persons as a class."*

On the issue of having good moral character to qualify for a license the United States Supreme Court took the position that *"... the violation of the penal laws of a State, has some relation to the question of character. It is not, as a rule, the good people who commit crime. When the legislature declares that whoever has violated the criminal laws of the State shall be deemed lacking in good moral character it is not laying down an arbitrary or fanciful rule – one having no relation to the subject-matter, but is only appealing to a well-recognized fact of human experience. So if the legislature enacts that one who has been convicted of crime shall no longer engage in the practice of medicine, it is simply applying the doctrine of res judicata and invoking the conclusive adjudication of the fact that the man has violated the criminal law, and is presumptively, therefore, a man of such bad character as to render it unsafe to trust the lives and health of citizens to his care."* The Court refused to recognize that a person's character may have changed since the time of the conviction stating that one who has violated the criminal law may thereafter reform and become in fact possessed of good moral character, but the legislature has power in cases of this kind to make a rule of universal application and concluded that once a felon, always a felon.

What makes this case rather interesting is that the act of performing an abortion, after the United States Supreme Court ruling in Roe v Wade, 410 U.S. 113 (1973), rendered such act legal and no longer results in a felony conviction and loss of licensure. What Dr. Hawker did that resulted in a justified question of how as a country we can continue to support barring people from a profession and never allowing them a chance to redeem themselves as time and societies morality changes. As a country we generally believe in second chances yet Dr. Hawker was stripped of his license for something that is no longer criminal but generally accepted medical practice. While the United States Supreme Court in 1898 felt that a universal application of a licensing bar was essential, such strict enforcement deprives individuals of an individualized assessment and their right to due process and makes sweeping assessments undermining equal protection arguments that could be made.[3]

What the court essentially did was establish in the last century that if there was a rational relationship between prior criminal behavior and professional disqualification the license should be denied and the state may rely on a conviction to presume bad moral character, even if that presumption is not universally valid. That bad moral character due to the conviction is the stain that can never be undone.

---

[2] *Baer v. City of Wauwatosa, 716 F.2d 1117, 1125 (1983)* ("[F]elons are not yet a protected class under the Fourteenth Amendment."); *Upshaw v. McNamara, 435 F.2d 1188, 1190 (1st Cir. 1970)* ("[A] classification based on criminal record is not a suspect classification."); *Kindem v. City of Alameda, 502 F. Supp. 1108, 1111 (N.D. Cal. 1980)* ("[E]x-felons are not thought to constitute a suspect class."); *Furst v. New York City Transit Authority, 631 F. Supp. 1331, 1336-37 (E.D.N.Y. 1986)* (noting that felons are not a suspect class, and that therefore rational basis review applies); *Hill v. Gill, 703 F. Supp. 1034, 1037 (D.R.I. 1989)* ("In this case, it is clear that the class in question (i.e. persons convicted of felonies) is not a protected one."); *Miller v. Carter, 547 F.2d 1314, 1321 (7th Cir. 1977)* (Campbell, J., concurring) (noting that the Supreme Court has defined a suspect class as one "saddled with such disabilities ... as to command extraordinary protection from the majoritarian political process," and finding that significant societal disabilities derive solely from the fact that a person has a criminal record, but deciding that, in light of Supreme Court's reluctance to expand the number of suspect classes, people with criminal records do not constitute a suspect class)

[3] *Smith v. Fussenich, 440 F. Supp. 1077, 1081 (D. Conn. 1977)*

In 1942, the United States Supreme Court decided to hear the case of Skinner v Oklahoma 316 U.S. 535 (1942) where it struck down Oklahoma's Habitual Criminal Sterilization Act on equal protection grounds because it impermissibly distinguished between embezzlers and thieves. The court rationalized that sterilization involves one of the basic rights of man and to pick one man over the other *"[w]hen the law lays an unequal hand on those who have committed intrinsically the same quality of offense and sterilizes one and not the other, it has made as invidious a discrimination as if it had selected a particular race or nationality for oppressive treatment."* Here the court gave the appearance that it would permit the sterilization of habitual offenders, so long as it is done equitably across offense classes. Judge Stone made a case that there must be due process involved in the decision: *"[T]he real question we have to consider is not one of equal protection, but whether the wholesale condemnation of a class to such an invasion of personal liberty, without opportunity to any individual to show that his is not the type of case which would justify resort to it, satisfies the demands of due process. There are limits to the extent to which the presumption of constitutionality can be pressed, especially where the liberty of the person is concerned and where the presumption is resorted to only to dispense with a procedure which the ordinary dictates of prudence would seem to demand for the protection of the individual from arbitrary action.... [T]he State does not contend – nor can there be any pretense – that either common knowledge or experience, or scientific investigation, has given assurance that the criminal tendencies of any class of habitual offenders are universally or even generally inheritable. In such circumstances, inquiry whether such is the fact in the case of any particular individual cannot rightly be dispensed with.... A law which condemns, without hearing, all the individuals of a class to so harsh a measure as the present because some or even many merit condemnation is lacking in the first principles of due process."*

The United States Supreme Court in 1954 was again faced with a licensing issue in New York in the case of <u>Barsky v Board of Regents of the University of the State of New York, 347 U.S. 442 (1954)</u>. Dr. Barksy was convicted of a criminal offense in the United States District Court for the District of Columbia of failing to produce before a Congressional Committee certain papers that were subpoenaed, but such offense was not criminal in New York. The court held that the New York law did not violate the Due Process Clause of the Fourteenth Amendment and that the state had the appropriate police power to regulate its high licensing standards and fix its terms of admission based on the disciplinary action and impose the 6 month suspension. The physician argued that, while the state has a legitimate right to regulate the practice of medicine, the standard adopted by New York exceeded reasonable supervision of the profession and deprived him of his property rights in his license and practice, without due process. The Court disagreed, upholding the statute on the grounds that New York had adopted a discretionary scheme that allowed it to "match the measure of the discipline to the specific case."

The Court clearly set out in its decision that the practice of medicine, as with a majority of licensures are a privilege granted by the State under its substantially plenary power to fix the terms of admission. *"The issue is not before us but it has not been questioned that the State could make it a condition of admission to practice that applicants shall not have been convicted of a crime.... It could at least require a disclosure of such convictions as a condition of admission and leave it to a competent board to determine, after opportunity for fair hearing, whether the convictions, if any, were of such a date and nature as to justify denial of admission to practice in light of all material circumstances before the board."*

Justice Douglas in his dissent noted that the right to work *"was the most precious liberty that man possesses."* The Justice argued that while a person does not have an affirmative right to any particular job, skill or profession, the state may also not deprive individuals of a job, skill, or profession, once acquired, making the question *"not what government must give, but rather what it may not take away."* Justice Douglas wisely recognized the slippery slope that would occur if there was no constitutional right to be a policeman or a doctor: *"[b]y the same reasoning a man has no constitutional right to teach, to work in a filling station, to be a grocery clerk, to mine coal, to tend a furnace, or to be on the assembly line. By that reasoning a man has no constitutional right to work."* Justice Douglas specifically commented about Dr. Barksy that his refusal to give documents resulting in a criminal conviction did not make him unfit to practice medicine because, *"The underlying conduct simply did not provide a "constitutional ground for taking away a man's right to work."* The court, even in its dissent made the distinction that the right to work is subject to regulation and that due process must be given before such a denial of a license can occur. The case firmly established that it is impermissible to automatically revoke licensure already granted because of a criminal conviction.

In 1957 the United States Supreme Court decided to hear the case of <u>Schware v. Board of Bar Examiners of New Mexico 353 U.S. 232 (1957)</u> where in 1953 Schware was not permitted to take the bar examination on the ground that he had not shown "good moral character," and thereby precluded his admission to the bar of that State even though he was qualified in all other respects. Schware had been a member of the Communist Party from 1932 to 1940, had been arrested but never convicted and used aliases from 1934 to 1937 and this formed the basis for denying his ability to practice law. The court found that arrests alone are insufficient to support a finding he had bad moral character at the time he took the bar examination or that conduct 20 years ago supported an inference of bad moral character at the time of licensing. The court chose to view Schware's prior conduct, including not just his arrests but also his use of aliases and membership in the communist party, as past youthful folly which "cannot be said to raise substantial doubts about his present good moral character." Schware stands for the proposition that occupational restrictions based on contact with the criminal justice system must be rationally related to the occupation in question, and must take into consideration the lapse of time and the nature of the offense. The Supreme Court in this decision tacitly rejected the conclusion in that case that a past criminal conviction, in and of itself, demonstrates a present lack of good moral character and justifies denial of a license. The court's decision has resonated with states in that they can establish qualifications for entry into particular professions, but "*any qualification must have a rational connection with the applicant's fitness or capacity to practice [his profession].*" This includes the nature of the offense and the lapse of time since the offense.[4]

The United States Supreme Court heard another New York based case in <u>DeVeau v. Braisted 363 U.S. 144 (1960)</u> where a statute prohibited waterfront unions from collecting dues if any agent or official of the union had a felony conviction. The law effectively prevented any felon from holding a union position. The appellant union member argued that barring all felons was not a reasonable means to eliminate waterfront corruption. The court deemed such legislation drastic but explained that, "*in the view of Congress and the two States involved the situation on the New York waterfront regarding the presence and influence of ex-convicts called for drastic action.... Duly mindful as we are of the promising record of rehabilitation by ex- felons, and of the emphasis on rehabilitation by modern penological efforts, it is not for this Court to substitute its judgment for that of Congress and the Legislatures of New York and New Jersey regarding the social surgery required by a situation as gangrenous as exposure of the New York waterfront ha[s] revealed.*" The justices applied the logic that, "*The Court, while noting that barring felons from certain jobs was "a familiar legislative device to insure against corruption in specified, vital areas," stressed that "New York was not guessing or indulging in airy assumptions that convicted felons constituted a deleterious influence on the waterfront," but "was acting on impressive if mortifying evidence[5] that the presence on the waterfront of ex- convicts was an important contributing factor to the corrupt waterfront situation.*"

Here the court reviewed the weight of the evidence and did not simply take the legislature's conclusion as fact but chose to support it because the situation called for it.

---

[4] *Lowe v. SEC, 472 U.S. 181, 229 (1985) (White, J., concurring)* quoting *Schware* for the proposition that "regulations on entry into a profession, as a general matter, are constitutional if they 'have a rational connection with the applicant's fitness or capacity to practice' the profession"); *Pordum v. Board of Regents, 491 F.2d 1281, 1287 n.14 (2d Cir. 1974)* (citing *Schware* for the proposition that exclusion of convicted persons from a profession can be justified only after a detailed and particularistic consideration of the relationship between the person involved and the purpose of exclusion); *Fussenich*, 440 F. Supp. at 1080 (citing *Schware* for the proposition that occupational restrictions must have a rational connection with the applicant's fitness or capacity to perform the job, and finding that an across-the-board disqualification of felons as security guards and private detectives did not meet this standard).

[5] *Fernandes v. Limmer, 663 F.2d 619, 630 (5th Cir. 1981)* (striking down a regulation prohibiting persons convicted of felonies from distributing literature or collecting funds at an airport because the airport had not shown "impressive" evidence to sustain the provision but was merely "indulging in assumptions"); *Smith v. Fussenich, 440 F. Supp.at 1081 (1977)* (striking down Connecticut's record-based bar to private detective and security guard work and distinguishing *DeVea v. Braisted 363 U.S. 144 (1960)* on the grounds that there the legislature had found impressive evidence regarding the dangers presented by convicted persons, while in the instant case there was "no evidence that prior to the passage of the statute the Connecticut legislature conducted an investigation which revealed that criminality was a serious problem in the regulated occupations"); *Pordum v Board of Regents State of New York, 491 F.2d at 1287 n.14 (1974)* (under *DeVeau*, a *per se* rule to exclude convicted person from certain occupations may be permissible, but only if that rule "was established after a comprehensive investigation into the relationship between the class of persons excluded ... and the evil sought to be avoided"). But see *Hill v. Gill, 703 F. Supp. 1034 (DRI 1989)* (upholding regulations prohibiting persons convicted of felonies from being licensed as school bus drivers and distinguishing *DeVeau* on the grounds that "[w]hile the Court did cite the extensive legislative investigations that led to enactment of the statute, it did not indicate that such investigations were a sine qua non of its validity").

B - New York Establishes the Executive Law
and Introduces Certificates of Rehabilitation in 1945

By 1945, New York sought to establish its own progressive Human Rights Law and it was originally known as *"The Law Against Discrimination"* located at Article 15 of the Executive Law and passed by the New York Legislature. It was recommended to the Legislature by the New York State Temporary Commission against Discrimination, an agency created by *Chapter 692 of the Laws of 1944*, in a report which contained the proposed statutory text and a study of the problem of discrimination and its background.[6] Along with the Human Rights Law, the legislature passed a Certificate of Rehabilitation document, obtainable under the Executive Law, which allowed an ex-offender a way to resume their life in society with the ability to get their rights restored. This rehabilitation concept which took effect in 1945 shaped the state's approach toward criminal justice reform and a new public policy emerged to support a way to give ex-offenders their rights back.[7] The earliest certificate was a more conservative version of today's Certificate of Good Conduct.[8]

The Board of Parole in the 1940's required a unanimous vote to award the certificate. By 1951, only a majority was necessary, by 1960 a majority of three members of the Board was acceptable, and in 1963 a unanimous vote of three Board members was required to grant a Certificate of Good Conduct.[9] The Certificate of Good Conduct statute was amended twice prior to its incorporation into Article 23. The first amendment to the statute extended the certificates to individuals with convictions outside New York but required that, a person had to also reside in New York for 5 years before applying for a Certificate of Good Conduct (in addition to five year post-conviction waiting period). This change intended to prevent forum shopping.

The second set of changes in the early 1950s required applicants to show deserving conduct, a burden that no longer exists.[10] Additionally the statute required good conduct for a "period of five consecutive years" after the completion of a criminal sentence or payment of a fine, regardless of the severity of the conviction. The statute also made clear that a person could not get a Certificate of Good Conduct while on parole which has not changed in today's version of the law.

Then in 1963, the statute clarified that issuing a certificate required three votes from members of the Board of Parole. A person with any level of conviction, even the most minor misdemeanor, was eligible for a Certificate of Good Conduct.[11] The legislature granted the Board of Parole broad discretion to issue a certificate, provided that they did so within "a reasonable time period."[12] Unlike the certificates that are issued since 1977, these Certificates of Good Conduct were granted only if they would end a specific disability affecting the applicant. The statute was not aimed at total civil reintegration.

---

[6] *N. Y. Legis. Doc., 1945, No. 6*

[7] *See New York Correction History Society, '100 Years of Progress' Book (1970)*

[8] *1945 Laws of New York Ch. 96 (64-65). See also Memorandum from Danielle D'Abate, Summer Intern, to Alan Rothstein, Corporate Counsel for the New York City Bar Association, Legislative History of Certificate Statutes*

[9] *1951 N.Y. Sess. Laws 1285-86 (McKinney).*

[10] *1951 N.Y. Sess. Laws 1285-86 (McKinney), 1960 N.Y. Sess. Laws 351 Ch. 610 (McKinney), 1963 Laws of N.Y. Ch. 356 (513) (McKinney).*

[11] *1945 Laws of New York Ch. 96*

[12] *1945 Laws of New York Ch. 96 §116 (3) (64-65).*

C - A Means To Be Rehabilitated:
The New Certificate of Relief Introduced in 1966

In 1966, the state legislature decided that New York would reconsider its ability to grant relief by passing a more expansive and easily obtainable and immediate certificate – a Certificate of Relief from Disabilities for "first offenders," which was added as Article 23 of New York's Correction Law. Governor Rockefeller's Special Committee on Criminal Offenders initiated a report as well as the creation of a bill to preserve the right to vote and prevent the forfeiture of other rights, "such as the right to retain or apply for licenses, which would otherwise follow automatically upon conviction. Rockefeller viewed the legislation as *"an important step beyond the previous system of automatic, indirect sanctions following upon a conviction without regard to the merits of the individual involved."* The Certificate of Relief committee report recommended that such a certificate would assist the individual in his rehabilitation process because it would enable certain first offenders to receive immediate consideration for available opportunities for which they are qualified, and thus to complete rehabilitation more rapidly and to contribute to the community in civic, social, economic and professional endeavors. The new standard for a Certificate of Relief that the sentencing court could issue was now *"consistent with the rehabilitation of the first offender and . . . with the public interest."*[13]

Article 23 of the Correction Law was added by Chapter 654 of the Laws of 1966. In approving enactment of the legislation Governor Nelson Rockefeller, noted that, *"This bill will reduce the automatic rejection and community isolation that often accompany conviction of crimes, and will thus contribute to the complete rehabilitation of first offenders and their successful return to responsible lives in the community. It is an important step beyond the previous system of automatic, indirect sanctions following upon a conviction without regard to the merits of the individual involved".* Governor's Approval Message No.44 on Senate bill 4875, June 21, 1966.

New York State Correction Law § 702.2(b) provides that a certificate should not issued unless *"[t]he relief to be granted by the certificate is consistent with the rehabilitation of the first offender . . . "* However, the proper construction of this requirement is that the certificate should be issued when it will be an aid to rehabilitation. It does not require a determination that the convict has already been rehabilitated. Governor's Memorandum Approval of L.1966, c. 654 in McKinney's 1966 Session Laws of New York 3003

---

[13] 1966 Regular Session Chapter 654 Article 23 §701, 791-94

D - The Scope of the Certificate Expands in 1972; Federal Convictions Covered

From 1966 to 1972 Correction Law Article 23 did not provide for the issuance of such certificates by the Board of Parole to persons not convicted in New York courts, and the Court based its decision on the proposition that the denial to a person who was convicted in a Federal court of the right to be relieved of disabilities, while granting that right to someone who was convicted in a New York State court, was an unconstitutional denial of equal protection of the law.

This changed when Michael DeGrossa, who filed suit against the state[14] sought to have equal standing to obtaining a certificate as those who pled in state court filed an Article 78 and the court concluded that, Subsequent to the DeGrossa decision, Correction Law Article 23 was amended to give the Board of Parole the authority to grant Certificates of Relief From Disabilities to persons convicted in courts of other jurisdictions.[15] In 1974 the scope of Certificates of Relief was further enlarged to allow the Board of Parole to issue a certificate to an individual *"whose judgment of conviction was rendered by a court in any other jurisdiction."*[16] One of the problems that the case presented was that the new amendment would appear to eliminate any justification for the issuance by a State court of a Certificate of Relief from Disabilities to a person who was convicted in a Federal court. The Court held that where a revocable sentence has been imposed by a Federal court a State court may issue a Certificate of Relief from Disabilities to the offender.[17]

The language of the statute, the legislative record and the Governor's report show that Certificates of Rehabilitation were now seen as a means to rehabilitation, not something solely for those who were already rehabilitated. Senator John Dunne in 1972 emphasized the advantages of a Certificates of Relief, which now could be issued a sentence of discharge, misdemeanor or one felony conviction and Certificates of Good Conduct which would be issued to parolees who had to serve several years in prison: *"Restrictions can be removed after five years of good conduct by the offender . . . but the intervening period is clearly the most critical in the rehabilitation process . . . Since our experience with the certificate of relief from disabilities has thus far been satisfactory, it is prudent that we take a step forward by expanding those qualified to receive the certificate."*[18] This change now relied on the ability of the sentencing court to directly issue a certificate of relief of civil disabilities. This dramatically enlarged the number of individuals eligible for immediate and automatic certificates because the standard of proof to obtain one was lowered from the "burden of deserving conduct" to "evidence of rehabilitation."

One of the major factors towards Senator Dunne's push to expand the certificate was because the studies showed that the percentage of people with misdemeanor convictions far exceeds the percentage with felony convictions. The Certificate of Relief of Disabilities was geared towards those type of offenses and the certificate of good conduct was geared towards the most serious of offenses.

New York State Article 23 of the Correction Law was significantly expanded by the New York Legislature by broadening those offenders eligible to receive a Certificate of Relief from first offenders to offenders who had not been convicted more than once of a felony (thus allowing offenders with multiple misdemeanor convictions to obtain a Certificate of Relief). In a Governor's Program Bill memorandum discussing the need for the legislation, the Governor's office noted that New York state laws *"are permeated with restrictions that deprive a criminal offender who has been allowed to remain in, or who has been returned to, the community of a wide variety of job opportunities."* A memorandum from the State Department of Correctional Services asserted that the bill would be a *"step forward in the humanization of the correction process."*

---

[14] *DeGrossa v. Goodman, 72 Misc.2d 806, 339 N.Y.S.2d 502, 505 (Sup.Ct.1972)*

[15] *(L. 1974 Ch. 475).*

[16] *1974 N.Y. Sess. Laws 630-631 (McKinney).*

[17] *Matter of Helmsley, 152 Misc.2d 215, 575 N.Y.S. 2d 1009 (1991)*

[18] *1972 N.Y. St. Legis. Ann. 13-14.*

E - Michael Meltsner and The Syracuse Law Review:
An Act To Promote The Rehabilitation of Criminal Offenders in New York State

Michael Meltsner was a Yale Law graduate and attorney who came of age in the sixties, utilizing lawsuits to integrate major southern institutions, representing Muhammad Ali in the restoration of his boxing license, and a staunch advocate of challenging the validity of the death penalty. A professor at Columbia University in 1973, Meltsner and his colleagues sought to find a sensible way of how the state and the legislature should deal with the increasing difficulty that ex- offenders found in employment. This lead to a Syracuse Law Review article that did just that along with authors March Caplan and William C. Lane. In the 1973 Syracuse Law Review publication "*An Act to Promote the Rehabilitation of Criminal Offenders in the State of New York*" the article stated that ex-offenders were encouraged upon release from prison as part of their rehabilitation to find employment, but could not find such employment because their criminal records caused great difficulty even though there was no connection between the job or license and the crime committed, its circumstances or that offender's background.[19]

Meltsner, with the help of statistics and sheer common sense, articulated that employers saw ex-offenders as a poor risk and were blinded by the very prejudice that they would not perform well in the workforce. He correctly pointed out that there was a high price to be paid on the tax payers by restricting so many licenses without doing any evaluation of the ex-offender's criminal offense to see if there was a direct relationship. With the burdens of poverty pushing down ex-offenders across the state, it created what Meltsner referred to as a "*double bind*" situation where the state wanted the ex-offender to be a part of an economic and social system that extols work ethic and on the other hand precludes, categorizes and bars ex-offenders from pursuing basic employment opportunities based on nothing more than the conviction itself. What Meltsner pointed out was that ex-offenders were shut out of public employment, specifically if they needed a security clearance or faced civil service regulations that established policies to prevent the hire of ex-offenders. At the time of his study, nearly one-third of New York State agencies would not hire ex-offenders and nearly half had placed restrictions on hiring. As Meltsner so aptly pointed out, "*those very entities responsible for rehabilitating prisoners--the states and the federal government--set a most unedifying example.*"[20]

In the private sector the problem was abundant and widespread. Employers, if given a choice, would seem to take the person without the conviction record over the person with the conviction record. While employers openly profess an open mind to hiring ex-offenders in 2019, they still hide guidelines and matrixes that categorize criminal behavior and stamp applicants eligible and ineligible based on nothing more than the conviction itself without any assessment required. The Syracuse Law Review article specifically pointed out that back then 75 percent of employment agencies would not hire an ex- offender and that joining a union to learn a trade or apprenticeship was near impossible due to exclusionary tactics. Getting bonded against theft through a fidelity bond was another common excuse for not hiring an ex-offender because such arrangements with bonding companies were made to automatically prevent "knowingly" hiring someone with a conviction record. Even in 2019 this is still a major issue but the Federal government since 1966 offers 6 months of free bonding for any job and any employer for hard to place job applicants. Most employers are unaware of this being available to them.[21]

One of the more pressing points Meltsner touched on was the high unemployment rates that often effect ex-offenders, documented at the time up to three times as bad as a person without a conviction record. Without a high skill level or education an ex-offender was left to fend for themselves and find whatever employment they could. The only other option presented as viable in the review was that if nothing were done a significant number of convicted criminals would return to a life of crime upon release from prison. As it is now the social services system is forced to support ex-offenders who cannot work because employers refuse to hire or consider them. Sadly not much has changed in this regard in 2019 as there is still a strong correlation between crime rates and unemployment. Without a future to look to, Meltsner correctly pointed out in 1973 that the ex-offender would become pessimistic and return to a deviant lifestyle because their employment possibilities have already been hindered by society's reflexive limitations.

---

[19] *Meltsner, Caplan and Lane, An Act to Promote the Rehabilitation of Criminal Offenders in the State of New York, 24 Syracuse L Rev 885, 905 [1973].*
[20] *President's Task Force on Prisoner Rehabilitation, The Criminal Offender-What Should Be Done? 10 (1970)*
[21] *Federal Bonding Program at url: http://www.bonds4jobs.com/individual-seeking-bonding.html*

The Model Act proposed by Meltnser sought to address major points that the legislature needed to act upon (1) find a way to promote stronger removal of civil disabilities imposed by statute (2) promote the rehabilitation of an ex-offender through direct relationship assessment (3) remove blanket policies by public and private employers (4) remove lifetime denial of licensing rights and opportunities (5) provide remedies for those denied opportunities on the basis of a criminal conviction. Meltnser established the direct relationship test, which had its basis in a Court of Appeals decision in 1972. Three judges of that court observed that a public employer may consider prior misconduct, *"but only to the extent that such misconduct is relevant to... fitness and qualifications for the position sought."*[22]

The Model act requested that New York adopt a "direct relationship" test. The purpose was that society has an interest in disabling an offender from employment in those occasions where the nature of the offense is such as to strongly suggest the offender will not lawfully pursue a particular occupation. Meltnser had firsthand experience in how easy a license can be lost when there is no direct relationship to the criminal offense when he represented Muhammad Ali, who was stripped of his boxing license because he was found guilty of violating the Selective Service Act.[23] Meltnser used this an example of the unfair rationale of denial of license on the presumption of general moral turpitude or bad character which flows from the adjudication of a criminal offense to show how irrational the decisions of taking away a license can be.

In creating the direct relationship test, the Model Act sought to establish that the crime must have a substantial and immediate connection between the criminal behavior and the functions and responsibilities which pertain to the particular right or opportunity. By forcing employers to prove a claimed relationship between job selection criteria and job performance the burden shifts away from the ex-offender and on to the employer to show that a prohibition is necessary to the safe and efficient operation of the business or that a state or local licensing law or regulation prohibits the employment of such individual. Meltnser went so far as to point out that the "direct relationship" test is constitutionally required. Such a presumption he argues violates due process unless there is a rational basis by which the fact presumed can be inferred from the fact proved.

Many of the problems with Certificates of Relief outlined in the 1973 review were dealt with in the proposed new law taking shape that would be passed in 1976. Many of the proposals of the Model Act, including the waiting periods for parolees to get a certificate were adopted to broaden the scope of the Certificates to more than first offenders. The Model Act also proposed the Division of Human Rights take jurisdiction to ensure compliance and for appeal of such final order.

While these were great proposed steps taken to broaden the rights of ex-offenders, committees were formed by Senator Dunne between 1974 and the beginning of 1976 based on Meltnser's recommendations that evaluated the problem and sought to find a way that ex- offenders could be reintegrated back into the workforce while allowing for employers to properly deny ex-offenders who have crimes that directly relate to the job duties or posed an unreasonable risk.

Not happy with the existing and limited Certificate system that had evolved, as Meltnser had pointed out correctly in his paper, the New York Legislature decided that the best course of action was an individualized analysis and sought to establish the Certificate of Rehabilitation, a fixture of the past 35 years, as one of the factors to be considered by private and public employers in an overall employment analysis before denial.

The introduction of a Certificate of Relief of Civil Disabilities and a Certificate of Good Conduct, as it is today, replaced the existing certificate system and became an integral part of introducing the legislature's new addition to the Human Rights Law: New York Correction Law Article 23-A.

---

[22] Cacchioli v Hoberman, 31 N.Y. 2d 287, 295, 291 N.E. 2d 117,121, 338 N.Y.S. 2d 865, 871 (1972) (concurring opinion).

[23] Ali v Division of State Athletic Commission, 308 F. Supp. 11, 16-17 (S.D.N.Y. 1969)

PART II

NEW YORK STATE CORRECTION LAW ARTICLE 23-A,
§750 -755 AND THE CERTIFICATE OF RELIEF OF CIVIL
DISABILITIES AND GOOD CONDUCT

In 1976, the New York legislature began efforts to pass a bill concerning the "Licensure and Employment of Persons Previously Convicted of One of More Criminal Offenses."[24] In a memorandum issued on approving the bill, Governor Hugh Carey declared that the new Human Rights Law, under Article 15 of the New York Executive Law, Section 296 and the revision of Correction Law Article 23 into Correction Law Article 23-A was "*designed to establish reasonable procedures to prevent the unfair discrimination against former criminal offenders in regard to licensure and employment. The bill in no way requires the hiring of former offenders, but provides reasonable standards to be applied by public agencies and private employers when considering applications by former offenders.*" Article 23-A was enacted to eliminate the practice of categorically rejecting any job applicant with a criminal record solely on that basis without an individualized assessment first.[25]

Under the provisions of *Article 23-A of the New York Correction Law*, a license or employment could not be denied to an individual on the basis of a previous criminal conviction, unless the criminal conduct of which he was convicted has a direct bearing upon his ability or fitness to perform one or more of the responsibilities or duties necessarily related to the license or employment sought,[26] or unless granting the application would pose an unreasonable risk to property or the health or safety of others.[27] Governor Carey added that, "*The great expense and time involved in successfully prosecuting and incarcerating the criminal offender is largely wasted if upon the individual's return to society his willingness to assume a law-abiding and productive role is frustrated by senseless discrimination.*"[28]

New York Executive Law 296.15 and 296.16 and the new Correction Law Article 23-A were designed to provide fair treatment to those ex-offenders who had already paid their debt to society, and those who were arrested but not convicted due to termination of pending charges. Governor Carey's thought was to have the legislature attempt to tackle a practical solution to the problem of criminal recidivism by giving an ex-offender a fair opportunity for a job and prohibiting arrests as a criteria where no conviction had resulted. Carey even correctly pointed out the burden on the state in that, "*For those who have committed crimes, being unemployed contributes to the escalating crime rates and imposed concomitant financial burdens upon New York State.*"[29]

It was clear that New York State saw the denial of ex-offenders as widespread, unfair and counterproductive with prejudice. In order to begin imposing obligations on employers to deal equitably with those with a conviction record, while protecting society's interest in hiring and employing reliable and trustworthy persons, New York developed what is today a model for other states in the area of Human Rights. Even the Court of Appeals has noted the intent of the legislature to protect ex-offenders from discrimination: "*Particularly with respect to the employment of ex-convicts — who are officially free to walk the streets, visit the playgrounds, and live and work in society without being branded or segregated — the opportunity for gainful employment may spell the difference between recidivism and rehabilitation.*"[30] After several months of intense discussion and legislature fine tuning, a final bill was proposed that eliminated *Article 23* by creating New York Correction Law Article 23-A §750-755, established New York Executive Law 296.15 and New York Executive Law 296.16 and created a separate section under New York Article 23 Correction Law §§ 700-706 to address Certificates of Relief of Civil Disabilities and Certificates of Good Conduct.

The provisions of New York Correction Law Article 23-A, §§ 750 - §755 were passed by the New York legislature and went into effect on January 1, 1977. Correction Law Article 23-A was incorporated into the Human Rights Law, and was codified at Article 15 of the New York State Executive Law 296 §15. Article 23-A of the New York Correction Law established itself as a landmark statute that articulates a broad and powerful public policy favoring employment opportunities for individuals who have previously been convicted of one or more criminal offenses. The stated purpose of Article 23-A of the New York Correction Law is not to give an ex-offender (re-entrants) preferred treatment, but to remove prejudice against former offenders in obtaining jobs, since this prejudice is not only widespread, but unfair and counterproductive to the people of New York.[31]

---

[24] *Legislative History-Bill Jacket, L. 1976, C. 931, § 5*

[25] As indicated by the *Governor's Bill Jacket, 1976, Ch. 931, Memorandum of Senator Marino and Assemblyman Fink in Support of S. 4222-C and A. 5393-C.*

[26] "The duties and responsibilities of the job must be inherent for a direct relationship to exist and if they do not then the first exception to the general prohibition of discrimination against persons previously convicted of criminal offenses cannot be claimed." *(Dellaporte v New York City Dept. of Bldgs., A.D. 3d, 2013 NY Slip Op 3281 [1st Dept 2013], Matter of Nuziale v LiMandri, 2013 NY Slip Op 4741 [1st Dept 2013])*

[27] Employers must offer more than "speculative inferences unsupported by the record" to raise an issue concerning any potential "unreasonable risk" to the public *(Matter of Nuziale v LiMandri, 2013 NY Slip Op 4741 [1st Dept 2013]) Matter of Marra v City of White Plains, 96 A.D. 2d 17, 25 [2d Dept 1983]*

[28] *(McKinney's Sess Laws, 1976, pp 2458-2459*; emphasis supplied).

[29] *Legislative History-Bill Jacket, L. 1976, C. 931, S.422-C, Memorandum of Hugh L. Carey*; ("Providing a former offender a fair opportunity for a job is ... one of the surest ways to reduce crime.").

[30] *Haddock v City of New York (75 N.Y.2d, supra, at 486 (1990),*

[31] *Peluso v. Smith, 540 N.Y.S.2d 631, 634 (Sup. Ct. 1989)* see also *Eiseman v. State, 511 N.E.2d 1128, 1132-33 (N.Y. 1987)* (discussing the strong public policy favoring rehabilitation of ex-convicts).

Article 23-A of the New York Correction Law was designed to be the most progressive law in the nation with respect to prohibiting employment discrimination against former offenders.[32] It applies to both public and private employers. The New York Division of Human Rights maintains jurisdiction over private employer complaints filed within a year, though the courts can have jurisdiction if filed within 3 years exclusively against a private employers based on New York Executive Law 297.9.[33] All public employer conviction record complaints must be filed under a CPLR Article 78 action (to be discussed later). The Court of Appeals is mandated to read the Human Rights Law in a manner that will accomplish its strong anti- discriminatory purpose.[34] The state has their objectives rehabilitating and reintegrating former inmates in the hope that they will spend their future years productively instead of returning to crime. To this end, the value of education — both as an escape from society's underclass and as a benefit to the public generally — is apparent.[35]

Unemployment is the greatest deterrence to rehabilitation. Statistics indicate that many ex-offenders return to lives of crime because other employment, including that of their choice, is unavailable.[36] Although ex-offenders were urged when released from prison to find employment as a part of their rehabilitation, they had great difficulty in doing so because of their criminal records and this difficulty existed even though there was an absence of any connection between the employment or license and the crime committed, its circumstances or the background of the offender.[37] Failure to find employment not only resulted in personal frustration but also injured society as a whole by contributing to a high rate of recidivism.[38]

The stated goal of the legislature by passing Article 23-A of the New York Correction Law and continuing to enforce it through agency/court decisions is to reduce recidivism by increasing employment opportunities for persons with criminal records.

A - Who Does Correction Law Article 23-A Cover?

It applies to any person who has a felony or misdemeanor and has already been convicted. It also applies to people currently working for an employer and those who are terminated from employment based on their conviction record. It also covers those perceived to have a conviction record, even if they do not actually have one or it is the wrong conviction record that the employer denies employment for.[39]

B - What Does Correction Law Article 23-A Contain?

Correction Law § 750 contains the definition of terms that are relied upon. Correction Law § 751 contains applicability concerning applications. Correction Law § 752 contains only two exemptions that an employer can claim in order to deny employment with Correction Law § 753 being the 8 factor mechanism that allows this to occur. Correction Law § 754 concerns the ability of the ex-offender to request a letter in 30 days setting forth the reasons for denial[40] and Correction Law § 755 clarifies where an action must be commenced against public agencies (Article 78) and private employers (City Commission or Division of Human Rights). Executive Law 296 § 15 covers Article 23-A and its provisions allowing for inclusion as one of the protected classes under the Human Rights Law and defining what entities are subject to its jurisdiction.

C - Correction Law Article 23-A
Prohibits Conviction Record Discrimination Outside of Two Exceptions

An employer may not deny or terminate employment on the basis of prior criminal convictions except in two narrowly defined circumstances. Correction Law § 752 expressly prohibits consideration of an individual's criminal convictions in employment decisions unless one of two exceptions applies: either that (1) there is a direct relationship between the criminal offense and the specific license or employment sought; or that (2)

---

[32] *Legislative History-Bill Jacket, L. 1976, C. 931, S.422-C, Memorandum of Hugh L. Carey*

[33] The Legislature has decreed that a person claiming to be aggrieved by unlawful discriminatory practices may elect to seek redress in either an administrative or a judicial forum *(Executive Law § 297 [9])*. The administrative forum offers a complainant remedies not available from a court *(see, e.g., Executive Law § 297 [3] [a])* and may be less expensive and time consuming than litigating in the State courts. However, a complainant has less time in which to seek administrative review — a complaint must be filed with the Division of Human Rights within one year of the accrual of the cause of action *(Executive Law § 297 [5])* while an action may be commenced in a court within three years of that time *(CPLR 214 [2])*. *Executive Law § 297 (9)* expressly precludes administrative review after the commencement of an action in a judicial forum. Similarly, once a complainant elects the administrative forum by filing a complaint with the Division of Human Rights, a subsequent judicial action on the same complaint is generally barred *(Executive Law § 297 [9])*.

[34] *Scheiber v. St. John's University, 1994, 84 N.Y.2d 120, 615 N.Y.S.2d 332, 638 N.E.2d 977(1994)*

[35] *Eiseman v. State of New York, 70 NY 2d 175, (see, Correction Law § 136; 1969 McKinney's Session Laws of NY, at 2579)*.

[36] *Memorandum in Support from Bill Jacket, Senate Bill No. 4222-C, 1976 amendment to Correction Law and Executive Law*

[37] *Meltsner, Caplan & Lane, An Act to Promote the Rehabilitation of Criminal Offenders in the State of New York, 24 Syracuse L Rev 885, 905*

[38] *1976 NY Legis Ann, at 50*

[39] *State Div. of Human Rights v. Sorrento Cheese Co., Inc., 115 A.D. 2d 323(1985)*

[40] This particular part of *Article 23-A of the Correction Law* has not been specifically defined by the legislature or court decisions concerning violations and remedies. No other protected class gets a written explanation of why they were denied directly by the employer.

the issuance or continuation of the license or the granting or continuation of the employment would involve an unreasonable risk to property or to the safety or welfare of specific individuals or the general public.

By allowing employers to consider an individual's criminal record only as an exception to a general prohibition, <u>Correction Law § 752</u> makes clear that agencies and other employers have the burden of justifying a denial of employment based on a criminal conviction.[41] Employers that deny or terminate employment based on one of the two exceptions may do so only after considering and applying all eight factors set forth in <u>Correction Law § 753</u>.[42] The Court of Appeals has consistently held that even if there is a direct relationship, the individualized assessment must be done by the employer before denial can occur, not after. A failure to review evidence provided by an applicant tending to show that he or she had reliably carried out duties similar to those contemplated in the license or employment in question would constitute a violation of <u>§ 753 (1) (b) and (g)</u>.[43] Without the regular application of the 8 factors listed in <u>Article 23-A of the Correction Law § 753'</u>s balancing test, New York's law ceases to be the distinguishing model of conviction record legislation to which scholars can point to as the most effective state statute at increasing employment opportunities for ex-offenders. The importance of employing former inmates, and reintegrating them back into society, without risk of absolute liability for those who open their doors to them, cannot be overstated.[44]

D - Applicants Must Be Truthful About Their Conviction Records

It is imperative on an ex-offender to be completely accurate during the employment application and hiring interview process. Concealment or deceptiveness on an employment application, including omitting criminal convictions is an acceptable basis for an employer or agency not to hire the applicant and terminate their application.[45] It also compromises the entire point of the analysis process if an applicant chooses to make false or misleading statements and cloak their prior criminal records in secrecy. The statute only protects an ex-offender if they are truthful and forthcoming about what they did in their past. Inaccuracies and omissions in a petitioner's employment application can constitute a sufficient basis for denial of employment by a potential employer.[46] Even a person who has never had a conviction record who is refused a job based on an erroneously perceived conviction record for a crime is protected by the statute.[47]

E - How Does New York Define A Criminal Offense?

Criminal offenses in New York occur in three classes: felony, misdemeanor and violation. Article 23-A covers those who have felonies and misdemeanors. A "felony" is the most serious type of criminal offense; those convicted can be imprisoned for more than one year. Imprisonment for a "misdemeanor" can be more than fifteen days, but no more than one year. A person is "convicted" of a criminal offense when found guilty by a court of law. It is a "conviction" whether it is based on a plea of guilty or on an evidentiary trial. A violation is not a criminal offense covered under New York Correction Law Article 23-A.

F - Standing and Jurisdiction

In order to have standing under the Human Rights Law, individuals must demonstrate that they have suffered an injury based upon their conviction record and that they fall within a zone of interest which the statute protects.[48] An employer is liable for discrimination pursuant to Correction Law Article 23-A and New York Executive Law 296 §15 as long as they have 10 employees or more.[49] As of October 27, 2015 the New York City Commission will take complaints if an employer has 4 or more employees based on arrest and conviction record.

---

[41] *Elmsford Transportation Corp. v. Schuler, 63 A.D.2d 1036, 1037 (3d Dep't 1978)* ("[It is ... firmly established that the burden of showing entitlement to an exemption from a statute rests on the party claiming its benefit.") (citing *Grace v. New York State Tax Comm'n, 37 N.Y.2d 193 (1975)*).

[42] ("In making a determination pursuant to Section [752], the public agency or private employer shall consider the [eight] factors[.]") (*citing Correction Law § 753*);

[43] *Matter of Luther Dempsey v New York City Department of Education, et al. 2015 NY Slip Op 04028*

[44] *Haddock v. New York, 553 N.E.2d 987, 992 (N.Y. 1990)*

[45] *Stewart v Civil Service Commission of New York City, 84 A.D. 2d 491, 493-94 (1st Dept. 1982)* "The purpose of the Executive Law and Correction Law provisions was not to give ex-convicts preferred treatment, not to cloak their prior criminal records in secrecy. Rather it was to create reasonable standards to be applied by potential employers....when considering applications by former offenders, no such standards having previously existed."

[46] *Grant v. State. Com. for Human Rights, 54 Misc.2d 775, 283 N.Y.S.2d 486*

[47] *State Division of Human Rights (Maymi) v. Sorrento Cheese Co., Inc., 115 A.D. 2d 323, 495 N.Y.S. 2d 865 (4th Dept. 1985).* "It is as much a violation of the Human Rights Law to discriminate against a person because of an arrest or conviction for a criminal offense as it is to discriminate against that person because of an erroneously perceived conviction for a crime.

[48] *Dunn v Fishbein, 123 A.D. 2d 659, 660, 507 N.Y.S. 2d 29 (2d Dept. 1986)*

[49] *Correction Law § 750(2)*

The Human Rights Laws require an individual to demonstrate the employers discriminatory actions if the company had an actual impact in New York.[50] New York Correction Law 23-A works in conjunction with The New York Human Rights Law, located at Executive Law 296, Section 15. The law states that *"It shall be an unlawful discriminatory practice for any person, agency, bureau, corporation or association, including the state and any political subdivision thereof, to deny any license or employment to any individual by reason of his or her having been convicted of one or more criminal offenses, or by reason of a finding of a lack of "good moral character"*[51] *which is based upon his or her having been convicted of one or more criminal offenses, when such denial is in violation of the provisions of article twenty- three-A of the correction law."*

G - The New York Division of Human Rights and Private Employers

The Division of Human Rights accepts complaints based on arrest and conviction record of private employers. It is the Division's responsibility, *"to receive, investigate and pass upon complaints alleging violations of this article."*[52] It is the Division's duty to determine if a potential complainant is actually an aggrieved person within the meaning of the Human Rights Law.[53] The Division has determined it does cover on the job training programs and apprenticeship programs where applicants with conviction records because these are entry points and Article 23-A specifically covers vocational and occupational employment.[54]

A person may file with the Division but not with the courts and vice versa on the same issue. This is referred to as an election of remedies. A person must choose where they file carefully. Actions in the Division of Human Rights must be within 1 year and actions against private employers are governed by the provisions of New York Executive Law 297 (9) for 3 years in court and against public employers by the guidelines established in Article 78 of the CPLR within 120 days of the adverse action. State agencies are considered public employers.

H - Who Does Correction Law Article 23-A Not Cover?

Cases where the Federal Law controls or bars an applicant based on acts of Congress from an employment position render Article 23-A unenforceable. This includes but is not limited to certain banking laws, federal post office jobs, federal employee jobs, jobs with the Navy, Marines or Army, certain Airport positions and federal government positions that can require clearance. The New York Human Rights Law does not apply to the Port Authority of New York and New Jersey because it is a bi-state agency created by compact.[55] New York Correction Law Article 23-A also cannot be used in appraising fitness of former criminal offenders who are in prison training programs.[56] New York Correction Law Article 23-A does not cover employers with less than 10 employees at anytime within a calendar year. This divests the Division and the courts of the proper jurisdiction under the statute to decide the case and is a defense that can be claimed by a Respondent at any time. New York Executive Law § 296.15 only applies to persons applying for employment previously convicted of a criminal offense and does not apply to those who have no conviction record.[57]

New York State Correction Law Article 23-A does not cover violations. A "violation" is the least serious type of criminal offense, and imprisonment can be for no more than fifteen days. While all three types are criminal offenses, only a felony or misdemeanor in New York may be referred to as a "crime" by operation of the explicit definition contained in the Penal Law and may be asked on an application for employment.[58] New York Law Correction Law Article 23-A does not cover arrests, as that is covered under a different section of the Human Rights Law.[59] This is because an arrest record is a separate class from conviction record in New York with different protections. A vacated conviction is not covered by New York Correction Law Article 23-A.[60]

---

[50] *Pearce v. Manhattan Ensemble Theater, Inc., 2007 WL 707068*
[51] *N.Y. Executive Law § 297.5*
[52] *New York Executive Law § 295.6.*
[53] *Cumberbatch v Lytle, 55 Misc. 2d 1041, 287 N.Y.S. 2d 132 Sup. Ct. Erie Co. 1967.*
[54] *General Counsel Legal Opinion 2010-04*
[55] *Mack v. Port Authority of New York and New Jersey, 225 F.Supp.2d 376 (2002)*
[56] *Brown v. Berry (3 Dept. 1989) 151 A.D.2d 882, 543 N.Y.S.2d 179, appeal dismissed 74 N.Y.2d 944, 550 N.Y.S.2d 277, 549 N.E.2d 479.*
[57] *Green v Wells Fargo Alarm Service 192 A.D. 463 ,596 N.Y.S. 2d 412 (1993)*
[58] *Penal Law § 10.00 (6)*
[59] *N.Y. Exec. Law § 296 (16)*
[60] *Markman v New York State Dept. of Educ., 131 A.D. 2d 908, 516 N.Y.S. 2d 359 (1987), Schwarz v. Consolidated Edison, Inc., 2015 NY Slip Op 25258*

I - 1976 Changes to the Certificate of Relief of Civil Disabilities and the Certificate of Good Conduct

In 1976, the current Certificates of Relief from Disabilities and Certificates of Good Conduct were chosen to be defined by the legislature at <u>N.Y. Corrections Law, Art. 23, §§700- 706</u> and its usage as a factor of employment was incorporated into the new provisions of the <u>New York Correction Law Article 23-A</u> in order *"to reduce the automatic rejection and community isolation that often accompany conviction of crimes"* and *"contribute to the complete rehabilitation of first offenders and their successful return to responsible lives in the community."* The purpose of the CRD or CGC since 1976 is to effectuate the public policy *"to encourage the licensure and employment"* of convicted individuals.

Additionally, <u>Correction Law §753(1)(a)</u> recognizes that it is the public policy of New York State to *"encourage the licensure and employment of persons previously convicted of one or more criminal offenses."* <u>Correction Law §753(2)</u> further establishes that with respect to a "public agency" or "private employer", a certificate "shall create a presumption of rehabilitation in regard to the offense or offenses specified therein." Such certificates are consistent with 2006 statutory change to the general purposes of the Penal Law (PL), specifically <u>PL§1.05(6)</u>, which added the concept of reentry and reintegration by referring to *"the promotion of ... successful and productive reentry and reintegration into society..."* of offenders. New York, through its public policy to encourage the reintegration of ex-offenders did not require a certificate because they did not pass bans on public assistance, food stamps or student loans for people with convictions. In addition, voting rights are automatically restored upon release from state prison and are never lost for those only sentenced to probation.[61]

J - Eligibility for Certificate of Relief and Certificate of Good Conduct

<u>Article 23 of the Correction Law §700</u> establishes that a person is eligible to receive a Certificate of Relief from Disabilities if he/she has been convicted of a crime or of an offense, but has not been convicted of more than one felony. A "felony" means a conviction of a felony in this state or of an offense in any other jurisdiction for which a sentence to a term of imprisonment in excess of one year, or a sentence of death, was authorized. Two or more convictions of felonies charged in separate counts of one indictment or information or two or more convictions of felonies charged in two or more indictments or informations, filed in the same court prior to judgment under any of them, shall be considered only one conviction. Additionally, a plea or verdict of guilty upon which a sentence or the execution of a sentence has been suspended or upon which a sentence of probation, conditional discharge or unconditional discharge has been imposed, shall be considered a conviction.

In general, <u>Correction Law §701</u> provides that a certificate may relieve an eligible offender of any forfeiture or disability, or remove any bar to employment, automatically imposed by law by reason of conviction of the crime or the offense. A conviction for a crime specified in a Certificate of Relief from Disabilities shall not cause automatic forfeiture of any license, permit, employment or franchise, including the right to register for or vote at an election, or automatic forfeiture of any other right or privilege, held by the eligible offender and covered by the certificate. A certificate also does not permit the convicted person to retain or be eligible for public office, nor does it void the conviction as if it were a pardon (see <u>Correction Law §§701 and 706</u>).

A certificate cannot in any way prevent any judicial, administrative, licensing or other body, board or authority from relying upon the conviction specified therein as the basis for exercise of its discretionary power to suspend, revoke, refuse to issue or refuse to renew any license, permit or other authority or privilege.[62] If the individual has one of these certificate documents, the employer must presume that the employee has been rehabilitated in regard to the prior conviction. The statutory presumption of rehabilitation resulting from a Certificate of Relief from Disabilities *"imposes a burden on respondents to come forward with evidence to rebut it."*[63] The same presumption of rehabilitation will result from a Certificate of Good Conduct.

K - Is A Certificate of Good Conduct The Same as a Certificate of Relief of Civil Disabilities?

Most recently under Governor David Patterson on June 22, 2010 the Certificate of Relief of Civil Disabilities and the Certificate of Good Conduct were made equivalent and now remove the exact same disabilities under law where either a CRD is specified or a COGC is specified. This includes Notary Public, which is a public office held to be originally only removed by a COGC.[64]

---

[61] Debbie A. Mukamal & Paul N. Samuels, *Statutory Limitations on Civil Rights of People with Criminal Records, 30 Fordham URB LJ. 1501 (2003).*

[62] *Correction Law §701(3)*

[63] *(Marra v City of White Plains, 96 A.D. 2d 17, 24 [2d Dept 1983]).(See Arrocha v Board of Educ. of City of New York, 93 N.Y. 2d 361, 365 [1999]; Peluso v Smith, 142 Misc 2d 642, 649 [Sup Ct, New York County 1989]; Camulaire, supra).*

[64] Legal Action Center: at url: *http://lac.org/index.php/lac/521*

A Certificate of Good Conduct is only issued by the Board of Parole. A Certificate of Good Conduct applies to those who have more than one felony and any number of misdemeanors. The only two things a Certificate of Good Conduct can do now that a Certificate of Relief of Civil Disabilities cannot do are restore the right to public office and the right to possess a firearm. In cases in which the most serious conviction is a misdemeanor, there must be at least one year of satisfactory community adjustment before a Certificate of Good Conduct can be considered. In cases in which the most serious conviction is a C, D or E felony, an applicant must wait at least three years. In cases in which the most serious conviction is an A or B felony, an applicant must wait at least five years.

If an applicant has been convicted of a felony, they lose the right to vote. This right is automatically restored when someone completes their maximum sentence or are discharged by the Board of Parole. If an applicant is issued a Certificate of Relief from Disabilities or a Certificate of Good Conduct while on parole, they may register to vote.

If a person is currently on probation or parole the certificate becomes permanent once they complete their probationary or parole mandated terms. It is also of note that only "persons" may obtain a certificate of relief, a business or corporation has no such ability to get a document if it is convicted of a felony under New York State Law.[65] It is also of note that there is no specific time frame as to when a judge or parole board must respond to the request for the Certificate. If a judge or parole board deny the Certificate, they must either grant (in whole or in part) or deny petitioner's application for a CRD and consider and apply the statutorily enumerated factors set forth in Correction Law § 702 (2). The absence of any mention of the statutory factors or the grounds for the denial precludes meaningful review of the rationality of the decision. The Appellate Court can review either a parole or individual courts Certificate denial if the basis is found to be arbitrary, capricious, one-sided or not rationally based on the record created.[66]

L - Presumption of Rehabilitation Only One Of 8 Factors To Consider

The presumption of rehabilitation created by the certificate of relief from disabilities applies even where the statutory definition of "direct relationship" (Correction Law § 750 [3]) has been satisfied. Thus the licensing agency or employer must consider the eight factors listed in Correction Law § 753 (1) (a)-(h) to determine whether, in fact, the "direct relationship" is sufficiently attenuated to warrant issuance of the license.[67] While the licensing agency is not required to conduct a public hearing, such may only deny a license after making the determinations required by the Legislature, under Correction Law § 752, after mandatory consideration of the eight factors under Correction Law § 753 (1) (a)-(h).

If the agency or employer considers all eight factors listed in Correction Law § 753 (1), it need not in every case produce independent evidence to rebut the presumption of rehabilitation before denying a license. In some cases, consideration of other factors such as the severity of the criminal offense(s), the passage of time (between the offenses and the application) and the nature of the license sought, can warrant denial of the license despite the absence of new specific evidence directed at overcoming the presumption of rehabilitation.

In other cases, the failure of the agency to rebut the presumption of rehabilitation with evidence suggesting no rehabilitation will result in an arbitrary and capricious determination.[68] The presumption of rehabilitation is an important factor in determining whether the license or employment will be granted. However, the factors in Correction Law § 753 must also be examined and considered well as used to rebut the presumption of rehabilitation.

Presumption of rehabilitation created by certificate of good conduct applies, even when applicant's prior conviction directly related to license or employment sought; because presumption applies, agency or employer must consider statutory factors to determine whether direct relationship is sufficiently attenuated to warrant issuance of license or employment.[69] A certificate of relief from disabilities does not authorize a job applicant with a criminal record to deny on an employment application that he has ever been convicted of a crime, but the employer must consider the certificate, which establishes a presumption of rehabilitation as to the criminal offenses specified in the certificate.[70] Unless a certificate of relief or good conduct is obtained, where a bar to employment is imposed by law, the provisions of Human Rights Law are not applicable.[71]

---

[65] *People of the State of New York v. Eastco Building Services 23 Misc.3d 864 (2009) 873 N.Y.S.2d 874.*

[66] *Jason Figel v Paul F. Dwyer, Town Justice 75 A.D.3d 802 (2010) 907 N.Y.S.2d 75*

[67] *Matter of Marra v City of White Plains, 96 A.D. 2d 17, 23 [2d Dept 1983]; 1985 Opns Atty Gen 14*

[68] *Matter of Bonacorsa v Van Lindt, 71 N.Y.2d 605, 614, supra*

[69] *Bonacorsa v. Van Lindt, 1988, 71 N.Y.2d 605, 528 N.Y.S.2d 519, 523 N.E.2d 806.*

[70] *1981 Op.Atty.Gen.(Inf.) 281.*

[71] *Dounn v. Ross (3 Dept. 1979) 71 A.D.2d 746, 419 N.Y.S.2d 251*

M - Applicability of Certificate of Relief To Remove Statutory Barriers

A certificate cannot overcome automatic forfeiture resulting from convictions for violations of Public Health Law §2806(5)[72] or Vehicle and Traffic Law (VTL) §1193(2) (b).[73] This is because these particular instances are limited by court cases that resulted in legislative amendments to the law. In 1983, New York's Article 23 of the Correction Law and the Public Health Law were amended to require automatic mandatory suspension of nursing home operator licenses when a person was convicted of an industry-related felony, regardless of whether the person held a Certificate of Relief.

In 1985, the legislature followed with an amendment preventing Certificates of Relief from removing the automatic suspension of a driver's license when a person is convicted of driving while intoxicated. Allowing a person with a certificate to maintain the license after a DWI conviction would have cost New York federal funding and was determined to run counter to the DMV policy concerning license rehabilitation. However, courts have found as a matter of law that a convicted felon who has been granted a certificate of relief under Correction Law § 701 may own and possess any firearm except those firearms requiring a New York State pistol permit (Penal Law § 400.00) or otherwise deemed illegal to possess by State law.[74]

Further, a conviction for a second or subsequent violation of any subdivision of VTL §1192 within the preceding 10 years imposes a disability to apply for or receive an operator's license during the period provided in such law. Under New York Banking Law§ 369 (6), which governs the licensing of those providing check cashing services, does retain an exception for those convicted of a crime who possess a certificate of relief in that they are not automatically denied a license. They must still, however, be approved by the Banking Department which may deny a license notwithstanding the applicant's possession of a certificate of relief.[75]

Consequently, applicants with an unpardoned felony conviction involving fraud, dishonesty or a breach of trust, as of July 11, 2009, the effective date of Article 12-E, cannot be licensed as an Mortgage Loan Officer in New York State.[76] The court has determined that Article 23-A of the Correction Law does not have any application to youthful offenders and was not intended to give them any rights.[77] Employment with a law enforcement agency is specifically exempted from the reach of the statute.[78] While Correction Law § 752 certainly permits employment of a person who has been convicted of a crime of dishonesty and extends so far as to prohibit denying employment to a person convicted of a crime of dishonesty except when specified considerations pertain, holding an office, public or private, is not an application for employment. Therefore, even if a union or agency pays wages for an individual to hold service in the office to which they were elected, the election, rather than application, places such issue outside the statutory confines of Correction Law § 752's scope.[79]

An ex-offender who gets a criminal history report (known as a "rap sheet") from the Division of Criminal Justice should see that a Certificate of Relief or the Certificate of Good Conduct has been granted if a public or private employer views a background check. This rap sheet can be obtained for a nominal fee for accuracy from the Division of Criminal Justice and is recommended before seeking employment to ensure truthfulness of one's conviction record.

[72] *Hodes v. Axelrod. 1983 N.Y. St. Legis. Ann 2629-31.*

[73] *1985 N.Y. ST. LEGIS. ANN. 258; Ex. 7*

[74] *People v Flook 164 Misc. 2d 284, 625 N.Y.S. 2d 405 (1995), Matter of Alarie, 168 Misc. 2d 329, 643 N.Y.S. 2d 926 (1996)* The applicants herein, by virtue of their respective certificates of relief, may own, possess and use long guns (shotguns and rifles) legally allowed for hunting in the State of New York and are not barred from taking the safety courses and obtaining a New York State hunting license. No special notations are needed on a certificate of relief for such activity.

[75] *Matter of City Servs., Inc. v Neiman, 77 A.D. 3d 505 [1st Dept 2010]*

[76] *RAMPOLLA v. State of New York, 31 Misc. 3d 161*

[77] *Correction Law, § 751; see, also, People v Doe, 52 Misc 2d 656.), Perez v New York State Human Rights Appeal Board 71 A.D.2d 150 (1979)*

[78] *Correction Law § 750 [5]*

[79] *Scarlino v Fathi 38 Misc.3d 883 , 57 N.Y.S.2d 565, 2012 NY Slip Op 22388 (2012)*

PART III

ELEMENTS OF A CORRECTION LAW ARTICLE 23-A CASE

In <u>Bonacorsa v Van Lindt</u>,[80] the Court provided the analytical framework that an employer must use in deciding whether to deny or terminate employment based on one of the exceptions. There, the Court confirmed <u>New York Correction Law Article 23-A</u>'s mandate that an employer must consider and apply all eight factors before finding that the "direct relationship"[81] and/or "unreasonable risk" exception applies. Plainly, in applying the eight factors, employers and agencies must make an individualized determination as to how each factor relates to the applicant.[82]

Under <u>Bonacorsa</u>, any policy or procedure that permits the denial of employment to a former offender before all eight factors are considered and applied violates the statute. The statute does not permit a Respondent to deny an application solely on the basis of an applicant's previous conviction of a crime without inquiry into the 8 factors set forth in <u>Correction Law § 753 [1]</u> and which also include the applicant's moral character and possible rehabilitation as required for <u>Correction Law § 753 [2]</u> before a denial of employment can be reached. The courts have stated that any automatic ban of an ex-offender must be eliminated. *"The thrust of article 23-A is the elimination of automatic bans to employment whichare imposed solely as the result of a conviction without regard to whether the offense bears any relation to the character and fitness of the individual involved."* [83]

The statute defines a "direct relationship" as one in which the "nature of criminal conduct for which the person was convicted has a direct bearing on his fitness or ability to perform one or more of the duties or responsibilities necessarily related to the license or employment sought" (<u>Correction Law § 750 [3]</u>). In context of statutory factors warranting denial of employment or license to ex-offenders, direct relationship between one or more of license applicant's previous criminal offenses and specific license or employment sought can be found where applicant's prior conviction was for offense related to industry or occupation at issue or elements inherent in nature of criminal offense have direct impact on applicant's duty to perform duties necessarily related to license or employment sought.[84] It contains no similar definition of "unreasonable risk" for the obvious reason that a finding of unreasonable risk depends upon a subjective analysis of a variety of considerations relating to the nature of the license or employment sought and the prior misconduct.

State policy favors employment of previously convicted individuals when there is no direct relationship between offense and employment sought, and the granting application for employment would not involve unreasonable risk to property or safety or welfare of individuals or general public.[85] Before denying a license or employment under either the direct relationship or unreasonable risk[86] exceptions, however, the agency must consider the factors in <u>Article 23- A § 753 of the Correction Law</u>: *(a) The public policy of this state, as expressed in this act, to encourage the licensure and employment of persons previously convicted of one or more criminal offenses. (b) The specific duties and responsibilities necessarily related to the license or employment sought. (c) The bearing, if any, the criminal offense or offenses for which the person was previously convicted will have on his fitness or ability to perform one or more such duties or responsibilities. (d) The time which has elapsed since the occurrence of the criminal offense or offenses. (e) The age of the person at the time of occurrence of the criminal offense or offenses. (f) The seriousness of the offense or offenses. (g) Any information produced by the person, or produced on his behalf, in regard to his rehabilitation and good conduct. (h) The legitimate interest of the public agency or private employer in protecting property, and the safety of and welfare of specific individuals or the general public.*

The weighing of these factors cannot be a sham by the employer or done after the fact. The review cannot be an artificial exercise in order to seemingly meet statutory requirements while actually seeking a predetermined conclusion.[87] An employer must be prepared to demonstrate that they used the factors before denying the applicant, including asking for all evidence of rehabilitation as going through each factor and applying it on a case by case basis to that particular applicant. The failure to take into consideration each

---

[80] *71 N.Y.2d at 613-14 (N.Y. 1988)*

[81] Section 750 of the Corrections Law defines "direct relationship" to mean that the nature of criminal conduct for which the person was convicted has a direct bearing on his fitness or ability to perform one or more of the duties or responsibilities necessarily related to the license, opportunity, or job in question.

[82] *City of New York v. State Division of Human Rights, 70 N.Y.2d 100, 107 (1987)* "Employment may not be denied based on speculation and mere possibilities, especially when such determination is premised solely on the fact of an applicant's inclusion in a class of persons with a particular disability rather than upon an individualized assessment of the specific individual."

[83] *People of the State of New York v Honeckman and Vall, 125 Misc.2d 1000 (1984)*

[84] *Marra v. City of White Plains (2nd Dept. 1983) 96 A.D.2d 17, 467 N.Y.S.2d 865)*

[85] *Soto-Lopez v. New York City Civil Service Com'n, 713 F.Supp. 677 (1989)*

[86] There is no statutory definition as to what shall constitute an "unreasonable risk" under *Article 23-A § 752*

[87] Boatright v N.Y. Off of Mental Ret. & Dev. Disabilities, 2007 N.Y. Misc. LEXIS 3399, 237 N.Y.L.J. 85 (Sup. Ct. N.Y. 2007)

of these factors results in a failure to comply with the Correction Law's mandatory directive.[88] When all eight factors are considered and the positive factors are balanced against the negative factors, the resulting decision is neither arbitrary nor capricious nor does it constitute an abuse of discretion and reviewing courts may not reweigh the factors and substitute their judgment for that of the agency or employer.[89] Employers cannot make a determination based on a "general catchall statement" nor penalize an applicant for not providing information that the employer or agency never requested.[90] The same public policy that prohibits discrimination in hiring on the basis of a criminal record prohibits discrimination in terminating employment on the basis of a criminal record.[91]

It is also recommended that before an applicant file a case with the courts or the New York Division of Human Rights based on conviction record that the denying public or private agency provide a written statement delineating the reasons for the denial of their employment application, pursuant to Correction Law, Article 23-A, § 754 within 30 days of request. While there are no formal decisions pertaining to this part of the Correction Law, it is clearly actionable in a state court proceeding in order to compel a Respondent to produce the reason for denial of the employment application.[92]

A - Cases of Conviction Record Discrimination Filed With The New York Division of Human Rights

The State Division of Human Rights accepts complaints from those who identify themselves as having one or more convictions. The only requirement is that a complaint have a notarization on it to be accepted for processing by the agency. The State Division of Human Rights can only review alleged unlawful discriminatory events that contain a notarization and investigate claims that occurred within a statutory year period.[93]

A dismissal by the Division for no probable cause is the administrative equivalent of a grant of summary judgment; and to obtain such a dismissal a respondent "must demonstrate either [complainant's] failure to establish every element of intentional discrimination, or, having offered legitimate, nondiscriminatory reasons for their challenged actions, the absence of a material issue of fact as to whether their explanations were pre-textual."

If the complainant demonstrates the existence of a material issue of fact, the case must proceed to a hearing. [94] Under New York law, a determination by the Division of Human Rights (DHR) that there is no probable cause is made by something less than proof by a preponderance of the evidence.[95] To appeal this Final Order dismissal by the agency, a person must file against all named parties and the Division of Human Rights (through its General Counsel) (known in the courts as Executive Law §298) which states that the court's review of a determination of the Division of Human Rights, consists of whether the determination (after the agency submits the complete record) was made in violation of lawful procedure, was affected by an error of law or was arbitrary and capricious or an abuse of discretion, including abuse of discretion as to the measure or mode of penalty imposed.[96] This must be done within 60 days from the date of the decision. Executive Law § 298 not Article 78 governs exclusively judicial review of Division final orders after dismissal and after a public hearing.[97] A challenge to a public agency's violation of Article 23-A of the Correction Law is raised by a CPLR Article 78 proceeding, not the Division of Human Rights.[98]

B - Preliminary Investigation and the Prima Facie Burden of Complainant

A claim of conviction record discrimination under the New York Human Rights Law is also subject to the burden-shifting analysis applied to discrimination claims under Title VII.[99] Under both laws the plaintiff (or the complainant) has to establish the "minimal" prima facie case defined by the Supreme Court in McDonnell

---

[88] *Matter of Arrocha v Board of Education of the City of New York, 93 N.Y.2d 361, 364 (1999)*

[89] *Matter of Gallo v. State of N.Y., Off. of Mental Retardation & Dev. Disabilities, 37 A.D. 3d at 985*

[90] *Black v. N.Y. State Office of Mental Retardation & Developmental Disabilities 858 N.Y.S.2d at 863-4*

[91] *Givens v.New York City Housing Authority (1 Dept. 1998) 249 A.D.2d 133, 671 N.Y.S.2d 479.*

[92] *Sinicropi v McCabe 123 A.D.2d 756 (1986)*

[93] *Miller v. General Elec. Co. (3 Dept. 1984) 102 A.D.2d 966, 477 N.Y.S.2d 834*

[94] *Falk v. Goodman, 7 N.Y.2d 87, 91 (1959)* ("It is well established that summary judgment may not be granted whenever the pleadings raise clear, well-defined and genuine issues; nor may it be granted whenever there is doubt as to the existence of a triable issue or when the issue is arguable since issue-finding, rather than issue- determination, is the key to the procedure. This is so because the granting of such a motion is the procedural equivalent of a trial.")

[95] *Kosakow v. New Rochelle Radiology Associates, P.C., C.A.2 (N.Y.) 274 F.3d 706 (2001)*

[96] *CPLR 7803(3); see Windsor Place Corp, v New York State DHCR, 161 A.D. 2d 279 [1st Dept 1990]; Mazel v DHCR, 138 A.D. 2d 600 [1st Dept 1988]; Bambeck v DHCR, 129 A.D. 2d 51 [1st Dept 1987], lv denied 70 N.Y. 2d 615 [1988]).*

[97] *Matter of State Commission for Human Rights v Lieber, 23 N.Y. 2d 253, 296, N.Y.S. 2d 319 (1968); Maloff v Commission on Human Rights 45 A.D.3d 834, 357 N.Y.S. 2d 513 (1st Dept 1974).*

[98] *Article 23-A § 755(1) of the Correction Law*

[99] *Spiegel v. Schulmann, 604 F.3d 72, 80 (2d CiT. 2010)*

Douglas Corp. v.Green, 411 U.S. 792 (1973). The specifics of a prima facie case will inevitably vary and are dependent upon the type and circumstances of the employment action under attack.[100] The New York State Court of Appeals adopted the Supreme Court's McDonnell Douglas Corp. v.Green, 411 U.S. 792 (1973) decision. As a result, the burden of proof outlined in the case applies to causes of action under the New York State Human Rights Law concerning conviction record.[101]

Where a plaintiff is alleging that he was denied employment based on conviction record, plaintiff must show that (1) he is a member of a protected class; (2) he was competent to perform the job in question, or was performing the job duties satisfactorily; (3) he suffered an adverse employment action; and (4) the action occurred under circumstances that give rise to an inference of discrimination.[102] The employer need only produce admissible evidence which would allow the Trier of Fact rationally to conclude that the employment decision had not been motivated by discriminatory animus. First, the defendant's explanation of its legitimate reasons must be clear and reasonably specific. Second, although the defendant does not bear a formal burden of persuasion, the defendant nevertheless retains an incentive to persuade the Trier of Fact that the employment decision was lawful.[103]

Once a prima facie case is established, the burden of production shifts to Respondent to rebut the presumption of unlawful discrimination by clearly articulating legitimate, nondiscriminatory reasons for Complainant's denial of employment. The ultimate burden rests with Complainant to show that Respondent's proffered explanations are a pretext for unlawful discrimination.[104] For a plaintiff to prevail, Plaintiff must point to evidence that reasonably supports a finding of prohibited discrimination otherwise the defendant is entitled to a dismissal of the case.[105]

Once a person establishes that they have a conviction record in New York, an applicant must be qualified for the position to have standing to bring a claim for discrimination unless they were deterred from the job for unlawful reasons or that doing so would be a futile gesture. If the applicant does not possess the qualifications for the job they are applying to they cannot perform the job duties and the employer can successfully argue that they do not meet the requirements for the position and that they can be denied on that legitimate non-discriminatory basis.[106] It has been established that for plaintiff to succeed they must show that he or she has a conviction, applied or was not required to apply, is qualified for the position and was rejected under circumstances giving rise to an inference of discrimination.[107]

To demonstrate that he/she was qualified for the position, a Title VII plaintiff need only show that he or she satisfied an employer's objective qualifications."[108] *"Where there are objective criteria for employment or promotion, ...[t]he plaintiff either has the qualifications or does not." Subjective criteria are given little to no weight. Allowing an employer to escape liability simply by articulating vague, inoffensive-sounding subjective criteria would disserve Title VII's goal of eradicating discrimination in employment."*[109] Furthermore, in a situation where an advertisement has chilled a member of a protected class and Respondent asserts that Plaintiff did not meet all the qualifications a Complainant could put forth that by so narrowly defining the acceptable work experience the Respondent was attempting to carry out their intent that no one with a criminal record would be named to the advertised job. *"Plaintiff's direct evidence of discrimination, together with the reasonable inferences from the discrepancy between the posted job responsibilities and ... narrow interpretation of the minimum qualifications, create a genuine issue of fact as to whether the defendants invented their narrow interpretation of the job qualifications with the intention of discriminating against...applicants."*[110]

---

[100] *See McDonnell Douglas, 411 U.S. at 802 n.13(1973)*

[101] *Miller Brewing Company v.New York State Division of Human Rights, 66 N.Y. 2d 937.*

[102] *McCoy v People Care Inc., Slip Copy, 2013 WL 5313433 [S.D.N.Y. 2013]* (finding no evidence from which to infer that decision not to hire plaintiff was due to her prior convictions where denial of employment was based on interviewer's interactions with plaintiff and observation of plaintiff's behavior while completing the job application, and no reference was made in employer's notes to plaintiff's convictions, but on her inability to follow instructions).

[103] *Texas Department of Community Affairs v. Burdine, 450 U.S. 248, --, 101 S.Ct. 1089, 1096, 67 L.Ed.2d 207 (1981) ("Burdine"). See also Furnco, supra, 438 U.S. at 577, 98 S.Ct. at 2949; Ste. Marie, supra, 650 F.2d at 399.*

[104] *Mittl v.New York State Div. of Human Rights, 100 N.Y.2d 326, 330, 763 N.Y.S.2d 518, 520 (2003).*

[105] *Fisher v. Vassar College, 114 F.3d 1332 (2d Cir.1997)); cf. Kravit v. Delta Air Lines, No. CV-92-0038, 1992 WL 390236, at 2 (E.D.N.Y. Dec.4, 1992) (applying the above legal framework to a Section 296(15) claim); 381 Ferrante v. Am. Lung Assoc., 90 N.Y.2d 623, 629-31, 665 N.Y.S.2d 25, 687 N.E.2d 1308 (1997).*

[106] *Bodley v New York Hosp.,1988 WKL 61976 at 4 (S.D.N.Y. June 8, 1988)* "An essential element of a prima facie case is that plaintiff must be qualified for the position."

[107] *Pelaez v. Life Alert, Inc., No. 09-CV-1688, 2011 U.S. Dist. LEXIS 34964, at 12-13 (E.D.N.Y. Mar. 30, 2011)*

[108] *Vessels v. Atlanta Independent School System, 408 F. 3d 763, 769 (11th Cir. 2005).*

[109] *Watson v. Fort Worth Bank & Trust, 487 U.S. 977, 1010 (1988). See also, Mandell v. County of Suffolk, 316 F.3d 368, 381 (2d Cir. 2003)* ("We have previously cautioned that an employer may not rely solely on wholly subjective and unarticulated standards as a basis for its promotion decisions.").

[110] *Burns v. Gadsden State Community College, 908 F. 2d 1512 (11th Cir. 1990)*

The next step if an applicant is qualified is to prove proof of the rejection, which can be obtained through use of a background check, interview denial or a letter of denial from the employer or agency (known as an adverse action letter) indicating the applicant will not be hired or offered the employment.

In many instances, an employer may be required by a government contract to perform a criminal background or security check on an applicant. A background check is legal and it serves the purpose of confirming the conviction record on the application. However, employers are not relieved of the obligation to comply with Corrections Law § 752 when conducting background checks or security checks. A third party background check company usually conducts the check and is the one that sends out the adverse action letter as required by law. As later discussed, a third party background check can be held liable under the Human Rights Law as an aider and abettor who participates in the unlawful conduct being made through the allegations.

An employer cannot use the background check or security check as the sole basis of denial or score a conviction a grade via a matrix or adjudication guideline if it fails to utilize the Correction Law in its analysis. In performing this analysis, the employer should consider all of the factors in Article 23-A of the Correction Law §753 that are relevant. All evidence submitted for consideration by the applicant or employee must be reviewed and considered, including Certificates of Relief of Civil Disabilities or Certificates of Good Conduct. Further, the applicant or employee should be given an opportunity to be heard. Finally, regardless of whether the decision is made to hire or not to hire the applicant, the employer should explain how it weighed the Corrections Law §753 factors and arrived at its conclusion in writing. Once a decision has been made and an ex-offender is denied they can ask for a written statement per Article 23-A of the Correction Law §754 within 30 days of the adverse employment decision.

The Division at its discretion will hold pre-hearing and settlement conferences. A Complainant is expected to participate in these proceedings and often times the matter can be resolved without a hearing. A Complainant before the hearing can ask for an Order of Annulment which allows a person to proceed in court as if the Division action never took place.

C - Limitations of the Courts and the Division of Human Rights

Under New York State Human Rights Law, direct filing of complaint with State Division of Human Rights by an aggrieved party constitutes election of remedies and results in loss of right to sue in state court.[111] If there is a protracted delay of more than seven years between filing of complaint against employer by State Division of Human Rights and determination of Hearing Commissioner, this can cause prejudice to an employer egregious enough to warrant a suasponte exercise of discretion which would procedurally grant the employer more protection than the petitioner as a matter of law and warrant a dismissal of complaint against employer.[112] Division's proceedings can be invalidated and its jurisdiction terminated where even four years and two months have elapsed.[113] There must, however, be some prejudice demonstrated that the employer is suffering because of the delay. The mere passage of time does not constitute substantial prejudice.[114]

Under New York law, a determination by the Division of Human Rights (DHR) that there is no probable cause to believe that a termination is the result of discrimination is made by something less than proof by a preponderance of the evidence.[115] Under the New York State Human Rights Law (NYSHRL), the employee bears the ultimate burden of proving intentional discrimination by a preponderance of the evidence; to satisfy this burden, employee must prove that the alleged impermissible consideration was a determinative factor in the adverse employment action about which she complains.[116] A Regional director of State Division of Human Rights has discretion to determine and conduct the most suitable investigation for a particular case; however, the complainant must be afforded an opportunity to rebut evidence submitted by or obtained from the respondents before the complaint may be dismissed for no probable cause.[117]

---

[111] *Long v. AT & T Information Systems, Inc., 733 F.Supp. 188 (1990)*

[112] *State Division of Human Rights on Complaint of Schilagi v. Bethlehem Steel Corp. (4 Dept. 1982) 86 A.D.2d 977, 448 N.Y.S.2d 331. Civil Rights 1708 (1982)*

[113] *State Division of Human Rights on Complaint of Eggers v. Board of Ed. of School Dist. of City of Niagara Falls (4 Dept. 1977) 59 A.D.2d 1048, 399 N.Y.S.2d 805. Civil Rights 1708 (1977)*

[114] *State Division of Human Rights v. City School Dist., Rochester, N. Y. (4 Dept. 1980) 75 A.D.2d 1009, 429 N.Y.S.2d 322 (1980)*

[115] *Kosakow v. New Rochelle Radiology Associates, P.C., C.A.2 (N.Y.) 274 F.3d 706. Civil Rights 1710 (2001) 116 Gross v. National Broadcasting Co., Inc., 232 F.Supp.2d 58. Civil Rights 1137; Civil Rights 1535; Civil Rights 1744 (2002)*

[116] *Gross v. National Broadcasting Co., Inc., 232 F.Supp.2d 58. Civil Rights 1137; Civil Rights 1535; Civil Rights 1744 (2002)*

[117] *Soellner v. State Div. of Human Rights (2nd Dept. 1984) 100 A.D.2d 876, 474 N.Y.S.2d 135 (1984)*

In order to get a hearing on a conviction record matter there must be probable cause based on the investigatory record established by the Division of Human Rights. Probable cause exists where there is a reasonable ground for suspicion founded on the facts and circumstances strong enough in themselves to warrant a cautious person to believe that the Human Rights Law is being violated.[118] It is no more than a determination by a Division regional director that there should be a formal hearing on the complaint.[119] The purpose of the hearing is to create a factual record as the basis for the Commissioner to render a final decision on the merits of the case. When in doubt, an administrative law judge will tend to allow a document rather than prevent its use in order to establish the most complete record. A hearing must be held, and a decision on the merits rendered based on the testimony and written record established. The public hearing is a quasi-judicial proceeding which the rules of evidence do not strictly apply.

The Court of Appeals has clearly established that New York favors broad and effective enforcement of the discrimination laws. The "`subtle and elusive'" methods which often characterize discriminatory practices and the strong State policy in favor of the eradication of discrimination, combined with the burden of proof placed on plaintiff in these actions, requires courts to insure that plaintiffs are afforded broad and thorough discovery.[120] In order to obtain a hearing on a charge of unlawful discriminatory practice, more than a simple question of fact must appear; hearing is required when questions of fact result from a conference and when, upon granting full credence, as the Division of Human Rights must, to complainant's version of the events, there is evidence of unlawful discrimination.[121]

D - What Can I Get if I Get A Probable Cause and Proceed To A Hearing?

Once a probable cause has been issued by the New York Division of Human Rights, a hearing is conducted. If a Respondent loses this hearing they can appeal through Executive Law §298[122] to challenge the Division of Human Rights decision in the matter, but so can the Complainant if he or she disagrees with the awarded amount of the basis of the decision. Courts reviewing a determination of the Division of Human Rights (DHR) made after a hearing in an employment discrimination case may not weigh the evidence or reject DHR's choice where the evidence is conflicting and room for a choice exists.[123]

Punitive damages are not awardable under the New York State Human Rights Law (SHRL) but are under the City Commission identical statute if the act occurs in the 5 boroughs of New York City.[124] A victim of employment discrimination has a duty to mitigate his or her damages by using reasonable diligence in finding other suitable employment. A victim need not accept employment that is not comparable to his or her previous position; but if he or she accepts less prestigious work, his or her earnings from that job are subtracted from his back pay award.

An employer must put forth any evidence during an employment discrimination case that suitable work existed or that a former employee did not make reasonable efforts to obtain it for them to prove the burden of a plaintiff's failure to mitigate.[125] Damages for emotional distress may not be presumed and are not established under New York law simply by evidence of a defendant's discriminatory conduct; however, such damages may be established by the plaintiff's testimony alone.[126] With respect to remedies for discriminatory practices, Commissioner of Human Rights has broad powers to adopt measures which he reasonably deems necessary to redress the injury including, but not limited to, directing reinstatement with back pay and awarding compensatory damages.[127] The remedial nature of the Human Rights Law evidences a legislative intent in New York to compensate fully victims of employment discrimination.[128] A policy which is not discriminatory in

---

[118] *Commissioner N.Y. State Dept of Civil Service v State Human Rights Appeal Board, 64. A.D. 2d 999, 408 N.Y.S. 2d 975 (3d Dep't 1978)*

[119] *Board of Educ.Of Tuxedo U.F.S.D. No. 3 v State Div. of Human Rights, 68 Misc. 2d 1035, 330 N.Y.S. 2d 274 (Sup Ct. Westch. Co 1972)*

[120] *State Div. of Human Rights v Kilian Mfg. Corp., supra, 35 NY2d, at 209*

[121] *State Division of Human Rights v. Buffalo Auto Glass Co., Inc. (4 Dept. 1973) 42 A.D.2d 678, 344 N.Y.S.2d 374. Civil Rights 1711 (1973)*

[122] This is used to appeal a no probable cause decision or to challenge a state agency final decision where a determination was made in violation of lawful procedure, was affected by an error of law or was arbitrary and capricious or an abuse of discretion, including abuse of discretion as to the measure or mode of penalty or discipline imposed. N.Y. CVP.LAW § 7803. There is a 60 day limit on actions brought through this appeal, even if dismissed by the Division of Human Rights.

[123] *Mittl v. New York State Div. of Human Rights, 100 N.Y.2d 326, 763 N.Y.S.2d 518, 794 N.E.2d 660, on remand 307 A.D.2d 881, 764 N.Y.S.2d 39. Civil Rights 1712 (2003)*

[124] *Tse v. UBS Financial Services, Inc., 568 F.Supp.2d 274. Civil Rights 1768 (2008)*

[125] *Epstein v. Kalvin-Miller Intern., Inc., 139 F.Supp.2d 469. Civil Rights 1573 (2001)*

[126] *Meacham v. Knolls Atomic Power Laboratory, 185 F.Supp.2d 193, affirmed 381 F.3d 56, vacated 125 S.Ct. 1731, 544 U.S. 957, 161 L.Ed.2d 596, on remand 461 F.3d 134 (2002), remanded 305 Fed.Appx. 748, 2009 WL 33609, on remand 627 F.Supp.2d 72. Damages 163(1); Damages 192*

[127] *Imperial Diner, Inc. v. State Human Rights Appeal Bd., 52 N.Y.2d 72, 436 N.Y.S.2d 231, 417 N.E.2d 525. Civil Rights 1711(1980)*

[128] *Boodram v. Brooklyn Developmental Center, 2 Misc.3d 574, 773 N.Y.S.2d 817 (2003)*

form or intent but which in actuality has that effect may constitute a violation of Article 15 of Executive Law 296.[129] A continuing violation of Human Rights Law may be found where there is proof of specific ongoing discriminatory policies or practices, or where specific and related instances of discrimination are permitted by the employer to continue remedied for so long as to amount to a discriminatory policy or practice.

A probable cause determination means that the investigator and director felt that there was enough to warrant a hearing on the matter. The legislature intends to give individuals who are victims of arrest and conviction discrimination the choice of either suing in court (a three year statute of limitations) and recovering all damages which they could establish including mental anguish, or electing to seek administrative relief under Human Rights Law (for which there is a one year statute of limitations) and take the matter to a hearing, if determined or annul the matter and then bring it into court.[130] The State Division attempts to conclude an investigation within 180 days of filing. Time limits applicable to the State Division of Human Rights are directory, not mandatory, and thus, absent any evidence of delay by petitioner or prejudice to petitioner's employer, an order of Division should not be annulled if it has exceeded statutory time limit from filing of complaint to date of its final order and determination.[131]

E - What is a CPLR Article 78 Proceeding?

In order to file a case against a public agency on the basis of conviction record you must file an Article 78 proceeding. New York CLS CPLR § 78 (known as an Article 78) encompasses three writs: mandamus, prohibition, and certiorari. The Article 78 must be brought within 120 days of the action in order to be timely with the court. At minimum, a Petitioner must file a Notice of Petition and Verified Petition. A writ is a formal, legal written order or document issued by an administrative body or judicial jurisdiction. An Article 78 proceeding serves as a uniform device to challenge the activities of an administrative agency in court, as well as an officer of the law, including town court and supreme court justices in the county where they reside and where the action took place.[132] It originated in 1937 as Article 78 of the Civil Practice Act, the CPLR's predecessor, to encompass the above mentioned 3 writs. By creating one proceeding to do the job of all three writs, the hope was to reduce the frequency of people accidentally doing the wrong writ. Mandamus compels action and only applies to purely ministerial duties. Prohibition prevents a body or officer from overstepping its jurisdiction. The third writ, certiorari, reviews Administrative determinations post hearing. Article 78 cases often straddle the line between these writs.

According to CPLR § 7803, the following are the only applicable questions that should be raised in an Article 78 proceeding: 1. whether the body or officer failed to perform a duty Enjoined upon it by law; or 2. whether the body or officer proceeded, is proceeding or is about to proceed without or in excess of jurisdiction; or 3. whether a determination was made in violation of lawful procedure, was affected by an error of law or was arbitrary and capricious or an abuse of discretion, including abuse of discretion as to the measure or mode of penalty or discipline imposed; or 4. whether a determination made as a result of a hearing held, and at which evidence was taken, pursuant to direction by law is, on the entire record, supported by substantial evidence.

The remedies of certiorari to review, mandamus and prohibition, which were three distinct remedies, each designed for a different type of wrong, were part of the law of England and became part of the law of New York. When the former Civil Practice Act was adopted and became effective in 1921, they were continued, but the writ practice was abolished in favor of an order. In 1937 the New York Legislature abolished these writs and combined the remedies under a proceeding against a body or officer in Article 78 of the Civil Practice Act. Article 78 of the Civil Practice Act was superseded in 1963 by the present Article 78 of the CPLR (23 Carmody-Wait 2d, New York Practice, § 145:1, page 423), CPLR 7801 being in part as follows:

"Relief previously obtained by writs of certiorari to review, mandamus or prohibition shall be obtained in a proceeding under this article. Wherever in any statute reference is made to a writ or order of certiorari, mandamus or prohibition, such reference shall, so far as applicable, be deemed to refer to the proceeding authorized by this article."

---

[129] *New York Institute of Technology v. State Div. of Human Rights (1 Dept. 1975) 48 A.D.2d 132, 368 N.Y.S.2d 207 (1975), appeal granted 37 N.Y.2d 709, 375 N.Y.S.2d 1028, 338 N.E.2d 330, reversed on other grounds 40 N.Y.2d 316, 386 N.Y.S.2d 685, 353 N.E.2d 598, on remand 54 A.D.2d 549, 387 N.Y.S.2d 541 (1977)*
[130] *State Division of Human Rights v. Luppino (2 Dept. 1970) 35 A.D.2d 107, 313 N.Y.S.2d 28 (1970), reversed on other grounds 29 N.Y.2d 555, 324 N.Y.S.2d 297, 272 N.E.2d 884, affirmed 29 N.Y.2d 558, 324 N.Y.S.2d 298, 272 N.E.2d 885.*
[131] *Baldwin v. State Division of Human Rights (1 Dept. 1980) 75 A.D.2d 745, 427 N.Y.S.2d 438 (1980). Civil Rights 1708; Civil Rights 1712*
[132] *C.P.L.R. 506 [b] [1].*

The purpose and effect of the present article 78 of the CPLR, and article 78 of the former Civil Practice Act was to simplify, and unify the procedure in connection with the three old remedies of, certiorari to review, mandamus and prohibition. They were merely remedial on the practice side. The substantive side of the remedies was left unaffected, there being no intention to extend, limit, or abolish the various remedies in substance. (23 Carmody-Wait 2d, § 145:2, pp. 424 and 425; Matter of Newbrand v. City of Yonkers, 285 N.Y. 164.) Thus, the relief formerly obtained by certiorari to review remains unchanged in reference to its function and the conditions under which it is granted. (Matter of Barber v. Richardson, 175 Misc. 210; Matter of Browne v. Rice, 171 Misc. 695, affd. 259 App. Div. 847.)

The "ancient and just" writ of prohibition is rooted deep in the common law. Originally used by the English king to curb the powers of ecclesiastical courts, prohibition has evolved into a basic protection for the individual in his relations with the State.[133] The gravity of the harm which would be caused by an excess of power is an important factor to be weighed. "[134] A writ of prohibition may be obtained only when a clear legal right of a petitioner is threatened by a body or officer acting in a judicial or quasi-judicial capacity and "*is never available merely to correct or prevent trial errors of substantive law or procedure, however grievous*"[135] The courts have concluded that even in those rare circumstances where an arrogation of power [this case does not nearly qualify for that ranking] would justify burdening the judicial process with collateral intervention and summary correction, "*the writ of prohibition nonetheless does not issue as of right, but only in the sound discretion of the court*" Matter of Rush v Mordue, 68 N.Y.2d 348, 354, supra [emphasis supplied]).

A petitioner seeking a writ of prohibition must demonstrate that: (1) a body or officer is acting in a judicial or quasi-judicial capacity, (2) that body or officer is proceeding or threatening to proceed in excess of its jurisdiction and (3) petitioner has a clear legal right to the relief requested.[136] Concerning public agencies and conviction record decisions, a writ of prohibition is petitioner's only specified remedy to stop a public agency who exceeds its power or authority. If need be this can include a non-final order of the Division of Human Rights.[137] A writ of mandamus would not be obtainable in these situations if a public agency establishes a conviction record blanket policy because "*The only relief we could grant to petitioner would be to annul the determination and remit the matter to the administrative agency for, which would be a futile gesture because of petitioner's ineligibility.*" Matter of McCormack v. Posillico, 213 AD 2d 913 (1995).

An article 78 proceeding in the nature of mandamus states that the aggrievement arises from the refusal of the body or officer to act or to perform a duty enjoined by law. Accordingly, it is necessary to make a demand and await a refusal before bringing a proceeding in the nature of mandamus and in the latter type of proceeding the Statute of Limitations does not run out until four months after the refusal. The period begins from the date of the refusal of which the action took place.

Traditionally, "[m]andamus lies to compel the performance of a purely ministerial act where there is a clear legal right to the relief sought"[138] The long-established law is that "*[w]hile a mandamus is an appropriate remedy to enforce the performance of a ministerial duty, it is well settled that it will not be awarded to compel an act in respect to which the officer may exercise judgment or discretion*"[139] Mandamus for such purpose, however, lies only where the right to relief is "clear" and the duty sought to be enjoined is performance of an act commanded to be performed by law and involving no exercise of discretion.[140] The review of a determination in such proceedings is in the nature of mandamus, on which the standard is the rationality of the administrative act. Matter of Sled Hill Cafe v. Hostetter, 22 N Y 2d 607, 612; cf. Matter of Colton v. Berman, 21 N Y 2d 322, 329; see 1 N. Y. Jur., Administrative Law, §§ 121, 178, 184, 185). Nevertheless, the determination must have a reasonable or rational basis and be based on substantial evidence. It is firmly established that the remedy of mandamus is not available to compel a judicial officer to render a decision with a particular outcome where the decision involves the exercise of discretion or judgment and is not merely a ministerial act that is required by law.[141]

---

[133] *Appo v People, 20 N.Y. 531, 541-542 (1860); Wolfram, The "Ancient and Just" Writ of Prohibition in New York, 52 Col L Rev 334, 338-353 (1927); Third Annual Report of N. Y. Judicial Council, 1937, p 137.*

[134] *Matter of Culver Contr. Corp. v Humphrey, 268 N.Y. 26, 40 (1935) supra; see, also, 23 Carmody-Wait, 2d, New York Practice, op. cit., § 145:216, pp 793-794 (1983).*

[135] *Matter of Morgenthau v Erlbaum, 59 N.Y.2d 143, 147 (1983) [emphasis supplied]), (La Rocca v Lane, 37 N.Y.2d 575, 579, supra (1975)).*

[136] *Garner v. Correctional Services, 889 N.E.2d 467, 859 N.Y.S.2d 590, 889 N.E. 2d 467(2008)*

[137] (Trial Judge proceeded in excess of his jurisdiction when he barred the entire public from entire proceeding when Petitioners' had a clear statutory right. Prohibition was petitioners' only remedy.) *Matter of United Press Associations et al v. Francis L. Valente, Individually and as Judge of The Court of General Sessions of the County of New York, 308 N.Y. 71 (1954)*

[138] *Matter of Legal Aid Soc. v Scheinman, 53 N.Y.2d 12, 16 (1981)*

[139] *Matter of Gimprich v Board of Educ., 306 N.Y. 401, 406 (1954)*

[140] *Weinstein-Korn-Miller, CPLR Manual [rev ed], par 32.02, subd [b].)*

[141] Matter of Crain Communications v Hughes, 74 N.Y.2d 626; see also, Matter of Brusco v Braun, 84 N.Y.2d 674, 679; Klostermann v Cuomo, 61 N.Y.2d 525, 539-540; Matter of Hamptons Hosp. & Med. Ctr. v Moore, 52 N.Y.2d 88, 96; Matter of United States of Mexico v Schmuck, 294 N.Y. 265, 271-272; Matter of Abbott v Conway, 148 AD2d 909, lv denied 74 N.Y.2d 608; Matter of Kahn v Backer, 21 A.D.2d 171, 173; Matter of Lorberblatt v McDonald, 10 A.D.2d 641).

Certiorari is the writ by which the court reviews an action of an administrative agency, public body or officer for the purpose of establishing whether a determination made as a result of a hearing held, and at which evidence was taken, pursuant to direction by law is, on the entire record, supported by substantial evidence (CPLR § 7803 [4]) The purpose of an Article 78 proceeding in the nature of certiorari is to seek judicial review of a final agency decision.

Article 78 proceedings are generally intended to be limited in scope to seeking the relief previously obtained by writs of certiorari to review, mandamus or prohibition. A provision exists in Article 78, however, which creates a hybrid form of relief that encompasses certiorari and mandamus, incorporating elements of both. In practice, many Article 78 proceedings seek the relief provided by this provision. This hybrid form of relief is provided in CPLR § 7803 (3), which authorizes the court to make a finding as to whether a determination of an administrative agency, public body or officer was made in violation of lawful procedure, was affected by an error of law or was arbitrary and capricious or an abuse of discretion, including abuse of discretion as to the measure or mode of penalty or discipline imposed. Monetary damages, such as restitution, are obtainable in Article 78 proceedings. Any restitution or damages granted to the petitioner, however, must be incidental to the primary relief sought by the petitioner, and must be such as he might otherwise recover on the same set of facts in a separate action or proceeding suable in New York State Supreme Court against the same administrative agency, public body or officer in its or his official capacity. CPLR § 7806

Only where the evidence submitted by the claimant fails, as a matter of law, to reveal any merit to the complaint may the Division make a determination of no probable cause without holding a hearing.[142] And before that determination may be reached, New York requires the Division to make a full investigation, wherein the complainant has full opportunity to present his evidence.

When you are challenging an agency action of denial, whether the Division of Human Rights or simply any "public agency" you will be doing so through an Article 78 Writ of Mandamus action where the court will have the agency submit the record. This is why it is important that a person keeps a paper trail, especially as the decision of the agency is often given preference over the allegations that the decision has no merit or lacks rationality. Simply put the review process of a final decision never favors a Complainant unless such decision is arbitrary and capricious or lacks rationality. When it does, remand is often the limited remedy ordered by the court to correct the Respondent's error of law or basis of its determination.

In a mandamus to review proceeding, however, no quasi-judicial hearing is required; the petitioner need only be given an opportunity "to be heard" and to submit whatever evidence he or she chooses and the agency may consider whatever evidence is at hand, whether obtained through a hearing or otherwise. The standard of review in such a proceeding is whether the agency determination was arbitrary and capricious or affected by an error of law.

On review of an Article 78 petition, the law is well settled that the courts may not overturn the decision of an administrative agency which has a rational basis and was not arbitrary and capricious simply because it disagrees with how the agency reached that conclusion.[143] Nothing in the law requires an agency to reach a particular result on any issue, or permits the courts to second-guess the agency's choice unless such decision is arbitrary and capricious. In applying the "arbitrary and capricious" standard, a court inquires whether the determination under review had a rational basis.[144] The arbitrary or capricious test chiefly *"relates to whether a particular action should have been taken or is justified . . . and whether the administrative action is without foundation in fact."* Arbitrary action is defined as being without sound basis in reason and is generally taken without regard to facts."[145] Under this standard, a final agency determination should not be disturbed unless the record shows that the agency's action was "*arbitrary, unreasonable, irrational or indicative of bad faith*"[146] New issues not in the record may not be raised for the first time before the courts in an article 78 proceeding. [147]

---

[142] *Flah's, Inc. v. Schneider, 71 App. Div. 2d 993, 420 N. Y. S. 2d 283, 284 (1979).*

[143] *Goldstein v Lewis, 90 A.D.2d 748, 749 (1st Dep't 1982).*

[144] *Halperin v City of New Rochelle, 24 A.D.3d 768, 770 (2d Dep't 2005); see Pell v Board. of Educ. of Union Free School Dist. No. 1 of Towns of Scarsdale & Mamaroneck, Westchester County, 34 N.Y.2d, 222, 231 (1974)* ("[r]ationality is what is reviewed under both the substantial evidence rule and the arbitrary and capricious standard.")

[145] *Pell v Board of Education, 34 N.Y.2d at 231 (1974)*

[146] *Matter of Cowan v. Kern, 41 N.Y. 2d 591, 599 [1977]*

[147] *Matter of Yonkers Gardens Co. v State of N.Y. Div. of Hous. & Community Renewal, 51 N.Y. 2d 966, 967 [1980]),*

In fact, the court may not substitute its judgment for that of the [NYHRD][148] and the court is "not empowered to find new facts or take a different view of the weight of the evidence if the [NYHRD's] determination is supported by substantial evidence."[149] Usually the courts find the agency's conclusion "was a reasonable one and thus may not be set aside by the courts although a contrary decision may have been reasonable and also sustainable."[150]

F - What Happens If I Get A No Probable Cause and Appeal?

Where determination of no probable cause is rendered by New York State Division of Human Rights without holding a public hearing against a private employer, the standard to be applied is whether determination was arbitrary and capricious or lacking rational basis through the right of appeal within 60 days specified in New York Executive Law 298.[151] Generally the court must uphold an administrative agency's determination if supported by substantial evidence.[152] A finding is supported by the evidence only when the evidence is so substantial that from it an inference of the existence of a fact may be drawn reasonably. A mere scintilla of evidence sufficient to justify a suspicion is not sufficient to support a finding upon which legal rights and obligations are based. That requires such relevant evidence as a reasonable mind might accept as adequate to support a conclusion.[153]

The role of the court in reviewing the record for substantial evidence ceases if there exists in the whole record a rational basis for the findings of fact upon which the administrative agency's determination is based.[154] When an administrative agency's determination is based upon speculative inferences unsupported in the record, its determination is a nullity.[155] As long as investigation is sufficient and claimant afforded a full opportunity to present his claims, it is within discretion of State Division of Human Rights to decide method or methods to be employed in investigating discrimination claim.[156]

If the record before the court demonstrates that State Division of Human Rights conducted a one-sided and abbreviated investigation of discrimination complaint, its determination of no probable cause will be overturned as capricious.[157] The Investigation by the Division of Human Rights of a complaint cannot be so one-sided and abbreviated as to render Division's determination of no probable cause capricious, where investigation consisted of no more than examination of papers submitted by parties and employer presented no proof, aside from own self-serving statements.[158] An investigation of an employment discrimination complaint can be deemed by the court to be inadequate if it recommended dismissal of complaint without studying employer's entire policy in relationship to the stated allegations put forth.[159] The Regional director of State Division of Human Rights has discretion to determine and conduct the most suitable investigation for a particular case; however, the complainant must be afforded an opportunity to rebut evidence submitted by or obtained from the respondents before the complaint may be dismissed for no probable cause.[160] When all statutory factors are considered in determining whether issuance of a license or employment application would post unreasonable risk in light of prior convictions, and the positive factors are balanced against the negative factors for license or employment, the resulting decision is neither arbitrary nor capricious nor does it constitute an abuse of discretion, and reviewing courts may not reweigh the factors and substitute their judgment for that of the agency.[161]

Where the agency's determination involves factual evaluation within an area of the agency's expertise and is amply supported by the record, the determination must be accorded great weight and judicial deference.[162] Courts are required to "resolve [any] reasonable doubts in favor of the administrative findings and decisions" of

---

[148] *State Division of Human Rights v. Mecca Kendall Corp.*, 53 App. Div. 2d 201, 203-204, 385 N. Y. S. 2d 665, 666-667 (1976);

[149] *State Division of Human Rights v. Columbia University*, 39 N. Y. 2d 612, 616, 350 N. E. 2d 396, 398 (1976), cert. denied sub nom. *Gilinsky v. Columbia University*, 429 U. S. 1096 (1977).

[150] *Imperial Diner, Inc. v. State Human Rights Appeal Bd.*, 52 N. Y. 2d, at 79, 417 N. E. 2d, at 529, quoting *Mize v. State Division of Human Rights*, 33 N. Y. 2d 53, 56, 304 N. E. 2d 231, 233 (1973).

[151] *Metz v. County of Suffolk*, 2004, 4 Misc.3d 914, 782 N.Y.S.2d 552. Civil Rights 1712

[152] *Matter of Pell v Board of Educ.*, 34 N.Y.2d 222; *Matter of Society for Ethical Culture in City of N. Y. v Spatt*, 68 AD2d 112

[153] *Consolidated Edison Co. v. National Labor Relations Board*, 305 U. S. 197, 229

[154] *300 Gramatan Ave. Assoc. v State Div. of Human Rights*, 45 N.Y.2d 176; *Matter of Flynn v Flacke*, 87 AD2d 930

[155] *Matter of Sled Hill Cafe v Hostetter*, 22 N.Y.2d 607; 924, *Matter of Stanwood Pub v New York State Liq. Auth.*, 82 AD2d 865.)

[156] *McFarland v. New York State Div. of Human Rights (1 Dept. 1998) 241 A.D.2d 108, 671 N.Y.S.2d 461. Civil Rights 1709*

[157] *Bachman v. State Div. of Human Rights (1 Dept. 1984) 104 A.D.2d 111, 481 N.Y.S.2d 858. See, also, Piekielniak v. New York State Dept. of Health, 1982, 90 A.D.2d 585, 456 N.Y.S.2d 128. Civil Rights 1712*

[158] *Hendel v. New York State Div. of Human Rights (2 Dept. 1985) 114 A.D.2d 897, 495 N.Y.S.2d 135. Civil Rights 1711*

[159] *Nanuet School Dist. v. New York State Human Rights Appeal Bd. (2 Dept. 1979) 67 A.D.2d 724, 412 N.Y.S.2d 656. Civil Rights 1709*

[160] *Soellner v. State Div. of Human Rights (2 Dept. 1984) 100 A.D.2d 876, 474 N.Y.S.2d 135. Civil Rights 1710*

[161] *Boatman v.New York State Dept. of Educ. (3 Dept. 2010) 72 A.D.3d 1467, 900 N.Y.S.2d 174.*

[162] *Flacke v Onondaga Landfill Systems, Inc.*, 69 NY2d 355, 363, 514 NYS2d 689, 693 [1987]

the responsible agency.[163] Likewise, the "construction given statutes and regulations by the agency responsible for their administration, if not irrational or unreasonable, should be upheld."[164] Where, however, the question is one of pure statutory reading and analysis, dependent only on accurate apprehension of legislative intent, "there is little basis to rely on any special competence or expertise of the administrative agency and its interpretive regulations are therefore to be accorded much less weight. And, of course, if the regulation runs counter to the clear wording of a statutory provision, it should not be accorded any weight"[165] If the agency's implementation of its powers violates the clear enablement of the statute, the Court need accord it no weight; the Court's exclusive judicial reviewing duty in such instances requires it to act autonomously.[166]

G - Aiding and Abetting and Retaliation

Aiding and Abetting is a cause of action under Human Rights Law Executive Law § 296 (6).[167] Retaliation is protected under the Human Rights Law Executive Law § 296 (7). Both can be used as formidable causes of action against Respondent(s) who violate the law.

Human Rights Law Executive Law § 296(6) states that it shall be an unlawful discriminatory practice "*for any person to aid, abet, incite, compel or coerce the doing of any of the acts forbidden under this article or attempt to do so.*"A defendant who actually participates in the conduct giving rise to a discrimination claim may be held personally liable under the Human Rights Law.[168] In order for a Complainant to recover against an aider or abettor of NYHRL violations pursuant to § 296.6, he or she must establish "(1) that [the aider and abettor] engaged in conduct protected by the NYHRL; (2) there is a causal connection between the protected conduct and the alleged [violations] of the NYHRL; and (3) that [the aider and abettor] 'actually participated' in the discrimination."[169] Further, plaintiff must show that the Respondent, "aided or abetted a primary violation of the NYHRL committed by (another employee or) the business itself."[170] Individuals cannot be held liable under New York Human Rights Law for aiding and abetting their own violations of Human Rights Law.[171]

Human Rights Law Executive Law § 296(7) states that, "*It shall be an unlawful discriminatory practice for any person engaged in any activity to which this section applies to retaliate or discriminate against any person because he or she has opposed any practices forbidden under this article or because he or she has filed a complaint, testified or assisted in any proceeding under this article.*"

The Court of Appeals has held that "*it is unlawful to retaliate against an employee or applicant for opposing discriminatory practices.*"[172] When analyzing claims for retaliation, courts apply the burden shifting test as set forth in McDonnell Douglas Corp. v Green (411 US 792, 802 [1973]), which places the "initial burden" for establishing a prima facie case of retaliation on the plaintiff. Claims for retaliation under the NYSHRL and the NYCHRL are analyzed in same manner as those under Title VII.[173] "*[B]ecause both the Human Rights Law and title VII address the same type of discrimination, afford victims similar forms of redress, are textually similar and ultimately employ the same standards of recovery, federal case law in this area also proves helpful...*"[174] Of course, in searching the Division record for the presence of substantial evidence in a case premised on an alleged violation of a statute purposed to counter retaliation or other discrimination, we must keep in mind that those engaged in such conduct rarely broadcast their intentions to the world. Rather, employers who practice retaliation may be expected to seek to avoid detection, and it is hardly to be supposed that they will not try to accomplish their aims by subtle rather than obvious methods.[175]

---

[163] *Town of Henrietta v Department of Envtl. Conservation, 76 A.D. 2d 215, 224, 430 N.Y.S. 2d 440, 448 [4th Dept 1980]; see also Jackson, 67 N.Y. 2d at 417, 503 N.Y.S. 2d at 305; City of Rome v Department of Health Dept., 65 AD2d 220, 225, 441 N.Y.S. 2d 61, 64 [4th Dept 1978], lv denied 46 N.Y. 2d 713, 416 N.Y.S. 2d 1027 [1979]).*

[164] *(In re Barie v Lavine, 40 N.Y. 2d 565, 568, 388 N.Y.S. 2d 878 [1976]).*

[165] *(Kurcsics v Merchants Mutual Ins. Co., 49 NY2d 451, 459, 426 NYS2d 454 [1980]; see Tze Chun Liao v New York State Banking Dept., 74 N.Y. 2d 505 1989).*

[166] *Tze Chun Liao v New York State Banking Dept, 74 NY2d 505 [1989] citing Kurcsics, at 459*

[167] *Clark v. State (4 Dept. 2003) 302 A.D.2d 942, 754 N.Y.S.2d 814, appeal and reargument denied 305 A.D.2d 1127, 758 N.Y.S.2d 251*

[168] *See, e.g., Poulsen v. City of North Tonawanda, N.Y., 811 F.Supp. 884, 900 (W.D.N.Y.1993); Bridges, 800 F.Supp. at 1180-81; Wanamaker v. Columbian Rope Co., 740 F.Supp. 127, 135-36 (N.D.N.Y.1990); but see Falbaum v. Pomerantz, 891 F.Supp. 986 (S.D.N.Y.1995).*

[169] *See Tomka v Seiler Corp. 66 F.Supp.2d 1295 (2nd Cir. 1995) and Beattie, 124 F.Supp.2d at 805, citing Tomka, 66 F.3d at 1317.*

[170] *Jordan v. Cayuga County, No. 01-CV-1037, 2004 WL 437459, at *4 (N.D.N.Y. Feb. 9, 2004), quoting Bennett v. Progressive Corp., 225 F.Supp.2d 190, 213 (N.D.N.Y. 2002) (internal quotation and emphasis omitted).*

[171] *Goldin v. Engineers Country Club (2 Dept. 2008) 54 A.D.3d 658, 864 N.Y.S.2d 43, leave to appeal dismissed in part, denied in part 13 N.Y.3d 763, 886 N.Y.S.2d 864, 915 N.E.2d 1160*

[172] *Forrest v Jewish Guild for the Blind, 3 N.Y.3d at 312*

[173] *Middleton v Metropolitan College of New York, 545 F Supp 2d 369, 373 (S.D.N.Y. 2008).*

[174] *Matter of Aurecchione v New York State Div. of Human Rights, 98 NY2d 21, 26 [2002] [citation omitted]).*

[175] *(see, generally, Matter of Holland v Edwards, 307 N.Y. 38, 45; State Div. of Human Rights v Kilian Mfg. Corp., 35 N.Y.2d 201, 209-210).*

In order to make out a prima facie case of retaliation against a Respondent, a complainant must show by a preponderance of the evidence that: "[1] He or she participated in a protected activity; [2] Defendant knew that he was participating in the protected activity; [3] Defendant took adverse action against him or her which disadvantaged Plaintiff and [4] There was a causal connection between the protected activity and the adverse employment action taken by the Defendant."

A "protected activity" refers to "*actions taken to protest or oppose statutorily prohibited discrimination.*"[176] To prove that he engaged in protected activity, the plaintiff need not establish that the conduct he opposed was in fact a violation of the Human Rights Law. However, the plaintiff must demonstrate a "good faith, reasonable belief that the underlying challenged actions of the employer violated the law."[177]

Adverse actions are those which affect the "*terms, privileges, duration, or conditions of employment*"[178] The courts have determined "because there are no bright-line rules, courts must pore over each case to determine whether the challenged employment action reaches the level of `adverse.'"[179] Courts have construed the anti-retaliation provision to "*prohibit a wide variety of employer conduct that is intended to restrain, or that has the likely effect of restraining, employees in the exercise of protected activities.*"[180] An adverse employment action requires a materially adverse change in the terms and conditions of employment. "*To be `materially adverse' a change in working conditions must be `more disruptive than a mere inconvenience or an alteration of job responsibilities.'. . . `A materially adverse change might be indicated by a termination of employment, a demotion evidenced by a decrease in wage or salary, a less distinguished title, a material loss of benefits, significantly diminished material responsibilities, or other indices . . . unique to a particular situation*"[181]

However natural it may be for an employer to be reluctant to hire someone who has brought suit against him, it is every citizen's right to resort to the judicial system, and Title VII makes illegal an employment decision based on an applicant's exercise of this right as it applies to actual or perceived employment discrimination. Essentially, this is retaliation. Title VII would be chilled to a freeze by allowing the icy finger of job discharge or refusal to touch an individual who claims his Title VII rights.[182] Not offering employment can be considered a sufficient adverse employment action.[183]

As for the fourth required element, a causal connection can be established directly, through evidence of retaliatory animus, such as verbal or written remarks[184] or indirectly, by showing that the adverse action closely followed in time the protected activity.[185] The elements of retaliation under the New York City Human Rights Law differ from those required under the State Human Rights Law only in "that the plaintiff need not prove any adverse' employment action; instead, he [she] must prove that something happened that would be reasonably likely to deter a person from engaging in protected activity.'"[186] To establish a causal connection between the protected activity and alleged retaliatory hostility, "some increase in the discrimination or harassment-either a `ratcheting up' of the preexisting behavior or new, additional forms of harassment-must occur for the employee to make out a viable retaliation claim.

---

[176] *Aspilaire v Wyeth Pharmaceuticals, Inc.,* 612 F Supp 2d 289, 308 (S.D.N.Y .2009).

[177] *See, e.g., Abel v. Bonfanti,* 625 F.Supp.263, 267 (S.D.N.Y.1985); *Francoeur v. Corroon& Black Co.,* 552 F.Supp.403, 412 (S.D.N.Y.1982). See Parker v. *Baltimore & Ohio Railroad,* 652 F.2d 1012, 1020 (D.C.Cir.1981).

[178] *Dortz v City of New York,* 904 F Supp 127, 156 [S.D.N.Y. 1995]

[179] *Wanamaker v Columbian Rope Co.,* 108 F.3d at 466 (1997).

[180] *Bill Johnson's Restaurants, Inc. v. NLRB,* 461 U. S. 731, 740 (1983)

[181] (*Galabya v New York City Bd. of Educ.,* 202 F.3d 636, 640 [2d Cir 2000], quoting *Crady v Liberty Natl. Bank & Trust Co. of Ind.,* 993 F2d 132, 136 [7th Cir 1993]).

[182] *Pace University v Human Rights* 200 A.D. 2d 173, 611 NYS 2d 835 See also *East v Romine, Inc.,* 518 F.2d 332, 342 [5th Cir 1975]

[183] *Pace Univ. v. Human Rights,* 200 A.D. 2d 173 (1994) (Refusal to offer Ms. Mittleman a teaching contract constituted an adverse employment action.) also see*Matter of Board of Education of the New Paltz Central School District v Donaldson,* 41 AD 3d 1138 (Adverse employment action taken when Bell denied offer of further employment that would secure tenure.)

[184] (see, e.g. *Mandell v County of Suffolk,* 316 F.3d 368, 383 [2003])

[185] (See, *Gorzynski v JetBlue Airways Corp.,* 596 F.3d 93, 110-11 [2010]; *Dubois v Brookdale Univ. Hosp.,* 6 Misc 2d 1023[A] [2004], affirmed 29 AD3d 731 [2006]); *McCoy v State of New York,* 16 Misc 3d 1128[A] [2007]; *Gordon v New York City Bd. of Educ.,* 232 F3d 111, 117 [2001]).

[186] *Jimenez v City of New York,* 605 F Supp 2d 485, 528 [2009], quoting Administrative Code of the City of New York § 8-107[7]; *Gorokhovsky v City of New York,* 2011 US Dist LEXIS 54941 [2011])

If, however, "the discrimination was just as bad before the employee complained as it was afterwards, then the employee's complaints cannot be said to have led to that discriminatory behavior."[187] A causal connection between a protected activity and an adverse employment action can be inferred from evidence that the protected activity was followed closely by discriminatory treatment.[188] Courts have recognized that proof of causal connection can be established indirectly by showing that protected activity is followed by discriminatory treatment.[189] The close proximity of the termination and complaints can arguably suggest that there may have been non-permissible reasons for the firing.[190] It is, of course, true that temporal proximity can demonstrate a causal nexus.[191]

If the plaintiff succeeds in making out a prima facie case the burden of production shifts to the defendant to articulate a legitimate, non-retaliatory reason for the adverse employment action. If the defendant meets that burden, the plaintiff has the opportunity to demonstrate that the defendant's proffered reason was merely a pretext for retaliation.[192] A violation may be found if the adverse employment action was based in part on a retaliatory purpose, even if that was not the sole motive.[193] Once the plaintiff demonstrates that a retaliatory factor played a "motivating part" in the adverse employment decision, the defendant must demonstrate that it would have made the same decision based on the legitimate factor alone.[194]

An individual may be held liable under Executive Law § 296 (6) and (7) for aiding and abetting discriminatory conduct.[195] Aiding and abetting claims can only survive if plaintiff has successfully raised a question of fact as to any of the original discrimination claims. An employer cannot be held liable for an employee's discriminatory act unless the employer became a party to it by encouraging, condoning or approving it.[196] Condonation, which may sufficiently implicate an employer in the discriminatory acts of its employee to constitute a basis for employer liability under the Human Rights Law, contemplates a knowing, after-the- fact forgiveness or acceptance of an offense. An employer's calculated inaction in response to discriminatory conduct may, as readily as affirmative conduct, indicate condonation. An employer may be liable for a single act of discrimination to which the employer is a party, [197] It can be rationally concluded that an employer is guilty of discrimination whenever an employee at any level commits an approved and anticipated discriminatory act. In order to hold the employer responsible the Division must demonstrate that the employer approved of, or acquiesced in, the employee's conduct."[198]

---

[187] *Hall v. Parker Hannifan Corp.*, No. 08-CV-6033, 2009 U.S. Dist. LEXIS 108663, at *15 (W.D.N.Y. Nov. 20, 2009) (citation omitted); see also Gregory v. Daly, 243 F.3d 687, 690 (2d Cir. 2001) (holding that plaintiff adequately stated a retaliation claim based on her allegation that her supervisor's conduct significantly worsened after she complained about his sexual harassment and filed a lawsuit against him in state court). See Hall, 2009 U.S. Dist. LEXIS 108663, at 15.

[188] (DeCintio v Westchester County Med. Ctr., 821 F.2d 111, 115 [2d Cir 1987], cert denied 484 US 965 [1987]; see Velez v Frion Realty Corp., 300 A.D.2d 103 [2002]).

[189] *Aguirre v. Chula Vista Sanitary Service*, 542 F.2d 779, 781 (9th Cir. 1976)

[190] (see Reeves v Sanderson Plumbing Products, Inc., 530 US 133, 148 [2000] ("appellant's prima facie case, combined with sufficient evidence to find that the employer's asserted justification is false, may permit the trier of fact to conclude that the employer unlawfully discriminated").

[191] *See Manoharan v. Columbia Univ.*, 842 F.2d 590, 593 (2d Cir.1988).

[192] *See Richardson v. New York State Dep't of Corr. Serv.*, 180 F.3d 426, 443 (2d Cir.1999); Quinn v. Green Tree Credit Corp., 159 F.3d 759, 768-69 (2d Cir.1998).

[193] *See Cosgrove, 9 F.3d at 1039; Davis v. State Univ. of New York,* 802 F.2d 638, 642 (2d Cir.1986); Iannone v. Frederic R. Harris, Inc., 941 F.Supp. 403, 410 (S.D.N.Y.1996).

[194] *Cosgrove, 9 F.3d at 1040*

[195] *D'Amico v Commodities Exch.*, 235 AD2d 313, 315 [1997], citing Peck v Sony Music Corp., 221 AD2d 157 [1995]

[196] *Youth Action Homes v State Div. of Human Rights*, 231 A.D. 2d 7, 13 [1997]

[197] *Matter of Imperial Diner v State Div. of Human Rights*, 52 N.Y.2d 72

[198] *Matter of Totem Taxi v State Human Rights Appeal Bd.*, 65 N.Y.2d 300, 305.

PART IV

THE FUTILE GESTURE IN ADVERTISING, MIXED MOTIVES
AND BACKGROUND CHECKS

A - The Futile Gesture Doctrine and Correction Law Article 23-A

With the rise of the internet in the last 20 years, the ability for an agency or employer to advertise for an employee has resulted in employers specifying direct limitations on those who apply with a conviction record. The National Employment Law Project, as recently as 2011, published a report called "*65 Million Need Not Apply: The Case of Reforming Criminal Background Checks for Employers.*" In this published overview[199] N.E.L.P. points out a continuing problem across the nation where employers create written blanket policies in advertisements (think Careerbuilder, Craigslist etc.) ensuring that ex-offenders do not apply for the position and makes the case that Title VII is being damaged with such Respondent's bars going unchecked. In states outside New York, where there is no protection there is little recourse if one is white and not a minority, other than ban the box laws (which often do not have private causes of action outside Massachusetts, Washington D.C., Rhode Island, Minnesota and California).

In New York State though, the Division of Human Rights has considered advertisements that create a chilling effect upon applications for employment to be a violation of the statute and clearly bar a person who is otherwise qualified simply because they have a conviction record without doing any of the analysis required by the statute.

There are numerous companies and ads on the internet that specify that an applicant have, **"no felonies"**, **"no misdemeanors"**, **"a clean criminal record"**, **"a clear background check"** , **" a clear criminal record"**, **"no criminal record"**, **"no criminal history"**, **"no prior arrests"**, **"no arrests"**, **"no arrest record"**, **"no criminal convictions"** or **"no crimes of dishonesty"** or simply, **"do not apply if you have a criminal record."** These terms discourage an application for employment because they create a chilling effect and render an application futile and do not include individualized factor assessments of the applicant as <u>Article 23-A of the Correction Law</u> mandate.[200]

The New York State Division of Human Rights has been proactive and dealt with the problem of advertising direct limitations on conviction record since such basis is not specified in <u>New York Executive Law 296 (1) (d)</u> where the other prohibitions on advertising are included. General Counsel has decided that <u>New York Executive Law 296 § 15</u> covers conviction record protection (and <u>New York Executive Law 296 § 16</u> arrest record), including limitations in advertising and that, "*…Respondent may not advertise job postings with language that deters people with prior convictions from applying. The Division has determined that advertising that has a chilling effect on applications by persons with prior convictions may be considered evidence of an unlawful hiring policy.*"[201] The person who sees the ad and attaches it to their complaint can state a valid claim pursuant to the Human Rights Law if they were deterred from applying for a position for which they met the minimum qualifications and they are a bona fide job seeker and have searched for jobs within the same area. The complaint would then be investigated to determine whether Complainant was otherwise qualified for the position and has standing as an aggrieved person who is injured.

New York courts found that where an employer's words or actions show that an application would be futile, a prospective plaintiff need not take the step of actually completing a formal application.[202] For example, the futility doctrine has been applied where an employer is aware that the individual intends to apply for a position or benefits, but nevertheless specifically tells them not to apply, allegedly for discriminatory reasons. The Courts have already found that an employer's denial of a tuition reimbursement could constitute an adverse employment action even though the plaintiff had not applied for such reimbursement.[203] One of the defendant's employees had told the plaintiff that her reimbursement had been denied because of the plaintiff's use of Family and Medical Leave Act ("FMLA") leave. The employee claimed that she in fact had no authority over reimbursement, but the court excused the plaintiff's failure to apply for the reimbursement on the ground that the plaintiff had reason to believe that applying would be a futile act. An employer's calculated inaction in response to discriminatory conduct may, as readily as affirmative conduct, indicate

---

199 Available at the url: http://www.nelp.org/page/-/SCLP/2011/65_Million_Need_Not_Apply.pdf?nocdn=1

200 New York State Division of Human Rights General Counsel Legal Opinion 2010-04 and 2010-19

201New York State Division of Human Rights General Counsel Legal Opinion 2010-04 and 2010-19

202Brown v. McLean, 159 F.3d 898, 902 (4th Cir.1998); Malarkey v. Texaco, Inc., 983 F.2d 1204, 1213 (2d Cir. 1993) (applying futile gesture doctrine to ADEA claim); Pinchback v. Armistead Homes Corp., 907 F.2d 1447, 1451 (4th Cir. 1990) (applying doctrine to claim of housing discrimination); Vargas v. Chubb Group of Ins. Companies, No. 99 CIV. 4916(GEL), 2002 WL 31175233, at *4 & n.10 (S.D.N.Y. September 30,2002) (applying logic of Teamsters where plaintiff was told she would not be considered for positions, allegedly for discriminatory reasons, before she had had a chance to formally apply for them); McDermott v. Lehman, 594 F. Supp. 1315 (D. Me. 1984) (allowing Title VII action for a failure to hire to proceed where plaintiff did not complete formal application process but contacted employer and was informed employer wanted to hire a younger engineer).

203Breneisen v. Motorola, Inc., 512 F.3d at 972, 980 (7th Cir, 2008)

condonation of that conduct, as would subject employer to liability under Human Rights Law.[204]

Once an employer learns of claims of discriminatory acts, it cannot rest idly on hopes that such acts will not be repeated, whether by same employee or any other.[205] An employer who has notice of a discriminatorily abusive environment in the work place has a duty to take reasonable steps to eliminate it.[206]

Even though a complainant did not apply, an applicant can become discouraged by the company's advertised policy of open discrimination. The proposition of discouraging an applicant from employment for discriminatory reasons can be an unlawful discriminatory practice under the Human Rights Law. In support of this position, one only need look to Holland v Edwards[207] decided by the Court of Appeals which stated: *"One intent on violating the Law Against Discrimination cannot be expected to declare or announce his purpose. Far more likely is it that he will pursue his discriminatory practice in ways that are devious, be methods subtle and elusive- for we deal with an area in which 'subtleties of conduct play no small part'."*

Facing discriminatory advertising, a person with a conviction record has the burden of proof to demonstrate that they would have applied but for accurate knowledge of an employer's discrimination and they would have been discriminatorily rejected had they actually applied.[208] In order to succeed on a case of discriminatory advertising in the New York Courts, a Complainant must show a direct tie between knowledge of a protected status (ie, conviction record) and the statement in question (ie. the ad limitation), evincing proof of an intent to discriminate in fact.[209] Executive Law 296 prohibits unlawful discriminatory practices; it is not necessary to find that discrimination was a regular practice, nor to wait and see if it would become one.[210] Concerning the advertisement itself, an employer cannot be held liable [under state law] for an employee's discriminatory act unless the employer became a party to it by encouraging, condoning, or approving it."[211]

The futile gesture doctrine[212] first explored by the United States Supreme Court spoke about such discouragement of a protected class of individuals. The court assumes that the futile gesture doctrine applies to non-applicant plaintiffs in individual suits.[213] The court reinforced the effects of and the injuries suffered from discriminatory employment practice in Teamsters that are not always confined to those who were expressly denied a requested employment opportunity. A consistently enforced discriminatory policy can surely deter job applications from those who are aware of it and are unwilling to subject themselves to the humiliation of explicit and certain rejection.[214]

The Supreme Court then explained its rationale that, *"If an employer should announce his policy of discrimination by a sign reading "Whites Only" on the hiring-office door, his victims would not be limited to the few who ignored the sign and subjected themselves to personal rebuffs. The same message can be communicated to potential applicants more subtly but just as clearly by an employer's actual practices-by his consistent discriminatory treatment of actual applicants, by the manner in which he publicizes vacancies, his recruitment techniques, his responses to casual or tentative inquiries, and even by the racial or ethnic composition of that part of his work force from which he has discriminatorily excluded members of minority groups. When a person's desire for a job is not translated into a formal application solely because of his unwillingness to engage in a futile gesture he is as much a victim of discrimination as is he who goes through the motions of submitting an application."* Even if a company chooses to pull down a discriminatory and chilling advertisement, *"The Company's later changes in its hiring and promotion policies could be of little comfort to the victims of the earlier ... discrimination, and could not erase its previous illegal conduct or its obligation to afford relief to those who suffered because of it."*[215]

[204] *Wal-Mart Stores East, L.P. v. New York State Div. of Human Rights (4 Dept. 2010) 71 A.D.3d 1452, 897 N.Y.S.2d 348*

[205] *McIntyre v. Manhattan Ford, Lincoln-Mercury, Inc., 1997, 175 Misc.2d 795, 669 N.Y.S.2d 122, appeal dismissed 256 A.D.2d 269, 682 N.Y.S.2d 167, appeal dismissed 93 N.Y.2d 919, 691 N.Y.S.2d 383, 713 N.E.2d 418, leave to appeal denied 94 N.Y.2d 753, 700 N.Y.S.2d 427, 722 N.E.2d 507. Civil Rights 1149*

[206] *Murray v. NYU College of Dentistry, 57 F.3d 243, 249 (2d Cir. 1995). See also, Snell v. Suffolk County, 782 F.2d 1094, 1103-04 (2d Cir. 1986)* (finding liability because "defendants have ignored or failed to take steps to prevent these abuses") (emphasis in original). *Cf. DeGrace v. Rumsfeld, 614 F.2d 796, 805 (1st Cir. 1980),* discussing duty of employers to "take all reasonable measures" to eliminate discrimination they become aware of.

[207] *Holland v Edwards, 307 N.Y. 38, 45 (1954)*

[208] *Brown v. McLean, 159 F.3d 898,902 (4th Cir. 1998)*

[209] *Giovanni Pelaez v Life Alert 09-CV-1668 (2009)*

[210] *Imperial Diner, Inc. v. State Human Rights Appeal Bd., 1980, 52 N.Y.2d 72, 436 N.Y.S.2d 231, 417 N.E.2d 525*

[211] *Matter of State Div. of Human Rights v St. Elizabeth's Hosp., 66 NY2d 684, 687 [1985], quoting Matter of Totem Taxi, Inc. v New York State Human Rights Appeal Bd., 65 NY2d 300, 305 [1985]).*

[212] *International Brotherhood of Teamsters v. United States 431 U.S. 324 (1977)*

[213] *Giovanni Pelaez v Life Alert 09-CV-1668 (2009)*

[214] *Pime v. Loyola Univ. of Chicago, 803 F.2d 351, 353 n. 1 (7th Cir.1986) ("One does not have to apply for a job when it is obvious that it would be a futile act.")*

[215] *Teamsters v. United States, 431 U.S. 234, 241-42 (1977); U.S. v. City of New York, 683 F.Supp.2d 225, 255 (E.D.N.Y. 2010) (same, quoting Teamsters).*

It is clear the legislature has carved out only two exceptions to a prohibition against ex- offenders. Certain companies might argue that advertising a direct or indirect limitation against an ex-offender is an acceptable practice because it is not directly stated in the statute. The courts have already concluded that the terms expressed in Executive Law 296 are "intended to be interpreted in its accepted and dictionary meaning."[216] If one looks at Executive Law 296 § 15 an ex-offender cannot simply be denied employment because he or she has convictions or a lack of good moral character when such provisions are in violation of *Article 23-A of the Correction Law*. Once you go to Correction Law Article 23-A §751, its term applies only to the "application" for a license by a person previously convicted of a crime. While this may be true, if one is prevented from putting in an application for employment by clearly discriminatory language, a company would be making a whole class of protected people ineligible for employment. Therefore it is reasonable to conclude that the intent of the New York Legislature was to prevent ex-offenders from facing prejudice in employment, including direct advertising. Courts have consistently interpreted the Human Rights Law so to accord individuals with the fullest of civil rights and the fullest of protections from discrimination, including, specifically, in the area of conviction record. It is the duty of the courts to make sure that the salutary purposes of the legislative body in enacting the Human Rights Law are not thwarted by a combination of a strict construction of the Administrative Code and a battle over semantics.[217] Generally, before a plaintiff can complain of discrimination in not being hired, he must have first applied for a job.[218]

While there remains no mention of unlawful conviction based advertising within the provisions of New York Correction Law Article 23-A, New York Executive Law 296.15 and New York Executive Law 296.1(d)[219] that is clearly defined it would be contrary to the language of the Human Rights Law for employers (which expressly includes *"any person, agency, bureau, corporation, or association,"*) not to follow the public policy of New York and hire an ex-offender and to follow the intent of the Law (which is to remove the prejudice against ex-offenders during the application and hiring practices). It is fundamental that a court, in interpreting a statute, should attempt to effectuate the intent of the Legislature.[220] Where the statutory language is clear and unambiguous, the court should construe it so as to give effect to the plain meaning of the words used.[221] When the statute describes the particular situations in which it is to apply, *"an irrefutable inference must be drawn that what is omitted or not included was intended to be omitted or excluded."*[222] The legislature clearly intended to remove the unfair discrimination and prejudice that exists by having a conviction record. To allow employers to bar applicants with conviction records in print would be incorrectly reading the statutory language and defeating the purpose of prohibiting conviction record discrimination and only allowing one or two exemptions to be claimed by the employer. There the Division of Human Rights has correctly concluded that such blanket policies cannot be held to be within the permissibility of the Human Rights Law because it is not one of the stated two exemptions.

If conviction record advertising could not be properly investigated the Human Rights Law could be avoided by the expedient use of using carefully designed code words to discourage all ex-offenders. If an advertiser could use code words as a substitute for terms clearly proscribed by law, the law would be nullified for all practical purposes. Code words are discriminatory additions to otherwise complete advertisements; the purpose is to signal the existence of an unlawful criterion.[223] The words themselves are only relevant for what they reveal — the intent of the speaker.[224]

---

[216] *State Div. of Human Rights v. Board of Cooperative Education Services, 98 A.D.2d 958, 958, 470 N.Y.S.2d 209, 210 (4th Dept. 1983)*

[217] *cf. City of Schenectady v State Div. of Human Rights, 37 N.Y.2d 421, 428*

[218] *McDonnell Douglas Corp. v Green, 411 U.S. 792, 802 [1973]; Hettrick, Appellant v Stark 3 A.D.3d 471, 771 N.Y.S.2d 133, 2004 N.Y. Slip Op. 00131 and Hettrick, Appellant v Stark.*

[219] To print or circulate or cause to be printed or circulated any statement, advertisement or publication, or to use any form of application for such programs or to make any inquiry in connection with such program which expresses, directly or indirectly, any limitation, specification or discrimination as to race, creed, color, national origin, sexual orientation, military status, sex, age, disability or marital status, or any intention to make any such limitation, specification or discrimination, unless based on a bona fide occupational qualification.

[220] *Matter of Petterson v Daystrom Corp., 17 N.Y.2d 32, 38; see Matter of Carr v New York State Bd. of Elections, 40 N.Y.2d 556),*

[221] *(Bender v Jamaica Hosp., 40 N.Y.2d 560; New Amsterdam Cas. Co. v Stecker, 3 N.Y.2d 1; Meltzer v Koenigsberg, 302 N.Y. 523; Matter of De Peyster, 210 N.Y. 216)*

[222] *(McKinney's Cons Laws of NY, Book 1, Statutes, § 240). (Matter of Petterson v Daystrom Corp., 17 N.Y.2d 32, 38; see Matter of Carr v New York State Bd. of Elections, 40 N.Y.2d 556)*

[223] *United States v Hunter, 459 F.2d 205, 215, cert den 409 US 934*

[224] *See Futrell v. J.I. Case, 38 F.3d 342, 347 (7th Cir.1994)* (holding that statements like "sharp young people" and that the employee was not a "forward enough thinker" could reasonably be interpreted as evidence of bias under the ADEA).

The reality is that "discrimination today is rarely so obvious, or its practices so overt that recognition of the fact is instant and conclusive" and that "code" words, while innocuous on their face, nonetheless effectively convey a message of discrimination.[225] Accordingly, code words which achieve the connotative effect of communicating such discrimination may be dealt with as discriminatory, even where the denotative meaning of the words or phrases in issue is an innocent one.[226] A discriminatory code word adds nothing but invidious unfairness. Employer's will often will take down ads and remove discriminatory content from its website if confronted by letter, lawsuit or complaint. Announcing a policy of not hiring anyone with a criminal history who might apply or stating code words prevent applicants from applying. Taking it down does not make the discrimination any less painful, it just stops it from being advertised, while establishing an end date of the discrimination for the employer. The policy often remains intact because it is now hidden from public view. Therefore it is still the plaintiff's burden to prove by a preponderance of the evidence that even if the advertisement was inadvertent that, "the reason pro-offered by the defendant's was false and that discrimination was the real reason."[227] Even if employers state they follow Article 23-A of the Correction Law, the tendentious selection of the conviction record prohibitive term, "no criminal record" so plainly indicates a preference for those outside the class it cannot be neutralized by insisting that Respondent utilizes an Article 23-A policy.[228]

Even though the courts have frowned upon those who do not apply, a complainant who does not apply must make a minimum showing that he or she would have applied for an available position for which he or she was qualified, but was rejected under circumstances which give rise to an inference of unlawful discrimination.[229] The Division's confirmation of the existence of the truthfulness of the advertisement for employment and its stated limitation would satisfy the minimal showing of rejection based upon a policy making a protected class ineligible to apply for that particular position. A plaintiff's failure to demonstrate a tri-able issue of fact that he or she was the victim of discrimination (and is part of a protected class) will force the dismissal of a case.[230] The Division has found probable cause where a statement is made that a protected class will not be offered a chance to apply for a benefit. A wife was prevented from applying by an alleged statement that the employee of the car company would not rent to Puerto Ricans. Such actions prevented Perez from completing Hertz' application process, thereby precluding her from completing a contract to rent; as such, they give her standing to complain that her civil rights were violated and that Hertz breached any contract it might have had with her regarding the desired rental car.[231]

B - Advertisements Are Direct Evidence of Discrimination; Mixed Motive

Often employers who discriminate with unlawful advertising on the basis of conviction record will argue that an applicant is not qualified or there was no position available at the time the advertisement was up in an attempt to contradict the direct evidence of their policies. Direct evidence of discrimination is "*evidence which, if believed, would prove the existence of a fact [in issue] without inference or presumption.*"[232]

Direct evidence relates statements or actions of an employer reflecting a discriminatory attitude correlating to the discrimination complained of by the employee.[233] Even if an employer does not target his remarks directly at the plaintiff, "*when evidence establishes the employer's animus toward the class to which the plaintiff belongs, the inference to the fact of discrimination against the plaintiff is sufficiently small that we have treated the evidence as direct*"[234] When an employer summarily rejects an applicant without considering his or her qualifications, those qualifications are irrelevant to whether the Title VII plaintiff has raised a prima facie case of disparate treatment.[235] Respondent rejected Complainant at a time when it had no knowledge of, and no way of evaluating, his qualifications. Therefore, neither "*an absolute or relative lack of qualification*" nor "*the absence of a vacancy in the job sought*" was the reason for Complainant's rejection, and Complainant established his prima facie case.[236]

---

[225] *State Div. of Human Rights v Kilian Mfg. Corp.*, 35 N.Y.2d 201, 209
[226] *United States v Hunter, 459 F.2d 205, cert den 409 US 934; Camp-of-The-Pines v New York Times Co., 184 Misc 389 Hodgson v Approved Personnel Serv., 529 F.2d 760*
[227] *Ferrante, 90 N.Y. 2d at 630, quoting St. Mary's Honor Ctr. v Hicks, 509 US 502, 515 [1993]*
[228] *Hailes v. United Air Lines, 464 F. 2d 1006 (5th Cir. 1972)*
[229] *Ardent v General Electric Company 761 N.Y.S. 2d. 334*
[230] *Hettrick v Stark 3 A.D. 3d 471, 771 N.Y.S. 2d 133, 2004 N.Y. Slip Op. 00131*
[231] *Perez Rivera v. Hertz Corp., 1997, 990 F.Supp. 234.*
[232] *Earley v. Champion Int'l Corp., 907 F.2d 1077, 1081 (11th Cir.1990)*
[233] *Caban-Wheeler v. Elsea, 904 F.2d 1549, 1555 (11th Cir.1990)*
[234] *Coghlan v. Am. Seafoods Co., 413 F.3d 1090, 1095 (9th Cir.2005)*
[235] *See EEOC v. Ford Motor Co., 645 F.2d 183, 188 n.3, 198-99 (4th Cir.1981)*
[236] *Nanty v. Barrows Co., 660 F. 2d 1327 (9th Cir. 1981)*

Absent a prima facie showing of discrimination, the mixed-motive analysis of <u>Price Waterhouse v Hopkins 490 US 228 (1989)</u> is inapplicable.[237] When there is direct evidence of intentional discrimination available against the member of the protected class, the United States Supreme Court has held numerous times that a Petitioner may prevail without proving all the elements of a prima facie case.[238] It would be illogical, indeed ironic, to hold a conviction record complainant presenting direct evidence of a defendant's intent to discriminate to a more stringent burden of proof, or to allow a Respondent to meet that direct proof by merely articulating, but not proving, legitimate, nondiscriminatory reasons for its action.

If the evidence demonstrates that defendant acted with a discriminatory motive, and the trier of fact accepts this evidence, the ultimate issue of discriminatory animus is proved and the employer must show it would have reached the same conclusion even had there been no animus and a motion for summary judgment on this basis is denied.[239] Defendant cannot refute this evidence by mere articulation of other reasons; the legal standard changes dramatically.[240]

A complainant under the Human Rights Law may meet their burden by using a mixed- motive analysis. [241]To prove a mixed motive case, complainant must present direct proof of discrimination, proving that an illegitimate factor had a motivating or substantial role in the employment decision. If a complainant can prevail on a "mixed motive" theory, it follows that he or she need not prove that the reason proffered by the employer for the challenged action was actually false or entirely irrelevant. Rather, under this analysis, the employer's production of evidence of a legitimate reason for the challenged action shifts to the plaintiff the lesser burden of raising an issue as to whether the action was *"motivated at least in part by ... discrimination"*[242] The statement, "no criminal record" can *"constitute evidence of discriminatory motivation when a plaintiff demonstrates that a nexus exists between the allegedly discriminatory statements and a defendant's decision to discharge the plaintiff."*[243]

A complainant should prevail in an action under the NYHRL if he or she proves that unlawful discrimination was one of the motivating factors, even if it was not the sole motivating factor, for an adverse employment decision.[244] The McDonnell Douglas burden-shifting framework does not apply in a mixed-motive case in the way it does in a pretext case because the issue in a mixed-motive case is not whether discrimination played the dispositive role but merely whether it played "a motivating part" in an employment decision.

The defendant's burden when refuting direct evidence of discrimination is one of persuasion and not merely production.[245] Defendants can rebut direct evidence "only by showing by a preponderance of the evidence that they would have acted as they did without regard to the plaintiff's protected class."[246] This constitutes a mixed-motive theory, where Respondent could put forth that they never would have hired the member of the protected class for a legitimate business reason. However, this does not absolve Respondent of all liability.[247] Pursuant to the 1991 amendments (also known as the Civil Rights Act of 1991), a plaintiff succeeds on a mixed-motive claim if she *"demonstrates that the protected characteristic was a motivating factor for any employment practice, even though other factors also motivated the practice."* 42 U.S.C.A. § 2000e-2(m).

---

[237] *Matter of Matthews v. City of New York*, 270 AD 2d 45, 704 N.Y.S.2d 49 (2000)

[238] *Teamsters v. United States*, 431 U. S. 324, 358, n. 44 (1977), *Trans World Airlines, Inc. v. Thurston*, 469 U. S. 111, 121 (1985,) *Swierkiewicz v. Sorema NA*, 534 US 506 (2002)("[T]he McDonnell Douglas test is inapplicable where the plaintiff presents direct evidence of discrimination.") In cases of discrimination proven by direct evidence, no such inference or presumption is required. Taylor v Runyon, 175 F.3d at 867 n. 2 (11th Cir. 1999); Evans v. McClain of Georgia, Inc., 131 F.3d 957, 962 (11th Cir.1997)

[239] *Cruz v. New York City Human Resources Admin. Dept. of Soc. Servs.*, 82 F.3d 16, 23 (2d Cir. 1996.

[240] *Trotter v. Board of Trustees of the Univ. of Ala.*, 91 F.3d 1449, 1453 (11th Cir.1996) ("When there is direct evidence that discrimination was a motivating factor in the challenged employment decision, the appropriate analysis is different from that employed in a case where only circumstantial evidence is available.")

[241] (*Allen v Domus Dev. Corp.*, 273 AD2d 891 [4'b Dept 2000], citing Michaelis v State of New York, 258 A.D. 2d 693, 694 [3d Dept 1999]; Tyler, 958 F2d 1176; see also Card v Sielaff, 154 Misc 2d 239 [Sup Ct, NY County 1992]; Morris, 2003 WL 1739009, *3, citing de la Cruz v New York City Human Resources Admin. Dept. of Social Servs., 82 F3d 16, 23 [2d Cir 1996]).

[242] (*Estate of Hamilton v City of New York*, 627 F3d 50, 56 [2d Cir 2010] [internal quotation marks omitted]) or, stated otherwise, was "more likely than not based in whole or in part on discrimination" (Aulicino v New York City Dept. of Homeless Servs., 580 F3d 73, 80 [2d Cir 2009] [internal quotation marks omitted]).

[243] (*Schreiber v Worldco, LLC*, 324 F Supp 2d 512, 518 [S.D.N.Y. 2004]; see Tomassi v Insignia Fin. Group, Inc., 478 F3d 111, 115-116 [2nd Cir 2007]).

[244] (*Williams v New York City Hous. Auth.*, 61 AD3d 62, 78 n 27 [2009], lv denied 13 NY3d 702 [2009] ["In the`mixed motive' context, ... the question on summary judgment is whether there exist triable issues of fact that discrimination was one of the motivating factors for the defendant's conduct"]; Weiss v JPMorgan Chase & Co., 2010 WL 114248, 2010 US Dist LEXIS 2505 [S.D.N.Y. 2010]. The basis of a mixed-motive theory is that both a legitimate and discriminatory reason for an employment decision can co-exist. Watson v. Se. Pa. Transp. Auth., 207 F3d 207, 216 (3d Cir.2000) (recognizing that the point of a mixed-motive theory is that a plaintiff may suffer discrimination even though there may also be a legitimate reason for the adverse employment action).

[245] *Hill v. Metropolitan Atlanta Rapid Transit Auth.*, 841 F.3d 1533, 1539 (11th Cir.1988)

[246] *Guillory v. St. Landry Parish Police Jury*, 802 F.2d 822, 824 (5th Cir.1986), Vaughn v. Edel, 918 F.2d 517, 521 (5th Cir. 1990)

[247] *Desert Palace, Inc. v. Costa*, 539 U.S. 90, 95, 123 S.Ct. 2148, 156 L.Ed.2d 84 (2003)

Once such a showing has been made, the employer cannot escape liability. However, through use of a limited affirmative defense, if an employer can demonstrate that it *"would have taken the same action in the absence of the impermissible motivating factor,"* it can restrict a plaintiff's damages to injunctive and declaratory relief, and attorney's fees and costs. 42 U.S.C.A. § 2000e-5(g)(2)(B).[2]

C - Mixed Motives Under the Human Rights Law

This provision has no direct application to cases brought under the Human Rights Law, but similar logic might in an appropriate case bear upon the determination of a complainant's actual economic loss. The Court of Appeals has adopted a similar evidentiary standard in "mixed motive" cases arising under the Human Rights Law. An employer must make a showing that the employee was terminated for some independently legitimate reason which was neither a pretext for discrimination nor was substantially influenced by impermissible discrimination.[248] In New York, the reasoning in Batista above, should be applied in all cases, regardless of basis. The determining factor is the showing of a nexus between the protected classes status and the adverse action – i.e. showing that the action *"was substantially influenced by impermissible discrimination."* A "mixed-motives" case is one in which an employer has created uncertainty as to causation by knowingly giving substantial weight to an impermissible criterion in firing an employee. Once petitioner has made out a prima facie case of mixed motives, the burden shifts to the employer to show that its employment decision would have been the same absent the unlawful motive.[249]

The Division of Human Rights has the power to conduct a hearing and has a wide discretion in its choice of a remedy deemed adequate to cope with the unlawful practices in question, including ex-offenders and advertising limitations. The courts will not interfere except where the remedy selected has no reasonable relation to the unlawful practices found to exist.[250] The Division's goal is to prevent the bias that exists towards ex-offenders. By the Division exerting its authority to cover conviction record advertising through General Counsel it has developed a rational and non-arbitrary and non-capricious way of reasonably relating those goals to stopping Respondents who advertise limitations on ex-offenders. When a hiring standard adversely affects equal employment opportunity for protected class of persons, judicial scrutiny is warranted and it is incumbent upon the employer to show that the standard bears a rational relationship to, and is a valid predictor of, employee job performance and does not create an arbitrary, artificial and unnecessary barrier to employment operating invidiously to discriminate on the basis of an impermissible classification.[251]

The Division of Human Rights has also determined that a Respondent cannot through its advertising of a position tell a potential applicant with an arrest or a criminal conviction "do not apply." The reasoning by the Division is that a Respondent cannot properly weigh the factors required by Article 23-A of the Correction Law if a potential victim of discrimination follows the Respondent's instructions. If a Respondent clearly states it does not want an application for employment it is not a defense for the Respondent to come back and demand an application for employment. It is clear that the Division will not allow a Respondent to jeopardize a Complainant's ability to apply for and be considered for employment in compliance with the Human Rights Law in a fair and equitable manner as proscribed by the law.[252]

D - The NYFCRA and Criminal Background Checks

The legislature amended the law concerning New York's Fair Credit Reporting Act (NY FCRA) in February 2009 by requiring that whenever an investigative consumer report is requested in connection with an offer for employment, the notice required under the fair credit reporting act must include a copy of Correction Law Article 23-A. N.Y. GBL §380-c(b) (2). Also, the law proscribes that whenever a reporting agency provides to an employer a report that contains a criminal conviction, the employer must provide the employee or applicant with a copy of Correction Law Article 23-A. N.Y. GBL §380-g(d). Employers are also required to post a copy of Article 23-A of the New York Correction Law at their place of business on a poster as per the New York Labor Law 201-F since its passage on February 1, 2009.

---

[248] *New York City Board of Education v. Batista, 54 N.Y.2d 379, 384 n. 1, 446 N.Y.S.2d 1 (1981). See also Pace College v. Commission on Human Rights, 38 N.Y.2d 28, 40, 377 N.Y.S.2d 471, 480 (1975) (what the plaintiff did to cause her termination would not have been considered "troublesome" if she had not been a woman).*

[249] *Price Waterhouse v Hopkins, 490 US 228, 270-277(1989)*

[250] *Jacob Siegel Co. v. Federal Trade Comm., 327 U.S. 608, 611, 612-613, 66 S.Ct. 758, 760, 90 L.Ed. 888; see, also, National Labor Relations Board v. Cheney California Lumber Co., supra, 327 U.S. 385, 388, 66 S.Ct. 553, 554; Federal Trade Comm. v. Ruberoid Co., 343 U.S. 470, 473, 72 S.Ct. 800, 803, 96 L.Ed. 1081.*

[251] *City of Schenectady v. State Division of Human Rights, 1975, 37 N.Y.2d 421, 373 N.Y.S.2d 59, 335 N.E.2d 290, reargument denied 38 N.Y.2d 856, 382 N.Y.S.2d 1031, 345 N.E.2d 606.*

[252] *Jeremy D. Zielenski v Makotek Inc. SDHR 10152295*

An employer may properly condition employment on a background investigation.[253] Conducting a background investigation is a lawful and a useful tool in the employer's hiring process by properly verifying the information provided on the application for employment. A permitted practice, such as running a background check can result in an undesirable condition which conflicts with the objectives of the Human Rights Law if used as the sole basis of denial of an ex-offender rather than the statutory obligation under Correction Law Article 23-A.[254]

A background investigation can be deemed unlawful discriminatory practice based on prior criminal conviction if the denial of the job offer is based on the results of the background check investigation (ie. pass, fail, score, matrix, or grade) that do not utilize Correction Law Article 23-A § 752 and permit an individual analysis of the conviction record. Employers often refer to the process of analyzing a conviction record confirmed on a background check as an "adjudication guideline". An "adjudication guideline" that utilizes a pass, fail, score, matrix or grade to make a Complainant non-competitive is in violation of the Human Rights Law § 296(15) since Correction Law § 752 states only two exceptions for denying employment to an ex-offender on the basis of their conviction, neither of which is the results of a background investigation. The eight factor test that must be conducted under New York Correction Law § 753 also does not mention denial on the basis of a background check investigation or list it as one of the 8 factors to be considered.

An employer must produce evidence that it conducted the analysis where a criminal background check is failed and the individual is deemed non-competitive.[255] A failure to take into consideration each of these 8 factors results in a failure to comply with the Correction Law's mandatory directive.[256] In order to secure the offer for employment an ex-offender who submits to a criminal background has often resulted in the incorrect application of Correction Law Article 23-A during the hiring process. A background check investigation that "fails" the applicant and rescinds the offer is not what the legislature intended with the 2009 amendments. If "passing" the background check secures you the job, it can be reasoned that "failing" a background check results in denial of employment or services.[257] Based on the legislature and judicial case law a "failed" background check is clearly not in compliance with Article 23-A and its provisions and the public policy of New York to hire an ex-offender when the factors are improperly weighed and no evidence of rehabilitation is considered before rendering the adverse action.

E-New York State Attorney General Investigations

The Attorney General's Office, through investigation, found in 2008 that RadioShack, after providing applicants with conditional offers of employment, had a policy of conducting criminal background checks that eliminated those with any arrest (sealed convictions) or conviction record (felonies within 7 years) that was disclosed.[258] RadioShack withdrew offers of employment from conditional employees in New York State and required that applicants, "must pass a background check" before they could be hired. Over 100 applicants were turned away, and probably many more were discouraged because they could not complete the process.

In a similar investigation, the Attorney General also investigated Aramark because it would openly advertise, ""All Applicants must have a FULLY clean background for the past seven (7) years and pass a criminal background check."[259] During the investigation it was also discovered that Aramark had a policy of evaluating conditional employees with a criminal background history, Aramark's "5-point Rating System" (which did not utilize Correction Law Article 23-A in any capacity, but rather created an "adjudication guideline"). These two instances are just exemplifying what is occurring in the denial of ex-offenders across the State of New York when Respondent's advertise they want an ex-offender to "pass" a background check. Most recently in 2014, Bed Bath and Beyond was caught by the Attorney General discouraging felons and automatically denying applications

---

[253] *ATM Corporation of America v. Unemployment Board of Review*, 892 A.2d 859, 2006 Pa.Commw.LEXIS 21 (Pa.Commw.Ct. 2006).

[254] *State Div. of Human Rights v Kilian Mfg. Corp.*, 35 N.Y.2d 201, 209.

[255] *Ishmael Walker v Wal-Mart Stores East LP SDHR 10111967*, where Walker failed the background check and Wal-Mart did not produce any evidence it engaged in such Article 23-A considerations.

[256] *Matter of Arrocha v Board of Educ. of City of N.Y.*, 93 NY2d 361, 364 [1999] ["the Board must consider" (emphasis added) the Correction Law § 753 (1) factors]).

[257] *See Matter of Tara Cummiskey v Rhea 2011 NY Slip 401289/10* (Where Cummiskey failed a criminal background check run by N.Y.C.H.A.), *Black v New York State Office of Mental Retardation and Developmental Disabilities 20 Misc.3d 581 (2008)*, 858 N.Y.S. 2d 859 (Where Black was hired by Arc subject to her passing the mandatory criminal background check, which she failed), *Matter of Bello v Whole Foods Market Group, Inc. and the New York Division of Human Rights No. 2010 NY Slip 402958/09* (Whole Foods conducted a background check and failed Bello on the basis of criminal convictions revealed). *Enigwe v U.S. Airways/U.S. Airways Express; Piedmont Airlines D.C. Civ No. 10-cv-01003)*(Where Enigwe's conviction was past the 10 years stated on the application but he still failed the background check), *Levine v WalMart Stores Inc. No. 4:08-CV-114*, 2008 WL 203658 (Where Levine failed a background check and was refused hire).

[258] *Matter of Cuomo and RadioShack Corporation AOD No 09-148*.

[259] *Matter of Cuomo and Aramark Corporation AOD No 09-164*.

without following the provisions of Correction Law Article 23-A. The unlawful discriminatory practice was discovered during a job fair. In addition the Attorney General also discovered that Party City was discouraging ex-offenders by having their managers indicate they would not hire felons and fined them $125,000 and ordered them to cease their policy and start hiring those who are qualified and have felonies for employment.

There are, of course, cases which establish, quite rightly, the principle that the antidiscrimination laws cannot be avoided by the expedient of using carefully designed code words. Code words which achieve the connotative effect of communicating such discrimination may be dealt with as discriminatory, even where the denotative meaning of the words or phrases in issue is an innocent one.[260] Discrimination can be inferred from evidence that the decision-maker showed a preference for a person not of the protected class. Where no evidence giving rise to an inference of discrimination has been presented, the fact that a plaintiff is replaced with an individual within his protected class undermines his attempt to establish a prima facie case of employment discrimination.[261] The New York State Human Rights Law (NYSHRL) and New York City Human Rights Law (NYCHRL) apply when a discriminatory act is committed in New York, even if impact of that act is felt outside of New York. It would be contrary to purpose of both NYSHRL and NYCHRL to leave it to courts of other jurisdictions to appropriately respond to acts of discrimination that occurred in New York.[262] When a non- resident seeks to invoke the coverage of the New York City and State Human Rights Laws, he or she must show that the alleged discrimination occurred within New York City and New York State respectively.[263]

F - Arrest Record and the Human Rights Law

In pertinent part, Executive Law § 296 (16) provides: "*It shall be an unlawful discriminatory practice, unless specifically required or permitted by statute, for any person, agency, bureau, corporation or association, including the state and any political subdivision thereof, to make any inquiry about, whether in any form of application or otherwise, or to act upon adversely to the individual involved, any arrest or criminal accusation of such individual not then pending against that individual which was followed by a termination of that criminal action or proceeding in favor of such individual, as defined in subdivision two of section 160.50 of the criminal procedure law, in connection with the employment [of] such individual.*"

The legislative purpose for adding the arrest provision of the Human Rights Law was to ensure that the protections provided to exonerate accused be "consistent with the presumption of innocence, which simply means that no individual should suffer adverse consequences merely on the basis of an accusation, unless the charges were ultimately sustained in a court of law." (Governor's Approval Mem, 1976 McKinney's Session Law of NY, at 2451)

It is a per se discriminatory practice to inquire about prior arrests on an application for employment. Executive Law 296 (16) permits such inquiry of applicants for employment as peace officers, which includes correction officers (CPL 1.20 [33]; 2.10 [25]) based on a 1985 amendment (L 1985, Ch 208) Matter of New York State Dept. of Mental Hygiene v State Div. of Human Rights, 66 N.Y.2d 752 (1985), Sheriff's Department v State Division of Human Rights 129 A.D. 2d 789 (1987).

The Human Rights Law is explicit in its condemnation of employment related inquiries regarding arrest records and using it as a critical factor to deny employment. To establish a prima facie case of unlawful discrimination under N.Y. Executive Law § 296 (16) a complainant must show that (1) he was a member of a protected class (2) he was qualified for the position that he sought (3) he was not hired (4) the circumstances under which he was denied employment gave rise to an inference of unlawful discrimination. Pace College v Commission of the City of New York, 38 N.Y. 3d 28, 39-40, 377 N.Y.S. 3d 471 (1975). Once a complainant establishes a prima facie case, a Respondent must show that the action was non-discriminatory and for a legitimate business reason. St. Mary's Honor v Hicks, 50 U.S. 502 (1993). If Respondent articulates a legitimate non-discriminatory reason for the adverse employment decision, the burden is on the complainant to proffer why the reasons proffered were false and that the arrest was not the reason for adverse decision. Holt v Kmi-Continental, Inc. 95 F. 3d 123, 129 (2d Cir. 1996), cert. denied 520 U.S. 1228 (1997).

In Hynes v Karassik, 47 N.Y. 2d 659 (1979), the Court noted at p.662 that the intent behind the enactment of both Section 160.50 of the Criminal Procedure Law and Section 296 of the Executive Law, subdivision 16 was that the statute serves the laudable goal of insuring that one who is charged but not convicted of an

---

[260] *United States v Hunter, 459 F.2d 205, cert den 409 US 934; Camp-of-The-Pines v New York Times Co., 184 Misc 389 Hodgson v Approved Personnel Serv., 529 F.2d 760.*

[261] *Giannone v. Deutsche Bank Securities, Inc., 2005, 392 F.Supp.2d 576*

[262] *RobnPadmore, Inc. v. LC Play Inc., 2010, 679 F.Supp.2d 454.*

[263] *McKinney's Executive Law §§ 296(1)(a); N.Y.C. Admin. Rylott-Rooney v. Alitalia-Linee Aeree Italiane-Societa Per Azioni, 2008, 549 F.Supp.2d 549.*

offense suffers no stigma as a result of his having once been the object of an unsustained accusation.

That detriment to one's reputation and employment prospects often flows from merely having been subjected to criminal process has long been recognized as a serious and unfortunate by-product of even unsuccessful criminal prosecutions (see Menard v Mitchell, 430 F.2d 486, 490 [BAZELON, Ch. J.]; see, also, Schwartz & Skolnik, Two Studies of Legal Stigma, 10 Social Prob 133 [1962]; Hess & Le Poole, Abuse of the Record of Arrest Not Leading to Conviction, 13 Crime & Delinquency 494 [1967]). The statute's design is to lessen such consequences (see Governor's Approval Memorandum, 663*663 NY Legis Ann, 1976, p 408; see, generally, Gough, Expungement of Adjudication Records of Juvenile and Adult Offenders: A Problem of Status, 1966 Wash U LQ 147, 156, 157-162).

The broad thrust of the sealing requirement is further evidenced by CPL 160.60, which states in no uncertain terms that "*[t]he arrest or [unsuccessful] prosecution shall not operate as a disqualification of any person so accused to pursue or engage in any lawful activity, occupation, profession, or calling* . . . Consistent with the statute's remedial purpose, is its intended application to any criminal action or proceeding terminated in favor of the person accused. The broad definition thus encompasses an expansive class of dispositions, including acquittal and various specified dismissals and vacaturs, regardless of whether premised on grounds unrelated to guilt or innocence (see CPL 160.50, subd 2).

Although New York Executive Law § 296 (16) does not permit an employer "to act upon adversely" an applicant regarding a pending charge followed by a conviction for a violation, "it is permissible to consider the independent evidence of the conduct leading to the criminal charges."[264] Material in the sealed criminal records may lead to relevant evidence, independent of the fact of the conviction itself.[265] *CPL 160.50* creates a statutory privilege intended to ensure confidentiality and protect an individual from the potential stigma resulting from a criminal matter."[266] Where, however, an individual affirmatively places the underlying conduct at issue by bringing a civil suit, the courts have consistently held that the statutory protection is waived.[267] This also applies to *CPL 160.55*, which similarly provides for sealing of criminal records.

---

[264] *(Matter of Skyline Inn Corp. v New York State Liq. Auth.,* 44 N.Y. 2d 695, 696 [1978] [interpreting Executive Law § 296 (14), which has similar "act upon adversely" language]; *Matter of New York State Dept. of Mental Hygiene v State Div. of Human Rights,* 103 A.D. 2d 546, 549 [2d Dept 1984], affd 66 N.Y. 2d 752 [1985]).

[265] *See Matter of Weigand [Elbridge True Value Hardware—Hudacs],* 187 A.D. 2d 791 [3d Dept 1992] [Claimant was charged with two misdemeanors stemming from theft of cash and merchandise, and charges were adjourned in *contemplation of dismissal and dismissed. Unemployment Insurance Board properly considered signed statement contained in sealed records that employee had been stealing from his employer up until his termination and making false returns on the cash register].)*

[266] *Wright v Snow,* 175 A.D.2d 451, 452 [3rd Dept 1991]

[267] *Green v Montgomery,* 95 NY2d 693, 701 [2001]; *Rodriguez v Ford Motor Co.,* 301 A.D.2d 372 [1st Dept 2003].)

PART V

THE FUTURE OF NEW YORK CORRECTION LAW ARTICLE 23-A:
DISPARATE IMPACT AND BAN THE BOX

A - Disparate Impact and Conviction Record

As the Court of Appeals made clear an employment practice neutral on its face and in terms of intent which has a disparate impact upon a protected class of persons violates the Human Rights Law[268] unless the employer can show justification for the practice in terms of employee performance. A standard or practice *"fair in form but discriminatory in operation"* as to employment or promotional opportunity is within the reach of the Human Rights Law.[269]

Where a condition exists in fact which permits an objective test as to whether a practice operates invidiously against a particular group, if it be so found, such obstacle can and should be removed by appropriate action unless the practice can be justified by business necessity.[270] In the absence of conduct from which willful intent might be presumed, the question rather is whether an employer knows or should have known the ultimate result or effect of its hiring practice. The Human Rights Law, *inter alia*, aims at equality of job opportunity not discriminatory preference.

When a hiring standard, although neutral on its face or even neutral in terms of intent, adversely affects equal employment opportunity for a protected class of persons, judicial scrutiny of that hiring criterion is warranted.[271] It is then incumbent upon the employer to show that the standard or test bears a rational relationship to and is a valid predictor of employee job performance, and that it does not create an arbitrary, artificial and unnecessary barrier to employment which operates invidiously to discriminate on the basis of an impermissible classification.[272]

The premise of disparate impact theory is that some employment practices, adopted without a deliberately discriminatory motive, may be the functional equivalent of intentional discrimination. In essence, disparate impact theory is a doctrinal surrogate for eliminating unprovable acts of intentional discrimination hidden innocuously behind facially-neutral policies or practices.

Gender based conviction record disparate impact is supported by the Equal Employment Opportunity Commission (herein known as "EEOC"). In <u>EEOC v Freeman 09cv2573 (4th Cir. 2015)</u> the EEOC alleged that Freeman's use of criminal history as a hiring criterion has a disparate impact on Black, Hispanic and male job applicants. The EEOC also pointed out that Freeman's ban on criminal history is neither job-related nor consistent with business necessity and there are less discriminatory alternative selection procedures available. Since the EEOC supports disparate impact claims on male job applicants, the EEOC must consider the argument and establish a broad authority and responsibility to root out gender based conviction record discrimination in the American workplace. The EEOC has previously determined that the refusal to hire an applicant with an unacceptable criminal history is undoubtedly a discrete act of discrimination based on gender and actionable under Title VII. Such an argument can be put forth through a disparate impact gender argument.

The disparate impact framework under Title VII by now is well-settled. A plaintiff need not prove discriminatory intent to make out a claim of disparate impact.[273] Congress has codified the appropriate burdens of proof in a disparate impact case in <u>42 U.S.C. § 2000e-2(k) (1994)</u>, and a settled jurisprudence has arisen to implement the methodology. A permitted practice, (such as banning ex-offenders on the basis of conviction) can result in a undesirable condition which conflicts with the objectives of the Human Rights Law.[274]

In a case involving a criminal record exclusion, the Eighth Circuit in <u>Green v. Missouri Pacific Railroad 523 F.2d 1290 (1975)</u> held that it was discriminatory under Title VII for an employer to follow a policy or practice requiring an automatic, across-the-board exclusion from all employment opportunities because of any criminal conduct is inconsistent with the Green factors because it does not focus on the dangers of particular crimes and the risks in particular positions. As the court recognized in Green, *"[w]e cannot conceive of any business necessity that would automatically place every individual convicted of any offense, except a minor*

---

[268] *Matter of Sontag v Bronstein 33 N.Y.2d 197, 201 (1973),*

[269] *State Div. of Human Rights v Kilian Mfg. Corp., 35 N.Y.2d 201, 209; cf. Connecticut v Teal, 457 US 440, 446-447, 454-456 (1982).*

[270] *Griggs v Duke Power Co., 401 U.S. 424 (1971).*

[271] *New York State Div. of Human Rights v. New York-Pennsylvania Professional Baseball League, 36 A. D. 2d 364, affd. 29 N Y 2d 921 (1972); State Div. of Human Rights v. New York City Dept. of Parks & Recreation, 38 A. D. 2d 25, 26-28 (1971).*

[272] *New York State Div. of Human Rights v. New York-Pennsylvania Professional Baseball League, supra; State Div. of Human Rights (1972) v. New York City Dept. of Parks & Recreation, supra; cf. Weeks v. Southern Bell Tel. & Tel. Co., 408 F.2d 228, 235-236 [5th Cir.] (1969)*

[273] *Griggs v. Duke Power Co., 401 U.S. 424, 431, 91 S.Ct. 849, 853, 28 L.Ed.2d 158 (1971)*

[274] (the question rather is whether an employer knows or should have known the ultimate result or effect of its hiring practice.) *State Div. of Human Rights v Kilian Mfg. Corp., 35 N.Y.2d 201, 209; cf. Connecticut v Teal, 457 US 440, 446-447, 454-456.*

traffic offense, in the permanent ranks of the unemployed. To deny job opportunities to these individuals because of some conduct which may be remote in time or does not significantly bear upon the particular job requirements is an unnecessarily harsh and unjust burden."

While Title VII does not directly cover conviction record, the court reasoned that to render every applicant with a conviction record denied would not only destroy the purpose of Title VII but would put a harsh and unjust burden upon the protected classes by directly affecting the ability to be hired, especially upon male minorities. The Eighth Circuit identified three factors (the "Green factors") that were relevant to assessing whether exclusion is job related for the position in question and consistent with business necessity:

- **The nature and gravity of the offense or conduct;**

- **The time that has passed since the offense or conduct and/or completion of the sentence;**

- **The nature of the job held or sought.**

An employment criterion that bans all felons and certain misdemeanors must be examined for its operation on a gender exclusionary basis — thus its effect must be measured upon males separately and upon females separately as it would be measured in race upon whites and blacks separately.[275]

In order to prevail on a disparate impact discrimination claim, a Complainant must establish a prima facie case by first identifying the specific employment practice that is challenged, which is conviction record based. Next the Complainant must show an adverse effect caused by the employment practice by offering "*statistical evidence of a kind or degree sufficient to show that the practice in question has caused the exclusion of applicants for jobs or promotion because of their membership in a protected group.*"[276]

If a prima facie case is made out under disparate impact, the burden of showing nondiscrimination shifts to the employer, and the employer is required to consider whatever reasons that might be offered to justify the allegedly discriminatory action.[277] To satisfy its burden an employer's explanation must consist of not only a nondiscriminatory reason for its conviction record ban, but also credible evidence indicating that the reasons advanced were the real reasons for the action and not merely a pretext for discriminatory conduct. As the finder of fact, the EEOC has the critical and sensitive function of determining whether the proffered reason is the genuine explanation for the employer's conduct.[278]

Once a Complainant establishes a prima facie case of disparate impact by statistical evidence, the Respondent must articulate a legitimate, non-discriminatory reason for the employment practice. At that point, the burden shifts back to the plaintiff to show either that the employer's reason is a pretext for discrimination, or that there exists an alternative employment practice which would achieve the same.

Disparate impact has not proved immensely useful in efforts to shield ex-offenders from continual discrimination by employers. Whether it be by race or sex, since Green in 1975 there has not been a winning federal disparate impact case, even though minorities are more disproportionately excluded now than they were then, and males are still convicted at higher rates than females. From the time Article 23-A of the Correction Law was passed only two states had passed anti-discrimination statutes protecting ex-offenders, Wisconsin and Pennsylvania.

B - Conviction Record Protection Outside New York Prior to 1998: Pennsylvania and Wisconsin

Keeping in mind that few states protected criminal conviction histories in anyway prior to 1998, Pennsylvania passed its own statute in 1979. The Criminal History Record Information Act ("CHIRA"), of July 16, 1979, *P.L. 116, No. 47*, <u>18 Pa. C.S.A. §§ 9101</u> *et seq.* (effective January 1, 1980), was passed to limit the use of criminal records by employers when making employment decisions. All employers with 1 or more employees are subject to Section 9125 and there is nothing about stated "qualifications" within the statute. It provides a limited right to action in the courts but no stated financial remedy.

---

[275] *Griggs v. Duke Power Co., supra, 401 U.S. at 430 n.6, 91 S.Ct. 849, 28 L.Ed.2d 158; United States v. Georgia Power Co., supra, 474 F.2d at 918; Gregory v. Litton Systems, Inc., supra, 316 F.Supp. at 403; Johnson v. Pike Corp., supra, 332 F.Supp. at 494; cf.*

[276] *Watson v. Fort Worth Bank & Trust Co., 487 U.S. 977, Id. at 994, 108 S.Ct. at 2788 (1988)*

[277] *Smith College, supra at 229. See James v. Newspaper Agency Corp., 591 F.2d 579, 583 (10th Cir.1979) (McKay, J., dissenting).*

[278] *Sweeney v. Trustees of Keene State College, 569 F.2d 169, 180 (1st Cir.) (Campbell, J., concurring), vacated and remanded, 439 U.S. 24 (1978).*

The courts in Pennsylvania have concluded that convictions for felonies and misdemeanors may be considered only insofar as they relate to an applicant's suitability for the job. "*allows employers to consider, when relevant in hiring decisions, convictions but not arrests.*" Foxworth v. Pa. State Police, 228 F. App'x 151, 155 (3d Cir. 2007). An action can be brought on the basis of arrests as the term "criminal history record information", as defined by the Act, includes "notations of arrests". 18 Pa.C.S.A. § 9102.

There is a private right of action for Pa.C.S.A. § 9125. The Act provides that "*[a]ny person aggrieved by a violation of the provisions of this chapter . . . shall have the substantive right to bring an action for damages by reason of such violation in a court of competent jurisdiction.*" 18 Pa.C.S.A. § 9183(b)(1). The court assumes that the principle of considering only convictions that relate to the job duties is an expression of public policy against unnecessarily stigmatizing former offenders. It is against the public policy of the Commonwealth to summarily reject an individual for employment on the ground that the individual has a prior criminal record unless in doing so the employer is furthering a legitimate public objective. Cisco v. United Parcel Services, 328 Pa.Super. 300, 476 A.2d 1340 (1984); Hunter v. Port Authority of Allegheny County, 277 Pa.Super. 4, 12, 419 A.2d 631, 635 (1980).

Section 9125 restricts an employer's reliance on an applicant's criminal history in the hiring process. Section 9125 may be implicated and there is possibly of a public policy issue because termination that may occur after hiring, may have been a decision concerning an applicant's criminal background made within or during the hiring process. Smith v. USG Corporation No. 101 MDA 2013. Advertising the precludes ex-offenders appears to be unlawful. ("It is not simply a request to be hired as the employment contends, rather it seeks to pollute the hiring decision by introducing the prohibited consideration as a legitimate basis for denial.") Commonwealth of Pennsylvania. v. Pittsburgh Press Co., 483 Pa. 314 396 A.2d 1187 (1979).

The employer's reasoning that it has any legitimate employment rationale to bar felons and misdemeanors is wrong. Section 9125 specifically states the only exemption an employer is entitled to when denying someone with a felony or misdemeanor conviction. Because Section 9125 controls business necessity in Pennsylvania, a blanket policy that violates public policy as well could never be a "legitimate business reason." Because Section 9125 specifies permissible business judgment, Respondent has actually indicated a discriminatory reason for its actions, and failed to meet its burden.

Wisconsin in 1981 passed its own statute to protect arrest and conviction record at WL§ 111.321. Considered the "substantial relationship test" an employer cannot deny employment unless there is a substantial relationship between the job duties and the conviction record. An employer in Wisconsin is prevented from placing applications or ads which discourage or chill ex-offenders by statute. The Wisconsin Equal Rights Division enforces this law. The Wisconsin Fair Employment Act provides that it is an act of employment discrimination to terminate from employment, or to discriminate against any individual in terms, conditions or privileges of employment because of conviction record. Wis. Stats., secs. 111.322 and 111.321. Sec. 111.335(1)(c)1 provides an exception, however, whereby it is not employment discrimination because of conviction record to terminate any individual who has been convicted of any felony, misdemeanor or other offense the circumstances of which substantially relate to the circumstances of the particular job.

A determination of whether the circumstances of a criminal offense are substantially related to a particular job requires assessing whether the tendencies and inclinations to behave in a certain way in a particular context are likely to reappear later in a related context, based on the traits revealed. It is the circumstances which foster criminal activity that are important, e.g., the opportunity for criminal behavior, the reaction to responsibility, or the character traits of the person. County of Milwaukee v. LIRC, 139 Wis. 2d 805, 824, 407 N.W.2d 908 (1987); Goerl v. Appleton Papers, Inc. (LIRC, October 5, 1992). As a general rule, the circumstances of the offense are gleaned from a review of the elements of the crime, and an inquiry into the factual details of the specific offense is not required. County of Milwaukee, at 823-824.

Wisconsin's statutes allow for enforcement of chilling advertising and denials of employment which have no substantial relationship to the job duties. The entire state has not banned the box, so the conviction record question is lawful. This is why it is not included in the next section, but its procedures for preventing conviction record discrimination are on a level next to New York. However, Wisconsin does not have any certificates of relief and the substantial relationship test is undefined and left to the courts for interpretation. Not every case is so easily decided though.

C - What Is Ban The Box?

The "ban the box" initiatives typically remove the "**have you ever been convicted of a crime?**" question from the job application, can prevent advertisements from barring or discouraging applicants to apply for certain jobs and delay the asking of the question until later in the hiring process, mostly when the job offer has been secured and the applicant is deemed qualified. Over 100 jurisdictions and twelve states have some sort of "ban the box" policy. However, not all of these "ban the box" laws are the same and not all of them address the evils of employers concerning advertising and blanket policies in print. Most still apply to public employers, not private.

D - The First Ban The Box State: Hawaii

The first ban the box law, Hawaii House Bill 3528 located at HRS § 378-2.5, was passed in 1998 against public and private employers and they were prohibited from inquiring about an applicant's criminal conviction history until after a conditional offer of employment is made, whereas the offer may only be withdrawn if a conviction satisfies a "rational relationship" to the duties and responsibilities of the position and consider the applicant's most recent ten year conviction record. Although Hawaii's statute extends to private employers, prospective employees of the federal government are excluded. Employers who are expressly permitted to inquire into an individual's criminal history for employment purposes under other state or federal laws include the Department of Education, counties, armed security services, certain health care facilities, and detective and security guard agencies among others. An employer is limited to a 10 year scope for a conviction record, something not available in other ban the box laws.

E - Ban The Box After Hawaii

For the better part of the next decade, a majority of states continued to ask the employment question about conviction and chose to take no stance to encourage the interviewing or hire of ex-offenders. As some states pushed to make public employment compliant with ban the box, the issue came back into the forefront of current politics due to the recession and movements by not for profits who organized to get politicians to remove the question and promote fairness. Boston banned the box for public employers in 2006. Minnesota in 2009 banned the box for public employment by passing Chapter 364, titling it "Criminal Rehabilitation" and even going so far as to demand that public employment not be denied unless there was a direct relationship.

F - Massachusetts Bans The Box;
Incorporates Conviction Record Inquiries as Protected Class;
Ensures Background Check Accuracy

Then on November 4, 2010 Massachusetts became the second state to publically and privately ban the box by passing GBL 151B §9 and §9½. While Hawaii had completely prevented an employer from ascertaining anything about convictions until a conditional offer was put forth, Massachusetts incorporated a private right to action and accorded ex-offenders protected class status concerning any inquiries before an interview. Further, the legislature sought to make criminal history accurate and available to ensure that employers were utilizing one database. This resulted in passage of laws to ensure that C.O.R.I. (Criminal Offender Record Information) would be centralized and even third party background check companies would have to obtain the information from a central database. The Massachusetts Commission Against Discrimination enforces the ban the box provision and all rights and remedies available to other protected classes are available to ex-offenders.

G - Widespread Passage; California, New Jersey, Illinois and Oregon

In 2013 numerous states began banning the box against private employers, including Maryland, Rhode Island and Minnesota. Jurisdictions such as Philadelphia in 2012 and Seattle, Buffalo, Rochester and San Francisco in 2014 pushed through ban the box. San Francisco not only bans the box but bars any employer from inquiring into conviction record in any advertisement. On August 11, 2014 New Jersey announced that it was banning the box for public and private employers by removing the question and making advertisements in the state unlawful before an interview is conducted. While the New Jersey law has no private right of action it went into effect on March 1, 2015 and has fines of $1,000 to $5,000 for repeat offenders. Washington D.C banned the box privately in 2014 as well. On January 1, 2015 Illinois passed its own law and now privately bans the box. On October 27, 2015 New York City passed ban the box. More information about these laws and summaries of how each is applied can be found in the Appendix in this book. On January 1, 2016 Oregon will join states in ban the box, however, its law is the weakest of all. On January 1, 2018 California passed a strong ban the box law to rival New York City's, including prohibition of advertisements that discourage ex-offenders.

H - Equal Employment Opportunity Commission 2012 Guidelines

Spurred by the recent Ban the Box movement and seeing an opportunity to clarify its position after losing a case in court, the EEOC realized that its lack of established guidelines hurt its chances of proper enforcement of Title VII. On April 25, 2012 the EEOC released its updated conviction record guidelines. Many of these best practices show employers how to avoid disparate impact claims and claims that may conflict with enforcement of Title VII and its protection of other classes. There are two ways in which an employer's use of criminal history information may violate Title VII. First, Title VII prohibits employers from treating job applicants with the same criminal records differently because of their race, color, religion, sex, or national origin ("disparate treatment discrimination"). Second, even where employers apply criminal record exclusions uniformly, the exclusions may still operate to disproportionately and unjustifiably exclude people of a particular race or national origin ("disparate impact discrimination"). If the employer does not show that such an exclusion is "job related and consistent with business necessity" for the position in question, the exclusion is unlawful under Title VII. These guidelines are available as an appendix in this book.

Final Thoughts and Suggestions For Legislative Change in New York

It appears to this author that the standard of the New York Courts has now reverted back to pre-1976 where the current courts, including the Court of Appeals have always concluded a criminal conviction rendered a candidate ineligible for private and public work, regardless of the conviction record. Employers in today's hiring world are still concerned about negligible hiring practices and the imposition of liability but the state has already addressed this fear. Negligible hiring has been held by the Appellate Division to not be a valid excuse in denying employment to an ex-offender because it creates *"an unacceptably chilling effect on society's efforts to reintegrate ex-offenders into mainstream society, contract to precedent and the explicitly stated public policy of the State."*[279]

With ban the box spreading and more states and jurisdictions jumping on the proverbial bandwagon, the country will eventually adopt the policy that the conviction record question will cease to be asked on employment applications and employers will have to interview and conduct background checks in compliance with state and federal laws. This does not solve the immediate problem as the discrimination just moves to the back of the hiring process, rather than the front where it has been for decades.

Correction Law Article 23-A needs significant legislative upgrades. New York State, while having a progressive way to analyze conviction records, has no mechanism for the elimination of an individual's criminal record as a consideration in employment decisions similar to Hawaii's ban the box model, which excludes consideration beyond 10 years. New York allows employers to consider a conviction no matter how old it is to the detriment of the ex-offender.

Another major flaw is that private employers rarely ask or inquire about a Certificate of Relief or Good Conduct because they give little value to them since they only remove forfeitures and disabilities imposed by state law and most ex-offenders do not know how or where to obtain one. Judges upon conviction do not mention them and courts and the board of parole often check a box denying an ex-offender the certificate, without ever telling them what they need to do in violation of the enumerated factors set forth in Correction Law § 702 (2).[280]

The courts have severely and consistently restricted the direct relationship and unreasonable risk exemptions based on finding rationality allowing employers broad leeway to reject applicants under a catchall "lack of integrity" argument. The Court of Appeals in its decisions on Correction Law Article 23-A has rarely sided for the rehabilitated ex-offender unless a factor was missing from the analysis, forcing a remand. It is proposed that the direct relationship test should be limited to instances which an element of the crime itself directly parallels a duty or potential risk of the employment or license sought.[281]

For Article 23-A to work the way it needs to, private and public employers cannot be treated differently under the same legislative scheme. There are no back pay, wages or damages if an agency discriminates but if a private employer discriminates, all of the above is available. An Article 78 is never available to challenge

279 Ford v Gilden 200 A.D. 2d 224 (N.Y. App. Div. 1994)

280 Figel v Dwyer 75 AD 3d 802, 907 N.Y.S.2d 75 (2010) In rendering a determination to either grant (in whole or in part) or deny petitioner's application for a CRD, respondent is required to consider and apply the statutorily enumerated factors set forth in Correction Law § 702 (2). The absence in respondent's cursory letter decision of any mention of the statutory factors or the grounds for the denial precludes meaningful review of the rationality of the decision.

281 Proposed by Jocelyn Simonson, Page 306 in Rethinking "Rational Discrimination" Against Ex-Offenders

Georgetown Journal on Poverty Law & Policy Volume XIII, Number 2, Summer 2006 amongst other ideas adopted for this book by the author.

a decision of a private employer. A public employer must inform the applicant in writing of its analysis if requested, where a private employer will not disclose such analysis unless it's in court or appearing at a hearing at the Division of Human Rights or City Commission. For the law to have its full effect, public agencies and private employers must be held to equal standards of the same law.

One of the major problems that has not been fixed by the legislature since 1976 is that an unreasonable risk remains undefined whereas a direct relationship is specific enough to be interpreted in favor of the ex-offender. This renders the unreasonable risk exemption vague and it is clear the courts will rule in favor of the employer since it appears every conviction is a threat to the public safety. The Court of Appeals has consistently and strictly interpreted Correction Law Article 23-A in overruling the lower courts by allowing agencies to deny employment under all circumstances, even when evidence submitted by a petitioner is extensive and unblemished and clearly reduces the unreasonable risk.[282] For the law to be truly progressive, an unreasonable risk must be defined by the legislature not just allowed to be assumed by employers.

As a final note, the legislature should fully utilize Article 23-A § 754 by revising it to force all employers to a strict standard of written reasoning of their denial or an application acted upon adversely of their individual 8 factor analysis. In this way state agencies and private employers would have to have gathered all the information, spoke to the applicant and would have to justify a denial of employment rather than coasting along claiming exemptions through an automated application system that go unchallenged without actually having to carry their burden. If there were consequences to hiring decisions, employers would more likely protect themselves by demonstrating the 8 factors if the statute mandated more specific requirements about penalties for failure to show an analysis upon request. As it stands now, Article 23-A § 754 demands a "reason for denial" in 30 days but that reason could be that an applicant looked at the interviewer the wrong way as it is written vaguely. If the legislature changed it to force employers to demonstrate how they arrived at their conclusion, the way the recent Ban the Box addition to the New York City Human Rights Commission just did, it would benefit the state as a whole and applicants as it was intended since 1976. As it stands private employers are clearly able to skirt the law more so then public employers when it comes to the 8 factor analysis when they don't have to provide it to an applicant for review before an adverse action.

While ban the box is a great start, New York's factor test is the way states and the federal government should proceed to ensure that ex-offenders have a fair chance to obtain employment. While many individuals seem to think the federal government will pass such legislation conviction record remains outside the federal government's protection mandate always looking in. The bias towards ex-offenders remains because to provide equal status is to justify to many politicians giving rights to those who broke the law and rewarding them for doing so. Rather than get more tax payers, ex-offenders often have no voting rights and limited power. By limiting their voice and excising them from the workforce by way of their crimes, they prevent their reintegration and encourage their recidivism. As it stands now the number one problem of the ex-offender is the increasing bigotry that appears in advertisements, completely ignoring Article 23-A by openly discouraging ex-offenders without understanding the damage it does. The legislature could remedy the problem by adding arrest and conviction record advertising protection to Exec. Law 296 (1) (d) or additional wordage to Exec. Law 296 (15) or the New York City Administrative Code 8-107 (10) and 8-107 (11) to prevent employers from discriminating against all state residents but it has not addressed the problem.

It stands that New York's Certificate of Relief system is the only one that encourages restoration of rights for all offenses through the court and parole system. With so many professions barred and unavailable because of a felony crime, or rights lost because of a misdemeanor, this remains a procedure so revolutionary that it should be considered when expanding the rights of ex-offenders in addition to ban the box. Removing the conviction record question from applications is a great start, but there is a lots of work to be done. Men and minorities are clearly suffering the strain as part of the 75 million people who are part of what is now viewed as a flawed class of people. While no one is suggesting that someone with a conviction record get preferred treatment the fact is that too many doors close and too many rights are lost once a felony is pled to. If we continue to lead the world in people incarcerated per capita[283], it is essential that ex-offenders be allowed to reintegrate back into society and support themselves. The other major issue is that lawyers and

---

[282] *Arrocha v Bd. Of Educ. of the City of New York, 677 N.Y.S. 2d 584, 585 (N.Y. App. Div. 1998)*

[283] The United States incarcerates 716 per 100,000 of the national population. While the United States represents about 4.4 percent of the world's population, it houses around 22 percent of the world's prisoners and is number one is this regard. In the last 90 years how the problem has been increasing over time. Women make up 10 percent of incarcerated criminals, while men make up 90 percent. Minorities are convicted at a higher rate than whites and therefore policies which bar ex-offenders fall hardest on that group based on race.

judges at time of guilty plea do not inform defendant's of the collateral consequences of their plea[284] and do not inform newly convicted ex-offenders that a Certificate of Relief or of Good Conduct would restore any forfeitures or civil disabilities imposed by law. Without awareness of these documents, ex- offenders will have no available means to be aware of how to restore their rights.

Massachusetts took a bold step reorganizing its Criminal Offender Record Information, something that should be viewed as a necessary step in New York in order to eliminate background check companies misuse of criminal record reporting in the hiring process. While this step is crucial for states, it is costly and requires legislatures to justify spending at a time when such budgets have their attention elsewhere. New York State should ensure correct usage of criminal record reporting in all hiring decisions.

Title VII federal law may never make conviction record a class of its own. If we truly want to solve the problem the first step is recognizing the invisible punishment needs to be addressed on a national scale and restoration of rights needs to be a top priority. The next step is creating a federal individualized assessment system like New York where an employer has a checks and balance system to ensure it conducts individualized assessments. If we can find a way to address the issues it can only benefit the over 70 million people who have a conviction record in the United States and society as well.

---

284 In *Padilla v. Kentucky, 130 S. Ct. 1473 (2010)* The Supreme Court specifically made it clear that attorneys are bound to discuss not only the criminal consequences of a criminal plea but the civil consequences of a plea that could have additional civil and criminal consequences as part of their effective assistance of counsel.

NEW YORK CORRECTION LAW - ARTICLE 23-A

LICENSURE AND EMPLOYMENT OF PERSONS PREVIOUSLY CONVICTED OF ONE OR MORE CRIMINAL OFFENSES

§750. Definitions.

For the purposes of this article, the following terms shall have the following meanings:

(1) "Public agency" means the state or any local subdivision thereof, or any state or local department, agency, board or commission.

(2) "Private employer" means any person, company, corporation, labor organization or association which employs ten or more persons.

(3) "Direct relationship" means that the nature of criminal conduct for which the person was convicted has a direct bearing on his fitness or ability to perform one or more of the duties or responsibilities necessarily related to the license, opportunity, or job in question.

(4) "License" means any certificate, license, permit or grant of permission required by the laws of this state, its political subdivisions or instrumentalities as a condition for the lawful practice of any occupation, employment, trade, vocation, business, or profession. Provided, however, that "license" shall not, for the purposes of this article, include any license or permit to own, possess, carry, or fire any explosive, pistol, handgun, rifle, shotgun, or other firearm.

(5) "Employment" means any occupation, vocation or employment, or any form of vocational or educational training. Provided, however, that "employment" shall not, for the purposes of this article, include membership in any law enforcement agency.

§751. Applicability.

The provisions of this article shall apply to any application by any person for a license or employment at any public or private employer, who has previously been convicted of one or more criminal offenses in this state or in any other jurisdiction, and to any license or employment held by any person whose conviction of one or more criminal offenses in this state or in any other jurisdiction preceded such employment or granting of a license, except where a mandatory forfeiture, disability or bar to employment is imposed by law, and has not been removed by an executive pardon, certificate of relief from disabilities or certificate of good conduct. Nothing in this article shall be construed to affect any right an employer may have with respect to an intentional misrepresentation in connection with an application for employment made by a prospective employee or previously made by a current employee.

§752. Unfair discrimination against persons previously convicted of one or more criminal offenses prohibited.

No application for any license or employment, and no employment or license held by an individual, to which the provisions of this article are applicable, shall be denied or acted upon adversely by reason of the individual's having been previously convicted of one or more criminal offenses, or by reason of a finding of lack of "good moral character" when such finding is based upon the fact that the individual has previously been convicted of one or more criminal offenses, unless:

(1) There is a direct relationship between one or more of the previous criminal offenses and the specific license or employment sought or held by the individual; or

(2) The issuance or continuation of the license or the granting or continuation of the employment would involve an unreasonable risk to property or to the safety or welfare of specific individuals or the general public.

§753. Factors to be considered concerning a previous criminal conviction; presumption.

1. In making a determination pursuant to section seven hundred fifty-two of this chapter, the public agency or private employer shall consider the following factors:

(a) The public policy of this state, as expressed in this act, to encourage the licensure and employment of persons previously convicted of one or more criminal offenses.

(b) The specific duties and responsibilities necessarily related to the license or employment sought or held by the person.

(c) The bearing, if any, the criminal offense or offenses for which the person was previously convicted will have on his fitness or ability to perform one or more such duties or responsibilities.

(d) The time which has elapsed since the occurrence of the criminal offense or offenses.

(e) The age of the person at the time of occurrence of the criminal offense or offenses.

(f) The seriousness of the offense or offenses.

(g) Any information produced by the person, or produced on his behalf, in regard to his rehabilitation and good conduct.

(h) The legitimate interest of the public agency or private employer in protecting property, and the safety and welfare of specific individuals or the general public.

2. In making a determination pursuant to section seven hundred fifty-two of this chapter, the public agency or private employer shall also give consideration to a certificate of relief from disabilities or a certificate of good conduct issued to the applicant, which certificate shall create a presumption of rehabilitation in regard to the offense or offenses specified therein.

§754. Written statement upon denial of license or employment.

At the request of any person previously convicted of one or more criminal offenses who has been denied a license or employment, a public agency or private employer shall provide, within thirty days of a request, a written statement setting forth the reasons for such denial.

§755. Enforcement.

1. In relation to actions by public agencies, the provisions of this article shall be enforceable by a proceeding brought pursuant to article seventy-eight of the civil practice law and rules.

2. In relation to actions by private employers, the provisions of this article shall be enforceable by the division of human rights pursuant to the powers and procedures set forth in article fifteen of the executive law, and, concurrently, by the New York city commission on human rights.

*Effective February 1, 2009, employers must post a copy of the Correction Law relating to the use of prior convictions.

NEW YORK CORRECTION LAW §§700-706

New York Correction Law Article 23
Discretionary Relief From Forfeitures and Disabilities Automatically Imposed By Law

§700. Definitions and rules of construction. 1. As used in this article the following terms have the following meanings:

(a) "Eligible offender" shall mean a person who has been convicted of a crime or of an offense, but who has not been convicted more than once of a felony.

(b) "Felony" means a conviction of a felony in this state, or of an offense in any other jurisdiction for which a sentence to a term of imprisonment in excess of one year, or a sentence of death, was authorized.

(c) "Revocable sentence" means a suspended sentence or a sentence upon which execution was suspended pursuant to the penal law in effect prior to September first, nineteen hundred sixty-seven; or a sentence of probation or of conditional discharge imposed pursuant to the penal law in effect after September first, nineteen hundred sixty-seven.

2. For the purposes of this article the following rules of construction shall apply:

(a) Two or more convictions of felonies charged in separate counts of one indictment or information shall be deemed to be one conviction;

(b) Two or more convictions of felonies charged in two or more indictments or informations, filed in the same court prior to entry of judgment under any of them, shall be deemed to be one conviction; and

(c) A plea or a verdict of guilty upon which sentence or the execution of sentence has been suspended or upon which a sentence of probation, conditional discharge, or unconditional discharge has been imposed shall be deemed to be a conviction.

§701. Certificate of relief from disabilities. 1. A certificate of relief from disabilities may be granted as provided in this article to relieve an eligible offender of any forfeiture or disability, or to remove any bar to his employment, automatically imposed by law by reason of his conviction of the crime or of the offense specified therein. Such certificate may be limited to one or more enumerated forfeitures, disabilities or bars, or may relieve the eligible offender of all forfeitures, disabilities and bars. Provided, however, that no such certificate shall apply, or be construed so as to apply, to the right of such person to retain or to be eligible for public office.

* 2. Notwithstanding any other provision of law, except subdivision five of section twenty-eight hundred six of the public health law or paragraph (b) of subdivision two of section eleven hundred ninety-three of the vehicle and traffic law, a conviction of a crime or of an offense specified in a certificate of relief from disabilities shall not cause automatic forfeiture of any license, permit, employment or franchise, including

the right to register for or vote at an election, or automatic forfeiture of any other right or privilege, held by the eligible offender and covered by the certificate. Nor shall such conviction be deemed to be a conviction within the meaning of any provision of law that imposes, by reason of a conviction, a bar to any employment, a disability to exercise any right or a disability to apply for or to receive any license, permit or other authority or privilege, covered by the certificate; provided, however, a conviction for a second or subsequent violation of any subdivision of section eleven hundred ninety-two of the vehicle and traffic law committed within the preceding ten years shall impose a disability to apply for or receive an operator's license during the period provided in such law. A certificate of relief from a disability imposed pursuant to subparagraph (v) of paragraph b of subdivision two and paragraphs i and j of subdivision six of section five hundred ten of the vehicle and traffic law may only be issued upon a determination that compelling circumstances warrant such relief.

* NB Repealed October 1, 2003

* 2. Notwithstanding any other provision of law, except subdivision five of section twenty-eight hundred six of the public health law or paragraph (b) of subdivision two of section eleven hundred ninety-three of the vehicle and traffic law, a conviction of a crime or of an offense specified in a certificate of relief from disabilities shall not cause automatic forfeiture of any license, permit, employment or franchise, including the right to register for or vote at an election, or automatic forfeiture of any other right or privilege, held by the eligible offender and covered by the certificate. Nor shall such conviction be deemed to be a conviction within the meaning of any provision of law that imposes, by reason of a conviction, a bar to any employment, a disability to exercise any right or a disability to apply for or to receive any license, permit or other authority or privilege, covered by the certificate; provided, however, a conviction for a second or subsequent violation of any subdivision of section eleven hundred ninety-two of the vehicle and traffic law committed within the preceding ten years shall impose a disability to apply for or receive an operator's license during the period provided in such law.

* NB Effective October 1, 2003

3. A certificate of relief from disabilities shall not, however, in any way prevent any judicial, administrative, licensing or other body, board or authority from relying upon the conviction specified therein as the basis for the exercise of its discretionary power to suspend, revoke, refuse to issue or refuse to renew any license, permit or other authority or privilege.

§702. Certificates of relief from disabilities issued by courts. 1. Any court of this state may, in its discretion, issue a certificate of relief from disabilities to an eligible offender for a conviction that occurred in such court, if the court either (a) imposed a revocable sentence or (b) imposed a sentence other than one executed by commitment to an institution under the jurisdiction of the state department of correctional services. Such certificate may be issued (i) at the time sentence is pronounced, in which case it may grant relief from forfeitures as well as from disabilities, or (ii) at any time thereafter, in which case it shall apply only to disabilities.

2. Such certificate shall not be issued by the court unless the court is satisfied that:

(a) The person to whom it is to be granted is an eligible offender, as defined in section seven hundred;

(b) The relief to be granted by the certificate is consistent with the rehabilitation of the eligible offender; and

(c) The relief to be granted by the certificate is consistent with the public interest.

3. Where a certificate of relief from disabilities is not issued at the time sentence is pronounced it shall only be issued thereafter upon verified application to the court. The court may, for the purpose of determining whether such certificate shall be issued, request its probation service to conduct an investigation of the applicant, or if the court has no probation service it may request the probation service of the county court for the county in which the court is located to conduct such investigation, or if there be no such probation service the court may request the state director of probation and correctional alternatives to arrange for such investigation. Any probation officer requested to make an investigation pursuant to this section shall prepare and submit to the court a written report in accordance with such request.

4. Where the court has imposed a revocable sentence and the certificate of relief from disabilities is issued prior to the expiration or termination of the time which the court may revoke such sentence, the certificate shall be deemed to be a temporary certificate until such time as the court's authority to revoke the sentence has expired or is terminated. While temporary, such certificate (a) may be revoked by the court for violation of the conditions of the sentence, and (b) shall be revoked by the court if it revokes the sentence and commits the person to an institution under the jurisdiction of the state department of correctional services. Any such revocation shall be upon notice and after an opportunity to be heard. If the certificate is not so revoked, it shall become a permanent certificate upon expiration or termination of the court's authority to revoke the sentence.

5. Any court that has issued a certificate of relief from disabilities may at any time issue a new certificate to enlarge the relief previously granted, provided, however, that the provisions of subdivisions one through four of this section shall apply to the issuance of any such new certificate.

6. Any written report submitted to the court pursuant to this section is confidential and may not be made available to any person or public or private agency except where specifically required or permitted by statute or upon specific authorization of the court. However, it shall be made available by the court for examination by the applicant's attorney, or the applicant himself, if he has no attorney. In its discretion, the court may except from disclosure a part or parts of the report which are not relevant to the granting of a certificate, or sources of information which have been obtained on a promise of confidentiality, or any other portion thereof, disclosure of which would not be in theinterest of justice. The action of the court excepting information from disclosure shallbe subject to appellate review. The court, in its discretion, may hold a conference in open court or in chambers to afford an applicant an opportunity to controvert or to comment upon any portions of the report. The court may also conduct a summary hearing at the conference on any matter relevant to the granting of the application and may take testimony under oath.

§703. Certificates of relief from disabilities issued by the board of parole. 1. The state board of parole shall have the power to issue a certificate of relief from disabilities to:

(a) any eligible offender who has been committed to an institution under the jurisdiction of the state department of correctional services. Such certificate may be issued by the board at the time the offender is released from such institution under the board's supervision or otherwise or at any time thereafter;

(b) any eligible offender who resides within this state and whose judgment of conviction was rendered by a court in any other jurisdiction.

2. Where the board of parole has issued a certificate of relief from disabilities, the board may at any time issue a new certificate enlarging the relief previously granted.

3. The board of parole shall not issue any certificate of relief from disabilities pursuant to subdivisions one or two, unless the board is satisfied that:

(a) The person to whom it is to be granted is an eligible offender, as defined in section seven hundred;

(b) The relief to be granted by the certificate is consistent with the rehabilitation of the eligible offender; and

(c) The relief to be granted by the certificate is consistent with the public interest.

4. Any certificate of relief from disabilities issued by the board of parole to an eligible offender who at time of the issuance of the certificate is under the board's supervision, shall be deemed to be a temporary certificate until such time as the eligible offender is discharged from the board's supervision, and, while temporary, such certificate may be revoked by the board for violation of the conditions of parole or release. Revocation shall be upon notice to the parolee, who shall be accorded an opportunity to explain the violation prior to decision thereon. If the certificate is not so revoked, it shall become a permanent certificate upon expiration or termination of the board's jurisdiction over the offender.

5. In granting or revoking a certificate of relief from disabilities the action of the board of parole shall be by unanimous vote of the members authorized to grant or revoke parole. Such action shall be deemed a judicial function and shall not be reviewable if done according to law.

6. For the purpose of determining whether such certificate shall be issued, the board may conduct an investigation of the applicant.

§703-a. Certificate of good conduct. 1. A certificate of good conduct may be granted as provided in this section to relieve an individual of any disability, or to remove any bar to his employment, automatically imposed by law by reason of his conviction of the crime or of the offense specified therein. Such certificate may be limited to one or more enumerated disabilities or bars, or may relieve the individual of all disabilities and bars.

2. Notwithstanding any other provision of law, a conviction of a crime or of an offense specified in a certificate of good conduct shall not be deemed to be a conviction within the meaning of any provision of law that imposes, by reason of a conviction, a bar to any employment, a disability to exercise any right or a disability to apply for or to receive any license, permit or other authority or privilege, covered by the certificate.

3. A certificate of good conduct shall not, however, in any way prevent any judicial administrative, licensing or other body, board or authority from considering the conviction specified therein in accordance with the provisions of article twenty-three-a of this chapter.

§703-b. Issuance of certificate of good conduct. 1. The state board of parole, or any three members thereof by unanimous vote, shall have the power to issue a certificate of good conduct to any person previously convicted of a crime in this state, when the board is satisfied that:

(a) The applicant has conducted himself in a manner warranting such issuance for a minimum period in accordance with the provisions of subdivision three of this section;

(b) The relief to be granted by the certificate is consistent with the rehabilitation of the applicant; and

(c) The relief to be granted is consistent with the public interest.

2. The state board of parole, or any three members thereof by unanimous vote, shall have the power to issue a certificate of good conduct to any person previously convicted of a crime in any other jurisdiction, when the board is satisfied that:

(a) The applicant has demonstrated that there exist specific facts and circumstances, and specific sections of New York state law that have an adverse impact on the applicant and warrant the application for relief to be made in New York; and (b) The provisions of paragraphs (a), (b) and (c) of subdivision one of this section have been met.

3. The minimum period of good conduct by the individual referred to in paragraph (a) of subdivision one of this section, shall be as follows:

Where the most serious crime of which the individual was convicted is a misdemeanor, the minimum period of good conduct shall be one year; where the most serious crime of which the individual was convicted is a class C, D or E felony, the minimum period of good conduct shall be three years; and, where the most serious crime of which the individual was convicted is a class B or A felony, the minimum period of good conduct shall be five years. Criminal acts committed outside the state shall be classified as acts committed within the state based on the maximum sentence that could have been imposed based upon such conviction pursuant to the laws of such foreign jurisdiction. Such minimum period of good conduct by the individual shall be measured either from the date of the payment of any fine imposed upon him or the suspension of sentence, or from the date of his unrevoked release from custody by parole, commutation or termination of his sentence. The board shall have power and it shall be its duty to investigate all persons when such application is made and to grant or deny the same within a reasonable time after the making of the application.

4. Where the board of parole has issued a certificate of good conduct, the board may at any time issue a new certificate enlarging the relief previously granted.

5. Any certificate of good conduct by the board of parole to an individual who at time of the issuance of the certificate is under the board's supervision, shall be deemed to be a temporary certificate until such time as the individual is discharged from the board's supervision, and, while temporary, such certificate may be revoked by the board for violation of the conditions of parole or release. Revocation shall be upon notice to the parolee, who shall be accorded an opportunity to explain the violation prior to decision thereon. If the certificate is not so revoked, it shall become a permanent certificate upon expiration or termination of the board's jurisdiction over the individual.

§ 704. Effect of revocation; use of revoked certificate. 1. Where a certificate of relief from disabilities is deemed to be temporary and such certificate is revoked, disabilities and forfeitures thereby relieved shall be reinstated as of the date upon which the person to whom the certificate was issued receives written notice of such revocation. Any such person shall upon receipt of such notice surrender the certificate to the issuing court or board.

2. A person who knowingly uses or attempts to use, a revoked certificate of relief from disabilities in order to obtain or to exercise any right or privilege that he would not be entitled to obtain or to exercise without a valid certificate shall be guilty of a misdemeanor.

§705. Forms and filing. 1. All applications, certificates and orders of revocation necessary for the purposes of this article shall be upon forms prescribed pursuant to agreement among the state commissioner of correctional services, the chairman of the state board of parole and the administrator of the state judicial conference. Such forms relating to certificates of relief from disabilities shall be distributed by the director of the state division of probation and correctional alternatives and forms relating to certificates of good conduct shall be distributed by the chairman of the board of parole.

2. Any court or board issuing or revoking any certificate pursuant to this article shall immediately file a copy of the certificate, or of the order of revocation, with the New York state identification and intelligence system.

§706. Certificate not to be deemed to be a pardon. Nothing contained in this article shall be deemed to alter or limit or affect the manner of applying for pardons to the governor, and no certificate issued hereunder shall be deemed or construed to be a pardon.

NEW YORK STATE EXECUTIVE LAW ARTICLE 15 §§296, 297, 298

§ 296. Unlawful discriminatory practices.

1. It shall be an unlawful discriminatory practice:

(a) For an employer or licensing agency, because of an individual's age, race, creed, color, national origin, sexual orientation, military status, sex, disability, predisposing genetic characteristics, marital status, or domestic violence victim status, to refuse to hire or employ or to bar or to discharge from employment such individual or to discriminate against such individual in compensation or in terms, conditions or privileges of employment.

(b) For an employment agency to discriminate against any individual because of age, race, creed, color, national origin, sexual orientation, military status, sex, disability, predisposing genetic characteristics, or marital status, in receiving, classifying, disposing or otherwise acting upon applications for its services or in referring an applicant or applicants to an employer or employers.

(c) For a labor organization, because of the age, race, creed, color, national origin, sexual orientation, military status, sex, disability, predisposing genetic characteristics, or marital status of any individual, to exclude or to expel from its membership such individual or to discriminate in any way against any of its members or against any employer or any individual employed by an employer.

(d) For any employer or employment agency to print or circulate or cause to be printed or circulated any statement, advertisement or publication, or to use any form of application for employment or to make any inquiry in connection with prospective employment, which expresses directly or indirectly, any limitation, specification or discrimination as to age, race, creed, color, national origin, sexual orientation, military status, sex, disability, predisposing genetic characteristics, or marital status, or any intent to make any such limitation, specification or discrimination, unless based upon a bona fide occupational qualification; provided, however, that neither this paragraph nor any provision of this chapter or other law shall be construed to prohibit the department of civil service or the department of personnel of any city containing more than one county from requesting information from applicants for civil service examinations concerning any of the aforementioned characteristics, other than sexual orientation, for the purpose of conducting studies to identify and resolve possible problems in recruitment and testing of members of minority groups to insure the fairest possible and equal opportunities for employment in the civil service for all persons, regardless of age, race, creed, color, national origin, sexual orientation, military status, sex, disability, predisposing genetic characteristics, or marital status.

(e) For any employer, labor organization or employment agency to discharge, expel or otherwise discriminate against any person because he or she has opposed any practices forbidden under this article or because he or she has filed a complaint, testified or assisted in any proceeding under this article.

(f) Nothing in this subdivision shall affect any restrictions upon the activities of persons licensed by the state liquor authority with respect to persons under twenty-one years of age.

(g) For an employer to compel an employee who is pregnant to take a leave of absence, unless the employee is prevented by such pregnancy from performing the activities involved in the job or occupation in a reasonable manner.

1-a. It shall be an unlawful discriminatory practice for an employer, labor organization, employment agency or any joint labor-management committee controlling apprentice training programs:

(a) To select persons for an apprentice training program registered with the state of New York on any basis other than their qualifications, as determined by objective criteria which permit review;

(b) To deny to or withhold from any person because of race, creed, color, national origin, sexual orientation, military status, sex, age, disability, or marital status, the right to be admitted to or participate in a guidance program, an apprenticeship training program, on-the-job training program, executive training program, or other occupational training or retraining program;

(c) To discriminate against any person in his or her pursuit of such programs or to discriminate against such a person in the terms, conditions or privileges of such programs because of race, creed, color, national origin, sexual orientation, military status, sex, age, disability or marital status;

(d) To print or circulate or cause to be printed or circulated any statement, advertisement or publication, or to use any form of application for such programs or to make any inquiry in connection with such program which expresses, directly or indirectly, any limitation, specification or discrimination as to race, creed, color, national origin, sexual orientation, military status, sex, age, disability or marital status, or any intention to make any such limitation, specification or discrimination, unless based on a bona fide occupational qualification.

2. (a) It shall be an unlawful discriminatory practice for any person, being the owner, lessee, proprietor, manager, superintendent, agent or employee of any place of public accommodation, resort or amusement, because of the race, creed, color, national origin, sexual orientation, military status, sex, or disability or marital status of any person, directly or indirectly, to refuse, withhold from or deny to such person any of the accommodations, advantages, facilities or privileges thereof, including the extension of credit, or, directly or indirectly, to publish, circulate, issue, display, post or mail any written or printed communication, notice or advertisement, to the effect that any of the accommodations, advantages, facilities and privileges of any such place shall be refused, withheld from or denied to any person on account of race, creed, color, national origin, sexual orientation, military status, sex, or disability or marital status, or that the patronage or custom thereat of any person of or purporting to be of any particular race, creed, color, national origin, sexual orientation, military status, sex or marital status, or having a disability is unwelcome, objectionable or not acceptable, desired or solicited.

(b) Nothing in this subdivision shall be construed to prevent the barring of any person, because of the sex of such person, from places of public accommodation, resort or amusement if the division grants an exemption based on bona fide considerations of public policy; nor shall this subdivision apply to the rental of rooms in a housing accommodation which restricts such rental to individuals of one sex.

(c) For the purposes of paragraph (a) of this subdivision, "discriminatory practice" includes:

   (i) a refusal to make reasonable modifications in policies, practices, or procedures, when such modifications are necessary to afford facilities, privileges, advantages or accommodations to individuals with disabilities, unless such person can demonstrate that making such modifications would fundamentally alter the nature of such facilities, privileges, advantages or accommodations;

   (ii) a refusal to take such steps as may be necessary to ensure that no individual with a disability is excluded or denied services because of the absence of auxiliary aids and services, unless such person can demonstrate that taking such steps would fundamentally alter the nature of the facility, privilege, advantage or accommodation being offered or would result in an undue burden;

   (iii) a refusal to remove architectural barriers, and communication barriers that are structural in nature, in existing facilities, and transportation barriers in existing vehicles and rail passenger cars used by an establishment for transporting individuals (not including barriers that can only be removed through the retrofitting of vehicles or rail passenger cars by the installation of a hydraulic or other lift), where such removal is readily achievable; and

   (iv) where such person can demonstrate that the removal of a barrier under subparagraph

   (v) of this paragraph is not readily achievable, a failure to make such facilities, privileges, advantages or accommodations available through alternative methods if such methods are readily achievable.

(d) For the purposes of this subdivision:

   (i) "Readily achievable" means easily accomplishable and able to be carried out without much difficulty or expense. In determining whether an action is readily achievable, factors to be considered include:

      (A)) the nature and cost of the action needed under this subdivision;

(B)) the overall financial resources of the facility or facilities involved in the action; the number of persons employed at such facility; the effect on expenses and resources or the impact otherwise of such action upon the operation of the facility;

(C) the overall financial resources of the place of public accommodation, resort or amusement; the overall size of the business of such a place with respect to the number of its employees; the number, type and location of its facilities; and

(D)) the type of operation or operations of the place of public accommodation, resort or amusement, including the composition, structure and functions of the workforce of such place; the geographic separateness, administrative or fiscal relationship of the facility or facilities in question to such place.

(ii) "Auxiliary aids and services" include:

(A)) qualified interpreters or other effective methods of making aurally delivered materials available to individuals with hearing impairments;

(B)) qualified readers, taped texts or other effective methods of making visually delivered materials available to individuals with visual impairments;

(C) acquisition or modification of equipment or devices; and

(D)) other similar services and actions.

(iii) "Undue burden" means significant difficulty or expense. In determining whether an action would result in an undue burden, factors to be considered shall include:

(A) The nature and cost of the action needed under this article;

(B) The overall financial resources of the site or sites involved in the action; the number of persons employed at the site; the effect on expenses and resources; legitimate safety requirements that are necessary for safe operation, including crime prevention measures; or the impact otherwise of the action upon the operation of the site;

(C) The geographic separateness, and the administrative or fiscal relationship of the site or sites in question to any parent corporation or entity;

(D) If applicable, the overall financial resources of any parent corporation or entity; the overall size of the parent corporation or entity with respect to the number of its employees; the number, type, and location of its facilities; and

(E) If applicable, the type of operation or operations of any parent corporation or entity, including the composition, structure, and functions of the workforce of the parent corporation or entity.

(e)) Paragraphs (c) and (d) of this subdivision do not apply to any air carrier, the National Railroad Passenger Corporation, or public transportation facilities, vehicles or services owned, leased or operated by the state, a county, city, town or village, or any agency thereof, or by any public benefit corporation or authority.

2-a.   It shall be an unlawful discriminatory practice for the owner, lessee, sub-lessee, assignee, or managing agent of publicly-assisted housing accommodations or other person having the right of ownership or possession of or the right to rent or lease such accommodations:

(a) To refuse to sell, rent or lease or otherwise to deny to or withhold from any person or group of persons such housing accommodations because of the race, creed, color, disability, national origin, sexual orientation, military status, age, sex, marital status, or familial status of such person or persons, or to represent that any housing accommodation or land is not available for inspection, sale, rental or lease when in fact it is so available.

(b) To discriminate against any person because of his or her race, creed, color, disability, national origin, sexual orientation, military status, age, sex, marital status, or familial status in the terms, conditions or privileges of any publicly-assisted housing accommodations or in the furnishing of facilities or services in connection therewith.

(c) To cause to be made any written or oral inquiry or record concerning the race, creed, color, disability, national origin, sexual orientation, membership in the reserve armed forces of the United States or in the organized militia of the state, age, sex, marital status, or familial status of a person seeking to rent or lease any publicly-assisted housing accommodation; provided, however, that nothing in this subdivision shall prohibit a member of the reserve armed forces of the United States or in the organized militia of the state from voluntarily disclosing such membership.

(c-1) To print or circulate or cause to be printed or circulated any statement, advertisement or publication, or to use any form of application for the purchase, rental or lease of such housing accommodation or to make any record or inquiry in connection with the prospective purchase, rental or lease of such a housing accommodation which expresses, directly or indirectly, any limitation, specification or discrimination as to race, creed, color, national origin, sexual orientation, military status, sex, age, disability, marital status, or familial status, or any intent to make any such limitation, specification or discrimination.

(d) (1) To refuse to permit, at the expense of the person with a disability, reasonable modifications of existing premises occupied or to be occupied by the said person, if the modifications may be necessary to afford the said person full enjoyment of the premises, in conformity with the provisions of the New York state uniform fire prevention and building code, except that, in the case of a rental, the landlord may, where it is reasonable to do so, condition permission for a modification on the renter's agreeing to restore the interior of the premises to the condition that existed before the modification, reasonable wear and tear excepted.

(2) To refuse to make reasonable accommodations in rules, policies, practices, or services, when such accommodations may be necessary to afford a person with a disability equal opportunity to use and enjoy a dwelling, including reasonable modification to common use portions of the dwelling, or

(3) In connection with the design and construction of covered multi-family dwellings for first occupancy after March thirteenth, nineteen hundred ninety-one, a failure to design and construct dwellings in accordance with the accessibility requirements of the New York state uniform fire prevention and building code, to provide that:

(i) The public use and common use portions of the dwellings are readily accessible to and usable by disabled persons with disabilities;

(ii) All the doors are designed in accordance with the New York state uniform fire prevention and building code to allow passage into and within all premises and are sufficiently wide to allow passage by persons in wheelchairs; and

(iii) All premises within covered multi-family dwelling units contain an accessible route into and through the dwelling; light switches, electrical outlets, thermostats, and other environmental controls are in accessible locations; there are reinforcements in the bathroom walls to allow later installation of grab bars; and there are usable kitchens and bathrooms such that an individual in a wheelchair can maneuver about the space, in conformity with the New York state uniform fire prevention and building code.

(e) Nothing in this subdivision shall restrict the consideration of age in the rental of publicly- assisted housing accommodations if the division grants an exemption based on bona fide considerations of public policy for the purpose of providing for the special needs of a particular age group without the intent of prejudicing other age groups.

(f) Nothing in this subdivision shall be deemed to restrict the rental of rooms in school or college dormitories to individuals of the same sex.

3. (a) It shall be an unlawful discriminatory practice for an employer, licensing agency, employment agency or labor organization to refuse to provide reasonable accommodations to the known disabilities of an employee, prospective employee or member in connection with a job or occupation sought or held or participation in a training program.

(b) Nothing contained in this subdivision shall be construed to require provision of accommodations which can be demonstrated to impose an undue hardship on the operation of an employer's, licensing agency's, employment agency's or labor organization's business, program or enterprise. In making such a demonstration with regard to undue hardship the factors to be considered include:

(i) The overall size of the business, program or enterprise with respect to the number of employees, number and type of facilities, and size of budget;

(ii) The type of operation which the business, program or enterprise is engaged in, including the composition and structure of the workforce; and

(iii) The nature and cost of the accommodation needed.

3-a.   It shall be an unlawful discriminatory practice: (a) For an employer or licensing agency to refuse to hire or employ or license or to bar or to terminate from employment an individual eighteen years of age or older, or to discriminate against such individual in promotion, compensation or in terms, conditions, or privileges of employment, because of such individual's age.

(b) For any employer, licensing agency or employment agency to print or circulate or cause to be printed or circulated any statement, advertisement or publication, or to use any form of application for employment or to make any inquiry in connection with prospective employment, which expresses, directly or indirectly, any limitation, specification or discrimination on account of age respecting individuals eighteen years of age or older, or any intent to make any such limitation, specification, or discrimination.

(c) For any employer, licensing agency or employment agency to discharge or otherwise discriminate against any person because he or she has opposed any practices forbidden under this article or because he or she has filed a complaint, testified or assisted in any proceeding under this article.

(d) Notwithstanding any other provision of law, no employee shall be subject to termination or retirement from employment on the basis of age, except where age is a bona fide occupational qualification reasonably necessary to the normal operation of a particular business, where the differentiation is based on reasonable factors other than age, or as otherwise specified in paragraphs (e) and (f) of this subdivision or in article fourteen-A of the retirement and social security law.

(e) Nothing contained in this subdivision or in subdivision one of this section shall be construed to prevent the compulsory retirement of any employee who has attained sixty-five years of age, and who, for a two-year period immediately before retirement, is employed in a bona fide executive or a high policymaking position, if such employee is entitled to an immediate nonforfeitable annual retirement benefit from a pension, profit-sharing, savings, or deferred compensation plan, or any combination of such plans, of the employer of such employee, which equals, in the aggregate, at least forty-four thousand dollars; provided that for the purposes of this paragraph only, the term "employer" includes any employer as otherwise defined in this article but does not include (i) the state of New York, (ii) a county, city, town, village or any other political subdivision or civil division of the state, (iii) a school district or any other governmental entity operating a public school, college or university, (iv) a public improvement or special district, (v) a public authority, commission or public benefit corporation, or (vi) any other public corporation, agency, instrumentality or unit of government which exercises governmental power under the laws of the state. In applying the retirement benefit test of this paragraph, if any such retirement benefit is in a form other than a straight life annuity with no ancillary benefits, or if employees contribute to any such plan or make rollover contributions, such benefit shall be adjusted in accordance with rules and regulations promulgated by the division, after an opportunity for public hearing, so that the benefit is the equivalent of a straight life annuity with no ancillary benefits under a plan to which employees do not contribute and under which no rollover contributions are made.

(f) Nothing contained in this subdivision, in subdivision one of this section or in article fourteen-A of the retirement and social security law shall be construed to prevent the compulsory retirement of any employee who has attained seventy years of age and is serving under a contract for unlimited tenure, or a similar arrangement providing for unlimited tenure, at a nonpublic institution of higher education. For purposes of such subdivisions or article, the term "institution of higher education" means an educational institution which

    (i) admits as regular students only persons having a certificate of graduation from a school providing secondary education, or the recognized equivalent of such a certificate,

    (ii) is lawfully authorized to provide a program of education beyond secondary education, and

    (iii) provides an educational program for which it awards a bachelor's degree or provides not less than a two-year program which is acceptable for full credit toward such a degree.

 (g) In the event of a conflict between the provisions of this subdivision and the provisions of article fourteen-A of the retirement and social security law, the provisions of article fourteen-A of such law shall be controlling. But nothing contained in this subdivision, in subdivision one of this section or in article fourteen-A of the retirement and social security law shall be construed to prevent the termination of the employment of any person who, even upon the provision of reasonable accommodations, is physically unable to perform his or her duties or to affect the retirement policy or system of any employer where such policy or system is not merely a subterfuge to evade the purposes of said subdivisions or said article; nor shall anything in such subdivisions or such article be deemed to preclude the varying of insurance coverages according to an employee's age. The provisions of this subdivision shall not affect any restriction upon the activities of persons licensed by the state liquor authority with respect to persons under twenty- one years of age.

3-b.   It shall be an unlawful discriminatory practice for any real estate broker, real estate salesperson or employee or agent thereof or any other individual, corporation, partnership or organization for the purpose of inducing a real estate transaction from which any such person or any of its stockholders or members may benefit financially, to represent that a change has occurred or will or may occur in the composition with respect to race, creed, color, national origin, sexual orientation, military status, sex, disability, marital status, or familial status of the owners or occupants in the block, neighborhood or area in which the real property is located, and to represent, directly or indirectly, that this change will or may result in undesirable consequences in the block, neighborhood or area in which the real property is located, including but not limited to the lowering of property values, an increase in criminal or anti-social behavior, or a decline in the quality of schools or other facilities.

4. It shall be an unlawful discriminatory practice for an education corporation or association which holds itself out to the public to be non-sectarian and exempt from taxation pursuant to the provisions of article four of the real property tax law to deny the use of its facilities to any person otherwise qualified, or to permit the harassment of any student or applicant, by reason of his race, color, religion, disability, national origin, sexual orientation, military status, sex, age or marital status, except that any such institution which establishes or maintains a policy of educating persons of one sex exclusively may admit students of only one sex.

5. (a) It shall be an unlawful discriminatory practice for the owner, lessee, sub-lessee, assignee, or managing agent of, or other person having the right to sell, rent or lease a housing accommodation, constructed or to be constructed, or any agent or employee thereof:

    (1) To refuse to sell, rent, lease or otherwise to deny to or withhold from any person or group of persons such a housing accommodation because of the race, creed, color, national origin, sexual orientation, military status, sex, age, disability, marital status, or familial status of such person or persons, or to represent that any housing accommodation or land is not available for inspection, sale, rental or lease when in fact it is so available.

    (2) To discriminate against any person because of race, creed, color, national origin, sexual orientation, military status, sex, age, disability, marital status, or familial status in the terms, conditions or privileges of the sale, rental or lease of any such housing accommodation or in the furnishing of facilities or services in connection therewith.

    (3) To print or circulate or cause to be printed or circulated any statement, advertisement or publication, or to use any form of application for the purchase, rental or lease of such housing accommodation or to make any record or inquiry in connection with the prospective purchase, rental or lease of such a housing accommodation which expresses, directly or indirectly, any limitation, specification or discrimination as to race, creed, color, national origin, sexual orientation, military status, sex, age, disability, marital status, or familial status, or any intent to make any such limitation, specification or discrimination.

The provisions of this paragraph (a) shall not apply (1) to the rental of a housing accommodation in a building which contains housing accommodations for not more than two families living independently of each other, if the owner resides in one of such housing accommodations, (2) to the restriction of the rental of all rooms in a housing accommodation to individuals of the same sex or (3) to the rental of a room or rooms in a housing accommodation, if such rental is by the occupant of the housing accommodation or by the owner of the housing accommodation and the owner resides in such housing accommodation or (4) solely with respect to age and familial status to the restriction of the sale, rental or lease of housing accommodations exclusively to persons sixty-two years of age or older and the spouse of any such person, or for housing intended and operated for occupancy by at least one person fifty-five years of age or older per unit. In determining whether housing is intended and operated for occupancy by persons fifty-five years of age or older, Sec. 807(b) (2) (c) (42 U.S.C. 3607 (b) (2) (c)) of the federal Fair Housing Act of 1988, as amended, shall apply.

(b) It shall be an unlawful discriminatory practice for the owner, lessee, sub-lessee, or managing agent of, or other person having the right of ownership or possession of or the right to sell, rent or lease, land or commercial space:

(1) To refuse to sell, rent, lease or otherwise deny to or withhold from any person or group of persons land or commercial space because of the race, creed, color, national origin, sexual orientation, military status, sex, age, disability, marital status, or familial status of such person or persons, or to represent that any housing accommodation or land is not available for inspection, sale, rental or lease when in fact it is so available;

(2) To discriminate against any person because of race, creed, color, national origin, sexual orientation, military status, sex, age, disability, marital status, or familial status in the terms, conditions or privileges of the sale, rental or lease of any such land or commercial space; or in the furnishing of facilities or services in connection therewith;

(3) To print or circulate or cause to be printed or circulated any statement, advertisement or publication, or to use any form of application for the purchase, rental or lease of such land or commercial space or to make any record or inquiry in connection with the prospective purchase, rental or lease of such land or commercial space which expresses, directly or indirectly, any limitation, specification or discrimination as to race, creed, color, national origin, sexual orientation, military status, sex, age, disability, marital status, or familial status; or any intent to make any such limitation, specification or discrimination.

(4) With respect to age and familial status, the provisions of this paragraph shall not apply to the restriction of the sale, rental or lease of land or commercial space exclusively to persons

(5) fifty-five years of age or older and the spouse of any such person, or to the restriction of the sale, rental or lease of land to be used for the construction, or location of housing accommodations exclusively for persons sixty-two years of age or older, or intended and operated for occupancy by at least one person fifty-five years of age or older per unit. In determining whether housing is intended and operated for occupancy by persons fifty-five years of age or older, Sec. 807(b)(2)(c) (42 U.S.C. 3607(b)(2)(c)) of the federal Fair Housing Act of 1988, as amended, shall apply.

(c) It shall be an unlawful discriminatory practice for any real estate broker, real estate salesperson or employee or agent thereof:

(1) To refuse to sell, rent or lease any housing accommodation, land or commercial space to any person or group of persons or to refuse to negotiate for the sale, rental or lease, of any housing accommodation, land or commercial space to any person or group of persons because of the race, creed, color, national origin, sexual orientation, military status, sex, age, disability, marital status, or familial status of such person or persons, or to represent that any housing accommodation, land or commercial space is not available for inspection, sale, rental or lease when in fact it is so available, or otherwise to deny or withhold any housing accommodation, land or commercial space or any facilities of any housing accommodation, land or commercial space from any person or group of persons because of the race, creed, color, national origin, sexual orientation, military status, sex, age, disability, marital status, or familial status of such person or persons.

(2) To print or circulate or cause to be printed or circulated any statement, advertisement or publication, or to use any form of application for the purchase, rental or lease of any housing accommodation, land or commercial space or to make any record or inquiry in connection with the prospective purchase, rental or lease of any housing accommodation, land or commercial space which expresses, directly or indirectly, any limitation, specification, or discrimination as to race, creed, color, national origin, sexual orientation, military status, sex, age, disability, marital status, or familial status; or any intent to make any such limitation, specification or discrimination.

(3) With respect to age and familial status, the provisions of this paragraph shall not apply to the restriction of the sale, rental or lease of any land or commercial space exclusively to persons fifty-five years of age or older and the spouse of any such person, or to the restriction of the sale, rental or lease of any housing accommodation or land to be used for the construction or location of housing accommodations for persons sixty-two years of age or older, or intended and operated for occupancy by at least one person fifty-five years of age or older per unit. In determining whether housing is intended and operated for occupancy by persons fifty-five years of age or older, Sec. 807 (b)(2)(c) (42 U.S.C. 3607(b)(2)(c)) of the federal Fair Housing Act of 1988, as amended, shall apply.

(d) It shall be an unlawful discriminatory practice for any real estate board, because of the race, creed, color, national origin, sexual orientation, military status, age, sex, disability, marital status, or familial status of any individual who is otherwise qualified for membership, to exclude or expel such individual from membership, or to discriminate against such individual in the terms, conditions and privileges of membership in such board.

(e) It shall be an unlawful discriminatory practice for the owner, proprietor or managing agent of, or other person having the right to provide care and services in, a private proprietary nursing home, convalescent home, or home for adults, or an intermediate care facility, as defined in section two of the social services law, heretofore constructed, or to be constructed, or any agent or employee thereof, to refuse to provide services and care in such home or facility to any individual or to discriminate against any individual in the terms, conditions, and privileges of such services and care solely because such individual is a blind person. For purposes of this paragraph, a "blind person" shall mean a person who is registered as a blind person with the commission for the visually handicapped and who meets the definition of a "blind person" pursuant to section three of chapter four hundred fifteen of the laws of nineteen hundred thirteen entitled "An act to establish a state commission for improving the condition of the blind of the state of New York, and making an appropriation therefor".

(f) The provisions of this subdivision, as they relate to age, shall not apply to persons under the age of eighteen years.

(g) It shall be an unlawful discriminatory practice for any person offering or providing housing accommodations, land or commercial space as described in paragraphs (a), (b), and (c) of this subdivision to make or cause to be made any written or oral inquiry or record concerning membership of any person in the state organized militia in relation to the purchase, rental or lease of such housing accommodation, land, or commercial space, provided, however, that nothing   in this subdivision shall prohibit a member of the state organized militia from voluntarily disclosing such membership.

6. It shall be an unlawful discriminatory practice for any person to aid, abet, incite, compel or coerce the doing of any of the acts forbidden under this article, or to attempt to do so.

7. It shall be an unlawful discriminatory practice for any person engaged in any activity to which this section applies to retaliate or discriminate against any person because he or she has opposed any practices forbidden under this article or because he or she has filed a complaint, testified or assisted in any proceeding under this article.

8. It shall be an unlawful discriminatory practice for any party to a conciliation agreement made pursuant to section two hundred ninety-seven of this article to violate the terms of such agreement.

9. (a) It shall be an unlawful discriminatory practice for any fire department or fire company therein, through any member or members thereof, officers, board of fire commissioners or other body or office having power of appointment of volunteer firefighters, directly or indirectly, by ritualistic practice, constitutional or by-law prescription, by tacit agreement among its members, or otherwise, to deny to any individual membership in any volunteer fire department or fire company therein, or to expel or discriminate against any volunteer member of a fire department or fire company therein, because of the race, creed, color, national origin, sexual orientation, military status, sex or marital status of such individual.

(b) Upon a complaint to the division, as provided for under subdivision one of section two hundred ninety-seven of this article, and in the event the commissioner finds that an unlawful discriminatory practice has been engaged in, the board of fire commissioners or other body or office having power of appointment of volunteer firefighters shall be served with any order required, under subdivision four of section two hundred ninety-seven of this article, to be served on any or all respondents requiring such respondent or respondents to cease and desist from such unlawful discriminatory practice and to take affirmative action. Such board shall have the duty and power to appoint as a volunteer firefighter, notwithstanding any other statute or provision of law or by-law of any volunteer fire company, any individual whom the commissioner has determined to be the subject of an unlawful discriminatory practice under this subdivision. Unless such board has been found to have engaged in an unlawful discriminatory practice, service upon such board of such order shall not constitute such board or its members as a respondent nor constitute a finding of an unlawful discriminatory practice against such board or its members.

10.(a) It shall be an unlawful discriminatory practice for any employer, or an employee or agent thereof, to impose upon a person as a condition of obtaining or retaining employment, including opportunities for promotion, advancement or transfers, any terms or conditions that would require such person to violate or forego a sincerely held practice of his or her religion, including but not limited to the observance of any particular day or days or any portion thereof as a sabbath or other holy day in accordance with the requirements of his or her religion, unless, after engaging in a bona fide effort, the employer demonstrates that it is unable to reasonably accommodate the employee's or prospective employee's sincerely held religious observance or practice without undue hardship on the conduct of the employer's business. Notwithstanding any other provision of law to the contrary, an employee shall not be entitled to premium wages or premium benefits for work performed during hours to which such premium wages or premium benefits would ordinarily be applicable, if the employee is working during such hours only as an accommodation to his or her sincerely held religious requirements. Nothing in this paragraph or paragraph (b) of this subdivision shall alter or abridge the rights granted to an employee concerning the payment of wages or privileges of seniority accruing to that employee.

(b) Except where it would cause an employer to incur an undue hardship, no person shall be required to remain at his or her place of employment during any day or days or portion thereof that, as a requirement of his or her religion, he or she observes as his or her sabbath or other holy day, including a reasonable time prior and subsequent thereto for travel between his or her place of employment and his or her home, provided however, that any such absence from work shall, wherever practicable in the reasonable judgment of the employer, be made up by an equivalent amount of time and work at some other mutually convenient time, or shall be charged against any leave with pay ordinarily granted, other than sick leave, provided further, however, that any such absence not so made up or charged, may be treated by the employer of such person as leave taken without pay.

(c) It shall be an unlawful discriminatory practice for an employer to refuse to permit an employee to utilize leave, as provided in paragraph (b) of this subdivision, solely because the leave will be used for absence from work to accommodate the employee's sincerely held religious observance or practice.

(d) As used in this subdivision:

(1) "undue hardship" shall mean an accommodation requiring significant expense or difficulty (including a significant interference with the safe or efficient operation of the workplace or a violation of a bona fide seniority system). Factors to be considered in determining whether the accommodation constitutes an undue economic hardship shall include, but not be limited to:

   (i) the identifiable cost of the accommodation, including the costs of loss of productivity and of retaining or hiring employees or transferring employees from one facility to another, in relation to the size and operating cost of the employer;

   (ii) the number of individuals who will need the particular accommodation to a sincerely held religious observance or practice; and

   (iii) for an employer with multiple facilities, the degree to which the geographic separateness or administrative or fiscal relationship of the facilities will make the accommodation more difficult or expensive.

Provided, however, an accommodation shall be considered to constitute an undue hardship if it will result in the inability of an employee to perform the essential functions of the position in which he or she is employed.

(2) "premium wages" shall include overtime pay and compensatory time off, and additional remuneration for night, weekend or holiday work, or for standby or irregular duty.

(3) "premium benefit" shall mean an employment benefit, such as seniority, group life insurance, health insurance, disability insurance, sick leave, annual leave, or an educational or pension benefit that is greater than the employment benefit due the employee for an equivalent period of work performed during the regular work schedule of the employee.

In the case of any employer other than the state, any of its political subdivisions or any school district, this subdivision shall not apply where the uniform application of terms and conditions of attendance to employees is essential to prevent undue economic hardship to the employer. In any proceeding in which the applicability of this subdivision is in issue, the burden of proof shall be upon the employer. If any question shall arise whether a particular position or class of positions is excepted from this subdivision by this paragraph, such question may be referred in writing by any party claimed to be aggrieved, in the case of any position of employment by the state or any of its political subdivisions, except by any school district, to the civil service commission, in the case of any position of employment by any school district, to the commissioner of education, who shall determine such question and in the case of any other employer, a party claiming to be aggrieved may file a complaint with the division pursuant to this article. Any such determination by the civil service commission shall be reviewable in the manner provided by article seventy-eight of the civil practice law and rules and any such determination by the commissioner of education shall be reviewable in the manner and to the same extent as other determinations of the commissioner under section three hundred ten of the education law.

11. Nothing contained in this section shall be construed to bar any religious or denominational institution or organization, or any organization operated for charitable or educational purposes, which is operated, supervised or controlled by or in connection with a religious organization, from limiting employment or sales or rental of housing accommodations or admission to or giving preference to persons of the same religion or denomination or from taking such action as is calculated by such organization to promote the religious principles for which it is established or maintained.

12. Notwithstanding the provisions of subdivisions one, one-a and three-a of this section, it shall not be an unlawful discriminatory practice for an employer, employment agency, labor organization or joint labor-management committee to carry out a plan, approved by the division, to increase the employment of members of a minority group (as may be defined pursuant to the regulations of the division) which has a state-wide unemployment rate that is disproportionately high in comparison with the state-wide unemployment rate of the general population. Any plan approved under this subdivision shall be in writing and the division's approval thereof shall be for a limited period and may be rescinded at any time by the division.

13. It shall be an unlawful discriminatory practice (i) for any person to boycott or blacklist, or to refuse to buy from, sell to or trade with, or otherwise discriminate against any person, because of the race, creed, color, national origin, sexual orientation, military status, sex, or disability of such person, or of such person's partners, members, stockholders, directors, officers, managers, superintendents, agents, employees, business associates, suppliers or customers, or (ii) for any person willfully to do any act or refrain from doing any act which enables any such person to take such action. This subdivision shall not apply to:

(a) Boycotts connected with labor disputes; or

(b) Boycotts to protest unlawful discriminatory practices.

14. It shall be an unlawful discriminatory practice for any person engaged in any activity covered by this section to discriminate against a blind person, a hearing impaired person or a person with a disability on the basis of his or her use of a guide dog, hearing dog or service dog.

15. It shall be an unlawful discriminatory practice for any person, agency, bureau, corporation or association, including the state and any political subdivision thereof, to deny any license or employment to any individual by reason of his or her having been convicted of one or more criminal offenses, or by reason of a finding of a lack of "good moral character" which is based upon his or her having been convicted of one or more criminal offenses, when such denial is in violation of the provisions of article twenty-three-A of the correction law. Further, there shall be a rebuttable presumption in favor of excluding from evidence the prior incarceration or conviction of any person, in a case alleging that the employer has been negligent in hiring or retaining an applicant or employee, or supervising a hiring manager, if after learning about an applicant or employee's past criminal conviction history, such employer has evaluated the factors set forth in section seven hundred fifty-two of the correction law, and made a reasonable, good faith determination that such factors militate in favor of hire or retention of that applicant or employee.

16. It shall be an unlawful discriminatory practice, unless specifically required or permitted by statute, for any person, agency, bureau, corporation or association, including the state and any political subdivision thereof, to make any inquiry about, whether in any form of application or otherwise, or to act upon adversely to the individual involved, any arrest or criminal accusation of such individual not then pending against that individual which was followed by a termination of that criminal action or proceeding in favor of such individual, as defined in subdivision two of section 160.50 of the criminal procedure law, or by a youthful offender adjudication, as defined in subdivision one of section 720.35 of the criminal procedure law, or by a conviction for a violation sealed pursuant to section 160.55 of the criminal procedure law or by a conviction which is sealed pursuant to section 160.58 of the criminal procedure law, in connection with the licensing, employment or providing of credit or insurance to such individual; provided, further, that no person shall be required to divulge information pertaining to any arrest or criminal accusation of such individual not then pending against that individual which was followed by a termination of that criminal action or proceeding in favor of such individual, as defined in subdivision two of section 160.50 of the criminal procedure law, or by a youthful offender adjudication, as defined in subdivision one of section 720.35 of the criminal procedure law, or by a conviction for a violation sealed pursuant to section 160.55 of the criminal procedure law, or by a conviction which is sealed pursuant to section 160.58 of the criminal procedure law. The provisions of this subdivision shall not apply to the licensing activities of governmental bodies in relation to the regulation of guns, firearms and other deadly weapons or in relation to an application for employment as a police officer or peace officer as those terms are defined in subdivisions thirty-three and thirty-four of section 1.20 of the criminal procedure law; provided further that the provisions of this subdivision shall not apply to an application for employment or membership in any law enforcement agency with respect to any arrest or criminal accusation which was followed by a youthful offender adjudication, as defined in subdivision one of section 720.35 of the criminal procedure law, or by a conviction for a violation sealed pursuant to section 160.55 of the criminal procedure law, or by a conviction which is sealed pursuant to section 160.58 of the criminal procedure law.

17. Nothing in this section shall prohibit the offer and acceptance of a discount to a person sixty-five years of age or older for housing accommodations.

18. It shall be an unlawful discriminatory practice for the owner, lessee, sub-lessee, assignee, or managing agent of, or other person having the right of ownership of or possession of or the right to rent or lease housing accommodations:

(1) To refuse to permit, at the expense of a person with a disability, reasonable modifications of existing premises occupied or to be occupied by the said person, if the modifications may be necessary to afford the said person full enjoyment of the premises, in conformity with the provisions of the New York state uniform fire prevention and building code except that, in the case of a rental, the landlord may, where it is reasonable to do so, condition permission for a modification on the renter's agreeing to restore the interior of the premises to the condition that existed before the modification, reasonable wear and tear excepted.

(2) To refuse to make reasonable accommodations in rules, policies, practices, or services, when such accommodations may be necessary to afford said person with a disability equal opportunity to use and enjoy a dwelling, including reasonable modification to common use portions of the dwelling, or

(3) In connection with the design and construction of covered multi-family dwellings for first occupancy after March thirteenth, nineteen hundred ninety-one, a failure to design and construct dwellings in accordance with the accessibility requirements for multi-family dwellings found in the New York state uniform fire prevention and building code to provide that:

(i) The public use and common use portions of the dwellings are readily accessible to and usable by persons with disabilities;

(ii) All the doors are designed in accordance with the New York state uniform fire prevention and building code to allow passage into and within all premises and are sufficiently wide to allow passage by persons in wheelchairs; and

(iii) All premises within covered multi-family dwelling units contain an accessible route into and through the dwelling; light switches, electrical outlets, thermostats, and other environmental controls are in accessible locations; there are reinforcements in the bathroom walls to allow later installation of grab bars; and there are usable kitchens and bathrooms such that an individual in a wheelchair can maneuver about the space, in conformity with the New York state uniform fire prevention and building code.

19. (a) Except as provided in paragraph (b) of this subdivision, it shall be an unlawful discriminatory practice of any employer, labor organization, employment agency, licensing agency, or its employees, agents, or members:

(1) to directly or indirectly solicit, require, or administer a genetic test to a person, or solicit or require information from which a predisposing genetic characteristic can be inferred as a condition of employment, pre-employment application, labor organization membership, or licensure; or

(2) to buy or otherwise acquire the results or interpretation of an individual's genetic test results or information from which a predisposing genetic characteristic can be inferred or to make an agreement with an individual to take a genetic test or provide genetic test results or such information.

(c) An employer may require a specified genetic test as a condition of employment where such a test is shown to be directly related to the occupational environment, such that the employee or applicant with a particular genetic anomaly might be at an increased risk of disease as a result of working in said environment.

(d) Nothing in this section shall prohibit the genetic testing of an employee who requests a genetic test and who provides written and informed consent to taking a genetic test for any of the following purposes:

(1) pursuant to a workers' compensation claim;

(2) pursuant to civil litigation; or

(3) to determine the employee's susceptibility to potentially carcinogenic, toxic, or otherwise hazardous chemicals or substances found in the workplace environment only if the employer does not terminate the employee or take any other action that adversely affects any term, condition or privilege of employment pursuant to the genetic test results.

(d) If an employee consents to genetic testing for any of the aforementioned allowable reasons, he or she must be given and sign an authorization of consent form which explicitly states the specific purpose, uses and limitations of the genetic tests and the specific traits or characteristics to be tested.

20.[repealed]

21.Nothing in this section shall prohibit the offer and acceptance of a discount for housing accommodations to a person with a disability, as defined in subdivision twenty-one of section two hundred ninety-two of this article.

§296-a. Unlawful discriminatory practices in relation to credit.

1. It shall be an unlawful discriminatory practice for any creditor or any officer, agent or employee thereof:

(a) In the case of applications for credit with respect to the purchase, acquisition, construction, rehabilitation, repair or maintenance of any housing accommodation, land or commercial space to discriminate against any such applicant because of the race, creed, color, national origin, sexual orientation, military status, age, sex, marital status, disability, or familial status of such applicant or applicants or any member, stockholder, director, officer or employee of such applicant or applicants, or of the prospective occupants or tenants of such housing accommodation, land or commercial space, in the granting, withholding, extending or renewing, or in the fixing of the rates, terms or conditions of, any such credit;

(b) To discriminate in the granting, withholding, extending or renewing, or in the fixing of the rates, terms or conditions of, any form of credit, on the basis of race, creed, color, national origin, sexual orientation, military status, age, sex, marital status, disability, or familial status;

(c) To use any form of application for credit or use or make any record or inquiry which expresses, directly or indirectly, any limitation, specification, or discrimination as to race, creed, color, national origin, sexual orientation, military status, age, sex, marital status, disability, or familial status;

(d) To make any inquiry of an applicant concerning his or her capacity to reproduce, or his or her use or advocacy of any form of birth control or family planning;

(e) To refuse to consider sources of an applicant's income or to subject an applicant's income to discounting, in whole or in part, because of an applicant's race, creed, color, national origin, sexual orientation, military status, age, sex, marital status, childbearing potential, disability, or familial status;

(f) To discriminate against a married person because such person neither uses nor is known by the surname of his or her spouse. This paragraph shall not apply to any situation where the use of a surname would constitute or result in a criminal act.

2. Without limiting the generality of subdivision one of this section, it shall be considered discriminatory if, because of an applicant's or class of applicants' race, creed, color, national origin, sexual orientation, military status, age, sex, marital status or disability, or familial status, (i) an applicant or class of applicants is denied credit in circumstances where other applicants of like overall credit worthiness are granted credit, or (ii) special requirements or conditions, such as requiring co-obligors or reapplication upon marriage, are imposed upon an applicant or class of applicants in circumstances where similar requirements or conditions are not imposed upon other applicants of like overall credit worthiness.

3. It shall not be considered discriminatory if credit differentiations or decisions are based upon factually supportable, objective differences in applicants' overall credit worthiness, which may include reference to such factors as current income, assets and prior credit history of such applicants, as well as reference to any other relevant factually supportable data; provided, however, that no creditor shall consider, in evaluating the credit worthiness of an applicant, aggregate statistics or assumptions relating to race, creed, color, national origin, sexual orientation, military status, sex, marital status or disability, or to the likelihood of any group of persons bearing or rearing children, or for that reason receiving diminished or interrupted income in the future.

3-a. It shall not be an unlawful discriminatory practice to consider age in determining credit worthiness when age has a demonstrable and statistically sound relationship to a determination of credit worthiness.

4. (a) If so requested by an applicant for credit, a creditor shall furnish such applicant with a statement of the specific reasons for rejection of the applicant's application for credit.

   (b) If so requested in writing by an individual who is or was married, a creditor or credit reporting bureau shall maintain in its records a separate credit history for any such individual. Such separate history shall include all obligations as to which such bureau has notice with respect to which any such person is or was individually or jointly liable.

5. No provision of this section providing spouses the right to separately apply for credit, borrow money, or have separate credit histories maintained shall limit or foreclose the right of creditors, under any other provision of law, to hold one spouse legally liable for debts incurred by the other.

6. Any person claiming to be aggrieved by an unlawful discriminatory practice engaged in by a regulated creditor, in lieu of the procedure set forth in section two hundred ninety-seven of this article, may file a verified complaint with the superintendent, as provided hereinafter; provided, however, that the filing of a complaint with either the superintendent or the division shall bar subsequent recourse to the other agency, as well as to any local commission on human rights, with respect to the grievance complained of.

7. In the case of a verified complaint filed with the superintendent the following procedures shall be followed:

   (a) After receipt of the complaint, the superintendent shall make a determination within thirty days of whether there is probable cause to believe that the person named in the complaint has engaged in or is engaging in an unlawful discriminatory practice. If the superintendent determines there is no such probable cause, the complaint shall be dismissed. If the superintendent determines that there is such probable cause, he or she shall attempt to resolve such complaint by conference and conciliation. If conciliation is achieved, the terms shall be recorded in a written agreement signed by the creditor and complainant, a copy of which shall be forwarded to the commissioner.

   (b) If conciliation is not achieved, the superintendent or his or her designated representative shall conduct a hearing with respect to the alleged violation of this section. All interested parties shall be entitled to adequate and timely notice of the hearing. Such parties shall have the right to be represented by counsel or by other representatives of their own choosing; to offer evidence and witnesses in their own behalf and to cross-examine other parties and witnesses; to have the power of subpoena exercised in their behalf; and to have access to a written record of such hearing. The superintendent or his or her representative shall not be bound by the strict rules of evidence prevailing in courts of law or equity. The testimony taken shall be under oath and a record shall be made of the proceedings. A written decision shall be made by the superintendent or his or her designated representative separately setting forth findings of fact and conclusions of law. A copy of such decision shall be forwarded to the commissioner.

   (c) If the superintendent finds that a violation of this section has occurred, the superintendent shall issue an order which shall do one or more of the following:

      (1) impose a fine in an amount not to exceed ten thousand dollars for each violation, to be paid to the people of the state of New York;

      (2) award compensatory damages to the person aggrieved by such violation;

      (3) require the regulated creditor to cease and desist from such unlawful discriminatory practices;

      (4) require the regulated creditor to take such further affirmative action as will effectuate the purposes of this section, including, but not limited to, granting the credit which was the subject of the complaint.

   (d) Any complainant, respondent or other person aggrieved by any order or final determination of the superintendent may obtain judicial review thereof.

8. Where the superintendent makes a determination that a regulated creditor has engaged in or is engaging in discriminatory practices, the superintendent is empowered to issue appropriate orders to such creditor pursuant to the banking law. Such orders may be issued without the necessity of a complaint being filed by an aggrieved person.

9. Whenever any creditor makes application to the superintendent or the banking board to take any action requiring consideration by the superintendent or such board of the public interest and the needs and convenience thereof, or requiring a finding that the financial responsibility, experience, charter, and general fitness of the applicant, and of the members thereof if the applicant be a co-partnership or association, and of the officers and directors thereof if the applicant be a corporation, are such as to command the confidence of the community and to warrant belief that the business will be operated honestly, fairly, and efficiently, such creditor shall certify to the superintendent compliance with the provisions of this section. In the event that the records of the banking department show that such creditor has been found to be in violation of this section, such creditor shall describe what action has been taken with respect to its credit policies and procedures to remedy such violation or violations. The superintendent shall, in approving the foregoing applications and making the foregoing findings, give appropriate weight to compliance with this section.

10. Any complaint filed with the superintendent pursuant to this section shall be so filed within one year after the occurrence of the alleged unlawful discriminatory practice.

11. The superintendent is hereby empowered to promulgate rules and regulations hereunder to effectuate the purposes of this section.

12. The provisions of this section, as they relate to age, shall not apply to persons under the age of eighteen years.

§ **296-b.** Unlawful discriminatory practices relating to domestic workers.

1. For the purposes of this section: "Domestic workers" shall have the meaning set forth in section two of the labor law.

2. It shall be an unlawful discriminatory practice for an employer to:

(a) Engage in unwelcome sexual advances, requests for sexual favors, or other verbal or physical conduct of a sexual nature to a domestic worker when: (i) submission to such conduct is made either explicitly or implicitly a term or condition of an individual's employment; (ii) submission to or rejection of such conduct by an individual is used as the basis for employment decisions affecting such individual; or (iii) such conduct has the purpose or effect of unreasonably interfering with an individual's work performance by creating an intimidating, hostile, or offensive working environment.

(b) Subject a domestic worker to unwelcome harassment based on gender, race, religion or national origin, where such harassment has the purpose or effect of unreasonably interfering with an individual's work performance by creating an intimidating, hostile, or offensive working environment.

The following § 296-c is effective for discrimination occurring after July 22, 2014. Laws of 2014, chapter 97.

§ **296-c.** Unlawful discriminatory practices relating to interns.

1. As used in this section, "Intern" means a person who performs work for an employer for the purpose of training under the following circumstances:

(a) the employer is not committed to hire the person performing the work at the conclusion of the training period;

(b) the employer and the person performing the work agree that the person performing the work is not entitled to wages for the work performed; and

(c) the work performed:

(1) provides or supplements training that may enhance the employability of the intern;

(2) provides experience for the benefit of the person performing the work;

(3) does not displace regular employees; and

(4) is performed under the close supervision of existing staff.

2. It shall be an unlawful discriminatory practice for an employer to:

(a) refuse to hire or employ or to bar or to discharge from internship an intern or to discriminate against such intern in terms, conditions or privileges of employment as an intern because of the intern's age, race, creed, color, national origin, sexual orientation, military status, sex, disability, predisposing genetic characteristics, marital status, or domestic violence victim status;

(b) discriminate against an intern in receiving, classifying, disposing or otherwise acting upon applications for internships because of the intern's age, race, creed, color, national origin, sexual orientation, military status, sex, disability, predisposing genetic characteristics, marital status, or domestic violence victim status;

(c) print or circulate or cause to be printed or circulated any statement, advertisement or publication, or to use any form of application for employment as an intern or to make any inquiry in connection with prospective employment, which expresses directly or indirectly, any limitation, specification or discrimination as to age, race, creed, color, national origin, sexual orientation, military status, sex, disability, predisposing genetic characteristics, marital status or domestic violence victim status, or any intent to make any such limitation, specification or discrimination, unless based upon a bona fide occupational qualification; provided, however, that neither this paragraph nor any provision of this chapter or other law shall be construed to prohibit the department of civil service or the department of personnel of any city containing more than one county from requesting information from applicants for civil service internships or examinations concerning any of the aforementioned characteristics, other than sexual orientation, for the purpose of conducting studies to identify and resolve possible problems in recruitment and testing of members of minority groups to insure the fairest possible and equal opportunities for employment in the civil service for all persons, regardless of age, race, creed, color, national origin, sexual orientation, military status, sex, disability, predisposing genetic characteristics, marital status or domestic violence victim status;

(d) to discharge, expel or otherwise discriminate against any person because he or she has opposed any practices forbidden under this article or because he or she has filed a complaint, testified or assisted in any proceeding under this article; or

(e) to compel an intern who is pregnant to take a leave of absence, unless the intern is prevented by such pregnancy from performing the activities involved in the job or occupation in a reasonable manner.

3. It shall be an unlawful discriminatory practice for an employer to:

(a) engage in unwelcome sexual advances, requests for sexual favors, or other verbal or physical conduct of a sexual nature to an intern when:

(1) submission to such conduct is made either explicitly or implicitly a term or condition of the intern's employment;

(2) submission to or rejection of such conduct by the intern is used as the basis for employment decisions affecting such intern; or

(3) such conduct has the purpose or effect of unreasonably interfering with the intern's work performance by creating an intimidating, hostile, or offensive working environment; or

(b) subject an intern to unwelcome harassment based on age, sex, race, creed, color, sexual orientation, military status, disability, predisposing genetic characteristics, marital status, domestic violence victim status, or national origin, where such harassment has the purpose or effect of unreasonably interfering with the intern's work performance by creating an intimidating, hostile, or offensive working environment.

4. Nothing in this section shall affect any restrictions upon the activities of persons licensed by the state liquor authority with respect to persons under twenty-one years of age.

5. Nothing in this section shall create an employment relationship between an employer and an intern for the purposes of articles six, seven, eighteen or nineteen of the labor law.

§ 297. Procedure.

1. Any person claiming to be aggrieved by an unlawful discriminatory practice may, by himself or herself or his her attorney at law, make, sign and file with the division a verified complaint in writing which shall state the name and address of the person alleged to have committed the unlawful discriminatory practice complained of and which shall set forth the particulars thereof and contain such other information as may be required by the division. The commissioner of labor or the attorney general, or the chair of the commission on quality of care for the mentally disabled, or the division on its own motion may, in like manner, make, sign and file such complaint. In connection with the filing of such complaint, the attorney general is authorized to take proof, issue subpoenas and administer oaths in the manner provided in the civil practice law and rules. Any employer whose employees, or some of them, refuse or threaten to refuse to cooperate with the provisions of this article, may file with the division a verified complaint asking for assistance by conciliation or other remedial action.

2. (a) After the filing of any complaint, the division shall promptly serve a copy thereof upon the respondent and all persons it deems to be necessary parties, and make prompt investigation in connection therewith. Within one hundred eighty days after a complaint is filed, the division shall determine whether it has jurisdiction and, if so, whether there is probable cause to believe that the person named in the complaint, hereinafter referred to as the respondent, has engaged or is engaging in an unlawful discriminatory practice. If it finds with respect to any respondent that it lacks jurisdiction or that probable cause does not exist, the commissioner shall issue and cause to be served on the complainant an order dismissing such allegations of the said complaint as to such respondent.

   (b) Notwithstanding the provisions of paragraph a of this subdivision, with respect to housing discrimination only, after the filing of any complaint, the division shall, within thirty days after receipt, serve a copy thereof upon the respondent and all persons it deems to be necessary parties, and make prompt investigation in connection therewith. Within one hundred days after a complaint is filed, the division shall determine whether it has jurisdiction and, if so, whether there is probable cause to believe that the person named in the complaint, hereinafter referred to as the respondent, has engaged or is engaging in an unlawful discriminatory practice. If it finds with respect to any respondent that it lacks jurisdiction or that probable cause does not exist, the commissioner shall issue and cause to be served on the complainant an order dismissing such allegations of the said complaint as to such respondent.

3. (a) If in the judgment of the division the circumstances so warrant, it may, at any time after the filing of the complaint, endeavor to eliminate such unlawful discriminatory practice by conference, conciliation and persuasion. Each conciliation agreement shall include provisions requiring the respondent to refrain from the commission of unlawful discriminatory practices in the future and may contain such further provisions as may be agreed upon by the division, the complainant, and the respondent, including a provision for the entry in the supreme court in any county in the judicial district where the alleged unlawful discriminatory practice was committed, or where any respondent resides or maintains an office for the transaction of business, or where the housing accommodation, land or commercial space specified in the complaint is located, of a consent decree embodying the terms of the conciliation agreement. The division shall not disclose what has transpired in the course of such endeavors.

   (b) If a conciliation agreement is entered into, the division shall issue an order embodying such agreement and serve a copy of such order upon all parties to the proceeding, and if a party to any such proceeding is a regulated creditor, the division shall forward a copy of the order embodying such agreement to the superintendent.

   (c) If the division finds that noticing the complaint for hearing would be undesirable, the division may, in its unreviewable discretion, at any time prior to a hearing before a hearing examiner, dismiss the complaint on the grounds of administrative convenience. However, in cases of housing discrimination only, an administrative convenience dismissal will not be rendered without the consent of the complainant. The division may, subject to judicial review, dismiss the complaint on the grounds of untimeliness if the complaint is untimely or on the grounds that the election of remedies is annulled.

4. (a) Within two hundred seventy days after a complaint is filed, or within one hundred twenty days after the court has reversed and remanded an order of the division dismissing a complaint for lack of jurisdiction or for want of probable cause, unless the division has dismissed the complaint or issued an order stating

the terms of a conciliation agreement not objected to by the complainant, the division shall cause to be issued and served a written notice, together with a copy of such complaint, as the same may have been amended, requiring the respondent or respondents to answer the charges of such complaint and appear at a public hearing before a hearing examiner at a time not less than five nor more than fifteen days after such service and at a place to be fixed by the division and specified in such notice. The place of any such hearing shall be the office of the division or such other place as may be designated by the division. The case in support of the complaint shall be presented by one of the attorneys or agents of the division and, at the option of the complainant, by his or her attorney. With the consent of the division, the case in support of the complainant may be presented solely by his or her attorney. No person who shall have previously made the investigation, engaged in a conciliation proceeding or caused the notice to be issued shall act as a hearing examiner in such case. Attempts at conciliation shall not be received in evidence. At least two business days prior to the hearing the respondent shall, and any necessary party may, file a written answer to the complaint, sworn to subject to the penalties of perjury, with the division and serve a copy upon all other parties to the proceeding. A respondent who has filed an answer, or whose default in answering has been set aside for good cause shown may appear at such hearing in person or otherwise, with or without counsel, cross examine witnesses and the complainant and submit testimony. The complainant and all parties shall be allowed to present testimony in person or by counsel and cross examine witnesses. The hearing examiner may in his or her discretion permit any person who has a substantial personal interest to intervene as a party, and may require that necessary parties not already parties be joined. The division or the complainant shall have the power reasonably and fairly to amend any complaint, and the respondent and any other party shall have like power to amend his or her answer. The hearing examiner shall not be bound by the strict rules of evidence prevailing in courts of law or equity. The testimony taken at the hearing shall be under oath and a record made.

(b) If the respondent fails to answer the complaint, the hearing examiner designated to conduct the hearing may enter the default and the hearing shall proceed on the evidence in support of the complaint. Such default may be set aside only for good cause shown upon equitable terms and conditions.

(c) Within one hundred eighty days after the commencement of such hearing, a determination shall be made and an order served as hereinafter provided. If, upon all the evidence at the hearing, the commissioner shall find that a respondent has engaged in any unlawful discriminatory practice as defined in this article, the commissioner shall state findings of fact and shall issue and cause to be served on such respondent an order, based on such findings and setting them forth, and including such of the following provisions as in the judgment of the division will effectuate the purposes of this article: (i) requiring such respondent to cease and desist from such unlawful discriminatory practice;(ii) requiring such respondent to take such affirmative action, including (but not limited to) hiring, reinstatement or upgrading of employees, with or without back pay, restoration to membership in any respondent labor organization, admission to or participation in a guidance program, apprenticeship training program, on the job training program or other occupational training or retraining program, the extension of full, equal and unsegregated accommodations, advantages, facilities and privileges to all persons, granting the credit which was the subject of any complaint, evaluating applicants for membership in a place of accommodation without discrimination based on race, creed, color, national origin, sex, disability or marital status, and without retaliation or discrimination based on opposition to practices forbidden by this article or filing a complaint, testifying or assisting in any proceeding under this article; (iii) awarding of compensatory damages to the person aggrieved by such practice; (iv) awarding of punitive damages, in cases of housing discrimination only, in an amount not to exceed ten thousand dollars, to the person aggrieved by such practice; (v) requiring payment to the state of profits obtained by a respondent through the commission of unlawful discriminatory acts described in subdivision three b of section two hundred ninety six of this article; and (vi) assessing civil fines and penalties in an amount not to exceed fifty thousand dollars, to be paid to the state by a respondent found to have committed an unlawful discriminatory act, or not to exceed one hundred thousand dollars to be paid to the state by a respondent found to have committed an unlawful discriminatory act which is found to be willful, wanton or malicious; (vii) requiring a report of the manner of compliance. If, upon all the evidence, the commissioner shall find that a respondent has not engaged in any such unlawful discriminatory practice, he or she shall state findings of fact and shall issue and cause to be served on the complainant an order based on such findings and setting them forth dismissing the said complaint as to such respondent. A copy of each order issued by the commissioner shall be delivered in all cases to the attorney general, the secretary of state, if he or she has issued a license to the respondent, and such other public officers as the division deems proper, and if any such order issued by the commissioner concerns a regulated creditor, the commissioner shall forward a copy of any such order to the superintendent. A copy of any complaint filed against any respondent who has previously entered into a conciliation agreement pursuant to paragraph a of subdivision three of this section or as to whom an order of the division has previously been entered pursuant to this paragraph shall be delivered to the attorney general, to the secretary of state if he or she has issued a license to the respondent and to such other public officers as the division deems proper, and if any such respondent is a regulated creditor, the commissioner shall forward a copy of any such complaint to the superintendent.

(d) The division shall establish rules of practice to govern, expedite and effectuate the foregoing procedure and its own actions thereunder.

(e) Any civil penalty imposed pursuant to this subdivision shall be separately stated, and shall be in addition to and not reduce or offset any other damages or payment imposed upon a respondent pursuant to this article. In cases of employment discrimination where the employer has fewer than fifty employees, such civil fine or penalty may be paid in reasonable installments, in accordance with regulations promulgated by the division. Such regulations shall require the payment of reasonable interest resulting from the delay, and in no case permit installments to be made over a period longer than three years.

5. Any complaint filed pursuant to this section must be so filed within one year after the alleged unlawful discriminatory practice.

6. At any time after the filing of a complaint with the division alleging an unlawful discriminatory practice under this article, if the division determines that the respondent is doing or procuring to be done any act tending to render ineffectual any order the commissioner may enter in such proceeding, the commissioner may apply to the supreme court in any county where the alleged unlawful discriminatory practice was committed, or where any respondent resides or maintains an office for the transaction of business, or if the complaint alleges an unlawful discriminatory practice under subdivision two a or paragraph (a), (b) or (c) of subdivision five of section two hundred ninety six of this article, where the housing accommodation, land or commercial space specified in the complaint is located, or, if no supreme court justice is available is such county, in any other county within the judicial district, for an order requiring the respondents or any of them to show cause why they should not be enjoined from doing or procuring to be done such act. The order to show cause may contain a temporary restraining order and shall be served in the manner provided therein. On the return date of the order to show cause, and after affording all parties an opportunity to be heard, if the court deems it necessary to prevent the respondents from rendering ineffectual an order relating to the subject matter of the complaint, it may grant appropriate injunctive relief upon such terms and conditions as it deems proper.

7. Not later than one year from the date of a conciliation agreement or an order issued under this section, and at any other times in its discretion, the division shall investigate whether the respondent is complying with the terms of such agreement or order. Upon a finding of non compliance, the division shall take appropriate action to assure compliance.

8. No officer, agent or employee of the division shall make public with respect to a particular person without his consent information from reports obtained by the division except as necessary to the conduct of a proceeding under this section.

9. Any person claiming to be aggrieved by an unlawful discriminatory practice shall have a cause of action in any court of appropriate jurisdiction for damages, including, in cases of housing discrimination only, punitive damages, and such other remedies as may be appropriate, including any civil fines and penalties provided in subdivision four of this section, unless such person had filed a complaint hereunder or with any local commission on human rights, or with the superintendent pursuant to the provisions of section two hundred ninety six a of this chapter, provided that, where the division has dismissed such complaint on the grounds of administrative convenience, on the grounds of untimeliness, or on the grounds that the election of remedies is annulled, such person shall maintain all rights to bring suit as if no complaint had been filed

with the division. At any time prior to a hearing before a hearing examiner, a person who has a complaint pending at the division may request that the division dismiss the complaint and annul his or her election of remedies so that the human rights law claim may be pursued in court, and the division may, upon such request, dismiss the complaint on the grounds that such person's election of an administrative remedy is annulled. Notwithstanding subdivision (a) of section two hundred four of the civil practice law and rules, if a complaint is so annulled by the division, upon the request of the party bringing such complaint before the division, such party's rights to bring such cause of action before a court of appropriate jurisdiction shall be limited by the statute of limitations in effect in such court at the time the complaint was initially filed with the division. Any party to a housing discrimination complaint shall have the right within twenty days following a determination of probable cause pursuant to subdivision two of this section to elect to have an action commenced in a civil court, and an attorney representing the division of human rights will be appointed to present the complaint in court, or, with the consent of the division, the case may be presented by complainant's attorney. A complaint filed by the equal employment opportunity commission to comply with the requirements of 42 USC 2000e 5(c) and 42 USC 12117(a) and 29 USC 633(b) shall not constitute the filing of a complaint within the meaning of this subdivision. No person who has initiated any action in a court of competent jurisdiction or who has an action pending before any administrative agency under any other law of the state based upon an act which would be an unlawful discriminatory practice under this article, may file a complaint with respect to the same grievance under this section or under section two hundred ninety six a of this article.

10. With respect to cases of housing discrimination only, in an action or proceeding at law under this section or section two hundred ninety eight of this article, the commissioner or the court may in its discretion award reasonable attorney's fees to any prevailing or substantially prevailing party; provided, however, that a prevailing respondent or defendant in order to recover such reasonable attorney's fees must make a motion requesting such fees and show that the action or proceeding brought was frivolous; and further provided that in a proceeding brought in the division of human rights, the commissioner may only award attorney's fees as part of a final order after a public hearing held pursuant to subdivision four of this section. In no case shall attorney's fees be awarded to the division, nor shall the division be liable to a prevailing or substantially prevailing party for attorney's fees, except in a case in which the division is a party to the action or the proceeding in the division's capacity as an employer. In order to find the action or proceeding to be frivolous, the court or the commissioner must find in writing one or more of the following:

(a)) the action or proceeding was commenced, used or continued in bad faith, solely to delay or prolong the resolution of the litigation or to harass or maliciously injure another; or

(b) the action or proceeding was commenced or continued in bad faith without any reasonable basis and could not be supported by a good faith argument for an extension, modification or reversal of existing law. If the action or proceeding was promptly discontinued when the party or attorney learned or should have learned that the action or proceeding lacked such a reasonable basis, the court may find that the party or the attorney did not act in bad faith.

§ 298. Judicial review and enforcement.

Any complainant, respondent or other person aggrieved by an order of the commissioner which is an order after public hearing, a cease and desist order, an order awarding damages, an order dismissing a complaint, or by an order of the division which makes a final disposition of a complaint may obtain judicial review thereof, and the division may obtain an order of court for its enforcement and for the enforcement of any order of the commissioner which has not been appealed to the court, in a proceeding as provided in this section. Such proceeding shall be brought in the Supreme Court in the county wherein the unlawful discriminatory practice which is the subject of the order occurs or wherein any person required in the order to cease and desist from an unlawful discriminatory practice or to take other affirmative action resides or transacts business. Such proceeding shall be initiated by the filing of a notice of petition and petition in such court. Thereafter, at a time and in a manner to be specified by rules of court, the division shall file with the court a written transcript of the record of all prior proceedings. Upon the filing of a notice of petition and petition, the court shall have jurisdiction of the proceeding and of the questions determined therein, except that where the order sought to be reviewed was made as a result of a public hearing held pursuant to paragraph a of subdivision four of section two hundred ninety seven of this article, the court shall make an order directing that the proceeding be transferred for disposition to the appellate division of the supreme court in the judicial department embracing the county in which the proceeding was commenced. The court shall have power to grant such temporary relief or restraining order as it deems just and proper, and to make and enter upon the pleadings, testimony, and proceedings set forth in such transcript an order enforcing, modifying, and enforcing as so modified, or setting aside in whole or in part such order. No objection that has not been urged in prior proceedings shall be considered by the court, unless the failure or neglect to urge such objection shall be excused because of extraordinary circumstances. Any party may move the court to remit the case to the division in the interests of justice for the purpose of adducing additional specified and material evidence and seeking findings thereon, provided he or she shows reasonable grounds for the failure to adduce such evidence in prior proceedings. The findings of facts on which such order is based shall be conclusive if supported by sufficient evidence on the record considered as a whole. All such proceedings shall be heard and determined by the court and any appeal taken from its judgment or order shall be reviewed by the appropriate appellate court as expeditiously as possible and with lawful precedence over other matters. The jurisdiction of the courts over these proceedings, as provided for herein, shall be exclusive and their judgments and orders shall be final, subject to appellate review in the same manner and form and with the same effect as provided for appeals from a judgment in a special proceeding. The division's copy of the testimony shall be available at all reasonable times to all parties for examination without cost and for the purposes of judicial review of such order. Any appeal under this section and any proceeding, if instituted under article seventy eight of the civil practice law and rules to which the division or the board is a party shall be heard on the record without requirement of printing. The division may appear in court by one of its attorneys. A proceeding under this section when instituted by any complainant, respondent or other person aggrieved must be instituted within sixty days after the service of such order.

§ 298-a. Application of article to certain acts committed outside the state of New York.

1. The provisions of this article shall apply as hereinafter provided to an act committed outside this state against a resident of this state or against a corporation organized under the laws of this state or authorized to do business in this state, if such act would constitute an unlawful discriminatory practice if committed within this state.

2. If a resident person or domestic corporation violates any provision of this article by virtue of the provisions of this section, this article shall apply to such person or corporation in the same manner and to the same extent as such provisions would have applied had such act been committed within this state except that the penal provisions of such article shall not be applicable.

3. If a non-resident person or foreign corporation violates any provision of this article by virtue of the provisions of this section, such person or corporation shall be prohibited from transacting any business within this state. Except as otherwise provided in this subdivision, the provisions of section two hundred ninety-seven of this article governing the procedure for determining and processing unlawful discriminatory practices shall apply to violations defined by this subdivision insofar as such provisions are or can be made applicable. If the division of human rights has reason to believe that a non-resident person or foreign corporation has committed or is about to commit outside of this state an act which if committed within this state would constitute an unlawful discriminatory practice and that such act is in violation of any provision of this article by virtue of the provisions of this section, it shall serve a copy of the complaint upon such person or corporation by personal service either within or without the state or by registered mail, return receipt requested, directed to such person or corporation at his or her or its last known place of residence or business, together with a notice requiring such person or corporation to appear at a hearing, specifying the time and place thereof, and to show cause why a cease and desist order should not be issued against such person or corporation. If such person or corporation shall fail to appear at such hearing or does not show sufficient cause why such order should not be issued, the division shall cause to be issued and served upon such person or corporation an order to cease or desist from the act or acts complained of. Failure to comply with any such order shall be followed by the issuance by the division of an order prohibiting such person or corporation from transacting any business within this state. A person or corporation who or which transacts business in this state in violation of any such order is guilty of a class A misdemeanor. Any order issued pursuant to this subdivision may be vacated by the division upon satisfactory proof of compliance with such order. All orders issued pursuant to this subdivision shall be subject to judicial review in the manner prescribed by article seventy-eight of the civil practice law and rules.

TITLE 8 OF THE ADMINISTRATIVE CODE OF THE CITY OF NEW YORK

§ 8-107 Unlawful discriminatory practices.

1. Employment. It shall be an unlawful discriminatory practice:

(a) For an employer or an employee or agent thereof, because of the actual or perceived age, race, creed, color, national origin, gender, disability, marital status, partnership status, caregiver status, sexual orientation or alienage or citizenship status of any person, to refuse to hire or employ or to bar or to discharge from employment such person or to discriminate against such person in compensation or in terms, conditions or privileges of employment.

(b) For an employment agency or an employee or agent thereof to discriminate against any person because of such person's actual or perceived age, race, creed, color, national origin, gender, disability, marital status, partnership status, caregiver status, sexual orientation or alienage or citizenship status in receiving, classifying, disposing or otherwise acting upon applications for its services or in referring an applicant or applicants for its services to an employer or employers.

(c) For a labor organization or an employee or agent thereof, because of the actual or perceived age, race, creed, color, national origin, gender, disability, marital status, partnership status, caregiver status, sexual orientation or alienage or citizenship status of any person, to exclude or to expel from its membership such person or to discriminate in any way against any of its members or against any employer or any person employed by an employer.

(d) For any employer, labor organization or employment agency or an employee or agent thereof to declare, print or circulate or cause to be declared, printed or circulated any statement, advertisement or publication, or to use any form of application for employment or to make any inquiry in connection with prospective employment, which expresses, directly or indirectly, any limitation, specification or discrimination as to age, race, creed, color, national origin, gender, disability, marital status, partnership status, caregiver status, sexual orientation or alienage or citizenship status, or any intent to make any such limitation, specification or discrimination.

(e) The provisions of this subdivision and subdivision two of this section:

(i) As they apply to employee benefit plans, shall not be construed to preclude an employer from observing the provisions of any plan covered by the federal employment retirement income security act of nineteen hundred seventy-four that is in compliance with applicable federal discrimination laws where the application of the provisions of such subdivisions to such plan would be preempted by such act;

(ii) Shall not preclude the varying of insurance coverage according to an employee's age;

(iii) Shall not be construed to affect any retirement policy or system that is permitted pursuant to paragraph (e) and (f) of subdivision three-a of section two hundred ninety-six of the executive law;

(iv) Shall not be construed to affect the retirement policy or system of an employer where such policy or system is not a subterfuge to evade the purposes of this chapter.

(f) The provisions of this subdivision shall not govern the employment by an employer of his or her parents, spouse, or children; provided, however, that such family members shall be counted as persons employed by an employer for the purposes of subdivision five of section 8-102 of this chapter.

2. Apprentice training programs. It shall be an unlawful discriminatory practice for an employer, labor organization, employment agency or any joint labor-management committee controlling apprentice training programs or an employee or agent thereof:

(a) To select persons for an apprentice-training program registered with the State of New York on any basis other than their qualifications, as determined by objective criteria which permit review.

(b) To deny to or withhold from any person because of his or her actual or perceived race, creed, color, national origin, gender, age, disability, marital status, partnership status, sexual orientation or alienage or citizenship status the right to be admitted to or participate in a guidance program, an apprentice training program, on-the-job training program, or other occupational training or retraining program.

(c) To discriminate against any person in his or her pursuit of such program or to discriminate against such a person in the terms, conditions or privileges of such program because of actual or perceived race, creed, color, national origin, gender, age, disability, marital status, partnership status, sexual orientation or alienage or citizenship status.

(d) To declare print or circulate or cause to be declared, printed or circulated any statement, advertisement or publication, or to use any form of application for such program or to make any inquiry in connection with such program which expresses, directly or indirectly, any limitation, specification or discrimination as to race, creed, color, national origin, gender, age, disability, marital status, partnership status, sexual orientation or alienage or citizenship status, or any intent to make any such limitation, specification or discrimination.

3. Employment; religious observance. (a) It shall be an unlawful discriminatory practice for an employer or an employee or agent thereof to impose upon a person as a condition of obtaining or retaining employment any terms or conditions, compliance with which would require such person to violate, or forego a practice of, his or her creed or religion, including but not limited to the observance of any particular day or days or any portion thereof as a Sabbath or holy day or the observance of any religious custom or usage, and the employer shall make reasonable accommodation to the religious needs of such person. Without in any way limiting the foregoing, no person shall be required to remain at his or her place of employment during any day or days or portion thereof that, as a requirement of such persons religion he or she observes as a Sabbath or other holy day, including a reasonable time prior and subsequent thereto for travel between his or her place of employment and his or her home, provided, however, that any such absence from work shall, wherever practicable in the judgment of the employer, be made up by an equivalent amount of time at some other mutually convenient time.

(b) "Reasonable accommodation", as used in this subdivision, shall mean such accommodation to an employee's or prospective employee's religious observance or practice as shall not cause undue hardship in the conduct of the employer's business. The employer shall have the burden of proof to show such hardship.

"Undue hardship" as used in this subdivision shall mean an accommodation requiring significant expense or difficulty (including a significant interference with the safe or efficient operation of the workplace or a violation of a bona fide seniority system). Factors to be considered in determining whether the accommodation constitutes an undue economic hardship shall include, but not be limited to:

(i) the identifiable cost of the accommodation, including the costs of loss of productivity and of retaining or hiring employees or transferring employees from one facility to another, in relation to the size and operating cost of the employer;

(ii) the number of individuals who will need the particular accommodation to a sincerely held religious observance or practice; and

(iii) for an employer with multiple facilities, the degree to which the geographic separateness or administrative or fiscal relationship of the facilities will make the accommodation more difficult or expensive.

Provided, however, an accommodation shall be considered to constitute an undue hardship, for purposes of this subdivision, if it will result in the inability of an employee who is seeking a religious accommodation to perform the essential functions of the position in which he or she is employed.

4. Public accommodations.

(a) It shall be an unlawful discriminatory practice for any person, being the owner, lessee, proprietor, manager, superintendent, agent or employee of any place or provider of public accommodation because of the actual or perceived race, creed, color, national origin, age, gender, disability, marital status, partnership status, sexual orientation or alienage or citizenship status of any person directly or indirectly, to refuse, withhold from or deny to such person any of the accommodations, advantages, facilities or privileges thereof, or, directly or indirectly, to make any declaration, publish, circulate, issue, display, post or mail any written or printed communication, notice or advertisement, to the effect that any of the accommodations, advantages, facilities and privileges of any such place or provider shall be refused, withheld from or denied to any person on account of race, creed, color, national origin, age, gender, disability, marital status, partnership status, sexual orientation or alienage or citizenship status or that the patronage or custom of any person belonging to, purporting to be, or perceived to be, of any particular race, creed, color, national origin, age, gender, disability, marital status, partnership status, sexual orientation or alienage or citizenship status is unwelcome, objectionable or not acceptable, desired or solicited.

(b) Notwithstanding the foregoing, the provisions of this subdivision shall not apply, with respect to age or gender, to places or providers of public accommodation where the commission grants an exemption based on bona fide considerations of public policy.

(c) The provisions of this subdivision relating to discrimination on the basis of gender shall not prohibit any educational institution subject to this subdivision from making gender distinctions which would be permitted (i) for educational institutions which are subject to section thirty-two hundred one-a of the education law or any rules or regulations promulgated by the state commissioner of education relating to gender or (ii) under sections 86.32, 86.33 and 86.34 of title forty-five of the code of federal regulations for educational institutions covered thereunder.

(d) Nothing in this subdivision shall be construed to preclude an educational institution—other than a publicly operated educational institution— which establishes or maintains a policy of educating persons of one gender exclusively from limiting admissions to students of that gender.

(e) The provisions of this subdivision relating to disparate impact shall not apply to the use of standardized tests as defined by section three hundred forty of the education law by an educational institution subject to this subdivision provided that such test is used in the manner and for the purpose prescribed by the test agency which designed the test.

(f) The provisions of this subdivision as they relate to unlawful discriminatory practices by educational institutions shall not apply to matters that are strictly educational or pedagogic in nature.

5. Housing accommodations, land, commercial space and lending practices.

(a) Housing accommodations. It shall be an unlawful discriminatory practice for the owner, lessor, lessee, sublessee, assignee, or managing agent of, or other person having the right to sell, rent or lease or approve the sale, rental or lease of a housing accommodation, constructed or to be constructed, or an interest therein, or any agency or employee thereof:

(1) To refuse to sell, rent, lease approve the sale, rental or lease or otherwise deny to or withhold from any person or group of persons such a housing accommodation or an interest therein because of the actual or perceived race, creed, color, national origin, gender, age, disability, sexual orientation, marital status, partnership status, or alienage or citizenship status of such person or persons, or because of any lawful source of income of such person, or because children are, may be or would be residing with such person or persons.

(2) To discriminate against any person because of such person's actual or perceived race, creed, color, national origin, gender, age, disability, sexual orientation, marital status, partnership status, or alienage or citizenship status, or because of any lawful source of income of such person, or because children are, may be or would be residing with such person, in the terms, conditions or privileges of the sale, rental or lease of any such housing accommodation or an interest therein or in the furnishing of facilities or services in connection therewith.

(3) To declare, print or circulate or cause to be declared, printed or circulated any statement, advertisement or publication, or to use any form of application for the purchase, rental or lease of such a housing accommodation or an interest therein or to make any record or inquiry in conjunction with the prospective purchase, rental or lease of such a housing accommodation or an interest therein which expresses, directly or indirectly, any limitation, specification or discrimination as to race, creed, color, national origin, gender, age, disability, sexual orientation, marital status, partnership status, or alienage or citizenship status, or because of any lawful source of income of such person, or whether children are, may be, or would be residing with a person, or any intent to make such limitation, specification or discrimination.

(4) The provisions of this paragraph

(a) shall not apply:

(1) To the rental of a housing accommodation, other than a publicly-assisted housing accommodation, in a building which contains housing accommodations for not more than two families living independently of each other, if the owner or a member of the owner's family reside in one of such housing accommodations, and if the available housing accommodation has not been publicly advertised, listed, or otherwise offered to the general public; or

(2) To the rental of a room or rooms in a housing accommodation, other than a publicly-assisted housing accommodation, if such rental is by the occupant of the housing accommodation or by the owner of the housing accommodation and the owner or members of the owner's family reside in such housing accommodation.

(b) Land and commercial space. It shall be an unlawful discriminatory practice for the owner, lessor, lessee, sublessee, or managing agent of, or other person having the right of ownership or possession of or the right to sell, rent, or lease, or approve the sale, rental or lease of land or commercial space or an interest therein, or any agency or employee thereof:

(1) To refuse to sell, rent, lease, approve the sale, rental or lease or otherwise deny or to withhold from any person or group of persons land or commercial space or an interest therein because of the actual or perceived race, creed, color, national origin, gender, age, disability, sexual orientation, marital status, partnership status, or alienage or citizenship status of such person or persons, or because children are, may be or would be residing with such person or persons.

(2) To discriminate against any person because of actual or perceived race, creed, color, national origin, gender, age, disability, sexual orientation, marital status, partnership status, or alienage or citizenship status, or because children are, may be or would be residing with such person, in the terms, conditions or privileges of the sale, rental or lease of any such land or commercial space or an interest therein or in the furnishing of facilities or services in connection therewith.

(3) To declare, print or circulate or cause to be declared, printed or circulated any statement, advertisement or publication, or to use any form of application for the purchase, rental or lease of such land or commercial space or an interest therein or to make any record or inquiry in connection with the prospective purchase, rental or lease of such land or commercial space or an interest therein which expresses, directly or indirectly, any limitation, specification or discrimination as to race, creed, color, national origin, gender, age, disability, sexual orientation, marital status, partnership status, or alienage or citizenship status, or whether children are, may be or would be residing with such person, or any intent to make any such limitation, specification or discrimination.

(c) Real estate brokers. It shall be an unlawful discriminatory practice for any real estate broker, real estate salesperson or employee or agent thereof:

(1) To refuse to sell, rent or lease any housing accommodation, land or commercial space or an interest therein to any person or group of persons or to refuse to negotiate for the sale, rental or lease, of any housing accommodation, land or commercial space or an interest therein to any person or group of persons because of the actual or perceived race, creed, color, national origin, gender, age, disability, sexual orientation, marital status, partnership status, or alienage or citizenship status of such person or persons, or because of any lawful source of income of such person, or because children are, may be or would be residing with such person or persons, or to represent that any housing accommodation, land or commercial space or an interest therein is not available for inspection, sale, rental or lease when in fact it is so available, or otherwise to deny or withhold any housing accommodation, land or commercial space or an interest therein or any facilities of any housing accommodation, land or commercial space or an interest therein from any person or group of persons because of the actual or perceived race, creed, color, national gender, age, disability, sexual orientation, marital status, partnership status, or alienage or citizenship status of such person or persons, or because of any lawful source of income of such person, or because children are, may be or would be residing with such person or persons.

(2) To declare, print or circulate or cause to be declared, printed or circulated any statement, advertisement or publication, or to use any form of application for the purchase, rental or lease of any housing accommodation, land or commercial space or an interest therein or to make any record or inquiry in connection with the prospective purchase, rental or lease of any housing accommodation, land or commercial space or an interest therein which expresses, directly or indirectly, any limitation, specification or discrimination as to race, creed, color, national origin, gender, age, disability, sexual orientation, marital status, partnership status, or alienage or citizenship status, or any lawful source of income, or to whether children are, may be or would be residing with a person, or any intent to make such limitation, specification or discrimination.

(3) To induce or attempt to induce any person to sell or rent any housing accommodation, land or commercial space or an interest therein by representations, explicit or implicit, regarding the entry or prospective entry into the neighborhood or area of a person or persons of any race, creed, color, gender, age, disability, sexual orientation, marital status, partnership status, national origin, alienage or citizenship status, or a person or persons with any lawful source of income, or a person or persons with whom children are, may be or would be residing.

(d) Lending practices. It shall be an unlawful discriminatory practice for any person, bank, trust company, private banker, savings bank, industrial bank, savings and loan association, credit union, investment company, mortgage company, insurance company, or other financial institution or lender, doing business in the city and if incorporated regardless of whether incorporated under the laws of the state of New York, the United States or any other jurisdiction, or any officer, agent or employee thereof to whom application is made for a loan, mortgage or other form of financial assistance for the purchase, acquisition, construction, rehabilitation, repair or maintenance of any housing accommodation, land or commercial space or an interest therein:

(1) To discriminate against such applicant or applicants because of the actual or perceived race, creed, color, national origin, gender, disability, sexual orientation, age, marital status, partnership status, or alienage or citizenship status of such applicant or applicants or of any member, stockholder, director, officer or employee of such applicant or applicants, or of the occupants or tenants or prospective occupants or tenants of such housing accommodation, land or commercial space, or because children are, may be or would be residing with such applicant, or other person in the granting, withholding, extending or renewing, or in the fixing of rates, terms or conditions of any such financial assistance or in the appraisal of any housing accommodation, land or commercial space or an interest therein.

(2) To use any form of application for a loan, mortgage, or other form of financial assistance, or to make any record or inquiry in connection with applications for such financial assistance, or in connection with the appraisal of any housing accommodation, land or commercial space or an interest therein, which expresses, directly or indirectly, any limitation, specification or discrimination as to race, creed, color, national origin, gender, disability, sexual orientation, age, marital status or alienage or citizenship status, or whether children are, may be, or would be residing with a person.

(e) Real estate services. It shall be an unlawful discriminatory practice to deny a person access to, or membership in or participation in, a multiple listing service, real estate brokers' organization, or other service because of the actual or perceived race, creed, color, national origin, gender, disability, sexual orientation, age, marital status, partnership status, or alienage or citizenship status of such person or because children are, may be or would be residing with such person.

(f) Real estate related transactions. It shall be an unlawful discriminatory practice for any person whose business includes the appraisal of housing accommodations, land or commercial space or interest therein or an employee or agent thereof to discriminate in making available or in the terms or conditions of such appraisal on the basis of the actual or perceived race, creed, color, national origin, gender, disability, sexual orientation, age, marital status, partnership status, or alienage or citizenship status of any person or because children are, may be or would be residing with such person.

(g) Applicability; persons under eighteen years of age. The provisions of this subdivision, as they relate to unlawful discriminatory practices in housing accommodations, land and commercial space or an interest therein and lending practices on the basis of age, shall not apply to unemancipated persons under the age of eighteen years.

(h) Applicability; discrimination against persons with children. The provisions of this subdivision with respect to discrimination against persons with whom children are, may be or would be residing shall not apply to housing for older persons as defined in paragraphs two and three of subdivision (b) of section thirty-six hundred seven of title forty-two of the United States code and any regulations promulgated thereunder.

(i) Applicability; senior citizen housing. The provisions of this subdivision with respect to discrimination on the basis of age shall not apply to the restriction of the sale, rental or lease of any housing accommodation, land or commercial space or an interest therein exclusively to persons fifty- five years of age or older. This paragraph shall not be construed to permit discrimination against such persons fifty-five years of age or older on the basis of whether children are, may be or would be residing in such housing accommodation or land or an interest therein unless such discrimination is otherwise permitted pursuant to paragraph (h) of this subdivision.

(j) Applicability; dormitory residence operated by educational institution. The provisions of this subdivision relating to discrimination on the basis of gender in housing accommodations shall not prohibit any educational institution from making gender distinctions in dormitory residences which would be permitted under sections 86.32 and 86.33 of title forty-five of the code of federal regulations for educational institutions covered thereunder.

(k) Applicability; dormitory-type housing accommodations. The provisions of this subdivision which prohibit distinctions on the basis of gender and whether children are, may be or would be residing with a person shall not apply to dormitory-type housing accommodations including, but not limited, to shelters for the homeless where such distinctions are intended to recognize generally accepted values of personal modesty and privacy or to protect the health, safety or welfare of families with children.

(l) Exemption for special needs of particular age group in publicly assisted housing accommodations. Nothing in this subdivision shall restrict the consideration of age in the rental of publicly-assisted housing accommodations if the State Division of Human Rights grants an exemption pursuant to section two hundred ninety-six of the executive law based on bona fide considerations of public policy for the purpose of providing for the special needs of a particular age group without the intent of prejudicing other age groups; provided however that this paragraph shall not be construed to permit discrimination on the basis of whether children are, may be or would be residing in such housing accommodations unless such discrimination is otherwise permitted pursuant to paragraph (h) of this section.

(m) Applicability; use of criteria or qualifications in publicly assisted housing accommodations. The provisions of this subdivision shall not be construed to prohibit the use of criteria or qualifications of eligibility for the sale, rental, leasing or occupancy of publicly-assisted housing accommodations where such criteria or qualifications are required to comply with federal or state law, or are necessary to obtain the benefits of a federal or state program, or to prohibit the use of statements, advertisements, publications, applications or inquiries to the extent that they state such criteria or qualifications or request information necessary to determine or verify the eligibility of an applicant, tenant, purchaser, lessee or occupant.

(n) Discrimination on the basis of occupation prohibited in housing accommodations. Where a housing accommodation or an interest therein is sought or occupied exclusively for residential purposes, the provisions of this subdivision shall be construed to prohibit discrimination in the sale, rental, or leasing of such housing accommodation or interest therein and in the terms, conditions and privileges of the sale, rental or leasing of such housing accommodation or interest therein and in the furnishing of faculties or services in connection therewith, on account of a person's occupation.

(o)Applicability; lawful source of income. The provisions of this subdivision, as they relate to unlawful discriminatory practices on the basis of lawful source of income, shall not apply to housing accommodations that contain a total of five or fewer housing units, provided, however:

(i) the provisions of this subdivision shall apply to tenants subject to rent control laws who reside in housing accommodations that contain a total of five or fewer units at the time of the enactment of this local law; and provided, however

(ii) the provisions of this subdivision shall apply to all housing accommodations, regardless of the number of units contained in each, of any person who has the rights to sell, rent or lease or approve the sale, rental or lease of at least one housing accommodation within New York City that contains six or more housing units, constructed or to be constructed, or an interest therein.

6. Aiding and abetting. It shall be an unlawful discriminatory practice for any person to aid, abet, incite, compel or coerce the doing of any of the acts forbidden under this chapter, or to attempt to do so.

7. Retaliation. It shall be an unlawful discriminatory practice for any person engaged in any activity to which this chapter applies to retaliate or discriminate in any manner against any person because such person has (i) opposed any practice forbidden under this chapter, (ii) filed a complaint, testified or assisted in any proceeding under this chapter, (iii) commenced a civil action alleging the commission of an act which would be an unlawful discriminatory practice under this chapter, (iv) assisted the commission or the corporation counsel in an investigation commenced pursuant to this title, or (v) provided any information to the commission pursuant to the terms of a conciliation agreement made pursuant to section 8-115 of this chapter. The retaliation or discrimination complained of under this subdivision need not result in an ultimate action with respect to employment, housing or a public accommodation or in a materially adverse change in the terms and conditions of employment, housing, or a public accommodation, provided, however, that the retaliatory or discriminatory act or acts complained of must be reasonably likely to deter a person from engaging in protected activity.

8. Violation of conciliation agreement. It shall be an unlawful discriminatory practice for any party to a conciliation agreement made pursuant to section 8-115 of this chapter to violate the terms of such agreement.

9. Licenses, registrations and permits.

(a) It shall be an unlawful discriminatory practice:

(1)Except as otherwise provided in paragraph (c) of this subdivision, for an agency authorized to issue a license, registration or permit or an employee thereof to discriminate against an applicant for a license, registration or permit because of the actual or perceived race, creed, color, national origin, age, gender, marital status, partnership status, disability, sexual orientation or alienage or citizenship status of such applicant.

(2)Except as otherwise provided in paragraph (c) of this subdivision, for an agency authorized to issue a license, registration or permit or an employee thereof to declare, print or circulate or cause to be declared, printed or circulated any statement, advertisement or publication, or to use any form of application for a license, registration or permit or to make any inquiry in connection with any such application, which expresses, directly or indirectly, any limitation, specification or discrimination as to race, creed, color, national origin, age, gender, marital status, partnership status, disability, sexual orientation or alienage or citizenship status, or any intent to make any such limitation, specification or discrimination.

(3)For any person to deny any license, registration or permit to any applicant, or act adversely upon any holder of a license, registration or permit by reason of his or her having been convicted of one or more criminal offenses, or by reason of a finding of a lack of "good moral character" which is based on his or her having been convicted of one or more criminal offenses, when such denial or adverse action is in violation of the provisions of article twenty-three-a of the correction law.

(4)For any person to deny any license, registration or permit to any applicant, or act adversely upon any holder of a license, registration or permit by reason of his or her having been arrested or accused of committing a crime when such denial or adverse action is in violation of subdivision 16 of section 296 of article 15 of the New York state executive law.

(5) For any person to make any inquiry, in writing or otherwise, regarding any arrest or criminal accusation of an applicant for any license, registration or permit when such inquiry is in violation of subdivision 16 of section 296 of article 15 of the New York state executive law.

(b) (1) Except as otherwise provided in this paragraph, it shall be an unlawful discriminatory practice for an agency to request or use for licensing, registration or permitting purposes information contained in the consumer credit history of an applicant, licensee, registrant or permittee for licensing or permitting purposes.

(2) Subparagraph (1) of this paragraph shall not apply to an agency required by state or federal law or regulations to use an individual's consumer credit history for licensing, registration or permitting purposes.

(3) Subparagraph (1) of this paragraph shall not be construed to affect the ability of an agency to consider an applicant's, licensee's, registrant's or permittee's failure to pay any tax, fine, penalty, or fee for which liability has been admitted by the person liable therefor, or for which judgment has been entered by a court or administrative tribunal of competent jurisdiction, or any tax for which a government agency has issued a warrant, or a lien or levy on property.

(4) Nothing in this paragraph shall preclude a licensing agency from requesting, receiving, or using consumer credit history information obtained pursuant to a lawful subpoena, court order or law enforcement investigation.

(c) The prohibition of this subdivision relating to inquiries, denials or other adverse action related to a person's record of arrests or convictions shall not apply to licensing activities in relation to the regulation of explosives, pistols, handguns, rifles, shotguns, or other firearms and deadly weapons. Nothing contained in this subdivision shall be construed to bar an agency authorized to issue a license, registration or permit from using age, disability, criminal conviction or arrest record as a criterion for determining eligibility or continuing fitness for a license, registration or permit when specifically required to do so by any other provision of law.

(d) (1) Except as otherwise provided in this paragraph, it shall be an unlawful discriminatory practice for an agency to request or use for licensing or permitting purposes information contained in the consumer credit history of an applicant, licensee or permittee for licensing or permitting purposes.

(2) Subparagraph (1) of this paragraph shall not apply to an agency required by state or federal law or regulations to use an individual's consumer credit history for licensing or permitting purposes.

(3) Subparagraph (1) of this paragraph shall not be construed to affect the ability of an agency to consider an applicant's, licensee's, registrant's or permittee's failure to pay any tax, fine, penalty, or fee for which liability has been admitted by the person liable therefor, or for which judgment has been entered by a court or administrative tribunal of competent jurisdiction, or any tax for which a government agency has issued a warrant, or a lien or levy on property.

(4) Nothing in this paragraph shall preclude a licensing agency from requesting, receiving, or using consumer credit history information obtained pursuant to a lawful subpoena, court order or law enforcement investigation.

(e) The provisions of this subdivision shall be enforceable against public agencies and employees thereof by a proceeding brought pursuant to article 78 of the civil practice law and rules.

10. Criminal conviction; employment. (a) It shall be an unlawful discriminatory practice for any employer, employment agency or agent thereof to deny employment to any person or take adverse action against any employee by reason of such person or employee having been convicted of one or more criminal offenses, or by reason of a finding of a lack of "good moral character" which is based on such person or employee having been convicted of one or more criminal offenses, when such denial or adverse action is in violation of the provisions of article twenty-three-a of the correction law.

(b) For purposes of this subdivision, "employment" shall not include membership in any law enforcement agency.

(c) Pursuant to section seven hundred fifty-five of the correction law, the provisions of this subdivision shall be enforceable against public agencies by a proceeding brought pursuant to article seventy-eight of the Civil Practice Law and Rules, and the provisions of this subdivision shall be enforceable against private employers by the commission through the administrative procedure provided for in this chapter or as provided in chapter five of this title. For purposes of this paragraph only, the terms "public agency" and "private employer" shall have the meaning given such terms in section seven hundred fifty of the correction law.

11. Arrest record; employment. It shall be an unlawful discriminatory practice, unless specifically required or permitted by any other law, for any person to:

(a) deny employment to any applicant or act adversely upon any employee by reason of an arrest or criminal accusation of such applicant or employee when such denial or adverse action is in violation of subdivision 16 of section 296 of article 15 of the New York state executive law; or

(b) make any inquiry in writing or otherwise, regarding any arrest or criminal accusation of an applicant or employee when such inquiry is in violation of subdivision 16 of section 296 of article 15 of the New York state executive law.

11-a. Arrest and conviction records; employer inquiries.

(a) In addition to the restrictions in subdivision 11 of this section, it shall be an unlawful discriminatory practice for any employer, employment agency or agent thereof to:

(1) Declare, print or circulate or cause to be declared, printed or circulated any solicitation, advertisement or publication, which expresses, directly or indirectly, any limitation, or specification in employment based on a person's arrest or criminal conviction; or

(2) Make any inquiry or statement related to the pending arrest or criminal conviction record of any person who is in the process of applying for employment with such employer or agent thereof until after such employer or agent thereof has extended a conditional offer of employment to the applicant. For purposes of this subdivision, with respect to an applicant for temporary employment at a temporary help firm as such term is defined by subdivision five of section 916 of article 31 of the New York labor law, an offer to be placed in the temporary help firm's general candidate pool shall constitute a conditional offer of employment. For purposes of this subdivision, "any inquiry" means any question communicated to an applicant in writing or otherwise, or any searches of publicly available records or consumer reports that are conducted for the purpose of obtaining an applicant's criminal background information. For purposes of this subdivision, "any statement" means a statement communicated in writing or otherwise to the applicant for purposes of obtaining an applicant's criminal background information regarding: (i) an arrest record; (ii) a conviction record; or (iii) a criminal background check.

(b) After extending an applicant a conditional offer of employment, an employer, employment agency or agent thereof may inquire about the applicant's arrest or conviction record if before taking any adverse employment action based on such inquiry, the employer, employment agency or agent thereof:

(i) provides a written copy of the inquiry to the applicant in a manner to be determined by the commission;

(ii) performs an analysis of the applicant under article twenty-three-a of the correction law and provides a written copy of such analysis to the applicant in a manner to be determined by the commission, which shall include but not be limited to supporting documents that formed the basis for an adverse action based on such analysis and the employer's or employment agency's reasons for taking any adverse action against such applicant; and

(iii) after giving the applicant the inquiry and analysis in writing pursuant to subparagraphs (i) and (ii) of this paragraph, allows the applicant a reasonable time to respond, which shall be no less than three business days and during this time, holds the position open for the applicant.

(c) Nothing in this subdivision shall prevent an employer, employment agency or agent thereof from taking adverse action against any employee or denying employment to any applicant for reasons other than such employee or applicant's arrest or criminal conviction record.

(d) An applicant shall not be required to respond to any inquiry or statement that violates paragraph (a) of this subdivision and any refusal to respond to such inquiry or statement shall not disqualify an applicant from the prospective employment.

(e) This subdivision shall not apply to any actions taken by an employer or agent thereof pursuant to any state, federal or local law that requires criminal background checks for employment purposes or bars employment based on criminal history. For purposes of this paragraph federal law shall include rules or regulations promulgated by a self-regulatory organization as defined in section 3(a)(26) of the securities exchange act of 1934, as amended.

(f) This subdivision shall not apply to any actions taken by an employer or agent thereof with regard to an applicant for employment:

(1) as a police officer or peace officer, as those terms are defined in subdivisions thirty-three and thirty-four of section 1.20 of the criminal procedure law, respectively, or at a law enforcement agency as that term is used in article 23-a of the correction law, including but not limited to the police department, the fire department, the department of correction, the department of investigation, the department of probation, the division of youth and family services, the business integrity commission, and the district attorneys' offices; or

(2) listed in the determinations of personnel published as a commissioner's calendar item and listed on the website of the department of citywide administrative services upon a determination by the commissioner of citywide administrative services that the position involves law enforcement, is susceptible to bribery or other corruption, or entails the provision of services to or safeguarding of persons who, because of age, disability, infirmity or other condition, are vulnerable to abuse. If the department takes adverse action against any applicant based on the applicant's arrest or criminal conviction record, it shall provide a written copy of such analysis performed under article twenty- three a of the correction law to the applicant in a form and manner to be determined by the department.

(g) The provisions of this subdivision shall be enforceable against public agencies by a proceeding brought pursuant to article seventy-eight of the Civil Practice Law and Rules, and the provisions of this subdivision shall be enforceable against private employers by the commission through the administrative procedure provided for in this chapter or as provided in chapter five of this title. For purposes of this paragraph only, the terms "public agency" and "private employer" shall have the meaning given such terms in section seven hundred fifty of the correction law.

11-b. Arrest record; credit application. For purposes of issuing credit, it shall be an unlawful discriminatory practice, unless specifically required or permitted by any other law, to:

(a) deny or act adversely upon any person seeking credit by reason of an arrest or criminal accusation of such person when such denial or adverse action is in violation of subdivision 16 of section 296 of article 15 of the New York state executive law; or

(b) make any inquiry in writing or otherwise, regarding any arrest or criminal accusation of a person seeking credit when such inquiry is in violation of subdivision 16 of section 296 of article 15 of the New York state executive law.

12. Religious principles. Nothing contained in this section shall be construed to bar any religious or denominational institution or organization or any organization operated for charitable or educational purposes, which is operated, supervised or controlled by or in connection with a religious organization from limiting employment or sales or rental of housing accommodations or admission to or giving preference to persons of the same religion or denomination or from making such selection as is calculated by such organization to promote the religious principles for which it is established or maintained.

13.Employer liability for discriminatory conduct by employee, agent or independent contractor.

(a) An employer shall be liable for an unlawful discriminatory practice based upon the conduct of an employee or agent which is in violation of any provision of this section other than subdivisions one and two of this section.

(b) An employer shall be liable for an unlawful discriminatory practice based upon the conduct of an employee or agent which is in violation of subdivision one or two of this section only where:

(1)The employee or agent exercised managerial or supervisory responsibility; or

(2)The employer knew of the employee's or agent's discriminatory conduct, and acquiesced in such conduct or failed to take immediate and appropriate corrective action; an employer shall be deemed to have knowledge of an employee's or agent's discriminatory conduct where that conduct was known by another employee or agent who exercised managerial or supervisory responsibility; or

(3)The employer should have known of the employee's or agent's discriminatory conduct and failed to exercise reasonable diligence to prevent such discriminatory conduct.

(c) An employer shall be liable for an unlawful discriminatory practice committed by a person employed as an independent contractor, other than an agent of such employer, to carry out work in furtherance of the employer's business enterprise only where such discriminatory conduct was committed in the course of such employment and the employer had actual knowledge of and acquiesced in such conduct.

(d) Where liability of an employer has been established pursuant to this section and is based solely on the conduct of an employee, agent, or independent contractor, the employer shall be permitted to plead and prove that prior to the discriminatory conduct for which it was found liable it had:

(1)Established and complied with policies, programs and procedures for the prevention and detection of unlawful discriminatory practices by employees, agents and persons employed as independent contractors, including but not limited to:

(i) A meaningful and responsive procedure for investigating complaints of discriminatory practices by employees, agents and persons employed as independent contractors and for taking appropriate action against those persons who are found to have engaged in such practices;

(ii) A firm policy against such practices which is effectively communicated to employees, agents and persons employed as independent contractors;

(iii) A program to educate employees and agents about unlawful discriminatory practices under local, state and federal law; and

(iv) Procedures for the supervision of employees and agents and for the oversight of persons employed as independent contractors specifically directed at the prevention and detection of such practices; and

(2)A record of no, or relatively few, prior incidents of discriminatory conduct by such employee, agent or person employed as an independent contractor or other employees, agents or persons employed as independent contractors.

(e) The demonstration of any or all of the factors listed above in addition to any other relevant factors shall be considered in mitigation of the amount of civil penalties to be imposed by the commission pursuant to this chapter or in mitigation of civil penalties or punitive damages which may be imposed pursuant to chapter four or five of this title and shall be among the factors considered in determining an employer's liability under subparagraph three of paragraph (b) of this subdivision.

(f) The commission may establish by rule policies, programs and procedures which may be implemented by employers for the prevention and detection of unlawful discriminatory practices by employees, agents and persons employed as independent contractors. Notwithstanding any other provision of the law to the contrary, an employer found to be liable for an unlawful discriminatory practice based solely on the conduct of an employee, agent or person employed as an independent contractor who pleads and proves that such policies, programs and procedures had been implemented and complied with at the time of the unlawful conduct shall not be liable for any civil penalties which may be imposed pursuant to this chapter or any civil penalties or punitive damages which may be imposed pursuant to chapter four or five of this title for such unlawful discriminatory practice.

14.Applicability; alienage or citizenship status. Notwithstanding any other provision of this section, it shall not be an unlawful discriminatory practice for any person to discriminate on the ground of alienage or citizenship status, or to make any inquiry as to a person's alienage or citizenship status, or to give preference to a person who is a citizen or a national of the United States over an equally qualified person who is an alien, when such discrimination is required or when such preference is expressly permitted by any law or regulation of the United States, the State of New York or the City of New York, and when such law or regulation does not provide that state or local law may be more protective of aliens; provided, however, that this provision shall not prohibit inquiries or determinations based on alienage or citizenship status when such actions are necessary to obtain the benefits of a federal program. An applicant for a license or permit issued by the City of New York may be required to be authorized to work in the United States whenever by law or regulation there is a limit on the number of such licenses or permits which may be issued.

15.Applicability; persons with disabilities.

(a) Requirement to make reasonable accommodation to the needs of persons with disabilities. Except as provided in paragraph (b), any person prohibited by the provisions of this section from discriminating on the basis of disability shall make reasonable accommodation to enable a person with a disability to satisfy the essential requisites of a job or enjoy the right or rights in question provided that the disability is known or should have been known by the covered entity.

(b) Affirmative defense in disability cases. In any case where the need for reasonable accommodation is placed in issue, it shall be an affirmative defense that the person aggrieved by the alleged discriminatory practice could not, with reasonable accommodation, satisfy the essential requisites of the job or enjoy the right or rights in question.

(c) Use of drugs or alcohol. Nothing contained in this chapter shall be construed to prohibit a covered entity from (i) prohibiting the illegal use of drugs or the use of alcohol at the workplace or on duty impairment from the illegal use of drugs or the use of alcohol, or (ii) conducting drug testing which is otherwise lawful.

16.Repealed.

17.Disparate impact.

(a) An unlawful discriminatory practice based upon disparate impact is established when:

(1)The Commission or a person who may bring an action under chapter four or five of this title demonstrates that a policy or practice of a covered entity or a group of policies or practices of a covered entity results in a disparate impact to the detriment of any group protected by the provisions of this chapter; and

(2)The covered entity fails to plead and prove as an affirmative defense that each such policy or practice bears a significant relationship to a significant business objective of the covered entity or does not contribute to the disparate impact; provided, however, that if the commission or such person who may bring an action demonstrates that a group of policies or practices results in a disparate impact, the commission or such person shall not be required to demonstrate which specific policies or practices within the group results in such disparate impact; provided further, that a policy or practice or group of policies or practices demonstrated to result in a disparate impact shall be unlawful where the commission or such person who may bring an action produces substantial evidence that an alternative policy or practice with less disparate impact is available to the covered entity and the covered entity fails to prove that such alternative policy or practice would not serve the covered entity as well. "Significant business objective" shall include, but not be limited to, successful performance of the job.

(b) The mere existence of a statistical imbalance between a covered entity's challenged demographic composition and the general population is not alone sufficient to establish a prima facie case of disparate impact violation unless the general population is shown to be the relevant pool for comparison, the imbalance is shown to be statistically significant and there is an identifiable policy or practice or group of policies or practices that allegedly causes the imbalance. (c) Nothing contained in this subdivision shall be construed to mandate or endorse the use of quotas, provided, however, that nothing contained in this subdivision shall be construed to limit the scope of the commission's authority pursuant to sections 8-115 and 8-120 of this chapter or to affect court-ordered remedies or settlements that are otherwise in accordance with law.

18.Unlawful boycott or blacklist. It shall be unlawful discriminatory practice (i) for any person to discriminate against, boycott or blacklist or to refuse to buy from, sell to or trade with, any person, because of such person's actual or perceived race, creed, color, national origin, gender, disability, age, marital status, partnership status, sexual orientation or alienage or citizenship status or of such person's partners, members, stockholders, directors, officers, managers, superintendents, agents, employees, business associates, suppliers or customers, or (ii) for any person willfully to do any act or refrain from doing any act which enables any such person to take such action. This subdivision shall not apply to:

(a) Boycotts connected with labor disputes;

(b) Boycotts to protest unlawful discriminatory practices; or

(c) Any form of expression that is protected by the First Amendment.

19.Interference with protected rights. It shall be an unlawful discriminatory practice for any person to coerce, intimidate, threaten or interfere with, or attempt to coerce, intimidate, threaten or interfere with, any person in the exercise or enjoyment of, or on account of his or her having aided or encouraged any other person in the exercise or enjoyment of, any right granted or protected pursuant to this section.

20.Relationship or association. The provisions of this section set forth as unlawful discriminatory practices shall be construed to prohibit such discrimination against a person because of the actual or perceived race, creed, color, national origin, disability, age, sexual orientation or alienage or citizenship status of a person with whom such person has a known relationship or association.

21.Employment; an individual's unemployment.

(a) Prohibition of discrimination based on an individual's unemployment.

(2)Except as provided in paragraphs b and c of this subdivision, an employer, employment agency, or agent thereof shall not base an employment decision with regard to hiring, compensation or the terms, conditions or privileges of employment on an applicant's unemployment.

(3)Unless otherwise permitted by city, state or federal law, no employer, employment agency, or agent thereof shall publish, in print or in any other medium, an advertisement for any job vacancy in this city that contains one or more of the following:

(a)Any provision stating or indicating that being currently employed is a requirement or qualification for the job;

(b)Any provision stating or indicating that an employer, employment agency, or agent thereof will not consider individuals for employment based on their unemployment.

(b) Effect of subdivision.

(1)Paragraph a of this subdivision shall not be construed to prohibit an employer, employment agency, or agent thereof from

(a)considering an applicant's unemployment, where there is a substantially job-related reason for doing so; or

(b)inquiring into the circumstances surrounding an applicant's separation from prior employment.

(2)Nothing set forth in this subdivision shall be construed as prohibiting an employer, employment agency, or agent thereof, when making employment decisions with regard to hiring, compensation, or the terms, conditions or privileges of employment, from considering any substantially job-related qualifications, including but not limited to: a current and valid professional or occupational license; a certificate, registration, permit, or other credential; a minimum level of education or training; or a minimum level of professional, occupational, or field experience.

(3)Nothing set forth in this subdivision shall be construed as prohibiting an employer, employment agency, or agent thereof from publishing, in print or in any other medium, an advertisement for any job vacancy in this city that contains any provision setting forth any substantially job-related qualifications, including but not limited to: a current and valid professional or occupational license; a certificate, registration, permit, or other credential; a minimum level of education or training; or a minimum level of professional, occupational, or field experience.

(4)(a) Nothing set forth in this subdivision shall be construed as prohibiting an employer, employment agency, or agent thereof, when making employment decisions with regard to hiring, compensation, or the terms, conditions or privileges of employment, from determining that only applicants who are currently employed by the employer will be considered for employment or given priority for employment or with respect to compensation or terms, conditions or privileges of employment. In addition, nothing set forth in this subdivision shall prevent an employer from setting compensation or terms or conditions of employment for a person based on that person's actual amount of experience.

(b) For the purposes of this subparagraph, all persons whose salary or wages are paid from the city treasury, and all persons who are employed by public agencies or entities headed by officers or boards including one or more individuals appointed or recommended by officials of the city of New York, shall be deemed to have the same employer.

(c) Applicability of subdivision.

(1) This subdivision shall not apply to:

(a) actions taken by the New York city department of citywide administrative services in furtherance of its responsibility for city personnel matters pursuant to chapter thirty-five of the charter or as a municipal civil service commission administering the civil service law and other applicable laws, or by the mayor in furtherance of the mayor's duties relating to city personnel matters pursuant to chapter thirty-five of the charter, including, but not limited to, the administration of competitive examinations, the establishment and administration of eligible lists, and the establishment and implementation of minimum qualifications for appointment to positions;

(b) actions taken by officers or employees of other public agencies or entities charged with performing functions comparable to those performed by the department of citywide administrative services or the mayor as described in paragraph one of this subdivision;

(c) agency appointments to competitive positions from eligible lists pursuant to subsection one of section sixty-one of the state civil service law; or

(d) the exercise of any right of an employer or employee pursuant to a collective bargaining agreement.

(2) This subdivision shall apply to individual hiring decisions made by an agency or entity with respect to positions for which appointments are not required to be made from an eligible list resulting from a competitive examination.

(d) Public education campaign. The commission shall develop courses of instruction and conduct ongoing public education efforts as necessary to inform employers, employment agencies, and job applicants about their rights and responsibilities under this subdivision.

(e) Disparate impact. An unlawful discriminatory practice based on disparate impact under this subdivision is established when:

(1) the commission or a person who may bring an action under chapter four or five of this title demonstrates that a policy or practice of an employer, employment agency, or agent thereof, or a group of policies or practices of such an entity results in a disparate impact to the detriment of any group protected by the provisions of this subdivision; and

(2) such entity fails to plead and prove as an affirmative defense that each such policy or practice has as its basis a substantially job-related qualification or does not contribute to the disparate impact; provided, however, that if the commission or such person who may bring an action demonstrates that a group of policies or practices results in a disparate impact, the commission or such person shall not be required to demonstrate which specific policies or practices within the group results in such disparate impact; provided further, that a policy or practice or group of policies or practices demonstrated to result in a disparate impact shall be unlawful where the commission or such person

who may bring an action produces substantial evidence that an alternative policy or practice with less disparate impact is available to such entity and such entity fails to prove that such alternative policy or practice would not serve such entity as well. A "substantially job-related qualification" shall include, but not be limited to, a current and valid professional or occupational license; a certificate, registration, permit, or other credential; a minimum level of education or training; or a minimum level of professional, occupational, or field experience.

22. Employment; Pregnancy, childbirth, or a related medical condition.

(a) It shall be an unlawful discriminatory practice for an employer to refuse to provide a reasonable accommodation, as defined in subdivision eighteen of section 8-102 of this chapter, to the needs of an employee for her pregnancy, childbirth, or related medical condition that will allow the employee to perform the essential requisites of the job, provided that such employee's pregnancy, childbirth, or related medical condition is known or should have been known by the employer. In any case pursuant to this subdivision where the need for reasonable accommodation is placed in issue, it shall be an affirmative defense that the person aggrieved by the alleged discriminatory practice could not, with reasonable accommodation, satisfy the essential requisites of the job.

(b) Notice of rights.

   (i) An employer shall provide written notice in a form and manner to be determined by the commission of the right to be free from discrimination in relation to pregnancy, childbirth, and related medical conditions pursuant to this subdivision to:

      (1) new employees at the commencement of employment; and

      (2) existing employees within one hundred twenty days after the effective date of the local law that added this subdivision. Such notice may also be conspicuously posted at an employer's place of business in an area accessible to employees.

   (ii) The commission shall develop courses of instruction and conduct ongoing public education efforts as necessary to inform employers, employees, employment agencies, and job applicants about their rights and responsibilities under this subdivision.

(c) This subdivision shall not be construed to affect any other provision of law relating to sex discrimination or pregnancy, or in any way to diminish the coverage of pregnancy, childbirth, or a medical condition related to pregnancy or childbirth under any other provision of this section.

23. The provisions of this chapter relating to employees shall apply to interns.

24. Employment; consumer credit history.

(a) Except as provided in this subdivision, it shall be an unlawful discriminatory practice for an employer, labor organization, employment agency, or agent thereof to request or to use for employment purposes the consumer credit history of an applicant for employment or employee, or otherwise discriminate against an applicant or employee with regard to hiring, compensation, or the terms, conditions or privileges of employment based on the consumer credit history of the applicant or employee.

(b) Paragraph (a) of this subdivision shall not apply to:

   (1) an employer, or agent thereof, that is required by state or federal law or regulations or by a self-regulatory organization as defined in section 3(a)(26) of the securities exchange act of 1934, as amended to use an individual's consumer credit history for employment purposes;

   (2) persons applying for positions as or employed:

      (A) as police officers or peace officers, as those terms are defined in subdivisions thirty-three and thirty-four of section 1.20 of the criminal procedure law, respectively, or in a position with a law enforcement or investigative function at the department of investigation;

      (B) in a position that is subject to background investigation by the department of investigation, provided, however, that the appointing agency may not use consumer credit history information for employment purposes unless the position is an appointed position in which a high degree of public trust, as defined by the commission in rules, has been reposed.

(C) in a position in which an employee is required to be bonded under City, state or federal law;

(D) in a position in which an employee is required to possess security clearance under federal law or the law of any state

(E) in a non-clerical position having regular access to trade secrets, intelligence information or national security information;

(F) in a position: (i) having signatory authority over third party funds or assets valued at $10,000 or more; or (ii) that involves a fiduciary responsibility to the employer with the authority to enter financial agreements valued at $10,000 or more on behalf of the employer.

(G) in a position with regular duties that allow the employee to modify digital security systems established to prevent the unauthorized use of the employer's or client's networks or databases.

(c) Paragraph (a) of this subdivision shall not be construed to affect the obligations of persons required by section 12-110 of this code or by mayoral executive order relating to disclosures by city employees to the conflicts of interest board to report information regarding their creditors or debts, or the use of such information by government agencies for the purposes for which such information is collected.

(d) As used in this subdivision:

(1) The term "intelligence information" means records and data compiled for the purpose of criminal investigation or counterterrorism, including records and data relating to the order or security of a correctional facility, reports of informants, investigators or other persons, or from any type of surveillance associated with an identifiable individual, or investigation or analysis of potential terrorist threats.

(2) The term "national security information" means any knowledge relating to the national defense or foreign relations of the United States, regardless of its physical form or characteristics, that is owned by, produced by or for, or is under the control of the United States government and is defined as such by the United States government and its agencies and departments.

(3) The term "trade secrets" means information that:

(a) derives independent economic value, actual or potential, from not being generally known to, and not being readily ascertainable by proper means by other persons who can obtain economic value from its disclosure or use;

(b) is the subject of efforts that are reasonable under the circumstances to maintain its secrecy; and

(c) can reasonably be said to be the end product of significant innovation. The term "trade secrets" does not include general proprietary company information such as handbooks and policies. The term "regular access to trade secrets" does not include access to or the use of client, customer or mailing lists.

(e) Nothing in this subdivision shall preclude an employer from requesting or receiving consumer credit history information pursuant to a lawful subpoena, court order or law enforcement investigation.

ARTICLE 23-A OF THE N.Y. CORRECTION LAW COURT DECISIONS

New York Court of Appeals

Eiseman v. State, 511 N.E.2d 1128, 1132-33 (N.Y. 1987) discussing the right to be free of unfair conviction based discrimination and the strong public policy which has its objectives rehabilitating and reintegrating former inmates in the hope that they will spend their future years productively instead of returning to crime and are mandated by law as well as by public policy.

Bonacorsa v Van Lindt, 71 N.Y.2d 605, 614 (1988) If an agency relies on the "direct relationship" exception, the "agency... must consider the factors mentioned in section 753 (1) to determine whether in fact the direct relationship is sufficiently attenuated to warrant issuance of the license." If an agency relies on the "unreasonable risk" exception, it must consider and apply the factors in section 753(1) "to determine if in fact an unreasonable risk exists. If the agency considers *all* eight factors listed in Correction Law § 753 (1), it need not in every case produce independent evidence to rebut the presumption of rehabilitation before denying a license, since it is only one of eight factors. The failure of a Respondent to rebut the presumption of rehabilitation with evidence suggesting no rehabilitation will result in an arbitrary and capricious determination.

Malverty v. Waterfront Com'n of New York Harbor, 71 N.Y.2d 977, 529 N.Y.S.2d 67, 524 N.E.2d 421, reargument denied 72 N.Y.2d 910, 532 N.Y.S.2d 758, 528 N.E.2d 1231 (1988) Provisions of Article 23-A concerning employment of former inmates do not apply to New York/New Jersey Waterfront Commission since the absence from the text and legislative history do not make reference to the Waterfront Commission or the Interstate Compact.

Arrocha v Board of Educ. of City of N.Y., 93 NY2d 361, 363 (1999) a finding of "unreasonable risk" involves "a subjective analysis of a variety of considerations," the analysis must be rationally based on a correct understanding of the facts in the record. Agency analyzed and balanced all 8 factors per Correction Law § 753 [1] and the presumption of rehabilitation afforded by Correction Law § 753 [2]. Giving greater weight to the statutory factors adversely affected by the fact and circumstances of his conviction than to the statutory factors favorably affected by his subsequent accomplishments and the presumption of rehabilitation is permitted.

Al Turi Landfill, Inc. v. New York State Dept. of Environmental Conservation, 98 N.Y.2d 758, 751 N.Y.S.2d 827, 781 N.E.2d 892 (2002) The admitted criminal histories of petitioner and its principals—involving deceit in the operation of their business over several years on their taxes—provides ample basis for denying the application of an expansion permit by the DEC. Commissioner's finding upheld that the benefit to the State of the landfill expansion does not outweigh the Applicant's poor fitness after the factors had established a direct relationship and willingness to mislead the government in duties inherent in the license sought.

Acosta v. New York City Dep't of Educ., 16 N.Y.3d 309, 316 (2011) An agency's failure to consider each of the factors in Correction Law § 753 (1), "results in a failure to comply with the Correction Law's mandatory directive." City department of education's failure to consider all statutory factors in determining whether "unreasonable risk" exception to rule barring adverse treatment of an application for license or employment because of a prior criminal conviction applied to application for employment at a special education contractor rendered its denial of the application based on applicant's 13-year-old robbery conviction arbitrary and capricious; department relied on applicant's failure to provide references from previous employers, but did not ask her to provide such references, which were available and favorable to applicant, and did not consider other supporting documentation that applicant submitted.

Matter of Dellaporte v. New York City Dept. of Bldgs., 2014 NY Slip Op 01211, 2013 NY Slip Op 3281, 2012 NY Slip Op 30750(U) Respondent arbitrarily concluded that petitioner's federal conviction for theft of funds bore a direct relationship to the duties and responsibilities attendant to a stationary engineer, the license for which he sought renewal after having his license renewed 15 consecutive times. Petitioner disclosed his 2006 conviction, based on acts occurring in 2005 and earlier, on his license renewal applications from 2007 through 2010, all of which were granted. Respondent declared that petitioner's evidence of rehabilitation was insufficient, in clear contravention of the statutory presumption, but did not raise any independent evidence in rebuttal and provided only speculative inferences to claim its exception based on unreasonable risk.

Matter of Luther Dempsey v New York City Department of Education, Et AL. 2015 NY Slip Op 04028 Respondent's decision to deny petitioner's certification for a school bus driver is not arbitrary or capricious where all factors were considered and all evidence of rehabilitation was submitted and reviewed by the agency and Petitioner does not meet burden to show such decision is not rational. While not applicable in this case. the court held that a failure to review evidence provided by an applicant tending to show that he or she had reliably carried out duties similar to those contemplated in the license or employment in question would constitute a violation of *§ 753 (1) (b) and (g).*

Matter of Griffin v Sirva 29 N.Y.3d 174 (2017), 76 N.E.3d 106, 54 N.Y.S.3d 360, 2017 NY Slip Op 03557 The court was faced for the first time with deciding if N.Y. Exec. Law 296 (15) limits liability to an aggrieved party's `employer'. The court stated that liability under section 296 (15) arises only upon a violation of article 23-A and reading Correction Law §§ 751, 752, and 753 together, article 23-A limits liability for employment discrimination to an employer — either public or private. The court, after limiting liability to an employer then asked how should the court determine whether an entity is the aggrieved party's `employer' for the purposes of a claim under Section 296(15). The court cited four relevant factors that were set forth by the Appellate Division in NYSDHR v GTE Corp 109 A.D.2d 1082 (1985): "`(1) the selection and engagement of the servant; (2) the payment of salary or wages; (3) the power of dismissal; and (4) the power of control of the servant's conduct" The court then answered a third question as to whether section 296 (6) extends liability to an out-of-state nonemployer who aids or abets employment discrimination against individuals with a prior criminal conviction. The court affirmed and stated that Section 296 (6) extends liability to persons and entities beyond joint employers and the goal of the section was "to furnish protection to all persons, whether employers, labor organizations or employment agencies, who find themselves subjected from any source to compulsion or coercion to adopt any forbidden employment practices."

New York Appellate Division

Matter of Glucksman 57 A.D.2d 205, 394 N.Y.S.2d 191, appeal denied 42 N.Y.2d 804, 398 N.Y.S.2d 1025, 367 N.E.2d 658 (1977) Attorney who was licensed, but forfeited same upon conviction for a crime deemed a felony, sought reinstatement after obtaining a Certificate of Relief. Article 23-A provides no legal basis for making application for reinstatement of a law license, only Subdivision 5 of section 90 of the Judiciary Law provides relief of reinstatement for a disbarred attorney on the basis of reversal of the conviction by a court or issuance of a pardon.

Mosner v. Ambach, 1978, 66 A.D.2d 912, 410 N.Y.S.2d 937 (1978) It is not against public policy to suspend a chiropractor's license on the basis of a conviction having no connection with the practice of the profession because Article 23-A by its terms applies only to the "application" for a license by a person previously convicted of a crime (see Correction Law, § 751); it has no bearing on disciplinary proceedings against persons already licensed.

Glucksman v. Cuomo 62 A.D.2d 978, 403 N.Y.S.2d 328(1978) Denial of petitioner's application for real estate broker's license was warranted by determination that there was direct relationship between petitioner's criminal offenses and license sought.

Perez v. New York State Human Rights Appeal Bd. 71 A.D.2d 150 422 N.Y.S.2d 767 (1979) Proper dismissal by Division of Human Rights since agency does not have jurisdiction over public agencies concerning conviction record complaints based on direct reading of Correction Law, § 755, subd 1. Article 23-A of the Correction Law § 751 does not have any application to youthful offenders and was not intended to give them any rights as they are not mentioned within its provisions.

Durante v. Board of Regents of State University of New York 70 A.D.2d 692, 416 N.Y.S.2d 401 (1979), appeal dismissed 48 N.Y.2d 654, 421 N.Y.S.2d 1034, 396 N.E.2d 490 (Article 23-A applies only to the "application" for a license by a person previously convicted of a crime and not to the discipline of a person already licensed)

Cantor v New York State Racing & Wagering Bd., 73 AD2d 544 (1979) (Although determination of the weight to be given evidence of rehabilitation is the responsibility of the licensing authority, that responsibility must be exercised within the law, consonant with the policy of this State to assist in the rehabilitation of ex-offenders and to avoid discrimination against such persons in licensed professions and occupations).

Pietranico v. Ambach, 82 A.D.2d 625, 442 N.Y.S.2d 827, affirmed 55 N.Y.2d 861, 447 N.Y.S.2d 924, 432 N.E.2d 796 (1981) Nurse who registered for lapsed license after 10 year break disclosed conviction record but was disciplined a 3 year suspension where "Article 23-A by its terms applies only to the `application' for a license by a person previously convicted of a crime (see Correction Law, § 751); it has no bearing on disciplinary proceedings against persons already licensed"

Ribotsky v. Lupkin, 114 Misc.2d 913, 452 N.Y.S.2d 806 (1982) New York City department of investigation directive Q-104, which prohibited city marshals from employing any former marshal convicted of crime related to his office when such employment bore direct relationship to such conviction, was not bound by definitional limitation of public agency in this section prohibiting unfair discrimination against persons previously convicted of one or more criminal offenses, where directive was merely conceptually based and sought to prevent the same individuals from taking advantage of the exact situation which caused their conviction record.

Stewart v. Civil Service Commission of City of New York 84 A.D.2d 491, 446 N.Y.S.2d 948 (1982) Misstatement of a material fact about one's personal history warrants disqualification, The purpose of the 1976 legislation was not to give ex-convicts preferred treatment, nor to cloak their prior criminal records in secrecy. Rather, it was to create reasonable standards to be applied by potential employers, including public agencies, when considering applications by former offenders, no such standards having previously existed.

Sinclair v. Division of Licensing of Dept. of State 96 A.D.2d 1130, 467 N.Y.S.2d 719, appeal denied 60 N.Y.2d 559, 470 N.Y.S.2d 1025, 458 N.E.2d 385 (1983) Article 23-A of the Correction Law, and subdivision 15 of section 296 of the Executive Law do not apply "where a mandatory forfeiture, disability or bar to employment is imposed by law, and has not been removed by an executive pardon or certificate of good conduct" (Correction Law, § 751). Here, section 130 of the Executive Law stands as such a mandatory forfeiture and thus no violation of the recited provisions is present in denial of a notary public licensure.

Pisano v. McKenna, 120 Misc.2d 536, 466 N.Y.S.2d 231 (1983) Article 23-A does not prevent dismissal of fireman, a position of honesty and integrity, for convictions related to state sales tax matter arising out of private business unrelated to his position as fireman because Correction Law by its terms applies only to the "application" for a license by a person previously convicted of a crime (see Correction Law, § 751); it has no bearing on disciplinary proceedings against persons already licensed.

New York City Transit Authority v. State Human Rights Appeal Bd. 97 A.D.2d 825, 468 N.Y.S.2d 708 (1983) An Article 78 proceeding is the exclusive remedy available to a petitioner charging a public agency with an unfair discriminatory practice based upon his prior criminal convictions.

Marra v City of White Plains, 96 A.D. 2d 17, 25 (1983) Decision to deny license to Petitioner found arbitrary and capricious based on "speculative inferences unsupported by the record" where reliance on direct relationship on his ability to perform duties is belied by facts showing Petitioner already has been granted a similar license with responsibilities that are close in relationship to those being sought for current license. Correction Law article 23-A was enacted to promote the policy of encouraging the rehabilitation of persons previously convicted of criminal offenses by prohibiting unfair discrimination against such persons in licensed professions and occupations.

State Div. of Human Rights on Complaint of Maymi v. Sorrento Cheese Co., Inc. 115 A.D.2d 323, 495 N.Y.S.2d 865 (1985) Evidence that employee who had been convicted of disorderly conduct, a "violation," truthfully indicated on employment application that he had not been convicted of a crime and was terminated after employer learned of employee's conviction was sufficient to demonstrate probable cause to believe that employee was unlawfully discriminated against on account of his conviction rather than for giving false information on employment application. It is as much a violation of the Human Rights Law to discriminate against a person because of an arrest (see, Executive Law § 296 [16]) or a conviction for a criminal offense (see, Executive Law § 296 [15]) as it is to discriminate against that person because of an erroneously perceived conviction for a crime.

Markman v. New York State Dept. of Educ. 131 A.D.2d 908, 516 N.Y.S.2d 359. (1987) Since Petitioner's acts did not trigger a criminal prosecution and a resulting conviction, article 23-A is inapplicable. Article 23-A by its terms applies only to the "application" for a license by a person previously convicted of a crime (see Correction Law, § 751); it has no bearing on disciplinary proceedings against persons already licensed. Dentist's repeated history over three-year period of use and improper prescription of controlled substances justified denial of application for license to practice dentistry due to failure to meet good moral character requirement, even though dentist provided evidence of rehabilitation.

Matter of Meth v. Manhattan & Bronx Surface Transit Operating Auth., 134 AD 2d 431 (1987) Appellants have not met the burden of rebutting the presumption of rehabilitation. The appellants have not demonstrated the existence of a direct relationship between driving a bus and a bribe receiving conviction nor have the appellants shown that the petitioner would pose an unreasonable risk to the general public. Correction Law article 23-A was enacted to promote the policy of encouraging the rehabilitation of persons previously convicted of criminal offenses by prohibiting unfair discrimination against such persons in licensed professions and occupations

Hughes v. Shaffer 154 A.D.2d 467, 546 N.Y.S.2d 25 (1989) Rebuttable presumption raised by certificate of relief from disabilities was only one of several factors to be considered by administrative law judge denying applications to renew license as private investigator and commission as notary public.

Rodgers v. New York City Human Resources Admin., Dept. of Social Services 154 A.D.2d 233, 154 A.D.2d 236, 546 N.Y.S.2d 581 (1989) The very purpose of Certificates of Relief is to permit an individual who has made mistakes but has been rehabilitated to begin anew and become a productive member of society. Evidence raised fact issue as to whether termination of caseworker for city department of social services based on his alleged failure to disclose two prior misdemeanor convictions was arbitrary and capricious, where evidence indicated that caseworker had obtained certificates of relief from civil disabilities and had notified department of his involvement with criminal justice system at time he was hired. Termination seems contrary to the intent of both the Legislature which enacted the statutory relief for the furtherance of public interest (*Correction Law § 702 [2] [c]),* and the courts which saw fit to grant petitioner a second chance at life.

Brown v. Berry 151 A.D.2d 882, 543 N.Y.S.2d 179, appeal dismissed 74 N.Y.2d 944, 550 N.Y.S.2d 277, 549 N.E.2d 479 (1989) Statutory standards to be used by public agencies and private employers in appraising fitness of former criminal offender for particular job or license did not apply to prison training programs based on Governor's mem, 1976 McKinney's Session Laws of NY, at 2459)

Stanton Corp. v. Department of Labor of State of N.Y. 166 A.D.2d 331, 561 N.Y.S.2d 6 (1990) The Department of Labor acted outside the scope of its authority in refusing to process requests for targeted jobs, tax credits and future requests for credit certification by employers which used a particular job applicant screening questionnaire which asked questions about the applicant's theft of cash or merchandise; the state Division of Human Rights was the only agency with the authority to determine that use of the survey by prospective employers, having determined that the use of The Stanton Survey or certain portions thereof by prospective employers would violate the State's Ex-Offender Law (Correction Law §§ 752-753; Executive Law § 296 [15]).

Grafer v. New York City Civil Service Com'n 181 A.D.2d 614, 581 N.Y.S.2d 337, leave to appeal denied 80 N.Y.2d 752, 587 N.Y.S.2d 904, 600 N.E.2d 631 (1992) Drunken driving offenses by applicant for position of fire fighter involved unreasonable risk to property and to safety and welfare of general public and, therefore, could be basis for denial of application .

Green v. Wells Fargo Alarm Service, a Div. of Baker Protective Services, Inc. 192 A.D.2d 463, 596 N.Y.S.2d 412 (1993) Employee's termination due to his arrest for driving while intoxicated and possession of unlicensed firearm did not violate Executive Law prohibiting employment discrimination based on prior conviction for criminal offense; provision of Executive Law § 296 [15]) applied only to persons applying for employment who were previously convicted of criminal offense.

Ford v. Gildin 200 A.D.2d 224, 613 N.Y.S.2d 139 (1994) Any negligence in residential landlord's hiring employee who pleaded guilty to manslaughter was not proximate cause some 18 years later of injuries sustained by minor resident of building who was allegedly sexually abused by employee; passage of 18 years from time employee was hired until his wrongful acts against minor, severed the causal nexus between the two events, it was not foreseeable, as a matter of law, that employee who had committed manslaughter would molest child 27 years later, and employee's sexual assaults upon minor had nothing to do with his employment in building, but rather it was circumstance that employee resided in building that provided setting for his relationship with minor.

Okoro v. City of New York Human Resources Admin. 219 A.D.2d 506, 631 N.Y.S.2d 342 (1995) Probationary child case worker's termination was supported by evidence that he misrepresented to parole authorities that his violation of curfew provisions of work release program was due to employment with agency and that failure to be reliable and truthful demonstrated his unfitness for position; there was no material issue of fact raised by his assertion that he was terminated because of prior conviction for criminal possession of controlled substance, and no hearing was required.

Givens v. New York City Housing Authority 249 A.D.2d 133, 671 N.Y.S.2d 479 (1998) The same public policy that prohibits discrimination in hiring on the basis of a criminal record (Correction Law §§ 752, 753) prohibits discrimination in terminating employment on the basis of a criminal record. The three nonviolent convictions that a city housing authority's employee failed to disclose in his employment application, in conjunction with a robbery conviction that he did disclose, did not, as a matter of law, give the housing authority reason to know that the employee had a propensity for violence, or was otherwise unsuited for employment as a caretaker under the statutory factors, and thus, the housing authority could not be held liable for negligent retention of the employee.

Alston v. City of New York 270 A.D.2d 3, 703 N.Y.S.2d 186 (2000) City did not violate 296.15 of the Executive Law when it failed to promote an employee of a city agency from caseworker to supervisor, despite his claim that he was denied the promotion because of his prior conviction for Federal mail fraud; his claim was speculative, given evidence of his mediocre performance and his prior attempt to obtain a medical leave when he had actually taken a job with another agency, and in any event, the conviction raised legitimate issues about his fitness for the supervisory position.

Rosa v. City University of New York 13 A.D.3d 162, 789 N.Y.S.2d 4, leave to appeal denied 5 N.Y.3d 705, 801 N.Y.S.2d 252, 834 N.E.2d 1262(2004) Collective bargaining agreement under which arbitrator upheld public university's discharge of a tenured professor of business law and business ethics who was also an attorney, after he was convicted of stealing money from a client, did not violate public policy by discriminating against felons, in view of statutes which expressly permit employment discrimination against felons where there is a direct relationship between the criminal offense and the specific employment being sought.

City of New York v. New York City Civil Service Com'n 30 A.D.3d 227, 817 N.Y.S.2d 254(2006) City civil service commission's reinstatement of city employee, whose employment was terminated based upon his past criminal record, was neither irrational nor arbitrary; commission rationally concluded that there was no direct relationship or unreasonable risk between employee's convictions for attempted robbery in the second degree, sexual abuse in the first degree, criminal possession of a weapon, and theft of transportation services, and the position of watershed maintainer within the DEP where the position was supervised and did not interact with the general public.

Smith v. Kingsboro Psychiatric Center (KPC) 35 A.D.3d 751, 828 N.Y.S.2d 419 (2006) State psychiatric center's termination of probationary employee, based upon employee's failure to disclose his criminal record completely and truthfully does not implicate Correction Law §§ 752.

Gallo v State of N.Y., Off. of Mental Retardation & Dev. Disabilities, 37 AD3d at 985 830 N.Y.S. 2d 796 (2007) Respondent is required by statute to obtain criminal background checks for employees under Mental Hygiene Law §§ 16.33, 31.35 and Executive Law § 845-b. When all eight factors are considered and the positive factors are balanced against the negative factors, the resulting decision is neither arbitrary nor capricious nor does it constitute an abuse of discretion and reviewing courts may not reweigh the factors and substitute their judgment for that of the agency. State's denial of application for employment as bus driver for provider of services for developmentally disabled persons was arbitrary, despite applicant's prior conviction for second degree assault, where applicant had received early discharge of his sentence of probation, demonstrating rehabilitation and the public policy factor (Correction Law § 753 [1] [a]) was not amongst one of the factors considered.

Glover v. Augustine 38 A.D.3d 364, 832 N.Y.S.2d 184 (2007) Genuine issues of fact as to whether elevator operator's attack on office worker in building where he was employed was unforeseeable, and whether operator's hiring entailed an unreasonable risk to the safety or welfare of specific individuals or the general public, given that operator had a lengthy criminal record, including convictions for sexual abuse in the first degree, and that he was a registered sex offender, precluded summary judgment in office worker's action against operator's employer for negligent hiring and negligent premises security.

Matter of Little v. County of Westchester 36 AD 3d 616, 827 NYS 2d (2007) Commissioner was not required to consider the factors set forth in Correction Law article 23-A before disqualifying the petitioner, since employment with a law enforcement agency is specifically exempted from the reach of that statute (see *Correction Law § 750 [5]*).

Association of Surrogates, and Supreme Court Reporters v. State of New York Unified Court System 48 A.D.3d 228, 851 N.Y.S.2d 170 (2008) Court Reporter's criminal conviction in New Jersey, bore a direct relationship to her employment in New York, since as an officer of the court, she was charged with producing a true, accurate and complete record of court proceedings. Therefore there was substantial evidence in the record to support her termination.

Formica Construction, Inc. v. Mintz 65 A.D.3d 686, 885 N.Y.S.2d 298 (2009) Agency denied the license based on Petitioner's recent felony conviction. DCA did not set forth its reasoning for its determination until it was compelled to do so by the commencement of proceeding. The reasoning that the DCA articulated in its answer to the petition does not reflect that it considered all eight statutory factors set forth in *Correction Law § 753 (1)* and therefore the matter must be remanded for consideration of the statutory factors.

Elgart v. New York City Dept. of Educ, 25 Misc. 3d 1231(A), 906 N.Y.S.2d 772 (2009) According When the petitioner applied to become a teacher she had not been convicted of a criminal offense. Respondents rely on this fact to dismiss the petition pursuant to CPLR §§ 7804(f) and 3211(a)(7). Respondents correctly contend that the statutory protection contemplated by Correction Law Article 23-A and Executive Law 296(15) are for people convicted of a criminal offense and since she has no convictions they do not apply to her.

Boatman v New York State Department of Education 72 AD 3d 1467 900 N.Y.S. 2d 174 (2010) Decision found rational and upheld to deny clearance for custodian position after eight factors considered where Petitioner, other than the certificate of relief from disabilities submitted to Respondent, failed to respond to a written request to submit any additional information regarding his prior convictions, the underlying circumstances or further evidence of rehabilitation.

Figel v Dwyer 75 A.D.3d 802 907 N.Y.S.2d 75 (2010) In rendering a determination to either grant (in whole or in part) or deny petitioner's application for a Certificate of Relief of Civil Disabilities, respondent is required to consider and apply the statutorily enumerated factors set forth in Correction Law § 702 (2). The absence in respondent's cursory letter decision of any mention of the statutory factors or the grounds for the denial of a certificate of relief precludes meaningful review of the rationality of the decision.

Wunderlich v. New York State Educ. Dept. 82 A.D.3d 1345, 918 N.Y.S.2d 257 (2011) Applicant lacked the requisite good moral character, based on previous illegal financial transactions and failure to amend tax returns to correct income obtained from conviction, for licensure as a certified public accountant (CPA) when such conviction directly related to the duties after state gave proper weighting to Certificate of Relief of Civil Disabilities.

Rampolla v. Banking Dept. of State 93 AD 3d 526 31 Misc.3d 161 916 N.Y.S.2d 492 (2012) Respondent's determination denying petitioner's application for a mortgage loan origination license was not arbitrary and capricious where federal law mandates denial without pardon. Banking Law § 599-e controls the licensing decision federally, where Article 23-A controls state licensing decisions.

Martino v. Consolidated Edison Co. of New York, Inc., 105 AD 3d 575, 965 N.Y.S.2d 86, 2013 NY Slip Op 2657 Correction Law § 751 specifically states that "[t]he provisions of this article shall apply ... to any ... employment held by any person whose conviction of one or more criminal offenses ... preceded such employment" (emphasis added; see also *L 2007, ch 284; Senate Introducer Mem in Support, Bill Jacket, L 2007, ch 284)*. Because plaintiff's conviction, and an additional subsequent arrest, occurred when he was already employed by Consolidated Edison, they do not provide a basis for a claim under Correction Law article 23-A. The statutory protections contemplated by Correction Law Article 23-A are for people convicted of a criminal offense.

Matter of Gil v New York City Dept. of Bldgs., 107 AD3d 632 (2013) Respondents arbitrarily concluded that petitioner's convictions of mail fraud and money laundering bore a direct relationship to the duties and responsibilities attendant to a stationary engineer. Respondents provided no evidence suggesting that petitioner has not been rehabilitated but instead offered only "speculative inferences unsupported by the record" to raise an issue concerning potential risk to the public arising out of conduct similar to that for which petitioner had been previously convicted. Actions that bear no direct relationship to the equipment maintenance duties and responsibilities inherent in the stationary engineer license cannot satisfy the first exception to the general prohibition against discrimination against persons previously convicted of criminal offenses (see Correction Law § 752 [1]). There was no evidence in the record that petitioner ever submitted false documents that related to his stationary engineer responsibilities or implicated public safety, and he disclosed his 2002 conviction on at least two prior license renewal applications, each of which was granted. It is also undisputed that petitioner lived a law-abiding life in the decade after the conviction,

Matter of Bovich v. LiMandri, 116 AD3d 489, 490 (2014) Denial of petitioner's application to renew his stationary engineer license based upon his prior federal conviction for theft of funds was arbitrary, lacked rational basis, and violated Article 23-A of Correction Law where it bore no direct relationship to his duties and posed no unreasonable risk to public safety, particularly in light of his being employed as a stationary engineer without incident for several years.

Matter of Costco Wholesale Corp. v. New York State Div. of Human Rights, 2015 NY Slip Op 4587[Leave to Appeal Denied] Division's determination of unlawful discriminatory practice by Respondent not based on substantial evidence where there was no rejection by employers, application was still considered by the automated system and employer has a non-mandatory guideline to evaluate criminal convictions that is only applied at the background check stage. The evidence further established that the answer to the prior conviction question was specifically not an automatic bar to employment, as stated in the application itself. The court noted that the fact that none of the 13 applicants with convictions (out of 625 total) advanced in the hiring process does not establish that there was an illegal automatic disqualifier.

Belgrave v City of New York 137 A.D.3d 439 (2016), 27 N.Y.S.3d 2, 2016 NY Slip Op 01548 Article 23-A of the Correction Law is "a remedial statute, enacted to eliminate the effect of bias against ex-offenders that prevented them from obtaining employment, while also protecting society's interest in assuring performance by reliable and trustworthy persons." Court found that the protections of article 23-A do not apply to a civilian seeking to be hired by NYPD because "membership in any law enforcement agency" is expressly exempted from the statutory definition of "employment" pursuant to section 750 (5) of the Correction Law. Had the legislature intended that the exemption from article 23-A only apply to persons seeking to enforce laws (i.e. uniformed police officers or peace officers), but not the civilians employed by the same agencies or departments, it could have specifically so provided. Correction Law § 751 did not apply and the law enforcement agency could transfer him out of that position, solely on the basis that the police dispatcher had been convicted of a felony, even though he had obtained a certificate of relief from disabilities, the court referenced *1981 Ops Atty Gen No. 81-7* as authority.

Schwarz v Consolidated Edison 147 A.D.3d 447 (2017), 47 N.Y.S.3d 9, 2017 NY Slip Op 00927 The assault-related convictions on which plaintiff was retried, and the jury deadlocked, are not covered by article 23-A, since the article applies only to individuals who "previously have been convicted," and the vacatur of plaintiff's prior assault convictions rendered those convictions nullities. The complaint was dismissed because Complainant failed to show that he was terminated under circumstances giving rise to an inference of discrimination based on his perjury conviction.

New York Supreme Court

Maloney v. Waterfront Commission of New York Harbor, 96 Misc.2d 688, 409 N.Y.S.2d 573 (1978) Commission is bound to consider and apply the public policy of both New York and New Jersey, as enunciated in article 23-A of the Correction Law and in section 2A:168A of the New Jersey Statutes. (No longer precedent based on *Malverty v. Waterfront Com'n of New York Harbor)*

People v Honeckman 125 Misc.2d 1000 (1984) In enacting article 23 of the Correction Law, the Legislature sought to encourage the rehabilitation of first offenders by improving employment opportunities *(NY Legis Ann, 1966, pp 18, 19)*. The thrust of article 23 is the elimination of automatic bans to employment which are imposed solely as the result of a conviction without regard to whether the offense bears any relation to the character and fitness of the individual involved.

Sinicropi v. McCabe 123 A.D.2d 756, 507 N.Y.S.2d 229, appeal dismissed 69 N.Y.2d 821, 513 N.Y.S.2d 964, 506 N.E.2d 535, appeal denied 70 N.Y.2d 728, 519 N.Y.S.2d 644, 513 N.E.2d 1305(1986) Former employee of county probation department, who was dismissed from tenured position after it was determined that she was guilty of certain specifications of misconduct, was not "convicted criminal" so as to be entitled to written statement delineating reasons for denial of subsequent employment application under Correction Law § 754, where charges were litigated in civil forum and did not result in initiation of any criminal proceedings.

Peluso v. Smith, 142 Misc.2d 642, 540 N.Y.S.2d 631 (1989) Former felon with certificate of relief from disability was entitled to procedural due process reasonable opportunity to present supportive evidence and witnesses to negate both Correction Law § 752 (1) and (2) exceptions through a fact-finding evidentiary hearing under CPLR 7804 (h), to examine the eight factors set forth in Correction Law § 753 with regard to the presumption of rehabilitation created by his certificate of relief from disabilities on his application for site safety manager license to determine whether direct relationship between his bribery conviction and license was sufficiently attenuated to warrant issuance of the license.

Matter of La Cloche v. Daniels, 195 Misc. 2d 329, 755 N.Y.S. 2d. 827 (2003) Contrary to respondent's contention, nothing in General Business Law article 28 or article 23-A of the Correction Law (see Correction Law § 750 et. seq. permits respondent to deny an application solely on the basis of an applicant's previous conviction of a crime without inquiry into the factors set forth in Correction Law § 753(2) which include the applicant's moral character and possible rehabilitation. A denial based solely on such ground would be contradictory to the goals of the barbering vocational programs present in many of this state's correctional facilities. To refuse to certify an applicant as a barber apprentice solely because of a previous criminal conviction would be to deny the applicant the opportunity to practice a trade which the State itself taught him/her. An applicant must be given an opportunity to present evidence of good moral character.

Black v New York State Office of Mental Retardation and Development Disabilities, 20 Misc.3d 581, 586 (2008) Respondent's position that interaction would involve "regular and substantial unsupervised or unrestricted physical contact with consumers" is a general catchall statement without any attempt to address the specific employment duties involved in the employment and is therefore arbitrary and capricious. When all statutory factors are considered in determining whether issuance of a license or employment application would post unreasonable risk in light of prior convictions, and the positive factors are balanced against the negative factors for license or employment, the resulting decision is neither arbitrary nor capricious nor does it constitute an abuse of discretion, and reviewing courts may not reweigh the factors and substitute their judgment for that of the agency. Corrections law did not require employee to request written statement setting forth reasons for termination prior to commencing article 78 proceeding challenging revocation of temporary work approval.

Matter of Hollingshed v N.Y.S. Off. of Mental Retardation & Dev. Disabilities, NYLJ, Feb. 22, 2008, at 27, col 1 (Respondent's denial arbitrary and capricious where denial is based in part on the failure of petitioner to submit information in regard to her parole and probation supervision. Respondent, however, did not request such information from petitioner nor did it advise petitioner that her failure to do so could lead to her denial.

El v New York State Department of Education 2009 NY Slip Op 30883 (U) Petitioner's criminal history is the only evidence detailed in any meaningful respect. Thus, the decision on the whole, as drafted, suggests that it was based primarily, if not entirely, on petitioner's criminal history, with little consideration of the other evidence and statutory factors.

Matter of Exum v. New York City Health & Hosps. Corp., 964 N.Y.S.2d 58, *2012 NY Slip Op 52078* Agency decision arbitrary, capricious and abuse of discretion where petitioner was disqualified on grounds that were factually incorrect and in error, respondent also failed to specify the bearing, if any, that petitioner's convictions, which have had on his fitness or ability to perform such duties or responsibilities and the position at issue called for. Failing to address the eight obligatory Correction Law § 753 factors and give proper consideration to evidence of petitioner's rehabilitation and good conduct including his Certificate of Relief from Disabilities, or Certificate of Good Conduct. The direct relationship' exception and the unreasonable risk' exception to this general rule may be resorted to only upon a consideration of each of the eight factors as required by Correction Law § 753.

Godbolt v. Verizon New York, Inc., 2013 NY Slip Op 30100 It is not a violation of Corrections Law § 752 to terminate employment based on an employee's failure to disclose a criminal record truthfully and completely. Plaintiff has failed to offer competent evidence to show that defendant's discriminatory intent, as opposed to plaintiff's falsification of his employment applications, was the basis for plaintiff's termination.

Tesker v. New York City Taxi & Limousine Commn., 2013 NY Slip Op 33270 Petitioner's prior conviction is not related to the job and license of operating a vehicle for hire. Remand of Commissioner's decision as it does not set forth how the prior conviction would interfere with petitioner's driving duties. "Remorse" is not one of the statutory factors to be considered before denying the license. Evidence of rehabilitation, including early probation termination and 7 letters of recommendation must be weighed accordingly.

Levine v McDonald 2014 NY Slip Op 30649(U) Petitioner failed to demonstrate that Respondent was operating in excess of their jurisdiction by imposing a bar for felonies and misdemeanor A convictions for HELP truck positions, that Petitioner is a suitable candidate or has a clear right to the relief request. Failure to apply or exhaust administrative remedies creates no record for which the court can determine fitness.

Matter of Thomas v. New York City Dept. of Educ., 2014 NY Slip Op 24338 DOE erroneously concluded that the crime, and the facts which surrounded petitioner's plea, bore a "direct relationship" to the license's requirement of working with children, and, failed to give effect to the presumption to which petitioner was entitled. Decision to deny is arbitrary and capricious as there is no evidence in the record concerning this "direct relationship" nor does DOE ever articulate how petitioner's crime or his prior acts bear a "direct relationship" with the job duties of a paraprofessional. Instead the denial appears to be based simply on supposition unsupported by facts. Such decision-making does not comport with the Correction Law, and runs athrwart the presumption of rehabilitation afforded by Correction Law § 753 (2). Lack of trust that petitioner is, in fact, rehabilitated is antithetical to the letter, spirit and purpose of the Correction Law which is meant to protect an ex-offender whose crime bears no direct relationship to the employment he seeks. Therefore, the law mandates that petitioner is entitled to a second chance.

Matter of Mcmillan v. Department of Citywide Admin. Serv., 2015 NY Slip Op 25114 Record does not show consideration of how petitioner's conviction history related to the duties and responsibilities of working as a DCAS Special Officer. Because Respondents did not satisfy their statutory responsibilities under Correction Law Article 23-A, and because they improperly based their decision on the original crime for which petitioner was charged, their determination must be annulled and remanded to DCAS. The provisions of Correction Law § 753 were enacted to prevent the potential discriminatory practices of employers as against ex-offenders by positing that those employers could not presume a direct relationship between one's past conduct and future employment and the potential safety risk that one may pose as a result of past conduct. Instead, the employers had to evaluate the factors enumerated in Correction Law § 753 before reaching that conclusion. Those factors guide a rational evaluation of a person's criminal history by, for instance, measuring how long ago and how serious one's prior conviction was, a person's age at the time, and any evidence of a person's rehabilitation since then, among other factors.

Schwarz v. Consolidated Edison, Inc., 2015 NY Slip Op 25258 A vacated conviction cannot serve as a basis for plaintiff's claims under the New York State and City Human Rights laws, incorporating Article 23-A. Plaintiff's termination had nothing to do with the fact that he was convicted of perjury in 2002. His notoriety stemmed from his record as a police officer, not his record as a "criminal" as plaintiff claims. Article 23-A does not apply where the ex-offender is terminated for reasons other than a previous conviction. Under the facts as alleged however, the stigma attached to plaintiff does not arise from any "conviction." No mention is made in the 1976 Memoranda of any intent to protect against employment decisions based on one's reputation or notoriety arising from events that gave rise to the conviction; quite simply, the statute extends to unfair discrimination based on one's "convictions."

Matter of Dudley v City of New York 56 Misc.3d 448 (2017), 50 N.Y.S.3d 856, 2017 NY Slip Op 27129 Petitioner asserts that respondents' revocation of his license, security clearance, and denial of his continued employment violates article 23-A of the Correction Law for failing to render a fair and reasoned decision based on the factors required to be considered for a determination as to whether petitioner's prior criminal record is directly related to his duties as a substance abuse counselor or whether his continued employment in that position would pose an unreasonable risk to persons or property. The court did not consider a security clearance to be membership in a law enforcement agency and noted that the license was at issue here. The court reasoned that had the legislature intended that employment and membership in a law enforcement agency include the grant of access to a facility owned or managed by a law enforcement agency, or that the protections of article 23-A not extend to one with access to or working at a facility owned or managed by a law enforcement agency, regardless of whether the applicant seeks a license or employment, it could have enacted such an exemption, along with a provision that one seeking a license for access to or working at a law enforcement facility or a license issued by a law enforcement agency is not protected by article 23-A. It did not.

Matter of Tinsley v Taxi and Limousine Commission 58 Misc.3d 941 (2017), 62 N.Y.S.3d 769, 2017 NY Slip Op 51341(U) Tinsley applied for a Taxi License after spending much of his adult life in prison and was destitute, living off a small social security. He was denied by TLC based on his extensive criminal record from the 1960's and 1970's and appealed. Here the court found that the ALJ who presided over the hearing failed properly to apply, weigh, and balance the eight factors contained in Correction Law § 753 (1). Significantly, the ALJ failed to consider documents offered by Tinsley that would have an effect on the balancing and weighing of such factors, including the public policy of the state to promote the hire of an ex-offender. ALJs and hearing examiner often fail to recognize that the legislature and the Court of Appeals mandate hearings specifically to provide law offenders with a forum in which the opportunity is presented for them to justify the obtaining of employment that will make them self-supportive. Here, in the present case, competing with this vital public policy to protect the public it is the State's interest in rehabilitating, whenever possible, formerly incarcerated individuals, reintegrating them both into society and to productive jobs, and showing them different and better opportunities than their past experiences and histories unfortunately permitted.

N.Y.S. DIVISION OF HUMAN RIGHTS
FINAL ORDER SUMMARIES: CONVICTION RECORD

Name of Case: **Peterman v Kelly Services, Inc.**

Case No: <u>6-E-V-00-4704621 (2006)</u>

Summary: Complainant has a violent felony conviction for second degree attempted murder on June 4, 1991. He applied for work with Kelly Services, Inc. on June 29, 1999, a staffing company, and was denied employment based on the corporate criminal conviction policy, which denied employment regardless of the type of work complaint would be doing. Complainant was never requested to submit evidence of rehabilitation.

Issue: Has Respondent violated the Human Rights Law on the basis of conviction when it shifted responses and blamed Complainant for not submitting evidence of rehabilitation after it already stated it denied employment through a blanket nationwide policy?

Rule: To deny employment lawfully to someone with a felony conviction, an employer must establish a direct relationship to the position or that the nature of the his conviction posed an unreasonable risk under *Correction Law Article 23-A § 752.*

Analysis: Respondent found Complainant to be ineligible for employment and could not hire him based on their existing conviction record policy, which changed after Peterman filed a complaint with the Division. Respondent's later claim that it chose not to hire Complainant because he failed to provide documents is not credible. Respondent's offer of "shifting responses alone, especially when the first proffered explanation proves baseless, may give rise to an inference that the latter justifications are pre-textual." <u>State Division of Human Rights v County of Onondaga Sheriff's Dept., 71 N.Y. 2d 623, 528 N.Y.S. 2d 802 (1988).</u>

Conclusion: Kelly Services, Inc. was found to be in violation of the Human Rights Law. Peterman's employment was temporary and therefore speculative and he could not get awarded back pay. He was awarded $10,000 in mental anguish for his testimony.

Name of Case: **Baez v Collins Building Services, Inc.**

Case No: <u>1A-E-V-99-2306648 (2007)</u>

Summary: Complainant was convicted of criminal possession of stolen property in the fifth degree and a misdemeanor conviction more than 10 years before he filled out the application. He was truthful on the application and had to undergo a fingerprinting criminal background check because he was a temporary worker at Chase's One Chase Manhattan Plaza location that had become permanent. Chase's background check revealed the convictions and he was not permitted by Chase to have security clearance resulting in his termination.

Issue: Has Respondent violated the Human Rights Law on the basis of conviction by terminating Baez's employment since it now claims Baez lied on his application?

Rule: To deny employment lawfully to someone with conviction, an employer must establish a direct relationship to the position or that the nature of his conviction posed an unreasonable risk under *Correction Law Article 23-A § 752*. There was probable cause of discrimination because a complainant's conviction rather than for giving false information where employee truthfully indicated on employment application that he had not been convicted of a crime for disorderly conduct. <u>State Division of Human Rights v. Sorrento Cheese Co., 115 A.D. 2d 323, 495 N.Y.S. 2d 865 (4th Dep't 1985).</u>

Analysis: Respondent made a belated attempt to rehire Complainant upon discovering its mistake, but made belated attempts to justify the termination with a claim that Complainant lied when he Respondent to an oral vague inquiry from a manager. Respondent had 12 other locations and could have assigned Baez but refused. The Unemployment Insurance Appeals Board determined that Respondent's managers inquiry was too broad and vague and did not put Complainant on notice that if he did not disclose his convictions he would be fired.

Conclusion: Collins Building Services, Inc. was found to be in violation of the Human Rights Law. Baez was awarded $11,244.06 in lost wages.

Name of Case: **Knight v Kelly Services, Inc.**

Case No: 7-E-RV-04-7905792-E (2007)

Summary: Complainant was convicted of third degree assault, a misdemeanor on September 10, 1997. Complainant earned a Bachelor Degree. Complainant then sought work with Respondent Kelly Services, Inc. for a substitute teacher position that required him to be cleared for employment by the State of New York Education Department. After a review, Respondent chose not to hire Knight based on his 1997 misdemeanor.

Issue: Has Respondent violated the Human Rights Law on the basis of conviction by denying employment after balancing the factors enumerated in § 753 by finding Complainant an unreasonable risk to students, teachers and parents?

Rule: To deny employment lawfully to someone with conviction, an employer must establish a direct relationship to the position or that the nature of his conviction posed an unreasonable risk under *Correction Law Article 23-A § 752*. Then a balancing of the factors under Correction Law Article 23-A § 753 must take place once an exemption is claimed.

Analysis: Respondent gathered its information and considered all the factors, including the underlining arrest charge which was more serious. When balancing the positive with the negative, the negative factors amounted to five and the positive factors three, that it had been 7 years since the offense and that the safety and welfare of children in a classroom is a priorty.

Conclusion: Complainant's claims were dismissed, even though the Division argued that there was no hard copy of the analysis showing the factors in the record.

Name of Case: **Walker v Wal-Mart Stores East, L.P.,**

Case No: <u>10111967 (2008)</u>

Summary: Complainant applied for a position as unloader with Respondent. He was convicted of felony assault in 1993 and for possession of a controlled substance in 1998. He had two interviews with Respondent. The background check came back and deemed Complainant non- competitive and denied employment.

Issue: Has Respondent violated the Human Rights Law on the basis of conviction by denying employment based on determining Complainant to be non-competitive based entirely on the results of the background check?

Rule: To deny employment lawfully to someone with conviction, an employer must establish a direct relationship to the position or that the nature of the his conviction posed an unreasonable risk under *Correction Law Article 23-A § 752*. An employer must consider the factors outlined in Correction Law Article 23-A to determine if an offer of employment should be made. <u>Bonacorsa v Van Lindt, 71 N.Y. 2d 605, 528 N.Y.S. 2d 519 (1988)</u>.

Analysis: Respondent failed to produce any evidence that it or its agent had engaged in such balancing considerations under New York Correction Law Article 23-A before denying employment even though it identified Complainant as noncompetitive in the two areas referencing his criminal convictions based entirely on the background check results.

Conclusion: Walmart Stores East L.P. was found to be in violation of the Human Rights Law. Walker was awarded $1,537.50 in lost wages and $10,000 in mental anguish.

Name of Case: **Price v Sutherland Global Services, Inc.**

Case No: <u>10114890 (2009)</u>

Summary: Complainant was convicted on December 17, 1999 of possession of a firearm in furtherance of a drug trafficking crime, a federal felony. He applied for a position with Respondent's Hewlett-Packard Program and disclosed his conviction. In the interview he discussed his criminal record, sentence and supervised release. Complainant's credit check disqualified him from the HP program.

Issue: Has Respondent violated the Human Rights Law on the basis of conviction by denying employment to Price based on his federal felony drug conviction?

Rule: To deny employment lawfully to someone with conviction, an employer must establish a direct relationship to the position or that the nature of the his conviction posed an unreasonable risk under *Correction Law Article 23-A § 752*. An employer must consider the factors outlined in Correction Law Article 23-A to determine if an offer of employment should be made. <u>Bonacorsa v Van Lindt, 71 N.Y. 2d 605, 528 N.Y.S. 2d 519 (1988).</u>

Analysis: The record showed that Respondent reviewed and analyzed the factors before denying employment to Complainant and was concerned about the relationship of the conviction and to a youthful work force which already had drug and disciplinary problems.

Conclusion: Complainant's claims were dismissed.

Name of Case: **Byrd v Kaleida Health**

Case No: <u>10117256 (2008)</u>

Summary: Complainant was convicted of a crime. She indicated originally on her application with Respondent that she was not convicted of any crime. She then indicated she has been convicted of a crime and filled out a consent to run a background check form that is required by the Department of Health. The record recovered was not of Complainant's. Respondent determined that Complainant was dishonest in filling out the application and terminated employment.

Issue: Has Respondent violated the Human Rights Law on the basis of conviction by denying employment based on Complainant disclosing the conviction later but lying originally on the application for employment?

Rule: Inaccuracies or omissions in an employment application can constitute a legitimate nondiscriminatory basis for the denial of employment. <u>Grant v State Com. for Human Rights , 54</u> <u>Misc. 2d 775, 283 N.Y.S. 2d</u> <u>486 (Sup. Ct. New York Co. 1967)</u>

Analysis: Complainant failed to prove the reason proffered by Respondent was merely a pretext for discrimination and offered no evidence to prove Respondent's legitimate discriminatory reason to terminate was not valid, thus nullifying the prima facie case established.

Conclusion: Complainant's claims were dismissed.

Name of Case: **Belle v Milan Maintenance, Inc.**

Case No: 10121725 (2011)

Summary: Complainant was convicted of third degree robbery in 2001, and served an eight month sentence which ended in September 2001. He applied for a position with Respondent for a cleaning/janitorial job at an Adidas Store and was never asked on the application about his conviction record. Another employee told the manager that he had a conviction and he was confronted on it. Respondent terminated employment immediately and walked him out.

Issue: Has Respondent violated the Human Rights Law by terminating employment when it refused to engage in an Article 23-A analysis after it discovered that Complainant had a conviction record?

Rule: To deny employment lawfully to someone with conviction, an employer must establish a direct relationship to the position or that the nature of the his conviction posed an unreasonable risk under *Correction Law Article 23-A § 752*. An employer must consider the factors outlined in Correction Law Article 23-A to determine if an offer of employment should be made. Bonacorsa v Van Lindt, 71 N.Y. 2d 605, 528 N.Y.S. 2d 519 (1988).

Analysis: Respondent failed to produce any evidence that it or its agent had engaged in such balancing considerations under New York Correction Law Article 23-A before denying employment based on the fact he had a prior conviction.

Conclusion: Milian was found to be in violation of the Human Rights Law. Belle was awarded

$10,000 in mental anguish.

Name of Case: **Burvenich v Town of Huntington**

Case No: <u>10121794 (2008)</u>

Summary: Complainant has been employed by Respondent since May of 2005. On May 18, 2007 Complainant pled guilty to driving while impaired. He received a conditional driver license but his CDL remain suspended for one year. Upon returning to work May 23, 2007 he was demoted to a Grade 9 because he no longer had a CDL. Complainant's CDL was restored on May 8, 2008. He was not restored to his prior position.

Issue: Has Respondent violated the Human Rights Law on the basis of conviction by insisting that it had a policy that all employees above Grade 9 must possess a CDL and applying it to Complainant upon his return?

Rule: Article 23-A of the Correction Law only protects persons previously convicted of a criminal offense. <u>Goodman v Family Home Care, Inc. DHR Case No. 10121974,</u> dismissed during investigation for lack of jurisdiction)

Analysis: Complainant's conviction occurred while on the job and therefore the Division correctly dismissed the matter for lack of jurisdiction.

Conclusion: Complainant's claims were dismissed.

Name of Case: **Amaretey v Morningside House Co. Inc.**

Case No: <u>10121904 (2009)</u>

Summary: Complainant has a criminal history that dates back to 1975 and has a recent conviction in 1998 for assault. On March 19, 2001 Respondent hired Complainant as a driver. Respondent terminated and rehired Complainant several times. After receiving a complaint and it being investigated by police concerning an incident at Morningside House, Complainant was cleared of any wrongdoing, and Respondent rehired Complainant but did not reinstate her to the original job she had before the complaint, which decreased her income. In December, Complainant has an issue with Respondent's customers. Once she was brought in to discuss the matter she had a yelling match and the President of the company terminated her employment on January 4, 2008 based on adversarial and insubordination.

Issue: Has Respondent violated the Human Rights Law on the basis of conviction by terminating employment of Complainant after several incidents and a yelling match resulted in her firing?

Rule: Respondent hired Complainant in 2001, fully aware of Complainant's conviction history and Complainant failed to establish a prima facie case and meet her burden under the Human Rights Law of an unlawful failure to hire.

Analysis: Respondent demonstrated that its decisions were made for legitimate non- discriminatory reasons and Complainant could not demonstrate that Respondent retaliated against her.

Conclusion: Complainant's claims were dismissed.

Name of Case: **Kun v Rockland County Chapter, NYSARC Inc.**

Case No: <u>10123803 (2010)</u>

Summary: Complainant was arrested in 2000 for reckless endangerment. In 2001, the charges against her were dismissed and her record expunged. In 2007 upon an application to a job she answered no to being convicted of a crime. The job offer stated that it was contingent upon "a satisfactory background investigation including criminal history record search." The background check revealed that Complainant had a reckless endangerment conviction and Respondent terminated employment immediately after OMRDD directed so even though Complainant proved that it was not a conviction weeks later.

Issue: Has Respondent violated the Human Rights Law on the basis of conviction by denying employment based on a sealed arrest record that appeared as a conviction on a background check?

Rule: Respondent's conditional offer of employment required her to pass a criminal background check. As a result of OMRDD's determination she was automatically precluded from being hired by Complainant. By the time it was cleared the position had been filled.

Analysis: While Complainant did establish she had a perceived conviction record, the Respondent had to fill the position due to the needs of consumers and New York State law and therefore such judgment was based on need and a determination by OMRDD.

Conclusion: The case was dismissed.

Name of Case: **Stranahan v Verizon New York, Inc.**

Case No: <u>10124420 (2010)</u>

Summary: Complainant pled guilty to the crime of criminal possession of a controlled substance and sentenced to probation in 1992. In 1995, Complainant was convicted of the crime of conspiracy to commit murder in the second degree. Complainant applied for a service representative position to Respondent in 2008. Complainant did not disclose her complete conviction record. The background check flagged her recent conviction as an area of concern, Respondent indicated they do not hire anyone released from parole until 7 years after and that Complainant was not eligible until October 2010 and the job offer was withdrawn.

Issue: Has Respondent violated the Human Rights Law on the basis of conviction by withdrawing its job offer because of Complainant's conspiracy conviction?

Rule: The weighing of the factors cannot be a sham. The review cannot merely be an artificial exercise in order to seemingly meet statutory requirements while actually seeking a predetermined conclusion. <u>Boatwright v N.Y. Off. of Mental Ret. & Dev. Disabilities, 2007 N.Y. Misc. LEXIS 3399, 237 N.Y.L.J. 85 (Sup. Cot. N.Y. 2007).</u>

Analysis: Respondent inaccurately informed Complainant that Respondent's NYS policy was to hire individuals who were within seven years of ending parole. Respondent cannot claim it refused to hire Complainant later because of overlapping dates when that was not the actual reason at the time of denial. The factors were applied after the employment denial, not before. Respondent did not weight all the Correction Law factors when they were considered. Respondent essentially was already predisposed to not hire Complainant because she committed a crime. Respondent also ignored Complainant's successful work history.

Conclusion: Verizon was found to be in violation of the Human Rights Law. Stranahan was awarded $7,500 in mental anguish but did not get back pay based on after-acquired evidence and the concealment, which was of severity to cause termination and Respondent would have dismissed upon discovery.

Name of Case: **Cox v Monroe Muffler Brake, Inc.**

Case No: 10134207 (2012)

Summary: Complainant applied in 2005 and was hired for a position with Respondent as a service technician. He attempted numerous times to apply for a manager position but was told that because he had a conviction on the enumerated crimes list, he was ineligible for promotion. After June 2, 2008 management made it clear that he would never be promoted.

Issue: By establishing an employment policy to preclude an individual from being hired or promoted to a manager position based on a list of enumerated crimes, did Respondent violate the Human Rights Law?

Rule: The Division is barred from considering discriminatory claims past a year of the complaint, which were prior to June 2, 2008. By failing to allow an application for promotion, Respondent failed to make an individualized assessment of Complainant's circumstance under

N.Y.S Correction Law Section 753-1. The weighing of the factors cannot be a sham. The review cannot merely be an artificial exercise in order to seemingly meet statutory requirements while actually seeking a predetermined conclusion. Boatwright v N.Y. Off. of Mental Ret. & Dev. Disabilities, 2007 N.Y. Misc. LEXIS 3399, 237 N.Y.L.J. 85 (Sup. Cot. N.Y. 2007).

Analysis: The Division finds that Respondent clearly violated the Human Rights Law by not allowing Complainant to apply for a branch manager position and rendering such application a futile gesture by the policy and the company's comments to him. Here a mixed motive case is established because even though Complainant established he was in a protected class, the employer would have made the same decision even if it had not taken the protected class into account since more qualified applicants were hired.

Conclusion: Monroe Muffler was found to be in violation of the Human Rights Law based on establishing a blanket policy against certain conviction records. Cox was awarded $5,000 in mental anguish.

Name of Case: **Harris v Action for A Better Community, Inc.**

Case No: <u>10146479 (2012)</u>

Summary: Complainant has a criminal record of felony aggravated criminal contempt. He applied for a food service assistant and was hired by Respondent on August 18, 2010 contingent upon successful results from a background check and New York State Central Registry Clearance. OCFS imposed a restriction of no unsupervised contact upon his hire. Respondent thereafter determined that constant supervision would disrupt its service and might result in loss of its license if it were unable to observe the restriction and terminated employment.

Issue: Did Respondent's decision to terminate employment based upon his conviction render made in accordance with the provisions of Article 23-A of the Correction Law?

Rule: To deny employment lawfully to someone with conviction, an employer must establish a direct relationship to the position or that the nature of his conviction posed an unreasonable risk under *Correction Law Article 23-A § 752*. An employer must consider the factors outlined in Correction Law Article 23-A to determine if an offer of employment should be made. <u>Bonacorsa v Van Lindt, 71 N.Y. 2d 605, 528 N.Y.S. 2d 519 (1988).</u>

Analysis: The Respondent utilized the Correction Law correctly and considered the factors before terminating employment and determined it could not provide the level of security required by OCFS to maintain employment. The Division determined that continued employment of Complainant would disrupt Respondent's business and that the restriction imposed by OCFS would prevent Complainant from performing a significant number of the duties required of him as a food service assistant and would disrupt operations.

Conclusion: The case was dismissed.

Name of Case: **Levine v Costco Wholesale Corporation**

Case No: <u>10145205 (2013)</u>

Summary: Complainant applied for any position in Respondent's warehouse. Complainant was convicted of a felony and 3 misdemeanors. Respondent utilized an adjudication guideline called Costco Grading Criteria whichdetermined which convictions were "ineligible" and "eligible" for employment. Respondent further utilized the conviction record question to knock out applicants and its employees did not conduct any Article 23-A analysis or ask for any evidence of rehabilitation during the interview and pre-background check stages.

Issue: Has Respondent violated the Human Rights Law on the basis of conviction by automatically rendering an applicant's application ineligible when they click yes to having a felony conviction record?

Rule: To deny employment lawfully to someone with conviction, an employer must establish a direct relationship to the position or that the nature of his conviction posed an unreasonable risk under *Correction Law Article 23-A § 752.* An employer must consider the factors outlined in Correction Law Article 23-A to determine if an offer of employment should be made. <u>Bonacorsa v Van Lindt, 71 N.Y. 2d 605, 528 N.Y.S. 2d 519 (1988).</u>

Analysis: Respondent automatically disqualified Complainant based on his checking yes on the application for employment and then failed to produce his actual employment application. Respondent failed to forward the applications to hiring managers so they could conduct individualized assessments but based its entire decision on the results of a background check.

Conclusion: Costco Wholesale Corporation was found to be in violation of the Human Rights Law. Levine was not awarded anything being self-employed, but Costco was fined $40,000 for their discriminatory actions by the State.

Name of Case: **Fabre v Me Fein Inc.**

Case No: <u>10152270 (2013)</u>

Summary: Complainant was discouraged during a phone call to Respondent from obtaining employment with Respondent. Complainant was discouraged by Respondent when she truthfully disclosed her conviction record on the phone for the position.

Issue: Has Respondent violated the Human Rights Law on the basis of conviction by discouraging Complainant once she disclosed she had a conviction record?

Rule: To deny employment lawfully to someone with conviction, an employer must establish a direct relationship to the position or that the nature of her conviction posed an unreasonable risk under *Correction Law Article 23-A § 752*. An employer must consider the factors outlined in Correction Law Article 23-A to determine if an offer of employment should be made. <u>Bonacorsa v Van Lindt, 71 N.Y. 2d 605, 528 N.Y.S. 2d 519 (1988).</u>

Analysis: Respondent failed to produce any evidence that it or its agent had engaged in such balancing considerations under New York Correction Law Article 23-A before discouraging employment. Respondent had made a blanket statement that they do not hire people with criminal records to Complainant.

Conclusion: Me Fein, Inc. was found to be in violation of the Human Rights Law. Fabre was awarded $1,500 in mental anguish.

Name of Case: **Daniels v Blossom Health Care Center Inc. AKA Brighton Manor**

Case No: <u>10164247 (2014)</u>

Summary: Complainant sought an LPN position with Respondent. He was hired then terminated when the background check revealed a conviction that had not been disclosed. Complainant was not convicted of a felony or misdemeanor, which was not a criminal offense. Respondent demanded that Complainant leave the premises and refused to allow him to submit documentation to substantiate his claim he did not lie.

Issue: Has Respondent violated the Human Rights Law by basing its decision to terminate Complainant entirely on the basis of a perceived conviction that was not disclosed on the application for employment?

Rule: Respondent's legitimate reason for terminating Complainant is not a legitimate business reason at all because it is simply not true, and therefore amounts to discrimination on the basis of the erroneously perceived conviction itself. *Division of Human Rights v Sorrento Cheese Co. Inc. 115 A.D. 2d 323, 495 N.Y.S. 2d 865 (1985)*

Analysis: Respondent used the results of the background check rather than gathering the 8 factors required by the Correction Law before denying employment to Complainant and refused to allow Complainant a chance to explain why the report was inaccurate and why he did not disclose it when asked on the application.

Conclusion: Blossom Health Care Center, Inc. was found to be in violation of the Human Rights Law. Daniels was awarded $3,212 in backpay and $2,500 in mental anguish.

Name of Case: **Dearaujo v 677 New Loudon Corporation, Stephen Dick, Jr.**

Case No: <u>10166237 (2016)</u>

Summary: Complainant sought a position as a nude dancer at a strip club. During the interview process she was asked directly if she had any legal issues by the General Manager. She denied having any arrest or criminal convictions. At the time she applied she had a criminal record in 2013 for possession of stolen property. Respondent was told by another employee that Complainant was lying and was convicted of a drug related offense. Respondent decided to run a criminal background check on Complainant. Because Complainant was calling every day to begin work, Respondent's General Manager then googled her name and found the misdemeanor conviction and pending arrest case based on her failure to adhere to a court order to submit DNA. Respondent then terminated employment based on the arrest and conviction misrepresentation.

Issue: Has Respondent violated the Human Rights Law by basing its decision to terminate Complainant on the failure to disclose a pending arrest and a criminal conviction?

Rule: A pending arrest is not protected under the Human Rights Law unless it is terminated in the Complainant's favor or dismissed. The misrepresentation of not having a criminal record is a lawful reason to terminate employment. A material misrepresentation of fact is a legitimate, non-discriminatory reason for employment disqualification<u>. *Smith v. Kingsboro Psychiatric Center, 35 A.D.3d 751, 828 N.Y.S.2d 419* </u><u>*(2d Dept. 2006); Stewart v. Civil Service Commission, 84 A.D.2d 491, 446 N. Y .S.2d 948 (1st Dept. 1982);* </u><u>*Moran v. Baxter. 193 A.D.2d 460,597 N.Y.S.2d 688 (I st Dept. 1993); see also N.Y.S. Correction Law§ 751.* </u>

Analysis: Complainant was not covered under the protection of the Human Rights Law when she lied about having pending arrests or convictions. Respondent was justified in terminating employment based on failure to disclose a pending arrest. The arrest had not been terminated or dismissed at that time in Complainant's favor and therefore the inquiry and subsequent termination were lawfully done based on the misrepresentation of Araujo.

Conclusion: Case Dismissed.

Name of Case: **Bonner v Cardinal Mccloskey School and Home for Children**

Case No: <u>10171975 (2016)</u>

Summary: Complainant sought a Case Planner position with Respondent. She was hired as a probationary employee for several months then terminated when the background check revealed a conviction for a misdemeanor of Intent to Cause Injury. Respondent argued that Complainant was terminated because her conviction showed her inability to potentially defuse a tense situation, which was one of the direct job duties she would be facing and that the conviction was recent.

Issue: Has Respondent violated the Human Rights Law by basing its decision to terminate Complainant entirely on the basis of her misdemeanor conviction?

Rule: Respondent determined that the risk to its clients of employing Bonner was too high. Even though she had performed the duties of the position for several months, Respondent felt that its decision to terminate after it found a direct relationship between the job duties and her conviction and after reviewing the 8 factors was justified. The Division should not sit as a "super-personnel department" that reexamines an entity's business decisions. *Baldwin v Cable Systems Corp., 65 A.D. 3d 961, 966, 988 N.Y.S 2d 1, 5 (2009) leave to appeal denied, 14 N.Y. 3d 701 (2010)*

Analysis: Respondent correctly used Correction Law before denying employment to Complainant and found a direct relationship and correctly used the factors rather than the background check itself. Its choice to rescind employment was justified.

Conclusion: Case Dismissed.

Name of Case: **Spindler v Joann Fabric & Craft Stores**

Case No: <u>10179788 (2017)</u>

Summary: Complainant, a person with a sex offense conviction, was offered a position as a team member contingent on successful completion of a criminal background check. Respondent has a policy of stating that sex offenses are incompatible with hire at Respondent's stores and must be evaluated on a case by case basis. Respondent rescinded employment and sent out an adverse action letter and gave him 7 days to dispute the contents of the report which he did not dispute the report. Respondent argued that Complainant did not provide any evidence of rehabilitation or any additional relevant information about his recent felony.

Issue: Has Respondent violated the Human Rights Law by basing its decision to terminate Complainant entirely on the basis of his felony conviction?

Rule: An employer is allowed to deny employment when there is a direct relationship and an 8 factor test is performed and evidence of rehabilitation is requested per Correction Law Article 23-A Section <u>*N.Y.S. Correction Law§ 752, 753 (a-b)*</u>.

Analysis: Respondent determined that the risk to its clients of employing Spindler was too high and found a direct relationship. It then did an 8 factor test. It allowed submission by Spindler, who declined to add anything.

Conclusion: Case Dismissed.

OFFICE OF THE ATTORNEY GENERAL LEGAL OPINIONS: CONVICTION RECORD

1981 N.Y. Op. Atty. Gen (Inf.) 96, 1981 WL 137956 (N.Y.A.G) (January 19, 1981)

CORRECTIONS LAW §§ 701 (1), 750 (5), 751, 753 (2).

The Police Department of the Village of Malone may request the transfer of a CETA employee who is assigned to work as a dispatcher in the Police Department upon discovering that he has been convicted of a felony even though the employee had obtained a certificate of relief from disabilities.

Hon. Robert G. Main, Jr.
Village Attorney
Village of Malone
Holland & Main, P.C.
298 East Main Street
Malone, New York
12953

Dear Mr. Main:

You have asked whether the Police Department of the Village of Malone may, after the Department discovers that he has been convicted of a felony, request the transfer of a CETA employee who is assigned to work as a dispatcher in the Police Department. The CETA employee contends that the transfer is improper because he had obtained a certificate of relief of from disabilities.

Section 701 (1) of the Correction Law provides:

' A certificate of relief from disabilities may be granted *** to relieve an eligible offender of any forfeiture or disability, or to remove any bar to his employment, automatically imposed by law by reason of his conviction of the crime or the offense specified therein.'

Section 751 of the Corrections Law prohibits the denial of an application for public employment upon the fact that the applicant has been convicted of one or more criminal offenses unless there is a direct relationship between the criminal offense and the employment sought or the granting of employment involves an unreasonable risk to property or persons. The public agency must give consideration to a certificate of relief from disabilities (§ 753 [2]). However, the Corrections Law explicitly exempts membership in a law enforcement agency from the definition of employment (§ 750 [5]). Therefore, a law enforcement agency may consider an application's conviction of one or more criminal offenses in determining whether to accept his application for employment in a law enforcement agency without regard to the criteria set forth in section 751.

We conclude that the Police Department of the Village of Malone may request the transfer of a CETA employee upon discovering that he has been convicted of a felony even though the employee had obtained a certificate of relief of disabilities.

Very Truly Yours,

Robert Abrams, Attorney General By: James D. Cole, Assistant Attorney General

1981 N.Y. Op. Atty. Gen (Inf.) 281, 1981 WL 145776 (N.Y.A.G) (November 9, 1981)

CORRECTIONS LAW §§ 701 (1), 750 (5), 752, 753

A certificate of relief from disability does not authorize a job applicant with a criminal record to deny on an employment application that he has ever been convicted of a crime. The employer must consider the certificate, which establishes a presumption of rehabilitation as to the criminal offenses specified in the certificate.

Robert G. Lyman,
Esq. County Attorney
County of Albany
County Court House

Albany, New York 12207

Dear Mr. Lyman:
You have asked whether a 'certificate of relief from disability' authorizes a job applicant with a criminal record to deny on an employment application that he has ever been convicted of a crime.

A 'certificate of relief from disability' (certificate) removes forfeitures, disabilities, or bars to employment automatically imposed by law by reason of a person's conviction of a crime or offense (Correction Law § 701). The certificate may remove all forfeitures, disabilities and bars or it may be limited to specific ones (ibid).

No person applying for a license or employment with a private employer or public agency may be denied a license or employment on account of the applicant's conviction of one or more criminal offenses unless:
   (1) there is a direct relationship between one or more of the previous criminal offenses and the specific license or employment sought; or
   (2) the issuance of the license or the granting of the employment would involve an unreasonable risk to property or to the safety or welfare of specific individuals or the general public. (Id. §752)

We note that the term 'employment' as used in this context excludes membership in any law enforcement agency (id.
§750 [5]). In making a determination under section 752 the public agency must consider a certificate of relief from disabilities, which creates a presumption of rehabilitation in regard to the offense or offenses specified in the certificate (id. §753).

We believe it clear from these provisions that a certificate does not in effect eliminate a conviction, thereby justifying a statement by an applicant for public employment that he has not been convicted of a crime. The certificate establishes a presumption of rehabilitation which must be overcome by an employer based upon the required findings under section 752. In other words, the certificate is to be used to mitigate the impact of a criminal record, not to eliminate it. We believe that the applicant must, upon request, list his convictions and should note that he has a certificate of relief from disability.

We conclude that a certificate of relief from disability does not authorize a job applicant with a criminal record to deny on an employment application that he has ever been convicted of a crime. The employer must consider the certificate, which establishes a presumption of rehabilitation as to the criminal offenses specified in the certificate.

Very Truly Yours,
Robert Abrams, Attorney General By: James D. Cole, Assistant Attorney General

1983 N.Y. Op. Atty. Gen (Inf.) 200, 1982 WL 178304 (N.Y.A.G) (September 23, 1982)

CORRECTIONS LAW §§ 750 (1) (2) and (3) 752 and 753, PUBLIC OFFICERS LAW § 30 (1) (e)

A local government may not deny an application for licensure or employment on account of the commission by the applicant of a criminal offense, except upon making certain required findings based upon statutory criteria. It is the policy of the State to encourage the licensure and employment of persons previously convicted of one or more criminal offenses.

S. Robert Putterman, Esq.
   VillageAttorney
Village of Atlantic Beach
   65 The Plaza

Atlantic Beach, New York 11509

Dear Mr. Putterman,
You have asked whether a village officer who has resigned on account of his conviction of a felony may be hired as an employee or consultant to the village.

Upon being convicted of a felony, a public officer by operation of law vacates his office (Public Officers Law, § 30 [1][e].

A 'private employer' or 'public agency' (including a local government) may not deny an application for a licensure or employment:

by reason of the applicant's having been previously convicted of one or more criminal offenses, or by reason of a finding of lack of 'good moral character' when such finding is based upon the fact that the applicant has previously been convicted of one or more criminal offenses, unless:

(1) there is a direct relationship between one or more of the previous criminal offenses and the specific license or employment sought; or

(2) the issuance of the license or the granting of the employment would involve an unreasonable risk to property or to the safety or welfare of specific individuals or the general public. (Correction Law, §§ 750 [1] and [2] and 752.)

'Employment' in this context excludes membership in any law enforcement agency (id., § 750[5]). In making this determination the private employer or public agency is required to consider certain factors (id. § 753). Among them is the public policy of the state 'to encourage the licensure and employment of persons previously convicted of one or more criminal offenses' (id. § 753[1][a]. The private employer or public agency is required to consider a certificate of relief from disabilities or a certificate of good conduct issued to the applicant, which create a presumption of rehabilitation regarding the offense(s) specified in these certificates (id., § 753[2]; Informal Opinions of the Attorney General No. 81-124, copy enclosed).

We conclude that a local government may not deny an application for licensure or employment on account of the commission by the applicant of a criminal offense, except upon making certain required findings based upon statutory criteria. It is the policy of the state to encourage the licensure and employment of persons previously convicted of one or more criminal offenses.

Very Truly Yours,
James D. Cole, Assistant Attorney General

1984 N.Y. Op. Atty. Gen (Inf.) 126, 1984 WL 186573 (N.Y.A.G) (August 28, 1984)

CIVIL PRACTICE LAW AND RULES, Art. 78; CORRECTIONS LAW §§ 752, 753, 754, 755; EXECUTIVE LAW §§ 296 (15), 837 (8-a); GENERAL CITY LAW, §§ 20 (27), 44; LABOR LAW, § 201-a; MUNICIPAL HOME RULE LAW, § 10 (1) (ii) (a) (12); TOWN LAW, § 137

Licensing official are authorized to consider the fitness of an applicant. In considering the effect of a prior conviction, the licensing officer may deny a license only after making the determination required by the Legislature. No public hearing is required in making such a licensing determination.

William W. Oliver, Esq.
Assistant Corporation Counsel
City of Schenectady
Office of the Corporation Counsel
Schenectady, New York 12305

Dear Mr. Oliver,

You have asked several questions in relation to the licensing of plumbers and electricians.

Your first question is whether a city may deny a license based upon moral turpitude and/or prior criminal conviction of an applicant. Cities are authorized to enact ordinances to "examine, license and regulate" electricians (General City Law, § 20[27]). They may also license and regulate plumbers and may in the licensing process determine the "fitness and character" of applicants (id., Art 4, §44). All local governments are authorized to adopt and amend local laws providing for the licensing and regulation of occupations or businesses (Municipal Home Rule Law, § 10[1][ii][a][12]. You regulations have been adopted under the provisions of the General City Law.

The general rule is that discretionary powers exercised by an administrative officer must be delegated to him by statute with sufficient standards to exercise these powers. (Mtr. Of Barton Trucking Corp. v. O' Connell, 7 N.Y. 2d 299, 307 [1959]. However, it is well settled with respect to licensing officials, that the power to withhold a license for good cause and the standards defining such decisions need not be expressly delegated where by fair implication in light of the statutory purpose, such power has been implicitly delegated (ibid.). Licensing officials have implicit discretion to pass upon the fitness of the applicant (ibid; Matter of Howell v Benson, 90 A.D. 2d 903 [3d Dept, 1982]). Where the enabling statute authorizes the licensing official to examine applicants, and in his judgment deny licensure, the power to determine fitness of the applicant is necessarily implied (ibid.). Thus, we believe that under the above-cited provisions of the General City Law, the licensing official may deny a license to a plumber or an electrician if in his judgment the person is unfit. Certainly the moral character of an applicant for a plumbing or electrical license is relevant in determining fitness since the licensee would be dealing wit hteh public on matters affecting health and safety.

The authority to consider a previous criminal offense in determining the character and fitness of an applicant for a license has been circumscribed by the Legislature (Stewart v Civil Service Commission, 84 AD2d 491 [1st Dept, 1982]; Correction Law, Art 23-A; Executive Law § 296[15]. The legislature has established a State policy to encourage the licensure and employment of persons previously convicted of one or more criminal offenses (ibid.) A private employer or agency may not deny a license or employment

*2 by reason of the applicant's having been previously convicted of one or more criminal offenses, or by reason of a finding of lack of 'good moral character' when such finding is based upon the fact that the applicant has previously been convicted of one or more criminal offenses, unless:

(1) there is a direct relationship between one or more of the previous criminal offenses and the specific license or employment sought; or

(2) the issuance of the license or the granting of the employment would involve an unreasonable risk to property or to the safety or welfare of specific individuals or the general public. (Correction Law, §§ 752)

In making this determination the private employer or public agency is required to consider certain factors (see id. § 753). One factor is the public policy of the state 'to encourage the licensure and employment of persons previously convicted of one or more criminal offenses' (id. § 753[1][a]. Consideration must be given to a certificate of relief from disabilities or a certificate of good conduct issued to the applicant, which create a presumption of rehabilitation regarding the offense(s) specified in these certificates (id., § 753[2]; See also, Op.Atty.Gen. [Inf] 81-7, 82-73).

You also ask whether in considering the effect of a prior conviction or moral turpitude a public hearing must be held. Article 23-A of the Correction Law does not require a hearing per se but requires that specific determinations be made § 753. As a practical matter, it may be necessary to make findings of fact and conduct investigations in order to make the required findings. In determining the effect of a prior conviction, the employer is required to consider any information produced by the job or license applicant regarding his rehabilitation and good conduct. (id.
§ 753[1][g]. Upon the request of a person denied a license or employment, the employer is required to indicate in writing the reasons for denial. (id. § 754). Denial of a license or employment is subject to judicial review under Article 79 of the CPLR (id., § 755). We note that a public hearing is not required in relation to an original application for a plumbing or electrician's license but is required prior to revocation (General City Law §§20[27][a], 47). Town officials are not required to conduct hearing in deciding whether to issue a license but must hold a hearing prior to revocation (Town Law §137; see Hempstead T-W Corp. V Town of Hempstead, 13 Misc. 2d 1054, 1061 [Sup Ct., Nassau Co. 1958], affd7 AD2d 637 ([2d Dept, 1958]).

Finally you ask whether the city may require the fingerprinting of an applicant, and forward the prints to the State Division of Criminal Services for a check on whether the individual as any outstanding convictions. Section 201-a of the Labor Law provides that no person as a condition of securing employment or of continuing employment, may be required to be fingerprinted. Exempted from coverage under this provision are employees of the State or any municipal subdivision of the State (ibid). We are not aware of any prohibition on requiring fingerprinting as a condition of licensure. However, local regulations should authorize such actions. A representative of the Division of Criminal Justice Services has informed us that the Division will make a criminal history search on behalf of a local government involved in a licensing matter. However, we recommend that you contact the Division since they require the local regulations specifically authorize fingerprinting and other related activities. Section 837 (8-a) of the Executive Law authorizes the Division to conduct a search of its criminal history records and report thereon in connection with an application for employment or for a license or permit.

*3 We conclude that licensing officials are authorized to consider the fitness of an applicant. In considering the effect of a prioer conviction, the licesning offiver may deny a license only after making the determination required by the Legislature. No public hearing is required in making a licensing determination.

Very Truly Yours, James
D. Cole
Assistant Attorney General in Charge of Opinions

1985 N.Y. Op. Atty. Gen 14 , 1985 WL 194015 (N.Y.A.G) (April 30, 1985) (F2)

CORRECTIONS LAW §§ 752, TAX LAW, § 1603 § 1604 § 1605 § 1607; CPLR Article 78

Denial of an application for a license to sell New York State Lottery Tickets because of a criminal conviction is permitted under section 752 of the Correction Law, dependent on a finding by the Division of the State Lottery that there is a direct relationship between the previous criminal offense and the specific license sought. Denial of sales licenses or revocation of sales licenses to the franchisees of a franchisor who was convicted of a crime is permissible under certain circumstances.

Honorable John D. Quinn
Director, New York State
Lottery Swan Street Building
Empire State Plaza
Albany, New York 12223

Dear Mr. Quinn,

Your counsel has requested an opinion regarding the licensing of lottery ticket sellers in New York State. According to her letter, the Division of the Lottery currently licenses thirteen independent franchisees of the Southland Corporation to sell lottery tickets in New York State. The licenses have been issued to the franchisees, not to Southland. Twenty more of these store have individually applied for the agent licenses. Counsel's letter states that Southland was convicted of taking an unauthorized business deduction of $96,000 to further an attempt to bribe New York State tax officials, which was never carried out. The Division does not wish to penalize independent franchisees for a matter over which they had no control and yet hesitates to do business with them under these circumstances. The questions are whether the conviction of the franchisor necessitates (1) the revocation of the licenses currently held by the franchisees; and (2) the denial of applications for licenses by other franchisees. Counsel has also inquired whether the Division could be subject to lawsuit if it decides to revoke licenses or deny application for licenses on the ground of the conviction.

Article 234 of the Tax Law is the statutory authorization for New York's lotteries (Tax Law §§ 1600-1616). The various lotteries are administered by the Division of the Lottery, which is part of the Department of Taxation and Finance (id.. § 1603). The Division is responsible for licensing agents to sell lottery tickets throughout the state (id.
§§ 1604, 1605. The decision to license a person as a sales agent is based on the Division's opinion as to whether the agent "will best service public convenience" (id. § 1605). The Division considers the following factors when deciding whether to grant a license:

1. Financial responsibility and security of the business or activity in which such person is engaged.

2. Accessibility of the place of business or activity to the public.

3. Sufficiency of existing licensees to service public convenience.

4. Whether place of business or activity is predominantly frequented by persons under the age of eighteen years.

*2 5. Volume of expected sales. (Ibid.)

In addition to these specific standards, it is well settled that the power to withhold a license for good cause and the standards defining such decisions need not be expressly delegated, where by fair implication lin light of the statutory purpose such power has been implicitly delegated (Matter of Barton Trucking Corp. v. O'Connell, 7 NY2d 299, 307 [1959]; Licensing officials have implicit discretion to pass on the fitness of the applicant (ibid: Matter of Howell v Benson, 90 AD2d903 3rd Department, 1982]). Where the enabling statute authorizes the licensing official to examine applicants, and as a matter of judgment deny licensure, the power to determine fitness of the applicant is necessarily implied. (ibid.).

The standards governing the suspension and revocation of licenses are also set forth by statute. Licenses can be suspended or revoked for several reasons, including failure to comply with instructions and standards established by the Division (see Neidich v Quinn, 90 AD2d 614 [3d Dept, 1982]), conviction of any offense as defined in the Penal Law and fraud, deceit, misrepresentation or "conduct prejudicial to public confidence in the state lottery." (Tax Law § 1607).

Authority to determine fitness, however is not absolute. Article 23-A of the Correction Law is designed to prevent unfair discrimination against persons who have been convicted of one or more criminal offenses (Correction Law,
§§ 750-755). Section 752 is applicable to private and public employers and licensors, and provides as follows:

No application for any license or employment, to which the provisions of this article are applicable, shall be denied by reason of the applicant's having been previously convicted of one or more criminal offenses, or by reason of a finding of lack of "good moral character" when such finding is based upon the fact that the applicant has previously been convicted of one or more criminal offenses, unless:

(1) there is a direct relationship between one or more of the previous criminal offenses and the specific license or employment sought; or

(2) the issuance of the license or the granting of the employment would involve an unreasonable risk to property or to the safety or welfare of specific individuals or the general public.

As we have indicated, in determining a license application the Division may consider the fitness of the applicant (Barton, supra; Op Atty Gen No. 84-37). Under section 752 of the Corrections Law, an applicant for a license may not be found unfit on account of a criminal conviction or based on a finding of bad moral character resulting from a conviction unless there is a direct relationship between one or more of the previous criminal offenses and the specific license sought. If the application for licensure had come directly from Southland, it is clear that it would be within the Division's discretion to deny the application on the ground that Southland's conviction of a crime involving dishonesty is directly related to its ability to act as a lottery ticket agent. It follows that if the Division were to make this finding, it may also be within its discretion to deny licenses to the franchisees. As your letter indicates, Southland receives 52% of the profit from the operation of each franchisee's store. Although the franchise agreement refers to the franchisee as an independent contractor, such an arrangement in fact may be more in the nature of a partnership. If that were the case, it might give credence to the argument that licensure of a franchisee is, in effect, also the licensure of Southland, the party who was convicted of the crime in question. Under these circumstances, the Division would have discretion to deny licensure of the franchisee on the basis of conviction of a crime involving dishonesty and to suspend or revoke a license for conviction of an "offense defined in the penal law." (Tax Law § 1607).

*3 If the Division were to find from the character of the business relationship between Southland and its franchisees that licensure of a franchisee were not the indirect licensure of Southland, the Division could still consider the general fitness of the franchisee, along with the factors set forth in sections 1605 and 1607 of the Tax Law, in determining the licensure applications and whether to revoke existing licenses. As we have indicated such factors would include determining whether licensees have engaged in conduct prejudicial to public confidence in the lottery. Section 1607 provides that a license may be suspended or revoked for the reasons contained therein, indicating that the decision to suspend or revoke is not mandatory, but is within the Division's discretion.

With regard to counsel's concern as to potential lawsuit liability, the denial of an application, or the revocation of license would be reviewable under Article 78 of the CPLR.

Accordingly, we conclude that denial of an application for a license to sell New York State lottery tickets because of a criminal conviction is permitted under section 752 of the Correction Law, dependent on a finding by the Division that there is a direct relationship between the previous criminal offense and the specific license sought. Denial of sales licenses or revocation of sales licenses as to franchisees of a franchisor who is convicted of a crime is permissible under certain circumstances.

Very Truly Yours,
Robert Abrams,
Attorney General

1996 N.Y. Op. Atty. Gen 1086 , 1996 WL 639886 (N.Y.A.G) (September 30, 1996) (35)

CORRECTION LAW, ART 23-A; GENERAL BUSINESS LAW, ART 7-A, §§ 89-f, 89-g(1), 89-h, 89-k, 89-l, 89-r; L 1992, CH 336.

The security guard act does not preclude the Nassau County Civil Service Commission from considering a job applicant's criminal history. That consideration, however, must be in accord with the requirements of Correction Law Article 23-A.

Owen B. Walsh, Esq. Informal Opinion
County Attorney No. 96-35
County of Nassau
County Executive Building
One West Street

Mineola, NY 11501

Dear Mr. Walsh:

You ask whether the Nassau County Civil Service Commission, which is considering the qualifications of an applicant for a security guard position, may disqualify the candidate based upon a criminal conviction notwithstanding that the Secretary of State, under General Business Law Article 7-A, has reviewed the applicant's criminal record and registered the individual as eligible for employment as a security guard within New York State. You state that the conviction in question was a misdemeanor and involved the discharge of an unlicensed weapon during a social event. Article 7-A, known as the security guard act, was enacted in 1992. It provides that only individuals registered by the Department of State, or those whose application is pending, may be employed as security guards. General Business Law § 89-g(1).

In order to be registered, an individual must satisfy the requirements set forth in section 89-h of the act, which include a provision that the applicant must not have been convicted of a serious offense, or of a misdemeanor in the state or of any offense in any other jurisdiction which, if committed in this state, would constitute a misdemeanor, and which, in the discretion of the secretary [of the Department of State], bears such a relationship to the performance of the duties of a security guard, as to constitute a bar to employment. Id. § 89-h(5). "Serious offense" is defined in the act to include certain felonies. Id. , § 89-f(13). 2 The act provides that the Department must issue a registration card unless it determines that the applicant does not meet the requirements of section 89-h or is unable to perform security guard functions. Id. , § 89-k(1). Registration may be suspended or revoked in circumstances described in the act. Id. § 89-l The security guard act also provides: The provisions of this article shall govern notwithstanding any other law to the contrary and further, no local law shall be enacted which shall require any fee or license for the licensure [or] registration [of] security guards. Id. § 89-r. (Footnote omitted.)

Accordingly, you ask whether the Commission is free to reject a candidate based upon the candidate's criminal history when the Secretary has concluded, as evidenced by registration of the candidate, that the past conviction does not bar the candidate from employment as a security guard. We conclude that the Legislature did not intend to preclude employers from establishing hiring standards for security guards that exceed the registration standards of the act. It simply established minimum requirements for employment as a security guard and preempted local registration or licensing provisions.

In 1992, the Legislature set forth its findings on the necessity for enacting the act. L 1992, ch 336, § 1. It noted that the provision of security guard services was a rapidly growing industry in the State. At that time guards were not regulated, licensed, required to complete minimum training or required to undergo a criminal history check as a condition of hiring. The Legislature went on to state: The legislature further finds that the proper screening, hiring and training of security guards is a matter of state concern and compelling state interest to ensure that such security guards meet certain minimum recruitment and training standards as this industry and the demands placed upon it grows daily. Therefore, the legislature hereby finds and declares that because of the large number of unregulated and unlicensed security guards who may lack sufficient training and their nexus to the general public, the state should establish uniform standards for the employment, registration, training, 3 enforcement and liability insurance coverage of security guards and the security guard industry within the state. Id.

Counsel to the Secretary of State has advised us that, in his opinion, these legislative findings indicate that the Legislature intended the security guard act to establish minimum qualifications for a person to be registered, and, therefore, employed as a security guard and that nothing in the findings or in the act itself suggests that the Legislature intended to pre-empt the discretion of an employer to impose higher standards, including higher standards regarding the applicant's criminal history. September 17, 1996 letter from Michael
E. Stafford, Esq. to James D. Cole, Esq., attached. Legislative history also supports the conclusion that the Legislature intended to establish minimum standards and not to bar employers from imposing more stringent requirements. The aim of the legislation was to protect the public by restricting security guard status to those qualified to perform security guard functions properly and to remove those who, due to criminal history or other reasons, should not be employed in the field. Bill Jacket, L 1992, ch 336, Memorandum in Support from Department of State, pp 26-27. It is consistent with this purpose for an employer to use hiring standards that are more stringent than the registration requirements of the act. The sponsor's memorandum in support of the legislation states that there is a compelling State interest to establish a Statewide minimum standard for hiring and training security guards. Bill Jacket, L 1992 ch 336, Memorandum in Support, pp 7 -8. A separate letter from the Senate sponsor also emphasizes that the public interest requires enactment of minimum standards. Id. , pp 11-12, June 25, 1992 letter from Senator Mega to Elizabeth Moore, Counsel to the Governor.

Accordingly, the Commission may evaluate the candidate's criminal history as it bears on fitness for employment as a security guard notwithstanding that the Department has registered the candidate. We also note that the Legislature has established a State policy to encourage the licensure and employment of persons previously convicted of one or more criminal offenses. A private employer or public agency may not deny a license or employment by reason of the applicant's having been previously convicted of one or more criminal offenses, or by reason of a finding of lack of "good moral character" when such finding is based upon the fact that the applicant has previously been convicted of one or more criminal offenses, unless:

(1) there is a direct relationship between one or more of the previous criminal offenses and the specific license or employment sought; or (2) the issuance of the license or the granting of the employment would involve an unreasonable risk to property or to the safety or welfare of specific individuals or the general public. Correction Law § 752.

In a prior opinion, we stated: In making this determination, the licensing officer or employer is required to consider certain factors (see , id. , § 753). One factor is the public policy of the State "to encourage the licensure and employment of persons previously convicted of one or more criminal offenses" (id. § 753[1][a]). Consideration must be given to a certificate of relief from disabilities or a certificate of good conduct issued to the applicant, which creates a presumption of rehabilitation in regard to the offenses ccovered by these certificates (id. , § 753[2]). (See also Op Atty Gen [Inf] 81-7, 82-73; Op Atty Gen [Inf] 84- 37). Accordingly, we conclude that the security guard act does not preclude the Commission from considering the applicant's criminal history and denying employment. That decision, however, must be in accord with the requirements of Correction Law Article 23-A.

Very truly yours,
SIOBHAN S. CRARY
Assistant Attorney General

1998 N.Y. Op. Atty. Gen 23 , 1998 WL 643362 (N.Y.A.G) (July 30, 1998) (F8)

CIVIL RIGHTS LAW § 79; CIVIL SERVICE LAW § 50(4)(d); CORRECTION LAW §§ 30, 700(1)(a), 701(3), 752; CRIMINAL PROCEDURE LAW § 2.10; ELECTION LAW § 5-106; JUDICIARY LAW §

510; PENAL LAW §§ 10.00(5), 265.20(a)(1)(c), 400.00; PUBLIC OFFICERS LAW §§ 3-b, 30; PUB L 90-351, TITLE VII §§ 1201-1203; PUB L 105-61 (111 Stat 1277); 18 USC §§ 921, et seq. ; 18 USCA § 922(g); 18 USCA § 925.

Analysis of whether persons convicted of State felonies or misdemeanor crimes of domestic violence may be appointed as peace officers or whether their convictions preclude such appointments because they are prohibited from possessing firearms under the federal Gun Control Act and/or State law.

Hon. Kenneth J. Connolly Formal Opinion
Division of Criminal
Justice Services
Executive Park Tower
Stuyvesant Plaza

Albany, New York 12203-3764

Dear Mr. Connolly:
You have requested a formal opinion as to whether individuals convicted of either felonies or misdemeanor crimes of domestic violence may be appointed as peace officers. You have asked that we consider whether their convictions preclude such appointment by virtue of the provisions of the federal Gun Control Act (GCA), 18 USC §§ 921, et seq. The Division of Criminal Justice Services certifies peace officers upon successful completion of the training required by law. Criminal Procedure Law § 2.30.

The only State statutory requirements for appointment as a peace officer are that an individual be a United States citizen, a State resident, and possess the right to vote. Public Officers Law § 3-b. A felon under sentence would be disqualified from appointment because he/she does not possess the right to vote. Election Law § 5-106(2). Accordingly, the question narrows to whether an individual convicted of a felony, who has completed his/her sentence, or an individual convicted of a misdemeanor crime of domestic violence, may possess a firearm.

We will first consider whether a felon may possess a firearm under the federal GCA. We will then consider whether a person convicted of a misdemeanor crime of domestic violence may possess a firearm under the Federal Act. Finally, we will discuss the discretion of appointing authorities regarding the appointment of peace officers.

I. THE POSSESSION OF FIREARMS BY STATE FELONS UNDER THE FEDERAL GUN CONTROL ACT

The GCA provides, in pertinent part, as follows:

It shall be unlawful for any person . . . who has been convicted in any court of a crime punishable by imprisonment for a term exceeding one year . . . to ship or transport in interstate or foreign commerce, or possess in or affecting commerce, any firearm or ammunition; or to receive any firearm or ammunition which has been shipped or transported in interstate or foreign commerce." 18 USCA § 922(g).

However, "[t]he provisions of this chapter . . . shall not apply with respect to the transportation, shipment, receipt, possession, or importation of any firearm or ammunition imported for, sold or shipped to, or issued for the use of, the United States or any department or agency thereof or any State or any department, agency, or political subdivision thereof." 18 USCA § 925(a)(1). In New York, Criminal Procedure Law § 2.10 provides an exclusive list of persons designated as "peace officers." Many of the peace officers on this list are employed by the State and local governments and, therefore, the firearms they are issued by their employers would be "for the use of . . . the State or any department, agency or political subdivision thereof," thus falling within the statutory exception. 18 USCA § 925(a)(1). Accordingly, these peace officers come within the exception from the federal prohibitions on possessing a firearm. See , Hyland v Fukuda , 580 F2d 977, 979 (9th Cir 1978); United States v Kozerski 518 F Supp 1082, 1090-91 (DNH 1981), affd , 740 F2d 952 (1st Cir), cert denied , 469 US 842 (1984).

Appointing authorities in New York must analyze the applicability of the GCA to persons convicted in other jurisdictions, looking to the law of those jurisdictions for guidance. Other peace officers are employed privately and, therefore, are not covered by the governmental employment exception contained in the GCA. For this class of peace officer, we must determine whether, in its reference to crimes punishable by imprisonment for a term exceeding one year, the GCA applies to individuals convicted of felonies. As a preliminary matter, under the GCA persons convicted of a covered crime are only prohibited from shipping, transporting, possessing, or receiving firearms or ammunition that have been shipped or transported "in interstate or foreign commerce" or possessed "in or affecting commerce." 18 USCA § 922(g). In Scarborough v United States , 431 US 563 (1977), the Supreme Court of the United States held that proof that the possessed firearm previously traveled in interstate commerce was sufficient to satisfy the statutorily required nexus between the possession of the firearm by the convicted felon and interstate commerce. The Court found "no indication that Congress intended to require any more than the minimal nexus that the firearm have [sic] been, at some time, in interstate commerce." Scarborough , 431 US at 575.

Based on Scarborough, courts have held that manufacture of firearms or ammunition outside of the state or previous travel in interstate commerce is sufficient to satisfy the commerce requirement. See , United States v Sanders , 35 F3d 61 (2d Cir), cert denied , 513 US 994 (1994); United States v Carter , 981 F2d 645 (2d Cir 1992), cert denied , 507 US 1023 (1993); United States v Ray , 41 F3d 1504 (4th Cir 1994). Whether an individual with a conviction falls within the prohibitions of the GCA depends upon the "law of the jurisdiction in which the proceedings were held." 18 USCA § 921(20). Therefore, we should look to the law of the jurisdiction in which the conviction occurred for guidance regarding the designation of crimes with terms of imprisonment exceeding one year. For purposes of this opinion, we will limit our analysis to persons convicted under New York law.

Under New York law a felony is defined as "an offense for which a sentence to a term of imprisonment in excess of one year may be imposed." Penal Law § 10.00(5). Thus, as a general matter, under the GCA a New York felon may not possess a firearm if the required nexus to interstate commerce is present.

However, under the GCA, "[a]ny conviction which has been expunged, or set aside or for which a person has been pardoned or has had civil rights restored shall not be considered a conviction for purposes of this chapter, unless such pardon, expungement, or restoration of civil rights expressly provides that the person may not ship, transport, possess or receive firearms." 18 USCA § 921(20). Under this statute, the "civil rights restored" must include at least the right to vote, to hold public office, and to serve as a juror. See , McGrath v United States , 60 F3d 1005, 1007 (2d Cir 1995), cert denied, 516 US 1121 (1996). These have been described as the core civil rights for purposes of the GCA. Id. Additionally, for the exception to apply, the person must not be prohibited under any State statutory provision from shipping, transporting, possessing or receiving firearms. 18 USCA § 921(20).

A. The Core Civil Rights
In New York, an individual convicted of a felony, who has been sentenced to imprisonment in a State correctional facility for a term less than for life or for an indeterminate term having a minimum of one day and a maximum of natural life, forfeits all of his/her civil rights, including, inter alia , the right to vote, to hold public office, and to serve as a juror. Civil Rights Law § 79. The right to vote and to hold public office are automatically restored to New York felons upon the completion of their sentences, including all parole. Election Law § 5-106(2); Civil Rights Law § 79. Such automatic restoration is sufficient to constitute a restoration of these rights within the meaning of the GCA. See , McGrath v United States , supra , at 1008. However, New York felons are statutorily prohibited from serving as jurors. Judiciary Law § 510. This statutory bar may be removed by obtaining a Certificate of Relief from Disabilities issued pursuant to Correction Law § 701. See 1991 Op Atty Gen 10 ("In our view, the language defining the relief granted by these certificates is

sufficiently broad to include the right of a felon to serve as a juror . . .". "A certificate of relief from disabilities may be granted as provided in this article to relieve an eligible offender of any forfeiture or disability, or remove any bar to his employment, automatically imposed by law by reason of his conviction of the crime or offense specified therein." Correction Law § 701. A Certificate of Relief from Disabilities, removing the statutory bar to serve as a juror, is sufficient to restore that right within the meaning of the GCA. See , McGrath v United States , supra , at 1008.

Accordingly, under the GCA, a State felon whose conviction has been expunged or set aside, or who has been pardoned or has had his/her civil rights restored, including the right to serve as a juror pursuant to a Certificate of Relief from Disabilities, may possess a firearm under the GCA, absent any State prohibition preventing the possession of firearms.

B. Firearms Licenses Under State Law

Under the GCA, a felon may not possess a firearm if he/she is prohibited, under any State statutory provision, from shipping, transporting, possessing or receiving firearms. 18 USCA § 921(20). Some peace officers are authorized to possess firearms by virtue of their peace officer status. Penal Law § 265.20(a)(1)(c); Criminal Procedure Law § 2.10. However, others must obtain firearms licenses under Penal Law § 400.00 prior to possessing, repairing or disposing of firearms. Criminal Procedure Law § 2.10. Penal Law § 400.00 governs the licensing of firearms in New York. Under Penal Law § 400.00, individuals convicted "anywhere of a felony" may not be issued a firearms license. Under decisional law, this disability may be removed if an individual obtains a Certificate of Relief from Disabilities pursuant to Correction Law § 701. See , Hines v Kelly, 222 AD2d 277, 278 (1st Dept 1995) (Certificate of Relief from Disabilities sufficient to remove automatic bar to licensure), lv denied 87 NY2d 810 (1996); People v Flook , 164 Misc 2d 284, 285 (NY County Ct 1995); 1975 Op Atty Gen 306; 1971 Op Atty Gen 8. But see , Matter of Alarie , 168 Misc 2d 329, 330 (NY County Ct 1996) (declining to follow dicta in People v Flook supra that a Certificate of Relief from Disabilities may remove the statutory bar to apply for or receive a firearms license). Although a Certificate of Relief from Disabilities might remove an absolute statutory bar to licensure, the licensing officer is still vested with broad discretion to deny a felon a firearms license. A Certificate of Relief from Disabilities does not prevent "any judicial, administrative, licensing or other body, board or authority from relying upon the conviction specified therein as the basis for the exercise of its discretionary power to suspend, revoke, refuse to issue or refuse to renew any license, permit or other authority or privilege." Correction Law § 701(3) (emphasis added). See , Hines v Kelly supra, at 278 (although Certificate of Relief from Disabilities might remove the automatic bar to licensure, it did not "prevent respondent from relying on the convictions in the exercise of his statutory discretion to deny a license for 'lack of good moral character' or 'good cause'"). Therefore, under both the GCA and State law, a State felon may be appointed as a peace officer, where such appointment requires the issuance of a firearms license, if he/she is issued a Certificate of Relief from Disabilities and the licensing officer grants a firearms license under Penal Law § 400.00.

II. THE POSSESSION OF FIREARMS BY PERSONS CONVICTED OF MISDEMEANOR CRIMES OF DOMESTIC VIOLENCE UNDER THE FEDERAL GUN CONTROL ACT

The 1996 amendments to the GCA (the "domestic violence amendments") provide, in pertinent part, as follows: It shall be unlawful for any person-- . . . (9) who has been convicted in any court of a misdemeanor crime of domestic violence, to ship or transport in interstate or foreign commerce, or possess in or affecting commerce, any firearm or ammunition; or to receive any firearm or ammunition which has been shipped or transported in interstate or foreign commerce. 18 USCA § 922(g)(9).

A "misdemeanor crime of domestic violence" means an offense that:
(A) . . . (i) is a misdemeanor under Federal or State law; and (ii) has, as an element, the use or attempted use of physical force, or the threatened use of a deadly weapon, committed by a current or former spouse, parent, or guardian of the victim, by a person with whom the victim shares a child in common, by a person who is cohabiting with or has cohabited with the victim as a spouse, parent, or guardian, or by a person similarly situated to a spouse, parent, or guardian of the victim.

. . .

(B). . . (ii) A person shall not be considered to have been convicted of such an offense for purposes of this chapter if the conviction has been expunged or set aside, or is an offense for which the person has been pardoned or has had civil rights restored (if the law of the applicable jurisdiction provides for the loss of civil rights under such an offense) unless the pardon, expungement, or restoration of civil rights expressly provides that the person may not ship, transport, possess, or receive firearms. 18 USCA § 921(a)(33).

As stated above, the GCA, including the domestic violence amendments, applies only to firearms or ammunition that have been shipped or transported "in interstate or foreign commerce" or possessed "in or affecting commerce." 18 USCA § 922(g). The domestic violence amendments do not contain the exception for those engaged in governmental employment as discussed above with respect to crimes punishable for a term in prison of more than one year. The statutory language regarding the issuance of firearms for the use of the "United States or any department or agency thereof or any State or any department, agency, or political subdivision thereof" is not made applicable to convictions of misdemeanor crimes of domestic violence. 18 USCA § 925(a)(1). Appointing authorities in New York must analyze the applicability of the GCA to persons convicted of misdemeanor crimes of domestic violence in other jurisdictions, looking to the law of those jurisdictions for guidance. We note that pursuant to Public Officers Law § 30, a public officer convicted of a misdemeanor which violates the officer's oath of office will forfeit that public office. See , e.g., Matter of Duffy v Ward , 81 NY2d 127 (1993). Under the Correction Law, a Certificate of Relief from Disabilities cannot restore a public office. Correction Law § 701(1). However, the domestic violence amendments do exempt persons convicted of misdemeanor crimes of domestic violence who have had their civil rights restored from the provisions of the GCA. Under the statute, whether a person's civil rights can be "restored" depends upon whether the person ever lost any civil rights as a result of the subject conviction. This seems clear from the parenthetical language "(if the law of the applicable jurisdiction provides for the loss of civil rights under such an offense)." 18 USCA § 921(a)(33). For this purpose, federal courts consider the core civil rights to be the right to vote, to serve on a jury, and to hold public office. See , McGrath v United States , supra , at 1007. The question is whether State law "provides for the loss of civil rights under such an offense." 18 USCA § 921(a)(33). For purposes of this opinion, we will limit our analysis to persons convicted under New York law.

Under New York law, a person convicted of a misdemeanor does not forfeit these core civil rights. See Civil Rights Law § 79; Public Officers Law § 30; People v Ahearn , 196 NY 221, 232 (1909). In McGrath v United States , the United States Court of Appeals for the Second Circuit held that a state's failure to divest felons of their civil rights does not qualify as a "restoration" under the federal statute. McGrath v United States , supra, at 1008. In McGrath , the court was interpreting a similar provision of the GCA, 18 USCA § 921(a)(20), which provides, in pertinent part: Any conviction which has been expunged, or set aside or for which a person has been pardoned or has had civil rights restored shall not be considered a conviction for purposes of this chapter, unless such pardon, expungement, or restoration of civil rights expressly provides that the person may not

Other courts have held that a person's civil rights are deemed "restored" for purposes of the federal statute, even if they were never taken away. See , United States v Indelicato 97 F3d 627 (1st Cir 1996), cert denied , __ US __, 117 S Ct 1013 (1997); United States v Cassidy , 899 F2d 543, 549 n13 (6th Cir 1990). It should be noted, however, that these courts were not analyzing the "restoration" language in the domestic violence amendments. Additionally, one court has suggested that "[s]uch an interpretation would . . . be nonsensical in the context of [the domestic violence amendments] for it would have the effect of prohibiting very few domestic violence misdemeanants from possessing a firearm." National Association of Government Employees, Inc. v Barrett , 968 F Supp 1564, 1575 n15 (ND Ga 1997). ship, transport, possess, or receive firearms. Although the court was sympathetic to the potential for injustice created by the restoration language, it noted that "the role of the court is to give effect to the legislation Congress has passed, not to legislation it might pass, if it further studied the question." McGrath v United States , supra at 1009. The domestic violence amendments, including the parenthetical language within the exemption provisions of these amendments, were enacted subsequent to McGrath . Therefore, a logical inference can be made that Congress, upon further study of the question, intended to make it clear that persons convicted of misdemeanor crimes of domestic violence would not have their civil rights "restored" if they had never been lost, by inserting the parenthetical language in 18 USCA § 921(a)(33), providing that a person shall not be considered to have been convicted of such an offense for purposes of this chapter if the conviction has been expunged or set aside, or is an offense for which the person has been pardoned or has had civil rights restored (if the law of the applicable jurisdiction provides for the loss of civil rights under such an offense). 18 USCA § 921(a)(33)(emphasis added). Moreover, the legislative history of these amendments states that because the We note that Congress is not currently appropriating funds for the investigation and review of individual requests for relief from federal firearms disabilities under 18 USCA § 925(c). Pub L 105-61 (111 Stat 1277). [l]oss of these [core civil] rights generally does not flow from a misdemeanor conviction, .\ . . [the] language [on civil rights restoration] is probably irrelevant to most, if not all, of those offenders covered . . .[by] the new ban. 142 Cong Rec S11877-78 (September 30, 1996) (statement of Sen. McCain).

In further support of this proposition, in United States v Smith , No. CR 96-2140 (ND Iowa July 14, 1997), the United States District Court for the Northern District of Iowa recently held that: [s]ection 921(a)(33)(B)(ii) specifically provides that the restoration of civil rights exception applies only where the "applicable jurisdiction provides for the loss of civil rights under such an offense". Thus, where a defendant's civil rights are not affected by the conviction . . . the defendant cannot have his civil rights restored for purposes of section 921(a)(33)(B)(ii). See also , National Association of Government Employees, Inc. v Barrett , 968 F Supp 1564, 1575 (ND Ga 1997) ("the fact that states' laws differ, with some failing to divest a misdemeanant of his or her civil rights such that they cannot be restored, does not render . . . [the domestic violence amendments] unconstitutional").

We note that an individual convicted of a misdemeanor crime of domestic violence may apply to the Secretary of the Treasury for relief from the disabilities imposed by the GCA. Such relief may be granted if it is satisfactorily established "that the circumstances regarding the disability, and the applicant's record and reputation, are such that the applicant will not be likely to act in a manner dangerous to public safety and that the granting of the relief would not be contrary to the public interest." 18 USCA § 925(c).

Therefore, a person convicted in New York of a misdemeanor crime of domestic violence may not be issued a firearm under the GCA unless the conviction has been expunged or set aside, or is an offense for which the person has been pardoned or unless the person has received, upon an application to the Secretary of the Treasury, relief from federal firearms disabilities.

III. DISCRETION OF APPOINTING AUTHORITIES

Although certain persons convicted of either State felonies or misdemeanor crimes of domestic violence may be issued firearms, the appointing authority can still use its discretion in appointing peace officers and may take into account an applicant's prior convictions. Civil Service Law § 50(4)(d); Matter of Golimowski v Bellamy , AD2d , 668 NYS2d 968(4th Dept 1997); Matter of Frederick v Civil Service Commission , 175 AD2d 428 (3d Dept 1991). However, the appointing authority may not deny an application for employment solely by reason of the applicant's having been previously convicted of one or more criminal offenses, or by reason of finding of lack of "good moral character" when such finding is based upon the fact that the applicant has previously been convicted of one or more criminal offenses, unless: (1) there is a direct relationship between one or more of the previous criminal offenses and the specific license or employment sought; or (2) the issuance of the license or the granting of the employment would involve an unreasonable risk to property or to the safety or welfare of specific individuals or the general public. Correction Law § 752. Therefore, State, local governments and other employers of peace officers may exercise some discretion in making employment decisions regarding persons convicted of criminal offenses.

Very truly yours,
DENNIS C. VACCO
Attorney General

APPLICATION FOR CERTIFICATE OF RELIEF
OF CIVIL DISABILITIES

STATE OF NEW YORK APPLICATION BY AN ELIGIBLE OFFENDER FOR CERTIFICATE OF RELIEF FROM DISABILITIES	FOR COURT OR BOARD OF PAROLE Docket, File or other Identifier

1. Applicant's Last Name   First Name   Initial | 3. NYSID (if known)

2. Address (Street and House Number, City, State, ZIP)

4. Sex ☐ Male ☐ Female	5. Race	6. Height Ft In.	7. Date of Birth (Month/Day/Year)
8. Offense for which convicted		9. Date of arrest	10. Date of sentence

11. Court of Disposition (Court, Part, Term, Venue)	12. Certificate issued by: ☐ Court indicated in box 11 ☐ State Board of Parole
	13. ☐ Certificate is intended to replace an existing certificate, issued on: ☐ Not applicable

14. Application is hereby made for a grant of a *Certificate of Relief from Disabilities* which will
☐ a. relieve the holder of all forfeitures, and of all disabilities and bars to employment, excluding the right to retain or to be eligible for public office, by virtue of the fact that the certificate is issued at the time of sentence.
☐ b. relieve the holder of all disabilities and bars to employment, excluding the right to be eligible for public office.
☐ c. relieve the holder of the forfeitures, disabilities or bars to employment hereinafter enumerated

15. The applicant agrees to allow an investigation to be made to determine his or her fitness for a certificate of relief from disabilities, pursuant to Correction Law Article 23.

Applicant's Signature _____   Date _____
sign in the presence of a notary

16.   State of New York)
         County of _____)   ss.:

_____, being duly sworn, deposes and says that __he is the applicant named in the within application; that __he has read the foregoing application and knows the contents thereof; that the same is true to   his   own knowledge, except as to the matters therein stated to be alleged on information and belief, and that as to those matters __he believes it to be true.

Sworn to before me this _____ day of _____ 20___

_____
Notary Public
affix stamp, seal

DC-DPCA-52 (6-05)

STATE OF NEW YORK
CERTIFICATE OF RELIEF FROM DISABILITIES

FOR COURT OR BOARD OF PAROLE
Docket, File or other Identifier

This certificate is issued to the holder from all or certain enumerated disabilities, forfeitures, or bars to his employment automatically imposed by law by reason of his conviction of the crime or of the offense specified herein.

This certificate shall NOT be deemed nor constructed to be a pardon.

See reverse side for explanation of the law governing this certificate, or http://courts.state.ny.us/courts/10jd/suffolk/dist/RCD.shtml
The original certificate is to be presented to the person to whom awarded. One copy is to be retained by the issuing agency, and one copy is to be filed with the NYS Division of Criminal Justice Services, 4 Tower Place, Albany, NY 12203-3702

1. Used by DCJS	Holder of Certificate 2. Last Name, First Name, Initial	3. NYSID (If unknown, supply fingerprints to DCJS. If fingerprints are unobtainable, complete 15-18 below)

4. Crime or Offense for which convicted	5. Date of arrest	6. Date of sentence

7. Court of Disposition (Court, Part, Term, Venue)	8. Certificate issued by: ☐ Court indicated in box 7 ☐ State Board of Parole

9. Date this certificate issued	10. ☐ Certificate replaces an existing Certificate of Relief from Disabilities, previously issued on: ☐ Not applicable

11. This certificate shall

☐ a. relieve the holder of all forfeitures, and of all disabilities and bars to employment, excluding the right to retain or to be eligible for public office, by virtue of the fact that the certificate is issued at the time of sentence.

☐ b. relieve the holder of all disabilities and bars to employment, excluding the right to be eligible for public office.

☐ c. relieve the holder of the forfeitures, disabilities or bars hereinafter enumerated

12. ☐ This certificate shall be considered permanent.

☐ This certificate shall be considered temporary until _____. After this date, unless revoked earlier by issuing court or parole board, this certificate shall be considered permanent. A person who knowingly uses or attempts to use a revoked certificate in order to obtain or exercise any right or privilege that he/she would not be entitled to obtain or to exercise without valid certificate shall be guilty of a misdemeanor.

13.

14.

Signature of issuing official	Name of issuing official	title of issuing official

15. Sex ☐ Male ☐ Female	16. Race	17. Height Ft___ In.___	18. Date of Birth (Month/Day/Year)

DC- DPCA-53 (6/05) Proposed Certificate submitted with DC- DPCA-52   original   copy to file   copy to DCJS

CERTIFICATE OF GOOD CONDUCT FORM

STATE OF NEW YORK
DEPARTMENT OF CORRECTIONS AND COMMUNITY SUPERVISION
CERTIFICATE REVIEW UNIT
The Harriman State Campus – Building 2
1220 Washington Avenue
Albany, NY 12226-2050
(518) 485-8953

In response to your recent request, attached is an application for a Certificate of Relief from Disabilities or Certificate of Good Conduct. **Return the completed original application form (not a copy), with all signatures notarized, to the Certificate Review Unit at the above address.**

You must submit, with the original application, proof of payment of income taxes for the last three years. Satisfactory proof will be copies (do not sent originals – they will not be returned) of your federal income tax returns, plus statements of wages (W-2 Forms), and copies of all statements of Miscellaneous Income (Form 1099). If you do not have copies, you may contact the IRS at 1-800-829-1040, and they will provide you with transcripts. If you have received Public Assistance or Social Security for any or all of this three-year period, a printout from the agency providing you with support must be submitted, showing all benefits received.

If you were convicted of a felony in a state other than New York, or in a Federal Court, you may need to be fingerprinted. You will be notified by mail if this applies to you.

An investigation into your circumstances is required and will include, but not necessarily be limited to, the following:

1. Employment history and means of support
2. Proof of payment of income taxes for the last three years
3. Proof of payment of any fines or restitution

After all necessary documents and records have been received, a field representative will contact you and arrange for an interview at your residence to clarify any questions and verify your current circumstances. The New York State Department of Corrections and Community Supervision will then evaluate your application to determine whether a certificate will be granted. Statute permits the Department of Corrections and Community Supervision to remove one, more than one, or all allowable disabilities.

This is a lengthy process, therefore, your cooperation is essential.

If, during the process, you move or change your phone number, contact this office as soon as possible.

If you desire restoration of firearms privileges and were convicted of a felony in Federal Court, you must seek relief from the Bureau of Alcohol, Tobacco and Firearms. If you were convicted of a felony in another state, you must seek relief from that state for restoration of firearms privileges.

IMPORTANT INFORMATION (Detach and retain for your records)

Granting of a Certificate removes disabilities you incurred but does not remove the underlying conviction. Neither does it limit a prospective employer or licensing agency from exercising lawful discretion to refuse employment, or to refuse to grant or renew any license, permit, or privilege.

The information below is for your guidance in determining your eligibility and the authority to which you should apply. For more specific information, consult Article 23 (Sections 700-706) of New York State Correction Law.

I. <u>Eligibility</u>

    A. **CERTIFICATE OF RELIEF FROM DISABILITIES:** An eligible offender is one who has been convicted of any number of misdemeanors and up to one felony.

    B. **CERTIFICATE OF GOOD CONDUCT:** This certificate is reserved for an individual who has been convicted of two or more separate felonies or an individual seeking the removal of a disability pertaining to a specific public office. One must have demonstrated a minimum period of good conduct in the community. The statutory waiting period is five years (if the highest felony on your criminal history record is an A or B) or three years (if the highest felony on your criminal history record is a C, D or E) or one year (if you have only misdemeanors on your criminal history record). The waiting period begins at the time of your last release from incarceration to community supervision, or discharge from incarceration by maximum expiration, or your last criminal conviction (which ever comes later).

II. <u>Issuing Authority (who to apply to)</u>

    A. **CERTIFICATE OF RELIEF FROM DISABILITIES:**

        The sentencing court is the issuing authority in all instances except where a conviction:

        1. results in commitment to a New York State correctional facility, or

        2. was in a federal court or court of another state and the applicant is presently a resident of New York State.

        Certificates in these cases shall be issued by the New York State Department of Corrections and Community Supervision.

    B. **CERTIFICATES OF GOOD CONDUCT:**

        Only the Department of Corrections and Community Supervision is authorized to issue this certificate.

Determine which certificate you are eligible for and submit your application to the appropriate issuing authority. An investigation into your circumstances is required.

<u>Sentencing Court</u>	<u>NYS Department of Corrections and Community Supervision</u>
Consult the local telephone directory for address	State of New York Department of Corrections and Community Supervision Certificate Review Unit The Harriman State Campus – Building 2 1220 Washington Avenue Albany, NY 12226-2050

Rev. 11/2012

NEW YORK STATE
DEPARTMENT OF CORRECTIONS AND COMMUNITY SUPERVISION
CERTIFICATE REVIEW UNIT

1. **Purpose for the certificate (be specific):** _____

    _____

IDENTIFYING

2. **Name:** _____

               (Last)   (First)   (Middle)   (Jr., Sr.)

3: **Date of Birth:** _____   4:   **Birth Place**_____

                                                            (City, State)

5. **Sex:** ( ) Male   ( ) Female

6. **Race:** ( ) African/American   ( ) Native American   ( ) Caucasian

          ( ) Chinese   ( ) Hispanic   ( ) Japanese   ( ) Other

7. **Social Security Number:**   _____-_____-_____

8. **Height:** _____ **9. Weight:** _____ **10. Eye Color:** _____ **11. Hair Color:** _____

12. **Have you ever been known by any other name? If yes, indicate below and state reason(s) for change of name.**

    Name: **Reason for Change of Name:**

    _____   _____

    _____   _____

RESIDENCE

13. **Present Address:**

    _____

         (Street)   (City)   (State)   (Zip Code)

    _____

       (Apt. No.)   (Home Phone/Cell Phone)   (County)

14. **For your present residence, list all members of your household below:**

Name	Age	Relationship
_____	_____	_____
_____	_____	_____
_____	_____	_____
_____	_____	_____

15. **List below ALL previous residences which when added to your present residence equal 5 years.**

Address (Include City and State)   From – To

_____   _____

_____   _____

_____   _____

_____   _____

[If additional space is required, use reverse side of this page]

Employment Record

16. **List your occupations and employers for the last 5 years or back to the time you left school. Do not omit any. Start with your present employer and work back. For each period you were unemployed, give dates of the period.**

Dates (mo. & yr.) From To	Occupation/ Position	Name & Address of Employer	Full P/T	Immediate Supervisor	Weekly Salary
_____ Present	_____		_____	_____	_____
_____ _____	_____	_____	_____	_____	_____
_____ _____	_____	_____	_____	_____	_____
_____ _____	_____	_____	_____	_____	_____
_____ _____	_____	_____	_____	_____	_____
_____ _____	_____	_____	_____	_____	_____
_____ _____	_____	_____	_____	_____	_____

[If additional space is required, use reverse side of this page]

CITIZENSHIP

17. **Are you a citizen of the United States? (check one)**

( ) Yes, by birth;   ( ) Yes, by Naturalization, Certificate Number _____

If not a citizen, provide _____   _____
                                        Alien Registration Number   Country

18. **If you were ever in the Armed Forces of the United States, indicate the following:**

Branch of Service:_____   Date of Entry into Active Duty: _____

Date of Discharge: _____   Honorable Discharge: ( ) Yes   ( ) No

Veterans Administration Claim Number (if any):   _____

SOCIAL STATUS

19. **Marital Status:** ( ) Single ( ) Married ( ) Separated ( ) Divorced
( ) Widow(er) ( ) Annulled

20. **How many times have you been married?:**_____**For each marriage, give the following information:**

Name Used	Wife's Maiden Name or Husband's full name	Date Married/ Divorced
_____	_____	_____
_____	_____	

21. **Address of your present spouse:** _____

22. **How many children do you have?:** _____

Give the following information about them:

Name	Age	Address	Currently resides with
_____	_____	_____	_____
_____	_____	_____	_____
_____	_____	_____	_____
_____	_____	_____	_____

23. **If at any time you cohabited with a person or persons to whom you were not legally married, give name(s) and present address(es). [If additional space is required, use reverse side of this page]**

Name	Address
_____	_____

24. **LICENSES held by you (Motor Vehicle, Trade, Professional or Pistol Permit). [If additional space is required, use reverse side of this page]**

Type of License	Licensing Agency	License Number	Date Issued	Expires
_____	_____	_____	_____	_____

25. **REFERENCES: Provide the complete names and mailing addresses of 2 people who will be contacted to provide character references on your behalf.**

Name	Address	Phone
_____	_____	_____
_____	_____	_____

CRIMINAL HISTORY

26. **If known:** NYSID#_____ FBI#_____ PRISON#_____

27. **RECORD OF CONVICTIONS: ALL CONVICTIONS MUST BE LISTED. ANY WILLFUL OMISSION WILL BE CONSTRUED AS A FALSIFICATION. You should rely on your own information. If any uncertainty exists, a statement to that effect will remove grounds for rejection of your application on the basis of falsification.**

Date	Court and Location	Charge – do not use codes	Sentence
_____	_____	_____	_____
_____	_____	_____	_____
_____	_____	_____	_____
_____	_____	_____	_____
_____	_____	_____	_____
_____	_____	_____	_____

28. **If you have been on probation and/or parole/community supervision, check:**
    ( ) **Probation**   ( ) **Parole/Community Supervision**

    From   To   Parole/Community Supervision Officer/Probation Officer's Name and Address where you reported

    _____ _____ _____

    _____ _____ _____

29. **If you have ever been committed to prison, reformatory, penitentiary or other institution, furnish the following:**

Date Committed	Charge	Name of Institution and Location	Date of Release
_____	_____	_____	_____
_____	_____	_____	_____
_____	_____	_____	_____
_____	_____	_____	_____
_____	_____	_____	_____

30. **If you previously applied for a Certificate of Relief from Disabilities, furnish:**

    Place: _____ Date: _____ Was it granted? _____

31. **If you previously applied for a Certificate of Good Conduct, furnish:**

    Place: _____ Date: _____ Was it granted? _____

32. I agree to allow an investigation to be made to determine my fitness for a certificate pursuant to Article 23 of the NYS Correction Law. I hereby certify that I have fully and truthfully answered all of the above questions.

Applicant's Signature: _____ Date: _____

YOU MUST HAVE BOTH #33 AND #34 SIGNED BY A NOTARY PUBLIC

33. State of New York
County of_____

_____ being duly sworn, deposes and says that he/she is the applicant named within the application: that he/she has read the foregoing application and knows the contents thereof; that the same is true to his/her own knowledge, except as to the matters therein stated to be alleged on information and belief, and that as to those matters he/she believes it to be true.

_____

Notary Public

34. **AUTHORIZATION FOR RELEASE OF INFORMATION**

I,_____, have applied to the New York State Department of Corrections and Community Supervision for a Certificate of Relief from Disabilities/Good Conduct. To facilitate the investigation of my application, I hereby authorize any individual, private business concern, state or federal agency to release to any authorized representative of the Department of Corrections and Community Supervision any information such person, private business concern, state or federal agency may have in its possession concerning me or my activities.

_____

Signature   Date

_____

Notary Public   Date

EEOC Enforcement Guidance	**Number** 915.002 **Date** 4/25/2012

1.   **SUBJECT**: Enforcement Guidance on the Consideration of Arrest and Conviction Records in Employment Decisions Under Title VII of the Civil Rights Act of 1964, *as amended*, 42 U.S.C. § 2000e *et seq*.

2.   **PURPOSE**: The purpose of this Enforcement Guidance is to consolidate and update the U.S. Equal Employment Opportunity Commission's guidance documents regarding the use of arrest or conviction records in employment decisions under Title VII of the Civil Rights Act of 1964, as amended, 42 U.S.C. § 2000e *et seq*.

3.   **EFFECTIVE DATE**: Upon receipt.

4.   **EXPIRATION DATE**: This Notice will remain in effect until rescinded or superseded.

5.   **ORIGINATOR**: Office of Legal Counsel.

Consideration of Arrest and Conviction Records
in Employment Decisions Under Title VII
of the Civil Rights Act of 1964

Table of Contents

I. Summary

- An employer's use of an individual's criminal history in making employment decisions may, in some instances, violate the prohibition against employment discrimination under Title VII of the Civil Rights Act of 1964, as amended.

- The Guidance builds on longstanding court decisions and existing guidance documents that the U.S. Equal Employment Opportunity Commission (Commission or EEOC) issued over twenty years ago.

- The Guidance focuses on employment discrimination based on race and national origin. The Introduction provides information about criminal records, employer practices, and Title VII.

- The Guidance discusses the differences between arrest and conviction records.

  - The fact of an arrest does not establish that criminal conduct has occurred, and an exclusion based on an arrest, in itself, is not job related and consistent with business necessity. However, an employer may make an employment decision based on the conduct underlying an arrest if the conduct makes the individual unfit for the position in question.

  - In contrast, a conviction record will usually serve as sufficient evidence that a person engaged in particular conduct. In certain circumstances, however, there may be reasons for an employer not to rely on the conviction record alone when making an employment decision.

- The Guidance discusses disparate treatment and disparate impact analysis under Title VII.

  - A violation may occur when an employer treats criminal history information differently for different applicants or employees, based on their race or national origin (disparate treatment liability).

  - An employer's neutral policy (e.g., excluding applicants from employment based on certain criminal conduct) may disproportionately impact some individuals protected under Title VII, and may violate the law if not job related and consistent with business necessity (disparate impact liability).

    o National data supports a finding that criminal record exclusions have a disparate impact based on race and national origin. The national data provides a basis for the Commission to investigate Title VII disparate impact charges challenging criminal record exclusions.

o Two circumstances in which the Commission believes employers will consistently meet the "job related and consistent with business necessity" defense are as follows:

- The employer validates the criminal conduct exclusion for the position in question in light of the Uniform Guidelines on Employee Selection Procedures (if there is data or analysis about criminal conduct as related to subsequent work performance or behaviors); or

- The employer develops a targeted screen considering at least the nature of the crime, the time elapsed, and the nature of the job (the three factors identified by the court in *Green v. Missouri Pacific Railroad*, 549 F.2d 1158 (8th Cir. 1977)). The employer's policy then provides an opportunity for an individualized assessment for those people identified by the screen, to determine if the policy as applied is job related and consistent with business necessity. (Although Title VII does not require individualized assessment in all circumstances, the use of a screen that does not include individualized assessment is more likely to violate Title VII.).

- Compliance with other federal laws and/or regulations that conflict with Title VII is a defense to a charge of discrimination under Title VII.

- State and local laws or regulations are preempted by Title VII if they "purport[] to require or permit the doing of any act which would be an unlawful employment practice" under Title VII. 42 U.S.C. § 2000e-7.

- The Guidance concludes with best practices for employers.

II.   Introduction

The EEOC enforces Title VII of the Civil Rights Act of 1964 (Title VII) which prohibits employment discrimination based on race, color, religion, sex, or national origin.[1] This Enforcement Guidance is issued as part of the Commission's efforts to eliminate unlawful discrimination in employment screening, for hiring or retention, by entities covered by Title VII, including private employers as well as federal, state, and local governments.[2]

In the last twenty years, there has been a significant increase in the number of Americans who have had contact[3] with the criminal justice system[4] and, concomitantly, a major increase in the number of people with criminal records in the working-age population.[5] In 1991, only 1.8% of the adult population had served time in prison.[6] After ten years, in 2001, the percentage rose to 2.7% (1 in 37 adults).[7] By the end of 2007, 3.2% of all adults in the United States (1 in every 31) were under some form of correctional control involving probation, parole, prison, or jail.[8] The Department of Justice's Bureau of Justice Statistics (DOJ/BJS) has concluded that, if incarceration rates do not decrease, approximately 6.6% of all persons born in the United States in 2001 will serve time in state or federal prison during their lifetimes.[9]

Arrest and incarceration rates are particularly high for African American and Hispanic men.[10] African Americans and Hispanics[11] are arrested at a rate that is 2 to 3 times their proportion of the general population.[12] Assuming that current incarceration rates remain unchanged, about 1 in 17 White men are expected to serve time in prison during their lifetime;[13] by contrast, this rate climbs to 1 in 6 for Hispanic men; and to 1 in 3 for African American men.[14]

The Commission, which has enforced Title VII since it became effective in 1965, has well-established guidance applying Title VII principles to employers' use of criminal records to screen for employment.[15] This Enforcement Guidance builds on longstanding court decisions and policy documents that were issued over twenty years ago. In light of employers' increased access to criminal history information, case law analyzing Title VII requirements for criminal record exclusions, and other developments,[16] the Commission has decided to update and consolidate in this document all of its prior policy statements about Title VII and the use of criminal records in employment decisions. Thus, this Enforcement Guidance will supersede the Commission's previous policy statements on this issue.

The Commission intends this document for use by employers considering the use of criminal records in their selection and retention processes; by individuals who suspect that they have been denied jobs or promotions, or have been discharged because of their criminal records; and by EEOC staff who are investigating discrimination charges involving the use of criminal records in employment decisions.

III. Background

The contextual framework for the Title VII analysis in this Enforcement Guidance includes how criminal record information is collected and recorded, why employers use criminal records, and the EEOC's interest in such criminal record screening.

A. Criminal History Records

Criminal history information can be obtained from a wide variety of sources including, but not limited to, the following:

- Court Records. Courthouses maintain records relating to criminal charges and convictions, including arraignments, trials, pleas, and other dispositions.[17] Searching county courthouse records typically provides the most complete criminal history.[18] Many county courthouse records must be retrieved on-site,[19] but some courthouses offer their records online.[20] Information about federal crimes such as interstate drug trafficking, financial fraud, bank robbery, and crimes against the government may be found online in federal court records by searching the federal courts' Public Access to Court Electronic Records or Case Management/Electronic Case Files.[21]

- Law Enforcement and Corrections Agency Records. Law enforcement agencies such as state police agencies and corrections agencies may allow the public to access their records, including records of complaints, investigations, arrests, indictments, and periods of incarceration, probation, and parole.[22] Each agency may differ with respect to how and where the records may be searched, and whether they are indexed.[23]

- Registries or Watch Lists. Some government entities maintain publicly available lists of individuals who have been convicted of, or are suspected of having committed, a certain type of crime. Examples of such lists include state and federal sex offender registries and lists of individuals with outstanding warrants.[24]

- State Criminal Record Repositories. Most states maintain their own centralized repositories of criminal records, which include records that are submitted by most or all of their criminal justice agencies, including their county courthouses.[25] States differ with respect to the types of records included in the repository,[26] the completeness of the records,[27] the frequency with which they are updated,[28] and whether they permit the public to search the records by name, by fingerprint, or both.[29] Some states permit employers (or third-parties acting on their behalf) to access these records, often for a fee.[30] Others limit access to certain types of records,[31] and still others deny access altogether.[32]

- The Interstate Identification Index (III). The Federal Bureau of Investigation (FBI) maintains the most comprehensive collection of criminal records in the nation, called the "Interstate Identification Index" (III). The III database compiles records from each of the state repositories, as well as records from federal and international criminal justice agencies.[33]

The FBI's III database may be accessed for employment purposes by:

- the federal government;[34]

- employers in certain industries that are regulated by the federal government, such as "the banking, nursing home, securities, nuclear energy, and private security guard industries; as well as required security screenings by federal agencies of airport workers, HAZMAT truck drivers and other transportation workers";[35] and

- employers in certain industries "that the state has sought to regulate, such as persons employed as civil servants, day care, school, or nursing home workers, taxi drivers, private security guards, or members of regulated professions."[36]

Recent studies have found that a significant number of state and federal criminal record databases include incomplete criminal records.

➢ A 2011 study by the DOJ/BJS reported that, as of 2010, many state criminal history record repositories still had not recorded the final dispositions for a significant number of arrests.[37]

➢ A 2006 study by the DOJ/BJS found that only 50% of arrest records in the FBI's III database were associated with a final disposition.[38]

Additionally, reports have documented that criminal records may be inaccurate.

➢ One report found that even if public access to criminal records has been restricted by a court order to seal and/or expunge such records, this does not guarantee that private companies also will purge the information from their systems or that the event will be erased from media archives.[39]

➢ Another report found that criminal background checks may produce inaccurate results because criminal records may lack "unique" information or because of "misspellings, clerical errors or intentionally inaccurate identification information provided by search subjects who wish to avoid discovery of their prior criminal activities."[40]

Employers performing background checks to screen applicants or employees may attempt to search these governmental sources themselves or conduct a simple Internet search, but they often rely on third-party background screening businesses.[41] Businesses that sell criminal history information to employers are "consumer reporting agencies" (CRAs)[42] if they provide the information in "consumer reports"[43] under the Fair Credit Reporting Act, 15 U.S.C. § 1681 *et seq*. (FCRA). Under FCRA, a CRA generally may not report records of arrests that did not result in entry of a judgment of conviction, where the arrests occurred more than seven years ago.[44]

However, they may report convictions indefinitely.[45]

CRAs often maintain their own proprietary databases that compile information from various sources, such as those described above, depending on the extent to which the business has purchased or otherwise obtained access to data.[46] Such databases vary with respect to the geographic area covered, the type of information included (e.g., information about arrests, convictions, prison terms, or specialized information for a subset of employers such as information about workplace theft or shoplifting cases for retail employers[47]), the sources of information used (e.g., county databases, law enforcement agency records, sex offender registries), and the frequency with which they are updated. They also may be missing certain types of disposition information, such as updated convictions, sealing or expungement orders, or orders for entry into a diversion program.[48]

B.   Employers' Use of Criminal History Information

In one survey, a total of 92% of responding employers stated that they subjected all or some of their job candidates to criminal background checks.[49] Employers have reported that their use of criminal history information is related to ongoing efforts to combat theft and fraud,[50] as well as heightened concerns about workplace violence[51] and potential liability for negligent hiring.[52] Employers also cite federal laws as well as state and local laws[53] as reasons for using criminal background checks.

C.   The EEOC's Interest in Employers' Use of Criminal Records in Employment Screening

The EEOC enforces Title VII, which prohibits employment discrimination based on race, color, religion, sex, or national origin. Having a criminal record is not listed as a protected basis in Title VII. Therefore, whether a covered employer's reliance on a criminal record to deny employment violates Title VII depends on whether it is part of a claim of employment discrimination based on race, color, religion, sex, or national origin. Title VII liability for employment discrimination is determined using two analytic frameworks: "disparate treatment" and "disparate impact." Disparate treatment is discussed in Section IV and disparate impact is discussed in Section V.

IV.   Disparate Treatment Discrimination and Criminal Records

A covered employer is liable for violating Title VII when the plaintiff demonstrates that it treated him differently because of his race, national origin, or another protected basis.[54] For example, there is Title VII disparate treatment liability where the evidence shows that a covered employer rejected an African American applicant based on his criminal record but hired a similarly situated White applicant with a comparable criminal record.[55]

> **Example 1: Disparate Treatment Based on Race.** John, who is White, and Robert, who is African American, are both recent graduates of State University. They have similar educational backgrounds, skills, and work experience.   They each pled guilty to charges of possessing and

distributing marijuana as high school students, and neither of them had any subsequent contact with the criminal justice system.

After college, they both apply for employment with Office Jobs, Inc., which, after short intake interviews, obtains their consent to conduct a background check. Based on the outcome of the background check, which reveals their drug convictions, an Office Jobs, Inc., representative decides not to refer Robert for a follow-up interview. The representative remarked to a co-worker that Office Jobs, Inc., cannot afford to refer "these drug dealer types" to client companies. However, the same representative refers John for an interview, asserting that John's youth at the time of the conviction and his subsequent lack of contact with the criminal justice system make the conviction unimportant. Office Jobs, Inc., has treated John and Robert differently based on race, in violation of Title VII.

Title VII prohibits "not only decisions driven by racial [or ethnic] animosity, but also decisions infected by stereotyped thinking . . . ."[56] Thus, an employer's decision to reject a job applicant based on racial or ethnic stereotypes about criminality—rather than qualifications and suitability for the position—is unlawful disparate treatment that violates Title VII.[57]

Example 2: Disparate Treatment Based on National Origin. Tad, who is White, and Nelson, who is Latino, are both recent high school graduates with grade point averages above 4.0 and college plans. While Nelson has successfully worked full-time for a landscaping company during the summers, Tad only held occasional lawn-mowing and camp-counselor jobs. In an interview for a research job with Meaningful and Paid Internships, Inc. (MPII), Tad discloses that he pled guilty to a felony at age 16 for accessing his school's computer system over the course of several months without authorization and changing his classmates' grades. Nelson, in an interview with MPII, emphasizes his successful prior work experience, from which he has good references, but also discloses that, at age 16, he pled guilty to breaking and entering into his high school as part of a class prank that caused little damage to school property. Neither Tad nor Nelson had subsequent contact with the criminal justice system.

The hiring manager at MPII invites Tad for a second interview, despite his record of criminal conduct. However, the same hiring manager sends Nelson a rejection notice, saying to a colleague that Nelson is only qualified to do manual labor and, moreover, that he has a criminal record. In light of the evidence showing that Nelson's and Tad's educational backgrounds are similar, that Nelson's work experience is more extensive, and that Tad's criminal conduct is more indicative of untrustworthiness, MPII has failed to state a legitimate, nondiscriminatory reason for rejecting Nelson. If Nelson filed a Title VII charge alleging disparate treatment based on national origin and the EEOC's investigation confirmed these facts, the EEOC would find reasonable cause to believe that discrimination occurred.

There are several kinds of evidence that may be used to establish that race, national origin, or other protected characteristics motivated an employer's use of criminal records in a selection decision, including, but not limited to:

- <u>Biased statements</u>. Comments by the employer or decisionmaker that are derogatory with respect to the charging party's protected group, or that express group-related stereotypes about criminality, might be evidence that such biases affected the evaluation of the applicant's or employee's criminal record.

- <u>Inconsistencies in the hiring process</u>. Evidence that the employer requested criminal history information more often for individuals with certain racial or ethnic backgrounds, or gave Whites but not racial minorities the opportunity to explain their criminal history, would support a showing of disparate treatment.

- <u>Similarly situated comparators (individuals who are similar to the charging party in relevant respects, except for membership in the protected group)</u>. Comparators may include people in similar positions, former employees, and people chosen for a position over the charging party. The fact that a charging party was treated differently than individuals who are not in the charging party's protected group by, for example, being subjected to more or different criminal background checks or to different standards for evaluating criminal history, would be evidence of disparate treatment.

- <u>Employment testing</u>. Matched-pair testing may reveal that candidates are being treated differently because of a protected status.[58]

- <u>Statistical evidence</u>. Statistical analysis derived from an examination of the employer's applicant data, workforce data, and/or third party criminal background history data may help to determine if the employer counts criminal history information more heavily against members of a protected group.

V.   Disparate Impact Discrimination and Criminal Records

A covered employer is liable for violating Title VII when the plaintiff demonstrates that the employer's neutral policy or practice has the effect of disproportionately screening out a Title VII-protected group and the employer fails to demonstrate that the policy or practice is job related for the position in question and consistent with business necessity.[59]

In its 1971 *Griggs v. Duke Power Company* decision, the Supreme Court first recognized that Title VII permits disparate impact claims.[60] The *Griggs* Court explained that "[Title VII] proscribes . . . practices that are fair in form, but discriminatory in operation. The touchstone is business necessity. If an employment practice which operates to exclude [African Americans] cannot be shown to be related to job performance, the practice is prohibited."[61] In 1991,

Congress amended Title VII to codify this analysis of discrimination and its burdens of proof.[62] Title VII, as amended, states:

> An unlawful employment practice based on disparate impact is established . . . if a complaining party demonstrates that an employer uses a particular employment practice that causes a disparate impact on the basis of race, color, religion, sex, or national origin and the respondent fails to demonstrate that the challenged practice is job related for the position in question and consistent with business necessity [63]

With respect to criminal records, there is Title VII disparate impact liability where the evidence shows that a covered employer's criminal record screening policy or practice disproportionately screens out a Title VII-protected group and the employer does not demonstrate that the policy or practice is job related for the positions in question and consistent with business necessity.

A. Determining Disparate Impact of Policies or Practices that Screen Individuals Based on Records of Criminal Conduct

1. Identifying the Policy or Practice

The first step in disparate impact analysis is to identify the particular policy or practice that causes the unlawful disparate impact. For criminal conduct exclusions, relevant information includes the text of the policy or practice, associated documentation, and information about how the policy or practice was actually implemented. More specifically, such information also includes which offenses or classes of offenses were reported to the employer (e.g., all felonies, all drug offenses); whether convictions (including sealed and/or expunged convictions), arrests, charges, or other criminal incidents were reported; how far back in time the reports reached (e.g., the last five, ten, or twenty years); and the jobs for which the criminal background screening was conducted.[64] Training or guidance documents used by the employer also are relevant, because they may specify which types of criminal history information to gather for particular jobs, how to gather the data, and how to evaluate the information after it is obtained.

2. Determining Disparate Impact

Nationally, African Americans and Hispanics are arrested in numbers disproportionate to their representation in the general population. In 2010, 28% of all arrests were of African Americans,[65] even though African Americans only comprised approximately 14% of the general population.[66] In 2008, Hispanics were arrested for federal drug charges at a rate of approximately three times their proportion of the general population.[67] Moreover, African Americans and Hispanics were more likely than Whites to be arrested, convicted, or sentenced for drug offenses even though their rate of drug use is similar to the rate of drug use for Whites.[68]

African Americans and Hispanics also are incarcerated at rates disproportionate to their numbers in the general population. Based on national incarceration data, the U.S. Department of Justice estimated in 2001 that 1 out of every 17 White men (5.9% of the White men in the U.S.)

is expected to go to prison at some point during his lifetime, assuming that current incarceration rates remain unchanged.[69] This rate climbs to 1 in 6 (or 17.2%) for Hispanic men.[70] For African American men, the rate of expected incarceration rises to 1 in 3 (or 32.2%).[71] Based on a state-by-state examination of incarceration rates in 2005, African Americans were incarcerated at a rate 5.6 times higher than Whites,[72] and 7 states had a Black-to-White ratio of incarceration that was 10 to1.[73] In 2010, Black men had an imprisonment rate that was nearly 7 times higher than White men and almost 3 times higher than Hispanic men.[74]

National data, such as that cited above, supports a finding that criminal record exclusions have a disparate impact based on race and national origin. The national data provides a basis for the Commission to further investigate such Title VII disparate impact charges. During an EEOC investigation, the employer also has an opportunity to show, with relevant evidence, that its employment policy or practice does not cause a disparate impact on the protected group(s). For example, an employer may present regional or local data showing that African American and/or Hispanic men are not arrested or convicted at disproportionately higher rates in the employer's particular geographic area. An employer also may use its own applicant data to demonstrate that its policy or practice did not cause a disparate impact. The Commission will assess relevant evidence when making a determination of disparate impact, including applicant flow information maintained pursuant to the Uniform Guidelines on Employee Selection Procedures,[75] workforce data, criminal history background check data, demographic availability statistics, incarceration/conviction data, and/or relevant labor market statistics.[76]

An employer's evidence of a racially balanced workforce will not be enough to disprove disparate impact. In *Connecticut v. Teal*, the Supreme Court held that a "bottom line" racial balance in the workforce does not preclude employees from establishing a prima facie case of disparate impact; nor does it provide employers with a defense.[77] The issue is whether the policy or practice deprives a disproportionate number of Title VII-protected individuals of employment opportunities.[78]

Finally, in determining disparate impact, the Commission will assess the probative value of an employer's applicant data. As the Supreme Court stated in *Dothard v. Rawlinson*, an employer's "application process might itself not adequately reflect the actual potential applicant pool since otherwise qualified people might be discouraged from applying" because of an alleged discriminatory policy or practice.[79] Therefore, the Commission will closely consider whether an employer has a reputation in the community for excluding individuals with criminal records. Relevant evidence may come from ex-offender employment programs, individual testimony, employer statements, evidence of employer recruitment practices, or publicly posted notices, among other sources.[80] The Commission will determine the persuasiveness of such evidence on a case-by-case basis.

B. Job Related For the Position in Question and Consistent with Business Necessity

1. Generally

After the plaintiff in litigation establishes disparate impact, Title VII shifts the burdens of production and persuasion to the employer to "demonstrate that the challenged practice is job related for the position in question and consistent with business necessity."[81] In the legislative history of the 1991 Civil Rights Act, Congress referred to *Griggs* and its progeny such as *Albemarle Paper Company v. Moody*[82] and *Dothard*[83] to explain how this standard should be construed.[84] The *Griggs* Court stated that the employer's burden was to show that the policy or practice is one that "bear[s] a demonstrable relationship to successful performance of the jobs for which it was used" and "measures the person for the job and not the person in the abstract."[85] In both *Albemarle*[86] and *Dothard*,[87] the Court emphasized the factual nature of the business necessity inquiry. The Court further stated in *Dothard* that the terms of the exclusionary policy must "be shown to be necessary to safe and efficient job performance."[88]

In a case involving a criminal record exclusion, the Eighth Circuit in its 1975 *Green v. Missouri Pacific Railroad* decision, held that it was discriminatory under Title VII for an employer to "follow[] the policy of disqualifying for employment any applicant with a conviction for any crime other than a minor traffic offense."[89] The Eighth Circuit identified three factors (the "*Green* factors") that were relevant to assessing whether an exclusion is job related for the position in question and consistent with business necessity:

- The nature and gravity of the offense or conduct;[90]
- The time that has passed since the offense or conduct and/or completion of the sentence;[91] and
- The nature of the job held or sought.[92]

In 2007, the Third Circuit in *El v. Southeastern Pennsylvania Transportation Authority*[93] developed the statutory analysis in greater depth. Douglas El challenged SEPTA's policy of excluding everyone ever convicted of a violent crime from the job of paratransit driver.[94] El, a 55 year-old African American paratransit driver-trainee, was terminated from employment when SEPTA learned of his conviction for second-degree murder 40 years earlier; the conviction involved a gang fight when he was 15 years old and was his only disqualifying offense under SEPTA's policy.[95] The Third Circuit expressed "reservations" about a policy such as SEPTA's (exclusion for all violent crimes, no matter how long ago they were committed) "in the abstract."[96]

Applying Supreme Court precedent, the *El* court observed that some level of risk is inevitable in all hiring, and that, "[i]n a broad sense, hiring policies . . . ultimately concern the management of risk."[97] Recognizing that assessing such risk is at the heart of criminal record exclusions, the Third Circuit concluded that Title VII requires employers to justify criminal record exclusions by demonstrating that they "accurately distinguish between applicants [who] pose an unacceptable level of risk and those [who] do not."[98]

The Third Circuit affirmed summary judgment for SEPTA, but stated that the outcome of the case might have been different if Mr. El had, "for example, hired an expert who testified that there is a time at which a former criminal is no longer any more likely to recidivate than the average person, . . . [so] there would be a factual question for the jury to resolve."[99] The Third Circuit reasoned, however, that the recidivism evidence presented by SEPTA's experts, in conjunction with the nature of the position at issue—paratransit driver-trainee with unsupervised access to vulnerable adults—required the employer to exercise the utmost care.[100]

In the subsections below, the Commission discusses considerations that are relevant to assessing whether criminal record exclusion policies or practices are job related and consistent with business necessity. First, we emphasize that arrests and convictions are treated differently.

2.   Arrests

The fact of an arrest does not establish that criminal conduct has occurred.[101] Arrests are not proof of criminal conduct. Many arrests do not result in criminal charges, or the charges are dismissed.[102] Even if an individual is charged and subsequently prosecuted, he is presumed innocent unless proven guilty.[103]

An arrest, however, may in some circumstances trigger an inquiry into whether the conduct underlying the arrest justifies an adverse employment action. Title VII calls for a fact-based analysis to determine if an exclusionary policy or practice is job related and consistent with business necessity. Therefore, an exclusion based on an arrest, in itself, is not job related and consistent with business necessity.

Another reason for employers not to rely on arrest records is that they may not report the final disposition of the arrest (e.g., not prosecuted, convicted, or acquitted). As documented in Section III.A., *supra*, the DOJ/BJS reported that many arrest records in the FBI's III database and state criminal record repositories are not associated with final dispositions.[104] Arrest records also may include inaccuracies or may continue to be reported even if expunged or sealed.[105]

> **Example 3: Arrest Record Is Not Grounds for Exclusion.** Mervin and Karen, a middle-aged African American couple, are driving to church in a predominantly white town. An officer stops them and interrogates them about their destination. When Mervin becomes annoyed and comments that his offense is simply "driving while Black," the officer arrests him for disorderly conduct. The prosecutor decides not to file charges against Mervin, but the arrest remains in the police department's database and is reported in a background check when Mervin applies with his employer of fifteen years for a promotion to an executive position. The employer's practice is to deny such promotions to individuals with arrest records, even without a conviction, because it views an arrest record as an indicator of untrustworthiness and irresponsibility. If Mervin filed a Title VII charge based on these facts, and disparate impact based on race were established, the EEOC would find reasonable cause to believe that his employer violated Title VII.

Although an arrest record standing alone may not be used to deny an employment opportunity, an employer may make an employment decision based on the conduct underlying the arrest if the conduct makes the individual unfit for the position in question. The conduct, not the arrest, is relevant for employment purposes.

Example 4: Employer's Inquiry into Conduct Underlying Arrest. Andrew, a Latino man, worked as an assistant principal in Elementary School for several years. After several ten and eleven-year-old girls attending the school accused him of touching them inappropriately on the chest, Andrew was arrested and charged with several counts of endangering the welfare of children and sexual abuse. Elementary School has a policy that requires suspension or termination of any employee who the school believes engaged in conduct that impacts the health or safety of the students. After learning of the accusations, the school immediately places Andrew on unpaid administrative leave pending an investigation. In the course of its investigation, the school provides Andrew a chance to explain the events and circumstances that led to his arrest. Andrew denies the allegations, saying that he may have brushed up against the girls in the crowded hallways or lunchroom, but that he doesn't really remember the incidents and does not have regular contact with any of the girls. The school also talks with the girls, and several of them recount touching in crowded situations. The school does not find Andrew's explanation credible. Based on Andrew's conduct, the school terminates his employment pursuant to its policy.

Andrew challenges the policy as discriminatory under Title VII. He asserts that it has a disparate impact based on national origin and that his employer may not suspend or terminate him based solely on an arrest without a conviction because he is innocent until proven guilty. After confirming that an arrest policy would have a disparate impact based on national origin, the EEOC concludes that no discrimination occurred. The school's policy is linked to conduct that is relevant to the particular jobs at issue, and the exclusion is made based on descriptions of the underlying conduct, not the fact of the arrest. The Commission finds no reasonable cause to believe Title VII was violated.

3. Convictions

By contrast, a record of a conviction will usually serve as sufficient evidence that a person engaged in particular conduct, given the procedural safeguards associated with trials and guilty pleas.[106] However, there may be evidence of an error in the record, an outdated record, or another reason for not relying on the evidence of a conviction. For example, a database may continue to report a conviction that was later expunged, or may continue to report as a felony an offense that was subsequently downgraded to a misdemeanor.[107]

Some states require employers to wait until late in the selection process to ask about convictions.[108] The policy rationale is that an employer is more likely to objectively assess the relevance of an applicant's conviction if it becomes known when the employer is already knowledgeable about the applicant's qualifications and experience.[109] As a best practice, and consistent with applicable laws,[110] the Commission recommends that employers not ask about convictions on job applications and that, if and when they make such inquiries, the inquiries be limited to convictions for which exclusion would be job related for the position in question and consistent with business necessity.

4. Determining Whether a Criminal Conduct Exclusion Is Job Related and Consistent with Business Necessity

To establish that a criminal conduct exclusion that has a disparate impact is job related and consistent with business necessity under Title VII, the employer needs to show that the policy operates to effectively link specific criminal conduct, and its dangers, with the risks inherent in the duties of a particular position.

Two circumstances in which the Commission believes employers will consistently meet the "job related and consistent with business necessity" defense are as follows:

o The employer validates the criminal conduct screen for the position in question per the Uniform Guidelines on Employee Selection Procedures (Uniform Guidelines) standards (if data about criminal conduct as related to subsequent work performance is available and such validation is possible); [111] or

o The employer develops a targeted screen considering at least the nature of the crime, the time elapsed, and the nature of the job (the three *Green* factors), and then provides an opportunity for an individualized assessment for people excluded by the screen to determine whether the policy as applied is job related and consistent with business necessity.

The individualized assessment would consist of notice to the individual that he has been screened out because of a criminal conviction; an opportunity for the individual to demonstrate that the exclusion should not be applied due to his particular circumstances; and consideration by the employer as to whether the additional information provided by the individual warrants an exception to the exclusion and shows that the policy as applied is not job related and consistent with business necessity. *See* Section V.B.9, *infra* (examples of relevant considerations in individualized assessments).

Depending on the facts and circumstances, an employer may be able to justify a targeted criminal records screen solely under the *Green* factors. Such a screen would need to be narrowly tailored to identify criminal conduct with a demonstrably tight nexus to the position in question. Title VII thus does not necessarily require individualized assessment in all circumstances. However, the use of individualized assessments can help employers avoid Title VII liability by allowing them to consider more complete information on individual applicants or employees, as part of a policy that is job related and consistent with business necessity.

5. Validation

The Uniform Guidelines describe three different approaches to validating employment screens.[112] However, they recognize that "[t]here are circumstances in which a user cannot or need not utilize" formal validation techniques and that in such circumstances an employer "should utilize selection procedures which are as job related as possible and which will minimize or eliminate adverse impact as set forth [in the following subsections]."[113] Although there may be social science studies that assess whether convictions are linked to future behaviors, traits, or conduct with workplace ramifications,[114] and thereby provide a framework for validating some employment exclusions, such studies are rare at the time of this drafting.

6. Detailed Discussion of the *Green* Factors and Criminal Conduct Screens

Absent a validation study that meets the Uniform Guidelines' standards, the *Green* factors provide the starting point for analyzing how specific criminal conduct may be linked to particular positions. The three *Green* factors are:

- The nature and gravity of the offense or conduct;
- The time that has passed since the offense, conduct and/or completion of the sentence; and
- The nature of the job held or sought.

a. The Nature and Gravity of the Offense or Conduct

Careful consideration of the nature and gravity of the offense or conduct is the first step in determining whether a specific crime may be relevant to concerns about risks in a particular position. The nature of the offense or conduct may be assessed with reference to the harm caused by the crime (e.g., theft causes property loss). The legal elements of a crime also may be instructive. For example, a conviction for felony theft may involve deception, threat, or intimidation.[115] With respect to the gravity of the crime, offenses identified as misdemeanors may be less severe than those identified as felonies.

b. The Time that Has Passed Since the Offense, Conduct and/or Completion of the Sentence

Employer policies typically specify the duration of a criminal conduct exclusion. While the *Green* court did not endorse a specific timeframe for criminal conduct exclusions, it did acknowledge that permanent exclusions from all employment based on any and all offenses were not consistent with the business necessity standard.[116] Subsequently, in *El*, the court noted that the plaintiff might have survived summary judgment if he had presented evidence that "there is a time at which a former criminal is no longer any more likely to recidivate than the average person . . . ."[117] Thus, the court recognized that the amount of time that had passed since the plaintiff's criminal conduct occurred was probative of the risk he posed in the position in question.

Whether the duration of an exclusion will be sufficiently tailored to satisfy the business necessity standard will depend on the particular facts and circumstances of each case. Relevant and available information to make this assessment includes, for example, studies demonstrating how much the risk of recidivism declines over a specified time.[118]

c. The Nature of the Job Held or Sought

Finally, it is important to identify the particular job(s) subject to the exclusion. While a factual inquiry may begin with identifying the job title, it also encompasses the nature of the job's duties (e.g., data entry, lifting boxes), identification of the job's essential functions, the circumstances under which the job is performed (e.g., the level of supervision, oversight, and interaction with co-workers or vulnerable individuals), and the environment in which the job's duties are performed (e.g., out of doors, in a warehouse, in a private home). Linking the criminal conduct to the essential functions of the position in question may assist an employer in demonstrating that its policy or practice is job related and consistent with business necessity because it "bear[s] a demonstrable relationship to successful performance of the jobs for which it was used."[119]

7. Examples of Criminal Conduct Exclusions that Do Not Consider the *Green* Factors

A policy or practice requiring an automatic, across-the-board exclusion from all employment opportunities because of any criminal conduct is inconsistent with the *Green* factors because it does not focus on the dangers of particular crimes and the risks in particular positions. As the court recognized in *Green*, "[w]e cannot conceive of any business necessity that would automatically place every individual convicted of any offense, except a minor traffic offense, in the permanent ranks of the unemployed."[120]

> **Example 5: Exclusion Is Not Job Related and Consistent with Business Necessity.** The National Equipment Rental Company uses the Internet to accept job applications for all positions. All applicants must answer certain questions before they are permitted to submit their online application, including "have you ever been convicted of a crime?" If the applicant answers "yes," the online application process automatically terminates, and the applicant sees a screen that simply says "Thank you for your interest. We cannot continue to process your application at this time."
>
> The Company does not have a record of the reasons why it adopted this exclusion, and it does not have information to show that convictions for all offenses render all applicants unacceptable risks in all of its jobs, which range from warehouse work, to delivery, to management positions. If a Title VII charge were filed based on these facts, and there was a disparate impact on a Title VII-protected basis, the EEOC would find reasonable cause to believe that the blanket exclusion was not job related and consistent with business necessity because the risks associated with all convictions are not pertinent to all of the Company's jobs.
>
> **Example 6: Exclusion Is Not Job Related and Consistent with Business Necessity.** Leo, an African American man, has worked

successfully at PR Agency as an account executive for three years. After a change of ownership, the new owners adopt a policy under which it will not employ anyone with a conviction. The policy does not allow for any individualized assessment before exclusion. The new owners, who are highly respected in the industry, pride themselves on employing only the "best of the best" for every position. The owners assert that a quality workforce is a key driver of profitability.

Twenty years earlier, as a teenager, Leo pled guilty to a misdemeanor assault charge. During the intervening twenty years, Leo graduated from college and worked successfully in advertising and public relations without further contact with the criminal justice system. At PR Agency, all of Leo's supervisors assessed him as a talented, reliable, and trustworthy employee, and he has never posed a risk to people or property at work. However, once the new ownership of PR Agency learns about Leo's conviction record through a background check, it terminates his employment. It refuses to reconsider its decision despite Leo's positive employment history at PR Agency.

Leo files a Title VII charge alleging that PR Agency's conviction policy has a disparate impact based on race and is not job related for the position in question and consistent with business necessity. After confirming disparate impact, the EEOC considers PR Agency's defense that it employs only the "best of the best" for every position, and that this necessitates excluding everyone with a conviction. PR Agency does not show that all convictions are indicative of risk or danger in all its jobs for all time, under the *Green* factors. Nor does PR Agency provide any factual support for its assertion that having a conviction is necessarily indicative of poor work or a lack of professionalism. The EEOC concludes that there is reasonable cause to believe that the Agency's policy is not job related for the position in question and consistent with business necessity. [121]

8. Targeted Exclusions that Are Guided by the *Green* Factors

An employer policy or practice of excluding individuals from particular positions for specified criminal conduct within a defined time period, as guided by the *Green* factors, is a targeted exclusion. Targeted exclusions are tailored to the rationale for their adoption, in light of the particular criminal conduct and jobs involved, taking into consideration fact-based evidence, legal requirements, and/or relevant and available studies.

As discussed above in Section V.B.4, depending on the facts and circumstances, an employer may be able to justify a targeted criminal records screen solely under the *Green* factors. Such a screen would need to be narrowly tailored to identify criminal conduct with a demonstrably tight nexus to the position in question. Title VII thus does not necessarily require individualized assessment in all circumstances. However, the use of individualized assessments can help employers avoid Title VII liability by allowing them to consider more complete information on individual applicants or employees, as part of a policy that is job related and consistent with business necessity.

9. Individualized Assessment

Individualized assessment generally means that an employer informs the individual that he may be excluded because of past criminal conduct; provides an opportunity to the individual to demonstrate that the exclusion does not properly apply to him; and considers whether the individual's additional information shows that the policy as applied is not job related and consistent with business necessity.

The individual's showing may include information that he was not correctly identified in the criminal record, or that the record is otherwise inaccurate. Other relevant individualized evidence includes, for example:

- The facts or circumstances surrounding the offense or conduct;
- The number of offenses for which the individual was convicted;
- Older age at the time of conviction, or release from prison; [122]
- Evidence that the individual performed the same type of work, post conviction, with the same or a different employer, with no known incidents of criminal conduct;
- The length and consistency of employment history before and after the offense or conduct; [123]
- Rehabilitation efforts, e.g., education/training; [124]
- Employment or character references and any other information regarding fitness for the particular position; [125] and
- Whether the individual is bonded under a federal, state, or local bonding program. [126]

If the individual does not respond to the employer's attempt to gather additional information about his background, the employer may make its employment decision without the information.

> **Example 7: Targeted Screen with Individualized Assessment Is Job Related and Consistent with Business Necessity.** County Community Center rents meeting rooms to civic organizations and small businesses, party rooms to families and social groups, and athletic facilities to local recreational sports leagues. The County has a targeted rule prohibiting anyone with a conviction for theft crimes (e.g., burglary, robbery, larceny, identity theft) from working in a position with access to personal financial

information for at least four years after the conviction or release from incarceration. This rule was adopted by the County's Human Resources Department based on data from the County Corrections Department, national criminal data, and recent recidivism research for theft crimes. The Community Center also offers an opportunity for individuals identified for exclusion to provide information showing that the exclusion should not be applied to them.

Isaac, who is Hispanic, applies to the Community Center for a full-time position as an administrative assistant, which involves accepting credit card payments for room rentals, in addition to having unsupervised access to the personal belongings of people using the facilities. After conducting a background check, the County learns that Isaac pled guilty eighteen months earlier, at age twenty, to credit card fraud, and that he did not serve time in prison. Isaac confirms these facts, provides a reference from the restaurant where he now works on Saturday nights, and asks the County for a "second chance" to show that he is trustworthy. The County tells Isaac that it is still rejecting his employment application because his criminal conduct occurred eighteen months ago and is directly pertinent to the job in question. The information he provided did nothing to dispel the County's concerns.

Isaac challenges this rejection under Title VII, alleging that the policy has a disparate impact on Hispanics and is not job related and consistent with business necessity. After confirming disparate impact, the EEOC finds that this screen was carefully tailored to assess unacceptable risk in relevant positions, for a limited time period, consistent with the evidence, and that the policy avoided overbroad exclusions by allowing individuals an opportunity to explain special circumstances regarding their criminal conduct. Thus, even though the policy has a disparate impact on Hispanics, the EEOC does not find reasonable cause to believe that discrimination occurred because the policy is job related and consistent with business necessity. [127]

Example 8: Targeted Exclusion Without Individualized Assessment Is Not Job Related and Consistent with Business Necessity. "Shred 4 You" employs over 100 people to pick up discarded files and sensitive materials from offices, transport the materials to a secure facility, and shred and recycle them. The owner of "Shred 4 You" sells the company to a competitor, known as "We Shred." Employees of "Shred 4 You" must reapply for employment with "We Shred" and undergo a background check. "We Shred" has a targeted criminal conduct exclusion policy that prohibits the employment of anyone who has been convicted of any crime related to theft or fraud in the past five years, and the policy does not provide for any individualized consideration. The company explains that its clients entrust it with handling sensitive and confidential information and materials; therefore, it cannot risk employing people who pose an above-average risk of stealing information.

Jamie, who is African American, worked successfully for "Shred 4 You" for five years before the company changed ownership. Jamie applies for his old job, and "We Shred" reviews Jamie's performance appraisals, which include high marks for his reliability, trustworthiness, and honesty. However, when "We Shred" does a background check, it finds that Jamie pled guilty to misdemeanor insurance fraud five years ago, because he exaggerated the costs of several home repairs after a winter storm. "We Shred" management informs Jamie that his guilty plea is evidence of criminal conduct and that his employment will be terminated. Jamie asks management to consider his reliable and honest performance in the same job at "Shred 4 You," but "We Shred" refuses to do so. The employer's conclusion that Jamie's guilty plea demonstrates that he poses an elevated risk of dishonesty is not factually based given Jamie's history of trustworthiness in the same job. After confirming disparate impact based on race (African American), the EEOC finds reasonable cause to believe that Title VII was violated because the targeted exclusion was not job related and consistent with business necessity based on these facts.

C.   Less Discriminatory Alternatives

If an employer successfully demonstrates that its policy or practice is job related for the position in question and consistent with business necessity, a Title VII plaintiff may still prevail by demonstrating that there is a less discriminatory "alternative employment practice" that serves the employer's legitimate goals as effectively as the challenged practice but that the employer refused to adopt.[128]

VI.   Positions Subject to Federal Prohibitions or Restrictions on Individuals with Records of Certain Criminal Conduct

In some industries, employers are subject to federal statutory and/or regulatory requirements that prohibit individuals with certain criminal records from holding particular positions or engaging in certain occupations. Compliance with federal laws and/or regulations is a defense to a charge of discrimination. However, the EEOC will continue to coordinate with other federal departments and agencies with the goal of maximizing federal regulatory consistency with respect to the use of criminal history information in employment decisions.[129]

A.   Hiring in Certain Industries

Federal laws and regulations govern the employment of individuals with specific convictions in certain industries or positions in both the private and public sectors. For example, federal law excludes an individual who was convicted in the previous ten years of specified crimes from working as a security screener or otherwise having unescorted access to the secure areas of an airport.[130] There are equivalent requirements for federal law enforcement officers,[131] child care workers in federal agencies or facilities,[132] bank employees, [133] and port workers,[134] among other positions.[135] Title VII does not preempt these federally imposed restrictions. However, if an employer decides to impose an exclusion that goes beyond the scope of a federally imposed restriction, the discretionary aspect of the policy would be subject to Title VII analysis.

> **Example 9: Exclusion Is Not Job Related and Consistent with Business Necessity.** Your Bank has a rule prohibiting anyone with convictions for any type of financial or fraud-related crimes within the last twenty years from working in positions with access to customer financial information, even though the federal ban is ten years for individuals who are convicted of any criminal offense involving dishonesty, breach of trust, or money laundering from serving in such positions.
>
> Sam, who is Latino, applies to Your Bank to work as a customer service representative. A background check reveals that Sam was convicted of a misdemeanor for misrepresenting his income on a loan application fifteen years earlier. Your Bank therefore rejects Sam, and he files a Title VII charge with the EEOC, alleging that the Bank's policy has a disparate impact based on national origin and is not job related and consistent with business necessity. Your Bank asserts that its policy does not cause a disparate impact and that, even if it does, it is job related for the position in question because customer service representatives have regular access to financial information and depositors must have "100% confidence" that their funds are safe. However, Your Bank does not offer evidence showing that there is an elevated likelihood of committing financial crimes for someone who has been crime-free for more than ten years. After establishing that the Bank's policy has a disparate impact based on national origin, the EEOC finds that the policy is not job related for the position in question and consistent with business necessity. The Bank's justification for adding ten years to the federally mandated exclusion is insufficient because it is only a generalized concern about security, without proof.

B.   Obtaining Occupational Licenses

Title VII also does not preempt federal statutes and regulations that govern eligibility for occupational licenses and registrations. These restrictions cover diverse sectors of the economy including the transportation industry,[136] the financial industry,[137] and import/export activities,[138] among others.[139]

C.   Waiving or Appealing Federally Imposed Occupational Restrictions

Several federal statutes and regulations provide a mechanism for employers or individuals to appeal or apply for waivers of federally imposed occupational restrictions. For example, unless a bank receives prior written consent from the Federal Deposit Insurance

Corporation (FDIC), an individual convicted of a criminal offense involving dishonesty, breach of trust, money laundering, or another financially related crime may not work in, own, or control "an insured depository institution" (e.g., bank) for ten years under the Federal Deposit Insurance Act.[140] To obtain such FDIC consent, the insured institution must file an application for a waiver on behalf of the particular individual.[141] Alternatively, if the insured institution does not apply for the waiver on the individual's behalf, the individual may file a request directly with the FDIC for a waiver of the institution filing requirement, demonstrating "substantial good cause" to grant the waiver.[142] If the FDIC grants the individual's waiver request, the individual can then file an application directly with the FDIC for consent to work for the insured institution in question.[143] Once the institution, or the individual, submits the application, the FDIC's criminal record waiver review process requires consideration of mitigating factors that are consistent with Title VII, including evidence of rehabilitation, and the nature and circumstances of the crime.[144]

Additionally, port workers who are denied the Transportation Workers Identification Credential (TWIC) based on their conviction record may seek a waiver for certain permanently disqualifying offenses or interim disqualifying offenses, and also may file an individualized appeal from the Transportation Security Administration's initial determination of threat assessment based on the conviction.[145] The Maritime Transportation Security Act, which requires all port workers to undergo a criminal background check to obtain a TWIC,[146] provides that individuals with convictions for offenses such as espionage, treason, murder, and a federal crime of terrorism are permanently disqualified from obtaining credentials, but those with convictions for firearms violations and distribution of controlled substances may be temporarily disqualified.[147] Most offenses related to dishonesty are only temporarily disqualifying.[148]

> **Example 10: Consideration of Federally Imposed Occupational Restrictions.** John Doe applies for a position as a truck driver for Truckers USA. John's duties will involve transporting cargo to, from, and around ports, and Truckers USA requires all of its port truck drivers to have a TWIC. The Transportation Security Administration (TSA) conducts a criminal background check and may deny the credential to applicants who have permanently disqualifying criminal offenses in their background as defined by federal law. After conducting the background check for John Doe, TSA discovers that he was convicted nine years earlier for conspiracy to use weapons of mass destruction. TSA denies John a security card because this is a permanently disqualifying criminal offense under federal law.[149] John, who points out that he was a minor at the time of the conviction, requests a waiver by TSA because he had limited involvement and no direct knowledge of the underlying crime at the time of the offense. John explains that he helped a friend transport some chemical materials that the friend later tried to use to damage government property. TSA refuses to grant John's waiver request because a conviction for conspiracy to use weapons of mass destruction is not subject to the TSA's waiver procedures.[150] Based on this denial, Truckers USA rejects John's application for the port truck driver position. Title VII does not override Truckers USA's policy because the policy is consistent with another federal law.

While Title VII does not mandate that an employer seek such waivers, where an employer does seek waivers it must do so in a nondiscriminatory manner.

D. Security Clearances

The existence of a criminal record may result in the denial of a federal security clearance, which is a prerequisite for a variety of positions with the federal government and federal government contractors.[151] A federal security clearance is used to ensure employees' trustworthiness, reliability, and loyalty before providing them with access to sensitive national security information.[152] Under Title VII's national security exception, it is not unlawful for an employer to "fail or refuse to hire and employ" an individual because "such individual has not fulfilled or has ceased to fulfill" the federal security requirements.[153] This exception focuses on whether the position in question is, in fact, subject to national security requirements that are imposed by federal statute or Executive Order, and whether the adverse employment action actually resulted from the denial or revocation of a security clearance.[154] Procedural requirements related to security clearances must be followed without regard to an individual's race, color, religion, sex, or national origin.[155]

E. Working for the Federal Government

Title VII provides that, with limited coverage exceptions, "[a]ll personnel actions affecting employees or applicants for employment . . . shall be made free from any discrimination based on race, color, religion, sex, or national origin."[156] The principles discussed above in this Guidance apply in the federal employment context. In most circumstances, individuals with criminal records are not automatically barred from working for the federal government.[157] However, the federal government imposes criminal record restrictions on its workforce through "suitability" requirements for certain positions.[158] The federal government's Office of Personnel Management (OPM) defines suitability as "determinations based on a person's character or conduct that may have an impact on the integrity or efficiency of the service."[159] Under OPM's rules, agencies may bar individuals from federal employment for up to three years if they are found unsuitable based on criminal or dishonest conduct, among other factors.[160] OPM gives federal agencies the discretion to consider relevant mitigating criteria when deciding whether an individual is suitable for a federal position.[161] These mitigating criteria, which are consistent with the three *Green* factors and also provide an individualized assessment of the applicant's background, allow consideration of: (1) the nature of the position for which the person is applying or in which the person is employed; (2) the nature and seriousness of the conduct; (3) the circumstances surrounding the conduct; (4) the recency of the conduct; (5) the age of the person involved at the time of the conduct; (6) contributing societal conditions; and (7) the absence or presence of rehabilitation or efforts toward rehabilitation.[162] In general, OPM requires federal agencies and departments to consider hiring an individual with a criminal record if he is the best candidate for the position in question and can comply with relevant job requirements.[163] The EEOC continues to coordinate with OPM to achieve employer best practices in the federal sector.[164]

VII. Positions Subject to State and Local Prohibitions or Restrictions on Individuals with Records of Certain Criminal Conduct

States and local jurisdictions also have laws and/or regulations that restrict or prohibit the employment of individuals with records of certain criminal conduct.[165] Unlike federal laws or regulations, however, state and local laws or regulations are preempted by Title VII if they "purport[] to require or permit the doing of any act which would be an unlawful employment practice" under Title VII.[166] Therefore, if an employer's exclusionary policy or practice is *not* job related and consistent with business necessity, the fact that it was adopted to comply with a state or local law or regulation does not shield the employer from Title VII liability.[167]

> **Example 11: State Law Exclusion Is Job Related and Consistent with Business Necessity.** Elijah, who is African American, applies for a position as an office assistant at Pre-School, which is in a state that imposes criminal record restrictions on school employees. Pre-School, which employs twenty-five full- and part-time employees, uses all of its workers to help with the children. Pre-School performs a background check and learns that Elijah pled guilty to charges of indecent exposure two years ago. After being rejected for the position because of his conviction, Elijah files a Title VII disparate impact charge based on race to challenge Pre-School's policy. The EEOC conducts an investigation and finds that the policy has a disparate impact and that the exclusion is job related for the position in question and consistent with business necessity because it addresses serious safety risks of employment in a position involving regular contact with children. As a result, the EEOC would not find reasonable cause to believe that discrimination occurred.

> **Example 12: State Law Exclusion Is Not Consistent with Title VII.** County Y enforces a law that prohibits all individuals with a criminal conviction from working for it. Chris, an African American man, was convicted of felony welfare fraud fifteen years ago, and has not had subsequent contact with the criminal justice system. Chris applies to County Y for a job as an animal control officer trainee, a position that involves learning how to respond to citizen complaints and handle animals. The County rejects Chris's application as soon as it learns that he has a felony conviction. Chris files a Title VII charge, and the EEOC investigates, finding disparate impact based on race and also that the exclusionary policy is not job related and consistent with business necessity. The County cannot justify rejecting everyone with any conviction from all jobs. Based on these facts, County Y's law "purports to require or permit the doing of an[] act which would be an unlawful employment practice" under Title VII.

VIII. Employer Best Practices

The following are examples of best practices for employers who are considering criminal record information when making employment decisions.

General

- Eliminate policies or practices that exclude people from employment based on any criminal record.

- Train managers, hiring officials, and decisionmakers about Title VII and its prohibition on employment discrimination.

Developing a Policy

- Develop a narrowly tailored written policy and procedure for screening applicants and employees for criminal conduct.

    - Identify essential job requirements and the actual circumstances under which the jobs are performed.

    - Determine the specific offenses that may demonstrate unfitness for performing such jobs.

        o Identify the criminal offenses based on all available evidence.

    - Determine the duration of exclusions for criminal conduct based on all available evidence.

        o Include an individualized assessment.

    - Record the justification for the policy and procedures.

    - Note and keep a record of consultations and research considered in crafting the policy and procedures.

- Train managers, hiring officials, and decisionmakers on how to implement the policy and procedures consistent with Title VII.

Questions about Criminal Records

- When asking questions about criminal records, limit inquiries to records for which exclusion would be job related for the position in question and consistent with business necessity.

Confidentiality

- Keep information about applicants' and employees' criminal records confidential. Only use it for the purpose for which it was intended.

Approved by the Commission:

_____   _____

Chair Jacqueline A. Berrien   Date

ENDNOTES

[1]   42 U.S.C. § 2000e *et seq.* The EEOC also enforces other anti-discrimination laws including: Title I of the Americans with Disabilities Act of 1990, as amended (ADA), and Section 501 of the Rehabilitation Act, as amended, which prohibit employment discrimination on the basis of disability; the Age Discrimination in Employment Act of 1967, as amended (ADEA), which prohibits discrimination on the basis of age 40 or above; Title II of the Genetic Information Nondiscrimination Act of 2008 (GINA), which prohibits discrimination on the basis of genetic information; and the Equal Pay Act of 1963, as amended (EPA), which requires employers to pay male and female employees at the same establishment equal wages for equal work.

[2]   All entities covered by Title VII are subject to this analysis. *See* 42 U.S.C. § 2000e-2 (anti-discrimination provisions); 42 U.S.C. § 2000e(b)–(e) (defining "employer," "employment agency," and "labor organization"); 42 U.S.C. § 2000e-16(a) (prohibiting discriminatory employment practices by federal departments and agencies). For purposes of this Guidance, the term "employer" is used in lieu of listing all Title VII-covered entities. The Commission considers other coverage questions that arise in particular charges involving, for example, joint employment or third party interference in *Compliance Manual Section 2: Threshold Issues,* U.S. EQUAL EMP'T OPPORTUNITY COMM'N, § 2-III B., *Covered Entities,* http://www.eeoc.gov/policy/docs/threshold.html#2-III-B (last visited April 23, 2012).

[3]   For the purposes of this Guidance, references to "contact" with the criminal justice system may include, for example, an arrest, charge, indictment, citation, conviction, incarceration, probation, or parole.

[4]   *See* THOMAS P. BONCZAR, BUREAU OF JUSTICE STATISTICS, U.S. DEP'T OF JUSTICE, PREVALENCE OF IMPRISONMENT IN THE U.S. POPULATION, 1974–2001, at 3 (2003), http://bjs.ojp.usdoj.gov/content/pub/pdf/piusp01.pdf [hereinafter PREVALENCE OF IMPRISONMENT] ("Between 1974 and 2001 the number of former prisoners living in the United States more than doubled, from 1,603,000 to 4,299,000."); SEAN ROSENMERKEL ET AL., BUREAU OF JUSTICE STATISTICS, U.S. DEP'T OF JUSTICE, FELONY SENTENCES IN STATE COURTS, 2006 – STATISTICAL TABLES 1 (2009), http://bjs.ojp.usdoj.gov/content/pub/pdf/fssc06st.pdf (reporting that between 1990 and 2006, there has been a 37% increase in the number of felony offenders sentenced in state courts); *see also* PEW CTR. ON THE STATES, ONE IN 31: THE LONG REACH OF AMERICAN CORRECTIONS 4 (2009), http://www.pewcenteronthestates.org/uploadedFiles/PSPP_1in31_report_FINAL_WEB_3-26-09.pdf [hereinafter ONE IN 31] ("During the past quarter-century, the number of prison and jail inmates has grown by 274 percent . . . .[bringing] the total population in custody to 2.3 million. During the same period, the number under community supervision grew by a staggering 3,535,660 to a total of 5.1 million."); PEW CTR. ON THE STATES, ONE IN 100: BEHIND BARS IN AMERICA 2008, at 3 (2008), http://www.pewcenteronthestates.org/uploadedFiles/8015PCTS_Prison08_FINAL_2-1-1_FORWEB.pdf ("[M]ore than one in every 100 adults is now confined in an American jail or

prison."); Robert Brame, Michael G. Turner, Raymond Paternoster, & Shawn D. Bushway, *Cumulative Prevalence of Arrest From Ages 8 to 23 in a National Sample*, 129 PEDIATRICS 21, 25, 26 (2012) (finding that approximately 1 out of 3 of all American youth will experience at least 1 arrest for a nontraffic offense by the age of 23).

[5]   *See* JOHN SCHMITT & KRIS WARNER, CTR. FOR ECON. & POLICY RESEARCH, EX-OFFENDERS AND THE LABOR MARKET 12 (2010), www.cepr.net/documents/publications/ex-offenders-2010-11.pdf ("In 2008, ex-prisoners were 2.9 to 3.2 percent of the total working-age population (excluding those currently in prison or jail) or about one in 33 working-age adults. Ex-felons were a larger share of the total working-age population: 6.6 to 7.4 percent, or about one in 15 working-age adults [not all felons serve prison terms]."); *see id.* at 3 (concluding that "in the absence of some reform of the criminal justice system, the share of ex-offenders in the working-age population will rise substantially in coming decades").

[6]   PREVALENCE OF IMPRISONMENT, *supra* note 4, at 4, Table 3.

[7]   *Id.*

[8]   ONE IN 31, *supra* note 4, at 5 (noting that when all of the individuals who are probationers, parolees, prisoners or jail inmates are added up, the total is more than 7.3 million adults; this is more than the populations of Chicago, Philadelphia, San Diego, and Dallas combined, and larger than the populations of 38 states and the District of Columbia).

[9]   PREVALENCE OF IMPRISONMENT, *supra* note 4, at 7.

[10]   *Id.* at 5, Table 5; *cf.* PEW CTR. ON THE STATES, COLLATERAL COSTS: INCARCERATION'S EFFECT ON ECONOMIC MOBILITY 6 (2010), http://www.pewcenteronthestates.org/uploadedFiles/Collateral_Costs.pdf?n=8653 ("Simply stated, incarceration in America is concentrated among African American men. While 1 in every 87 white males ages 18 to 64 is incarcerated and the number for similarly-aged Hispanic males is 1 in 36, for black men it is 1 in 12."). Incarceration rates are even starker for 20-to-34-year-old men without a high school diploma or GED: 1 in 8 White males in this demographic group is incarcerated, compared to 1 in 14 Hispanic males, and 1 in 3 Black males. PEW CTR. ON THE STATES, *supra*, at 8, Figure 2.

[11]   This document uses the terms "Black" and "African American," and the terms "Hispanic" and "Latino," interchangeably.

[12]   *See infra* notes 65–67 (citing data for the arrest rates and population statistics for African Americans and Hispanics).

[13]   PREVALENCE OF IMPRISONMENT, *supra* note 4, at 1.

[14]   *Id.* at 8.

[15]   *See Policy Statement on the Issue of Conviction Records Under Title VII of the Civil Rights Act of 1964*, U.S. EQUAL EMP'T OPPORTUNITY COMM'N (Feb. 4, 1987), http://www.eeoc.gov/policy/docs/convict1.html; *EEOC Policy Statement on the Use of Statistics in Charges Involving the Exclusion of Individuals with Conviction Records from Employment*, U.S. EQUAL EMP'T OPPORTUNITY COMM'N (July 29, 1987), http://www.eeoc.gov/policy/docs/convict2.html; *Policy Guidance on the Consideration of Arrest Records in Employment Decisions Under Title VII*, U.S. EQUAL EMP'T OPPORTUNITY COMM'N (Sept. 7, 1990), http://www.eeoc.gov/policy/docs/arrest_records.html; *Compliance Manual Section 15: Race & Color Discrimination*, U.S. EQUAL EMP'T OPPORTUNITY COMM'N, § 15-VI.B.2 (April 19, 2006), http://www.eeoc.gov/policy/docs/race-color.pdf. *See also* EEOC Decision No. 72-1497 (1972) (challenging a criminal record exclusion policy based on "serious crimes"); EEOC Decision No. 74-89 (1974) (challenging a policy where a felony conviction was considered an adverse factor that would lead to disqualification); EEOC Decision No. 78-03 (1977) (challenging an exclusion policy based on felony or misdemeanor convictions involving moral turpitude or the use of drugs); EEOC Decision No. 78-35 (1978) (concluding that an employee's discharge was reasonable given his pattern of criminal behavior and the severity and recentness of his criminal conduct).

[16]   In 2011, U.S. Attorney General Eric Holder assembled a Cabinet-level interagency Reentry Council to support the federal government's efforts to promote the successful reintegration of ex-offenders back into their communities. *National Reentry Resource Center – Federal Interagency Reentry Council*, http://www.nationalreentryresourcecenter.org/reentry-council (last visited April 23, 2012). As a part of the Council's efforts, it has focused on removing barriers to employment for ex-offenders to reduce recidivism by publishing several fact sheets on employing individuals with criminal records. *See, e.g.*, FED. INTERAGENCY REENTRY COUNCIL, REENTRY MYTHBUSTER! ON FEDERAL HIRING POLICIES (2011), http://www.nationalreentryresourcecenter.org/documents/0000/1083/Reentry_Council_Mythbuster_Fed_Employment.pdf; FED. INTERAGENCY REENTRY COUNCIL, REENTRY MYTHBUSTER! ON HIRING/CRIMINAL RECORDS GUIDANCE (2011), http://www.nationalreentryresourcecenter.org/documents/0000/1082/Reentry_Council_Mythbuster_Employment.pdf; FED. INTERAGENCY REENTRY COUNCIL, REENTRY MYTHBUSTER! CRIMINAL HISTORIES AND EMPLOYMENT BACKGROUND CHECKS (2011), http://www.nationalreentryresourcecenter.org/documents/0000/1176/Reentry_Council_Mythbuster_FCRA_Employment.pdf; FED. INTERAGENCY REENTRY COUNCIL, REENTRY MYTHBUSTER! ON FEDERAL BONDING PROGRAM (2011), http://www.nationalreentryresourcecenter.org/documents/0000/1061/Reentry_Council_Mythbuster_Federal_Bonding.pdf.

In addition to these federal efforts, several state law enforcement agencies have embraced initiatives and programs that encourage the employment of ex-offenders. For example, Texas' Department of Criminal Justice has a Reentry and Integration Division and within that Division, a Reentry Task Force Workgroup. *See Reentry and Integration Division-Reentry Task Force*, TEX. DEP'T OF CRIMINAL JUSTICE, http://www.tdcj.state.tx.us/divisions/rid/rid_texas_reentry_task_force.html (last visited April 23, 2012). One of the Workgroups in this Task Force specifically focuses on identifying employment opportunities for ex-offenders and barriers that affect ex-offenders' access to employment or vocational training programs. *Reentry and Integration Division – Reentry Task Force Workgroups*, TEX. DEP'T OF CRIMINAL JUSTICE, http://www.tdcj.state.tx.us/divisions/rid/r_workgroup/rid_workgroup_employment.html (last visited April 23, 2012). Similarly, Ohio's Department of Rehabilitation and Correction has an Offender Workforce Development Office that "works with departmental staff and correctional institutions within the Ohio Department of Rehabilitation and Correction to prepare offenders for employment and the job search process." *Jobs for Ohio Offenders*, OHIO DEP'T OF REHAB. AND CORR. OFFENDER WORKFORCE DEV., http://www.drc.ohio.gov/web/JOBOFFEN.HTM (last updated Aug. 9, 2010). Law enforcement agencies in other states such as Indiana and Florida have also recognized the importance of encouraging ex-offender employment. *See, e.g.*, *IDOC: Road to Re-Entry*, IND. DEP'T OF CORR., http://www.in.gov/idoc/reentry/index.htm (last visited April 23, 2012) (describing various services and programs that are available to ex-offenders to help them to obtain employment); FLA. DEP'T OF CORRS., RECIDIVISM REDUCTION STRATEGIC PLAN: FISCAL YEAR 2009-2014, at 11, 12 (2009), http://www.dc.state.fl.us/orginfo/FinalRecidivismReductionPlan.pdf (identifying the lack of employment as one of the barriers to successful ex-offender reentry).

[17]   CARL R. ERNST & LES ROSEN, "NATIONAL" CRIMINAL HISTORY DATABASES 1 (2002), http://www.brbpub.com/articles/CriminalHistoryDB.pdf.

[18]   LEXISNEXIS, CRIMINAL BACKGROUND CHECKS: WHAT NON-PROFITS NEED TO KNOW ABOUT CRIMINAL RECORDS 4 (2009), http://www.lexisnexis.com/risk/nonprofit/documents/Volunteer_Screening_White_Paper.pdf.

[19]   *Id.*

[20]   ERNST & ROSEN, *supra* note 17, at 1; NAT'L ASS'N OF PROF'L BACKGROUND SCREENERS, CRIMINAL BACKGROUND CHECKS FOR EMPLOYMENT PURPOSES 5, http://www.napbs.com/files/public/Learn_More/White_Papers/CriminalBackgroundChecks.pdf.

[21]   LEXISNEXIS, *supra* note 18, at 6. *See also* NAT'L ASS'N OF PROF'L BACKGROUND SCREENERS, *supra* note 20 at 5.

[22]   ERNST & ROSEN, *supra* note 17, at 1.

[23]   *Id.*

[24]   *See* SEARCH, THE NATIONAL TASK FORCE ON THE CRIMINAL BACKGROUNDING OF AMERICA 3, 4 (2005), http://www.search.org/files/pdf/ReportofNTFCBA.pdf. Registries and watch lists can also include federal and international terrorist watch lists, and registries of individuals who are being investigated for certain types of crimes, such as gang-related crimes. *Id. See also* LEXISNEXIS, *supra* note 18, at 5 (reporting that "all 50 states currently have a publicly available sex offender registry").

[25]   *See* U.S. DEP'T OF JUSTICE, THE ATTORNEY GENERAL'S REPORT ON CRIMINAL HISTORY

BACKGROUND CHECKS 4 (2006), http://www.justice.gov/olp/ag_bgchecks_report.pdf [hereinafter BACKGROUND CHECKS]. *See also* ERNST & ROSEN, *supra* note 17, at 2.

[26] *See* NAT'L ASS'N OF PROF'L BACKGROUND SCREENERS, *supra* note 20, at 5. *See also* LEXISNEXIS, *supra* note 18, at 5.

[27] LEXISNEXIS, *supra* note 18, at 5. *See also* AM. ASS'N OF COLLS. OF PHARMACY, REPORT OF THE AACP CRIMINAL BACKGROUND CHECK ADVISORY PANEL 6–7 (2006), http://www.aacp.org/resources/academicpolicies/admissionsguidelines/Documents/AACPBackgroundChkRpt.pdf.

[28] AM. ASS'N OF COLLS. OF PHARMACY, *supra* note 27, at 6–7.

[29] BACKGROUND CHECKS, *supra* note 25, at 4.

[30] *Id.*

[31] NAT'L ASS'N OF PROF'L BACKGROUND SCREENERS, *supra* note 20, at 5.

[32] BACKGROUND CHECKS, *supra* note 25, at 4.

[33] *Id.* at 3.

[34] *See id.* ("Non-criminal justice screening using FBI criminal history records is typically done by a government agency applying suitability criteria that have been established by law or the responsible agency.").

[35] *Id.* at 5.

[36] *Id.* at 4.

[37] DENNIS A. DEBACCO & OWEN M. GREENSPAN, BUREAU OF JUSTICE STATISTICS, U.S. DEP'T OF JUSTICE, SURVEY OF STATE CRIMINAL HISTORY INFORMATION SYSTEMS, 2010, at 2 (2011), https://www.ncjrs.gov/pdffiles1/bjs/grants/237253.pdf [hereinafter STATE CRIMINAL HISTORY].

[38] *See* BACKGROUND CHECKS, *supra* note 25, at 17.

[39] SEARCH, REPORT OF THE NATIONAL TASK FORCE ON THE COMMERCIAL SALE OF CRIMINAL JUSTICE RECORD INFORMATION 83 (2005), www.search.org/files/pdf/RNTFCSCJRI.pdf; *see also* Douglas Belkin, *More Job Seekers Scramble to Erase Their Criminal Past*, WALL ST. J., Nov. 11, 2009, at A1, *available at* http://online.wsj.com/article/SB125789494126242343.html?KEYWORDS=Douglas+Belkin ("Arrests that have been legally expunged may remain on databases that data-harvesting companies offer to prospective employers; such background companies are under no legal obligation to erase them.").

If applicants deny the existence of expunged or sealed records, as they are permitted to do in several states, they may appear dishonest if such records are reported in a criminal background check. *See generally* Debbie A. Mukamal & Paul N. Samuels, *Statutory Limitations on Civil Rights of People with Criminal Records*, 30 FORDHAM URB. L.J. 1501, 1509–10 (2003) (noting that 29 of the 40 states that allow expungement/sealing of arrest records permit the subject of the record to deny its existence if asked about it on employment applications or similar forms, and 13 of the 16 states that allow the expungement/sealing of adult conviction records permit the subject of the record to deny its existence under similar circumstances).

[40]   *See* SEARCH, INTERSTATE IDENTIFICATION NAME CHECK EFFICACY: REPORT OF THE NATIONAL TASK FORCE TO THE U.S. ATTORNEY GENERAL 21–22 (1999), www.search.org/files/pdf/III_Name_Check.pdf ("A so-called 'name check' is based not only on an individual's name, but also on other personal identifiers such as sex, race, date of birth and Social Security Number. . . . [N]ame checks are known to produce inaccurate results as a consequence of identical or similar names and other identifiers."); *id.* at 7 (finding that in a sample of 82,601 employment applicants, 4,562 of these individuals were *inaccurately* indicated by a "name check" to have criminal records, which represents approximately 5.5% of the overall sample).

[41]   BACKGROUND CHECKS, *supra* note 25, at 2.

[42]   A "consumer reporting agency" is defined by FCRA as "any person which, for monetary fees, dues, or on a cooperative nonprofit basis, regularly engages in whole or in part in the practice of assembling or evaluating consumer credit information *or other information* on consumers for the purposes of furnishing consumer reports to third parties . . . ." 15 U.S.C. § 1681a(f) (emphasis added); *see also* BACKGROUND CHECKS, *supra* note 25, at 43 (stating that the records that CRAs collect include "criminal history information, such as arrest and conviction information").

[43]   A "consumer report" is defined by FCRA as "any written, oral, or other communication of any information by a consumer reporting agency bearing on a consumer's credit worthiness, credit standing, credit capacity, *character, general reputation, personal characteristics*, or mode of living which is used or expected to be used or collected in whole or in part for the purpose of serving as a factor in establishing the consumer's eligibility for . . . employment purposes . . . ." 15 U.S.C. § 1681a(d)(1) (emphasis added).

[44]   *See* 15 U.S.C. § 1681c(a)(2) ("[N]o consumer reporting agency may make any consumer report containing . . . records of arrest that, from date of entry, antedate the report by more than seven years or until the governing statute of limitations has expired, whichever is the longer period."). *But see id.* §1681c(b)(3) (stating that the reporting restrictions for arrest records do not apply to individuals who will earn "an annual salary which equals, or which may reasonably be expected to equal $75,000 or more").

[45]   15 U.S.C. § 1681c(a)(5) ("[N]o consumer reporting agency may make any consumer report containing . . . [a]ny other adverse item of information, other than records of convictions of crimes which antedates the report by more than seven years.").

[46]   BACKGROUND CHECKS, *supra* note 25, at 2.

[47]   *See* Adam Klein, *Written Testimony of Adam Klein*, U.S. EQUAL EMP'T OPPORTUNITY COMM'N, http://www.eeoc.gov/eeoc/meetings/7-26-11/klein.cfm (last visited April 23, 2012) (describing how "several data-collection agencies also market and sell a retail-theft contributory database that is used by prospective employers to screen applicants"). *See also Retail Theft Database, ESTEEM, Workplace Theft Contributory Database*, LEXISNEXIS, http://www.lexisnexis.com/risk/solutions/retail-theft-contributory-database.aspx (last visited April 23, 2012) (stating that their database has "[t]heft and shoplifting cases supplied by more than 75,000 business locations across the country"). These databases may contain inaccurate and/or misleading information about applicants and/or employees. *See generally* Goode v. LexisNexis Risk & Info. Analytics Grp., Inc., No. 2:11-CV-2950-JD, 2012 WL 975043 (E.D. Pa. Mar. 22, 2012) (unpublished).

[48]   BACKGROUND CHECKS, *supra* note 25, at 2.

[49]   SOC'Y FOR HUMAN RES. MGMT., BACKGROUND CHECKING: CONDUCTING CRIMINAL BACKGROUND CHECKS, slide 3 (Jan. 22, 2010), http://www.slideshare.net/shrm/background-check-criminal?from=share_email [hereinafter CONDUCTING CRIMINAL BACKGROUND CHECKS] (73% of the responding employers reported that they conducted criminal background checks on all of their job candidates, 19% reported that they conducted criminal background checks on selected job candidates, and a mere 7% reported that they did not conduct criminal background checks on any of their candidates). The survey excluded the "not sure" responses from its analysis, which may account for the 1% gap in the total number of employer responses. *Id.*

[50]   CONDUCTING CRIMINAL BACKGROUND CHECKS, *supra* note 49, at slide 7 (39% of the surveyed employers reported that they conducted criminal background checks "[t]o reduce/prevent theft and embezzlement, other criminal activity"); *see also* Sarah E. Needleman, *Businesses Say Theft by Their Workers is Up*, WALL ST. J., Dec. 11, 2008, at B8, *available at* http://online.wsj.com/article/SB122896381748896999.html.

[51]   CONDUCTING CRIMINAL BACKGROUND CHECKS, *supra* note 49, at slide 7 (61% of the surveyed employers reported that they conducted criminal background checks "[to] ensure a safe work environment for employees"); *see also* ERIKA HARRELL, BUREAU OF JUSTICE STATISTICS, U.S. DEP'T OF JUSTICE, WORKPLACE VIOLENCE, 1993–2009, at 1 (2011), http://bjs.ojp.usdoj.gov/content/pub/pdf/wv09.pdf (reporting that in 2009, "[n]onfatal violence in the workplace was about 15% of all nonfatal violent crime against persons age 16 or older"). *But see id.* (noting that from "2002 to 2009, the rate of nonfatal workplace violence has declined by 35%, following a 62% decline in the rate from 1993 to 2002"). Studies indicate that most workplace violence is committed by individuals with no relationship to the business or its employees. *See id.* at 6 (reporting that between 2005 and 2009, strangers committed the majority of workplace violence against individuals (53% for males and 41% for females) while violence committed by co-workers accounted for a much smaller percentage (16.3% for males and 14.3% for females)); *see also* NAT'L INST. FOR OCCUPATIONAL SAFETY & HEALTH, CTR. FOR DISEASE CONTROL & PREVENTION, WORKPLACE VIOLENCE PREVENTION STRATEGIES AND RESEARCH

NEEDS 4, Table 1 (2006), http://www.cdc.gov/niosh/docs/2006-144/pdfs/2006-144.pdf (reporting that approximately 85% of the workplace homicides examined were perpetrated in furtherance of a crime by persons with no relationship to the business or its employees; approximately 7% were perpetrated by employees or former employees, 5% were committed by persons with a personal relationship to an employee, and 3% were perpetrated by persons with a customer-client relationship to the business).

[52]   CONDUCTING CRIMINAL BACKGROUND CHECKS, *supra* note 49, at slide 7 (55% percent of the surveyed employers reported that they conducted criminal background checks "[t]o reduce legal liability for negligent hiring"). Employers have a common law duty to exercise reasonable care in hiring to avoid foreseeable risks of harm to employees, customers, and the public. If an employee engages in harmful misconduct on the job, and the employer has not exercised such care in selecting the employee, the employer may be subject to liability for negligent hiring. *See, e.g.*, Stires v. Carnival Corp., 243 F. Supp. 2d 1313, 1318 (M.D. Fla. 2002) ("[N]egligent hiring occurs when . . . the employer knew or should have known of the employee's unfitness, and the issue of liability primarily focuses upon the adequacy of the employer's pre-employment investigation into the employee's background.").

[53]   CONDUCTING CRIMINAL BACKGROUND CHECKS, *supra* note 49, at slide 4 (40% of the surveyed employers reported that they conducted criminal background checks for "[j]ob candidates for positions for which state law requires a background check (e.g., day care teachers, licensed medical practitioners, etc.)"); *see id.* at slide 7 (20% of the employers reported that they conducted criminal background checks "[t]o comply with the applicable State law requiring a background check (e.g., day care teachers, licensed medical practitioners, etc.) for a particular position"). The study did not report the exact percentage of employers that conducted criminal background checks to comply with applicable federal laws or regulations, but it did report that 25% of the employers conducted background checks for "[j]ob candidates for positions involving national defense or homeland security." *Id.* at slide 4.

[54]   *See* 42 U.S.C. § 2000e-2(a).

[55]   Disparate treatment based on the race or national origin of job applicants with the same qualifications and criminal records has been documented. For example, a 2003 study demonstrated that White applicants with the same qualifications and criminal records as Black applicants were three times more likely to be invited for interviews than the Black applicants. *See* Devah Pager, *The Mark of a Criminal Record*, 108 AM. J. SOC. 937, 958, Figure 6 (2003), www.princeton.edu/~pager/pager_ajs.pdf. Pager matched pairs of young Black and White men as "testers" for her study. The "testers" in Pager's study were college students who applied for 350 low-skilled jobs advertised in Milwaukee-area classified advertisements, to test the degree to which a criminal record affects subsequent employment opportunities. The same study showed that White job applicants with a criminal record were called back for interviews more often than equally-qualified Black applicants who *did not have* a criminal record. *Id.* at 958. *See also* Devah Pager et al., *Sequencing Disadvantage: The Effects of Race and Criminal Background for Low Wage Job Seekers*, 623 ANNALS AM. ACAD. POL. & SOC. SCI., 199 (2009), www.princeton.edu/~pager/annals_sequencingdisadvantage.pdf (finding that among Black and

White testers with similar backgrounds and criminal records, "the negative effect of a criminal conviction is substantially larger for blacks than whites. . . . the magnitude of the criminal record penalty suffered by black applicants (60 percent) is roughly double the size of the penalty for whites with a record (30 percent)"); *see id.* at 200–201 (finding that personal contact plays an important role in mediating the effects of a criminal stigma in the hiring process, and that Black applicants are less often invited to interview, thereby having fewer opportunities to counteract the stigma by establishing rapport with the hiring official); Devah Pager, *Statement of Devah Pager, Professor of Sociology at Princeton University*, U.S. EQUAL EMP'T OPPORTUNITY COMM'N, http://www.eeoc.gov/eeoc/meetings/11-20-08/pager.cfm (last visited April 23, 2012) (discussing the results of the *Sequencing Disadvantage* study); DEVAH PAGER & BRUCE WESTERN, NYC COMMISSION ON HUMAN RIGHTS, RACE AT WORK, REALITIES OF RACE AND CRIMINAL RECORD IN THE NYC JOB MARKET 6, Figure 2 (2006), http://www.nyc.gov/html/cchr/pdf/race_report_web.pdf (finding that White testers *with* a felony conviction were called back 13% of the time, Hispanic testers *without* a criminal record were called back 14% of the time, and Black testers *without* a criminal record were called back 10% of the time).

[56] *Race & Color Discrimination, supra* note 15, § V.A.1.

[57] A 2006 study demonstrated that employers who are averse to hiring people with criminal records sometimes presumed, in the absence of evidence to the contrary, that African American men applying for jobs have disqualifying criminal records. Harry J. Holzer et al., *Perceived Criminality, Criminal Background Checks, and the Racial Hiring Practices of Employers*, 49 J.L. & ECON. 451 (2006), http://www.jstor.org/stable/pdfplus/10.1086/501089.pdf; *see also* HARRY HOLZER ET AL., URBAN INST., EMPLOYER DEMAND FOR EX-OFFENDERS: RECENT EVIDENCE FROM LOS ANGELES 6–7 (2003), http://www.urban.org/UploadedPDF/410779_ExOffenders.pdf (describing the results of an employer survey where over 40% of the employers indicated that they would "probably not" or "definitely not" be willing to hire an applicant with a criminal record).

[58] The Commission has not done matched-pair testing to investigate alleged discriminatory employment practices. However, it has issued an Enforcement Guidance that discusses situations where individuals or organizations file charges on the basis of matched-pair testing, among other practices. *See generally Enforcement Guidance: Whether "Testers" Can File Charges and Litigate Claims of Employment Discrimination*, U.S. EQUAL EMP'T OPPORTUNITY COMM'N (May 22, 1996), http://www.eeoc.gov/policy/docs/testers.html.

[59] 42 U.S.C. § 2000e-2(k)(1)(A)(i). If an employer successfully demonstrates that its policy or practice is job related for the position in question and consistent with business necessity, a Title VII plaintiff may still prevail by demonstrating that there is a less discriminatory "alternative employment practice" that serves the employer's legitimate goals as effectively as the challenged practice but that the employer refused to adopt. *Id.* § 2000e-2(k)(1)(A)(ii).

[60] 401 U.S. 424, 431–32 (1971).

[61]   *Id.* at 431.

[62]   The Civil Rights Act of 1991, Pub. L. No. 102-166, § 105; *see also* Lewis v. City of Chicago, 130 S. Ct. 2191 (2010) (reaffirming disparate impact analysis); Ricci v. DeStefano, 557 U.S. 557 (2009) (same).

[63]   42 U.S.C. § 2000e-2(k)(1)(A)(i).

[64]   The Commission presumes that employers use the information sought and obtained from its applicants and others in making an employment decision. *See* Gregory v. Litton Sys. Inc.,316 F. Supp. 401, 403 (C.D. Cal.1970). If an employer asserts that it did not factor the applicant's or employee's known criminal record into an employment decision, the EEOC will seek evidence supporting this assertion. For example, evidence that the employer has other employees from the same protected group with roughly comparable criminal records may support the conclusion that the employer did not use the applicant's or employee's criminal record to exclude him from employment.

[65]   UNIF. CRIME REPORTING PROGRAM, FED. BUREAU OF INVESTIGATION, CRIME IN THE U.S. 2010, at Table 43a (2011), http://www.fbi.gov/about-us/cjis/ucr/crime-in-the-u.s/2010/crime-in-the-u.s.-2010/tables/table-43/10tbl43a.xls.

[66]   U.S. CENSUS BUREAU, THE BLACK POPULATION: 2010, at 3 (2011), http://www.census.gov/prod/cen2010/briefs/c2010br-06.pdf (reporting that in 2010, "14 percent of all people in the United States identified as Black, either alone, or in combination with one or more races").

[67]   Accurate data on the number of Hispanics arrested and convicted in the United States is limited. *See* NANCY E. WALKER ET AL., NAT'L COUNCIL OF LA RAZA, LOST OPPORTUNITIES: THE REALITY OF LATINOS IN THE U.S. CRIMINAL JUSTICE SYSTEM 17–18 (2004), http://www.policyarchive.org/handle/10207/bitstreams/20279.pdf (explaining why "[i]t is very difficult to find any information – let alone accurate information – on the number of Latinos arrested in the United States"). The Department of Justice's Bureau of Justice Statistics' (BJS) *Sourcebook of Criminal Justice Statistics* and the FBI's Crime Information Services Division do not provide data for arrests by ethnicity. *Id.* at 17. However, the U.S. Drug Enforcement Administration (DEA) disaggregates data by Hispanic and non-Hispanic ethnicity. *Id.* at 18. According to DOJ/BJS, from October 1, 2008 to September 30, 2009, 45.5% of drug arrests made by the DEA were of Hispanics or Latinos. MARK MOTIVANS, BUREAU OF JUSTICE STATISTICS, U.S. DEP'T OF JUSTICE, FEDERAL JUSTICE STATISTICS, 2009 – STATISTICAL TABLES, at 6, Table 1.4 (2011), http://bjs.ojp.usdoj.gov/content/pub/pdf/fjs09.pdf. Accordingly, Hispanics were arrested for drug offenses by the DEA at a rate of three times their numbers in the general population. *See* U.S. CENSUS BUREAU, OVERVIEW OF RACE AND HISPANIC ORIGIN: 2010, at 3 (2011), http://www.census.gov/prod/cen2010/briefs/c2010br-02.pdf (reporting that in 2010, "there were 50.5 million Hispanics in the United States, composing 16 percent of the total population"). However, national statistics indicate that Hispanics have similar or lower drug usage rates compared to Whites. *See, e.g.,* SUBSTANCE ABUSE & MENTAL HEALTH SERVS.

ADMIN., U.S. DEP'T OF HEALTH & HUMAN SERVS., RESULTS FROM THE 2010 NATIONAL SURVEY ON DRUG USE AND HEALTH: SUMMARY OF NATIONAL FINDINGS 21, Figure 2.10 (2011), http://oas.samhsa.gov/NSDUH/2k10NSDUH/2k10Results.pdf (reporting, for example, that the usage rate for Hispanics in 2009 was 7.9% compared to 8.8% for Whites).

[68] *See, e.g.*, HUMAN RIGHTS WATCH, DECADES OF DISPARITY: DRUG ARRESTS AND RACE IN THE UNITED STATES 1 (2009), http://www.hrw.org/sites/default/files/reports/us0309web_1.pdf (noting that the "[t]he higher rates of black drug arrests do not reflect higher rates of black drug offending . . . . blacks and whites engage in drug offenses - possession and sales - at roughly comparable rates"); SUBSTANCE ABUSE & MENTAL HEALTH SERVS. ADMIN., U.S. DEP'T OF HEALTH & HUMAN SERVS., RESULTS FROM THE 2010 NATIONAL SURVEY ON DRUG USE AND HEALTH: SUMMARY OF NATIONAL FINDINGS 21 (2011), http://oas.samhsa.gov/NSDUH/2k10NSDUH/2k10Results.pdf (reporting that in 2010, the rates of illicit drug use in the United States among persons aged 12 or older were 10.7% for African Americans, 9.1% for Whites, and 8.1% for Hispanics); HARRY LEVINE & DEBORAH SMALL, N.Y. CIVIL LIBERTIES UNION, MARIJUANA ARREST CRUSADE: RACIAL BIAS AND POLICE POLICY IN NEW YORK CITY, 1997–2007, at 13–16 (2008), www.nyclu.org/files/MARIJUANA-ARREST-CRUSADE_Final.pdf (citing U.S. Government surveys showing that Whites use marijuana at higher rates than African Americans and Hispanics; however, the marijuana arrest rate of Hispanics is nearly three times the arrest rate of Whites, and the marijuana arrest rate of African Americans is five times the arrest rate of Whites).

[69] PREVALENCE OF IMPRISONMENT, *supra* note 4, at 1, 8. Due to the nature of available data, the Commission is using incarceration data as a proxy for conviction data.

[70] *Id.*

[71] *Id.*

[72] MARC MAUER & RYAN S. KING, THE SENTENCING PROJECT, UNEVEN JUSTICE: STATE RATES OF INCARCERATION BY RACE AND ETHNICITY 10 (2007), www.sentencingproject.org/Admin%5CDocuments%5Cpublications%5Crd_stateratesofincbyraceandethnicity.pdf.

[73] *Id.*

[74] PAUL GUERINO ET AL., BUREAU OF JUSTICE STATISTICS, U.S. DEP'T OF JUSTICE, PRISONERS IN 2010, at 27, Table 14 (2011), http://bjs.ojp.usdoj.gov/content/pub/pdf/p10.pdf (reporting that as of December 31, 2010, Black men were imprisoned at a rate of 3,074 per 100,000 Black male residents, Hispanic men were imprisoned at a rate of 1,258 per 100,000 Hispanic male residents, and White men were imprisoned at a rate of 459 per 100,000 White male residents); *cf.* ONE IN 31, *supra* note 4, at 5 ("Black adults are four times as likely as whites and nearly 2.5 times as likely as Hispanics to be under correctional control. One in 11 black adults -- 9.2 percent -- was under correctional control [probation, parole, prison, or jail] at year end 2007.").

[75]   The Uniform Guidelines on Employee Selection Procedures, 29 C.F.R. part 1607, provide that "[employers] should maintain and have available . . . information on [the] adverse impact of [their employment selection procedures]." 29 C.F.R. § 1607.15A. "Where [an employer] has not maintained [such records, the EEOC] may draw an inference of adverse impact of the selection process from the failure of [the employer] to maintain such data . . . ." *Id.* § 1607.4D.

[76]   *See, e.g.,* El v. SEPTA, 418 F. Supp. 2d 659, 668–69 (E.D. Pa. 2005) (finding that the plaintiff established a prima facie case of disparate impact with evidence from the defendant's personnel records and national data sources from the U.S. Bureau of Justice Statistics and the Statistical Abstract of the U.S.), *aff'd on other grounds,* 479 F.3d 232 (3d Cir. 2007); Green v. Mo. Pac. R.R., 523 F.2d 1290, 1294–95 (8th Cir. 1975) (concluding that the defendant's criminal record exclusion policy had a disparate impact based on race by evaluating local population statistics and applicant data), *appeal after remand,* 549 F.2d 1158, 1160 (8th Cir. 1977).

[77]   457 U.S. 440, 442 (1982).

[78]   *Id.* at 453–54

[79]   433 U.S. 321, 330 (1977).

[80]   *See, e.g.,* Int'l Bhd. of Teamsters v. United States, 431 U.S. 324, 365 (1977) (stating that "[a] consistently enforced discriminatory policy can surely deter job applications from those who are aware of it and are unwilling to subject themselves to the humiliation of explicit and certain rejection").

[81]   42 U.S.C. § 2000e-2(k)(1)(A)(i). *See* Griggs v. Duke Power Co., 401 U.S. 424 (1971). *See also* 42 U.S.C. § 2000e(m) (defining the term "demonstrates" to mean "meets the burdens of production and persuasion").

[82]   422 U.S. 405 (1975).

[83]   433 U.S. 321 (1977).

[84]   137 Cong. Rec. 15273 (1991) (statement of Sen. Danforth) ("[T]he terms 'business necessity' and 'job related' are intended to reflect the concepts enunciated by the Supreme Court in *Griggs v. Duke Power Co,* and in the other Supreme Court decisions prior to *Wards Cove Packing Co. v. Atonio.*" (citations omitted)). Section 105(b) of the Civil Rights Act of 1991 provides that only the interpretive memorandum read by Senator Danforth in the Congressional Record may be considered legislative history or relied upon in construing or applying the business necessity standard.

[85]   401 U.S. at 431, 436.

[86]   422 U.S. at 430–31 (endorsing the EEOC's position that discriminatory tests are impermissible unless shown, by professionally acceptable methods, to predict or correlate with "'important elements of work behavior which comprise or are relevant to the job or jobs for which candidates are being evaluated'" (quoting 29 C.F.R. § 1607.4(c))).

[87]   433 U.S. at 331–32 (concluding that using height and weight as proxies for strength did not satisfy the business necessity defense because the employer failed to establish a correlation between height and weight and the necessary strength, and also did not specify the amount of strength necessary to perform the job safely and efficiently).

[88]   *Id.* at 331 n.14.

[89]   523 F.2d 1290, 1293 (8th Cir. 1975). "In response to a question on an application form, Green [a 29-year-old African American man] disclosed that he had been convicted in December 1967 for refusing military induction. He stated that he had served 21 months in prison until paroled on July 24, 1970." *Id.* at 1292–93.

[90]   Green v. Mo. Pac. R.R., 549 F.2d 1158, 1160 (8th Cir. 1977) (upholding the district court's injunction prohibiting the employer from using an applicant's conviction record as an absolute bar to employment but allowing it to consider a prior criminal record as a factor in making individual hiring decisions, as long as the defendant took these three factors into account).

[91]   *Id.* (referring to completion of the sentence rather than completion of parole).

[92]   *Id.*

[93]   479 F.3d 232 (3d Cir. 2007).

[94]   *Id.* at 235.

[95]   *Id.* at 235, 236.

[96]   *Id.* at 235.

[97]   *Id.* at 244.

[98]   *Id.* at 244–45.

[99]   *Id.* at 247. *Cf.* Shawn Bushway et al., *The Predictive Value of Criminal Background Checks: Do Age and Criminal History Affect Time to Redemption?*, 49 CRIMINOLOGY 27, 52 (2011) [hereinafter *The Predictive Value of Criminal Background Checks*] ("Given the results of the current as well as previous [recidivism] studies, the 40-year period put forward in *El v. SEPTA* (2007) . . . seems too old of a score to be still in need of settlement.").

100   *El*, 479 F.3d at 248.

101   Some states have enacted laws to limit employer inquiries concerning all or some arrest records. *See* BACKGROUND CHECKS, *supra* note 25, at 48–49. At least 13 states have statutes explicitly prohibiting arrest record inquiries and/or dissemination subject to certain exceptions. *See, e.g.*, Alaska (ALASKA STAT. § 12.62.160(b)(8)); Arkansas (ARK. CODE ANN. § 12-12-1009(c)); California (CAL. LAB. CODE § 432.7(a)); Connecticut (CONN. GEN. STAT. § 46a-80(e)); Illinois (775 ILL. COMP. STAT. § 5/2-103(A)) (dealing with arrest records that have been ordered expunged, sealed, or impounded); Massachusetts (MASS. GEN. LAWS ch. 151B § 4(9)); Michigan (MICH COMP. LAWS § 37.2205a(1) (applying to misdemeanor arrests only)); Nebraska (NEB. REV. STAT. § 29-3523(2)) (ordering no dissemination of arrest records under certain conditions and specified time periods)); New York (N.Y. EXEC. LAW § 296(16)); North Dakota (N.D. CENT. CODE § 12-60-16.6(2)); Pennsylvania (18 PA. CONS. STAT. § 9121(b)(2)); Rhode Island (R.I. GEN. LAWS § 28-5-7(7)), and Wisconsin (WIS. STAT. §§ 111.321, 111.335a).

102   *See* United States v. Armstrong, 517 U.S. 456, 464 (1996) (discussing federal prosecutors' broad discretionary authority to determine whether to prosecute cases and whether to bring charges before a grand jury); Bordenkircher v. Hayes, 434 U.S. 357, 364 (1978) (explaining same for state prosecutors); *see also* THOMAS H. COHEN & TRACEY KYCKELHAHN, BUREAU OF JUSTICE STATISTICS, U.S. DEP'T OF JUSTICE, FELONY DEFENDANTS IN LARGE URBAN COUNTIES, 2006, at 10, Table 11 (2010), http://bjs.ojp.usdoj.gov/content/pub/pdf/fdluc06.pdf (reporting that in the 75 largest counties in the country, nearly one-third of the felony arrests did not result in a conviction because the charges against the defendants were dismissed).

103   Schware v. Bd. of Bar Exam'rs, 353 U.S. 232, 241 (1957) ("The mere fact that a [person] has been arrested has very little, if any, probative value in showing that he has engaged in any misconduct."); United States. v. Hynes, 467 F.3d 951, 957 (6th Cir. 2006) (upholding a preliminary jury instruction that stated that a "defendant is presumed to be innocent unless proven guilty. The indictment against the Defendant is only an accusation, nothing more. It's not proof of guilt or anything else."); *see* Gregory v. Litton Sys. Inc., 316 F. Supp. 401, 403 (C.D. Cal. 1970) ("[I]nformation concerning a prospective employee's record of arrests without convictions, is irrelevant to [an applicant's] suitability or qualification for employment."), *modified on other grounds*, 472 F.2d 631 (9th Cir. 1972); Dozier v. Chupka, 395 F. Supp. 836, 850 n.10 (S.D. Ohio 1975) (stating that the use of arrest records was too crude a predictor of an employee's predilection for theft where there were no procedural safeguards to prevent reliance on unwarranted arrests); City of Cairo v. Ill. Fair Empl. Prac. Comm., 8 Empl. Prac. Dec. (CCH) & 9682 (Ill. App. Ct. 1974) (concluding that, where applicants sought to become police officers, they could not be absolutely barred from appointment solely because they had been arrested, as distinguished from convicted); *see also* EEOC Dec. 74-83, ¶ 6424 (CCH) (1983) (finding no business justification for an employer's unconditional termination of all employees with arrest records (all five employees terminated were Black), purportedly to reduce thefts in the workplace; the employer produced no evidence that these particular employees had been involved in any of the thefts, or that all people who are arrested but not convicted are prone towards crime in the future); EEOC Dec. 76-87, ¶ 6665 (CCH) (1983) (holding that an applicant who sought to become a police officer could not be rejected based on one arrest five years earlier

for riding in a stolen car when he asserted that he did not know that the car was stolen and the charge was dismissed).

[104]   *See* STATE CRIMINAL HISTORY, *supra* note 37, at 2; *see also* BACKGROUND CHECKS, *supra* note 25, at 17.

[105]   *See supra* notes 39–40.

[106]   S*ee* Clark v. Arizona, 548 U.S. 735, 766 (2006) ("The first presumption [in a criminal case] is that a defendant is innocent unless and until the government proves beyond a reasonable doubt each element of the offense charged. . . ."). *See also* FED. R. CRIM P 11 (criminal procedure rule governing pleas).   The Supreme Court has concluded that criminal defendants have a Sixth Amendment right to effective assistance of counsel during plea negotiations. *See generally* Lafler v. Cooper, 132 S. Ct. 1376 (2012); Missouri v. Frye, 132 S. Ct. 1399 (2012).

[107]   *See supra* text accompanying note 39.

[108]   *See e.g.*, HAW. REV. STAT. § 378-2.5(b). Under this provision, the employer may withdraw the offer of employment if the prospective employee has a conviction record "that bears a rational relationship to the duties and responsibilities of the position." *Id. See also* CONN. GEN. STAT. § 46a-80(b) ("[N]o employer . . . shall inquire about a prospective employee's past convictions until such prospective employee has been deemed otherwise qualified for the position."); MINN. STAT. § 364.021(a) ("[A] public employer may not inquire or consider the criminal record or criminal history of an applicant for public employment until the applicant has been selected for an interview by the employer.").   State fair employment practices agencies have information about applicable state law.

[109]   *See generally* NAT'L LEAGUE OF CITIES & NAT'L EMP'T LAW PROJECT, CITIES PAVE THE WAY: PROMISING REENTRY POLICIES THAT PROMOTE LOCAL HIRING OF PEOPLE WITH CRIMINAL RECORDS (2010), www.nelp.org/page/-/SCLP/2010/CitiesPavetheWay.pdf?nocdn=1 (identifying local initiatives that address ways to increase employment opportunities for individuals with criminal records, including delaying a background check until the final stages of the hiring process, leveraging development funds, and expanding bid incentive programs to promote local hiring priorities); NAT'L EMP'T LAW PROJECT, CITY AND COUNTY HIRING INITIATIVES (2010), www.nelp.org/page/-/SCLP/CityandCountyHiringInitiatives.pdf (discussing the various city and county initiatives that have removed questions regarding criminal history from the job application and have waited until after a conditional offer of employment has been made to conduct a background check and inquire about the applicant's criminal background).

[110]   Several federal laws automatically prohibit employing individuals with certain felony convictions or, in some cases, misdemeanor convictions. *See, e.g.*, 5 U.S.C. § 7371(b) (requiring the mandatory removal of any federal law enforcement officer who is convicted of a felony); 46 U.S.C. § 70105(c)(1)(A) (mandating that individuals who have been convicted of espionage, sedition, treason or terrorism be permanently disqualified from receiving a biometric transportation security card and thereby excluded from port work employment); 42 U.S.C.

§ 13726(b)(1) (disqualifying persons with felony convictions or domestic violence convictions from working for a private prisoner transport company); 25 U.S.C. § 3207(b) (prohibiting individuals with a felony conviction, or any of two or more misdemeanor convictions, from working with Indian children if their convictions involved crimes of violence, sexual assault, molestation, exploitation, contact or prostitution, crimes against persons, or offenses committed against children); 18 U.S.C. § 922(g)(1), (9) (prohibiting an individual convicted of a felony or a misdemeanor for domestic violence from possessing a firearm, thereby excluding such individual from a wide range of jobs that require such possession); 18 U.S.C. § 2381 (prohibiting individuals convicted of treason from "holding any office under the United States"). Other federal laws prohibit employing individuals with certain convictions for a defined time period. *See, e.g.*, 5 U.S.C. § 7313(a) (prohibiting individuals convicted of a felony for inciting a riot or civil disorder from holding any position in the federal government for five years after the date of the conviction); 12 U.S.C. § 1829 (requiring a ten-year ban on employing individuals in banks if they have certain financial-related convictions); 49 U.S.C. § 44936(b)(1)(B) (imposing a ten-year ban on employing an individual as a security screener for an air carrier if that individuals has been convicted of specified crimes).

[111]   *See* 29 C.F.R. § 1607.5 (describing the general standards for validity studies).

[112]   *Id.*

[113]   *Id.* § 1607.6B. The following subsections state:

> (1) *Where informal or unscored procedures are used.* When an informal or unscored selection procedure which has an adverse impact is utilized, the user should eliminate the adverse impact, or modify the procedure to one which is a formal, scored or quantified measure or combination of measures and then validate the procedure in accord with these guidelines, or otherwise justify continued use of the procedure in accord with Federal law.
> (2) *Where formal and scored procedures are used.* When a formal and scored selection procedure is used which has an adverse impact, the validation techniques contemplated by these guidelines usually should be followed if technically feasible. Where the user cannot or need not follow the validation techniques anticipated by these guidelines, the user should either modify the procedure to eliminate adverse impact or otherwise justify continued use of the procedure in accord with Federal law.

> *Id.* § 1607.6A, B(1)–(2).

[114]   *See, e.g.,* Brent W. Roberts et al., *Predicting the Counterproductive Employee in a Child-to-Adult Prospective Study*, 92 J. APPLIED PSYCHOL. 1427, 1430 (2007), http://internal.psychology.illinois.edu/~broberts/Roberts,%20Harms,%20Caspi,%20&%20Moffit t,%202007.pdf (finding that in a study of New Zealand residents from birth to age 26, "[a]dolescent criminal convictions were unrelated to committing counterproductive activities at work [such as tardiness, absenteeism, disciplinary problems, etc.]. In fact, according to the

[results of the study], people with an adolescent criminal conviction record were less likely to get in a fight with their supervisor or steal things from work.").

[115]   *See* OHIO REV. CODE ANN. § 2913.02.

[116]   523 F.2d at 1298 (stating that "[w]e cannot conceive of any business necessity that would automatically place every individual convicted of any offense, except a minor traffic offense, in the permanent ranks of the unemployed").

[117]   479 F.3d at 247.

[118]   *See, e.g.*, Keith Soothill & Brian Francis, *When do Ex-Offenders Become Like Non-Offenders?*, 48 HOWARD J. OF CRIM. JUST., 373, 380–81 (2009) (examining conviction data from Britain and Wales, a 2009 study found that the risk of recidivism declined for the groups with prior records and eventually converged within 10 to 15 years with the risk of those of the nonoffending comparison groups); Alfred Blumstein & Kiminori Nakamura, *Redemption in the Presence of Widespread Criminal Background Checks,* 47 CRIMINOLOGY 327 (2009) (concluding that there may be a "point of redemption" (i.e., a point in time where an individual's risk of re-offending or re-arrest is reasonably comparable to individuals with no prior criminal record) for individuals arrested for certain offenses if they remain crime free for a certain number of years); Megan C. Kurlychek, Robert Brame & Shawn D. Bushway, *Enduring Risk? Old Criminal Records and Predictions of Future Criminal Involvement*, 53 CRIME & DELINQUENCY 64 (2007) (analyzing juvenile police contacts and Racine, Wisconsin police contacts for an aggregate of crimes for 670 males born in 1942 and concluding that, after seven years, the risk of a new offense approximates that of a person without a criminal record); Megan C. Kurlychek et al., *Scarlet Letters and Recidivism: Does an Old Criminal Record Predict Future Offending?*, 5 CRIMINOLOGY & PUB. POL'Y 483 (2006) (evaluating juvenile police contacts and arrest dates from Philadelphia police records for an aggregate of crimes for individuals born in 1958, a 2006 study concluded that the risk of recidivism decreases over time and that, six or seven years after an arrest, an individual's risk of re-arrest approximates that of an individual who has never been arrested).

[119]   *Griggs*, 401 U.S. at 431.

[120]   523 F.2d at 1298; *see also* Field v. Orkin Extermination Co., No. Civ. A. 00-5913, 2002 WL 32345739, at *1 (E.D. Pa. Feb. 21, 2002) (unpublished) ("[A] blanket policy of denying employment to any person having a criminal conviction is a [*per se*] violation of Title VII."). The only exception would be if such an exclusion were required by federal law or regulation. *See, e.g., supra* note 110.

[121]   *Cf. Field*, 2002 WL 32345739, at *1. In *Field*, an employee of ten years was fired after a new company that acquired her former employer discovered her 6-year-old felony conviction. The new company had a blanket policy of firing anyone with a felony conviction less than 10 years old. The court granted summary judgment for the employee because the employer's argument that her conviction was related to her job qualifications was "weak at best," especially

given her positive employment history with her former employer. *Id.*

122   Recidivism rates tend to decline as ex-offenders' ages increase. A 2011 study found that an individual's age at conviction is a variable that has a "substantial and significant impact on recidivism." *The Predictive Value of Criminal Background Checks, supra* note 99, at 43. For example, the 26-year-olds in the study, with no prior criminal convictions, had a 19.6% chance of reoffending in their first year after their first conviction, compared to the 36-year-olds who had an 8.8% chance of reoffending during the same time period, and the 46-year-olds who had a 5.3% of reoffending. *Id.* at 46. *See also* PATRICK A. LANGAN & DAVID J. LEVIN, BUREAU OF JUSTICE STATISTICS, U.S. DEP'T OF JUSTICE, SPECIAL REPORT: RECIDIVISM OF PRISONERS RELEASED IN 1994, at 7 (2002), http://bjs.ojp.usdoj.gov/content/pub/pdf/rpr94.pdf (finding that, although 55.7% of ex-offenders aged 14–17 released in 1994 were reconvicted within three years, the percentage declined to 29.7% for ex-offenders aged 45 and older who were released the same year).

Consideration of an applicant's age at the time the offense occurred or at his release from prison would benefit older individuals and, therefore, would not violate the Age Discrimination in Employment Act of 1967, *as amended,* 29 U.S.C. § 621 *et seq. See* Age Discrimination in Employment Act, 29 C.F.R. § 1625.2 ("Favoring an older individual over a younger individual because of age is not unlawful discrimination under the ADEA, even if the younger individual is at least 40 years old."); *see also* Gen. Dynamics Land Sys., Inc. v. Cline, 540 U.S. 581, 600 (2004) (concluding that the ADEA does not preclude an employer from favoring an older employee over a younger one within the protected age group).

123   *See* Laura Moskowitz, *Statement of Laura Moskowitz, Staff Attorney, National Employment Law Project's Second Chance Labor Project*, U.S. EQUAL EMP'T OPPORTUNITY COMM'N, http://www.eeoc.gov/eeoc/meetings/11-20-08/moskowitz.cfm (last visited April 23, 2012) (stating that one of the factors that is relevant to the assessment of an ex-offender's risk to a workplace and to the business necessity analysis, is the "length and consistency of the person's work history, including whether the person has been recently employed"; also noting that various studies have "shown a strong relationship between employment and decreases in crime and recidivism"). *But see* Stephen J. Tripodi et al., *Is Employment Associated With Reduced Recidivism?: The Complex Relationship Between Employment and Crime*, 54 INT'L J. OF OFFENDER THERAPY AND COMP. CRIMINOLOGY 716, 716 (2010) (finding that "[b]ecoming employed after incarceration, although apparently providing initial motivation to desist from crime, does not seem to be on its own sufficient to prevent recidivism for many parolees").

124   *See* WENDY ERISMAN & JEANNE BAYER CONTARDO, INST. FOR HIGHER EDUC. POLICY, LEARNING TO REDUCE RECIDIVISM: A 50 STATE ANALYSIS OF POSTSECONDARY CORRECTIONAL EDUCATION 5 (2005), http://www.ihep.org/assets/files/publications/g-l/LearningReduceRecidivism.pdf (finding that increasing higher education for prisoners enhances their prospects for employment and serves as a cost-effective approach to reducing recidivism); *see also* John H. Laud & Robert J. Sampson, *Understanding Desistance from Crime*, 28 CRIME & JUST. 1, 17–24 (2001), http://www.ncjrs.gov/pdffiles1/Digitization/192542-192549NCJRS.pdf (stating that factors associated with personal rehabilitation and social

stability, such as stable employment, family and community involvement, and recovery from substance abuse, are correlated with a decreased risk of recidivism).

[125] Some employers have expressed a greater willingness to hire ex-offenders who have had an ongoing relationship with third party intermediary agencies that provide supportive services such as drug testing, referrals for social services, transportation, child care, clothing, and food. *See* Amy L. Solomon et al., *From Prison to Work: The Employment Dimensions of Prisoner Reentry*, 2004 URBAN INST. 20, http://www.urban.org/UploadedPDF/411097_From_Prison_to_Work.pdf. These types of services can help ex-offenders avoid problems that may interfere with their ability to obtain and maintain employment. *Id.*; *see generally* Victoria Kane, *Transcript of 7-26-11 Meeting*, U.S. EQUAL EMP'T OPPORTUNITY COMM'N, http://www.eeoc.gov/eeoc/meetings/7-26-11/transcript.cfm#kane (last visited April 23, 2012) (describing why employers should partner with organizations that provide supportive services to ex-offenders).

[126] *See generally* REENTRY MYTHBUSTER! ON FEDERAL BONDING PROGRAM, *supra* note 16; *Work Opportunity Tax Credit (WOTC)*, EMP'T & TRAINING ADMIN., U.S. DEP'T OF LABOR, http://www.doleta.gov/business/incentives/opptax/ (last visited April 3, 2012); *Directory of State Bonding Coordinators*, EMP'T & TRAINING ADMIN., U.S. DEP'T OF LABOR, http://www.doleta.gov/usworkforce/onestop/FBPContact.cfm (last visited April 3, 2012); *Federal Bonding Program - Background*, U.S. DEP'T OF LABOR, http://www.bonds4jobs.com/program-background.html (last visited April 3, 2012); *Bureau of Prisons: UNICOR's Federal Bonding Program*, http://www.bop.gov/inmate_programs/itb_bonding.jsp (last visited April 3, 2012).

[127] This example is loosely based on a study conducted by Alfred Blumstein and Kiminori Nakamura measuring the risk of recidivism for individuals who have committed burglary, robbery, or aggravated assault. *See* Blumstein & Nakamura, *supra* note 118.

[128] 42 U.S.C. § 2000e-2(k)(1)(A)(ii), (C). *See also* Watson v. Fort Worth Bank & Trust, 487 U.S. 977, 998 (1988).

[129] *See* Exec. Order No. 12,067, 3 C.F.R. 206 (1978 Comp.).

[130] *See* 49 U.S.C. §§ 44935(e)(2)(B), 44936(a)(1), (b)(1). The statute mandates a criminal background check.

[131] *See* 5 U.S.C. § 7371(b) (requiring mandatory removal from employment of law enforcement officers convicted of felonies).

[132] *See* 42 U.S.C. § 13041(c) ("Any conviction for a sex crime, an offense involving a child victim, or a drug felony may be grounds for denying employment or for dismissal of an employee. . . .").

[133] 12 U.S.C. § 1829.

[134]   46 U.S.C. § 70105(c).

[135]   Other jobs and programs subject to federally-imposed restrictions based on criminal convictions include the business of insurance (18 U.S.C. § 1033(e)), employee benefits employee (29 U.S.C. § 1111(a)), participation in Medicare and state health care programs (42 U.S.C. § 1320a-7(a)–(b)), defense contractor (10 U.S.C. § 2408(a)), prisoner transportation (42 U.S.C. § 13726b(b)(1)), and court-imposed occupational restrictions (18 U.S.C. §§ 3563(b)(5), 3583(d)). This list is not meant to be exhaustive.

[136]   *See, e.g.*, federal statutes governing commercial motor vehicle operator's licenses (49 U.S.C. § 31310(b)-(h)), locomotive operator licenses (49 U.S.C. § 20135(b)(4)(B)), and certificates, ratings, and authorizations for pilots, flight instructors, and ground instructors (49 U.S.C. §§ 44709(b)(2), 44710(b), 4711(c); 14 C.F.R. § 61.15).

[137]   *See, e.g.*, federal statutes governing loan originator licensing/registration (12 U.S.C. § 5104(b)(2)), registration of brokers and dealers (15 U.S.C. § 78o(b)(4)(B)), registration of commodity dealers (7 U.S.C. § 12a(2)(D), (3)(D), (E), (H)), and registration of investment advisers (15 U.S.C. § 80b-3(e)(2)-(3), (f)).

[138]   *See, e.g.*, custom broker's licenses (19 U.S.C. § 1641(d)(1)(B)), export licenses (50 U.S.C. App. § 2410(h)), and arms export (22 U.S.C. § 2778(g)).

[139]   *See, e.g.*, grain inspector's licenses (7 U.S.C. § 85), merchant mariner's documents, licenses, or certificates of registry (46 U.S.C. § 7503(b)), licenses to import, manufacture, or deal in explosives or permits to use explosives (18 U.S.C. § 843(d)), and farm labor contractor's certificates of registration (29 U.S.C. § 1813(a)(5)). This list of federally-imposed restrictions on occupational licenses and registrations for individuals with certain criminal convictions is not meant to be exhaustive. For additional information, please consult the relevant federal agency or department.

[140]   *See* 12 U.S.C. § 1829(a)(1). The statute imposes a ten-year ban for individuals who have been convicted of certain financial crimes such as corruption involving the receipt of commissions or gifts for procuring loans (18 U.S.C. § 215), embezzlement or theft by an officer/employee of a lending, credit, or insurance institution (18 U.S.C § 657), false or fraudulent statements by an officer/employee of the federal reserve or a depository institution (18 U.S.C. § 1005), or fraud by wire, radio, or television that affects a financial institution (18 U.S.C. § 1343), among other crimes. *See* 12 U.S.C. § 1829(a)(2)(A)(i)(I), (II). Individuals who have either been convicted of the crimes listed in § 1829(a)(2)(A), or conspiracy to commit those crimes, will not receive an exception to the application of the 10-year ban from the FDIC. 12 U.S.C. § 1829(a)(2)(A).

[141]   *See* FED. DEPOSIT INS. CORP., FDIC STATEMENT OF POLICY FOR SECTION 19 OF THE FDI ACT, § C, "PROCEDURES" (amended May 13, 2011), http://www.fdic.gov/regulations/laws/rules/5000-1300.html [hereinafter FDIC POLICY]; *see also*

Statement of Policy, 63 Fed. Reg. 66,177, 66,184 (Dec. 1, 1998); Clarification of Statement of Policy, 76 Fed. Reg. 28,031 (May 13, 2011) (clarifying the FDIC's Statement of Policy for Section 19 of the FDI Act).

"Approval is automatically granted and an application [for a waiver] will not be required where [an individual who has been convicted of] the covered offense [criminal offenses involving dishonesty, breach of trust, or money laundering] . . . meets all of the ["*de minimis*"] criteria" set forth in the FDIC's Statement of Policy. FDIC POLICY, *supra*, § B (5). These criteria include the following: (1) there is only one conviction or program of record for a covered offense; (2) the offense was punishable by imprisonment for a term of one year or less and/or a fine of $1,000 or less, and the individual did not serve time in jail; (3) the conviction or program was entered at least five years prior to the date an application would otherwise be required; and (4) the offense did not involve an insured depository institution or insured credit union. *Id.* Additionally, an individual's conviction for writing a "bad" check will be considered a *de minimis* offense, even if it involved an insured depository institution or insured credit union, if: (1) all other requirements of the *de minimis* offense provisions are met; (2) the aggregate total face value of the bad or insufficient funds check(s) cited in the conviction was $1000 or less; and (3) no insured depository institution or insured credit union was a payee on any of the bad or insufficient funds checks that were the basis of the conviction. *Id.*

[142]   *See* FDIC POLICY, *supra* note 141, § C, "PROCEDURES."

[143]   *Id. But cf.* NAT'L H.I.R.E. NETWORK, PEOPLE WITH CRIMINAL RECORDS WORKING IN FINANCIAL INSTITUTIONS: THE RULES ON FDIC WAIVERS, http://www.hirenetwork.org/FDIC.html ("Institutions rarely seek a waiver, except for higher level positions when the candidate is someone the institution wants to hire. Individuals can only seek FDIC approval themselves if they ask the FDIC to waive the usual requirement. Most individuals probably are unaware that they have this right."); FED. DEPOSIT INSUR. CORP. 2010 ANNUAL REPORT, § VI.A: KEY STATISTICS, FDIC ACTIONS ON FINANCIAL INSTITUTION APPLICATIONS 2008–2010 (2011), http://www.fdic.gov/about/strategic/report/2010annualreport/chpt6-01.html (reporting that between 2008 and 2010, the FDIC approved a total of 38 requests for consent to employ individuals with covered offenses in their background; the agency did not deny any requests during this time period).

[144]   FDIC POLICY, *supra* note 141, § D, "EVALUATION OF SECTION 19 APPLICATIONS" (listing the factors that are considered in this waiver review process, which include: (1) the nature and circumstances underlying the offense; (2) "[e]vidence of rehabilitation including the person's reputation since the conviction . . . the person's age at the time of conviction . . . and the time which has elapsed since the conviction"; (3) the position to be held in the insured institution; (4) the amount of influence/control the individual will be able to exercise over management affairs; (5) management's ability to control and supervise the individual's activities; (6) the degree of ownership the individual will have in the insured institution; (7) whether the institution's fidelity bond coverage applies to the individual; (8) the opinion of the applicable federal and/or state regulators; and (9) any other relevant factors).

[145]   *See* 49 C.F.R. §§ 1515.7 (describing the procedures for waiver of criminal offenses, among other standards), 1515.5 (explaining how to appeal the Initial Determination of Threat Assessment based on a criminal conviction). In practice, some worker advocacy groups have criticized the TWIC appeal process due to prolonged delays, which leaves many workers jobless; especially workers of color. *See generally* MAURICE EMSELLEM ET AL., NAT'L EMP'T LAW PROJECT, A SCORECARD ON THE POST-911 PORT WORKER BACKGROUND CHECKS: MODEL WORKER PROTECTIONS PROVIDE A LIFELINE FOR PEOPLE OF COLOR, WHILE MAJOR TSA DELAYS LEAVE THOUSANDS JOBLESS DURING THE RECESSION (2009), http://nelp.3cdn.net/2d5508b4cec6e13da6_upm6b20e5.pdf.

The Patient Protection and Affordable Care Act, Pub. L. No. 111-148, § 6201, 124 Stat. 721 (2010) (the Act) includes a process to appeal or dispute the accuracy of information obtained from criminal records. The Act requires participating states to perform background checks on applicants and current employees who have direct access to patients in long-term care facilities, such as nursing homes, to determine if they have been convicted of an offense or have other disqualifying information in their background, such as a finding of patient or resident abuse, that would disqualify them from employment under the Social Security Act or as specified by state law. *See* 42 U.S.C. § 1320a-7l(a)(3)(A), (a)(4)(B), (6)(A)–(E). The background check involves an individualized assessment of the relevance of a conviction or other disqualifying information. The Act protects applicants and employees in several ways, for example, by: (1) providing a 60-day provisional period of employment for the prospective employee, pending the completion of the criminal records check; (2) providing an independent process to appeal or dispute the accuracy of the information obtained in the criminal records check; and (3) allowing the employee to remain employed (subject to direct on-site supervision) during the appeals process. 42 U.S.C. § 1320a-7l(a)(4)(B)(iii), (iv).

[146]   *See* 46 U.S.C. § 70105(d); *see generally* TWIC Program, 49 C.F.R. § 1572.103 (listing the disqualifying offenses for maritime and land transportation security credentials, such as convictions and findings of not guilty by reason of insanity for espionage, murder, or unlawful possession of an explosive; also listing temporarily disqualifying offenses, within seven years of conviction or five years of release from incarceration, including dishonesty, fraud, or misrepresentation (expressly excluding welfare fraud and passing bad checks), firearms violations, and distribution, intent to distribute, or importation of controlled substances).

[147]   46 U.S.C. § 70105(c)(1)(A)–(B).

[148]   46 U.S.C. § 70105(c)(1)(B)(iii).

[149]   *See* 46 U.S.C. § 70105(c)(1)(A)(iv) (listing "Federal crime of terrorism" as a permanent disqualifying offense); *see also* 18 U.S.C. § 2332b(g)(5)(B) (defining "Federal crime of terrorism" to include the use of weapons of mass destruction under § 2332a).

[150]   *See* 49 C.F.R. § 1515.7(a)(i) (explaining that only certain applicants with disqualifying crimes in their backgrounds may apply for a waiver; these applicants do not include individuals

who have been convicted of a Federal crime of terrorism as defined by 18 U.S.C. § 2332b(g)).

[151]   These positions are defined as "national security positions" and include positions that "involve activities of the Government that are concerned with the protection of the nation from foreign aggression or espionage, including development of defense plans or policies, intelligence or counterintelligence activities, and related activities concerned with the preservation of the military strength of the United States" or "require regular use of, or access to, classified information." 5 C.F.R. § 732.102(a)(1)–(2). The requirements for "national security positions" apply to competitive service positions, Senior Executive Service positions filled by career appointment within the Executive Branch, and excepted service positions within the Executive Branch. *Id.* § 732.102(b). The head of each Federal agency can designate any position within that department or agency as a "sensitive position" if the position "could bring about, by virtue of the nature of the position, a material adverse effect on the national security." *Id.* § 732.201(a). Designation of a position as a "sensitive position" will fall under one of three sensitivity levels: Special-Sensitive, Critical-Sensitive, or Noncritical-Sensitive. *Id.*

[152]   *See* Exec. Order No. 12,968, § 3.1(b), 3 C.F.R. 391 (1995 Comp.):

> [E]ligibility for access to classified information shall be granted only to employees who are United States citizens for whom an appropriate investigation has been completed and whose personal and professional history affirmatively indicates loyalty to the United States, strength of character, trustworthiness, honestly, reliability, discretion, and sound judgment, as well as freedom from conflicting allegiances and potential for coercion, and willingness and ability to abide by regulations governing the use, handling, and protection of classified information. A determination of eligibility for access to such information is a discretionary security decision based on judgments by appropriately trained adjudicative personnel. Eligibility shall be granted only where facts and circumstances indicate access to classified information is clearly consistent with the national security interests of the United States, and any doubt shall be resolved in favor of the national security.

[153]   42 U.S.C. § 2000e-2(g); *see, e.g.*, Bennett v. Chertoff, 425 F.3d 999, 1001 (D.C. Cir. 2005) ("[E]mployment actions based on denial of a security clearance are not subject to judicial review, including under Title VII."); Ryan v. Reno, 168 F.3d 520, 524 (D.C. Cir. 1999) ("[A]n adverse employment action based on denial or revocation of a security clearance is not actionable under Title VII.").

[154]   *See Policy Guidance on the use of the national security exception contained in § 703(g) of Title VII of the Civil Rights Act of 1964, as amended,* U.S. EQUAL EMP'T OPPORTUNITY COMM'N, § II, *Legislative History* (May 1, 1989), http://www.eeoc.gov/policy/docs/national_security_exemption.html ("[N]ational security requirements must be applied equally without regard to race, sex, color, religion or national origin."); *see also* Jones v. Ashcroft, 321 F. Supp. 2d 1, 8 (D.D.C. 2004) (indicating that the

national security exception did not apply because there was no evidence that the government considered national security as a basis for its decision not to hire the plaintiff at any time before the commencement of the plaintiff's lawsuit, where the plaintiff had not been forthright about an arrest).

[155]   Federal contractor employees may challenge the denial of a security clearance with the EEOC or the Office of Contract Compliance Programs when the denial is based on race, color, religion, sex, or national origin. *See generally* Exec. Order No. 11,246, 3 C.F.R. 339 (1964–1965 Comp.).

[156]   42 U.S.C. § 2000e-16(a).

[157]   Robert H. Shriver, III, *Written Testimony of Robert H. Shriver, III, Senior Policy Counsel for the U.S. Office of Personnel Management*, U.S. EQUAL EMP'T OPPORTUNITY COMM'N, http://www.eeoc.gov/eeoc/meetings/7-26-11/shriver.cfm (last visited April 23, 2012) (stating that "with just a few exceptions, criminal convictions do not automatically disqualify an applicant from employment in the competitive civil service"); *see also* REENTRY MYTHBUSTER! ON FEDERAL HIRING POLICIES, *supra* note 16 ("The Federal Government employs people with criminal records with the requisite knowledge, skills and abilities."). *But see supra* note 110, listing several federal statutes that prohibit individuals with certain convictions from working as federal law enforcement officers or port workers, or with private prisoner transport companies.

[158]   OPM has jurisdiction to establish the federal government's suitability policy for competitive service positions, certain excepted service positions, and career appointments in the Senior Executive Service. *See* 5 C.F.R. §§ 731.101(a) (stating that OPM has been directed "to examine 'suitability' for competitive Federal employment"), 731.101(b) (defining the covered positions within OPM's jurisdiction); *see also* Shriver, *supra* note 157.

OPM is also responsible for establishing standards that help agencies decide whether to grant their employees and contractor personnel long-term access to federal facilities and information systems. *See* Homeland Security Presidential Directive 12: Policy for a Common Identification Standard for Federal Employees and Contractors, 2 PUB. PAPERS 1765 (Aug. 27, 2004) ("establishing a mandatory, Government-wide standard for secure and reliable forms of identification issued by the Federal Government to its employees and contractors [including contractor employees]"); *see also* Exec. Order No. 13,467, § 2.3(b), 3 C.F.R. 196 (2009 Comp.) ("[T]he Director of [OPM] . . . [is] responsible for developing and implementing uniform and consistent policies and procedures to ensure the effective, efficient, and timely completion of investigations and adjudications relating to determinations of suitability and eligibility for logical and physical access."); *see generally* Shriver, *supra* note 157.

[159]   5 C.F.R. § 731.101(a).

[160]   *See* 5 C.F.R. §§ 731.205(a) (stating that if an agency finds applicants unsuitable based on the factors listed in 5 C.F.R. § 731.202, it may, in its discretion, bar those applicants from federal employment for three years), § 731.202(b) (disqualifying factors from federal civilian

employment may include: misconduct or negligence in employment; material, intentional false statement, or deception or fraud in examination or appointment; refusal to furnish testimony as required by 5 C.F.R. § 5.4; alcohol abuse without evidence of substantial rehabilitation; illegal use of narcotics, drugs, or other controlled substances; and knowing and willful engagement in acts or activities designed to overthrow the U.S. Government by force).

[161] *See id.* § 731.202(c).

[162] *Id.*

[163] *See generally* Shriver, *supra* note 157. *See also* REENTRY MYTHBUSTER! ON FEDERAL HIRING POLICIES, *supra* note 16 ("Consistent with Merit System Principles, [federal] agencies [and departments] are required to consider people with criminal records when filling positions if they are the best candidates and can comply with requirements.").

[164] *See generally EEOC Informal Discussion Letter* (March 19, 2007), http://www.eeoc.gov/eeoc/foia/letters/2007/arrest_and_conviction_records.html#N1 (discussing the EEOC's concerns with changes to OPM's suitability regulations at 5 CFR part 731).

[165] *See* Stephen Saltzburg, *Transcript of 7-26-11 Meeting*, U.S. EQUAL EMP'T OPPORTUNITY COMM'N, http://www.eeoc.gov/eeoc/meetings/7-26-11/transcript.cfm#saltzburg (last visited April 23, 2012) (discussing the findings from the American Bar Association's (ABA) Collateral Consequences of Conviction Project, which found that in 17 states that it has examined to date, 84% of the collateral sanctions against ex-offenders relate to employment). For more information about the ABA's project, visit: Janet Levine, *ABA Criminal Justice Section Collateral Consequences Project*, INST. FOR SURVEY RESEARCH, TEMPLE UNIV., http://isrweb.isr.temple.edu/projects/accproject/ (last visited April 20, 2012). In April 2011, Attorney General Holder sent a letter to every state Attorney General, with a copy to every Governor, asking them to "evaluate the collateral consequences" of criminal convictions in their state, such as employment-related restrictions on ex-offenders, and "to determine whether those [consequences] that impose burdens on individuals . . . without increasing public safety should be eliminated." Letter from Eric H. Holder, Jr., Att'y Gen., Dep't of Justice, to state Attorney Generals and Governors (April 18, 2011), http://www.nationalreentryresourcecenter.org/documents/0000/1088/Reentry_Council_AG_Letter.pdf.

Most states regulate occupations that involve responsibility for vulnerable citizens such as the elderly and children. *See* STATE CRIMINAL HISTORY, *supra* note 37, at 10 ("Fifty states and the District of Columbia reported that criminal history background checks are legally required" for several occupations such as nurses/elder caregivers, daycare providers, caregivers in residential facilities, school teachers, and nonteaching school employees). For example, Hawaii's Department of Human Services may deny applicants licensing privileges to operate a childcare facility if: (1) the applicant or any prospective employee has been convicted of a crime other than a minor traffic violation or has been confirmed to have abused or neglected a child or threatened harm; and (2) the department finds that the criminal history or child abuse record of the applicant or prospective employee may pose a risk to the health, safety, or well-being of children. *See* HAW. REV. STAT. § 346-154(e)(1)–(2).

[166]   42 U.S.C. § 2000e-7.

[167]   *See* Int'l Union v. Johnson Controls, Inc., 499 U.S. 187, 210 (1991) (noting that "[i]f state tort law furthers discrimination in the workplace and prevents employers from hiring women who are capable of manufacturing the product as efficiently as men, then it will impede the accomplishment of Congress' goals in enacting Title VII"); Gulino v. N.Y. State Educ. Dep't, 460 F.3d 361, 380 (2d Cir. 2006) (affirming the district court's conclusion that "the mandates of state law are no defense to Title VII liability").

SAMPLE COMPLAINT APPLICATION

STATE OF NEW YORK
DIVISION OF HUMAN RIGHTS

NEW YORK STATE DIVISION OF HUMAN RIGHTS on the Complaint of _____ Complainant, v. _____ . Respondent.	**VERIFIED COMPLAINT** *N.Y. EXEC. LAW ART. 15* *N.Y. CORR.LAW ART. 23-A* SDHR CASE NO. _____

Complainant, _____ submits the following as and for a complaint of unlawful discrimination against Respondent, _____ on the basis of unlawful discriminatory practices in violation of state employment laws. Respondent has perpetrated and continues to perpetrate (1) a pattern and practice of systematically discriminating against persons with a criminal record (2) taking an adverse action or in the alternative acting upon adversely applicants with convictions records (3) upon information and belief an automatic blanket conviction record exclusion through its application and background check policy that is a prima facie violation of *New York Corr. Law Art. 23-A* and *New York Exec. Law.* § *296 (15)*.

The claims in this complaint are set forth as follows and require an answer to each allegation:

<u>PARTIES</u>

1.   Complainant is an aggrieved person who brings this proceeding against Respondent. I am a resident of New York and have an address of_____.

2.   Upon information and belief, Respondent hires in New York and conducts business in New York State, employing a minimum of 10 individuals under the provisions of *New York Correction Law Article 23-A §§ 750-755* and *New York Executive Law Article 15 § 296.15*.

3.   Respondent has a principal business address of

_____.

FACTS

4.   Respondent was seeking applicants for a position of _____.

5.   Respondent sought these applicants through application **via printed form or website submission at the following url:** (choose one) _____.

6.   I filled out an application on or about _____, 20_____.

7.   I **handed/submitted** (choose one) the application to **an employee/automated system** (choose one).

8.   Respondent described the qualifications for the position it sought applicants for as (attach description):

_____

_____

9.   Respondent **did/did not** (choose one) interview me for the position.

10.   Respondent **did/did not** (choose one) hand me a copy of Article 23-A of the New York State Correction Law when I signed the last page of the application for employment and agreed to a background check consent for the job I applied to.

RESPONDENT DENIED EMPLOYMENT OF MY APPLICATION WITHOUT ASSESSING MY INDIVIDUAL QUALIFICATIONS AND BASED ITS DECISION ENTIRELY ON MY CONVICTION RECORD

11.   Respondent asks on its application for employment the following conviction record question: **Have you ever been convicted of a crime?, Have you ever been convicted of a criminal offense?, Have you ever been convicted of a felony?, Have you ever been convicted of a misdemeanor?, Have you ever been convicted of a violation? Have you ever been convicted of any crime since the age of 18? Have you ever been convicted of any felonies or misdemeanors in the last 7 years? Have you ever been convicted of a criminal offense in the last 7 years? Have you ever had any arrests that led to a conviction?** (Circle One That Applies, if not type here):_____

_____)

12.   I checked "yes" and listed my convictions. I answered the question truthfully.

13.   Respondent **made/did not make** (choose one) a statement *that "a conviction record is not a bar to employment."* on its application.

14.   Respondent did not ask me if I had any rehabilitation anywhere in the application.

15.   I had a background check run on me on the following date:_____, 20__. (only if applicable). I have attached such background check to this complaint as Exhibit A.

16.   I received an adverse action letter from the background check company, _____ on or about _____, 20_____(only if applicable). I have attached such letter to this complaint as Exhibit B.

17.   I was interviewed on_____, 20_____. The person who interviewed me was _____ and their position was _____. (fill out if applicable)

18.   I **did/did not** discuss my conviction record during the interview with Respondent's employee. (fill out if applicable)

19.   I was denied employment on _____, 20_____. I know this because I received from the Respondent a **letter/email/notice** (circle all that apply). I have attached that document as Exhibit C.

20.   The only thing I was asked during the entire application and interview process was whether I had a conviction record or not. Respondent did not gather anything else, including my rehabilitation since my conviction(s) before it denied me employment.

21.   Upon information and belief Respondent utilizes a grading criteria through its background check third party vendor which would eliminate me from obtaining positions with the company.

COMPLAIANT, WHO HAS A CRIMINAL RECORD, EXCEEDS THE
QUALIFICATIONS FOR THE POSITION BEING SOUGHT

22.   Complainant is a person with a conviction record consisting of:

_____

_____

_____

_____ (indicate each conviction

by name, date you pled guilty. Look up the Penal Law for each conviction §§ and include here.)

23.   Because I have a conviction record, I am part of a protected class in New York State.

24.   Complainant is an eligible offender who possesses a Certificate of Relief of Civil Disabilities under the provisions of *Article 23 § 701(1)* for the following conviction listed above: _____ and is therefore entitled to a presumption of rehabilitation at all times.

25.   I can meet the stated requirements of the position of _____ that I applied to Respondent for.

26.   Therefore I put forth that I am qualified for the job that I applied to.

27.   I was denied employment for this job and it is upon information and belief that Respondent continued hiring people who did not have any conviction record and less qualifications than me.

28.   Therefore, I have standing to exert a claim of discrimination because I have met my prima facie case in that I am part of a protected class, I am qualified for the position I applied to, I was denied employment and other people who have no convictions who were less qualified than me were hired after me.

DIVISION MUST ISSUE A PROBABLE CAUSE;
COMPLAINANT MEETS MINIMUM JOB QUALIFICATIONS AND MEETS PRIMA FACIE CASE

29.   Article 23-A of the Correction Law, which is incorporated into Human Rights Law 296.15, specifically provides the basis upon which to evaluate an employer's actions with respect to persons with prior conviction records. Correction Law Art. 23-A permits consideration of prior convictions based on an employer' analysis of business necessity. Article 23-A provides that this business judgment must be exercised in such a way that the State's public policy encouraging employment and licensure of persons with prior convictions is observed.

30.   Article 23-A establishes the specific lawful, job-related factors that must be considered in evaluating conviction records of applicants and employees, and therefore establishes by statute the parameters of permissible business judgment.

31.   The law specifically provides that employers may consider an applicant's record of prior convictions, such as myself, so long as the determination whether or not to hire is made in accordance with the factors set forth in *New York Correction Law Article 23-A § 752* either by a "direct relationship" or an "unreasonable risk."

32.   Respondent's failure to ask me any additional questions about my conviction record and the seriousness of my criminal offense(s) indicates that they already came to a pre-determined conclusion not to hire me. One would think that an employer would want to ask me questions in order to gather the appropriate information to determine if it wanted to claim either a direct relationship or unreasonable risk exemption.

33.   Respondent cannot adequately show how my conviction record is directly relevant to the position or how it would an unreasonable risk if I was interfacing with the public.

34.   The background check revealed nothing that I did not disclose during the hiring process. The information in the report should only be relevant if it revealed something I failed to disclose.

35.   Respondent upon information and belief cannot provide any evidence that it at any time applied the eight factors under *Article 23-A of the Correction Law* before it denied me employment.

36.   When Respondent denied employment by not hiring me because I have a conviction record, the decision was made in accordance with an unlawfully stated blanket policy and therefore failed to utilize *New York Correction Law Article 23-A § 752* to determine if a "direct relationship" or an "unreasonable risk" exists. This explains why I was not hired and why I was denied the chance to submit evidence of rehabilitation.

37.   Respondent was aware at the time of the discrimination that it needed to follow *New York Correction Law Article 23-A* because *New York Labor Law 201-F* and *General Business Law 380* require that a company that operates in New York and runs background checks for New York applicants post and give a copy of *New York Correction Law Article 23-A* to anyone it hires.

38.   Respondent did not claim either of the two exemptions stated in *New York Correction Law Article 23-A* at the time of my denial. By not utilizing a proper denial, Respondent has promoted the unfair discrimination that the New York legislature sought to eradicate by removing barriers to employment by passing the statute over 35 years ago.

FIRST CAUSE OF ACTION: VIOLATION OF EXECUTIVE LAW § 296 (15)

39.   Paragraphs 1 through 38 are re-alleged and fully set forth.

40.   The public policy of New York is to encourage the hire of an ex-offender.

41.   I was automatically denied employment since Respondent based its entire decision on my conviction record and did not conduct an individualized analysis before denying me employment.

42.   Respondent does not encourage the hire of individuals with conviction records.

43.   I am facially ineligible for employment with Respondent because of my conviction record.

44.   Denying me employment based on nothing more than my background check or application for employment is a denial based on the mere existence of their conviction record, a practice forbidden by *N.Y. Executive Law § 296(15)*.

45.   Respondent has violated *New York Executive Law § 296 (15)* by not properly considering me for employment in accordance with the provisions of *New York Article 23-A of the Correction Law*.

SECOND CAUSE OF ACTION: VIOLATION OF ARTICLE 23-A § 752

46.   Paragraphs 1 through 38 are re-alleged and fully set forth.

47.   Upon information and belief, Respondent has not properly claimed exemptions for a direct relationship or/and an unreasonable risk.

48.   Upon information and belief Respondent utilizes an adjudication or matrix guideline that allows for the automatic prohibition of anyone with a felony or misdemeanor conviction record.

49.   Respondent's own failure to gather an individualized assessment prevented a weighing of my conviction record to determine if an exemption is required as mandated by the statute.

50.   I was honest and checked "yes" to a conviction record question and was eliminated from the hiring process. The conviction record question promoted unfair discrimination because it gathered nothing else from me, including my rehabilitation before denying me employment.

51.   Respondent's own action prevented any assessment of qualifications, job duties, skills or education because it could not properly conduct an Article 23-A § 752 analysis at the time of denial.

52.   Respondent has violated Article 23-A § 752 because it has disqualified me and removed me from consideration in its applicant pool rather than properly analyze a direct relationship or unreasonable risk analysis as required by statute that included the qualifications, job duties, skills and education of an applicant.

THIRD CAUSE OF ACTION: VIOLATION OF ARTICLE 23-A § 753-1

53.   Paragraphs 1 through 38 are re-alleged and fully set forth.

54.   Complainant has been barred from consideration in the application process entirely because of the existence of his conviction record.

55.   Respondent does not consider the relevant eight factors under Article 23-A § 753-1 before denying an ex-offender with a conviction record because they have denied employment without properly conducting an individualized assessment.

56.   Respondent violated Correction Law §753 by failing to evaluate and consider the following required factors when refusing to hire me for a position due to my prior criminal record:

   a.   The public policy of this state; and

   b.   The specific duties and responsibilities necessarily related to working in the position; and

   c.   The bearing, if any, of Complainant's convictions on his fitness or ability to perform one or more of his duties or responsibilities for the position; and

   d.   The time which has elapsed since the occurrence of Complainant's offenses; and

   e.   Complainant's age at the time of the offenses; and

   f.   The seriousness of Complainant's offenses; and

   g.   Information produced by Complainant or produced on his behalf, with respect to his rehabilitation and good conduct; and

   h.   The safety and welfare of individuals and the general public, and the protection of property.

57.   Respondent denied employment and in the alternative, acted upon adversely my application for employment because it gathered nothing more than my conviction itself.

58.   Respondent has violated Article 23-A § 753-1 by not establishing at the time of denial it asked information concerning the 8 factors as specified in the statute before denying employment.

59.   Respondent's policies and practices of barring persons with felony conviction records from employment violate *NY Exec. Law §296 (15), NY Corr. Law §752, NY Corr. Law §753-1 and NY Corr. Law §753-2.*

FOURTH CAUSE OF ACTION: VIOLATION OF ARTICLE 23-A § 753-2

60.   Paragraphs 1 through 38 are re-alleged and fully set forth.

61.   I have a Certificate of Relief for my conviction. The presumption of rehabilitation created by the certificate of relief from disabilities applies even where the statutory definition of "direct relationship" (Correction Law § 750 [3]) has been satisfied.

62.   Respondent must consider the eight factors listed in Correction Law § 753 (1) (a)-(h) to determine whether, in fact, the "direct relationship" is sufficiently attenuated to warrant issuance of employment and not ignore an applicant simply because they checked yes to having a criminal record.

63.   The issuance of a certificate of relief from disabilities creates a presumption of rehabilitation which Respondent's must rebut.

64.   Respondent violated Article 23-A § 753-2 by never rebutting the presumption of rehabilitation before denying employment on the basis that no such request was made to me to gather such information for a proper analysis.

FIFTH CAUSE OF ACTION: RESPONDENT'S CONDUCT WAS WILLFUL, WANTON AND/OR MALICIOUS AND MUST BE FINED PURSUANT TO NEW YORK EXECUTIVE LAW §297(4)(c)(vi)

65.   Paragraphs 1 through 38 are re-alleged and fully set forth.

66.   Each and every act and omission by Respondent constituting unlawful discrimination is and was done willfully, wantonly and/or maliciously and justifies the imposition of civil penalties.

67.   New York Executive Law § 297 (4)(c)(vi) permits the Division to assess civil fines and penalties, "in an amount not to exceed fifty thousand dollars, to be paid to the state by a respondent found to have committed an unlawful discriminatory act, or not to exceed one hundred thousand dollars to be paid to the state by a Respondent found to have committed an unlawful discriminatory act which is found to be willful, wanton or malicious.

PRAYER FOR RELIEF

WHEREFORE, Complainant respectfully requests:

A. A declaration that Respondent has violated *NY Exec. Law §§ 296 (15), NY Corr. Law §752, NY Corr. Law §753-1 and NY Corr. Law §753-2* and an order to cease and desist the unlawful conduct described above.

B. A declaration that Respondent does not follow *New York Correction Law Article 23-A* during the employment, interview and background check policies by denying me employment.

C. Back Pay and Compensatory Damages since I have been denied a position and discouraged from applying simply based entirely on having a criminal record.

D. Requiring Respondent to comply with the provisions of the Human Rights Law and Correction Law Article 23-A, including but not limited to developing and implementing practices, policies and procedures for the pre-employment process in order to fully comply with the Human Rights Law and encourage the hire of ex-offenders.

E. That the Division recognize that no other similar relief has been requested by myself and no other complaint stating such set of allegations has been verified to before any other state agency complainant of the exact same practice.

F. Such other and further relief as may be deemed just and proper, including imposing civil fines and awarding such additional relief as may be just and proper.

Dated: _____   _____

                                                NAME OF COMPLAINANT

VERIFICATION

STATE OF NEW YORK   )
)   SS:
COUNTY OF _____)

     I, _____, being duly sworn, deposes and says: that I am the Complainant herein, and that I have read the foregoing complaint and know the content thereof; that the same is true and correct of my own knowledge except as to the matters therein stated on information and belief; and that as to those matters, I believe the same to be true.

                                      _____

                                         NAME OF COMPLAINANT

Subscribed and sworn to
before me this _____ day
of _____ in the year 20___

_____
Signature of Notary Public

SAMPLE AD COMPLAINT

STATE OF NEW YORK
DIVISION OF HUMAN RIGHTS

NEW YORK STATE DIVISION OF HUMAN RIGHTS on the Complaint of _____ Complainant, v. _____ . Respondent.	**VERIFIED COMPLAINT** *N.Y. EXEC. LAW ART. 15* *N.Y. CORR.LAW ART. 23-A* SDHR CASE NO. _____

Complainant, _____ submits the following as and for a complaint of unlawful discrimination against Respondent, _____ on the basis of unlawful discriminatory practices in violation of state employment laws. Respondent has perpetrated and continues to perpetrate (1) a pattern and practice of systematically discriminating against persons with a criminal record (2) advertisements for jobs which chill and discriminate against ex-offenders based on nothing more than having a criminal record (3) an automatic blanket conviction record exclusion that is a prima facie violation of *New York Corr. Law Art. 23-A* and *New York Exec. Law. § 296 (15)*.

The claims in this complaint are set forth as follows and require an answer to each allegation:

PARTIES

1.   Complainant is an aggrieved person who brings this proceeding against Respondent. I am a resident of New York and have an address of_____.

2.   Upon information and belief, Respondent hires in New York and conducts business in New York State, employing a minimum of 10 individuals under the provisions of *New York Correction Law Article 23-A §§ 750-755* and *New York Executive Law Article 15 § 296.15*.

3.   Respondent   has   a   principal   business   address   of _____.

FACTS

4.   Respondent was seeking applicants for a position of _____.

5. Respondent sought these applicants by placing an advertisement at the following url:
_____.

6. Respondent runs a website at the url:_____

7. Respondent's advertisement stated lawful qualifications which I can meet.

8. Respondent's advertisement contains a telephone number/address of _____ that belongs to this specific Respondent.

9. Respondent's advertisement contains a logo/application link/webpage that I saw that clearly identified Respondent.

RESPONDENT OPENLY STATES A POLICY THAT EFFECTIVELY DISCOURGES PERSONS IN NEW YORK STATE WITH CRIMINAL HISTORIES FROM APPLYING AND BARS SUCH PERSON WITHOUT ASSESSING INDIVIDUAL QUALIFICATIONS

10. Respondent paid for and placed an advertisement on or about _____, 20_____ which I viewed and attached as Exhibit A. This advertisement was placed within the last year of this complaint.

11. Respondent then listed a job requirement that included a qualification of one of the following : **no felonies, no felony conviction, clean criminal background, no misdemeanors, clear criminal background, no criminal history, no criminal convictions, no theft convictions, clean criminal history, clear criminal history, no prior convictions, no criminal offenses.** *(Circle all that apply)*

12. Respondent clearly did not want to hire anyone with a criminal record. It is impossible for me to meet this stated qualification since I have a criminal conviction record.

13. Respondent directed me to not apply for the position. I was not able to apply for the position because of this limitation stated by Respondent to potential applicants.

14. If Respondent had not discouraged and chilled me through a blanket policy I would have had a fair chance to obtain the position and been a valuable employee.

15. I am not the right person for Respondent because I have a criminal background. I was therefore discouraged from applying based on Respondent's unlawfully stated qualification.

16. Upon information and belief Respondent utilizes a grading criteria through its background check third party vendor which eliminates ex-offenders from obtaining positions with the company as indicated in its open policy displayed in advertisements it posts in New York State.

COMPLAIANT, WHO HAS A CRIMINAL RECORD, EXCEEDS THE QUALIFICATIONS FOR THE POSITION BEING SOUGHT

17. Complainant is a person with a conviction record consisting of:

_____

_____

_____

_____ (indicate each

conviction by name, date you pled guilty. Look up the Penal Law for each conviction §§ and include here.)

18.   Complainant is an eligible offender who possesses a Certificate of Relief of Civil Disabilities under the provisions of *Article 23 § 701(1)* for the following conviction listed above: _____ and is therefore entitled to a presumption of rehabilitation at all times.

19.   I can meet the lawful requirements of the position of _____ stated in the advertisement.

20.   I was discouraged by Respondent from employment on the sole basis that I have a criminal record. I did not apply for employment because Respondent openly stated a policy qualification of **no felonies, no felony conviction, clean criminal background, no misdemeanors, clear criminal background, no criminal history, no criminal convictions, no theft convictions, clean criminal history, clear criminal history, no prior convictions, no criminal offenses.** *(Circle all that apply)* which rendered any potential application for employment a futile gesture.

21.   I have standing to exert a claim of discrimination because I was qualified for the position and chilled from applying based on an unlawfully stated qualification.

22.   Upon information and belief Respondent has no justification to impose a bar based on any state or federal statute by denying all ex-offenders a position based on nothing more than the conviction itself.

DIVISION MUST ISSUE A PROBABLE CAUSE; NO LEGITIMATE BUSINESS NECESSITY FOR POSTING SUCH CHILLINING JOB QUALIFICATIONS AGAINST PROTECTED CLASS

23.   Article 23-A of the Correction Law, which is incorporated into Human Rights Law 296.15, specifically provides the basis upon which to evaluate an employer's actions with respect to persons with prior conviction records. Correction Law Art. 23-A permits consideration of prior convictions based on an employer' analysis of business necessity. Article 23-A provides that this business judgment must be exercised in such a way that the State's public policy encouraging employment and licensure of persons with prior convictions is observed.

24.   Openly stating an employment qualification that acts to bar all ex-offenders is not a business necessity or permissible business judgment in New York and has the effect of violating public policy by discouraging those with prior conviction records from obtaining employment.

25.   Article 23-A establishes the specific lawful, job-related factors that must be considered in evaluating conviction records of applicants and employees, and therefore establishes by statute the parameters of permissible business judgment.

26.   The practice of demanding such an unlawful qualification effectively discouraged me, a member of a protected class, and those with conviction record histories from applying for employment. This practice appears to violate the New York State Human Rights law, regardless of what Respondent claims its company practices to be.

27.   It is reasonable to believe that a job advertisement that lists such an unlawful requirement would have such a chilling effect on an applicant with a conviction record that the need to actually apply for the position would be obviated, as such application would appear to be futile.

28.   Respondent upon information and belief cannot provide any evidence that it does apply the eight factors under *Article 23-A of the Correction Law*, contrary to the posted advertisement.

29.   When Respondent advertised openly that it wanted applicants who did not have a conviction record as a qualification, the decision to not hire candidates who might wish to apply was made in accordance with an unlawfully stated blanket policy and therefore failed to utilize *New York Correction Law Article 23-A § 752* to determine if a "direct relationship" or an "unreasonable risk" because it automatically denied employment.

30.   Respondent's conviction record qualification stated in advertisements has disqualified, separated, segregated and branded away from the applicant pool potential applicants who have a criminal record, including myself.

31.   Respondent, based on its openly stated policy in the ad cannot determine that my conviction record would have resulted in my ineligibility for consideration for the position had I applied since Respondent deprived itself of my application by stating the unlawful qualification. Since I could not meet the unlawful criteria, I did not apply.

32.   Respondent is aware since February 1, 2009 that they are statutorily required to post *New York Correction Law Article 23-A* in their establishment under *New York Labor Law § 201 F* but yet have chosen to post to potential applicants that those with criminal convictions are not welcome to apply in violation of the public policy of New York.

FIRST CAUSE OF ACTION: VIOLATION OF EXECUTIVE LAW § 296 (15)

33.   Paragraphs 1 through 32 are re-alleged and fully set forth.

34.   The public policy of New York is to encourage the hire of an ex-offender.

35.   An automatic policy to exclude ex-offenders is a prima facie violation of the statute.

36.   Stating a blanket prohibition against an ex offender to not hire on the basis of criminal convictions regardless of circumstance is not consistent with the public policy of New York to encourage applications of employment from individuals with conviction records and constitutes a prima facie violation of the Human Rights Law where such automatic denial of employment occurs.

37.   Complainant is facially ineligible for employment because of a conviction record.

38.   Successfully barring a person from applying for a position solely because they have a conviction record effectively denies them employment based on the mere existence of their conviction record, a practice forbidden by *N.Y. Executive Law § 296(15).*

39.   Respondent has violated *New York Executive Law § 296 (15)* by openly stating chilling and discouraging qualification that discriminate by branding, segregating and separating ex-offenders if they have a criminal record from being considered for employment.

SECOND CAUSE OF ACTION: VIOLATION OF ARTICLE 23-A § 752

40.   Paragraphs 1 through 32 are re-alleged and fully set forth.

41.   Respondent in order to properly deny an ex-offender must claim exemptions for a direct relationship or/and an unreasonable risk.

42.   Respondent denied employment when it did not utilize any individualized analysis and chose to promote an openly stated automatic prohibition on anyone with a criminal record.

43.   Respondent's own action to state that ex-offenders need not apply prevented a weighing of my conviction record to determine if an exemption is required as mandated by the statute.

44.   Respondent's own action prevented any assessment of qualifications, job duties, skills or education because it could not properly conduct an Article 23-A § 752 analysis at the time of denial.

45.   Respondent has violated Article 23-A § 752 because it has disqualified anyone with a criminal record from consideration in its applicant pool rather than properly analyze a direct relationship or unreasonable risk analysis as required by statute that included the qualifications, job duties, skills and education of an applicant.

THIRD CAUSE OF ACTION: VIOLATION OF ARTICLE 23-A § 753-1

46.   Paragraphs 1 through 32 are re-alleged and fully set forth.

47.   I have been barred from consideration in the application process entirely because of the existence of his conviction record.

48.   Respondent does not consider the relevant eight factors under Article 23-A § 753-1 before denying an ex-offender with a conviction record because they have denied employment on the basis of a qualification which is unlawful as stated in there advertisement.

49.   Respondent violated Correction Law §753 by failing to evaluate and consider the following required factors when refusing to hire me for the position based on a prior criminal record:

        (a)   The public policy of this state; and

        (b)   The specific duties and responsibilities necessarily related to working in the position; and

        (c)   The bearing, if any, of Complainant's convictions on his fitness or ability to perform one or more of his duties or responsibilities of the position; and

        (d)   The time which has elapsed since the occurrence of Complainant's offenses; and

        (e)   Complainant's age at the time of the offenses; and

        (f)   The seriousness of Complainant's offenses; and

        (g)   Information produced by Complainant or produced on his behalf, with respect to his rehabilitation and good conduct; and

        (h)   The safety and welfare of individuals and the general public, and the protection of property.

50.   Respondent denied employment and in the alternative, acted upon adversely applicants because Complainant cannot meet the unlawful qualification for the position. This is an unlawful discriminatory practice that automatically denies employment without any individualized assessment and comes to a pre-determined conclusion which is a "sham."

51.   Respondent did not consider the facts or circumstances of the factors above surrounding the criminal conviction(s) before barring those with criminal histories from consideration.

52.   Respondent has violated Article 23-A § 753-1 by openly barring Complainant and failing to properly conduct an 8 factor analysis under the statute before denying employment.

FOURTH CAUSE OF ACTION: VIOLATION OF ARTICLE 23-A § 753-2

53.   Paragraphs 1 through 32 are re-alleged and fully set forth.

54.   Complainant has Certificates of Relief for his misdemeanor convictions. The presumption of rehabilitation created by the certificate of relief from disabilities applies even where the statutory definition of "direct relationship" (Correction Law § 750 [3]) has been satisfied.

55.   Respondent must consider the eight factors listed in Correction Law § 753 (1) (a)-(h) to determine whether, in fact, the "direct relationship" is sufficiently attenuated to warrant issuance of employment and not bar an applicant simply because they have a conviction record.

56.   The issuance of a certificate of relief from disabilities creates a presumption of rehabilitation which Respondent's must rebut.

57.   Respondent has violated Article 23-A § 753-2 by never rebutting the presumption of rehabilitation before denying employment on the basis of requiring applicants to have no criminal record as a qualification for employment.

FIFTH CAUSE OF ACTION: RESPONDENT'S CONDUCT WAS WILLFUL, WANTON AND/OR MALICIOUS AND MUST BE FINED PURSUANT TO NEW YORK EXECUTIVE LAW §297(4)(c)(vi)

58.   Paragraphs 1 through 32 are re-alleged and fully set forth.

59.   Respondent posted advertisements in New York State which specifically discouraged and chilled potential applicants with a qualification that stated: _____.

60.   New York Executive Law § 297 (4)(c)(vi) permits the Division to assess civil fines and penalties, "in an amount not to exceed fifty thousand dollars, to be paid to the state by a respondent found to have committed an unlawful discriminatory act, or not to exceed one hundred thousand dollars to be paid to the state by a Respondent found to have committed an unlawful discriminatory act which is found to be "willful, wanton or malicious."

61.   Stating such an unlawful qualification was done maliciously to prevent my application.

62.   Respondent's openly stated policies and practices of barring persons with conviction records from employment in its advertisements violates *NY Exec. Law § 296 (15), NY Corr. Law §752, NY Corr. Law §753-1 and NY Corr. Law §753-2.*

PRAYER FOR RELIEF

WHEREFORE, Complainant respectfully requests:

A.   A declaration that Respondent has violated *NY Exec. Law §§ 296 (15), NY Corr. Law §752, NY Corr. Law §753-1 and NY Corr. Law §753-2* and an order to cease and desist the unlawful conduct described above.

B.   A declaration that Respondent does not follow *New York Correction Law Article 23-A* but bars applicants with conviction records instead in an openly stated policy in its advertisements.

C.   Back Pay and Compensatory Damages since I have been denied a position and discouraged from applying simply based entirely on having a criminal record.

D.   Requiring Respondent to comply with the provisions of the Human Rights Law and Correction Law Article 23-A, including but not limited to developing and implementing practices, policies and procedures for the pre-employment process in order to fully comply with the Human Rights Law and encourage the hire of ex-offenders.

E.   That the Division recognize that no other similar relief has been requested by myself and no other complaint stating such set of allegations has been verified to before any other state agency complainant of the exact same practice.

F.   Such other and further relief as may be deemed just and proper, including imposing civil fines and awarding such additional relief as may be just and proper.

Dated: _____   _____

                                                                            NAME OF COMPLAINANT

VERIFICATION

STATE OF NEW YORK   )   SS:
COUNTY OF _____)

    I, _____, being duly sworn, deposes and says: that I am the Complainant herein, and that I have read the foregoing complaint and know the content thereof; that the same is true and correct of my own knowledge except as to the matters therein stated on information and belief; and that as to those matters, I believe the same to be true.

_____
NAME OF COMPLAINANT

Subscribed and sworn to
before me this _____ day
of _____ in the year 20___

_____
Signature of Notary Public

SAMPLE ARTICLE 23-A
SECTION 754 LETTER

NAME OF COMPLAINANT
ADDRESS 1
ADDRESS 2
DATE

NAME OF RESPONDENT
Att: Legal Counsel
ADDRESS 1
ADDRESS 2

To Whom It May Concern:

    My name is _____ and I was denied employment by _____ on or about _____, 20_____ for the _____ position in _____, New York. Because I was denied employment and disclosed my entire conviction record on my application and my application is no longer active I am requesting and you must produce the reasons for my denial/disqualification of employment within 30 days based on New York Correction Law Article 23-A Section 754 as stated below. The statute reads:

    754. Written statement upon denial of license or employment. At the request of any person previously convicted of one or more criminal offenses who has been denied a license or employment, a public agency or private employer shall provide, within thirty days of a request, a written statement setting forth the reasons for such denial.

    Please provide the reasons set forth for such denial with your detailed **New York Correction Law Article 23-A§ 752 (1) (2) and § 753 (1) (2)** analysis made on or about _____, 20___, the date you denied my employment. This information will be valuable in understanding the reasons and factors you applied when you took adverse action against my application for employment.

Thank you in advance and I look forward to your detailed response.

Sincerely,

SIGNATURE HERE

NAME OF COMPLAINANT

NEW YORK FELONY BASED LICENSING RESTRICTIONS

Occupation	Enforcing Agency	Statute	Bar?	Appeal
Accountant	State Ed. Dept.	*Art. 149, §7404 (1) (7), § 7405 (3)*	No[1]	Yes
Acupuncturist	State Ed. Dept.	*Article 160, §8214 (6)*	No[2]	Yes
Alcoholic Beverage	State Liquor Auth.	*Article 8, § 110 (d), § 126 (1)*	Yes[3]	Yes
Animal Health	Agr and Market Dept	*Article 5 § 61*	No[4]	Yes
Architect	State Ed Dept	*ADBD Educ Law § 7304*	No[5]	Yes
Attorney	Chara & Fitness Com	*CPLR § 9404*	No	No[6]
Baby Chick Seller	Dept of Agri & Mkts	*A & M Law § 175-n*	No	No
Bail Bondsman	State Ins Dept	*Insurance Law § 6802 (g)*	Yes[7]	Yes
Barber	Dept of State	*GBL § 434(b), 441*	No[8]	Yes
Barber Shop Owner	Dept of State	*GBL § 438 (3)*	No[9]	Yes
Bingo Distributor/Op	Racing Wagering Brd	*N.Y. Exec Law § 435 (2) (c) (1)*	Yes[10]	Yes
Blasters	Dept. of Labor	*GBL § 483(Fingerprinting)*	No	No
Boxer/Wrestler	State Athletic Comm	*Uncon L §§ 8911, 8912, 8917*	No[11]	No
Bus Driver	Dept of Mtr Vehicles	*V & TL§ 509-C*	Yes[12]	Yes
Cannabis Dispenser	Dept of Health	*10 NYCRR 1004.10(a)(10)(b)(8)*	Yes[13]	No
Check Cashier	State Banking Dept	*Banking Law § 369 (1)*	Yes[14]	No
Chiropractor	State Ed. Dept.	*Educ. Law § 6554 (7)*	No[15]	Yes
Civil Service NYC	Citywide Adm Serv	*NYC Civil Service R & R § 3.2.6*	No[16]	No
Comm Feed Dist	Agr and Market Dept.	*A & M Law§ 129*	Yes[17]	Yes
Controlled Sub Dist	Dept of Health	*PHL§ 3312 (1) (a) and (2) (b)*	No[18]	Yes

[1] Good Moral Character

[2] Good Moral Character

[3] Fingerprinting, bonding, Mandatory bar for felonies and specific misdemeanors for licenses and employees. Applicant must disclose whether spouse has been convicted of crimes listed in §126.

[4] Good Character and Responsibility

[5] Good Moral Character

[6] Must obtain permission from Appellate Division in order to refile application.

[7] Applicant must not have been convicted of any offense involving moral turpitude of any crime. Fingerprinting, good character and reputation, bonding.

[8] License may be suspended or revoked for one year if convicted of crime or offense involving moral turpitude or for habitual substance abuse.

[9] License may be suspended or revoked for one year if convicted of crime or offense involving moral turpitude or for habitual substance abuse.

[10] Bar for conviction of any time. Good Moral Character. No one who has been a professional gambler or gambling promoter may be licensed.

[11] Character and Fitness, Fingerprinting

[12] Felony bar for certain sex offenses and vehicular offenses. Bar may be waived if 5 years from sentence.

[13] Convictions less than 10 years including incarceration for conviction of any felony of sale or possession of drugs, narcotics, or controlled substances

[14] May be refused if convicted of a crime or if consorting with anyone who has been convicted of a crime. Character and Fitness.

[15] Good Moral Character

[16] Satisfactory Character and Reputation

[17] May be denied or revoked if convicted of a felony. Character and Responsibility.

[18] Must submit affidavit if ever convicted of drug offense.

Occupation	Enforcing Agency	Statute	Bar?	Appeal
Dental Hygienist	State Ed. Dept.	*ADBD Educ Law § 6609 (7)*	No[19]	Yes
Dentist	State Ed. Dept.	*ADBD Educ Law § 6604 (7)*	No[20]	Yes
Deputy Sheriff	County Sup Office	*County Law § 652(4)(Fingerprinting)*	No	No
Dietician	State Ed. Dept.	*Educ. Law § 8004*	No	No
Disposal Plant Oper	Agr and Market Dept.	*ADBC A & M Law § 96-z-2,3*	Yes[21]	Yes
Dry Milk Importer	Agr & Mkets Dept.	*A & M L §258dd, 1 NYCRR 13.2*	No	No
Electrician	Dept. of Buildings	*NYC Adm.Code § 27-3010, 3016*	No[22]	Yes
EMT	Emer Med Serv Cncl	*PHL§ 3005 (8)*	Yes[23]	No
Occupation	Enforcing Agency	Statute	Bar?	Appeal
Empl Agency Oper	Dept of Labor NYC	*GBL § 173, 174 (Fingerprinting)*	No[24]	No
Engineer	State Ed. Dept.	*ADBD Educ. Law § 7206*	No	Yes
Explosives Handler	Comm of Dept. Labor	*Labor Law § 458, 459*	Yes[25]	Yes
Farm Labor Contr	Labor Stand Dept.	*Labor Law § 212-a*	Yes[26]	Yes
Farm Products Dealer	Agr & Mkets Dep.t	*A & M Law § 248*	No[27]	Yes
Fertilizer Dist	Agr & Mkets Dept.	*A & M Law § 146*	No	No
Firearms Carrier	Lic Off of City	*Penal Law§ 400.00*	Yes[28]	No
Firefighter	Fire Dept.	*NYC Admin Code § 15-10, 113*	Yes[29]	Yes
Food Proc Plant Oper	Agri & Mkets Dep.t	*A & M Law § 251-z-3, 5(7)*	Yes[30]	Yes
Food Salvager	Agri & Mkets Dept.	*ADBC A & M Law § 219-221*	Yes[31]	Yes
Frozen Dessert	Agri & Mkets Dept.	*A & M Law § 71-d*	No[32]	Yes
Funeral Director	Dept. of Health	*PHL § 3450*	Yes[33]	Yes
Furniture Manuf	Dept. of State	*GBL § 388*	No	No
Harbor Pilot	State Bd of Pilots	*Nav Law § 92*	No[34]	No

[19] Good Moral Character

[20] Good Moral Character

[21] May be barred, suspended or revoked if convicted of a felony.

[22] Good Moral Character

[23] Mandatory bar for certain felonies (murder, manslaughter, theft, drug offenses, robbery, fraud, assault, sexual abuse and embezzlement)

[24] Good Moral Character

[25] Not confined as patient or inmate in institution for treatment of mental diseases. Fingerprinting may be waived if applicant has a gun license.

[26] May be denied or revoked if convicted of any crime or offense, except traffic violations.

[27] Good Character, Bonding

[28] Good Moral Character and never been confined to a mental hospital or have history of mental illness. Mandatory denial of applicant for felony and serious offenses, automatic revocation if convicted of felony or serious offense while licensed.

[29] Discretionary discipline or removal for conviction of any legal offense, conduct injurious to public peace or welfare, or immoral conduct.

[30] Good Character and Bonding

[31] Good Character

[32] Character and Experience

[33] May be revoked for habitual drunkenness or addiction to narcotics.

[34] Good Moral Character & Temperate Habits

Occupation	Enforcing Agency	Statute	Bar?	Appeal
Hairdresser	Dept. of State	GBL § 411	Yes[35]	Yes
Hearing Aid Dealer	Dept. of State	GBL § 790	Yes[36]	Yes
Horse Racing	State Wagering Bd	RPMWBL § 213 (2)	Yes[37]	No
Insurance Sec Sales	State Insurance Dept.	Insurance Law § 1204	No[38]	Yes
Insurance Sav Office	State Insurance Dept.	Insurance Law § 2202 (2)	No[39]	Yes
Inspector & Investig	Dept. of Agri & Mkts	A & M Law § 11	No	No
Junk Dealer	Mayor Office City	GBL § 61	No[40]	No
Land Surveyor	State Ed Dept	ADBD Educ Law § 7206-a(7)	No[41]	Yes
Liming Mater. Seller	Dept. Of Agr & Mkts	A& M Law § 142ee	No	Yes
Long-Shoreman	Waterfront Comm.	Uncon Law § 9829	Yes[42]	Yes
Masseur/Masseuse	State Ed Dept	ADBD Educ Law § 7804 (6)	No[43]	No
Melloream Mftr	Dept of Agri & Mkts	A & M Law § 50 (g)	No	No
Midwife	State Ed Dept	ADBD Educ Law § 6955	No	Yes
Milk Dealer	Dept of Agri & Mkts	A & M Law § 258 (c), (c) (i)	Yes[44]	Yes
Milk Tester	Dept of Agri & Mkts	A & M Law § 57 (a)	No[45]	No
Money Lender	State Banking Dept.	Banking Law § 342	No[46]	No
Money Transmitter	State Banking Dept.	Banking Law §642	No[47]	Yes
Notary Public	Dept. of State	Exec. Law and Banking Law § 130	Yes[48]	No
Nurse	State Ed Dept.	Educ. Law §§6905 (RN) 6906 (LPN)	No	Yes
Nursery Stock Seller	Dept of Agri & Mkts	A & M Law § 163 (a)	No	No
Occupational Therap.	State Ed Dept.	ADBD Educ. Law§ 7904	No[49]	Yes
Ophthalmic Dispenser	State Ed Dept.	ADBD Educ. Law § 7124	No[50]	Yes
Optometrist	State Ed Dept.	ADBD Educ. Law § 7104	No[51]	Yes

[35] Freedom from infectious or communicable disease. Good Moral Character.
[36] Good character, reputation & fitness
[37] Character and general fitness
[38] Public Interest
[39] Trustworthy and competent
[40] Applicant must not have been convicted of larceny or knowingly receiving stolen property.
[41] Good Moral Character
[42] Registration may be denied or revoked if convicted of treason, murder, manslaughter or of any felony or high misdemeanor.
[43] Good Moral Character
[44] May Be Denied, revoked or suspended if convicted of a felony. Good Character, no acts injurious to public health, bonding.
[45] Good Moral Character
[46] Good Character and General Fitness
[47] Good Character and General Fitness
[48] Mandatory Bar for felony and specific misdemeanors for applicants.
[49] Good Moral Character
[50] Good Moral Character
[51] Good Moral Character

Occupation	Enforcing Agency	Statute	Bar?	Appeal
Pawn Broker	Local Licen Auth	*GBL § 41*	No[52]	No
Pharmacist	State Ed Dept.	*ADBD Educ. Law § 6805*	No[53]	Yes
Physical Therapist	State Ed Dept.	*ADBD Educ. Law § 6734*	No[54]	Yes
Physician	State Ed. Dept.	*ADBD Educ. Law § 6524*	No[55]	Yes
Physician's Assistant	State Ed. Dept.	*ADBD Educ. Law § 6541*	No[56]	Yes
Pier Super/Hiring Ag	Waterfront Comm	*Uncon Law § 9814, 9818*	Yes[57]	Yes
Plant/Soil Seller	Dept of Agri & Mkts	*A & M Law § 147 (b)*	No	Yes
Plumber	Dept of Buildings	*NYC Admin Code § 26-133, 151*	No[58]	Yes
Podiatrist	State Ed Dept	*ADBD Educ. Law § 7004*	No[59]	Yes
Police Officer	Police Dept	*NYC Admin Code § 14-109*	Yes[60]	No
Private Investigator	Dept of State	*Article 7, GBL § 72, 74, 79, 81*	Yes[61]	Yes
Private Service Bureau	Dept of MV	*15 N.Y.C.R.R. 77.6*	Yes[62]	Yes
Process Server	NYC Dept Cons Aff	*Title 6, §2-231*	No[63]	No
Psychologist	Dept of State	*ADBD Educ. Law § 7603*	No[64]	Yes
Public Adjuster	State Ins Dept	*Insurance Law § 2108 (d) (3) & (4)*	Yes[65]	Yes
Radiologist	Bureau of Env Rad	*PHL § 3510*	Yes[66]	Yes
Real Estate Broker	Secret of State	*Real Prop Law § 440(a)*	Yes[67]	Yes
Ref War, Lock Pl Op	Dept of Agri & Mkts	*ADBC A & M Law § 231*	No[68]	Yes
Sanitation Worker	Sanitation Dept.	*NYC Admin Code § 16-106*	No	Yes
Scrap Processor	Mayor's Office	*GBL § 69 (f)*	No	No
Secur. Broker/Dealer	Dept of Law	*GBL§ 359-e (3) (a) (b) and e (12)*	No	No
Security Guard	Dept of State	*GBL § 89*	Yes[69]	Yes

[52] Good Moral Character, Bonding

[53] Good Moral Character

[54] Good Moral Character

[55] Good Moral Character

[56] Good Moral Character

[57] Mandatory felony and specific misdemeanor bar for applicants, good character and integrity

[58] Good Moral Character, Revocation for Poor moral character that adversely reflects on fitness to conduct plumbing business.

[59] Good Moral Character

[60] Mandatory permanent felony bar, Article 23-A of the Correction law not applicable

[61] Mandatory felony and specific misdemeanor bar (drug offenses, buying, receiving/possessing stolen property/unlawful entry) for applicants.

[62] Mandatory felony and misdemeanor bar, can be removed by DMV Commissioner if approved.

[63] Bond and Finger Printing Required if serving more than 5 times per year in NYC.

[64] Good Moral Character

[65] Mandatory felony and specific misdemeanor bar for convictions involving fraud or dishonest practices.

[66] Suspension/revocation if guilty of crime involving moral turpitude, forfeiture of license if convicted of any crime considered a felony in New York, Good Moral Character

[67] Mandatory must not have been convicted of a felony. Trustworthiness.

[68] Good Character, fiscal responsibility & competency

[69] Mandatory felony and certain misdemeanors if related to functions of job, fingerprinting, good character and fitness, criminal history investigation.

Occupation	Enforcing Agency	Statute	Bar?	Appeal
Shorthand Reporter	State Ed Dept	*ADBD Educ. Law § 7504*	No[70]	Yes
Social Worker	State Ed Dept	*ADBD Educ. Law § 7704*	No[71]	Yes
Speech Pathologist	State Ed Dept	*ADBD Educ. Law § 8206*	No[72]	Yes
Stevedore	Waterfront Comm	*Uncon Law§ 9821*	No[73]	Yes
Taxi Driver	Dept of Motor Veh	*V & T L § 510*	No[74]	Yes
Taxi Driver NYC	Taxi Limo Comm	*NYC Adm Code § 19-505*	No[75]	Yes
Teacher	State Dept of Ed	*Edu. Law § 3012,3020, 2590-h(20c)*	No[76]	Yes
Theatre Ticket Resell	County Lic Comm	*ACA Law § 25.03, 25.07*	No[77]	No
Truck Driver	Dept of Motor Veh	*V & T Law § 510*	No[78]	Yes
Veterinarian	State Ed Dept	*ADBD Educ. Law § 6704*	No[79]	Yes
Weighmaster	Dept of Agri & Mkts	*A & M Law 195*	No[80]	Yes

---

[70] Good Moral Character

[71] Good Moral Character

[72] Good Moral Character

[73] Good Character and Integrity

[74] Good Moral Character, Fingerprinting, no drug or alcohol addiction.

[75] Good Moral Character, Fingerprinting, no drug or alcohol addiction.

[76] Good moral character

[77] Good moral character, bonding

[78] Must report once per year all convictions for violations of vehicle laws and ordinances other then parking.

[79] Good Moral Character

[80] Good Character

N.Y. EXEC. LAW 296 (16) PRECEDENTS AND DECISIONS

New York Court of Appeals

Matter of New York State Department of Mental Hygiene v. State Div. of Human Rights, 66 NY 2d 752 (1985) Discharged probationary employee commenced proceeding before State Division of Human Rights. The Division found discrimination, and the Appeal Board affirmed. The Court of Appeals held that employer did not violate Executive Law section prohibiting, inter alia, inquiry into past criminal record, where, prior to effective date of statute, employer asked employee whether he had ever been arrested, employee informed employer that charge against him had been resolved by an adjournment in contemplation of dismissal. Complainant refused to cooperate in eliminating the discrepancy between information lawfully obtained from him at the interview and facts learned in the background investigation report, Respondent had reasonable and permissible grounds for terminating his probationary employment.

Matter of Joseph M. v New York City Board of Education 82 N.Y.2d 128, 623 N.E.2d 115, 603 N.Y.S.2d 804623 NE 2d 1154 (1993) Board of Education, a public agency not listed in CPL 160.50 (1) (d), is not entitled to obtain such sealed records based on an arrest record for use in a hearing under Education Law § 3020-a on charges brought against a tenured teacher for controlled substance drug possession where teacher was arrested and found not guilty by jury. Purpose of 1976 amendment was the protecting of exonerated individuals from the unwarranted stigma that their employers or others could attach to dismissed criminal charges.

Appellate Division

Sheriff's Dep't v. State Div. of Human Rights, 129 AD 2d 789 (1987) Division of Human Rights correctly determined that the petitioner discriminated against the respondent Withers based on his arrest record on its application for employment, which established that it is a prima facie discriminatory practice to inquire about prior arrests on an application when such denial is protected from inquiry. Backpay was not applicable since it would deprive the hiring authority of the power of selection. Mental anguish was reduced from $35,000 to $7,500.

Giles v. Lockport Sav. Bank, 142 AD 2d 943 (1988) Employer did not unlawfully discriminate against employee by firing her after entry of order adjourning criminal action against her in contemplation of dismissal; action was not actually dismissed until six months after firing. In order to be covered by the statute, an individual must have their adjournment "deemed entered" as stated in paragraph (b) of CPL 160.50 (2). The 1977 amendment realized that in instances of adjournments in contemplation of dismissal the accusatory instruments were not dismissed by an order entered, but were "deemed" dismissed and therefore added the words, "or deemed entered."

Matter of Bellacosa v. White, 145 AD 2d 342 (1988) Unsuccessful applicant for court officer's position claimed discriminatory refusal to hire him because of his arrest record in violation of statute that formerly precluded inquiry about or adverse action based upon arrest which was followed by termination of criminal proceeding in favor of individual in connection with employment. Administrative law judge determined that there could be inquiry as to underlying facts in arrest of applicant for criminal impersonation of public servant while in possession of court officer's badge since court officer was peace officer. Commissioner of State Division of Human Rights overruled ALJ, and chief administrative judge of the Courts of the Unified Court System of the State of New York petitioned. Court held that the statute did not preclude consideration of facts surrounding arrest of individual for criminal impersonation of public servant while in possession of court officer's badge in acting upon his application for employment as court officer.

New York City Department of Correction v. White, 163 AD 2d 250 (1990) Although it has since been amended to permit inquiry regarding any arrest or criminal accusation, not then pending, which was terminated in favor of an applicant for employment as a police officer or peace officer (L 1985, ch 208), Executive Law § 296 (16), in effect at the time, prohibited such inquiry and there is substantial evidence in the record that the complainant's arrest record and petitioner's misconception that he had been convicted were the primary reasons for petitioner's non-selection of complainant for the position of correction officer. However, the civil service eligibility list in question expired almost one year prior to respondent's determination. The list was not challenged and therefore it expired. There is also an insufficient basis for respondent's award of compensatory damages for hurt, humiliation and mental anguish, since there was no evidence supporting the complainant's claims of mental anguish other than his statement that he was very upset.

Matter of Olshan v. County of Dutchess, 233 AD 2d 448 (1996) The Commissioner of the Dutchess County Department of Social Services adopted hearing officer's recommendation on charge one and determined that case manager was guilty of improperly disclosing confidential information, and imposed penalty of demotion. The penalty of demotion is not so disproportionate to the offense, in light of all the circumstances, as to be shocking to one's sense of fairness. Charge two not permitted based on protections afforded in Executive Law § 296 (16).

Matter of Ruggiero, 263 AD 2d 554, 693 N.Y.S.2d 266 (1999) Prior to being hired at a banking and brokerage firm, claimant completed an employment application which included, pursuant to SEC rules, questions seeking information as to whether claimant had ever been arrested for, or charged with, any misdemeanor relating to acts of dishonesty, theft or fraud to which he answered no. Claimant was fired later for being untrustworthy after Respondent sought more information and Claimant provided unsigned disposition and facts that misstated both the 1989 and 1991 arrests. Claimant then applied for unemployment insurance and was denied based on disqualifying conduct of not disclosing arrests. Because claimant had no obligation, under the cited SEC rules, to disclose his 1991 arrest and because, under Executive Law § 296 (16) an employer may not inquire into an employee's arrest when the charge leading to that arrest has been dismissed, the court concluded that the Board's determination should be annulled and the matter remitted for a new hearing. Court could not locate any statute or rule which would override this State statutory prohibition, and the employer could not cite any precedents, statutes or regulations authorizing the inquiry which led to claimant's dismissal.

Johnson v. Brooklake Associates, 271 AD 2d 382 (2000) The motion court properly dismissed plaintiff's Executive Law § 296 (16) claim. Plaintiff's breach of contract claim was, however, properly sustained as against defendant's contention that, pursuant to the parties' contract, it was one properly to be pursued in arbitration. Defendant waived any right to arbitrate the claim by affirmatively participating in this lawsuit.

Annabi v. Cassino, 269 AD 2d 551, 703 NYS 2d 745 (2000) The Supreme Court properly denied the defendant's motion to dismiss the complaint on the ground that it failed to state a cause of action. The complaint alleged that the defendant took adverse employment actions against the plaintiff, based on the fact that the plaintiff, a police officer, was arrested, although the arrest had not resulted in a conviction. Accordingly, it properly stated a cause of action for a violation of Executive Law § 296 (16)

Iatauro v. St. John's University, 295 AD 2d 478, 744 N.Y.S.2d 347 (2002) The plaintiff pleaded guilty in the Superior Court of New Jersey to the charge of endangering the welfare of a child. That the charge was later ordered dismissed because the plaintiff subsequently completed treatment in a "Pretrial Intervention Program," does not constitute a favorable determination within the contemplation of CPL 160.50 (3). Accordingly, since the plaintiff was not a member of the class protected by Executive Law § 296(16) and New York City Administrative Code § 8–107(11), and thus cannot establish a prima facie case of discrimination pursuant to that statute and ordinance, respectively, the Supreme Court properly granted the defendant's motion and dismissed the amended complaint

Matter of Amaker v Fischer 120 AD 3d 988, 990 NYS 434, 2014 NY Slip Op 05750 CPL 160.50 and Executive Law § 296 (16) do not require respondent to remove any information concerning the 2006 incident from petitioner's inmate record. Those statutes provide protection only to petitioner's mother, not to petitioner. With respect to CPL 160.50, the Unusual Incident (UI) report, which is one of the documents found in petitioner's inmate record relating to the 2006 incident, is not a document that arises from a "criminal action or proceeding" (id.). As properly noted by the court, the UI report is an internal document prepared and used by respondent for administrative purposes, and it is "independent of, and unrelated to, the `arrest or prosecution' of the petitioner's mother"

New York Supreme Court

Matter of Brown v. Passidomo, 127 Misc. 2d 700 (1985) Brown was arrested and charged with violation of Vehicle and Traffic Law § 1192 (2) and (3) and § 1120 (a). He was convicted and upon appeal his conviction was overturned and then sealed in accordance with CPL law. Section 296(16) is only part of a comprehensive legislative scheme which also includes CPL sections 160.50 and 160.60. Under Criminal Procedure Law section providing that upon termination of a criminal action in favor of defendant, information pertaining to the arrest or prosecution may not be required to be divulged, the Commissioner of the Department of Motor Vehicles was prohibited from retaining petitioner's conviction record and disseminating it to insurance companies following reversal of petitioner's driving while impaired and failure to keep right convictions, notwithstanding Vehicle and Traffic Law section which provides that the Commissioner will provide to insurance companies the "operating record," including enumeration of any convictions.

Brown v. Fireman's Fund Ins., 131 Misc. 2d 525 (1986) Brown was arrested and charged with violation of Vehicle and Traffic Law § 1192 (2) and (3) and § 1120 (a) and his insurance was terminated. He was convicted and upon appeal his conviction was overturned and then sealed in accordance with CPL law. His insurance was reinstated upon reversal by the court, but then was terminated the last time on April 17, 1984. Respondent put forth that Insurance Law § 3425 demands suspension and termination of a driver's license upon conviction and therefore they acted accordingly. Court determined there is no authority for defendant to consider penalties flowing from criminal charges ultimately terminated in favor of plaintiff and there was no evidence that defendant considered any evidence leading to the charges independent of the driving record disseminated by DMV.

Matter of Anonymous, 174 Misc. 2d 333, 663 NYS 2d 492 (1997) CPL 160.60 and Executive Law § 296 (16) purpose was "to ensure that the protections provided to exonerated accused's be `consistent with the presumption of innocence, which simply means that no individual should suffer adverse consequences merely on the basis of an accusation, unless the charges were ultimately sustained in a court of law' (Governor's Approval Mem, 1976 McKinney's Session Laws of NY, at 2451)" Court concluded that the Legislature did not intend to extend the "presumption of innocence" to a person acquitted as a result of mental disease or defect. Such a person actually committed acts which are crimes and are deserving of punishment. Such persons are not set free to roam in society, but are kept in custody until they are no longer "dangerous" to themselves or to the public. The charges against such persons are not "unfounded", frivolous, or unproven. The court holds that insanity acquittals are not statutorily entitled to have their records sealed. They are not persons whose criminal actions have been terminated "favorably" under CPL 160.50.

Koleshnick v. ScotiaBank Group, 2012 NY Slip Op 31660 U (2012) Although Plaintiff was a resident of New Jersey at the time of termination based on New Jersey arrest record, he was terminated in New York City while in the employ of the Scotia Defendants, therefore nonresident plaintiff may invoke the protections of the NYCHRL and HRL by merely alleging and proving that the discriminatory decision to terminate was made in the city. Court finds that the legislature in enacting the aforementioned law, wanted to insure that a person in Plaintiff's position be protected from dissemination of the subject information, as well as from the acting upon the information so disseminated.

N.Y.S. DIVISION OF HUMAN RIGHTS FINAL ORDER SUMMARIES: ARREST RECORD

Name of Case: **Withers v Rockland County Sheriff Department**

Case No: <u>E-T-85879-82</u>

Summary: Complainant sought employment with the Rockland County Sheriff Department. He disclosed an arrest that was terminated in his favor and was denied employment on that basis after the Sheriff stated he lied on his application for employment.

Issue: Has Respondent violated the Human Rights Law on the basis of arrest when it used an arrest question (have you ever been arrested?) on its application to knock out potential applicants, including Complainant?

Rule: It is an unlawful discriminatory practice under *New York Executive Law § 296 (16)* to inquire or ask "have you ever been arrested" on an application for employment when such arrest terminates in favor of Complainant and there is no criminal conviction.

Analysis: Respondent found Complainant to be ineligible for employment based on a prior arrest that was terminated in his favor after Complainant submitted application for employment. He did not fully answer the question and proved the point of the statute, that by disclosing it, it would prejudice his ability to get the job.

Conclusion: The Rockland County Sherriff's Office was found to be in violation of the Human Rights Law. Withers was awarded about $2,000 back pay and $35,000 mental anguish. Upheld as rational by Appellate Division in <u>Sheriff's Dep't v. State Div. of Human Rights, 129 AD 2d 789 (1987)</u> but fine reduced to $7,500 with no back pay because it was a civil service position and the power of selection was by Rockland County Sheriff's Office and therefore cannot order hire.

Name of Case: **Acevedo v Yonkers Public Schools**

Case No: <u>1255309 (2007)</u>

Summary: Complainant was a custodial worker. Respondent received information about Complainant's arrest. Respondent terminated Complainant after the pending arrest was terminated in his favor after continuing to employ him by transferring him out of the school he was in and did not conduct its own investigation into the matter.

Issue: Has Respondent violated the Human Rights Law on the basis of conviction by terminating Acevedo's arrest based on nothing more than speculation after the charges were terminated in his favor?

Rule: It is an unlawful discriminatory practice under *New York Executive Law § 296 (16)* to base the denial of employment of an employee on an arrest that terminated in the employee's favor.

Analysis: Respondent failed to conduct any investigation, including talking to Complainant or victim or getting a police report. Instead it relied on hearsay evidence from a relative and the ADA in its decision to terminate employment after the arrest was sealed. The Division ordered reinstatement. If the Respondent refused reinstatement, it ordered that Acevedo be given front pay.

Conclusion: Yonkers Public Schools was found to be in violation of the Human Rights Law. Baez was awarded $107,984 in lost wages and $10,000 mental anguish. Decision upheld by the Appellate Division to be rational. <u>Matter of Board of Education of Pub. Schools v. New York State Div. of Human Rights, 2009 NY Slip Op 4897</u>

Name of Case: **Jenkins v Elite Investigations LTD.**

Case No: 10114293 (2008)

Summary: Complainant was arrested and held for 3 days and notified the employer. The District Attorney refused to prosecute and the charges were resolved in Jenkins favor. Respondent then terminated his employment without providing any explanation when he arrived and forced to sign a resignation letter.

Issue: Has Respondent violated the Human Rights Law on the basis of arrest by terminating Respondent as soon as he arrived back to work after the charges were resolved in his favor?

Rule: It is an unlawful discriminatory practice under *New York Executive Law § 296 (16)* to base the denial of employment of an employee on an arrest that terminated in the employee's favor.

Analysis: The closeness in time of the arrest to his termination provides an inference of discrimination. The Respondent provided no legitimate reason for the termination.

Conclusion: Complainant failed to mitigate his damages but got a $10,000 award in mental anguish.

Name of Case: **Patterson v MTA New York City Transit**

Case No: <u>10163438 (2014)</u>

Summary: Complainant was terminated during the time of pending charges immediately, even though the charges were dismissed in his favor months later. Respondent has already made a determination well in advance of any decision.

Issue: Has Respondent violated the Human Rights Law on the basis of arrest by terminating employment?

Rule: It is an unlawful discriminatory practice under *New York Executive Law § 296 (16)* to base the denial of employment of an employee on an arrest that terminated in the employee's favor.

Analysis: It is not required of an employer under *New York Executive Law § 296 (16)* to reinstate employment of an employee who was terminated and employed for that reason or reconsider a decision it previously made because the charges were in Complainant's favor. By acting quickly while the charges were pending, Respondent avoided liability.

Conclusion: Dismissed.

1976 LEGISLATIVE HISTORY

Chap 931

SENATE JOURNAL
JUN 27 1976
PAGE 9

1976 SENATE

The Senate Bill by Mr. MARINO *etal*   Calendar No. 720   Senate No. 4222-C   Assem. Rept. No. ____

Entitled: "

S. 4222-C
Cal. No. 720

A. 5393-C

AN ACT

to amend the correction law and the executive law, in relation to the removal
of disabilities of criminal offenders and repealing certain provisions thereof
relating thereto

" was read the third time

No. 1 (THREE DAY MESSAGE OF GOVERNOR)

The President put the question whether the Senate would agree to final passage of said bill, and the facts which necessitate an immediate vote thereon having been certified by the Governor, the same being upon the desks of the members in final form, it was decided in the affirmative, a majority of all the members elected voting in favor thereof and three-fifths being present as follows

AYE	Dist.		NAY	AYE	Dist.		NAY
	47	Mr. Anderson			15	Mr. Knorr	————
	49	Mr. Auer			29	Mr. Leichter	
	16	Mr. Babbush			8	Mr. Levy	
	45	Mr. Barclay			22	Mr. Lewis	
	18	Mr. Bartosiewicz			50	Mr. Lombardi	EXCUSED
	23	Mr. Beatty			24	Mr. Marchi	
	25	Ms. Bellamy			5	Mr. Marino	
	33	Mr. Bernstein			48	Mr. Mason	
	19	Mr. Bloom			28	Mr. McCall	
	12	Mr. Bronston			59	Mr. McFarland	————
	9	Ms. Burstein			42	Mr. Nolan	
	7	Mr. Caemmerer			27	Mr. Ohrenstein	
	34	Mr. Calandra			17	Mr. Owens	
	21	Mr. Conklin			11	Mr. Padavan	————
	46	Mr. Donovan			60	Mr. Paterson	
	6	Mr. Dunne			53	Mr. Perry	
	54	Mr. Eckert			36	Mr. Pisani	
	35	Mr. Flynn			57	Mr. Present	————
	32	Mr. Galiber			39	Mr. Rolison	EXCUSED
	30	Mr. Garcia			31	Mr. Ruiz	
	14	Mr. Gazzara			10	Mr. Santucci	
	1	Mr. Giuffreda	EXCUSED		40	Mr. Schermerhorn	
	3	Mr. Gold			2	Mr. Smith, B.C.	EXCUSED
	26	Mr. Goodman			51	Mr. Smith, W.T.	
	37	Mr. Gordon			43	Mr. Stafford	
	56	Mr. Griffin	————		55	Mr. Tauriello	
	20	Mr. Halperin			3	Mr. Trunzo	
	41	Mr. Hudson			58	Mr. Volker	————
	44	Mr. Isabella			52	Mr. Warder	
	4	Mr. Johnson			38	Mrs. Winikow	

AYES 50
NAYS 6

* Ordered, that the Secretary deliver said bill to the Assembly and request its concurrence therein.

AB AMERICAN BAR ASSOCIATION

S-4222-C

1800 M STREET, N.W., WASHINGTON, D.C. 20036 TELEPHONE (202) 331-2200

July 7, 1976

The Honorable Hugh Carey
Governor
State of New York
Albany, New York

Dear Governor Carey:

We are pleased to learn that S-4222-C, a bill designed to relieve discriminatory employment practices against ex-offenders, has passed the New York Legislature. We respectfully urge you to sign this important measure into law.

The American Bar Association, through the Corrections Commission, has been active since 1971 in assisting efforts to remove offender employment disabilities. The Association's House of Delegates last year endorsed remedial legislation concerning public employment and occupational licensing. A copy of the policy adopted is enclosed. Nearly half the states have now taken remedial action. We trust that New York, with its excellent S-4222-C, will add momentum in this critical area of criminal justice reform.

Sincerely,

Bob McKay

Robert B. McKay
Chairman

RBM/jp
Encl.

cc: Judah Gribetz, Counsel

STATE OF NEW YORK
EXECUTIVE CHAMBER
ALBANY 12224

MEMORANDUM filed with Senate Bill Number 4222-C, entitled:

"AN ACT to amend the correction law and the
executive law, in relation to the
removal of disabilities of criminal
offenders and repealing certain
provisions thereof relating thereto"

A P P R O V E D

The bill, which is part of my 1976 Legislative
Program, is designed to establish reasonable procedures
to prevent the unfair discrimination against former criminal
offenders in regard to licensure and employment, and establish
reasonable standards for the issuance of certificates of good
conduct.

The bill in no way requires the hiring of former
offenders, but provides reasonable standards to be applied
by public agencies and private employers when considering
applications by former offenders. No such standards presently
exist. Under the bill, a license or employment could not be
denied an individual on the basis of a previous criminal
conviction, unless the criminal conduct of which he was
convicted has a direct bearing upon his ability or fitness
to perform one or more of the responsibilities or duties
necessarily related to the license or employment sought, or
unless granting the application would pose an unreasonable
risk to property or the health or safety of others.

The bill would also make various changes in regard
to certificates of good conduct, which are issued by the
Parole Board to former offenders who have demonstrated their
ability to lead a productive and law-abiding life. The bill
would clarify the legal effect of a certificate; establish
clear guidelines for the Parole Board in regard to their
issuance; reduce the minimum period of good conduct required;
and allow the issuance of temporary certificates to individuals
on parole.

Observers of our criminal justice system agree that
the key to reducing crime is a reduction in recidivism (i.e.
repeated criminal conduct by the same individuals). The great
expense and time involved in successfully prosecuting and
incarcerating the criminal offender is largely wasted if upon
the individual's return to society his willingness to assume
a law-abiding and productive role is frustrated by senseless
discrimination.

Providing a former offender a fair opportunity for a
job is a matter of basic human fairness, as well as one of the
surest ways to reduce crime.

The bill is approved.

S 4222-C

C-931

7 '76

THE SENATE
STATE OF NEW YORK

RALPH J. MARINO
5th DISTRICT
CHAIRMAN
COMMITTEE ON CRIME AND CORRECTION

LEGISLATIVE OFFICE BUILDING
ALBANY, NEW YORK 12224

July 26, 1976

The Honorable Judah Gribetz
Counsel to the Governor
Executive Chamber
State Capitol
Albany, New York 12224

Dear Mr. Gribetz:

Re: S. 4222-C - A. 5393-C

The legislation is the product of long sought reform in the area of rehabilitation of persons subject to a disability due to conviction of a crime or of an offense.

This legislation would revamp "certificates of good conduct" issued by the State Board of Parole if said relief is consistent with the individual's rehabilitation and if consistent with public interest. The present five year period at which time relief may be considered is lowered to one year in a misdemeanor; three years for class C, D and E felonies; five years for A and B felonies.

This proposal would affect all public agencies and private employers who employ ten or more persons. It affects any bar due to previous criminal offenses with respect to the employment or licensing of an applicant. Such discrimination against a prior offender is permitted if there is a direct relationship between his previous criminal acts and the license or employment sought, or his employment or licensing which involves an unreasonable risk to property or to the safety of specific individuals or the general public. Furthermore, the legislation sets forth factors which must be considered by the entity in determining whether the individual should be employed.

Finally, the proposal sets forth built-in reviewing procedures based upon a denial of license or employment pursuant to a written statement setting forth the reasons.

I have worked carefully with your staff with respect to this legislation and other groups who are strongly in favor of this legislation.

It is respectfully requested that the Governor sign this bill.

Sincerely,

Ralph J. Marino

RJM;aff
Enclosure

S. 4222-C By Senator Marino
A. 5393-C By Mr. Fink

MEMORANDUM IN SUPPORT

AN ACT to amend the correction law and the
executive law, in relation to the
removal of disabilities of criminal
offenders and repealing certain provision
thereof relating thereto.

PURPOSE OF BILL: This bill is designed to facilitate the obtainment
of employment for ex-offenders and to aid their rehabilitation by
eliminating many of the obstacles to employment.

EXPLANATION OF BILL: This bill adds a new article 23-a to the
correction law dealing with the license and employment of persons
previously convicted of one or more criminal offenses. This amendment, applicable to all convicted in any jurisdiction and to any
employer whether private or public, prevents unfair discrimination
against those who had past convictions or were found to lack "good
moral character". A certificate of good conduct is issued to this
effect, carrying with it a presumption of rehabilitation as to
specified offenses. Exceptions to this rule exist, however, where
there is a direct relationship between the conviction and the specifi
license or employment sought or where there is an unreasonable risk
to the safety or welfare of the public.

If the ex-offender is denied employment, he can request the
employer to provide, within 30 days of request, a written statement
setting forth the reasons for such denial. Thereafter, proceedings
on appeal as to public agencies are to be instituted by filing
Article 78 and as to private employer by filing with the Division of
Human Rights.

Two new subsections are added to the current Article 23.
Section 703-a explains how a certificate of good conduct operates
to relieve an individual of any disability. Section 703-b then
lays out the procedure as to the issuance of these certificates by
the State Board of Parole based on action in accordance with the
minimum period of good conduct. These periods are one year after
release from suspended sentencing, probation, imprisonment, or
parole for a misdemeanor, three years for C, D, and E felonies,
and 5 years for A and B felonies.

The bill also would provide for the issuance of new certificates extending the relief of the original certificate and for the issuance of temporary certificates while the ex-offender is still under the Board's supervision, which are revocable for violation of parole.

Section 296 of the executive law is also amended by new subdivision 15 which states that any person, bureau, agency, etc. acting under article 23-a of the correction law cannot discriminate by the finding of a lack of "good moral character".

JUSTIFICATION: This legislation would undoubtedly remove many of the barriers facing ex-offenders in obtaining employment by the issuance of a certificate of good conduct with its underlying presumption of rehabilitation. Unemployment is the greatest deterrence to rehabilitation as statistics indicate that many of the ex-offenders return to lives of crime because other employment is not available. It would lift job restrictions from rehabilitated ex-offenders now deprived of over 125 licensing and employment categories because of their criminal records.

FISCAL IMPLICATIONS: None.

EFFECTIVE DATE: This act shall take effect on the first day of January next succeeding the date on which it shall have become a law.

7/76

`34222-C`

`20.`   BUDGET REPORT ON BILLS   Session Year: 19 76

SENATE   Introduced by: ASSEMBLY

No. 4222-C   Senator Marino et. al.   No.

Law: Correction   Sections: 6e; 702; 703; 703a and b (new)
                                              Article 23-A (new)
    Executive   296

Division of the Budget recommendation on the above bill:

Approved: ____X____   Veto: _____   No Objection: _____   No Recommendation: _____

1. Subject and Purpose: This bill modifies the State's current "certificate of good conduct" program relating to ex-offenders and also prohibits licensing and employment discrimination against such persons.

2. Summary of Provisions: The major provisions of this bill would:

   -- Repeal the current provisions of the Correction Law relating to certificates of good conduct; current law requires a five year waiting period in all cases and the certificate does not eliminate statutory bars to various types of licensure.

   -- Create new certificate of good conduct provisions which relieve ex-offenders of any legal disability or bar to employment or licensure; the new provisions also replace the five year waiting period with a sliding scale of one to five years based on the seriousness of the crime committed.

   -- Provide that no application for any license or employment can be denied because the applicant is an ex-offender, except where the job or license relates directly to the previous criminal offenses or where the licensing or employment would result in unreasonable risk to persons or property; these exceptions are clarified by a series of factors which must be considered by the employer or licensing agent.

   -- Require a written explanation to the applicant where an ex-offender is denied a license or employment.

   -- Provide that enforcement actions against public agencies be through Article 78 proceedings and those against private employers be through the State Division of Human Rights and concurrently, the New York City Commission on Human Rights.

   This bill would take effect on January 1, 1977.

3. Prior Legislative History: Similar legislation to restore the rights of former criminal offenders has a long history. The current bill was introduced in 1975 (S. 4222). In 1974, Senator Marino introduced similar legislation (S. 10114) which would have replaced

Date: _____   Examiner: _____

Disposition: Chapter No.   Vote No.

-2-

certificates of good conduct and certificates of relief from disabilities with a more comprehensive certificate of restoration of rights. No action was taken on that bill.

4. Arguments in Support:

A.   This legislation is needed to reverse the long history of employment discrimination against former criminal offenders. License restrictions currently in law bar the employment of ex-offenders in jobs ranging from taxi cab driver to teacher to stock exchange employee. In addition, blatant discrimination by employers in other areas of employment add to the problem that there is virtually no alternative for the ex-offender other than additional criminal activity.

B.   While it is extremely difficult to draft legislation which eliminates unjust job discrimination against ex-offenders while at the same time recognizing the legitimate concerns of employers and licensing agencies for protection of life and property, the Department of Correctional Services, Department of Labor and Division of Criminal Justice Services all argue that this bill represents a sound attempt at creating that balance.

5. Possible Objections:

A.   The Division of Human Rights has informed us of two possible objections to this bill. First, the Division argues that it should be responsible for enforcing actions against both public and private employers rather than just the latter group because of the need for consistency in the application of the law. Secondly, since the bill gives the New York City Commission on Human Rights concurrent jurisdiction, the bill should amend the New York City Administrative Code.

B.   This bill's effectiveness in eliminating job discrimination will be limited because of the severe backlog of cases currently in the State Division of Human Rights. It currently has an eight month (1300 case) backlog of complaints awaiting investigation and is working with a twenty percent vacancy freeze because of a reduced 1976-77 appropriation. Therefore, any increase in complaints resulting from this bill will only exacerbate the Division's problems and result in even less timely service to its clients.

-3-

6. **Other State Agencies Interested:** Although the Department of
   Correctional Services has not taken a position on this bill, it
   sees no problems with that portion of the bill relating to the
   State Parole Board. The Division of Human Rights recommends
   approval. The Department of Labor and the Division of Criminal
   Justice Services likewise support the bill.

7. **Known Position of Others:** None.

8. **Budgetary Implications:** See 5b above.

9. **Recommendation:** The bill would increase the likelihood that former
   criminal offenders will find employment by prohibiting job discrimination against such persons and liberalizing the current certificate
   of good conduct statutes. There is a need for this legislation
   because of the high level of unjustified discrimination against
   ex-offenders. According to spokesmen from all of the relevant
   State agencies, this bill represents the most rational balance
   between the rights of these individuals and employers that has been
   attempted during the many years in which similar legislation has
   been drafted.

   The only major problem associated with the bill is the limited
   ability of the Division of Human Rights to assume any additional
   enforcement responsibilities because of its severe case backlog.
   Despite this problem, there is a critical need for this legislation
   which should be an overriding consideration.

   We recommend approval.

   Paul J. Elston

STATE OF NEW YORK
EXECUTIVE DEPARTMENT
DIVISION OF HUMAN RIGHTS

TWO WORLD TRADE CENTER
NEW YORK, NEW YORK 10047

WERNER H. KRAMARSKY
Commissioner

July 12, 1976

Honorable Judah Gribetz
Counsel to the Governor
Executive Chamber
State Capitol
Albany, New York 12224

> Re: AN ACT to amend the correction law and the
> executive law, in relation to the
> removal of disabilities of criminal
> offenders and repealing certain pro-
> visions thereof relating thereto. S.4222-C

Dear Mr. Gribetz:

Reference is made to your memorandum relative to the
above-entitled Ten-Day bill of Senator Marino and others to
amend the Correction Law in regard to certificates of relief
from disabilities and of good conduct and provide in a new article
for the prevention of discrimination in licensing or employment
because of the previous conviction of one or more criminal offenses
with a complementary amendment to the Human Rights Law. Our
comments are requested.

The bill contains some inconsistencies with respect to
enforcement by the State Division of Human Rights. The proposed Section 755 of the Correction Law treats cases involving
public agencies differently from cases involving private employers,
while the proposed Section 296.15 of the Human Rights Law makes
no such distinction. In addition, Section 755 provides for concurrent jurisdiction in the New York City Commission on Human
Rights, but there is no amendment to the New York City Administrative Code to support such concurrent jurisdiction.

Despite these defects, the bill is a commendable effort to
deal with the employment problems of ex-offenders, and the State
Division of Human Rights recommends that the Governor approve
the bill. It would be desirable for the Governor to include in
his approval of the bill, a recommendation to the Legislature
to take corrective action to remedy the inconsistencies noted
above.

- 2 -

Please communicate with me again if I can be of assistance
to you.

Yours very truly,

Werner H. Kramarsky
Commissioner

S4222-C

C-931

7·76

THE SENATE
STATE OF NEW YORK

RALPH J. MARINO
5th DISTRICT
CHAIRMAN
COMMITTEE ON CRIME AND CORRECTION

July 26, 1976

LEGISLATIVE OFFICE BUILDING
ALBANY, NEW YORK 12224

The Honorable Judah Gribetz
Counsel to the Governor
Executive Chamber
State Capitol
Albany, New York 12224

Dear Mr. Gribetz:

Re: S. 4222-C - A. 5393-C

The legislation is the product of long sought reform in the area of rehabilitation of persons subject to a disability due to conviction of a crime or of an offense.

This legislation would revamp "certificates of good conduct" issued by the State Board of Parole if said relief is consistent with the individual's rehabilitation and if consistent with public interest. The present five year period at which time relief may be considered is lowered to one year in a misdemeanor; three years for class C, D and E felonies; five years for A and B felonies.

This proposal would affect all public agencies and private employers who employ ten or more persons. It affects any bar due to previous criminal offenses with respect to the employment or licensing of an applicant. Such discrimination against a prior offender is permitted if there is a direct relationship between his previous criminal acts and the license or employment sought, or his employment or licensing which involves an unreasonable risk to property or to the safety of specific individuals or the general public. Furthermore, the legislation sets forth factors which must be considered by the entity in determining whether the individual should be employed.

Finally, the proposal sets forth built-in reviewing procedures based upon a denial of license or employment pursuant to a written statement setting forth the reasons.

I have worked carefully with your staff with respect to this legislation and other groups who are strongly in favor of this legislation.

It is respectfully requested that the Governor sign this bill.

Sincerely,

Ralph J. Marino

RJM;aff
Enclosure

Hon. Judah Gribetz   - 2 -   July 15, 1976
Re: S. 4222-C

    The bill has the desirable purpose of aiding in the rehabilica-
tion of former convicts. It does not directly affect the provisions
of the Labor Law, and I have no objection to its approval.

        Sincerely,

        Philip Ross

STATE DEPARTMENT OF CIVIL SERVICE   JUL 1 1976   July 15, 1976

SENATE
4222-C   Introduced by Senator Marino, et al.

RECOMMENDATION: No Objection

STATUTES INVOLVED: Correction Law §§ 6-e (repeal), 702, 703, 703-a (new)
                     703-B (new), Art. 23-a (new);
                     Executive Law § 296(15) (new)

EFFECTIVE DATE: January 1, 1977

DISCUSSION:

          This bill would provide for the issuance of good conduct
certificates by the State Board of Parole to persons convicted of
crimes and would seek to prohibit unfair discrimination against
persons convicted of one or more criminal offenses. These good
conduct certificates together with certificates of relief from
disabilities must be given consideration by public and private
employers and create a presumption of rehabilitation.

          We note that this measure represents a substantial modification
of a prior version, Senate 4222-B, that we were consulted on by your
office earlier this year. We are glad to see that many of the
suggested changes that we proposed then have been incorporated into
this version of the bill.

          We consider this measure aptly drawn and we fully support
its intended purpose.

                                   Victor S. Bahou
                          President, Civil Service Commission

Attachment

STATE OF NEW YORK
EXECUTIVE DEPARTMENT
DIVISION OF HUMAN RIGHTS

TWO WORLD TRADE CENTER
NEW YORK, NEW YORK 10047

WERNER H. KRAMARSKY
Commissioner

April 22, 1976

Honorable Judah Gribetz
Counsel to the Governor
Executive Chamber
State Capitol
Albany, New York 12224

    Att: Clarence Sundram, Assistant Counsel

      Re: AN ACT to amend the correction law, in relation to rehabili-
          tation of criminal offenders and repealing certain
          provisions thereof relating thereto. S.4222-B/A. 5393-B.

Dear Mr. Gribetz:

      You have referred the above-numbered bill of Senator Marino and
Assemblyman Fink to amend the Correction Law to prohibit certain discrimination in connection with employment and licensing because of arrests,
accusatory statements or certain convictions which involve juveniles or for
which confinement was discontinued if after the lapse of fixed periods, with
the courts, the board of parole and the State Division of Human Rights given
jurisdiction in certain areas. Our comments are requested.

      We approve of the principle of this bill but the provisions re-
ferring to this Division would cause confusion.

      The proposed Section 908 does not mesh with the Human Rights Law
(Executive Law, Art. 15). The present enforcement jurisdiction of this
Division is limited to the trial and redress of "unlawful discriminatory
practices" specified in Executive Law §§ 296 and 296-a. Thus the matters
set forth in the proposed definition of "discriminatory practice" [§ 900(1)]
and in the exceptions thereto [§ 908(b)] should be integrated into Executive
Law § 296, subdivision 1. If this were done, the proposed § 908 would be
unnecessary.

      I will be glad to have my staff draft amendments along the lines
suggested if you approve of these changes.

- 2 -

It may also be brought to your attention that criminal matters have only been involved in a very secondary way in the work of the State Division of Human Rights and a substantial appropriation will be needed to enforce jurisdiction in this area.

Sincerely,

WERNER H. KRAMARSKY
Commissioner

FACILITIES DEVELOPMENT CORPORATION
44 HOLLAND AVENUE, ALBANY, N.Y. 12209

April 14, 1976

Hon. Judah Gribetz
Executive Chamber
State Capitol
Albany, New York 12224

Re: A5393-B/S4222-B

Dear Mr. Gribetz:

This proposal, which amends the Correction Law to remove economic and licensing barriers for ex-offenders, has no effect on this Corporation.

Therefore, the Corporation takes no position with respect to this legislation.

Sincerely,

JJS:bmr

JOHN J. SAUERWALD
Counsel

By Senator Marine

MEMORANDUM IN SUPPORT OF

4222
710

AN ACT to amend the correction law
in relation to rehabilitation of
criminal offenders and repealing
provisions thereof relating thereto.

PURPOSE OF BILL:

This bill is designed to make it easier for ex-offenders to obtain
employment and rehabilitate themselves by eliminating many of the obstacles to
employment.

EXPLANATION OF BILL:

This bill adds a new article 29 to the correction law removing disabilities arising from (a) conviction of a violation; (b) conviction or adjudication as a delinquent, person in need of supervision, youthful offender of the
Criminal Procedure Law, or an equivalent statute in another jurisdiction; (c) an
arrest, or the lodging of an accusatory instrument.

Employers, unions and other organizations seeking employment information
would be prohibited from inquiring of an applicant for any licensing or economic
right or employment opportunity as to (1) whether the applicant has a record of
arrests, (2) whether the applicant has been convicted of a felony, or released from
actual confinement, other than within the past seven years, or (3) whether the
applicant has been convicted of a misdemeanor, or released from actual confinement,
other than within the past three years.

Disabilities would also be removed following:

conviction of a felony if a period of more than seven years has
elapsed since the date of the last conviction of any crime or of the
release of the person from confinement;

conviction of a misdemeanor if a period of more than three years
has elapsed since the date of the last conviction of any crime
or of the release of the person from actual confinement;

conviction of any offense if the person has received an executive
pardon.

The bill would also prohibit regulations depriving ex-offenders of rights
unless the offense bears a direct relationship to the employment right sought. Provision is also made for discretionary relief from disabilities, the relief to be
granted by the sentencing court or the board of parole.

JUSTIFICATION:

This legislation would remove barriers facing ex-offenders in obtaining
employment. Statistics indicate that many ex-offenders return to lives of crime
because other employment is not available.

FISCAL IMPLICATIONS: None.

EFFECTIVE DATE: This act shall take effect on the first day of January next succeeding
the date on which it shall have become a law.

2/75

CALENDAR NO. RR 320

BILL NO. A. 5393-C   INTRODUCED BY: Mr. Fink

        S.

AN ACT
to amend the correction law and the executive law,
in relation to the removal of disabilities of
criminal offenders and repealing certain provisions thereof relating thereto

SUMMARY OF PROVISIONS -   This bill adds a new article 29 to the correction law removing
disabilities arising from (a) conviction of a violation; (b) conviction or adjudication as a
delinquent, person in need of supervision, youthful offender of the Criminal Procedure Law,
or an equivalent statute in another jurisdiction; (c) an arrest, or the lodging of an accusatory instrument.

    Employers, unions and other organizations seeking employment information would be
prohibited from inquiring of an applicant for any licensing or economic right or employment
opportunity as to (1) whether the applicant has a record of arrests, (2) whether the applicant
has been convicted of a felony, or released from actual confinement, other than within the
past seven years, or (3) whether the applicant has been convicted of a misdemeanor, or released
from actual confinement, other than within the past three years.

    Disabilities would also be removed following:

    conviction of a felony if a period of more than seven years has elapsed since the
date of the last conviction of any crime or of the release of the person from confinement;

    conviction of a misdemeanor if a period of more than three years has elapsed since
the date of the last conviction of any crime or of the release of the person from actual confinement;

    conviction of any offense if the person has received an executive pardon.

    The bill would also prohibit regulations depriving ex-offenders of rights unless the
offense bears a direct relationship to the employment right sought. Provision is also made
for discretionary relief from disabilities, the relief to be granted by the sentencing court
or the board of parole..

RATIONALE - Automatic prohibitions and reflexive limitations pertaining to the employment of
ex-offenders are arbitrary, irrational and dysfunctional. They only serve to increase the
frustration and desperation of such persons and to encourage their return to crime. To the
extent that this bill would help remove these employment barriers it is long overdue and should
be enacted.

LEGISLATIVE HISTORY -

PERTINENT CONSIDERATIONS - It has been reported that in at least fifty occupations, licenses
and privileges are, because of various New York Statutes, either totally closed or substantially
closed to persons who have been convicted of crimes. But even this figure does not accurately
reflect the extent of the legal barriers which consistently and cruelly deny employment opportunities to exoffenders. In fact, certain licensing provisions effectively prevent all conceivable employment of ex-offenders by any business that falls within the jurisdiction of
the licensing agency. For example, the Alcoholic Beverage Control Act prohibits the owner of
a restaurant which has a liquor license from employing most ex-felons, whether they be hired
as chefs, musicians or busboys, unless specific permission is secured from the State Liquor
Authority (S.L.A.)

Facet

Motor Components Division
Facet Enterprises, Inc.

Elmira, New York 14903
(607) 737-8011
Telex 93-2490
TWX 510-252-1594

July 16, 1976

Governor Hugh L. Carey
Governor of the State of New York
The Capitol
Albany, New York 12224

SUBJECT: Senate 4222-C (Marino)

Dear Governor Carey:

The above bill should be rejected. No potential employer, under forced attitudes from a prospective employee, can ever submit an acceptable reason for rejection of employment. Yet, there can be and are many wholly legitimate ones. Any that might be truly judged unfair would be in a definite minority.

The nature of accepting or rejecting applicants for employment is such that it might not relate in any way to past criminal offenses, yet a convicted person would naturally believe such to be the case and be hard to convince otherwise.

It would not be beneficial for a rejected applicant to force an employer to accept him through third party intervention. The normal employer - employee relationship would be seriously affected. Then the law has been of no benefit to either party.

Unfortunately, there may be some few recorded situations that gave rise to the proposed legislation, but I cannot believe it is a problem of sufficient magnitude to justify the problems such legislation will cause.

I respectfully urge a rejection of this bill.

Sincerely,

Robert T. Snowdon
Director of Industrial Relations

cc: Honorable Judah Gribetz, Counsel to the Governor
     Commissioner John Dyson, Department of Commerce
     William Redmond, Industrial Coordinator

THE ERASER CO. INC.

P.O. BOX 1342 · OLIVA DRIVE · SYRACUSE, NEW YORK 13201
PHONE (315) 454-3237   TELEX: 937442

July 20, 1976

The Honorable Judah Gribetz
Counsel to the Governor
The Executive Department
State Capitol Building
Albany, New York 12224

Dear Mr. Gribetz:

We understand that Senate bill No. 4222-C (Marino) has been significantly amended during the closing days of the Legislature and that the bill will shortly be submitted to the office of the Governor for further action. Obviously, the provisions of this bill and especially the amendments referred to would have profound influence on businesses considering moving into the State of New York, and might possibly tip the scales for those who are currently considering moving out of the State because of the poor business climate that already exists in the State.

It is inconceivable to me, and to several other businessmen with whom I have regular contact, and/or the Executive Branch of the State government can continue to burden business with these non-productive activities. The time and expense involved in complying with these literally thousands of requirements can only serve to create discouragement and frustration in the business environment and community.

This particular bill and its amendments not only are contrary to the best interests of the business community, but also the labor community. It impinges upon the dignity in general of the labor component of our economy and specifically upon those who would be affected by it.

I, therefore, enthusiastically and heartily urge you to deal negatively with this legislation in the best interest of the labor and business communities in the State of New York.

Sincerely,

Ralph E. BeVard
President

REB:cm

WIRE STRIPPING AND LEAD FORMING SPECIALIST

Penny Curtiss Baking Co., Inc.

1813 LEMOYNE AVENUE
SYRACUSE, N. Y. 13211

July 19, 1976

The Honorable Judah Gribetz
Counsel to the Governor
The Executive Department
State Capitol Bldg.
Albany, N. Y. 12224

Dear Sir:

Re: Bill Senate 4222-C (Marino)

We feel this bill will have a serious <u>unfavorable</u> impact on our

Corporate Personnel hiring practices.

We ask you to veto - destroy or do whatever is necessary to cancel

this bill as it now stands.

You - representing us must start to do a few things to make it

possible for us to remain our businesses in New York State.

Very, truly yours,

William A. Adamsen
President

WAA:br
cc: Manufacturers Assoc. of Syracuse
    770 James Street
    Syracuse, N. Y. 13203

MANUFACTURERS ASSOCIATION of Syracuse

ESTABLISHED 1913

770 JAMES STREET · SYRACUSE N Y 13203

TELEPHONE 474-4201

July 19, 1976

The Honorable Judah Gribetz
Counsel to the Governor
Executive Department
State Capitol
Albany, New York 12224

Dear Mr. Gribetz:

The Manufacturers Association of Syracuse wishes to call your attention to Senate Bill 4222-C, an act to amend the Correction Law and the Executive Law, in relation to the removal of disabilities of criminal offenders and repealing certain provisions thereof relating thereto.

A. This bill would create "favored treatment" for job applicants that have been convicted of one or more criminal offenses. These applicants, according to the bill, if denied employment, are entitled to receive a written statement from the employer setting forth the reasons for such a job denial.

 This appears to be a form of paperwork harrassment which carries the additional disability that the employer is guilty of misjudgment until proven innocent. In an era when New York State should be looking to lighten its regulatory as well as its tax load, the legislation referred to would seem to contravene the movement in those desired directions.

B. The fact is that business and industry have been and will continue to be most cooperative in the hiring of ex-offenders and in encouraging rehabilitation of criminals to make them once again useful members of society.

 The emphasis, therefore, in their behalf, should be on penal institutions and civil authorities working in cooperation with business and industry toward improving relevant occupational training, rehabilitation and placement programs, instead of taking a negative punitive approach toward employers as this legislation would do.

C. We strongly recommend, therefore, that S. 4222-C be vetoed.

Sincerely,

James B. Schneider
Executive Vice President

JBS:ak

July 20, 1976

Governor Hugh Carey
The Executive Department
State Capitol Building
Albany, NY   12224

Dear Governor Carey:

This letter is with respect to Senate Bill 4222-C which
seeks to make unlawful the refusal of an employer to
hire a convicted felon on the basis of such conviction.
No doubt this is an effort to minimize the rate of recidivism and thereby lower the crime rate. Unfortunately,
the method of approach to this problem is wrong.

The Human Rights Law, indeed the Constitution, is designed
to prevent employers from discriminating against individuals on the basis of irrational categorization such as
age, race, religion, etc. All of these categories are
irrational in the sense that any distinctions among people
have to do with what they are rather than who they are.
In the case of a convicted felon, the category is entirely
rational. The employer is basing his judgment entirely
on something that the individual seeking employment has unlawfully done. The refusal to hire in that instance is
not a case of the accident of birth, rather, it is based
upon the individual's performance record. It is a hard
fact that a convicted felon pays a serious penalty for
his misdeeds, but those misdeeds are his doing. Even the
state sees fit to take from such person, certain rights
of citizenship. An employer must not be required to
close his eyes, indeed ignore, a matter which goes to the
heart of an employer--employee relationship, namely trust
and confidence in the integrity of the individual to be
employed.

In some respects the proposed statute is almost incom-
prehensible. While the employer cannot accept the
criminal record of the prospective employee as evidence
with respect to moral character, presumptively the law
would leave untouched the employer's right to make that
judgment on the basis of rumor, innuendo and heresay.

Carrols Development Corporation • P.O. Box 1094 • 968 James Street • Syracuse New York 13201 • 315 471 3700

Governor Hugh Carey
July 20, 1976
Page 2

We do not question the motivation of this bill, we
seriously suggest that the problem cannot be solved and
must not be solved in the manner proposed. In the case
of a convicted felon, it is wholly unreasonable to place
upon the employer the burden of proving that the prospective employee lacks good moral character. Quite right-
fully, the burden of such proof must rest upon the convicted felon. It is for him to explain and for him to
satisfy the prospective employer. This is a problem of
ends and means, the ends sought to be achieved cannot
justify the means adopted by the prospective bill.

We urge that the bill be vetoed.

Very truly yours,

JACK B. TALSKY
VICE PRESIDENT - GENERAL COUNSEL

JBT:kw

New York State Coalition for Criminal Justice
c/o Rapid Communication Network
810 Madison Avenue, Albany, New York 12208
Phone 518-482-0214

July 9, 1976

Re: S.4222-C, to remove
licensing and employ-
ment disabilities for
ex-offenders

Governor Hugh L. Carey
Executive Chamber
New York State Capitol
Albany, New York 12224

Attention: Clarence Sundram

Dear Governor Carey:

We commend you and your staff on the difficult job of negotiating a bill
which could pass both houses of the Legislature and meet the requirements necessary to assure executive approval. We urge your signature on S.4222-C without
delay.

Members of the N. Y. S. Coalition for Criminal Justice have worked for
several years to remove legal barriers to ex-offender employment. We note that
S.4222-C contains protections for employers as well as ex-offenders. It is
particularly commendable that the bill expresses a public policy of the state
to encourage licensing and employment of persons previously convicted of criminal
offenses.

Although the passage of this bill sets the legal framework for licensing and
hiring of ex-offenders, we urge you to support continuing efforts toward instilling
positive public and employer attitudes and assuring positive hiring practices.

Sincerely,

Irene F. Jackson
Chairperson, Policy Committee

Policy Committee Members

James Cashen
N. Y. S. Council of Catholic
Charities Directors
Lynn Cobden
United Church of Christ
Pauline Feingold
New York Urban Coalition
Lenora Gittis
Legal Aid Society
Diana Gordon
Citizens' Inquiry on Parole
and Criminal Justice
Irene Jackson
N. Y. S. Council of Churches

DeWitt Lee, Jr.
BRIDGE
David Leven
Monroe County Legal Assistance Corp.
Ellen Flanders-Morrison
Quaker Prisons Committee NYYM
Barbara Shack
New York Civil Liberties Union
Stephen Shestakofsky
Citizens' Union
Basil Velez
Criminal Justice Consultant
Carol Whalen
Community Service Society

HAROLD BAER, JR   JUL 1   1976

July 16, 1976

Hon. Judah Gribetz
Executive Chamber
State Capitol
Albany, New York 12224

                              Re: S. 4222-C
                                  A. 5393-C

Dear Mr. Gribetz:

Amongst a series of bills I received during my vacation, this
one is by far the most significant in my view. I do hope that
the signing period has not elapsed or, in the alternative, that
the Governor has signed the above bill into law.

The proposal would broaden the scope of certificates of good
conduct and give simultaneous relief from civil disability.
Unless legislation of this type becomes law, we are doomed to
a continuance of high rates of recidivism amongst ex-offenders.

Frankly, the bill has one defect which is that the appellate
procedure is somewhat bulky and puts the onus of bringing a
proceeding on the shoulders of the ex-offender, rather than a requirement of a hearing, assuming that a license or an employment
opportunity is denied.

None the less, it is a step in the right direction and I would
highly endorse the measure.

                              Very truly yours,

                              Harold Baer, Jr.

tm
Enc.

Commission on Correctional Facilities and Services
1800 M Street, N.W. • Washington, D.C. 20036 • 202/331-2280

1975 CORRECTIONAL POLICY POSITIONS
OF
THE AMERICAN BAR ASSOCIATION

- Offender Employment Restrictions
- Legal Services to the Institutionalized Poor
- Development of United Nations Community Supervision
- Increased Recruitment of Minority and Female Staff
- Statewide Jail and Detention Standards

APPROVED BY THE HOUSE OF DELEGATES
OF THE AMERICAN BAR ASSOCIATION
AT THE
ASSOCIATION'S 98th ANNUAL MEETING
MONTREAL, CANADA—AUGUST 8-13, 1975

OFFENDER EMPLOYMENT RESTRICTIONS

RESOLVED, that the American Bar Association calls for the elimination of all laws which (a) deny government employment or occupational licensing of ex-offenders without consideration of the relationship between the offender's record and the position or license sought, and (b) permit adverse action against ex-offenders seeking government employment or occupational licensing based on arbitrary criteria, and further

RESOLVED, that the American Bar Association urges the federal, state and local governments to assure that ex-offenders receive full and fair consideration in hiring and licensing decisions subject to their control.

REPORT

Unemployment and crime have been positively correlated. [1] Although the extent of the causal link is unclear, both manpower and criminal justice experts accept that unemployment contributes heavily to the nation's persistently high recidivism and crime rates.

---

1. Glaser, The Effectiveness of a Prison and Parole System (1964); Pownall, Employment Problems of Released Prisoners (1969); Babst and Cowden, Program Research in Correctional Effectiveness (1967); Library of Congress, Prison Population and Costs - Illustrative Projections to 1980 (1974).

Cosponsored by ABA Corrections Commission and ABA Section of Criminal Justice

Of the many factors which contribute to high rates of ex-offender unemployment, one -- statutory law -- is uniquely remediable through governmental action. Many state laws impose unwarranted restrictions on the job opportunities of former offenders in two key areas: government employment and trades or occupations for which a state certificate or license is required. Government employment now totals 13 million workers, or some 15 percent of the work force. In 1960, an estimated 7 million persons worked in occupations requiring a license, a total which has no doubt risen substantially since then. In the main, these positions are in the ever expanding services sector of the economy. Conceptually for public protection, both of these job areas are extensively regulated by statute. These laws often automatically disqualify from occupational licensing, or revoke the licenses of, persons who have been convicted of a crime, any crime. Even more common is statutory language providing that the hiring or certifying entity "may reject" the applications of persons with felony convictions, or those persons convicted of "crimes of moral turpitude," or those persons lacking "good moral character," a condition often imputed to former felons.

Two studies completed in 1972 underscore the magnitude of the problem facing former offenders. In one, 2/ conducted by the National Clearinghouse on Offender Employment Restrictions (a joint project of the Section of Criminal Justice and the Commission on Correctional Facilities and Services), nearly 2,000 state laws were found which included provisions capable of adversely affecting the occupational licensing of ex-offenders. (For example, over 700 laws provide no license shall issue to one convicted of a criminal offense. 3/) The other study found that half the states have civil service laws which may automatically or arbitrarily exclude former felons from public employment. 4/

Since the Clearinghouse was created to disseminate such facts as these, over a third of the states have taken some remedial action. This has been in the form of legislation in 16 states, gubernatorial action in three others, and an attorney general's opinion in yet another. Legislation is pending this year in more than a dozen states to mitigate current restrictions.

Current ABA policy is consistent with the position stated in the resolution. Four prior actions seem relevant:

1. In 1970, the Association's Standards Relating to Probation were approved. They include a provision (Standard 4.3) that "[e]very jurisdiction should have a method by which the collateral effects of a criminal record can be avoided or mitigated following the successful completion of a term on probation and during its service."

---

2. Laws, Licenses and the Offender's Right to Work.

3. Id at 5.

4. Miller, The Closed Door: The Effect of a Criminal Record on Employment with State and Local Agencies, Table D, p. 191 (1972).

2. In 1971, the systematic treatment of sentencing in the Final Report of the National Commission on Reform of Federal Criminal Laws was endorsed in principle. Chapter 35 of the Commission's proposed code provided only for limited, temporary collateral consequences of convictions.

3. In 1973, the Association endorsed pending federal legislation which would authorize the setting aside of convictions in order to facilitate the reintegration of offenders into the community.

4. In 1974, the Association opposed federal procurement policies which limit the employability of work releasees.

Provisions in two model acts -- the Model Penal Code 5/ and the Model Act to Authorize Courts to Annul a Record of Conviction 6/ -- also support the thrust of the resolutions, as did the 1967 President's Commission on Law Enforcement and Administration of Justice. 7/

The most explicit such statement, however, is found in the Report on Corrections of the National Advisory Commission on Criminal Justice Standards and Goals:

Standard 16.17:
    Each State should enact by 1975 legislation repealing all mandatory provisions depriving persons convicted of criminal offenses of civil rights or other attributes of citizenship. Such legislation should include: . . . 3) Repeal of all mandatory provisions denying persons convicted of a criminal offense the right to engage in any occupation or obtain any license issued by the government. 4) Repeal of all statutory provisions prohibiting employment of ex-offenders by State and local government agencies.

The second resolution is not substantively different from the first. It calls upon governments at all levels to do more than simply articulate a policy favoring reintegration of former offenders. There must be action consistent with the law. This statement is doubly important, however, because it calls on government to set an example so that the private sector will have a model to emulate.

This matter has recently received presidential attention and impetus. In his June 19, 1975 crime message, President Ford noted that the U.S. Civil Service Commission "administers a program designed to prevent Federal employers from unjustly discriminating against ex-felons." President Ford continued:

---

5. American Law Institute, Model Penal Code Art. 306 (P.O.D. 1962).

6. National Council on Crime and Delinquency (1962).

7. Task Force Report: Corrections 92 (1967).

-3-

I am directing the Commission to review this program to ensure that it is accomplishing its objectives. I am also calling on the National Governors Conference to consider steps the States can take to eliminate unjustified discriminatory practices. Giving ex-offenders who have paid their penalty and seek to "go straight" a fair shake in the job market can be an effective means of reducing crime and improving our criminal justice system. 8/

Neither resolution, it should be noted, makes the employment or occupational licensing of an ex-offender automatic, nor provides a hiring or license preference for such individuals. They are rather aimed solely at assuring full and fair and consistent consideration for such persons.

8. Ford, Message on Crime 7, (White House Press Release, June 19, 1975).

-4-

NYCLU

New York Civil Liberties Union, 84 Fifth Avenue, New York, N.Y. 10011. Telephone (212) 924-7800

Legislative Department
Barbara Shack, Director
Arthur Eisenberg, Staff Counsel
Kenneth P. Norwick, Counsel

State Legislative Office
90 State Street
Albany, N.Y. 12207
(518) 436-8594

July 9, 1976

Governor Hugh Carey
Executive Chamber
State Capitol
Albany, N.Y. 12224

RE: S4222-e

Dear Governor Carey:

NYCLU supports this bill and urges your approval. It is an important
step towards relieving the irrational discrimination against ex-offenders
and should become law.

Automatic prohibitions and reflexive limitations pertaining to the
employment of ex-offenders are arbitrary, irrational and dysfunctional.
They only serve to increase the frustration and desperation of such
persons and to encourage their return to crime. To the extent that
this bill would help remove these employment barriers it is long overdue and should be enacted.

The doors to at least fifty occupations, licenses and privileges are,
because of various New York statutes, either totally closed or substantially closed to persons who have been convicted of crimes. But even
this figure does not accurately reflect the extent of the legal barriers
which consistently and cruelly deny employment opportunities to ex-
offenders. In fact, certain licensing provisions effectively prevent
all conceivable employment of ex-offenders by any business that falls
within the jurisdiction of the licensing agency. For example, the
Alcoholic Beverage Control Act prohibits the owner of a restaurant which
has a liquor license from employing most ex-felons, whether they be
hired as chefs, musicians or busboys, unless specific permission is
secured from the State Liquor Authority (S.L.A.). Such permission by
the S.L.A. is grudgingly granted. And in deciding whether or not to
grant permission, the S.L.A. is under no obligation to conduct a hearing.

See Bergansky v. State Liquor Authority, 39 A.D. 2d 849, 332 N.Y.S. 2d 783 (1st Dept., 1972). Such a process which effectively imposes a strong presumption against the employment of ex-offenders regardless of the job cannot be shown to advance any legitimate state interest. It merely suggests the absurdity of New York's employment barriers. Moreover, the spectrum of occupations from which ex-offenders are barred further reinforces the suggestion that such impediments are absurd and irrational. One who has been convicted of a crime is statutorily forbidden from employment as varied as a junk dealer, an X-ray technician, and the manager of a billiard parlor. An ex-offender may be denied a license as a podiatrist, an undertaker, or an operator of bingo games.

Some of the occupational disabilities which are statutorily imposed upon ex-offenders are seemingly and inextricably retained in perpetuity Thus, for example, an individual who engages in certain proscribed conduct may be found guilty of a misdemeanor and be "_forever_ disqualified from receiving a license to act as an auctioneer in this state". See _General Business Law_, Section 24 (emphasis supplied). Such an employment disability is unambiguously permanent.

Other statutory provisions, however, create occupational impediments for ex-offenders yet allow for the removal of such disabilities under certain narrow circumstances. But the removal procedures are unfamiliar to most persons; and difficult and burdensome even for those few who might possibly know about them. Such procedures, in fact, discourage the restoration of occupational opportunities and accord every presumption in favor of the retention of the disability. Thus Section 3510 of the Public Health Law provides for the restoration of the right to be licensed as an X-ray technician in the following manner:

> "If a person convicted of a felony...is subsequently pardoned by the governor of the state where such conviction was had, or by the president of the United States, or shall receive a certificate of good conduct granted by the board of parole...the commissioner may, in his discretion, on application of such person, and, on the submission to him of satisfactory evidence, restore to such person, the right to practice X-ray technology in this state."

It is well known that pardons by the governors are seldom granted; a pardon by the President of the United States is -- unless your middle name happens to be Milhous -- almost inconceivable; and a certificate of good conduct is circumscribed by so many procedural and substantive requirements that it is rarely obtained. Moreover, even if such rare muniments could be obtained by the ex-offender, the opportunity to work as an X-ray technician would not be guaranteed for even then such person must still apply to the commissioner; must still submit additional satisfactory evidence; and the commission may, in its discretion, restore or fail to restore the right to engage in that particular profession.

Among the procedures which attempt to ameliorate the loss of occupational opportunities, the most frequently utilized is the provision which permits the issuance of the certificate of relief from disabilities. But even this procedure is of limited application and assistance, for the certificate of relief from disabilities applies only to first offenders. Moreover, neither the certificate of relief from disabilities nor the certificate of good conduct expunges the criminal conviction. At best, the certificates assist in the removal of the statutory bars to employment. The individual employer (whether public or private) still retains the right to consider a person's conviction when evaluating his or her employment application. And most employers, when given the opportunity to choose between an ex-offender and one with a clean record, will not select the ex-offender regardless of how irrelevant the offense to the occupational responsibilities or how long ago the conviction took place.

In a job market as tight as is the present one, the ex-offender is indeed placed in a desperate situation. Statutory barriers combine with popular prejudice to deny such person any opportunity for the kind of economic security that is necessary for personal rehabilitation. Thus, the statutory policy and popular practice of discriminating against ex-offenders not only fail to achieve any legitimate societal interest, but they are, in fact, demonstrably dysfunctional. Such policies and practices present a fundamental cause for the disturbingly high rate of recidivism.

Moreover, any discussion of the inequities of the use of convictions as a bar to employment cannot overlook the racial aspects of the problem. It has long been recognized that the use of criminal records (whether it be of "arrests" or "convictions") to disqualify prospective employees imposes a particular hardship upon most non-white minorities. See, e.g., Gregory v. Litton Systems, Inc., 316 F. Supp. 411 (1970); Carter v. Callagher, 452 F.2d 315 (8th Cir., 1971).

Exhortations to employers are not enough. In 1614 Lord Coke announced: "Peona mori potest, culpa perennis erit" (punishment can terminate, guilt endures forever)". Brown v. Crashaw, 2 Bulst. 154, 80 Eng. Rep. 1028 [KB 1614]. The State of New York unfortunately mandates that its

Governor Carey   July 9, 1976
Page 4

punishment endures forever. The New York Civil Liberties Union
submits that punishment should end at the moment when the offender
completes the sentence imposed. A man's criminal conviction should
not pursue him for the remainder of his life. The elimination of or
the restriction of the statutorily mandated disabilities would substantially help in the effort to eliminate the perpetuity of punishment.

Accordingly, the New York Civil Liberties Union believes that all records
of criminal convictions be subject to sealing after a certain period of
time. The time might vary with the crime, as the sentence does, and
for certain crimes the sealing might be automatic. Ultimately, no one
should have to live forever incapable of shaking a past mistake. The
inability to escape one's past and make a new beginning has become a
critical problem in modern society where there are no frontiers and
where electronic storage in vast computers create indelible records
that follow you everywhere.

Our present system makes a mockery of the idea of rehabilitation. Im--
prisonment is not even called imprisonment any more; it's called correction. But even after the offender is presumably "corrected", the outside
world manages to block every attempt to begin anew. If that's the
system we mean to have, we should drop the hypocrisy about rehabilitation, and imprison everyone who commits a crime for life. In effect,
that is precisely what the present bars to employment accomplish.

This bill would substantially improve employment opportunities for
ex-offenders and strike a significant blow against recidivism. It
should be "law."

Sincerely,

Barbara Shack

Barbara Shack
Legislative Director

The Correctional Association of New York

FOUNDED 1844

135 EAST 15th STREET, NEW YORK, N.Y. 10003   (212) 254-5700

July 13, 1976

Hon. Hugh L. Carey
Governor of the State of New York
Executive Chamber
State Capitol
Albany, N.Y. 12224

RE: S 4222-C
SUPPORT

Dear Governor Carey:

The Correctional Association has long recommended in its Annual Reports to the Legislature that bars to the employment of ex-offenders be removed. It is the Association's firm conviction that the most effective deterrent to criminal behavior is meaningful employment at decent wages. Every step possible should be taken to assist the ex-offender in finding such employment.

The above bill would prohibit unfair discrimination against persons previously convicted of a crime so that their access to employment, public or private, would not be hampered. Exceptions would be based on a number of criteria that would in effect provide for individual judgement of applicants, eliminating blanket denials of employment, and requiring a written statement of reason for denial. It would further reduce the waiting time required for the issuance of a certificate of good conduct, except for Class A and B felony convictions, so that the ex-offender would be eligible for restricted jobs or licenses at an earlier date.

The Association urges strongly that this bill be signed into law.

Sincerely,

Adam F. McQuillan
President

AFM:dw

COMMUNITY SERVICE SOCIETY · 105 PARK AVENUE · NEW YORK, N.Y. 10016 · (212) 254-8900

July 6, 1976

Honorable Hugh L. Carey
Governor of New York
Executive Chamber
Albany, New York 12224

Re: S. 4222-C AN ACT to amend the correction law and the executive law,
in relation to the removal of disabilities of criminal offenders and
repealing certain provisions thereof
relating thereto

Dear Governor Carey:

In response to your request for our comments on this bill, we urge you to
sign S. 4222-C which would create for the first time in New York State
a uniform policy in relation to rights and disabilities of ex-offenders.
The bill provides a balance between protection of the public and prohibition of arbitrary discrimination.

Convicted offenders may not be denied a license or employment unless their
offense bears a "direct relationship" to the job sought, or would entail
unreasonable risk to the property, safety or welfare of individuals or the
public. The bill also permits the State Board of Parole to issue certificates removing civil disabilities for any convicted persons whether or
not under its jurisdiction. Appeals may be taken against public agencies
through an Article 78 proceeding under the Civil Practice Law and Rules.
The New York State Division of Human Rights is empowered to enforce the
provisions pertaining to private employers.

This bill represents a major advance in public policy; its vigorous
enforcement can remove the second class status to which former offenders
have been relegated regardless of their efforts to be lawabiding citizens.
We commend you for your active efforts and leadership in development of
this legislation.

Sincerely,

Eliot D. Hawkins, Chairman
Committee on Youth and Correction

EDH/ij

VEGA INDUSTRIES, INC.

Syracuse, New York 13205

July 22, 1976

The Honorable Judah Gribetz
Counsel to the Governor
The Executive Department
State Capitol Building
Albany, New York 12224

Re: S4222-C (Marino) Denial of Employment Ex-offenders

Dear Mr. Gribetz:

Another piece of legislation that is restrictive to business development in the state is Marino's bill that is on Governor Carey's desk.

This is a bad bill for business. It attempts to legislate employment standards in the private sector and my company is strongly opposed to it. It imposes personnel hiring practices that can adversely effect the quality of our work force. Further, the provision that require a corporate response in writing in a time period following rejection of employment is another burden of record keeping.

I urge that you recommend to Governor Carey that he veto this bill.

Very truly yours,

VEGA INDUSTRIES, INC.

Donald S. Jaquith
Executive Vice President

DSJ/jtt

INVESTMENT CASTINGS IN AIR AND VACUUM ALLOYS

Gray-Syracuse, Inc.

116 West Seneca Street
MANLIUS, N. Y. 13104

PHONE (315) 682-5111

July 22, 1976

Mr. William Redmond
State Economic Development Board
State Capitol Building
Albany, New York 12224

Dear Mr. Redmond:

Re: Senate Bill 4222-C

As a small businessman, I am surprised to learn about the contents of the above bill to make it illegal to deny employment to persons previously convicted of even serious criminal offenses.

This is a bad bill that I hope never becomes law.

It may be worthy to help a criminal to return to society, but many criminals become frequent offenders. It is not right to force employment at the expense of a larger and honest group of citizens; namely, the businesses and their employees. Judgment of the employer to hire or fire is a constitutional right to also be protected.

Thank you for reviewing my comments.

Sincerely yours,

GRAY-SYRACUSE, INC.

R. E. Gray
Chairman

REG/dhd

INVESTMENT CASTINGS IN AIR AND VACUUM ALLOYS

Gray-Syracuse, Inc.

116 West Seneca Street
MANLIUS, N. Y. 13104
PHONE (315) 682-5111

July 22, 1976

Mr. William Redmond
State Economic Development Board
State Capitol Building
Albany, New York 12224

Dear Mr. Redmond:

Re: Senate Bill 4222-C

As a small businessman, I am surprised to learn about the contents of the above bill to make it illegal to deny employment to persons previously convicted of even serious criminal offenses.

This is a bad bill that I hope never becomes law.

It may be worthy to help a criminal to return to society, but many criminals become frequent offenders. It is not right to force employment at the expense of a larger and honest group of citizens; namely, the businesses and their employees. Judgment of the employer to hire or fire is a constitutional right to also be protected.

Thank you for reviewing my comments.

Sincerely yours,

GRAY-SYRACUSE, INC.

R. E. Gray
Chairman

REG/dhd

C - 431

Colt Industries

Crucible Inc
Specialty Metals Division
Box 977
Syracuse, New York 13201
315/487-4111

July 23, 1976

The Honorable Hugh L. Carey
The Executive Department
State Capitol Building
Albany, New York 12224

Dear Governor Carey:

I am writing with regard to bill, Senate 4222-C (Marino), which I understand will shortly be transmitted to you for consideration. The provisions in this proposed legislation which are particularly disturbing deal with the additional unreasonable restrictions it would place on the employers of New York State in the area of personnel selection.

As I am sure you are well aware, the employment practices of the state's employers are already being scrutinized by the federal, state, and local governments in every personnel area possible. In fact, it is reaching a point where in some cases, the employer is hardly permitted the opportunity to make the best choice in the selection of its personnel, but the choice that must satisfy one or more, if not all, of these agencies. This creates a situation of constant concern that selection procedures may run afoul of a government rule somewhere. To add still more restrictions with such far reaching implications as those contained in this bill, it seems to me, cannot possibly serve the best interests of the Empire State's business community. I'm certain I'm speaking for many when I question how many more restrictions and regulations the employers of this state can endure and still remain financially healthy.

Because of the concerns noted, when you review the contents of this proposed legislation, I hope you will find it impossible to condone its passage into law.

Thank you for permitting me to share my thoughts on the subject with you.

Very truly yours,

COLT INDUSTRIES
CRUCIBLE SPECIALTY METALS DIVISION

T. J. Ward, Jr.
Vice President - Employee Relations

TJW/img
cc: The Hon. Judah Gribetz
     Commissioner John Dyson
     William Redmond, Industrial Coordinator

SYBRON

C-93?

July 29, 1976

The Honorable Hugh Carey
Governor of New York
State Capitol
Albany, NY 12224

Dear Governor Carey:

While Senate 4222-C was written to protect persons previously convicted of criminal offenses, it is my opinion that such persons are already adequately protected by Federal legislation.

This seems to be one more New York State Law that makes it so very difficult for industry to conduct business in this state.

We urge your careful consideration of this bill.

Sincerely,

Patricia L. Wild
Director of Community Relations

PLW:mjw
cc: The Hon. Judah Gribetz
     Commissioner John Dyson

N. Y. S. COALITION FOR CRIMINAL JUSTICE
c/o Rapid Communication Network
810 Madison Avenue
Albany, N. Y. 12208

FOR RELEASE May 8, 1975
10:00 a.m.

Contact: Irene Jackson
518-482-0214
518-449-7332

COALITION OF SIXTY GROUPS URGES ASSEMBLY ACTION
Endorses Prison Package: Cites Four Key Areas Omitted

The N. Y. S. Coalition for Criminal Justice, a coalition of over sixty civic, religious and professional organizations representing New Yorkers from all parts of the
state, has announced its support for the eleven-bill package of prison reform
measures now on the Assembly's Third Reading Calendar. While supporting the Assembly
package, the Coalition cited four more areas of concern where action is desired at
the 1975 Session.

The Coalition, in a letter sent to all members of the Assembly, called the eleven-bill
package "an acceptable baseline for correctional reform". The Coalition singled out
three Assembly members for special praise: Speaker Stanley Steingut, Codes Committee
Chairman Stanley Fink, and Saul Weprin, Chairman of the Subcommittee on Corrections.

The Coalition saw the need for further reform in four distinct areas:

- ex-offender employment disabilities
- prison health services
- parole revocation hearings
- non-classified civil service status for prison superintendents

According to Irene Jackson, Chairperson of the Coalition's Policy Committee, "at least
four key areas not covered by the package must be acted upon this session for real
correctional reform." In addition, Ms. Jackson noted that the Coalition felt that
major restructuring of the Commission of Correction is needed and should be considered
in this session.

COMMITTEE ON CIVIL RIGHTS
BARBARA ANN ROWAN
  Chairperson
  335 Broadway
  New York, N.Y. 10013

New York State Bar Association

July 7, 1976

Hon. Judah Gribetz
Executive Chambers
State Capitol
Albany, N.Y. 12224

        Re: S 4222 - C   Cal. No. 720
           A 5393 - C

Dear Sir:

    The Civil Rights Committee is delighted to comment
favorably on this proposed Act. We proposed a similar
but somewhat less comprehensive scheme in 1975, and again
in 1976, with no success. While some members of the
committee may feel that more aggressive legislation is
required, the general consensus is that this step is long
overdue and quite appropriate in the present punitive
political atmosphere.

                Yours very truly,

                BARBARA ANN ROWAN

2007 LEGISLATIVE AMENDMENTS

RF

CHAPTER **284**

LAWS OF 20 O7

SENATE BILL 1602   ASSEMBLY BILL _____

STATE OF NEW YORK

S. 1602--A   A. 3208-A
Cal. No. 1089   Cal. No. 49

2007-2008 Regular Sessions

SENATE - ASSEMBLY

January 23, 2007

IN SENATE -- Introduced by Sen. VOLKER -- read twice and ordered printed, and when printed to be committed to the Committee on Crime Victims, Crime and Correction -- reported favorably from said committee, ordered to first and second report, ordered to a third reading, passed by Senate and delivered to the Assembly, recalled, vote reconsidered, restored to third reading, amended and ordered reprinted, retaining its place in the order of third reading

IN ASSEMBLY -- Introduced by M. of A. AUBRY, COOK, GREENE, PERALTA, TITUS, WRIGHT, LAFAYETTE, BENJAMIN, D. GORDON -- Multi-Sponsored by M. of A. BOYLAND, COLTON, ORTIZ, PERRY, ROBINSON, WEISENBERG -- read once and referred to the Committee on Correction -- reported from committee, advanced to a third reading, amended and ordered reprinted, retaining its place on the order of third reading

AN ACT to amend the correction law, in relation to extending protection from discrimination to current employees and licensees

A3208 - AUBRY

DATE RECEIVED BY GOVERNOR:

JUL 0 6 2007

ACTION MUST BE TAKEN BY:

JUL 1 6 2007

DATE GOVERNOR'S ACTION TAKEN:
JUL 1 6 2007

SENATE VOTE 62 Y 0 N   HOME RULE MESSAGE ___ Y ___ N

DATE 6/14/07

ASSEMBLY VOTE 135 Y 14 N

DATE 6/20/07

RETRIEVE BILL

Yes Cole	Yes Colton	Yes Conte	Yes Cook
Yes Crouch	Yes Cusick	Yes Cymbrowitz	Yes DelMonte
Yes Destito	Yes Diaz L	Yes Diaz R	Yes Dinowitz
No Duprey	Yes Eddington	Yes Englebright	No Errigo
Yes Espaillat	Yes Farrell	Yes Fields	Yes Finch
No Fitzpatrick	Yes Gabryszak	Yes Galef	Yes Gantt
Yes Gianaris	Yes Giglio	Yes Glick	Yes Gordon D
Yes Gordon T	Yes Gottfried	Yes Greene	No Gunther A
Yes Hawley	Yes Hayes	Yes Heastie	Yes Hevesi
Yes Hikind	Yes Hooper	Yes Hoyt	Yes Hyer-Spencer
Yes Jacobs	Yes Jaffee	Yes Jeffries	No John
Yes Kavanagh	Yes Kellner	Yes Kirwan	No Kolb
No Koon	Yes Lafayette	Yes Lancman	Yes Latimer
Yes Lavine	Yes Lentol	Yes Lifton	No Lopez P
Yes Lopez V	Yes Lupardo	Yes Magee	No Magnarelli
Yes Maisel	Yes Markey	Yes Mayersohn	Yes McDonald
Yes McDonough	Yes McEneny	Yes McKevitt	Yes Miller
Yes Millman	Yes Molinaro	Yes Morelle	Yes Nolan
No Oaks	Yes O'Donnell	Yes O'Mara	Yes Ortiz
Yes Parment	Yes Paulin	Yes Peoples	Yes Peralta
Yes Perry	Yes Pheffer	Yes Powell	Yes Pretlow
No Quinn	Yes Rabbitt	Yes Raia	Yes Ramos
Yes Reilich	Yes Reilly	Yes Rivera J	Yes Rivera N
Yes Rivera P	Yes Robinson	Yes Rosenthal	Yes Saladino
No Sayward	Yes Scarborough	Yes Schimel	Yes Schimminger
Yes Schroeder	Yes Scozzafava	Yes Seminerio	Yes Spano
Yes Stirpe	Yes Sweeney	Yes Tedisco	Yes Thiele
Yes Titone	Yes Titus	Yes Tobacco	Yes Tonko
Yes Towns	Yes Townsend	Yes Walker	Yes Weinstein
ER Weisenberg	Yes Weprin	Yes Wright	Yes Young
Yes Zebrowski K	Yes Mr. Speaker		

Go to Top of Page
06/14/07 S1602-A Senate Vote Aye: 62 Nay: 0

Aye Adams	Aye Alesi	Aye Bonacic	Aye Breslin
Aye Bruno	Aye Connor	Aye DeFrancisco	Aye Diaz
Aye Dilan	Aye Duane	Aye Farley	Aye Flanagan
Aye Fuschillo	Aye Golden	Aye Gonzalez	Aye Griffo
Aye Hannon	Aye Hassell-Thompson	Aye Huntley	Aye Johnson C
Aye Johnson O	Aye Klein	Aye Krueger	Aye Kruger
Aye Lanza	Aye Larkin	Aye LaValle	Aye Leibell
Aye Libous	Aye Little	Aye Maltese	Aye Marcellino
Aye Maziarz	Aye Montgomery	Aye Morahan	Aye Nozzolio
Aye Onorato	Aye Oppenheimer	Aye Padavan	Aye Parker
Aye Perkins	Aye Rath	Aye Robach	Aye Sabini
Aye Saland	Aye Sampson	Aye Savino	Aye Schneiderman
Aye Serrano	Aye Seward	Aye Skelos	Aye Smith
Aye Stachowski	Aye Stavisky	Aye Stewart-Cousins	Aye Thompson
Aye Trunzo	Aye Valesky	Aye Volker	Aye Winner
Aye Wright	Aye Young		

Go to Top of Page
05/30/07 S1602   Senate Vote   Aye: 60   Nay: 0

Aye Adams	Aye Alesi	Aye Bonacic	Aye Breslin
Aye Bruno	Aye Connor	Aye DeFrancisco	Aye Diaz
Aye Dilan	Aye Duane	Aye Farley	Aye Flanagan
Aye Fuschillo	Aye Golden	Aye Gonzalez	Aye Griffo
Aye Hannon	Aye Hassell-Thompson	Exc Huntley	Aye Johnson C
Aye Johnson O	Aye Klein	Aye Krueger	Aye Kruger
Aye Lanza	Aye Larkin	Aye LaValle	Aye Leibell
Aye Libous	Aye Little	Aye Maltese	Aye Marcellino
Aye Maziarz	Aye Montgomery	Aye Morahan	Aye Nozzolio
Exc Onorato	Aye Oppenheimer	Aye Padavan	Aye Parker
Aye Perkins	Aye Rath	Aye Robach	Aye Sabini
Aye Saland	Aye Sampson	Aye Savino	Aye Schneiderman
Aye Serrano	Aye Seward	Aye Skelos	Aye Smith
Aye Stachowski	Aye Stavisky	Aye Stewart-Cousins	Aye Thompson
Aye Trunzo	Aye Valesky	Aye Volker	Aye Winner
Aye Wright	Aye Young		

RETRIEVE BILL

NEW YORK STATE SENATE
INTRODUCER'S MEMORANDUM IN SUPPORT
submitted in accordance with Senate Rule VI. Sec 1

BILL NUMBER: S1602A

SPONSOR: VOLKER

TITLE OF BILL:

An act to amend the correction law, in relation to extending protection from discrimination to current employees and licensees

PURPOSE:

The bill extends the provisions of Article 23-A of the Correction Law to prohibit unfair discrimination against current employees and license holders who have a previous criminal conviction that is unrelated to the employment or license.

SUMMARY OF PROVISIONS

Section 1 of the bill amends Section 750 of the Correction Law to make the definition of "direct relationship" applicable to current employees and license holders.

Section 2 of the bill amends Section 751 of the Correction Law to make Article 23-A applicable to current employees and license holders.

Section 3 of the bill amends Section 752 of the Correction Law to prohibit discrimination against current employees and license holders based on a previous criminal conviction or convictions unless there is a direct relationship between the conviction(s) and the duties or responsibilities of the employment or license.

Section 4 of the bill makes a conforming amendment to Section 753 of the Correction Law.

Section 5 of the bill provides that it shall take effect immediately.

JUSTIFICATION:

Article 23-A of the Correction Law currently prohibits unfair discrimination against individuals with criminal records whose convictions are unrelated to the job or license sought and do not constitute a threat to safety. The law further encourages "the licensure and employment of persons previously convicted of one or more criminal offenses." However, the statutes inapplicability to current employees and licensees have limited the intended protections of the law.

The anti-discrimination protections in Section 752 of the Correction Law currently apply only to applicants for employment or occupational licenses who have criminal convictions. The law provides no protection

RETRIEVE BILL

to current employees or license holders who face unfair discrimination based on criminal records that predate their employment or licensure. This bill extends the anti-discrimination protections to current employees and license holders whose convictions predate employment or licensure and were not improperly denied by the applicant in response to legal inquiries from the employer or licensing agent.

With the advent of the computer age and all the other means by which criminal history information can be obtained, employers have easy access to criminal history information, leading more employers to refuse to hire, or fire individuals with criminal records. This bill is necessary in order to ensure that New York's strong, long-standing policy of encouraging the employment of qualified individuals with criminal records is enforced.

LEGISLATIVE HISTORY:

Similar to S.7730A/A.10986A, Veto #401.

FISCAL IMPLICATIONS:

None.

EFFECTIVE DATE:
The bill takes effect immediately.

DIVISION OF THE BUDGET BILL MEMORANDUM

Session Year 2007

<u>SENATE:</u>
No. S1602-A

<u>ASSEMBLY:</u>
No.

Primary Sponsor: Volker

Law: Correction   Sections: 750-753

Division of the Budget recommendation on the above bill

APPROVE: __   VETO: __   NO OBJECTION: X

1.   Subject and Purpose

This bill extends the current protections against employment discrimination for those with a minor criminal record, from applicants only to those currently employed.

2.   Summary of Provisions

This bill would amend sections 750 - 753 of the Correction Law by extending the current provisions of Article 23-A of the Correction Law to current employees and occupational licensees who are convicted of a prior criminal offense.   Article 23-A currently provides protection against employment discrimination to job and occupational license (including licenses, permits, certificates and other grants of permission) applicants, convicted of a prior criminal offense, and whose convictions are unrelated to the job or license sought and do not constitute a threat to public safety. This bill would extend those same anti-discrimination protections to current employees and license holders whose convictions predate employment or licensure.

Exemptions to discrimination protection would still exist for persons whose criminal conviction has a direct relationship to their job or license or if their participation in a license or employment involves an unreasonable risk to property or to the safety or welfare of specific persons or to the general public. Persons experiencing such discrimination would not be protected either due to intentional misrepresentations made in job applications or due to other current legally mandated conditions for forfeiture of licenses. In regard to the nature of the direct relationship of the criminal offense to a job or license, consideration would also be given to the age of the person when the crime was committed, the length of time since the offense occurred, and information concerning the rehabilitation and good conduct of the individual.

Enforcement of these employment rights would continue to be sought by filing complaints, for private employees with the Division of Human Rights or in New York City with the NYC Office of Human Rights and for public employees with the Office of the Attorney General.

This bill will take effect immediately.

Validation Document ID 52740443 476
Paul F. Francis Director of the Budget and Senior Advisor to the Governor
By Susan F. Knapp
Date 7/13/2007 3.45.00 PM

3. Legislative History

Senate bill 7730-A was approved by the Legislature in 2006 but was vetoed by Governor Pataki (Message #401) This veto message focused on the issue of considering a prior criminal conviction that poses a potential risk to the public as grounds for an exemption from discrimination protection.

4. Arguments in Support:

Article 23-A of the Correction Law currently prohibits unfair discrimination against individuals with criminal records whose convictions are unrelated to the job or license sought and do not constitute a threat to safety. The law further encourages "the licensure and employment of persons previously convicted of one or more criminal offenses." However, the statute's inapplicability to current employees and licensees has limited the intended protections of the law.

Persons who are currently employed or hold an occupational license should not lose their employment or license for prior criminal convictions that have no direct relationship to their job or license unless an employee intentionally misrepresented their criminal history on an employment application. Employees or license holders should enjoy the same legal protections as job and license applicants, since it is consistent with a policy to facilitate the gainful and appropriate employment of ex-offenders thereby fostering their re-integration into society – a perspective that has been held by the courts. In fact, courts have held that a law to protect applicants, by its very nature, also is intended to protect those currently employed.

5. Arguments in Opposition:

This legislation could result in numerous time-demanding employment discrimination complaints for the NYC Office of Human Rights, the Division of Human Rights and the Office of the Attorney General.

Also, this bill does not provide for the withholding of employment discrimination protection for license holders who intentionally misrepresented their criminal record on their license applications or renewal application forms.

6. Other State Agencies Interested:

The Division of Human Rights supports this bill and projects that it would result in a small increase in their caseload that could be accommodated with a minimal impact on operations. The Division of Criminal Justice Services, the Division of Parole and the Office of the Attorney General may be interested in this legislation.

7. Other Interested Groups:

Organizations who jointly produced a report in 2006 on re-entry employment issues at the request of the Division of Criminal Justice may be interested in this bill, including: the Doe Fund, the Osborne Association, the Community Service Society of New York, Opportunities for a Better Tomorrow, the New York City Employment and Training Coalition, the Legal Action

Validation: Document ID: 52744443 476
Paul J. Francis, Director of the Budget and Senior Advisor to the Governor
By Susan E. Knapp
Date: 7/13/2007 3:45:00 PM

000009

Center and the Center for Employment Opportunities. The NYC Office of Human Rights objects to this bill but has not provided a rationale for this position, to our knowledge.

8.   Budget Implications:

This legislation could result in minimal increases of employment discrimination complaints filed with the Division of Human Rights, the NYC Office of Human Rights and the Office of the Attorney General. These additional complaints would not have a significant impact on the operations of these agencies and could likely be absorbed within their current budgets.

9.   Recommendation:

This bill would extend employment discrimination protections to employees and occupational license holders who were previously convicted of a non-related (to their employment or license) criminal offense. Enforcement agencies for this legislation, including the Division of Human Rights, the NYC Office of Human Rights and the Office of the Attorney General should be able to accommodate these additional complaints within their current budgets. For these reasons, the Division of the Budget does not object to this bill.

Validation: Document ID: 52740443-475
Paul E. Francis, Director of the Budget and Senior Advisor to the Governor
By Susan E. Knapp
Date: 7/13/2007 3:45:00 PM

STATE OF NEW YORK
DEPARTMENT OF STATE
41 STATE STREET
ALBANY, NY 12231-0001

ELIOT SPITZER
GOVERNOR

LORRAINE A. CORTES-VÁZQUEZ
SECRETARY OF STATE

MEMORANDUM

July 3, 2007

TO: Hon David Nocenti, Esq.
         Counsel to the Governor

FROM: William L. Sharp, Esq.
         Principal Attorney

SUBJECT: A.3208-A (M. of A. Aubry) / S.1602-A (Sen. Volker)
         Recommendation: No Objection

You have requested our comments on the above-referenced bill.

The proposed legislation would amend Article 23-A of the Correction Law to clarify that its provisions extend to current, as well as prospective, licensees and employees.

Article 23-A of the Correction Law provides protection to persons previously convicted of one or more criminal offenses. The statute prohibits the State and private employers (those employing ten or more persons) from denying a license or employment to persons based on their previous criminal conviction unless it is determined (1) there is a "direct relationship" between the crime and the license or employment sought or (2) the issuance of a license to or employment of the person would involve an unreasonable risk to property, safety or welfare of specific individuals or the general public. Section 753 of the Correction Law sets forth a list of factors which must be considered by the State or employer in making said determination.

The bill would amend Correction Law § 750 (3) to clarify that the phrase "direct relationship" applies to current employees/licensees as well as those who are applying for an initial license or employment. The bill makes corresponding amendments to Corrections Law §§751, 752 and 753 to ensure those statutes encompass those applying for a license or employment, and those currently employed or licensed. The bill also provides that the statute and its provisions shall not affect any right an employer may have with respect to an intentional misrepresentation in connection with an application

000011

for employment made by a prospective employee or previously made by a current employee.

The Department of State, Division of Licensing Services ("DLS"), routinely applies the provisions of Article 23-A of the Correction Law to any current licensee or license applicant who has been convicted of a crime which DLS believes is directly related to the duties and qualifications for licensure. In said cases, DLS will either commence an enforcement proceeding against a current licensee or notify the license applicant that it proposes to deny the application. Both procedures result in an administrative hearing where the provisions of the relevant statute and Correction Law are applied. Insofar as DLS already affords both current, and prospective licensees the protections of the Correction Law, the proposed legislation does not affect DLS or its established procedures.

The Department of State has no objection to the bill.

WLS/WC/mel

New York State Department of Labor
Eliot Spitzer, *Governor*
M. Patricia Smith, *Commissioner*

RF

June 26, 2007

The Honorable David Nocenti
Counsel to the Governor
The Capitol, Room 210
Albany, New York 12224

> **S.1602** - AN ACT to amend the correction law, in relation to extending protection from discrimination to current employees and licensees

Dear Mr. Nocenti:

The above-referenced legislation would extend provisions of Article 23-A of the Correction Law to prohibit unfair discrimination against current employees and license holders who have a previous criminal conviction that is unrelated to the employment or license.

This legislation would not have a direct impact on any of the programs that the Department administers; therefore the Department takes no position on its enactment.

Sincerely,

M. Patricia Smith

M. Patricia Smith

cc: David Weinstein
Department of Labor Counsel's Office

RF

STATE OF NEW YORK
DEPARTMENT OF CIVIL SERVICE
ALFRED E. SMITH STATE OFFICE BUILDING
ALBANY, NEW YORK 12239
www.cs.state.ny.us

ELIOT SPITZER
GOVERNOR

NANCY G. GROENWEGEN
COMMISSIONER

MEMORANDUM

TO: David Nocenti
Counsel to the Governor

FROM: Judith I. Ratner
Deputy Commissioner and Counsel

SUBJECT: A3208-A/S1602-A (Introduced by Senator Volker)

DATE: June 27, 2007

STATUES INVOLVED: Sections 750 (3), 751, 752 and 753(b)(1) of the Correction Law

EFFECTIVE DATE: Immediately

RECOMMENDATION: **No Comment**

DISCUSSION:

This bill would amend provisions of Article 23-A of the Correction Law, "Licensure and Employment of Persons Previously Convicted of One or More Criminal Offenses," to extend the protections of such Article to current employees and license holders who face unfair discrimination based upon previous criminal convictions that are unrelated to their employment or licensure.

A similar proposal was previously disapproved in Veto Message No. 401 of 2006.

This legislation does not impact the enforcement or administration of the Civil Service Law and Rules subject to the jurisdiction of the New York State Department of Civil Service. Accordingly, the Department has no comment regarding this legislation.

000014

NEW YORK STATE
DIVISION OF HUMAN RIGHTS
ONE FORDHAM PLAZA
FOURTH FLOOR
BRONX, NEW YORK 10458

(718) 741-8398
Fax: (718) 741-8102
www.dhr.state.ny.us

ELIOT SPITZER
GOVERNOR

KUMIKI GIBSON
COMMISSIONER

To: David Nocenti
        Counsel to the Governor

From: Caroline J. Downey
        Acting General Counsel

Re: S.1602

Date: July 29, 2007

Thank you for the opportunity to comment on the above-referenced legislation, which amends the Correction Law in reference to discrimination against current employees and licensees with previous criminal convictions. Although the amendment is to the Correction Law, the bill impacts upon the Human Rights Law ("HRL"), because HRL §296.15 specifically references Article 23-A of the Correction Law for the standards employers are to utilize to avoid discrimination against ex-offenders. Although HRL §296.15 itself states that employment is not to be denied under the circumstances set out, and is not, in our view, limited to applicants, this legislation will clarify the matter as to the Correction Law. Accordingly, the Division of Human Rights supports this legislation.

000015

RF
284

STATE OF NEW YORK
EXECUTIVE DEPARTMENT
DIVISION OF PROBATION AND CORRECTIONAL ALTERNATIVES
80 WOLF ROAD, ALBANY, NEW YORK 12205
TELEPHONE: (518) 485-7692
FAX: (518) 485-5140

ELIOT SPITZER
Governor

ROBERT M. MACCARONE
State Director

MEMORANDUM

TO: David Nocenti
           Counsel to the Governor

FROM: Linda J. Valenti
           Counsel, Division of Probation and Correctional Alternatives

DATE: July 17, 2007

RE: S.1602-A (Volker)

The above-referenced legislation, which amends Sections 750-753 of the Correction Law in relation to unlawful discriminatory employer practices, has passed both houses of the State Legislature and has been transmitted to the Executive Chamber for final Executive action. Specifically, it would extend protection from unlawful discrimination to current employees and licensees.

In general, the Division of Probation and Correctional Alternatives (DPCA) supports efforts to ensure those with criminal records are not unfairly discriminated by employers. DPCA has been at the forefront of expanded measures to help individuals with criminal records overcome barriers to employment as we recognize it as a critical component to successful reintegration of offenders into the community and to deter recidivism. Since 2003, DPCA in conjunction with the Department of Labor has worked to increase employment of individuals under community supervision through job preparation training as to the availability of federally-funded employee bonding and New York State tax credits for employers. In January 2005, a 6 member team from New York State, which included state staff and selected local probation officers, received intensive 3 week training by the National Institute of Corrections on the Offender Workforce Development Specialist Program. This culminated in development of two evidence based curricula to be used by both probation and community corrections staff as well as offenders. It further led to expanded regional training statewide which focused on securing and maintaining employment, educating participants on federal and state incentives to encourage employers to hire this population, and learning ways of overcoming barriers to employment. Trained officers have been able to work closely with local employers to secure employment opportunities and assist with job retention. DPCA is anticipating being awarded a federal grant to expand the number of offender workforce development specialist's trainers. Additionally, DPCA recently promoted the training of a 12 member team from New York City (NYC) and we firmly support NYC's new programmatic initiative by its Department of Small Business to work with NYC Department of Probation to implement workforce development strategies with selected contractors, the public workforce, and other key partners to strengthen the skills and address barriers and needs of jobseekers in order to achieve increase employment among its supervising population. DPCA further has disseminated to our constituent agencies and posted on our agency website a series of questions and answers with respect to certificates of relief from disabilities and certificates of good conduct to foster better understanding of certificates and the role they can play in facilitating and/or continuing employment or licensure. This coupled with recirculation and posting of a past legal opinion which DPCA received from the New York State Board of Elections as to voting rights of existing and ex-offenders has helped to ensure that probation officers and those under community supervision are knowledgeable in this area of law which is of utmost importance to promote citizenry.

This legislation still allows a licensing agency or employer to deny a license or employment where there exists a direct relationship with the previous criminal conviction and to commence disciplinary actions if necessary based on the past conviction. Further, it clearly recognizes any right that an employer may have as to intentional misrepresentation in connection with an employment application.

While DPCA is supportive of this legislation, in light of these provisions covering existing employees and that frequently the nature of the employment or business may change affecting the employee's job duties and responsibilities, it would appear that Correction Law Section 753 (b) also should have been amended. This section governs factors to be considered concerning a previous criminal conviction and paragraph b refers to the "specific duties and responsibilities necessarily related to the license or employment sought." It is recommended that future legislation be considered to ensure that the words "or held" are added.

As this legislation will better protect ex-offenders from unlawful discrimination, DPCA recommends that the Governor sign S.1602-A into law.

Cc: Robert Maccarone, State Director of Probation and Correctional Alternatives
Robin Forshaw, Assistant Counsel to the Governor

State of New York
Governor's Office of Employee Relations
Counsel's Office
2 Empire State Plaza, Suite 1201, Albany, New York 12223
(518) 474-4090 • (518) 486-7304 (Fax)

Eliot Spitzer
Governor

Gary Johnson
Director

MEMORANDUM

June 25, 2007

TO: David Nocenti

FROM: Walter Pellegrini

SUBJECT: S. 1602-a

The instant bill amends the Correction Law extending the protections from discrimination based on prior criminal convictions to current employees and licensees.

The current law prohibits unfair discrimination against individuals with criminal records whose prior convictions are unrelated to the job or license sought and do not constitute a threat to safety. This law currently applies to applicants for employment or occupational licenses. The bill extends the coverage to those currently employed or in possession of such licenses.

An unintended consequence of this bill with regard to current employees or license holders is that it provides the blanket of the employment or license they hold. Providing false information on an application for employment is a serious matter and the lines between coverage against unfair discrimination for convictions for non-job related activity and falsifying an application (even if about non-job related convictions) should not be blurred.

This Office does not support this bill.

/mc

000013

STATE OF NEW YORK
DEPARTMENT OF CORRECTIONAL SERVICES
THE HARRIMAN STATE CAMPUS - BUILDING 2
1220 WASHINGTON AVENUE
ALBANY N Y 12226-2050

BRIAN FISCHER
COMMISSIONER

June 25, 2007

Honorable David Nocenti
Counsel to the Governor
Executive Chamber
State Capitol
Albany New York 12224

RE S1602

Dear Mr Nocenti

With regard to the above-referenced bill S1602, the Department of Correctional Services has no objection to this legislation This bill would extend protection from discrimination to current employees and licensees

Should you have any questions, please do not hesitate to contact me

Sincerely.

Brian Fischer
Commissioner

cc   Anthony J. Annucci Deputy Commissioner & Counsel
      Michael A. L. Balboni, Deputy Secretary for Public Safety

000010

STATE OF NEW YORK
DIVISION OF CRIMINAL JUSTICE SERVICES
Four Tower Place
Albany, New York 12203-3764
http://criminaljustice.state.ny.us

ELIOT SPITZER
GOVERNOR

DENISE E. O'DONNELL
COMMISSIONER

June 25, 2007

Honorable David Nocenti
Counsel to the Governor
Executive Chamber
State Capitol
Albany, NY 12224

Via E-mail

RE: Senate Bill Number 1602-A
No Objection

Dear Mr. Nocenti:

This is in response to your request for comment on the above-referenced bill which would amend Article 23-A (§§750-753) of the Correction Law to extend the provisions regarding unfair discrimination against applicants for employment or licenses to current employees and licensees.

Currently, Correction Law §752 provides that no application for a license or employment may be denied based on the applicant's previous conviction for a crime unless there is a direct relationship between the previous crime and the license or employment sought, or the issuance of the license or the granting of employment would involve an unreasonable risk to property or to the safety or welfare of specific individuals to the general public. The memorandum in support of this bill asserts that there is no similar protection for current employees or license holders and, therefore, this legislation is necessary.

However, the courts have held that the same public policy that prohibits discrimination in hiring on the basis of a criminal record (as set forth in Correction Law §752) prohibits discrimination in terminating employment on the basis of a criminal record (see, Givens v.

000020

N.Y.C. Housing Authority, 249 A.D.2d 133 [1st Dept. 1998]). As such, it is not clear whether this legislation is necessary. We note, however, that this bill addresses and corrects the deficiency highlighted in our comment on similar legislation, S.7730, introduced during the last legislative session. The current legislation amends subdivision (2) of Correction Law §752 to permit a licensing authority or employer to consider a conviction as it relates to current licensees and employees when there is an unreasonable risk to property or public safety.

This bill does not directly impact the operations of this agency, and, thus, the Division has **no objection** to **S. 1602-A.**

Thank you for the opportunity to comment on this proposal.

Very truly yours,

Denise E. O'Donnell

New York State AFL-CIO

DENIS M. HUGHES
President

PAUL F. COLE
Secretary-Treasurer

ED DONNELLY
Legislative Director

June 28, 2007

Honorable Eliot Spitzer
Governor of the State of New York
State Capitol
Albany, New York 12224

ATT: David Nocenti, Counsel

RE: S1602 Volker/A3208 Aubrey, et al

Dear Governor Spitzer:

The New York State AFL-CIO, representing over 2 million union members, their families as well as our retirees and their families takes no position on the above referenced legislation.

For further information contact Ed Donnelly, Legislative Director at 518-436-8516.

Sincerely,

Ed Donnelly
Legislative Director

ED:eb
opeiu-153
Letter #31/2007

000022

STATE OF NEW YORK
EXECUTIVE DEPARTMENT
DIVISION OF PAROLE
97 CENTRAL AVENUE
ALBANY, NEW YORK 12206

ELIOT SPITZER
GOVERNOR

GEORGE B. ALEXANDER
CHAIRMAN

June 29, 2007

Honorable David Nocenti
Counsel to the Governor
Executive Chamber
The Capitol
Albany, New York 12224

    Re: S.1602-A

Dear Mr. Nocenti:

    The New York State Division of Parole has been asked to comment upon S.1602-A, a bill that amends the Correction Law to extend protections against discrimination to current employees and licensees. Please be advised that the Division of Parole has no opposition to this legislation.

    Thank you for your attention in this matter and for affording the Division the opportunity to comment on this legislation.

        Respectfully yours,

        Terrence X. Tracy
        Counsel

000023

STATE OF NEW YORK • EXECUTIVE DEPARTMENT

STATE COMMISSION OF CORRECTION

80 WOLF ROAD, 4TH FLOOR
ALBANY, NEW YORK 12205-2670
(518) 485-2346
FAX (518) 485-2467

CHAIRMAN
Daniel L. Stewart

COMMISSIONERS
Frederick C. Lamy
Frances T. Sullivan

June 25, 2007

David Nocenti, Esq.
Counsel to the Governor
Executive Chamber
State Capitol
Albany, NY 12224

Re: S.1602

Dear Mr. Nocenti:

The State Commission of Correction takes no position with respect to the above referenced bill which relates to extending protection from discrimination to current employees and licensees.

Very truly yours,

Michael F. Donegan
Counsel

000021

Memorandum

NEW YORK STATE POLICE

June 28, 2007

To   Honorable David Nocenti
            Counsel to the Governor

From   Glenn Valle
            Counsel to the Division of State Police

Subject   TEN DAY BILL – S1602-A

AN ACT to amend the correction law, in relation to extending protection from discrimination to current employees and licensees

Position:

The Division of State Police takes no position on this legislation

RF

199 WATER STREET NEW YORK, N.Y. 10038 TEL. 212-577-3300 FAX:212-809-1574 www.legal-aid.org

Alan Levine
Chairperson of the Board

Theodore A. Levine
President

July 13, 2007

Steven Banks
Attorney-in-Chief

David Nocenti, Esq.
Counsel to the Governor
Executive Chamber,
Albany, N.Y. 12224

Dear Mr. Nocenti:

We are writing to urge the Governor to sign S.1602-A/A.3208-A. This legislation amends Article 23-A of the Correction Law §§750-753. These provisions are intended to ensure that opportunities for employment, and licensure when necessary, are made available to qualified individuals with criminal records. The basic law has been on the books since 1976. This law prohibits discrimination based on convictions when there is no unreasonable risk to public safety, and there is no "direct relationship" between the crime committed and the job or license at issue.

This legislation corrects the problem caused by appellate rulings that have interpreted the existing law to afford protections to "applicants" for employment, but not to current employees who lose their jobs because of crimes that occurred before they were hired. This distinction is irrational and inconsistent with the underlying public policy. In recent years, the expansion of criminal background checks to numerous classes of employees whose backgrounds were not previously checked has resulted in discharge and unemployment for numerous solidly-performing employees as a result of conduct that occurred many years in the past. Our goal should be to expand opportunity for persons to rehabilitate themselves and participate in New York's economy, not to shrink such opportunities.

The legislation does not alter the substantive standards for determining when a job or license may be denied because of a criminal conviction, nor does it prevent discipline for misconduct in the course of current employment. The legislation also makes it clear that employees may dismiss employees for intentionally misrepresenting their past record. The only change in current law is that current employees and licensees will be treated the same as "applicants."

For all these reasons, we urge the Governor to sign this legislation.

Very truly yours,

STEVEN BANKS
Attorney-in-Chief

000028

Frank Vazquez
271 Prospect Park W. #3B
6/29/07   Brooklyn, NY., 11215
Home-718-788-9180

Honorable Gov. M. E. Spitzer

Exec. Chamber
State Capitol
Albany, NY., 12224

Honorable Gov. Mr. Elliott Spitzer:

I would like to encourage you to sign
the following "reentry bills:
1) S1602/A03208

2) S3092/A03379

3) S5875/A.8356

4) S.705-B/A.3397-B

5) S820/A1531
Thank you
Sincerely,
Frank Vazquez

000027

RF

LEGAL ACTION CENTER

June 22, 2007

David Nocenti, Esq.
Counsel to the Governor
Executive Chamber

Re: S1602

Dear Mr. Nocenti,

The Legal Action Center, an organization that for over three decades has worked to advance and protect the rights of qualified jobseekers with criminal records and assist them in reclaiming their lives and transitioning to self-sufficiency, **strongly urges the Governor to sign bill S1602.**

The existing anti-discrimination protections in Article 23-A §752 of the Correction Law, which prohibits unfair discrimination against individuals with criminal records whose convictions are unrelated to the job sought and do not constitute a threat to safety, apply only to *applicants* for employment or occupational licenses who have criminal convictions. However, the law provides no protection to current employees or license holders who face unfair discrimination based on criminal records that predate their employment or licensure. It is inconsistent to require employers to individually consider each person with a criminal history who applies for a job but not extend that protection to individuals who are already employed. S1602 corrects this oversight, thereby advancing New York's strong, longstanding policy of encouraging the employment of qualified individuals with criminal records.

This bill in particularly important given the advent of the computer age and all the other means by which employers can obtain criminal history information. Background checks conducted by private screening firms have increased at a record rate, with 80% of large employers in the U.S. now screening their workers for criminal records. Once this information is obtained, employers can act (and have acted) at will to terminate employees solely on the basis of their past criminal histories, when there has been no direct relationship between the criminal offense(s) and the job and no unreasonable risk to the safety of the public or property. S1602 ensures that the protections in Article 23-A §752 are implemented consistently, evenly and fairly across the board.

We greatly appreciate the opportunity to comment on this important piece of legislation. If you have any questions or concerns, please feel free to call us at 212-243-1313.

Thank you.

Paul N. Samuels   Anita Marton   Glenn E. Martin
Executive Director/President   Vice President   Co-Director/HIRE

New York
225 Varick Street New York, New York 10014
Phone 212-243-1313   Fax 212-675-0286
E-mail lacinfo@lac.org

Washington
236 Massachusetts Avenue, NE Suite 505 Washington, DC 20002
Phone 202-544-5478   Fax 202-544-5712
Email lacinfo@lac-dc.org

000023

RETRIEVE BILL

STATE OF NEW YORK

S. 1602--A   A. 3208--A
Cal. No. 1089   Cal. No. 45

2007-2008 Regular Sessions

SENATE - ASSEMBLY

January 23, 2007

IN SENATE -- Introduced by Sen. VOLKER -- read twice and ordered printed, and when printed to be committed to the Committee on Crime
Victims, Crime and Correction -- reported favorably from said committee, ordered to first and second report, ordered to a third reading,
passed by Senate and delivered to the Assembly, recalled, vote reconsidered, restored to third reading, amended and ordered reprinted,
retaining its place in the order of third reading

IN ASSEMBLY -- Introduced by M. of A. AUBRY, COOK, GREENE, PERALTA,
TITUS, WRIGHT, LAFAYETTE, BENJAMIN, D. GORDON -- Multi-Sponsored by --
M. of A. BOYLAND, COLTON, ORTIZ, PERRY, ROBINSON, WEISENBERG -- read
once and referred to the Committee on Correction -- reported from
committee, advanced to a third reading, amended and ordered reprinted,
retaining its place on the order of third reading

AN ACT to amend the correction law, in relation to extending protection
from discrimination to current employees and licensees

The People of the State of New York, represented in Senate and Assembly, do enact as follows:

1 Section 1. Subdivision 3 of section 750 of the correction law, as
2 added by chapter 931 of the laws of 1976, is amended to read as follows:
3 (3) "Direct relationship" means that the nature of criminal conduct
4 for which the person was convicted has a direct bearing on his fitness
5 or ability to perform one or more of the duties or responsibilities
6 necessarily related to the license [or employment sought], opportunity,
7 or job in question.
8 § 2. Section 751 of the correction law, as added by chapter 931 of the
9 laws of 1976, is amended to read as follows:
10 § 751. Applicability. The provisions of this article shall apply to
11 any application by any person for a license or employment at any public
12 or private employer, who has previously been convicted of one or more
13 criminal offenses[,] in this state or in any other jurisdiction, [to any

EXPLANATION--Matter in italics (underscored) is new; matter in brackets
[-] is old law to be omitted.

LBD05922-02-7

RIEVE BILL

S. 1602--A   2   A. 3208--A

1   [public agency or private employer for a license or employment] and to
2   any license or employment held by any person whose conviction of one or
3   more criminal offenses in this state or in any other jurisdiction
4   preceded such employment or granting of a license, except where a manda-
5   tory forfeiture, disability or bar to employment is imposed by law, and
6   has not been removed by an executive pardon, certificate of relief from
7   disabilities or certificate of good conduct. Nothing in this article
8   shall be construed to affect any right an employer may have with respect
9   to an intentional misrepresentation in connection with an application
10 for employment made by a prospective employee or previously made by a
11 current employee.
12   § 3. Section 752 of the correction law, as added by chapter 931 of
13 the laws of 1976, is amended to read as follows:
14   § 752. Unfair discrimination against persons previously convicted of
15 one or more criminal offenses prohibited. No application for any
16 license or employment, and no employment or license held by an individ-
17 ual, to which the provisions of this article are applicable, shall be
18 denied or acted upon adversely by reason of the [applicant's] individ-
19 ual's having been previously convicted of one or more criminal offenses,
20 or by reason of a finding of lack of "good moral character" when such
21 finding is based upon the fact that the [applicant] individual has
22 previously been convicted of one or more criminal offenses, unless:
23   (1) there is a direct relationship between one or more of the previous
24 criminal offenses and the specific license or employment sought or held
25 by the individual; or
26   (2) the issuance or continuation of the license or the granting or
27 continuation of the employment would involve an unreasonable risk to
28 property or to the safety or welfare of specific individuals or the
29 general public.
30   § 4. Paragraph (b) of subdivision 1 of section 753 of the correction
31 law, as added by chapter 931 of the laws of 1976, is amended to read as
32 follows:
33   (b) The specific duties and responsibilities necessarily related to
34 the license or employment sought or held by the person.
35   § 5. This act shall take effect immediately.

2008 LEGISLATIVE AMENDMENTS

reviewing the results, employers are often unwilling to hire an individual who has had a criminal conviction. As a result, potentially qualified candidates face unfair, illegal discriminatory hiring practices and are not considered for positions, even when their conviction has no connection to the job for which they are applying. By amending Section 380-g of the general business law, this type of blatant employment discrimination could be avoided. This bill would require potential employers to include a copy of article 23-A of the Correction Law, which delineates specific criteria by which a candidate must be considered for a job, when providing a consumer report including criminal conviction information to a third party. Employers who receive what they deem to be unsatisfactory information about a current or prospective employee could no longer feign ignorance, and would be forced to recognize that people with criminal histories are protected from discriminatory acts under New York State law. Obtaining a stable, decent-paying job is an essential first step in helping to reintegrate formerly incarcerated individuals into the workforce and the at-large community. Without these opportunities, our collective public safety may be compromised, and the likelihood of recidivism is greatly increased.

For the foregoing reasons, Community Service Society urges your favorable consideration of this legislation.

Sincerely,

David R. Jones
President and CEO

CHAPTER 465

LAWS OF 20 08

SENATE BILL 7638-A   ASSEMBLY BILL _____

STATE OF NEW YORK

Text A

IN SENATE

April 23, 2008

Introduced by Sen. VOLKER -- read twice and ordered printed, and when printed to be committed to the Committee on Consumer Protection -- committee discharged, bill amended, ordered reprinted as amended and recommitted to said committee

AN ACT to amend the general business law and the labor law, in relation to the provision of criminal record conviction information in certain instances

A 10288-A Aubry

DATE RECEIVED BY GOVERNOR

JUL 25 2008

ACTION MUST BE TAKEN BY

AUG 2008

DATE GOVERNOR'S ACTION TAKEN

AUG 05 2008

SENATE VOTE _62_ Y _0_ N HOME RULE MESSAGE ___ Y ___ N

DATE 6/23/08

ASSEMBLY VOTE _144_ Y _1_ N

DATE 6/23/08

Bill is missing

S7638-A VOLKER   Same as A 10288-A Aubry (MS)
06/23/08 S7638-A   Assembly Vote   Yes: 144 No : 1
06/23/08 S7638-A   Senate Vote   Aye: 62 Nay: 0

Go to Top of Page
06/23/08 S7638-A   Assembly Vote   Yes: 144 No : 1

Yes Abbate	Yes Alessi	Yes Alfano	Yes Amedore
ER Arroyo	Yes Aubry	Yes Bacalles	Yes Ball
Yes Barclay	Yes Barra	Yes Benedetto	Yes Benjamin
Yes Bing	Yes Boyland	Yes Boyle	Yes Bradley
Yes Brennan	Yes Brodsky	Yes Brook-Krasny	Yes Burling
Yes Butler	Yes Cahill	Yes Calhoun	Yes Camara
Yes Canestrari	Yes Carrozza	Yes Christensen	Yes Clark
No Cole	Yes Colton	Yes Conte	Yes Cook
Yes Crouch	Yes Cusick	Yes Cymbrowitz	Yes DelMonte
Yes Destito	Yes Diaz L	Yes Diaz R	Yes Dinowitz
Yes Duprey	Yes Eddington	Yes Englebright	Yes Errigo
Yes Espaillat	Yes Farrell	Yes Fields	Yes Finch
Yes Fitzpatrick	Yes Gabryszak	Yes Galef	Yes Gantt
Yes Gianaris	Yes Giglio	Yes Glick	Yes Gordon
Yes Gottfried	Yes Greene	Yes Gunther A	Yes Hawley
Yes Hayes	Yes Heastie	Yes Hevesi	Yes Hikind
Yes Hooper	Yes Hoyt	Yes Hyer-Spencer	Yes Jacobs
Yes Jaffee	Yes Jeffries	Yes John	Yes Kavanagh
Yes Kellner	Yes Kirwan	Yes Kolb	Yes Koon
Yes Lafayette	Yes Lancman	Yes Latimer	Yes Lavine
Yes Lentol	Yes Lifton	Yes Lopez P	Yes Lopez V
Yes Lupardo	Yes Magee	Yes Magnarelli	Yes Maisel
Yes Markey	Yes Mayersohn	Yes McDonald	Yes McDonough
Yes McEneny	Yes McKevitt	Yes Miller	Yes Millman
Yes Molinaro	Yes Morelle	ER Nolan	Yes Oaks
Yes O'Donnell	Yes O'Mara	Yes Ortiz	Yes Parment
Yes Paulin	Yes Peoples	Yes Peralta	Yes Perry
Yes Pheffer	Yes Powell	Yes Pretlow	Yes Quinn
Yes Rabbitt	Yes Raia	Yes Ramos	Yes Reilich
Yes Reilly	ER Rivera J	Yes Rivera N	Yes Rivera P
Yes Robinson	Yes Rosenthal	Yes Saladino Yes	Sayward
Yes Scarborough	Yes Schimel	Yes Schimminger	Yes Schroeder
Yes Scozzafava	Yes Seminerio	Yes Spano	Yes Stirpe
Yes Sweeney	Yes Tedisco	Yes Thiele	Yes Titone
Yes Titus	Yes Tobacco	Yes Towns	Yes Townsend
Yes Walker	Yes Weinstein	Yes Weisenberg	Yes Weprin
Yes Wright	Yes Young	Yes Zebrowski K	Yes Mr. Speaker

Go to Top of Page
06/23/08 S7638-A   Senate Vote   Aye: 62 Nay: 0

Aye Adams	Aye Alesi	Aye Aubertine	Aye Bonacic
Aye Breslin	Aye Bruno	Aye Connor	Aye DeFrancisco
Aye Diaz	Aye Dilan	Aye Duane	Aye Farley
Aye Flanagan	Aye Fuschillo	Aye Golden	Aye Gonzalez

Aye Griffo	Aye Hannon	Aye Hassell-Thompson	Aye Huntley
Aye Johnson C	Aye Johnson O	Aye Klein	Aye Krueger
Aye Kruger	Aye Lanza	Aye Larkin	Aye LaValle
Aye Leibell	Aye Libous	Aye Little	Aye Maltese
Aye Marcellino	Aye Maziarz	Aye Montgomery	Aye Morahan
Aye Nozzolio	Aye Onorato	Aye Oppenheimer	Aye Padavan
Aye Parker	Aye Perkins	Aye Rath	Aye Robach
Aye Sabini	Aye Saland	Aye Sampson	Aye Savino
Aye Schneiderman	Aye Serrano	Aye Seward	Aye Skelos
Aye Smith	Aye Stachowski	Aye Stavisky	Aye Stewart-Cousins
Aye Thompson	Aye Trunzo	Aye Valesky	Aye Volker
Aye Winner	Aye Young		

STATE OF NEW YORK
EXECUTIVE CHAMBER
ALBANY 12224

June 26, 2008

Honorable Dale M. Volker
New York State Senate
Legislative Office Building – Room 707
Albany, New York 12248

Honorable Jeffrion L. Aubry
New York State Assembly
Legislative Office Building – Room 526
Albany, New York 12248

Dear Senator Volker and Assemblyman Aubry:

As you know, legislation that you have sponsored (S.7638-A/A.10288) has now passed both houses of the Legislature, and will soon be sent to the Governor for action.

In order to assist the Governor in reviewing this legislation and deciding whether it should be signed into law, we would greatly appreciate receiving any relevant documents or information that you have on this bill. In particular, we would very much like to receive:

- copies of the sponsor's memorandum in support of this bill;

- copies of any comment letters in support of or in opposition to this bill that you received from outside organizations, individuals or other third parties;

- if hearings were held on the bill, copies of the transcripts of those hearings; and

- any other documents or information that you believe should be considered by the Governor.

The State Constitution gives the Governor only 10 days to act on bills after they have been forwarded by the Legislature, and we therefore would appreciate receiving the above information at your earliest convenience. Please send any materials you have to:

> Kristin Rosenstein
> Legislative Secretary's Office
> Executive Chamber
> State Capitol – Room 225
> Albany, New York 12224

Any information that you provide will be included in the bill jacket that is maintained by the State Archives and constitutes the legislative history of bills that have been signed into law.

Thank you for your consideration and assistance, and please feel free to contact this office if you have any questions.

Sincerely,

David M. Nocenti
Counsel to the Governor

cc: K. Rosenstein

DIVISION OF THE BUDGET BILL MEMORANDUM

Session Year 2008

SENATE: ASSEMBLY:
No. S7638A   No.

Primary Sponsor: Senator Volker

Law: General Business Law and Labor Law   Sections: 380-c, 380-g, and 201-f

Division of the Budget recommendation on the above bill:

NO RECOMMENDATION

1   Subject and Purpose:

This bill amends the General Business Law and the Labor Law to require that potential employers who request a consumer report as a condition of employment must also provide the applicant with a copy of Article 23-A of the Correction Law relating to licensure and employment of previously convicted persons. Additionally, this bill requires that all employers post a copy of Article 23-A of the Correction Law in a visually conspicuous manner at the workplace.

2.   Reason for No Recommendation:

There are no discernible fiscal implications associated with this bill. Accordingly, the Division of the Budget offers no recommendation on this legislation.

STATE OF NEW YORK
DEPARTMENT OF STATE
ONE COMMERCE PLAZA
99 WASHINGTON AVENUE
ALBANY, NY 12231-0001

DAVID A. PATERSON
GOVERNOR

LORRAINE A. CORTES-VAZQUEZ
SECRETARY OF STATE

MEMORANDUM

To: Honorable Terryl Brown Clemons, Esq
           Acting Counsel to the Governor

From: Matthew W. Febo, Esq
           Legislative Counsel

Date: July 1, 2008

Subject: S.7638-A (Sen. Volker)
           Recommendation: No comment

           The Department of State has no comment on the above referenced bill.

           If you have any questions or comments regarding our position on the bill, or if we can
otherwise assist you, please feel free to contact me at (518) 474-6740.

MWT mel

New York State Department of Labor
David A. Paterson, *Governor*
M. Patricia Smith, *Commissioner*

July 23, 2008

The Honorable Terryl Brown Clemons
Acting Counsel to the Governor
The Capitol, Room 210
Albany, New York 12224

> **S.7638-A** - AN ACT to amend the general business law and the labor law, in relation to the provision of criminal record conviction information in certain instances

Dear Ms. Brown Clemons:

The above-referenced bill would require employers that request consumer credit reports concerning job applicants who have a criminal conviction to provide the applicants with a copy of Article 23-A of the Correction Law relating to the employment rights of persons convicted of crimes. The bill would also amend the Labor Law to require every employer to post in an accessible place and in a visually conspicuous manner at the worksite a copy of Article 23-A of Correction Law and any regulations issued under that law.

This legislation reflects an effort to protect the employment rights of persons who may otherwise experience obstacles to obtaining a job because they have a criminal conviction. The Department of Labor is actively engaged in facilitating employment of ex-offenders through its various workforce programs and shares a keen interest in this goal with the bill sponsors. Should this bill become law, we will work with the Department of Corrections to ensure that employers can readily obtain access to Article 23-A and its regulations on our agency websites so that they may meet the posting requirements set forth in the bill. This will facilitate voluntary compliance by employers and ease the additional enforcement responsibility imposed upon the Department by this bill.

The Department of Labor supports this bill and urges its enactment into law.

Sincerely,

M. Patricia Smith

M. Patricia Smith

cc: David Weinstein
Department of Labor Counsel's Office

STATE OF NEW YORK
DEPARTMENT OF CORRECTIONAL SERVICES
THE HARRIMAN STATE CAMPUS - BUILDING 2
1220 WASHINGTON AVENUE
ALBANY, N.Y. 12226-2050

BRIAN FISCHER
COMMISSIONER

July 2, 2008

Honorable David Nocenti
Counsel to the Governor
Executive Chamber
State Capitol
Albany, New York 12244

RE: S7638-A

Dear Mr. Nocenti:

The above-captioned item of legislation would amend the general business law to require that whenever an investigative written report is requested in connection with an offer of employment, the requesting entity shall also provide the subject of the report with a copy of Article 23-A of the Correction Law, which is the provision of law dealing with the licensure and employment of persons previously convicted of one or more criminal offenses. In addition, this legislation would also amend the labor law to require that every employer post within his or her establishment in a visibly conspicuous manner, a copy of Article 23-A.

The Department of Correctional Services strongly supports this legislation since, ultimately, it will greatly assist released inmates to obtain employment and will also help ensure that all appropriate entities are placed on notice about the requirements of Article 23-A, and thereby help prevent any unlawful discrimination based upon a person's prior criminal record.

Should you have any questions, please do not hesitate to contact me.

Sincerely,

Brian Fischer
Commissioner

cc   Anthony J. Annucci, Executive Deputy Commissioner
        Michael A. L. Balboni, Deputy Secretary for Public Safety

NCC011

STATE OF NEW YORK
DIVISION OF CRIMINAL JUSTICE SERVICES
4 Tower Place
Albany, New York 12203-3764
http://criminaljustice.state.ny.us

DAVID A. PATERSON
GOVERNOR

DENISE E. O'DONNELL
COMMISSIONER

July 18, 2008

Honorable Terryl Brown Clemons
Acting Counsel to the Governor
Executive Chamber
State Capitol
Albany, NY 12224

Via E-mail

RE: Senate Bill Number 7638-A
         Recommend Approval

Dear Ms. Clemons:

This is in response to your request for comment on the above-referenced legislation that amends the General Business Law, and adds a new section 201-f to the Labor Law, to require employers to include a copy of Article 23-A of the Correction Law when providing a consumer report containing criminal conviction information and to post Article 23-A in various places of employment.

Obtaining employment after an individual is released from prison or has a criminal record is a pivotal step in an individual's successful reentry back into the community. Stable employment gives needed structure and financial support to an individual and can help lessen the chance of recidivism. It is currently illegal in New York State to bar an individual from employment or licensure solely because of a criminal record, unless "there is a direct relationship between one or more of the previous criminal offenses and the specific license or employment sought or held by the individual" or "the issuance or continuation of the license or the granting or continuation of the employment would involve an unreasonable risk to property or to the safety or welfare of specific individuals or the general public."

Some employers, however, may not be aware of current law and, consequently, may violate it if they are barring individuals from employment exclusively because of a criminal record. By mandating that a copy of Article 23-A be included in any report containing information on criminal records, this bill will help clarify current law to employers and additionally, inform those individuals who have a criminal history record of their rights under the law.

Although this bill will impose some additional responsibility on employers throughout New York State, it should not be overly burdensome given that State law already requires postings regarding minimum wage, workers' compensation laws, and other important information related to labor. Accordingly, due to the significant public policy concerns being addressed by this bill, the Division of Criminal Justice Services **recommends approval** of **S. 7638-A.**

Thank you for the opportunity to comment on this bill.

Very truly yours,

Denise E. O'Donnell

**NEW YORK STATE
DIVISION OF HUMAN RIGHTS**
ONE FORDHAM PLAZA, 4TH FLOOR
BRONX, NEW YORK 10458
(718) 741 - 8398
Fax (718) 741 - 8102
www.dhr.state.ny.us

DAVID A. PATERSON
GOVERNOR

GALEN D. KIRKLAND
COMMISSIONER

To: Terryl Brown Clemons
         Acting Counsel to the Governor

From: Caroline J. Downey
         General Counsel

Re: S. 7638A

Date: July 16, 2008

Thank you for the opportunity to comment on the above-referenced legislation, which amends the General Business Law Section 380c to provide that that the notice to the consumer of an "investigative consumer report" required by this section also includes a copy of Article 23-A of the Correction Law, when such a report is requested in connection with an offer of employment.

The proposed legislation also provides that when a consumer reporting agency provides a consumer report that contains criminal conviction information, the entity requesting such report shall provide the subject of the report with a copy of Article 23-A of the Correction Law. Additionally, the Labor Law is amended by the proposed legislation to provide that every employer shall post a copy of Article 23-A of the Correction Law in his or her establishment in a place accessible to employees.

The Division supports this legislation. Article 23-A of the Correction Law, specifically referenced in Human Rights Law section 296.15, sets out the factors to be considered by an employer considering employing an ex-offender. The Division then applies these standards, in complaint cases before it, when determining whether an employer weighed the appropriate factors before denying employment because of an individual's prior criminal convictions.

Additional notice and information about the analysis required by Article 23-A of the Correction Law will be helpful in educating both employers and prospective employees about these important safeguards and will aid in the enforcement of the Human Rights Law. The requirement that the provisions of Article 23-A be posted in the workplace will also complement the requirement in the Division's regulations that a Division poster, setting out the provisions of the Human Rights Law and the Division's procedures, be posted in each workplace. See 9 N.Y.C.R.R. Section 466.1.

2

New York State AFL-CIO
Helping Working Families Achieve A Better Life

Denis M. Hughes
President

50 Broadway, 35th Fl
New York, NY 10004
(212) 777-6040
Fax - (212) 777-8422

Terrence L. Melvin
Secretary-Treasurer

100 South Swan Street
Albany, NY 12210
(518) 436-8516
Fax - (518) 436-8470

July 14, 2008

Honorable David Paterson
Governor of the State of New York
State Capitol
Albany, New York 12224

ATT: Counsel   RE: S. 7638

Dear Governor Paterson:

The New York State AFL-CIO, representing over 2 million union members, their families as well as our retirees and their families takes no position on the above referenced legislation.

For further information contact Ed Donnelly, Legislative Director at 518-436-8516.

Sincerely,

Ed Donnelly
Legislative Director

ED:cb
opeiu-153
Letter #81/2008

000016

The
Business
Council

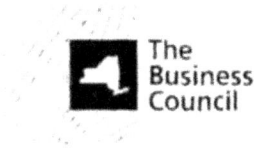

KENNETH ADAMS
President & CEO

August 1, 2008

Terryl Browns-Clemons, Esq.
Counsel
State of New York
Executive Chamber
State Capital
Albany, New York 12224

Dear Ms. Clemons:

The Business Council of New York State respectfully urges the gubernatorial veto of S.7638-A (Volker)/A.10288 A (Aubry). This bill would amend the labor law and general business law and require additional workplace postings by employers and a requirement that employers provide copies of article 23-A of the corrections law to certain job applicants.

In the workplace, employers are already required to post a minimum of seven separate federal notices; employee polygraph protection act, equal employment opportunity, minimum wage, occupational safety and health, family medical leave act, family medical leave for military leave and veterans' rights. Employers are also required to post a minimum of eight separate state notices in the workplace; no smoking, minimum wage, right to know, human rights, election law, workers' compensation, disability and unemployment insurance coverage. More notices are required based on industry or other activity such as employing minors in the workplace. This legislation would go far beyond the posting of another single poster to include the entire article 23-A of the corrections law. Accessing article 23-A of the corrections law through the laws of New York from the Assembly or Senate websites, requires one to access seven separate sections in order to cut and paste the entire article 23-A.

Furthermore, the legislation would also require the posting of " any regulations promulgated ..." related to the employment of persons previously convicted of a crime. Does the Legislature really expect the more than 550,000 employers in New York State to research related regulations and post them on a bulletin board along with the complete article 23-A of the corrections law?

If the Legislature is really concerned about employers' ignorance of the law with respect to criminal convictions and the rights of persons with convictions, they should turn to the Division of Human Rights. The Division has a two page brochure available on its website focusing on employers' obligations regarding employment of persons with a conviction record. It is easy to read and gives actual examples to assist the reader. A Division project to communicate with employers and employer groups around the state to achieve the same results

The Business Council of New York State, Inc.

should be attempted prior to authorizing this legislation. Successful results do not necessarily flow from more legislation.

The other objectionable provision of this legislation requires the employer to provide an applicant for employment with up to two copies of article 23-A of the corrections law if (i) the employer has requested an investigative consumer report on that applicant and (ii) if the completed report contains criminal conviction information. New York State employers already have significant disclosure requirements and other obligations under the federal Fair Credit Reporting Act and the state's general business law when it elects to order a consumer report on a job applicant. These involve, a separate notice informing the applicant of the possibility of a consumer report, securing the authorization of the applicant, disclosure of information from a consumer report and providing contact information on the firm conducting the investigative consumer report so the applicant may contact them. The job applicant already gets appropriate notices of any intent to secure an investigative consumer report and has the opportunity to review the contents. It is unrealistic to not only charge employers in New York State with disclosure but also require them to walk applicants through employment laws that may apply to them. This is not and should not be an employer responsibility.

Clearly, there are more effective and efficient ways to convey the information intended by this legislation. This letter suggests one example. Adding layer upon layer of additional administrative and legal obligations creates unrealistic expectations, a system of "gotcha" enforcement and yet another negative to the state's business environment.

For these reasons, The Business Council opposes S.7638-A/A.10288-A and respectfully urges that it not be enacted.

Sincerely,

tm

The Fortune Society

www.fortunesociety.org

DAVID ROTHENBERG CENTER FOR PUBLIC POLICY

July 9, 2008

Ms. Terryl Brown Clemons
Acting Counsel to the Governor
Executive Chamber
State Capitol
Albany, NY 12224

Re: S7638A / A10288-A

Dear Ms. Brown Clemons,

The Fortune Society (Fortune), founded in 1967, provides reentry services and alternatives to incarceration, and also advocates for an improved and more humane criminal justice system. In order to outfit people with criminal records with the necessary skills and supports for successful reentry, our direct services are provided through a holistic, one-stop model of service, which includes: career development, education, substance abuse treatment, counseling, housing, lifetime aftercare, and alternatives to incarceration, among other programs. Annually, Fortune's Career Development unit engages approximately 700 men and women with criminal histories, providing them with job training, counseling, and placement services.

The Fortune Society's David Rothenberg Center for Public Policy (DRCPP) strongly urges the Governor to sign bill S7638A / A10288-A. This bill, drafted by DRCPP, (1) requires employers and potential employers to include a copy of Article 23-A of the Correction Law when providing a consumer report containing criminal conviction information to a third party, and (2) requires the posting of Article 23-A in various places of employment. This bill will ensure that both employers and job seekers are properly informed of the relevant law, thereby enhancing public safety by facilitating the fair employment of qualified individuals with criminal histories.

The attainment of gainful employment is a critical factor in predicting the success of individuals returning home from incarceration or under community supervision. From a recent sample of individuals incarcerated in the New York City Department of Correction system, less than 25% were employed at the time of arrest and almost 23% had never been employed. Similarly, 70% of New York City probationers are unemployed at the time of re-arrest. Helping these and other individuals with criminal records enter or reenter the workforce is critical to promoting public safety, reducing recidivism rates and avoiding the high costs of incarceration.

While employment is critical for this population, many employers maintain blanket barriers to employment based solely on criminal conviction records — even when the conviction may be completely unrelated to the job sought and no threat to the public or property is present. As highlighted in a 2007 report, *The Independent Committee on Reentry and Employment. Report and Recommendations to New York State on Enhancing Employment opportunities for*

Formerly Incarcerated People, "ignorance - both ignorance about the law and ignorance about the population in question - poses a significant barrier to employment for individuals with a criminal record. Employers are largely unfamiliar with New York State laws governing employment discrimination and the hiring of individuals with a criminal record. Some employers consider arrests not leading to a conviction in the hiring practice and others conceal the findings of criminal background checks from potential employees."

With the recent proliferation of inexpensive commercial background checks, employers have easy access to criminal history information. Unfortunately, these employers often claim ignorance of the existence of Article 23-A of the Correction Law, which outlines standards for the consideration of job seekers with criminal records and makes it illegal to automatically deny employment based on a criminal conviction. For this reason, it is critical that both employers and applicants with criminal records are furnished with Article 23-A so that all relevant parties are equipped with a full understanding of how criminal history information can be appropriately and legally considered amidst the hiring process.

This bill will prove instrumental in advancing the efforts of thousands of job seekers with criminal records to enter the labor market and become productive, self-sufficient citizens of New York State.

We greatly appreciate the opportunity to comment on this important piece of legislation. If you have any questions or concerns, please feel free to call me at 347-510-3607.

All the best,

Glenn E. Martin
Associate Vice President of Policy and Advocacy
The Fortune Society
David Rothenberg Center for Public Policy (DRCPP)

CC: Senator Dale M. Volker
CC: Assemblyman Jeffrion L. Aubry

✉ send this to a friend

The Fortune Society
David Rothenberg Center for Public Policy
CHANGING MINDS & BUILDING LIVES

Hello Denise,

Last night, we spent the evening at Fishkill Correctional Facility, talking to the men about the work of DRCPP. Their ability to find and maintain employment after release was on top of their agenda for discussion. One thing we mentioned was the passage of the Employer Education Act, the first bill drafted by DRCPP, and how hard we intended to work to convince the Governor to sign the bill. Well, the bill was **delivered to Governor Paterson last Friday, July 25, 2008. Now we're counting on you to help us deliver good news!!**

The clock is ticking and we need your support: **the Governor has 10 days to either sign or veto this important piece of legislation**. It's up to you to make sure he makes the right decision and signs the Employer Education Act into law!

Please take a moment out of your busy schedule to **call the Governor's office at 518-474-8390 to voice your support for the Employer Education Act (S7638A/A10288A).** We must act now to make sure the Governor hears loud and clear that we care about fair hiring practices in New York State and want to safeguard the lawful employment of qualified job seekers with criminal records. We promised the men at Fishkill that we would work with you to convince the Governor to sign this bill. The last thing either of us wants is to have to tell them we didn't succeed.

About the Employer Education Act (S7638A/A10288A)

The Employer Education Act will require employers to:

- Include a copy of Article 23-A of the Correction law—which makes it illegal to automatically deny employment to qualified job seekers with criminal records and provides guidance on how criminal history information can be appropriately and legally considered amidst the hiring process—to job applicants if they run background checks during the interview process and;
- Post Article 23-A conspicuously in the workplace.

Discrimination against men and women with criminal records who want to work hurts our communities, threatens public safety, and contributes to recidivism. The Employer Education Act will prove instrumental in advancing the efforts of thousands of job seekers with criminal records to enter the labor market and become productive, self-sufficient citizens of New York State.

Please take a moment to let us know that you made a phone call by emailing one of us at jcolter@fortunesociety.org and/or gmartin@fortunesociety.org.

Thanks to you, Denise, we've come this far. Let's nail this one down by inundating the Governor's office with calls showing support.

Have a great day and we'll be sure to tell the guys at Fishkill about your efforts!

Best,

Jessica Colter
Director of Policy & Communications

Glenn E. Martin
Vice President

LEGAL ACTION CENTER

July 17, 2008

Terryl Brown Clemons, Esq.
Acting Counsel to the Governor
Executive Chamber

Re. S7638-A/A10288-A

Dear Ms. Clemons,

The Legal Action Center, an organization that for over three decades has worked to advance and protect the rights of people in recovery from drug dependence or alcoholism, individuals living with HIV/AIDS, and people with criminal records by assisting them in reclaiming their lives and transitioning to self-sufficiency, **strongly urges the Governor to sign bill S7638-A/A10288-A**

This bill requires employers and potential employers to include a copy of Article 23-A of the correction law when providing a consumer report containing criminal conviction information to a third party, and requires employers to post a copy of Article 23-A in their establishments. In this way, the bill helps ensure that employers do not illegally discriminate against people with criminal conviction records but rather apply the factors which must be considered by employers under Article 23-A

Employment is essential to individuals' successful re-entry into the community following incarceration, and is critical to reducing recidivism rates and protecting the public safety. The Legislature recognized this when it passed Article 23-A, which bars blanket barriers to employment that are based solely on the fact of a criminal conviction. However, employers are often unaware of the state's framework for considering jobseekers with criminal histories, which requires that they consider whether the job has a direct relationship to the criminal offense(s) and whether an unreasonable risk to the public or property exists. As a result, they repeatedly reject qualified applicants and dismiss employees based solely on their criminal records. As a 2007 report compiled by the Independent Committee on Reentry and Employment explained, ignorance ... poses a significant barrier to employment for individuals with a criminal record. Employers are largely unfamiliar with New York State laws governing employment discrimination and the hiring of individuals with a criminal record

By requiring employers to include a copy of Article 23-A of the correction law when providing a consumer report containing criminal conviction information to a third party, and post a copy of Article 23-A in their establishments, this bill ensures that employers will be educated about their responsibilities under Article 23-A, thereby facilitating reentry and improving employment opportunities for individuals with criminal histories, and thereby reducing recidivism rates and improving public safety.

We greatly appreciate the opportunity to comment on this important piece of legislation. If you have any questions or concerns, please feel free to call us at 212-243-1313.

Thank you.

Paul N. Samuels   Anita Marton   April L. Frazier
Executive Director/President   Vice President   Deputy Director/HIRE

400023

THE CITY OF NEW YORK
OFFICE OF THE MAYOR
NEW YORK, N.Y. 10007

July 28, 2008

S.7638-A — by Senator Volker

AN ACT to amend the General Business Law, in relation to the
provision of a consumer report that contains criminal
conviction information

APPROVAL RECOMMENDED

Hon. David Paterson
Governor of the State of New York
Executive Chamber
Albany, New York 12224

Dear Governor Paterson:

The above-referenced bill is now before you for executive action.

The bill amends the General Business Law to require consumer reporting agencies to include a copy of Article 23-A of the Correction Law when providing a consumer report including criminal conviction information to a third party.

Research shows that employment is a critical factor in predicting the success of individuals returning home from incarceration, or under community supervision. Without employment, the chances of success for these individuals are significantly reduced. From a recent sample of New York City Department of Correction inmates, less than 25% were employed at the time of arrest and almost 23% had never been employed. Similarly, 70% of New York City probationers are unemployed at the time of re-arrest. Helping these individuals enter or re-enter the workforce is critical to promoting public safety, reducing recidivism rates and avoiding the high costs of incarceration.

While employment is critical for this population, employers face a difficult challenge in determining when and how to take into account criminal convictions when making hiring decisions. Fortunately, in New York State, Article 23-A of the Correction Law provides standards and guidance for employers when making hiring decisions about job seekers with criminal records. The law also specifically prohibits employers from automatically denying employment to job seekers based solely on a criminal conviction, unless there is a material relation between the crime of conviction and the job position.

000024

Hon. David Paterson
July 28, 2008
Page 2

S.7638-A

With the recent increase in the availability of inexpensive commercial background checks, employers have easy access to criminal history information. Once this information is obtained, it is critical that employers also have Article 23A of the Correction Law on hand so that they are equipped to use criminal history information appropriately and legally. Including a copy of Article 23A with background check results will enhance public safety by facilitating the appropriate employment of qualified individuals with criminal histories and by providing a simple and effective means of ensuring that employers are informed of the relevant law.

Accordingly, it is urged that this bill be approved.

Very truly yours,

MICHAEL R. BLOOMBERG, Mayor

By: Michelle L. Goldstein
        Director

Legislative Secretary/NYEC
Sent by: Kristin
Rosenstein/NYEC

07/14/2008 09:35 AM

To: amarton@fac.org, bmahan@nysba.org,
rkennedy@nysba.org, kkerwin@nysba.org,
sbanks@legal-aid.org, ebridegroom@nysaflcio.org,
ebridegroom@nysaflcio.org, ken.pokalsky@bcnys.org,
mcmahon@nysedc.org, tedpotrikus@retailcouncilnys.com,
rwolken@macny.org, diana.ehrlich@nfib.org,
bnoylman@nycp.org, cdowney@dhr.state.ny.us,
trodriguez@dhr.state.ny.us, phidelson@nycbar.org

cc

bcc

Subject: s.7638-a

Community
Service | Fighting Poverty
Society | Strengthening
New York

July 28, 2008

Honorable David A. Paterson
Governor, State of New York
Executive Chamber
State Capitol Building
Albany, New York 12224

RE: S.7638-A Volker AN ACT to amend the general business law and the labor law, in relation to the provision of criminal record conviction information in certain instances

Dear Governor Paterson:

The above-referenced bill is now before you for Executive action.

This legislation would require employers and potential employers to include a copy of Article 23-A of the Correction Law when providing a consumer report containing criminal conviction information to a third party and to require the posting of Article 23-A in various places of employment.

The Community Service Society of New York (CSS) **strongly supports** this legislation, which requires that a consumer reporting agency provide a potential employer with a copy of New York State Law governing the licensure and employment of people with prior criminal offenses, when an applicant's report contains a criminal offense or conviction.

For over 160 years, CSS has been advocating for poor New Yorkers, and has tried to identify and address the root causes of poverty. In recent years we have begun to focus on employment as a pathway out of poverty, and have identified the formerly incarcerated as a vulnerable population in need of assistance. Toward that end, we have been convening monthly re-entry roundtable discussions since December 2005, to identify policies to help reintegrate those individuals into their communities. Removing barriers to employment is one of the New York Reentry Roundtable's primary legislative goals.

People with criminal records face innumerable hurdles when trying to secure employment. One such significant barrier is the tendency for employers to conduct criminal background checks without the consent or knowledge of the applicant, which serves to exclude formerly incarcerated individuals from getting certain jobs. Upon

206271.1

000027

NYC™

**Commission on
Human Rights**

FAIR CHANCE ACT

CRIMINAL RECORD?
YOU CAN WORK WITH THAT.
Criminal history can't be part of the hiring process until after a job offer. That means you get a fair chance, and employers get to consider more candidates.

Starting October 27, 2015, employers cannot ask you about your criminal history until after they offer you a job. After an employer offers you a job, they can ask about and consider your criminal history. If an employer decides that they no longer want to hire you after finding out about your record, the employer must follow a specific process. This guide explains that process and provides you with information about your rights both before and after getting a job offer. You have the same rights under this law in hiring or any other employment decision, like promotions. However, this guide focuses on the job application process.

BEFORE A JOB OFFER

Your criminal record is off-limits until an employer offers you a job.

Employers cannot place job ads that mention arrests, convictions, or having a clean record, such as "no felons," "background check required," or "must have clean record."

Job applications cannot have questions about criminal records and cannot ask you to authorize a background check. Employers cannot ask you questions about your criminal record. If you are asked about your record, your answer cannot be used against you. Employers cannot run a background check on you until after a conditional offer of employment.

AFTER A JOB OFFER

Once an employer offers you a job, they can ask about and consider your criminal record.

Employers can ask you if you have any criminal convictions. You must disclose felony and misdemeanor convictions, no matter how old they are.

Employers can require you to authorize a background check. If you do not authorize a background check, an employer can refuse to hire you.

There are two things **employers can never ask about, and you should not disclose even if asked:**

1. Any arrest where you were never convicted;

2. Any convictions that are sealed. Convictions are usually sealed when you:

   - Are convicted of a non-criminal violation, like disorderly conduct;

   - Complete a court-ordered drug treatment program; or

   - Are adjudicated as a youthful offender or juvenile delinquent.

Even if an employer finds out about this information, it cannot be used against you. The only exception is if you are applying to be a police or peace officer.

BEFORE A FINAL EMPLOYMENT DECISION

Once an employer finds out about your criminal record, the employer can decide not to hire you. But before making a final decision, an employer must do three things:

1. Give you a copy of any background check it did on you;

2. Evaluate you by considering specific factors and share that written evaluation with you; and

3. Hold the job open for at least three business days after the employer communicates its decision to you so that you can respond to the decision.

Employers cannot deny you work just because you have a criminal record. Before deciding not to hire you because of your criminal record, employers must consider these factors:

- That New York public policy encourages the employment of people with criminal records;

- The specific duties and responsibilities of the job;

- The bearing, if any, of your criminal record on your ability to do the job;

- The amount of time that has passed since the events that led to your criminal conviction;

- Your age when you engaged in criminal conduct;

- The seriousness of your conviction record;

- Any positive information you have in your favor. This includes evidence that you attended school, job training, or counseling; had past employment; or are involved with your community. These can include letters of recommendation from people who know you, like teachers, counselors, supervisors, clergy, and parole or probation officers.

- If you have a certificate of relief from disabilities or a certificate of good conduct, an employer **must** presume you are rehabilitated for your convictions.

After looking at these factors, an employer can decide to not hire you for one of two reasons:

1) because a **direct relationship** exists between your conviction and the job you want; or

2) because your conviction history creates an **unreasonable risk** to people or property.

The employer must send you its reasoning in writing, along with the background check it used. After receiving these materials, you have three business days to respond to address the employer's concerns.

Do all employers have to follow the Fair Chance Act?

No, some employers are required by law to check your criminal record. Other employers are required by law to not hire people with certain serious convictions. These employers do not have to follow the FCA. In addition, law enforcement-related city agencies do not have to follow the FCA.

Does this law apply to housing?

No, this law affects employment only. Criminal history can still be used by landlords to decide whether to rent property.

What should I do if I believe an employer did not follow the rules described here?

Call 311 and ask for the Commission on Human Rights. You can leave an anonymous tip, or you can file a complaint about what happened to you. If the employer is found to have broken the law, you could recover lost wages or other damages and the employer may have to pay a fine.

Article 23-A
Evaluation Form

_____
Applicant Name

FAIR CHANCE ACT NOTICE

After extending a conditional offer of employment, we checked your criminal record. Based on the enclosed check, we have reservations about hiring you for the position of _____, and may decide to retract our job offer. Below explains why. We invite you to provide us with any information that could help us decide to offer you the job. If you choose to provide us with additional information you have _____ days (must be at least three business days) from the date you receive this to do so.

If you wish to respond, please contact _____.

In your response, you may:
- Tell us about any errors on your criminal record;
- Give us any additional information you'd like us to consider after reviewing this notice.

The following factors were considered, as required by Article 23-A of the New York State Correction Law, before making our determination:

The government encourages employers to hire people with criminal records.

The specific duties and responsibilities of the job, which are:	How long ago your criminal activity, not your conviction, occurred:
1. _____	_____ years _____ months
2. _____	Your age when your criminal activity, not your conviction, occurred: _____ years old
3. _____	
4. _____	

We believe your record impairs your fitness or ability to perform these duties and responsibilities because:

1. _____
2. _____
3. _____
4. _____

The seriousness of the conduct that led to your criminal record. This is judged in part by how many felony and misdemeanor convictions you have, and whether your conduct involved violence or theft:

_____ Misdemeanors   _____ Felonies

a. _____ *involving violence*   a. _____ *involving violence*

b. _____ *involving theft*   b. _____ *involving theft*

Your evidence of rehabilitation and good conduct, which is listed below.

1. _____
2. _____
3. _____
4. _____

If you have additional documents we should consider, please send them, including evidence that you attended school, job training, or counseling; or are involved with your community. They can include letters from people who know you, like teachers, counselors, supervisors, clergy, and parole or probation officers.

Your certificate(s) of relief or certificate of good conduct shows that you are rehabilitated. If you did not have a certificate, we did not hold that against you.

Based on these factors, we may deny you a job because *(choose only one):*

We believe there is a direct relationship between your criminal record and the job we offered to you, and the factors listed above do not lessen that relationship because:	We believe there is no direct relationship, but your criminal record creates an unreasonable risk to specific persons, the general public, or our property because:

If you wish to respond, please contact _____.
Based on your response, we may hire you. If you do not contact us by then, we will withdraw the

NYC COMMISSION ON HUMAN RIGHTS
Legal Enforcement Guidance on the
Fair Chance Act, Local Law No. 63 (2015)

The New York City Human Rights Law (the "NYCHRL") prohibits discrimination in employment, public accommodations, and housing. It also prohibits discriminatory harassment and bias-based profiling by law enforcement. The NYCHRL, pursuant to the 2005 Civil Rights Restoration Act, must be construed "independently from similar or identical provisions of New York state or federal statutes," such that "similarly worded provisions of federal and state civil rights laws [are] a floor below which the City's Human Rights law cannot fall, rather than a ceiling above which the local law cannot rise."[1]

The New York City Commission on Human Rights (the "Commission") is the City agency charged with enforcing the NYCHRL. Individuals interested in vindicating their rights under the NYCHRL can choose to file a complaint with the Commission's Law Enforcement Bureau within one (1) year of the discriminatory act or file a complaint in New York State Supreme Court within three (3) years of the discriminatory act. The NYCHRL covers employers with four or more employees.

The Fair Chance Act ("FCA"), effective October 27, 2015, amends the NYCHRL by making it an unlawful discriminatory practice for most employers, labor organizations, and employment agencies to inquire about or consider the criminal history of job applicants until after extending conditional offers of employment. If an employer wishes to withdraw its offer, it must give the applicant a copy of its inquiry into and analysis of the applicant's conviction history, along with at least three business days to respond.

I. LEGISLATIVE INTENT

The FCA reflects the City's view that job seekers must be judged on their merits before their mistakes. The FCA is intended to level the playing field so that New Yorkers who are part of the approximately 70 million adults residing in the United States who have been arrested or convicted of a crime[2] "can be considered for a position among other equally qualified candidates," and "not overlooked during the hiring process simply because they have to check a box."[3]

Even though New York Correction Law Article 23-A ("Article 23-A") has long protected people with criminal records from employment discrimination,[4] the City determined that such discrimination still occurred when applicants were asked about their records before completing the hiring process because many employers were not weighing

---

1 Local Law No. 85 (2005). "The provisions of this title shall be construed liberally for the accomplishment of the uniquely broad and remedial purposes thereof, regardless of whether federal or New York State civil and human rights laws, including those laws with provisions comparably worded to provisions of this title have been so construed." N.Y.C. Admin. Code § 8-130.

2 Gov'tl Affairs Division of the N.Y. City Council, Committee Report on Int. No. 318-A, S. 2015-5, at 2 (June 9, 2015) ("Civil Rights Committee's Report"), *available at* http://legistar.council.nyc.gov/View.ashx?M=F&ID=3815856&GUID=59D912BA-68B5-429C-BF39-118EB4DFAAF5.

3 Testimony of Gale A. Brewer, Manhattan Borough President on Int. No. 318 to Prohibit Employment Discrimination Based on One's Arrest Record or Criminal Conviction at 2 (Dec. 3, 2014) (emphasis in original), *available at* http://legistar.council.nyc.gov/View.ashx?M=F&ID=3410802&GUID=7D143B7E-C532-41EF-9A97-04FD17854ED7.

4 Violating Article 23-A is an unlawful discriminatory practice under the NYCHRL. N.Y.C. Admin. Code § 8-107(10).

the factors laid out in Article 23-A.[5] For that reason, the FCA prohibits any discussion or consideration of an applicant's criminal history until after a conditional offer of employment. Certain positions are exempt from the FCA, as described in Section VII of this Guidance.

While the FCA does not require employers to hire candidates whose convictions are directly related to a job or pose an unreasonable risk, it ensures that individuals with criminal histories are considered based on their qualifications before their conviction histories. If an employer is interested enough to offer someone a job, it can more carefully consider whether or not that person's criminal history makes her or him unsuitable for the position. If the employer wishes to nevertheless withdraw its offer, it must first give the applicant a meaningful opportunity to respond before finalizing its decision.

II.   Definitions

The FCA applies to both licensure and employment, although this Guidance focuses on employment. The term "**applicant**," as used in this Guidance, refers to both potential and current employees. The FCA applies to all decisions that affect the terms and conditions of employment, including hiring, termination, transfers, and promotions; where this Guidance describes the "**hiring process**," it includes the process for making all of these employment decisions. Any time the FCA or this Guidance requires notices and disclosures to be printed or in writing, they may also be communicated by email, if such method of communication is mutually agreed on in advance by the employer and the applicant.

For the purpose of this Guidance, the following key terms are defined as follows:

Article 23-A Analysis
> The evaluation process mandated by New York Correction Law Article 23-A.

Article 23-A Factors
> The factors employers must consider concerning applicants' criminal conviction history under Section 753 of New York Correction Law Article 23-A.

Conditional Offer of Employment
> An offer of employment that can only be revoked based on:

1) The results of a criminal background check;

2) The results of a medical exam in situations in which such exams are permitted by the Americans with Disabilities Act;[6] or

3) Other information the employer could not have reasonably known before the conditional offer if, based on the information, the employer would not have made the offer and the employer can show the information is material to job performance.

> For temporary help firms, a conditional offer is the offer to be placed in a pool of applicants from which the applicant may be sent to temporary positions.

---

5   Transcript of the Minutes of the Committee on Civil Rights at 10 (Dec. 3, 2014) (statement of Council Member Jumaane Williams), *available at* http://legistar.council.nyc.gov/View.ashx?M=F&ID=3410594&GUID=5FE2433E-1A95-4FAA-AECC-D60D4016F3FB.

6   The Americans with Disabilities Act ("ADA") prohibits employers from conducting medical exams until after a conditional offer of employment. 42 U.S.C. § 12112(d)(3). To comply with the FCA and the ADA, employers may condition an offer of employment on the results of a criminal background check and then, after the criminal background check, a medical examination.

Conviction History

A previous conviction of a crime, either a felony or misdemeanor under New York law,[7] or a crime as defined by the law of another state.

Criminal Background Check

When an employer, orally or in writing, either:

1) Asks an applicant whether or not she or he has a criminal record; or

2) Searches public records, including through a third party, such as a consumer reporting agency ("CRA"), for an applicant's criminal history.

Criminal History

A previous record of criminal convictions or non-convictions or a currently pending criminal case.

Fair Chance Process

The post-conditional offer process mandated by the FCA, as outlined in Section V of this Guidance.

Inquiry

Any question, whether made in writing or orally, asked for the purpose of obtaining an applicant's criminal history, including, without limitation, questions in a job interview about an applicant's criminal history; and any search for an applicant's criminal history, including through the services of a third party, such as a consumer reporting agency.

Non-convictions

A criminal action, not currently pending, that was concluded in one of the following ways:

1) Termination in favor of the individual, as defined by New York Criminal Procedure Law ("CPL") § 160.50, even if not sealed;

2) Adjudication as a youthful offender, as defined by CPL § 720.35, even if not sealed;

3) Conviction of a non-criminal violation that has been sealed under CPL § 160.55; or

4) Convictions that have been sealed under CPL § 160.58.

Statement

Any words, whether made in writing or orally, for the purpose of obtaining an applicant's criminal history, including, without limitation, stating that a background check is required for a position.

Temporary Help Firms

A business which recruits, hires, and assigns its own employees to perform work at or services for other organizations, to support or supplement the other organization's workforce, or to provide assistance in special work situations such as, without limitation, employee absences, skill shortages, seasonal workloads, or special assignments or projects.[8]

---

7   A misdemeanor is an offense, other than a "traffic infraction," for which a person may be incarcerated for more than 15 days and less than one year. N.Y. Pen. L. § 10.00(4). A felony is an offense for which a person may be incarcerated for more than one year. *Id.* § 10.00(5).

8   N.Y. Lab. L. § 916(5).

III. *Per Se* Violations of the FCA

As of October 27, 2015, the following acts are separate, chargeable violations of the NYCHRL:

1. Declaring, printing, or circulating – or causing the declaration, printing, or circulation of – any solicitation, advertisement, or publication for employment that states any limitation or specification regarding criminal history, *even if no adverse action follows*. This includes, without limitation, advertisements and employment applications containing phrases such as: "no felonies," "background check required," and "must have clean record."

2. Making any statement or inquiry, as defined in Section II of this Guidance, before a conditional offer of employment, *even if no adverse action follows*.

3. Withdrawing a conditional offer of employment based on an applicant's criminal history before completing the Fair Chance Process as outlined in Section V of this Guidance. Each of the following is a separate, chargeable violation of the NYCHRL:
    a) Failing to disclose to the applicant a written copy of any inquiry an employer conducted into the applicant's criminal history;
    b) Failing to share with the applicant a written copy of the employer's Article 23-A analysis;
    c) Failing to hold the prospective position open for at least three business days, from an applicant's receipt of both the inquiry and analysis, to allow the applicant to respond.

4. Taking an adverse employment action because of an applicant's non-conviction.[9]

IV.   The Criminal Background Check Process Under the FCA

The FCA does not change what criminal history information employers may consider. Instead, it changes when employers may consider this information. No employer may seek, obtain, or base an adverse employment action on a non-conviction.[10] No employer may seek, obtain, or base an adverse employment action on a criminal conviction until after extending a conditional offer of employment. After a conditional offer of employment, an employer can only withdraw the offer after evaluating the applicant under Article 23-A and finding that the applicant's conviction history poses a direct relationship or unreasonable risk.

A. Before a Conditional Offer

The FCA prohibits the discovery and use of criminal history before a conditional offer of employment. During this time, an employer must not seek or obtain an applicant's criminal history. Consistent with Article 23-A, an employer's focus must instead be on an applicant's qualifications.

The following are examples of common hiring practices that are affected by the FCA.

   i. Solicitations, advertisements, and publications for employment cannot mention criminal history.

The FCA now explicitly prohibits employers from expressing any limitation or specification based on criminal history in their job advertisements,[11] even though

---

9   The FCA updates the NYCHRL's protections regarding non-conviction discrimination to match the New York State Human Rights Law. *See* Section XI of this Guidance.

10 Employers of police and peace officers can consider all non-convictions, except criminal actions terminated in favor of the applicant, as defined by New York Criminal Procedure Law § 160.50. N.Y.C. Admin. Code §§ 8-107(11)(a),(b).

11 *Id.* § 8-107(11-a)(a)(1).

such advertisements are already illegal under the existing NYCHRL.[12] Ads cannot say, for example, "no felonies," "background check required," or "clean records only." Solicitations, advertisements, and publications encompass a broad variety of items, including, without limitation, employment applications, fliers, handouts, online job postings, and materials distributed at employment fairs and by temporary help firms and job readiness organizations. Employment applications cannot ask whether an applicant has a criminal history or a pending criminal case or authorize a background check.

ii. Employers cannot inquire about criminal history during the interview process.

The FCA prohibits employers from making any inquiry or statement related to an applicant's criminal history until after a conditional offer of employment. Examples of prohibited statements and inquiries include, without limitation:

- Questions, whether written or oral, during a job interview about criminal history;

- Assertions, whether written or oral, that individuals with convictions, or certain convictions, will not be hired or cannot work at the employer; and

- Investigations into the applicant's criminal history, including using public records or the Internet, whether conducted by an employer or for an employer by a third party.

The FCA does not prevent employers from otherwise looking into an applicant's background and experience to verify her or his qualifications for a position, including asking for resumes and references and performing general Internet searches (e.g., Google, LinkedIn, etc.). Searching an applicant's name is legal, but trying to discover an applicant's conviction history is not. In connection with an applicant, employers cannot search for terms such as, "arrest," "mugshot," "warrant," "criminal," "conviction," "jail," or "prison." Nor can employers search websites that contain or purport to contain arrest, warrant, conviction, or incarceration information.

The FCA allows an applicant to refuse to respond to any prohibited inquiry or statement. Such refusal or response to an illegal question shall not disqualify the applicant from the prospective employment.

iii. Inadvertent disclosures of criminal record information before a conditional offer of employment do not create employer liability.

The FCA prohibits any inquiry or statement made for the purpose of obtaining an applicant's criminal history. If a legitimate inquiry not made for that purpose leads an applicant to reveal criminal history, the employer should continue its hiring process. It may not examine the applicant's conviction history information until after deciding whether or not to make a conditional offer of employment.

If the applicant raises her or his criminal record voluntarily, the employer should not use that as an opportunity to explore an applicant's criminal history further. The employer should state that, by law, it will only consider the applicant's record if it decides to offer her or him a job. Similarly, if an applicant asks an employer during the interview if she or he will be subject to a criminal background check, the employer may state that a criminal background check will be conducted only after a conditional offer of employment. It must then move the conversation to a different topic. Employers who make a good faith effort to exclude information regarding criminal history before extending a conditional offer of employment will not be liable under the FCA.

---

12 Advertisements excluding people who have been arrested violate the NYCHRL's complete ban on employment decisions based on an arrest that did not lead to a criminal conviction. *Id.* § 8-107(11). Employers whose advertisements exclude people with criminal convictions are not engaging in the individual analysis required by Article 23-A. *Id.* § 8-107(10).

B. After the Conditional Offer of Employment

After extending a conditional offer of employment, as defined in Section II of this Guidance, an employer may make the same inquiries into, and statements about, an applicant's criminal history as before the FCA became effective. An employer may:

- Ask, either orally or in writing, whether an applicant has a criminal conviction history or a pending criminal case;

- Run a background check itself or, after giving the applicant notice and getting her or his permission, use a consumer reporting agency to do so;[13] and

- Once an employer knows about an applicant's conviction, ask her or him about the circumstances that led to it.

Employers must never inquire about or act on non-conviction information, however. To guard against soliciting or considering non-conviction information, employers may frame inquiries by using the following language after a conditional offer is made:

> Have you ever been convicted of a misdemeanor or felony? Answer "NO" if your conviction: (a) was sealed, expunged, or reversed on appeal; (b) was for a violation, infraction, or other petty offense such as "disorderly conduct;" (c) resulted in a youthful offender or juvenile delinquency finding; or (d) if you withdrew your plea after completing a court program and were not convicted of a misdemeanor or felony.

If an employer hires an applicant after learning about her or his conviction history, the FCA does not require it to do anything more. An employer that wants to withdraw its conditional offer of employment, however, must first consider the Article 23-A factors. If, after doing so, an employer still wants to withdraw its conditional offer, it must follow the Fair Chance Process.

C. Evaluating the Applicant Using Article 23-A

Under Article 23-A, an employer cannot deny employment unless it can:

1. Draw a direct relationship between the applicant's criminal record and the prospective job; or

2. Show that employing the applicant "would involve an unreasonable risk to property or to the safety or welfare of specific individuals or the general public."[14]

An employer that cannot show the applicant meets at least one of the exceptions to Article 23-A cannot withdraw the conditional offer because of the applicant's criminal record.

An employer cannot simply presume a direct relationship or unreasonable risk exists because the applicant has a conviction record.[15] The employer must evaluate the Article 23-A factors using the applicant's specific information before reaching either conclusion.

- To claim the direct relationship exception, an employer must first draw some connection between the nature of conduct that led to the conviction(s) and the potential position. If a direct relationship exists, an employer must evaluate

---

13 The consumer report cannot contain credit information. Under the Stop Credit Discrimination in Employment Act, employers, labor organizations, and employment agencies cannot request or use the consumer credit history of an applicant or employee for the purpose of making any employment decisions, including hiring, compensation, and other terms and conditions of employment. Id. §§ 8-102(29); 8-107(24).

14 N.Y. Correct. L. § 752.

15 Bonacorsa v. Van Lindt, 71 N.Y.2d 605, 613-14 (N.Y. 1988).

the Article 23-A factors to determine whether the concerns presented by the relationship have been mitigated.[16]

- To claim the unreasonable risk exception, an employer must begin by assuming that no risk exists and then show how the Article 23-A factors combine to create an unreasonable risk.[17] Otherwise, this exception would cover all convictions not directly related.

The Article 23-A factors are:

- That New York public policy encourages the licensure and employment of people with criminal records;

- The specific duties and responsibilities of the prospective job;

- The bearing, if any, of the person's conviction history on her or his fitness or ability to perform one or more of the job's duties or responsibilities;

- The time that has elapsed since the occurrence of the events that led to the applicant's criminal conviction, not the time since arrest or conviction;

- The age of the applicant when the events that led to her or his conviction occurred, not the time since arrest or conviction;

- The seriousness of the applicant's conviction history;[18]

- Any information produced by the applicant, or produced on the applicant's behalf, regarding her or his rehabilitation or good conduct;

- The legitimate interest of the employer in protecting property and the safety and welfare of specific individuals or the general public.

Employers must also consider a certificate of relief from disabilities or a certificate of good conduct, which shall create a presumption of rehabilitation regarding the relevant conviction.[19]

Employers must carefully conduct the Article 23-A analysis. Before extending a conditional offer of employment, employers must define the job's duties and responsibilities, as required by Article 23-A. Employers cannot alter the job's duties and responsibilities after making a conditional offer of employment. Once an employer extends a conditional offer and learns of an applicant's criminal record, it must solicit the information necessary to properly consider each Article 23-A factor, including the applicant's evidence of rehabilitation.

The Commission will review private employers' adverse employment decisions to ensure that they correctly consider the Article 23-A factors and properly apply the exceptions. The Commission will begin with the purpose of Article 23-A: to create "a fair opportunity for a job is a matter of basic human fairness," one that should not be "frustrated by senseless discrimination."[20] The Commission will also consider Article

---

16 *Id.* at 613-14; *see Soto v. N.Y. State Office of Mental Retardation & Developmental Disabilities,* 907 N.Y.S.2d 104, 26 Misc. 3d 1215(A) at *9 (N.Y. Sup. Ct. 2010) (citing *Marra v. City of White Plains,* 467 N.Y.S.2d 865, 870 (N.Y. App. Div. 1983)).

17 *Bonacorsa,* 71 N.Y.2d at 613; *Exum v. N.Y. City Health & Hosps. Corp.,* 964 N.Y.S.2d 58, 37 Misc. 3d 1218(A) at *6 (N.Y. Sup. Ct. 2012) .

18 Employers may judge the seriousness of an applicant's criminal record based on the number of felony and misdemeanor convictions, along with whether the acts underlying those convictions involved violence or theft.

19 N.Y. Correct. L. § 753(2). An employer may not disfavor an applicant because she or he does not possess a certificate.

20 Governor's Approval Mem., Bill Jacket, L. 1976, ch. 931.

23-A case law.[21] Employers must evaluate each Article 23-A factor; they cannot ignore evidence favorable to the applicant;[22] and they cannot disproportionately weigh any one factor over another.[23] Employers should consider applicants' successful performance of their job duties in past employment, along with evidence that they have addressed the causes of their criminal activity.[24]

V. The Fair Chance Process

If, after evaluating the applicant according to Article 23-A, an employer wishes to decline employment because a direct relationship or unreasonable risk exists, it must follow the Fair Chance Process:

1. Disclose to the applicant a written copy of any inquiry it conducted into the applicant's criminal history;

2. Share with the applicant a written copy of its Article 23-A analysis; and

3. Allow the applicant at least three business days, from receipt of the inquiry and analysis, to respond to the employer's concerns.

A. Disclosing the Inquiry

The Commission requires an employer to disclose a complete and accurate copy of every piece of information it relied on to determine that an applicant has a criminal record, along with the date and time the employer accessed the information. The applicant must be able to see and challenge the same criminal history information relied on by the employer.

Employers who hire consumer reporting agencies to conduct background checks can fulfill this obligation by supplying a copy of the CRA's report on the applicant.[25] Because CRAs can be held liable for aiding and abetting discrimination under the NYCHRL, they should ensure that their customers only request criminal background reports after a conditional offer of employment. Employers who rely on criminal record information beyond what is contained in a criminal background report must also give that information to the applicant.

Employers who search the Internet to obtain criminal histories must print out the pages they relied on, and such printouts must identify their source so that the applicant can verify them. Employers who check public records must provide copies of those records. Employers who rely on oral information must identify the interlocutor and provide a written summary of their conversation. The summary must contain the same information the employer relied on in reaching its determination. Oral information includes anything the applicant revealed about her or his criminal record.

---

21 Nearly all reported cases concern public agencies' employment decisions, which cannot be reversed unless "arbitrary and capricious." N.Y. Correct. L. § 755; see C.P.L.R. § 7803(3). The "arbitrary and capricious" standard does not apply to private employers.

22 *Gallo v. N.Y. State Office of Mental Retardation & Developmental Disabilities,* 830 N.Y.S.2d 796, 798 (N.Y. App. Div. 2007).

23 *Soto,* 26 Misc. 3d 1215(A) at *7.

24 *Odems v. N.Y.C. Dep't of Educ.,* No. 400637/09 at *4, 2009 WL 5225201, at *5, 2009 N.Y. Misc. LEXIS 6480, at *5 (N.Y. Sup. Ct. Dec. 16, 2009); *El v. N.Y.C. Dep't of Educ.,* 23 Misc.3d 1121(A), at *4-5 (N.Y. Sup. Ct. 2009).

25 15 U.S.C. § 1681d; N.Y. Gen. Bus. L. § 380-b(b).

B. Sharing the Fair Chance Notice

The FCA directs the Commission to determine the manner in which employers inform applicants under Article 23-A and provide a written copy of that analysis to applicants.[26] The Commission has prepared a Fair Chance Notice (the "Notice")[27] that employers may use to comply with this requirement. As long as the material substance – considering specific facts in the Article 23-A analysis – does not change, the Notice may be adapted to an employer's preferred format.

The Notice requires employers to evaluate each Article 23-A factor and choose which exception – direct relationship or unreasonable risk – the employer relies on. The Notice also contains space for the employer to articulate its conclusion.[28] Boilerplate denials that simply list the Article 23-A factors violate the FCA. For example, an employer cannot simply say it considered the time since conviction; it must identify the years and/or months since the conviction. An employer also cannot list specific facts for each factor but then fail to describe how it concluded that the applicant's record met either the direct relationship or unreasonable risk exceptions to Article 23-A.

Finally, the Notice informs the applicant of her or his time to respond and requests evidence of rehabilitation and good conduct. The Notice provides examples of such information. Employers may identify specific examples of rehabilitation and good conduct that would be most relevant to the prospective position, but examples must be included.

C. Allowing Time to Respond

Employers must give applicants a reasonable time, which shall be no less than three business days, to respond to the employer's inquiry and Notice. During this time, the employer may not permanently place another person in the applicant's prospective position. This time period begins running when an applicant receives both the inquiry and Notice. Employers may therefore wish to confirm receipt, either by disclosing the information in person, electronically, or by registered mail. Such method of communication must be mutually agreed on in advance by the applicant and employer. Otherwise, the Commission will credit an applicant's recollection as to when she or he received the inquiry and Notice.

By giving an applicant at least three business days to respond, the FCA contemplates a process in which employers discuss their reasons for finding that an applicant's record poses a direct relationship or unreasonable risk. The process allows an applicant to respond either orally or in writing and provide additional information relevant to any of the Article 23-A factors.[29] After receiving additional information from an applicant, an employer must examine whether it changes its Article 23-A analysis. Employers may offer an applicant a similar position that mitigates the employer's concerns. If, after communicating with an applicant, the employer decides not to hire her or him, it must relay that decision to the applicant.

The three-day time period to respond also provides an opportunity for the applicant to address any errors on the employer's background report, including any discrepancies between the convictions she or he disclosed and the results of the background check. As detailed below, a discrepancy could be due to an error on the report or an applicant's intentional misrepresentation.

---

26 N.Y.C. Admin. Code § 8-107(11-a)(b)(ii).

27 The Notice is available on the Commission's website, http://www.nyc.gov/FairChanceNYC.

28 N.Y. Correct. L. § 753(1)(h).

29 N.Y.C. Admin. Code § 8-107(11-a)(b).

i. Handling Errors in the Background Check

An error on a background check might occur because, for example, it contains information that pertains to another person or is outdated. If an applicant is able to demonstrate an error on the background report, the employer must conduct the Article 23-A analysis based on the corrected conviction history information to ensure its decision is not tainted by the previous error. If the employer then finds a direct relationship or unreasonable risk and intends to take an adverse action on that basis, it must follow the Fair Chance Process: the applicant must be given a copy of the corrected inquiry, the employer's Article 23-A analysis, at least three business days to respond, with an opportunity to provide any additional information for the employer to review and re-examine its analysis.

ii. Handling Applicants' Misrepresentations of Their Conviction Histories

If an applicant cannot or does not demonstrate that any discrepancy between the information she or he disclosed and the employer's background report is due to an error, the employer can choose not to hire the individual based on the applicant's misrepresentation. It need not evaluate the applicant's record under Article 23-A.

VI. Temporary Help Firms Under the Fair Chance Act

Temporary help firms employ individuals, either as direct or joint employers, and place them in job assignments at the firms' clients. The FCA applies the same way to temporary help firms as it does to any other employer. The only difference is that, for these firms, a conditional offer of employment is an offer to place an applicant in the firm's labor pool, from which the applicant may be sent on job assignments to the firm's clients. Before a temporary help firm withdraws a conditional offer of employment after discovering an applicant's conviction history, it must follow the Fair Chance Process, according to Section V of this Guidance. To evaluate the job duties, a temporary help firm may only consider the basic skills necessary to be placed in its applicant pool.

Employers who accept placements from temporary help firms, and who wish to inquire about temporary workers' criminal histories, must follow the Fair Chance Act. They may not make any statements or inquiries about an applicant's criminal record until after the worker is assigned to the employer, and they must follow the Fair Chance Process if they wish to decline employment because of an applicant's criminal record.

As with any other type of discrimination, temporary help firms will be liable if they aid and abet an employer's discriminatory hiring preferences. For example, a temporary help firm cannot, based on an employer's instructions, refer only temporary workers who do not have criminal histories or who have "less serious" criminal histories.

VII. Positions Exempt from the FCA

Consistent with the Local Civil Rights Restoration Act of 2005,[30] all exemptions to coverage under the FCA's anti-discrimination provisions are to be construed narrowly. Employers may assert the application of an exemption to defend against liability, and they have the burden of proving the exemption by a preponderance of the evidence. Other than the employers described in Subsections C and D of this Section, the Commission does not assume that an entire employer or industry is exempt and will investigate how an exemption applies to a particular position or role. Positions that are exempt from the FCA are not necessarily exempt from Article 23-A.

---

30 N.Y.C. Local Law No. 85 (2005); N.Y.C. Admin. Code § 8-130.

A. Employers hiring for positions where federal, state, or local law requires criminal background checks or bars employment based on certain criminal convictions

The FCA does not apply to the actions of employers or their agents that are taken pursuant to any state, federal, or local law that requires criminal background checks for employment purposes or bars employment based on criminal history.[31] The purpose of this exemption is to not delay a criminal background inquiry when the results of that inquiry might legally prohibit an employer from hiring an applicant.

A network of federal, state, and local laws creates employment barriers for people with criminal records. The Commission characterizes these barriers as either mandatory or discretionary. Mandatory barriers require a licensing authority or employer to deny applicants with certain convictions enumerated in law. Discretionary barriers allow, but do not require, a licensing authority or employer to deny applicants with criminal records, and may or may not enumerate disqualifying convictions. The FCA controls any time an employer's decision is discretionary, meaning it is not explicitly mandated by law.

For example, state law contains mandatory barriers for – and requires background checks of – applicants to employers regulated by the state Department of Health ("DOH"), Office of Mental Health ("OMH"), and Office of People with Developmental Disabilities ("OPWDD").[32] These agencies require the employers they regulate to conduct background checks because the agencies are charged by state law to ensure that individuals with certain convictions are not hired to work with vulnerable people.[33] Employers regulated by DOH, OMH, and OPWDD are therefore exempt from the FCA when hiring for positions where a criminal history check is required by law. For positions that do not require a criminal history check, however, such employers have to follow the FCA.

The FCA applies when an employer hires people who require licensure, or approval by a government agency, even if the license has mandatory barriers. In that case, an employer can only ask whether an applicant has the required license or can obtain one within an acceptable period of time. Any inquiry into the applicant's criminal record – before a conditional offer of employment – is not allowed. An applicant who has a license has already passed any criminal record barriers and been approved by a government agency. An applicant who cannot, because of her or his conviction record, obtain a required license may have her or his conditional offer withdrawn or employment terminated for such legitimate nondiscriminatory reason.

B. Employers Required by a Self-Regulatory Organization to Conduct a Criminal Background Check of Regulated Persons

Employers in the financial services industry are exempt from the FCA when complying with industry-specific rules and regulations promulgated by a self-regulatory organization ("SRO").[34] This exemption only applies to those positions regulated by SROs; employment decisions regarding other positions must still comply with the FCA.

C. Police and Peace Officers, Law Enforcement Agencies, and Other Exempted City Agencies

Police and peace officers are limited to their definitions in CPL §§ 1.20(34) and 2.10, respectively. Employment decisions about such officers are exempt from the FCA, as

---

31 N.Y.C. Admin. Code § 8-107(11-a)(e).

32 N.Y. Exec. L. § 845-b.

33 *Id.* at 845-b(5)(a).

34 15 U.S.C. § 78c(a)(26).

are decisions about positions in law enforcement agencies exempted under New York Correction Law Article 23-A.[35]

As of the date of this Guidance, the following City agencies are also exempt from the FCA: the New York City Police Department, Fire Department, Department of Correction, Department of Investigation, Department of Probation, the Division of Youth and Community Development, the Business Integrity Commission, and the District Attorneys' offices in each borough.

D. City Positions Designated by the Department of Citywide Administrative Services ("DCAS") as Exempt

This exemption gives the Commissioner of DCAS the discretion to determine that employment decisions about some City positions, not already exempted pursuant to another provision, need not comply with the FCA because the position involves law enforcement; is susceptible to bribery or other corruption; or entails the provision of services to, or the safeguarding of, people vulnerable to abuse.

Once DCAS exempts a position, applicants may be asked about their conviction history at any time during the hiring process. Under this exemption, however, applicants who are denied employment because of their conviction history must receive a written copy of the DCAS's Article 23-A analysis.[36]

VIII. Best Practices for Employers

An employer claiming an exemption must be able to show that the position falls under one of the categories in Section VII of this Guidance. Employers availing themselves of exemptions to the FCA should inform applicants of the exemption they believe applies and keep a record of their use of such exemptions for a period of five (5) years from the date an exemption is used. Keeping an exemption log will help the employer respond to Commission requests for information.

The exemption log should include the following:

- Which exemption(s) is claimed;
- How the position fits into the exemption and, if applicable, the federal, state, or local law or rule allowing the exemption under Sections VII(A) or (B) of this Guidance;
- A copy of any inquiry, as defined by Section V(A) of this Guidance, along with the name of the employee who made it;
- A copy of the employer's Article 23-A analysis and the name of any employees who participated in it; and
- The final employment action that was taken based on the applicant's criminal history.

Employers may be required to share their exemption log with the Commission. Prompt responses to Commission requests may help avoid a Commission-initiated investigation into employment practices.

The Commission recommends that the results of any inquiry into an applicant's criminal history be collected and maintained on separate forms and kept confidential. An applicant's criminal history should not be used, distributed, or disseminated to any persons other than those involved in making an employment decision about an applicant.[37]

---

35 N.Y. Correct. L. § 750(5).

36 N.Y.C. Admin. Code § 8-107(11-a)(f)(2).

37 After hire, the employee's supervisor or manager may also be informed of the applicant's criminal

IX. Enforcement

The Commission will vigorously enforce the FCA. The amount of a civil penalty will be guided by the following factors, among others:

- The severity of the particular violation;

- The existence of additional previous or contemporaneous violations;

- The employer's size, considering both the total number of employees and its revenue; and

- Whether or not the employer knew or should have known about the FCA.

These penalties are in addition to the other remedies available to people who successfully resolve or prevail on claims under the NYCHRL, including, but not limited to, back and front pay, along with compensatory and punitive damages.

The Commission will presume, unless rebutted, that an employer was motivated by an applicant's criminal record if it revokes a conditional offer of employment, as defined in Section II of this Guidance. Consistent with that definition, the Commission will presume that any reason known to the employer before its conditional offer is not a legitimate reason to later withdraw the offer.

X. Criminal Record Discrimination in Obtaining Credit

The FCA additionally prohibits adverse actions regarding credit based on an individual's criminal record. No person can ask about non-convictions in connection with any application or evaluation for credit. Similarly, credit cannot be denied or affected adversely because of an individual's criminal record, unless the person's record is directly related to the extension of credit or otherwise creates an unreasonable risk that the person is not credit-worthy.

XI. Parity of Coverage with the State Human Rights Law

The FCA updates the NYCHRL's prohibition against discrimination based on non-convictions, linking the NYCHRL's protections to the New York State Human Rights Law's ("NYSHRL") protections. The NYCHRL now prohibits the same types of non-conviction discrimination as the NYSHRL. For employment,[38] licensing,[39] and credit[40] purposes, no person may make any inquiry, in writing or otherwise, or deny or take an adverse action against a person based on a non-conviction. Neither the NYCHRL nor the NYSHRL protections apply to firearm licenses and employment as a police or peace officer, nor does either law prohibit basing an employment decision on a pending criminal proceeding.

Parity in coverage does not mean parity in interpretation. While the NYCHRL has the same substantive prohibitions on non-conviction discrimination as the NYSHRL, the NYCHRL must be interpreted independently from state and federal employment discrimination laws, pursuant to the 2005 Civil Rights Restoration Act.

---

38 N.Y.C. Admin. Code § 8-107(11).

39 Id.

40 Id. § 8-107(11-b).

NYC UPDATED 2016 FAIR CHANCE ACT GUIDANCE

NYC Commission on Human Rights

Revised 06/24/2016

NYC Commission on Human Rights
Legal Enforcement Guidance on the
Fair Chance Act, Local Law No. 63 (2015)

6/24The New York City Human Rights Law (the "NYCHRL") prohibits discrimination in employment, public accommodations, and housing. It also prohibits discriminatory harassment and bias-based profiling by law enforcement. The NYCHRL, pursuant to the 2005 Civil Rights Restoration Act, must be construed "independently from similar or identical provisions of New York state or federal statutes," such that "similarly worded provisions of federal and state civil rights laws [are] a floor below which the City's Human Rights law cannot fall, rather than a ceiling above which the local law cannot rise."[1]

The New York City Commission on Human Rights (the "Commission") is the City agency charged with enforcing the NYCHRL. Individuals interested in vindicating their rights under the NYCHRL can choose to file a complaint with the Commission's Law Enforcement Bureau within one (1) year of the discriminatory act or file a complaint in New York State Supreme Court within three (3) years of the discriminatory act. The NYCHRL covers employers with four or more employees.

The Fair Chance Act ("FCA"), effective October 27, 2015, amends the NYCHRL by making it an unlawful discriminatory practice for most employers, labor organizations, and employment agencies to inquire about or consider the criminal history of job applicants until after extending conditional offers of employment. If an employer wishes to withdraw its offer, it must give the applicant a copy of its inquiry into and analysis of the applicant's conviction history, along with at least three business days to respond.

I Legislative Intent

The FCA reflects the City's view that job seekers must be judged on their merits before their mistakes. The FCA is intended to level the playing field so that New Yorkers who are part of the approximately 70 million adults residing in the United States who have been arrested or convicted of a crime[2] "can be considered for a position among other equally qualified candidates," and "not overlooked during the hiring process simply because they have to check a box."[3]

Even though New York Correction Law Article 23-A ("Article 23-A") has long protected people with criminal records from employment discrimination,[4] the City determined that such discrimination still occurred when applicants were asked about their records before completing the hiring process because many employers were

---

[1] Local Law No. 85 (2005). "The provisions of this title shall be construed liberally for the accomplishment of the uniquely broad and remedial purposes thereof, regardless of whether federal or New York State civil and human rights laws, including those laws with provisions comparably worded to provisions of this title have been so construed." N.Y.C. Admin. Code § 8-130.

[2] Gov'tl Affairs Division of the N.Y. City Council, Committee Report on Int. No. 318-A, S. 2015-5, at 2 (June 9, 2015) ("Civil Rights Committee's Report"), *available at* http://legistar.council.nyc.gov/View.ashx?M=F&ID=3815856&GUID=59D912BA-68B5-429C-BF39-118EB4DFAAF5.

[3] Testimony of Gale A. Brewer, Manhattan Borough President on Int. No. 318 to Prohibit Employment Discrimination Based on One's Arrest Record or Criminal Conviction at 2 (Dec. 3, 2014) (emphasis in original), *available at* http://legistar.council.nyc.gov/View.ashx?M=F&ID=3410802&GUID=7D143B7E-C532-41EF-9A97-04FD17854ED7.

[4] Violating Article 23-A is an unlawful discriminatory practice under the NYCHRL. N.Y.C. Admin. Code § 8-107(10).

NYC Commission on Human Rights

not weighing the factors laid out in Article 23-A.[5] For that reason, the FCA prohibits any discussion or consideration of an applicant's criminal history until after a conditional offer of employment. Certain positions are exempt from the FCA, as described in Section VII of this Guidance.

While the FCA does not require employers to hire candidates whose convictions are directly related to a job or pose an unreasonable risk, it ensures that individuals with criminal histories are considered based on their qualifications before their conviction histories. If an employer is interested enough to offer someone a job, it can more carefully consider whether or not that person's criminal history makes her or him unsuitable for the position. If the employer wishes to nevertheless withdraw its offer, it must first give the applicant a meaningful opportunity to respond before finalizing its decision.

II Definitions

The FCA applies to both licensure and employment, although this Guidance focuses on employment. The term **"applicant,"** as used in this Guidance, refers to both potential and current employees. The FCA applies to all decisions that affect the terms and conditions of employment, including hiring, termination, transfers, and promotions; where this Guidance describes the **"hiring process,"** it includes the process for making all of these employment decisions. Any time the FCA or this Guidance requires notices and disclosures to be printed or in writing, they may also be communicated by email, if such method of communication is mutually agreed on in advance by the employer and the applicant.

For the purpose of this Guidance, the following key terms are defined as follows:

Article 23-A Analysis

The evaluation process mandated by New York Correction Law Article 23-A.

Article 23-A Factors

The factors employers must consider concerning applicants' criminal conviction history under Section 753 of New York Correction Law Article 23-A.

Conditional Offer of Employment

An offer of employment that can only be revoked based on:

1. The results of a criminal background check;

2. The results of a medical exam in situations in which such exams are permitted by the Americans with Disabilities Act;[6] or

3. Other information the employer could not have reasonably known before the conditional offer if, based on the information, the employer would not have made the offer and the employer can show the information is material to job performance.

For temporary help firms, a conditional offer is the offer to be placed in a pool of applicants from which the applicant may be sent to temporary positions.

---

[5] Transcript of the Minutes of the Committee on Civil Rights at 10 (Dec. 3, 2014) (statement of Council Member Jumaane Williams), *available at* http://legistar.council.nyc.gov/View.ashx?M=F&ID=3410594&GUID=5FE2433E-1A95-4FAA-AECC-D60D4016F3FB.

[6] The Americans with Disabilities Act ("ADA") prohibits employers from conducting medical exams until after a conditional offer of employment. 42 U.S.C. § 12112(d)(3). To comply with the FCA and the ADA, employers may condition an offer of employment on the results of a criminal background check and then, after the criminal background check, a medical examination.

NYC Commission on Human Rights

Conviction History

A previous conviction of a crime, either a felony or misdemeanor under New York law,[7] or a crime as defined by the law of another state.

Criminal Background Check

When an employer, orally or in writing, either:

1. Asks an applicant whether or not she or he has a criminal record; or

2. Searches public records, including through a third party, such as a consumer reporting agency ("CRA"), for an applicant's criminal history.

Criminal History

A previous record of criminal convictions or non-convictions or a currently pending criminal case.

Fair Chance Process

The post-conditional offer process mandated by the FCA, as outlined in Section V of this Guidance.

Inquiry

Any question, whether made in writing or orally, asked for the purpose of obtaining an applicant's criminal history, including, without limitation, questions in a job interview about an applicant's criminal history; and any search for an applicant's criminal history, including through the services of a third party, such as a consumer reporting agency.

Non-convictions

A criminal action, not currently pending, that was concluded in one of the following ways:

1. Termination in favor of the individual, as defined by New York Criminal Procedure Law ("CPL") § 160.50, even if not sealed;

2. Adjudication as a youthful offender, as defined by CPL § 720.35, even if not sealed;

3. Conviction of a non-criminal violation that has been sealed under CPL § 160.55; or

4. Convictions that have been sealed under CPL § 160.58.

Statement

Any words, whether made in writing or orally, for the purpose of obtaining an applicant's criminal history, including, without limitation, stating that a background check is required for a position.

Temporary Help Firms

A business which recruits, hires, and assigns its own employees to perform work at or services for other organizations, to support or supplement the other organization's workforce, or to provide assistance in special work situations such as, without limitation, employee absences, skill shortages, seasonal workloads, or special assignments or projects.[8]

---

[7] A misdemeanor is an offense, other than a "traffic infraction," for which a person may be incarcerated for more than 15 days and less than one year. N.Y. Pen. L. § 10.00(4). A felony is an offense for which a person may be incarcerated for more than one year. *Id.* § 10.00(5).

[8] N.Y. Lab. L. § 916(5).

NYC Commission on Human Rights

III *Per Se* Violations of the FCA

As of October 27, 2015, the following acts are separate, chargeable violations of the NYCHRL:

1. Declaring, printing, or circulating – or causing the declaration, printing, or circulation of – any solicitation, advertisement, or publication for employment that states any limitation or specification regarding criminal history, *even if no adverse action follows.* This includes, without limitation, advertisements and employment applications containing phrases such as: "no felonies," "background check required," and "must have clean record."[9]

2. Making any statement or inquiry, as defined in Section II of this Guidance, before a conditional offer of employment, *even if no adverse action follows.*

3. Withdrawing a conditional offer of employment based on an applicant's criminal history before completing the Fair Chance Process as outlined in Section V of this Guidance. Each of the following is a separate, chargeable violation of the NYCHRL:

   a) Failing to disclose to the applicant a written copy of any inquiry an employer conducted into the applicant's criminal history;

   b) Failing to share with the applicant a written copy of the employer's Article 23-A analysis;

   c) Failing to hold the prospective position open for at least three business days, from an applicant's receipt of both the inquiry and analysis, to allow the applicant to respond.

4. Taking an adverse employment action because of an applicant's non-conviction.[10]

IV The Criminal Background Check Process Under the FCA

The FCA does not change what criminal history information employers may consider. Instead, it changes when employers may consider this information. No employer may seek, obtain, or base an adverse employment action on a non-conviction.[11] No employer may seek, obtain, or base an adverse employment action on a criminal conviction until after extending a conditional offer of employment. After a conditional offer of employment, an employer can only withdraw the offer after evaluating the applicant under Article 23-A and finding that the applicant's conviction history poses a direct relationship or unreasonable risk.

A. Before a Conditional Offer

The FCA prohibits the discovery and use of criminal history before a conditional offer of employment. During this time, an employer must not seek or obtain an applicant's criminal history. Consistent with Article 23-A, an employer's focus must instead be on an applicant's qualifications.

The following are examples of common hiring practices that are affected by the FCA.

i. *Solicitations, advertisements, and publications for employment cannot mention criminal history.*

---

[9] *See* discussion regarding language that encourages individuals with criminal history to apply *infra* p. 5.

[10] The FCA updates the NYCHRL's protections regarding non-conviction discrimination to match the New York State Human Rights Law. *See* Section XI of this Guidance.

[11] Employers of police and peace officers can consider all non-convictions, except criminal actions terminated in favor of the applicant, as defined by New York Criminal Procedure Law § 160.50. N.Y.C. Admin. Code §§ 8-107(11)(a),(b).

NYC Commission on Human Rights

The FCA now explicitly prohibits employers from expressing any limitation or specification based on criminal history in their job advertisements,[12] even though such advertisements are already illegal under the existing NYCHRL.[13] Ads cannot say, for example, "no felonies," "background check required," or "clean records only." Solicitations, advertisements, and publications encompass a broad variety of items, including, without limitation, employment applications, fliers, handouts, online job postings, and materials distributed at employment fairs and by temporary help firms and job readiness organizations. Employment applications cannot ask whether an applicant has a criminal history or a pending criminal case or authorize a background check.

Solicitations, advertisements, and publications may include language that welcomes people with criminal records, however. For example, solicitations, advertisements, or publications that include language such as "People with criminal histories are encouraged to apply," and "We value diverse experiences, including prior contact with the criminal legal system" are permissible. Stigmatizing language, like "ex-felon" and "former inmate," may not be used.

ii. Employers cannot inquire about criminal history during the interview process.

The FCA prohibits employers from making any inquiry or statement related to an applicant's criminal history until after a conditional offer of employment. Examples of prohibited statements and inquiries include, without limitation:

- Questions, whether written or oral, during a job interview about criminal history;

- Assertions, whether written or oral, that individuals with convictions, or certain convictions, will not be hired or cannot work at the employer; and

- Investigations into the applicant's criminal history, including using public records or the Internet, whether conducted by an employer or for an employer by a third party.

The FCA does not prevent employers from otherwise looking into an applicant's background and experience to verify her or his qualifications for a position, including asking for resumes and references and performing general Internet searches (e.g., Google, LinkedIn, etc.). Searching an applicant's name is legal, but trying to discover an applicant's conviction history is not. In connection with an applicant, employers cannot search for terms such as, "arrest," "mugshot," "warrant," "criminal," "conviction," "jail," or "prison." Nor can employers search websites that contain or purport to contain arrest, warrant, conviction, or incarceration information.

The FCA allows an applicant to refuse to respond to any prohibited inquiry or statement. Such refusal or response to an illegal question shall not disqualify the applicant from the prospective employment.

iii. Inadvertent disclosures of criminal record information before a conditional offer of employment do not create employer liability.

The FCA prohibits any inquiry or statement made for the purpose of obtaining an applicant's criminal history. If a legitimate inquiry not made for that purpose leads an applicant to reveal criminal history, the employer should continue its hiring process. It may not examine the applicant's conviction history information until after deciding whether or not to make a conditional offer of employment.

---

[12] Id. § 8-107(11-a)(a)(1).

[13] Advertisements excluding people who have been arrested violate the NYCHRL's complete ban on employment decisions based on an arrest that did not lead to a criminal conviction. Id. § 8-107(11). Employers whose advertisements exclude people with criminal convictions are not engaging in the individual analysis required by Article 23-A. Id. § 8-107(10).

NYC Commission on Human Rights

If the applicant raises her or his criminal record voluntarily, the employer should not use that as an opportunity to explore an applicant's criminal history further. The employer should state that, by law, it will only consider the applicant's record if it decides to offer her or him a job. Similarly, if an applicant asks an employer during the interview if she or he will be subject to a criminal background check, the employer may state that a criminal background check will be conducted only after a conditional offer of employment. It must then move the conversation to a different topic. Employers who make a good faith effort to exclude information regarding criminal history before extending a conditional offer of employment will not be liable under the FCA.

B. After the Conditional Offer of Employment

After extending a conditional offer of employment, as defined in Section II of this Guidance, an employer may make the same inquiries into, and statements about, an applicant's criminal history as before the FCA became effective. An employer may:

- Ask, either orally or in writing, whether an applicant has a criminal conviction history or a pending criminal case;

- Run a background check itself or, after giving the applicant notice and getting her or his permission, use a consumer reporting agency to do so;[14] and

- Once an employer knows about an applicant's conviction, ask her or him about the circumstances that led to it and begin to gather information relevant to every Article 23-A factor.

Employers must never inquire about or act on non-conviction information, however. To guard against soliciting or considering non-conviction information, employers may frame inquiries by using the following language after a conditional offer is made:

> Have you ever been convicted of a misdemeanor or felony? Answer "NO" if your conviction: (a) was sealed, expunged, or reversed on appeal; (b) was for a violation, infraction, or other petty offense such as "disorderly conduct;" (c) resulted in a youthful offender or juvenile delinquency finding; or (d) if you withdrew your plea after completing a court program and were not convicted of a misdemeanor or felony.

If an employer hires an applicant after learning about her or his conviction history, the FCA does not require it to do anything more. An employer that wants to withdraw its conditional offer of employment, however, must first consider the Article 23-A factors. If, after doing so, an employer still wants to withdraw its conditional offer, it must follow the Fair Chance Process.

C. Evaluating the Applicant Using Article 23-A

Under Article 23-A, an employer cannot deny employment unless it can:

1. Draw a direct relationship between the applicant's criminal record and the prospective job; or

2. Show that employing the applicant "would involve an unreasonable risk to property or to the safety or welfare of specific individuals or the general public."[15]

An employer that cannot show the applicant meets at least one of the exceptions to Article 23-A cannot withdraw the conditional offer because of the applicant's criminal record.

---

[14] The consumer report cannot contain credit information. Under the Stop Credit Discrimination in Employment Act, employers, labor organizations, and employment agencies cannot request or use the consumer credit history of an applicant or employee for the purpose of making any employment decisions, including hiring, compensation, and other terms and conditions of employment. *Id.* §§ 8-102(29); 8-107(24).

[15] N.Y. Correct. L. § 752.

NYC Commission on Human Rights

An employer cannot simply presume a direct relationship or unreasonable risk exists because the applicant has a conviction record.[16] The employer must evaluate the Article 23-A factors using the applicant's specific information before reaching either conclusion.

- To claim the direct relationship exception, an employer must first draw some connection between the nature of conduct that led to the conviction(s) and the potential position. If a direct relationship exists, an employer must evaluate the Article 23-A factors to determine whether the concerns presented by the relationship have been mitigated.[17]

- To claim the unreasonable risk exception, an employer must begin by assuming that no risk exists and then show how the Article 23-A factors combine to create an unreasonable risk.[18] Otherwise, this exception would cover all convictions not directly related.

The Article 23-A factors are:

- That New York public policy encourages the licensure and employment of people with criminal records;

- The specific duties and responsibilities of the prospective job;

- The bearing, if any, of the person's conviction history on her or his fitness or ability to perform one or more of the job's duties or responsibilities;

- The time that has elapsed since the occurrence of the events that led to the applicant's criminal conviction, not the time since arrest or conviction;

- The age of the applicant when the events that led to her or his conviction occurred, not the time since arrest or conviction;

- The seriousness of the applicant's conviction history;[19]

- Any information produced by the applicant, or produced on the applicant's behalf, regarding her or his rehabilitation or good conduct;

- The legitimate interest of the employer in protecting property and the safety and welfare of specific individuals or the general public.

Employers must also consider a certificate of relief from disabilities or a certificate of good conduct, which shall create a presumption of rehabilitation regarding the relevant conviction.[20]

Employers must carefully conduct the Article 23-A analysis. Before extending a conditional offer of employment, employers must define the job's duties and responsibilities, as required by Article 23-A. Employers cannot alter the job's duties and responsibilities after making a conditional offer of employment. Once an employer extends a conditional offer and learns of an applicant's criminal record, it must solicit the information necessary to properly consider each Article 23-A factor, including the applicant's evidence of rehabilitation.

The Commission will review private employers' adverse employment decisions to ensure that they correctly consider the Article 23-A factors and properly apply the exceptions. The Commission will begin with the

---

[16] *Bonacorsa v. Van Lindt,* 71 N.Y.2d 605, 613-14 (N.Y. 1988).

[17] *Id.* at 613-14; *see Soto v. N.Y. State Office of Mental Retardation & Developmental Disabilities,* 907 N.Y.S.2d 104, 26 Misc. 3d 1215(A) at *9 (N.Y. Sup. Ct. 2010) (citing *Marra v. City of White Plains,* 467 N.Y.S.2d 865, 870 (N.Y. App. Div. 1983)).

[18] *Bonacorsa,* 71 N.Y.2d at 613; *Exum v. N.Y. City Health & Hosps. Corp.,* 964 N.Y.S.2d 58, 37 Misc. 3d 1218(A) at *6 (N.Y. Sup. Ct. 2012)

[19] Employers may judge the seriousness of an applicant's criminal record based on the number of felony and misdemeanor convictions, along with whether the acts underlying those convictions involved violence or theft.

[20] N.Y. Correct. L. § 753(2). An employer may not disfavor an applicant because she or he does not possess a certificate.

NYC Commission on Human Rights

purpose of Article 23-A: to create "a fair opportunity for a job is a matter of basic human fairness," one that should not be "frustrated by senseless discrimination."[21] The Commission will also consider Article 23-A case law.[22] Employers must evaluate each Article 23-A factor; they cannot ignore evidence favorable to the applicant;[23] and they cannot disproportionately weigh any one factor over another.[24] Employers should consider applicants' successful performance of their job duties in past employment, along with evidence that they have addressed the causes of their criminal activity.[25]

V The Fair Chance Process

If, after evaluating the applicant according to Article 23-A, an employer wishes to decline employment because a direct relationship or unreasonable risk exists, it must follow the Fair Chance Process:

1. Disclose to the applicant a written copy of any inquiry it conducted into the applicant's criminal history;

2. Share with the applicant a written copy of its Article 23-A analysis; and

3. Allow the applicant at least three business days, from receipt of the inquiry and analysis, to respond to the employer's concerns.

A. Disclosing the Inquiry

The Commission requires an employer to disclose a complete and accurate copy of every piece of information it relied on to determine that an applicant has a criminal record, along with the date and time the employer accessed the information. The applicant must be able to see and challenge the same criminal history information relied on by the employer.

Employers who hire consumer reporting agencies to conduct background checks can fulfill this obligation by supplying a copy of the CRA's report on the applicant.[26] Because CRAs can be held liable for aiding and abetting discrimination under the NYCHRL, they should ensure that their customers only request criminal background reports after a conditional offer of employment. Employers who rely on criminal record information beyond what is contained in a criminal background report must also give that information to the applicant.

Employers who search the Internet to obtain criminal histories must print out the pages they relied on, and such printouts must identify their source so that the applicant can verify them. Employers who check public records must provide copies of those records. Employers who rely on oral information must provide a written summary of their conversation. The summary must contain the same information the employer relied on in reaching its determination, and it should identity whether that information was provided by the applicant.

B. Sharing the Fair Chance Notice

The FCA directs the Commission to determine the manner in which employers inform applicants under Article 23-A and provide a written copy of that analysis to applicants.[27] The Commission has prepared a Fair

---

[21] Governor's Approval Mem., Bill Jacket, L. 1976, ch. 931.

[22] Nearly all reported cases concern public agencies' employment decisions, which cannot be reversed unless "arbitrary and capricious." N.Y. Correct. L. § 755; see C.P.L.R. § 7803(3). The "arbitrary and capricious" standard does not apply to private employers.

[23] Gallo v. N.Y. State Office of Mental Retardation & Developmental Disabilities, 830 N.Y.S.2d 796, 798 (N.Y. App. Div. 2007).

[24] Soto, 26 Misc. 3d 1215(A) at *7.

[25] Odems v. N.Y.C. Dep't of Educ., No. 400637/09 at *4, 2009 WL 5225201, at *5, 2009 N.Y. Misc. LEXIS 6480, at *5 (N.Y. Sup. Ct. Dec. 16, 2009); El v. N.Y.C. Dep't of Educ., 23 Misc.3d 1121(A), at *4-5 (N.Y. Sup. Ct. 2009).

[26] 15 U.S.C. § 1681d; N.Y. Gen. Bus. L. § 380-b(b).

[27] N.Y.C. Admin. Code § 8-107(11-a)(b)(ii).

NYC Commission on Human Rights

Chance Notice (the "Notice")[28] that employers may use to comply with this requirement. As long as the material substance – considering specific facts in the Article 23-A analysis – does not change, the Notice may be adapted to an employer's preferred format.

The Notice requires employers to evaluate each Article 23-A factor and choose which exception – direct relationship or unreasonable risk – the employer relies on. The Notice also contains space for the employer to articulate its conclusion.[29] Boilerplate denials that simply list the Article 23-A factors violate the FCA. For example, an employer cannot simply say it considered the time since conviction; it must identify the years and/or months since the conviction. An employer also cannot list specific facts for each factor but then fail to describe how it concluded that the applicant's record met either the direct relationship or unreasonable risk exceptions to Article 23-A.

Finally, the Notice informs the applicant of her or his time to respond and requests evidence of rehabilitation and good conduct. The Notice provides examples of such information. Employers may identify specific examples of rehabilitation and good conduct that would be most relevant to the prospective position, but examples must be included.

C. Allowing Time to Respond

Employers must give applicants a reasonable time, which shall be no less than three business days, to respond to the employer's inquiry and Notice. During this time, the employer may not permanently place another person in the applicant's prospective position. This time period begins running when an applicant receives both the inquiry and Notice. Employers may therefore wish to confirm receipt, either by disclosing the information in person, electronically, or by registered mail. Such method of communication must be mutually agreed on in advance by the applicant and employer. Otherwise, the Commission will credit an applicant's recollection as to when she or he received the inquiry and Notice.

By giving an applicant at least three business days to respond, the FCA contemplates a process in which employers discuss their reasons for finding that an applicant's record poses a direct relationship or unreasonable risk. The process allows an applicant to respond either orally or in writing and provide additional information relevant to any of the Article 23-A factors.[30] After receiving additional information from an applicant, an employer must examine whether it changes its Article 23-A analysis. Employers may offer an applicant a similar position that mitigates the employer's concerns. If, after communicating with an applicant, the employer decides not to hire her or him, it must relay that decision to the applicant.

The three-day time period to respond also provides an opportunity for the applicant to address any errors on the employer's background report, including any discrepancies between the convictions she or he disclosed and the results of the background check. As detailed below, a discrepancy could be due to an error on the report or an applicant's intentional misrepresentation.

i. Handling Errors in the Background Check

An error on a background check might occur because, for example, it contains information that pertains to another person or is outdated. If an applicant is able to demonstrate an error on the background report, the employer must conduct the Article 23-A analysis based on the corrected conviction history information to ensure its decision is not tainted by the previous error. If the employer then finds a direct relationship or unreasonable risk and intends to take an adverse action on that basis, it must follow the Fair Chance Process: the applicant

---

[28] The Notice is available on the Commission's website, http://www.nyc.gov/FairChanceNYC.

[29] N.Y. Correct. L. § 753(1)(h).

[30] N.Y.C. Admin. Code § 8-107(11-a)(b).

NYC Commission on Human Rights

must be given a copy of the corrected inquiry, the employer's Article 23-A analysis, at least three business days to respond, with an opportunity to provide any additional information for the employer to review and re-examine its analysis.

ii. Handling Applicants' Misrepresentations of Their Conviction Histories

If an applicant cannot or does not demonstrate that any discrepancy between the information she or he disclosed and the employer's background report is due to an error, the employer can choose not to hire the individual based on the applicant's misrepresentation. It need not evaluate the applicant's record under Article 23-A.

VI Temporary Help Firms Under the Fair Chance Act

Temporary help firms employ individuals, either as direct or joint employers, and place them in job assignments at the firms' clients. The FCA applies the same way to temporary help firms as it does to any other employer. The only difference is that, for these firms, a conditional offer of employment is an offer to place an applicant in the firm's labor pool, from which the applicant may be sent on job assignments to the firm's clients. Before a temporary help firm withdraws a conditional offer of employment after discovering an applicant's conviction history, it must follow the Fair Chance Process, according to Section V of this Guidance. To evaluate the job duties, a temporary help firm may only consider the basic skills necessary to be placed in its applicant pool.

Employers who accept placements from temporary help firms, and who wish to inquire about temporary workers' criminal histories, must follow the Fair Chance Act. They may not make any statements or inquiries about an applicant's criminal record until after the worker is assigned to the employer, and they must follow the Fair Chance Process if they wish to decline employment because of an applicant's criminal record.

As with any other type of discrimination, temporary help firms will be liable if they aid and abet an employer's discriminatory hiring preferences. For example, a temporary help firm cannot, based on an employer's instructions, refer only temporary workers who do not have criminal histories or who have "less serious" criminal histories.

VII Positions Exempt from the FCA

Consistent with the Local Civil Rights Restoration Act of 2005,[31] all exemptions to coverage under the FCA's anti-discrimination provisions are to be construed narrowly. Employers may assert the application of an exemption to defend against liability, and they have the burden of proving the exemption by a preponderance of the evidence. Other than the employers described in Subsections C and D of this Section, the Commission does not assume that an entire employer or industry is exempt and will
investigate how an exemption applies to a particular position or role. Positions that are exempt from the FCA are not necessarily exempt from Article 23-A.

A. Employers hiring for positions where federal, state, or local law requires criminal background checks or bars employment based on certain criminal convictions

The FCA does not apply to the actions of employers or their agents that are taken pursuant to any state, federal, or local law that requires criminal background checks for employment purposes or bars employment

---

[31] N.Y.C. Local Law No. 85 (2005); N.Y.C. Admin. Code § 8-130.

NYC Commission on Human Rights

based on criminal history.[32] The purpose of this exemption is to not delay a criminal background inquiry when the results of that inquiry might legally prohibit an employer from hiring an applicant.

A network of federal, state, and local laws creates employment barriers for people with criminal records. The Commission characterizes these barriers as either mandatory or discretionary. Mandatory barriers require a licensing authority or employer to deny applicants with certain convictions enumerated in law. Discretionary barriers allow, but do not require, a licensing authority or employer to deny applicants with criminal records, and may or may not enumerate disqualifying convictions. The FCA controls any time an employer's decision is discretionary, meaning it is not explicitly mandated by law.

For example, state law contains mandatory barriers for – and requires background checks of – applicants to employers regulated by the state Department of Health ("DOH"), Office of Mental Health ("OMH"), and Office of People with Developmental Disabilities ("OPWDD").[33] These agencies require the employers they regulate to conduct background checks because the agencies are charged by state law to ensure that individuals with certain convictions are not hired to work with vulnerable people.[34] Employers regulated by DOH, OMH, and OPWDD are therefore exempt from the FCA when hiring for positions where a criminal history check is required by law. For positions that do not require a criminal history check, however, such employers have to follow the FCA.

The FCA applies when an employer hires people who require licensure, or approval by a government agency, even if the license has mandatory barriers. In that case, an employer can only ask whether an applicant has the required license or can obtain one within an acceptable period of time. Any inquiry into the applicant's criminal record – before a conditional offer of employment – is not allowed. An applicant who has a license has already passed any criminal record barriers and been approved by a government agency. An applicant who cannot, because of her or his conviction record, obtain a required license may have her or his conditional offer withdrawn or employment terminated for such legitimate nondiscriminatory reason.

B. Employers Required by a Self-Regulatory Organization to Conduct a Criminal Background Check of Regulated Persons

Employers in the financial services industry are exempt from the FCA when complying with industry-specific rules and regulations promulgated by a self-regulatory organization ("SRO").[35] This exemption only applies to those positions regulated by SROs; employment decisions regarding other positions must still comply with the FCA.

C. Police and Peace Officers, Law Enforcement Agencies, and Other Exempted City Agencies

Police and peace officers are limited to their definitions in CPL §§ 1.20(34) and 2.10, respectively. Employment decisions about such officers are exempt from the FCA, as are decisions about positions in law enforcement agencies exempted under New York Correction Law Article 23-A.[36]

As of the date of this Guidance, the following City agencies are also exempt from the FCA: the New York City Police Department, Fire Department, Department of Correction, Department of Investigation, Department of Probation, the Division of Youth and Community Development, the Business Integrity Commission, and the District Attorneys' offices in each borough.

---

[32] N.Y.C. Admin. Code § 8-107(11-a)(e).

[33] N.Y. Exec. L. § 845-b.

[34] Id. at 845-b(5)(a).

[35] 15 U.S.C. § 78c(a)(26).

[36] N.Y. Correct. L. § 750(5).

NYC Commission on Human Rights

D. City Positions Designated by the Department of Citywide Administrative Services ("DCAS") as Exempt

This exemption gives the Commissioner of DCAS the discretion to determine that employment decisions about some City positions, not already exempted pursuant to another provision, need not comply with the FCA because the position involves law enforcement; is susceptible to bribery or other corruption; or entails the provision of services to, or the safeguarding of, people vulnerable to abuse.

Once DCAS exempts a position, applicants may be asked about their conviction history at any time during the hiring process. Under this exemption, however, applicants who are denied employment because of their conviction history must receive a written copy of the DCAS's Article 23-A analysis.[37]

VIII Best Practices for Employers

An employer claiming an exemption must be able to show that the position falls under one of the categories in Section VII of this Guidance. Employers availing themselves of exemptions to the FCA should inform applicants of the exemption they believe applies and keep a record of their use of such exemptions for a period of five (5) years from the date an exemption is used. Keeping an exemption log will help the employer respond to Commission requests for information.

The exemption log should include the following:

- Which exemption(s) is claimed;

- How the position fits into the exemption and, if applicable, the federal, state, or local law or rule allowing the exemption under Sections VII(A) or (B) of this Guidance;

- A copy of any inquiry, as defined by Section V(A) of this Guidance, along with the name of the employee who made it;

- A copy of the employer's Article 23-A analysis and the name of any employees who participated in it; and

- The final employment action that was taken based on the applicant's criminal history.

Employers may be required to share their exemption log with the Commission. Prompt responses to Commission requests may help avoid a Commission-initiated investigation into employment practices.

The Commission recommends that the results of any inquiry into an applicant's criminal history be collected and maintained on separate forms and kept confidential. An applicant's criminal history should not be used, distributed, or disseminated to any persons other than those involved in making an employment decision about an applicant.[38]

IX Enforcement

The Commission will vigorously enforce the FCA. The amount of a civil penalty will be guided by the following factors, among others:

- The severity of the particular violation;

- The existence of additional previous or contemporaneous violations;

---

[37] N.Y.C. Admin. Code § 8-107(11-a)(f)(2).

[38] After hire, the employee's supervisor or manager may also be informed of the applicant's criminal record.

NYC Commission on Human Rights

- The employer's size, considering both the total number of employees and its revenue; and

- Whether or not the employer knew or should have known about the FCA.

These penalties are in addition to the other remedies available to people who successfully resolve or prevail on claims under the NYCHRL, including, but not limited to, back and front pay, along with compensatory and punitive damages.

The Commission will presume, unless rebutted, that an employer was motivated by an applicant's criminal record if it revokes a conditional offer of employment, as defined in Section II of this Guidance. Consistent with that definition, the Commission will presume that any reason known to the employer before its conditional offer is not a legitimate reason to later withdraw the offer.

X Criminal Record Discrimination in Obtaining Credit

The FCA additionally prohibits inquiries and adverse actions based on non-convictions when a person is seeking credit.

FCA SAMPLE COMPLAINT APPLICATION

CITY OF NEW YORK
COMMISSION ON HUMAN RIGHTS
In the Matter of the Complaint of:

COMPLAINANT (INSERT NAME)   Complaint No.:

                Complainant,

    - against –   **Verified Complaint**

RESPONDENT, (INSERT EMPLOYER)

                Respondent.

COMPLAINANT, complaining of Respondent, alleges as follows:

1. Complainant is a New York resident who has been previously convicted of one or more criminal offenses. His address is _____.

2. Respondent EMPLOYER employs four (4) or more individuals and is an employer as defined by Section 8-102 of the Administrative Code of the City of New York ("Code"). Its address for service of process is ADDRESS.

3. On or around DATE, Complainant obtained an application for employment at Respondent ("Respondent's Application"), and the application stated "ILLEGAL LANGUAGE." A copy of Respondent's Application is attached as Exhibit A.

4. Complainant charges that Respondent's Application expresses, directly or indirectly, a limitation or specification based on arrest or criminal conviction in violation of Section 8-107(11-a)(a)(1) of the Code.

5. Complainant charges that Respondent's Application contains an inquiry or statement related to Complainant's arrest or conviction record in violation of Section 8-107(11-a)(a)(2) of the Code.

Complainant being duly sworn, deposes and says: that I am the Complainant herein; I have read (or had read to me) the foregoing complaint and know the content thereof; that the same is true of my own knowledge except as to the matters therein stated on information and belief; and that as to those matters, I believe the same to be true.

_____
Complainant

Subscribed and sworn to me before this _____ day of_____, 20___

_____
Notary Public

FCA SAMPLE COMPLAINT ADVERTISEMENT

CITY OF NEW YORK
COMMISSION ON HUMAN RIGHTS
In the Matter of the Complaint of:

COMPLAINANT, (INSERT YOUR NAME)

Complaint No.:

Complainant,

Verified Complaint

- against –

RESPONDENT, (INSERT EMPLOYER)

Respondent.

Complainant, complaining of Respondent, alleges as follows:

1. Complainant is a New York resident who has been previously convicted of one or more criminal offenses. His address is _____

2. Respondent EMPLOYER ("SHORT NAME") employs four (4) or more individuals and is an employer as defined by Section 8-102 of the Code. Its address for service of process is ADDRESS.

3. On or around DATE, Respondent posted on the internet at WEBSITE an advertisement stating "ILLEGAL LANGUAGE." A copy of the ad is attached as Exhibit A.

4. Complainant charges that Respondent caused to be circulated an advertisement for employment that expresses, directly or indirectly, a limitation or specification based on arrest or criminal conviction in violation of Section 8-107(11-a)(a)(1) of the Code.

Complainant, being duly sworn, deposes and says: that I am the Complainant herein; I have read (or had read to me) the foregoing complaint and know the content thereof; that the same is true of my own knowledge except as to the matters therein stated on information and belief; and that as to those matters, I believe the same to be true.

_____
COMPLAINANT

Subscribed and sworn to me before this _____ day of_____, 20__

_____
Notary Public

NYC STOP CREDIT DISCRIMINATION & EMPLOYMENT ACT GUIDANCE

NYC COMMISSION ON HUMAN RIGHTS
Legal Enforcement Guidance on the
Stop Credit Discrimination in Employment Act,
N.Y.C. Admin. Code §§ 8-102(29), 8-107(9)(d), (24);
Local Law No. 37 (2015)

The New York City Human Rights Law (hereinafter the "NYCHRL") prohibits discrimination in employment, public accommodations, and housing. It also prohibits discriminatory harassment and bias-based policing by law enforcement. The NYCHRL, pursuant to the 2005 Civil Rights Restoration Act, must be construed "independently from similar or identical provisions of New York state or federal statutes," such that "similarly worded provisions of federal and state civil rights laws [are] a floor below which the City's Human Rights law cannot fall, rather than a ceiling above which the local law cannot rise."[1]

The New York City Commission on Human Rights (the "Commission") is the City agency charged with enforcing the NYCHRL. Individuals interested in vindicating their rights under the NYCHRL can choose to file a complaint with the Commission's Law Enforcement Bureau within one (1) year of the discriminatory act or file a complaint at New York State Supreme Court within three (3) years of the discriminatory act. The NYCHRL covers employers with four or more employees.

The Stop Credit Discrimination in Employment Act ("SCDEA"), which goes into effect on September 3, 2015, amends the NYCHRL by making it an unlawful discriminatory practice for employers, labor organizations, and employment agencies to request or use the consumer credit history of an applicant or employee for the purpose of making any employment decisions, including hiring, compensation, and other terms and conditions of employment. N.Y.C. Admin. Code §§ 8-102(29), 8-107(24). The SCDEA also makes it an unlawful discriminatory practice for a City agency to request or use, for licensing or permitting purposes, information contained in the consumer credit history of an applicant, licensee or permittee. *Id.* at § 8-107(9)(d)(1). As of September 3, 2015, this document serves as the Commission's interpretative enforcement guidance of the SCDEA's protections.[2]

I. LEGISLATIVE INTENT

The SCDEA reflects the City's view that consumer credit history is rarely relevant to employment decisions, and consumer reports should not be requested for individuals seeking most positions in New York City. In enacting the SCDEA, the City Council intended for it to "be the strongest bill of its type in the country prohibiting discriminatory employment credit checks."[3]

The SCDEA is intended to stop employers from using consumer credit history when making employment decisions—a practice that has a disproportionately negative effect on unemployed people, low income communities, communities of color, women, domestic violence survivors, families with children, divorced individuals, and

---

1 *Local Law No. 85 (2005); see also N.Y.C. Admin. Code § 8-130 ("The provisions of this title shall be construed liberally for the accomplishment of the uniquely broad and remedial purposes thereof, regardless of whether federal or New York State civil and human rights laws, including those laws with provisions comparably-worded to provisions of this title have been so construed.").*

2 *The Commission does not have jurisdiction to enforce federal and state fair credit reporting laws, which require employers to give applicants notice and get their permission before obtaining a consumer report about them. 15 U.S.C. § 1681d; N.Y. Gen. Bus. L. § 380-b(b).*

3 *Council Member Brad S. Lander, Hearing Transcript of the New York City Council Stated Meeting, 63 (Apr. 16, 2015), available at http://legistar.council.nyc.gov/Legislation.aspx (last accessed Aug. 12, 2015).*

NYC COMMISSION ON HUMAN RIGHTS
Legal Enforcement Guidance on the
Stop Credit Discrimination in Employment Act,
N.Y.C. Admin. Code §§ 8-102(29), 8-107(9)(d), (24);
Local Law No. 37 (2015)

The New York City Human Rights Law (hereinafter the "NYCHRL") prohibits discrimination in employment, public accommodations, and housing. It also prohibits discriminatory harassment and bias-based policing by law enforcement. The NYCHRL, pursuant to the 2005 Civil Rights Restoration Act, must be construed "independently from similar or identical provisions of New York state or federal statutes," such that "similarly worded provisions of federal and state civil rights laws [are] a floor below which the City's Human Rights law cannot fall, rather than a ceiling above which the local law cannot rise."[1]

The New York City Commission on Human Rights (the "Commission") is the City agency charged with enforcing the NYCHRL. Individuals interested in vindicating their rights under the NYCHRL can choose to file a complaint with the Commission's Law Enforcement Bureau within one (1) year of the discriminatory act or file a complaint at New York State Supreme Court within three (3) years of the discriminatory act. The NYCHRL covers employers with four or more employees.

The Stop Credit Discrimination in Employment Act ("SCDEA"), which goes into effect on September 3, 2015, amends the NYCHRL by making it an unlawful discriminatory practice for employers, labor organizations, and employment agencies to request or use the consumer credit history of an applicant or employee for the purpose of making any employment decisions, including hiring, compensation, and other terms and conditions of employment. N.Y.C. Admin. Code §§ 8-102(29), 8-107(24). The SCDEA also makes it an unlawful discriminatory practice for a City agency to request or use, for licensing or permitting purposes, information contained in the consumer credit history of an applicant, licensee or permittee. Id. at § 8-107(9)(d)(1). As of September 3, 2015, this document serves as the Commission's interpretative enforcement guidance of the SCDEA's protections.[2]

I. LEGISLATIVE INTENT

The SCDEA reflects the City's view that consumer credit history is rarely relevant to employment decisions, and consumer reports should not be requested for individuals seeking most positions in New York City. In enacting the SCDEA, the City Council intended for it to "be the strongest bill of its type in the country prohibiting discriminatory employment credit checks."[3]

The SCDEA is intended to stop employers from using consumer credit history when making employment decisions—a practice that has a disproportionately negative effect on unemployed people, low income communities, communities of color, women, domestic violence survivors, families with children, divorced individuals, and

---

1 Local Law No. 85 (2005); see also N.Y.C. Admin. Code § 8-130 ("The provisions of this title shall be construed liberally for the accomplishment of the uniquely broad and remedial purposes thereof, regardless of whether federal or New York State civil and human rights laws, including those laws with provisions comparably-worded to provisions of this title have been so construed.").

2 The Commission does not have jurisdiction to enforce federal and state fair credit reporting laws, which require employers to give applicants notice and get their permission before obtaining a consumer report about them. 15 U.S.C. § 1681d; N.Y. Gen. Bus. L. § 380-b(b).

3 Council Member Brad S. Lander, Hearing Transcript of the New York City Council Stated Meeting, 63 (Apr. 16, 2015), available at http://legistar.council.nyc.gov/Legislation.aspx (last accessed Aug. 12, 2015).

those with student loans and/or medical bills. The City Council noted that multiple studies have failed to demonstrate any correlation between individuals' credit history and their job performance.[4]

II. Definitions

The SCDEA defines *"consumer credit history"* to mean an individual's "credit worthiness, credit standing, credit capacity, or payment history, as indicated by:

(a) a consumer credit report;

(b) credit score; or

(c) information an employer obtains directly from the individual regarding

1. details about credit accounts, including the individual's number of credit accounts, late or missed payments, charged-off debts, items in collections, credit limit, prior credit report inquiries, or

2. bankruptcies, judgments or liens." N.Y.C. Admin. Code § 8-102(29).

Under the SCDEA, a *consumer credit report* includes "any written or other communication of any information by a consumer reporting agency that bears on a consumer's creditworthiness, credit standing, credit capacity or credit history." *Id.* Companies that provide reports containing information about people's payment history to creditors, the amount of people's credit and credit consumption, and information from debt buyers and collectors are considered consumer reporting agencies for purposes of the SCDEA, though the definition of a "consumer reporting agency" is not confined to such companies. *"Consumer reporting agency"* includes any person or entity that, for monetary fees, dues, or on a cooperative nonprofit basis, engages in whole or in part in the practice of assembling or evaluating consumer credit information or other information on consumers for the purpose of furnishing consumer reports or investigative consumer reports to third parties. Note that, unlike the definition of a "consumer reporting agency" under the New York State Fair Credit Reporting Act ("FCRA"), a person need not *regularly* engage in assembling or evaluating consumer credit history in order to be a "consumer reporting agency" under the SCDEA.

III. Violations of the SCDEA

After September 2, 2015, the following acts will be separate chargeable violations of the NYCHRL:

1. Requesting consumer credit history from job applicants or potential or current employees, either orally or in writing;

2. Requesting or obtaining consumer credit history of a job applicant or potential or current employee from a consumer reporting agency; and

3. Using consumer credit history in an employment decision or when considering an employment action.

All of the above are unlawful discriminatory practices, even if such practices do not lead to an adverse employment action. Whether or not an adverse employment action occurred as a result of considering credit history can be considered when determining damages or penalties, but is not relevant for finding liability.

The SCDEA does not prevent employers from researching potential employees' background and experience, evaluating their résumés and references, and conducting online searches (e.g., Google and LinkedIn).

---

4 *Report of the Governmental Affairs Division, Committee on Civil Rights, 4 (April 14, 2015) (available through http://legistar.council.nyc.gov/Legislation.aspx, last accessed Aug. 28, 2015).*

IV. Positions that are Exempted from the SCDEA's Anti-discrimination Provisions

Consistent with the broad scope of the NYCHRL, all exemptions to coverage under the SCDEA's anti-discrimination provisions are to be construed narrowly. Employers may claim an exemption to defend against liability, and they have the burden of proving the exemption by a preponderance of the evidence. No exemption applies to an entire employer or industry. Exemptions apply to positions or roles, not individual applicants or employees.

A. Employers Required by State or Federal Law or Regulations or by a Self-Regulatory Organization to Use an Individual's Consumer Credit History for Employment Purposes.

Employers in the financial services industry are exempt from the SCDEA when complying with industry-specific rules and regulations promulgated by a self-regulatory organization ("SRO"). This exemption only applies to those positions regulated by SROs; employment decisions regarding other positions must still comply with the SCDEA.

As of the date of this interpretive guidance, the only New York law requiring the evaluation of a current or potential employee's consumer credit history applies to licensed mortgage loan originators. N.Y. Bank. L. § 559-d(9). This law was enacted to comply with the requirements of the federal SAFE Mortgage Licensing Act of 2008. 12 U.S.C. § 5104(a)(2)(A).

B. Police officers, peace officers, or positions with a law enforcement or investigative function at the Department of Investigation ("DOI").

Police and peace officers are limited to their definitions in New York Criminal Procedure Law §§ 1.20(34) and 2.10, respectively. The SCDEA's anti-discrimination provisions still apply when making employment decisions about civilian positions; only positions for police or peace officers are exempt from the SCDEA.

The DOI has several positions that do not serve investigative functions. Certain operations and communications positions are examples of positions to which the SCDEA's anti-discrimination provisions still apply.

C. Positions subject to a DOI background investigation.

For certain positions with the City of New York, the DOI conducts background checks that involve collecting consumer credit history from the job applicant. The DOI may provide some of the information collected from the background check to the City agency interviewing or hiring the job applicant. Under the SCDEA, City agencies may not request or use consumer credit history collected by the DOI in making employment decisions unless:

1. The position is appointed; and

2. The position requires a high degree of public trust.

The Commission currently defines only the following positions as involving a **high degree of public trust:**

- Commissioner titles, including Assistant, Associate, and Deputy Commissioners;

- Counsel titles, including General Counsel, Special Counsel, Deputy General Counsel, and Assistant General Counsel, that involve high-level decision-making authority;

- Chief Information Officer and Chief Technology Officer titles; and

- Any position reporting to directly to an agency head.

D. Positions requiring bonding under federal, state, or City law or regulation.

In order for this exemption to apply, the specific position must be required to be bonded under City, state, or federal law, and bonding must be legally required, not simply permitted, by statute. For example, the following positions must be bonded: Bonded Carriers for U.S. Customs, 19 C.F.R. § 112.23; Harbor Pilot, N.Y. Nav. L. § 93; Pawnbrokers, N.Y. Gen. Bus. L. § 41; Ticket Sellers & Resellers, N.Y. Arts & Cult. Aff. L. §§ 25.15, 25.07; Auctioneers, N.Y. City Admin. Code § 20-279; and Tow Truck Drivers, § 20-499.

E. Positions requiring security clearance under federal or state law.

This exception only applies when the review of consumer credit history will be done by the federal or state government as part of evaluating a person for security clearance, and that security clearance is legally required for the person to fulfill the job duties. Having "security clearance" means the ability to access classified information, and does not include any other vetting process utilized by a government agency.

F. Non-clerical positions having regular access to trade secrets, intelligence information, or national security information.

The SCDEA defines *"trade secrets"* as "information that:

(a) Derives independent economic value, actual or potential, from not being generally known to, and not being readily ascertainable by proper means, by other persons who can obtain economic value from its disclosure or use;

(b) Is the subject of efforts that are reasonable under the circumstances to maintain its secrecy; and

(c) Can reasonably be said to be the end product of significant innovation."

The SCDEA limits the trade secret definition to exclude "general proprietary company information such as handbooks and policies" and "access to or the use of client, customer, or mailing lists."

Consistent with this definition and the broad scope of the NYCHRL, "trade secrets" do not include information such as recipes, formulas, customer lists, processes, and other information regularly collected in the course of business or regularly used by entry-level and non-salaried employees and supervisors or managers of such employees.

The SCDEA defines *"intelligence information"* as "records and data compiled for the purpose of criminal investigation or counterterrorism, including records and data relating to the order or security of a correctional facility, reports of informants, investigators or other persons, or from any type of surveillance associated with an identifiable individual, or investigation or analysis of potential terrorist threats." Positions having regular access to intelligence information shall be narrowly construed to include those law enforcement roles that must routinely utilize intelligence information.

The SCDEA defines *"national security information"* as "any knowledge relating to the national defense or foreign relations of the United States, regardless of its physical form or characteristics, that is owned by, produced by or for, or is under the control of the United States government and is defined as such by the United States government and its agencies and departments." Positions having regular access to national security information shall be narrowly construed to include those government or government contractor roles that require high-level security clearances.

The intelligence and national security exemptions encompass those few occupations not already subject to exemptions for police and peace officers or where credit checks are required by law.

G. Positions involving responsibility for funds or assets worth $10,000 or more.

In general, this exemption includes only executive-level positions with financial control over a company, including, but not limited to, Chief Financial Officers and Chief Operations Officers. This exemption does not include all staff in a finance department.

H. Positions involving digital security systems.

This exemption includes positions at the executive level, including, but not limited to, Chief Technology Officer or a senior information technology executive who controls access to all parts of a company's computer system. The exemption does not include any person who may access a computer system or network available to employees, nor does it include all staff in an information technology department.

V. Employers' Record of Exemption Use

An employer claiming an exemption must show that the position or role falls under one of the eight (8) exemptions in Part IV above. Employers availing themselves of exemptions to the SCDEA's anti-discrimination provisions should inform applicants or employees of the claimed exemption. Employers should also keep a record of their use of such exemptions for a period of five (5) years from the date an exemption is used. Keeping an exemption log will help the employer respond to Commission requests for information.

The exemption log should include the following:

1. The claimed exemption;
2. Why the claimed exemption covers the exempted position;
3. The name and contact information of all applicants or employees considered for the exempted position;
4. The job duties of the exempted position;
5. The qualifications necessary to perform the exempted position;
6. A copy of the applicant's or employee's credit history that was obtained pursuant to the claimed exemption;
7. How the credit history was obtained; and
8. How the credit history led to the employment action.

Employers may be required to share their exemption log with the Commission upon request. Prompt responses to Commission requests may help avoid a Commission-initiated investigation into employment practices.

VI. Penalties for administrative actions

The Commission takes seriously the SCDEA's prohibitions against asking about or using consumer credit history for employment purposes and will impose civil penalties up to $125,000 for violations, and up to $250,000 for violations that are the result of willful, wanton or malicious conduct. The amount of a civil penalty will be guided by the following factors, among others:

- The severity of the violation;
- The existence of subsequent violations;
- The employer's size, considering both the total number of employees and its revenue; and
- The employer's actual or constructive knowledge of the SCDEA.

These penalties are in addition to the other remedies available to people who successfully resolve or prevail on claims under the NYCHRL, including, but not limited to, back and front pay, along with compensatory and punitive damages.

BUFFALO BAN THE BOX

Chapter 154. Discrimination

Article V. Fair Employment Screening

[Adopted 5-28-2013]

§ 154-25. Prior criminal conviction consideration.

The City of Buffalo, its vendors, and any employer located within the City of Buffalo limits shall not ask questions regarding or pertaining to an applicant's prior criminal conviction on preliminary employment application. Consideration of the candidate's prior criminal convictions shall take place only after an application is submitted and to begin during an initial interview, or thereafter.

§ 154-26. Definitions.

For purposes of this article, the following terms shall have the following meanings:

APPLICANT
Any person considered or who requests to be considered for employment by an employer.

CITY
The City of Buffalo, its departments, administrative units and related agencies.

CONVICTION
Any sentence imposed by a court of competent jurisdiction arising from a verdict or plea of guilty, including a sentence of incarceration, a suspended sentence, a sentence of probation, an unconditional discharge, or diversion program.

EMPLOYER
The City or any person, partnership, corporation, labor organization, not-for-profit, or association having 15 or more employees.

EMPLOYMENT
An occupation, vocation, job, work for pay, including temporary or seasonal work, contracted work, contingent work, and work through the services of a temporary or other employment agency; or any form of vocational or educational training with or without pay. "Employment" shall not, for the purposes of this chapter, include employment by any government law enforcement agency.

INTERVIEW
Any direct contact by the employer with the applicant, whether in person or by telephone, to discuss the employment being sought or the applicant's qualifications.

VENDOR
Any vendor, contractor, or supplier of goods or services to the City of Buffalo, including vendors located outside the City of Buffalo limits.

§ 154-27. Fair employment screening standards.

A. Effective the first day of January 2014, it shall be an unlawful discriminatory practice for an employer to make any inquiry regarding, or to require any person to disclose or reveal, any criminal conviction during the application process. The application process shall begin when the applicant inquires about the employment sought and shall end when an employer has accepted an employment application.
[Amended 6-25-2013]

B. It shall be an unlawful discriminatory practice for an employer to make any inquiry regarding, or to require any person to disclose or reveal, any criminal conviction against such person before a first interview. If an employer does not conduct an interview, that employer must inform the applicant whether a criminal background check will be conducted before employment is to begin.

C. An employer hiring for licensed trades or professions, including positions such as interns and apprentices for such licensed positions, may ask applicants the same questions asked by the trade or professional licensing body, in accordance with New York State law.

D. An employer hiring for positions where certain convictions or violations are a bar to employment in that position under New York State or federal law shall not be constrained from asking questions about those convictions or violations.

E. An employer shall comply with Article 23-A of the New York State Correction Law when considering an applicant's prior criminal convictions in determining suitability for employment. In accordance with Article 23-A, nothing in this article shall be construed to limit an employer's authority to withdraw conditional offers of employment for any lawful reason, including the determination that the candidate has a conviction that bears a direct relationship to the duties and responsibilities of the position sought, or that hiring would pose an unreasonable risk to property or to the safety of individuals or the general public.

§ 154-28. Exceptions.

A. The prohibitions of this article shall not apply if the inquiries or adverse actions prohibited herein are specifically authorized by any other applicable law.

B. The prohibitions of this article shall not apply to the Department of Police or the Department of Fire, or to any other employer hiring for police officer and peace officer positions, as defined by Criminal Procedure Law §§ 1.20 and 2.10.

C. The prohibitions of this article shall not apply to any public or private school, nor to any public or private service provider of direct services specific to the care or supervision of children, young adults, senior citizens, or the physically or mentally disabled.

§ 154-29. Enforcement; penalties for offenses.

A. Any person aggrieved by a violation of this article may commence a civil action or proceeding for injunctive relief, damages, and other appropriate relief in law or equity against a person who violates this article. In any such action or proceeding, the court, in its discretion, may allow for the party commencing such action or proceeding, if such party prevails, a reasonable attorney's fee as part of the costs.

B. Any person or organization, whether or not an aggrieved party, may file with the Commission on Citizens' Rights and Community Relations a complaint alleging violation of this article. Such complaint shall be in writing on a form prescribed by the Commission on Citizens' Rights.

C. Upon certification by the Commission on Citizens' Rights and Community Relations Director that there has been an affirmative finding of probable cause of discriminatory practice, the Director may request the Corporation Counsel to commence an action against the accused party, in a court of competent jurisdiction, seeking the imposition of the following penalties or a combination thereof:

(1) A penalty of $500 for the first violation of this article; or

(2) A penalty of $1,000 for each subsequent violation of this article.

ROCHESTER BAN THE BOX

City of Rochester

City Clerks Office

Certified Ordinance

Rochester, N.Y., _____

TO WHOM IT MAY CONCERN:

I hereby certify that the following is a true copy of an ordinance which was duly passed by the Council of the City of Rochester on **May 20, 2014** and **Approved** by the Mayor of the City of Rochester, and was deemed duly adopted on **May 22, 2014** in accordance with the applicable provisions of law.

Ordinance No. 2014-155

Amending Chapter 63 Of The Municipal Code With
Regard to Fair Employment Screening, As
Amended

BE IT ORDAINED by the Council of the City of Rochester as follows:

Section 1. Chapter 63 of the Municipal Code of the City of Rochester is hereby amended by adding a new Article II thereto to read as follows:

Article II. Fair Employment Screening

§63-12 Fair Employment Screening

The City of Rochester, its vendors, and any employer located within the City of Rochester shall not make any inquiry regarding or pertaining to an applicant's prior criminal conviction on any initial employment application. Consideration of an applicant's prior criminal conviction(s) shall take place only after an employment application is submitted and after any initial employment interview.

§63-13 Definitions

For purposes of this article, the following terms shall have the following meanings:

A. "Applicant": Any person considered or who requests to be considered for employment by an employer.

B. "City": The City of Rochester, its departments, administrative units and agencies.

C. "Criminal Conviction": ~~Any judgment of conviction of a criminal offense in this state or any other jurisdiction, including but not limited to adjudication as a juvenile delinquent or youthful offender.~~ <u>Entry of a plea of guilty, or a verdict of guilty, for a misdemeanor or felony offense in this state or any other jurisdiction.</u>

D. "Employment": Any work for pay, including temporary or seasonal work, contracted work, contingent work, and work through the services of a temporary, job placement, referral, or other employment agency, for any work or position for which the primary place of work is located within the City of Rochester. "Employment" shall not, for the purposes of this article, include employment by any government law enforcement agency or any position classified as a police officer or peace officer pursuant to the Criminal Procedure Law.

E. "Employer": The City, its vendors, or any entity that employs persons in ~~a~~ <u>any</u> position for which the primary place of work is located within the City of Rochester including a person, partnership, company, business corporation, limited liability company, public corporation, labor organization, not-for-profit corporation, or association, ~~including but not limited to~~ <u>"Employer" shall also include</u> temporary, job placement, referral, or other employment agencies. "Employer" shall not include an employer with fewer than four persons in ~~his or her~~ <u>its</u> employ.

F. "Interview": Any direct contact by the employer with the applicant whether in person or by telephone, to discuss the employment being sought or the applicants' qualifications.

G. "Vendor": Any vendor, contractor, or supplier of goods or services to the City of Rochester, including vendors located outside the City of Rochester limits.

§63-14 Fair Employment Screening Standards

A. It shall be an unlawful discriminatory practice for the City, its vendors, and any employer located within City limits to make any inquiry regarding, or to require any person to disclose or reveal, any criminal conviction during the application process. The "application process" shall be deemed to begin when the applicant inquires about the employment sought and shall end when an employer has conducted an initial employment interview or made a conditional offer of employment.

B. If an employer does not conduct an interview, that employer must inform the applicant whether a criminal background check will be conducted before employment is to begin.

C. The City, its vendors, and any employer hiring for licensed trades or professions, including positions such as interns and apprentices for such licensed positions, may make an inquiry of applicants about prior criminal convictions if such inquiry is required by a licensing authority or by New York State or Federal Law.

D. The City, its vendors, and any employer hiring for positions where certain convictions are a bar to employment in that position under New York State or Federal Law, shall not be prohibited from making inquiries about those convictions during the application process.

E. The City, its vendors, and any employer shall comply with Article 23-A of the New York State Correction Law and the Fair Credit Reporting Act, 15 USC §1681, et seq. when considering an applicant's prior criminal convictions in determining suitability for employment. In accordance with Article 23-A, nothing in this ordinance shall be construed to limit an employer's authority to withdraw conditional offers of employment for any lawful reason, including the determination that the candidate has a conviction that bears a direct relationship to the duties and responsibilities of the position sought, or that hiring would pose an unreasonable risk to property or to the safety of individuals or the general public.

F. In compliance with Executive Law § 296 subdivision 16 (Human Rights Law) and the Family Court Act, employers are prohibited from asking at any time for applicants to disclose information about any arrest that resulted in a Youthful Offender Adjudication pursuant to Criminal Procedure Law § 720.35; any arrest that was processed as a Juvenile Delinquency proceeding in Family Court; any arrest that resulted in a sealing pursuant to Criminal Procedure Law (CPL) § 160.50 or CPL § 160.55; any conviction that was sealed pursuant to CPL § 160.58, unless said inquiry is specifically required or permitted by New York State or Federal law.

§63-15 Exceptions

A.   The prohibitions of this article shall not apply if the ~~inquires~~ inquiries prohibited herein are specifically authorized by any other applicable law.

B.   The prohibitions of this article shall not apply to applicants for positions in the City Police Department or the Fire Department, or to any other employer hiring for "police officer" and "peace officer" positions, as defined by Criminal Procedure Law §1.20 or §2.10.

§63-16 Enforcement

A.   Any person aggrieved by a violation of this Article may commence a civil action or proceeding for injunctive relief, damages, or other appropriate relief in law or equity against any person or employer who violates this Article. In any such action or proceeding, the ~~court, may~~ court may allow the party commencing such action or proceeding, if such party prevails, costs and reasonable attorney's fees as part of the relief granted.

B.   Any action brought for violation of this chapter must be commenced within one year after the alleged violation of this article.

C.   The remedies provided herein shall be separate and distinct from remedies provided in other laws, rules or regulations, and shall not be construed by any court to be a prerequisite to an action or proceeding commenced pursuant to such other laws, rules or regulations. The provisions of this ordinance shall not be construed to diminish the rights of an applicant under any other law.

D.   The Corporation Counsel may, in his or her discretion, bring an action to restrain or prevent any violation of this Article or any continuance of any such violation, in any court of competent jurisdiction and may further seek the imposition of the following penalties or a combination thereof:

   (1)   A penalty of five hundred dollars for the first violation of this Article;

   (2)   A penalty of one thousand dollars for each subsequent violation of this Article.

Section 2. The City shall make information about the provisions of this ordinance available to the public and to vendors and other persons who may be interested in it.

Section 3. The criminal history record checks in connection with employment required by Section 6B-2 of the City Charter shall be conducted in compliance with the provisions of this article.

Section 4. This ordinance shall take effect 180 days after it is adopted.

Strikeout indicates deleted text, new text is underlined

Passed by the following vote:

Ayes -   President Scott, Councilmembers Conklin, Haag, McFadden, Miller, Ortiz, Palumbo, Patterson, Spaull - 9.

Nays -   None - 0.

Attest   _Hazel L. Washington_
                     City Clerk

BAN THE BOX: PRIVATE EMPLOYER SUMMARIES

State: Hawaii

Effective Date: January 1, 1998

Known As: **Fair Employment Practices for Arrest and Conviction Record Act**

Located At: *Haw. Rev. Stat. § 378-2.5*

Applies to: "Employer" includes the state and all political subdivisions of the state, and any person in this state employing (4) or more individuals, and any person acting in the interest of an employer, acting directly or indirectly.

Prohibited Actions:

(1) Subject to subsection (b), an employer may inquire about and consider an individual's criminal conviction record concerning hiring, termination, or the terms, conditions, or privileges of employment; provided that the conviction record bears a rational relationship to the duties and responsibilities of the position.

(2) Inquiry into and consideration of conviction records for prospective employees shall take place only after the prospective employee has received a conditional offer of employment which may be withdrawn if the prospective employee has a conviction record that bears a rational relationship to the duties and responsibilities of the position. For purposes of this section, "conviction" means an adjudication by a court of competent jurisdiction that the defendant committed a crime, not including final judgments required to be confidential pursuant to section 571-84; provided that the employer may consider the employee's conviction record falling within a period that shall not exceed the most recent ten years, excluding periods of incarceration. If the employee or prospective employee claims that the period of incarceration was less than what is shown on the employee's or prospective employee's conviction record, an employer shall provide the employee or prospective employee with an opportunity to present documentary evidence of a date of release to establish a period of incarceration that is shorter than the sentence imposed for the employee's or prospective employee's conviction.

Exception:

[2008 amendment retroactive to July 1, 2006. L 2008, c 28, §43.] Notwithstanding subsections (b) and (c), the requirement that inquiry into and consideration of a prospective employee's conviction record may take place only after the individual has received a conditional job offer, and the limitation to the most recent ten-year period, excluding the period of incarceration, shall not apply to employers who are expressly permitted to inquire into an individual's criminal history for employment purposes pursuant to any federal or state law other than subsection (a), including:

Enforcement:

By: **Hawaii Civil Rights Commission**

Time Frame: **180 Days**

Filing: Aggrieved individuals may file an administrative charge with the Hawaii Civil Rights Commission (HCRC) and cannot file a court action until having done so.

Fines: HCRC has the authority to award an aggrieved applicant with a range of remedies including back pay, compensatory damages, punitive damages, and attorney's fees and costs. -

Jurisdiction: The law authorizes the Commission to enforce the State's anti-discrimination statutes or any of its orders, conciliation agreements, or predetermination settlements by commencing civil action in circuit court; by issuing "right to sue" authority to complainants; or by ordering appropriate legal and equitable relief or affirmative action when violations are found.

State:	Massachusetts
Effective Date:	November 4, 2010, May 4, 2012 for CORI
Known As:	**Reforming Criminal Offender Record Information Act (C.O.R.I.)**
Located At:	*G.L. c. 151B, § 4(9), (9½)*
Applies to:	"Employer" means any private person *(to include individuals, partnerships, associations, corporations, legal representatives, trustees, trustees in bankruptcy, receivers, and the commonwealth and all political subdivisions, boards and commissions)* labor organization or employment agency *(to include joint and temporary employers)*, which have 6 or more employees that does business and takes applications in Massachusetts. Public employers are included regardless of number of employees.

Prohibited Actions:

(1) An employer shall not prior to the interview, ask a job applicant to provide any information about his/her criminal history on a written application unless the employer or the position falls within a statutory exception. *G.L. c. 151B, § 4(9½)*.

(2) Prior to the interview, ask an applicant whether he or she has been convicted of a felony or a misdemeanor on a written application, unless the employer or the position falls within a statutory exception. *G.L. c. 151B, § 4(9½)*.

(3) Ask an applicant or current employee in writing or orally, about a conviction of a misdemeanor where the date of the conviction predates the inquiry by more than 5 years; sealed records or juvenile offenses and arrests that did not result in a conviction; A criminal detention or disposition that did not result in a conviction; A first conviction for any of the following misdemeanors: drunkenness, simple assault, speeding, minor traffic violations, affray, or disturbance of the peace. During an interview or thereafter, an employer can ask about convictions so long as the employer does not ask about any offenses in *G.L. c. 151B, § 4(9)*.

(4) Ask an applicant to obtain a copy of his or her CORI record for the employer. *G.L. c. 6, § 172*

Exception: There are two exceptions to the blanket prohibition against asking an applicant or Employee for criminal history information on a written application. An employer may ask about criminal convictions if: (1) The applicant is applying for a position where federal or state law or regulation creates a mandatory or presumptive disqualification based on a conviction for 1 or more types of criminal offenses, or (2) The employer or an affiliate is subject by federal or state law or regulation not to employ persons in 1 or more positions who have been convicted of 1 or more types of criminal offenses. A "regulation" will only create a mandatory or presumptive disqualification if it was promulgated in accordance with G.L. c. 30A, for state regulations, and 5 U.S.C. §§ 551 et seq. for federal regulations.

Enforcement:

By: **Massachusetts Commission Against Discrimination**

Time Frame: 300 Days

Filing: Can be sent in via mail, offices prefer intakes but not required.

Fines: An employer is subject to the same remedies and actions that are available for other protected classes for violations that include equitable relief, compensatory and punitive damages, interest, and attorney's fees.

Jurisdiction: The violation must first be filed with the MCAD, otherwise the person aggrieved has no standing in Superior Court to proceed. It can then be filed in Superior Court after being removed on the 91st day or thereafter. Overall, the legislative history unmistakably suggests that the Legislature's intent in enacting the 2010 reforms was to recalibrate the balance between protecting public safety and facilitating the reintegration of criminal defendants by removing barriers to housing and employment.

City: Philadelphia, Pennsylvania

Effective Date: July 12, 2011 (Updated in 2016)

Known As: **Philadelphia Fair Criminal Record Screening Standards Ordinance**

Located At: *Chapter 9-3500-3507*

Applies to: "Private employer" means any person, company, corporation, labor organization or association which employs one or more persons within the City of Philadelphia. It includes job placement and referral agencies and other employment agencies. Employment" means any occupation, vocation, job, work for pay or employment, including temporary or seasonal work, contracted work, contingent work and work through the services of a temporary or other employment agency; or any form of vocational or educational training with or without pay. Employment" shall not, for the purposes of this Chapter, include membership in any law enforcement agency.

Prohibited Actions:

(1) In connection with the licensing or employment of any person, it shall be an unlawful discriminatory practice for a City agency or private employer to make any inquiry regarding or to require any person to disclose or reveal any criminal convictions during the application process. The application process shall begin when the applicant inquires about the employment being sought and shall end when an employer has accepted an employment application.

(2) It shall further be an unlawful discriminatory practice for a City agency or private employer to make any inquiry regarding, or to require any person to disclose or reveal any criminal convictions against such person before and during the first interview. If an employer does not conduct an interview, that employer is prohibited from making any inquiries or gathering any information regarding the applicant's criminal convictions. If the applicant voluntarily discloses any information regarding his or her criminal convictions at the interview, the employer may discuss the criminal conviction disclosed by the applicant.

(3) Prohibits ANY questions about criminal records on job applications.

(4) Permits employers to consider criminal convictions within 7 years of date of application (not including times of incarceration)

(5) Prohibits employers from asking at any time about arrests or criminal accusations that did not lead to conviction

(6) Employers must screen applicants individually by considering:

- The type of offense and how much time has passed since it occurred

- The applicant's job history

- Duties of the job being sought

- Character or employment references

- Evidence of rehabilitation

(7) Allows employers to reject applicants based on a criminal records only IF the employer concludes that the person would be an unacceptable risk to the business or other people

(8) If rejecting the applicant, employers must notify the person in writing with the reason; provide the criminal history report AND allow 10 days for the applicant to respond

(9) compensatory damages and attorney's fees

(10) If PCHR dismisses the case, or does not settle it within 1 year, a complainant may file a case in court

- Employers must post the PCHR's informational poster in plain sight on the employer's website and premises

Exception:

There are three exceptions to the blanket prohibition against asking an applicant for criminal history information through an inquiry before interview or on a written application. An employer may ask about criminal convictions if: (1) The prohibitions of this Chapter shall not apply if the inquiries or adverse actions prohibited herein are specifically authorized by any other applicable law. (2) The prohibitions of this Chapter shall not apply to a Criminal Justice Agency as defined herein (3) Nothing in this Chapter shall modify or waive the requirements and limitations on the use of criminal records in Pennsylvania pursuant to 18 Pa. C.S. §9125.

Enforcement:

By: **Philadelphia Commission on Human Relations (PCHR)**

Time Frame: 300 Days

Filing: Form

Fines: A violation of the Ordinance is a "Class III" offense, subject to a fine of up to $2,000 per violation. All penalties assessed are payable to the City of Philadelphia. Those who report will not receive any compensation or other damages for a violation of Ban the Box.

Jurisdiction: No private cause of action. If person's complaint is based on unlawful questions asked on an employment application, you will not have to testify so long as the PCHR has a copy of the application. If your complaint is based on unlawful questions asked at an interview or adverse personnel actions, you will be required to testify. If you believe that you have been discriminated against on the basis of any category protected by the Fair Practices Ordinance (for example, race, ethnicity, or national origin), you must complete a separate Complaint of Discrimination to be filed with the Philadelphia Commission on Human Relations to pursue such a claim.

State:	Minnesota
Effective Date:	January 1, 2014
Known As:	**Minnesota Ban The Box Law**
Located At:	*Minn. Stat. 364.21*
Applies to:	"Private employer" is not defined by the statute. All businesses in Minnesota are considered covered by the statute there is no minimum threshold, including those mandated to perform background checks that are mandatory.

Prohibited Actions:

(1) Minn. Stat. 364.021 provides in part that all Minnesota public and private employers may not consider or require disclosure of the criminal record or criminal history of an applicant by inquiring into or considering or requiring disclosure of an applicant's criminal record or criminal history" until after the applicant has been selected for an interview. If there is no interview planned, the ban applies until a conditional offer of employment is made to the applicant. If an employer wants to screen employees' criminal records due to working with vulnerable populations or some other legal requirement they are still allowed to obtain necessary criminal background information. The change in statute does not preclude an employer from asking about an applicant's criminal history, it merely changes the timing of when that request can be made, including for occupations with legal requirements about criminal records.

Exception: There are two exceptions to the blanket prohibition against asking an applicant for criminal history information through an inquiry before interview or on a written application. An employer may ask about criminal convictions if: (1) The position is for the Department of Corrections or to employers who have a statutory duty to conduct a criminal history background check or otherwise take into consideration a potential employee's criminal history during the hiring process. (2) This section does not prohibit an employer from notifying applicants that law or the employer's policy will disqualify an individual with a particular criminal history background from employment in particular positions.

Enforcement:

By: **Minnesota Department of Human Rights** (MDHR)

Time Frame: One Year

Filing: Letter/Contact Agency to the Commissioner of Human Rights

Fines: For violations that occur in 2015, the penalties are as follows:

- For employers that employ 10 or fewer persons at a site, the penalty is up to $100 for each violation, not to exceed $100 in a calendar month.

- For employers that employ 11 to 20 persons at a site, the penalty is up to $500 for each violation, not to exceed $500 in a calendar month.

- For employers that employ more than 20 persons at one or more sites, the penalty is up to $500 for each violation, not to exceed $2,000 in a calendar month.

Jurisdiction: No private cause of action. The Ban the Box law applies to any business, even if a business is employed in another state but has a Minnesota location. Also, if the employer is multi-state employer and has one electronic application system, then that employer can continue to use the one electronic application system as long as there is language on the application that is clear and unambiguous that Minnesota law provides that applicants do not have to answer criminal background history questions.

If a facially neutral employment practice (one that does not appear to be discriminatory on its face) is challenged, and it is shown to have a statistically significant, adverse impact on a particular group within a protected class, an employer must justify that practice by demonstrating that it is manifestly related to the job or significantly furthers an important business purpose. If this justification is established, the practice may still be discriminatory if it is demonstrated that there is a comparably effective practice which would cause a significantly lesser adverse impact on people of the identified protected class status. Rejecting applicants on the basis of poor creditworthiness or history could have a disproportionate, adverse impact on applicants who received public assistance, or who are of particular races or marital status.

State: Rhode Island

Effective Date: January 1, 2014

Known As: **Fair Employment Practices for Arrest and Conviction Record Act**

Located At: *R.I. General Laws § 28-5-6, §28-5-7*

Applies to: "Employer" includes the state and all political subdivisions of the state, and any person in this state employing (4) or more individuals, and any person acting in the interest of an employer, acting directly or indirectly.

Prohibited Actions:

(1) For any employer to include on any application for employment, except applications for law enforcement agency positions or positions related to law enforcement agencies, a question inquiring or to otherwise inquire either orally or in writing whether the applicant has ever been arrested, or charged with or convicted of any crime.

(2) **Exception:** There are two exceptions to the blanket prohibition against asking an applicant or Employee for criminal history information on a written application. An employer may ask about criminal convictions: (i) if a federal or state law or regulation creates a mandatory or presumptive disqualification from employment based on a person's conviction of one or more specified criminal offenses, an employer may include a question or otherwise inquire whether the applicant has ever been convicted of any of those offenses; or (ii) If a standard fidelity bond or an equivalent bond is required for the position for which the applicant is seeking employment and his or her conviction of one or more specified criminal offenses would disqualify the applicant from obtaining such a bond, an employer may include a question or otherwise inquire whether the applicant has ever been convicted of any of those offenses; and (iii) Notwithstanding, any employer may ask an applicant for information about his or her criminal convictions at the first interview or thereafter, in accordance with all applicable state and federal laws.

Enforcement

By: **Rhode Island Commisson Against Discrimination**

Time Frame: 1 Year

Filing: Aggrieved individuals may file an administrative charge with the Rhode Island Commission for Human Rights (RICHR) or a civil action alleging a violation of the Fair Employment Practices law.

Fines: The RICHR and Rhode Island courts have the authority to award an aggrieved applicant with a range of remedies including back pay, compensatory damages, punitive damages, and attorney's fees and costs. -

Jurisdiction: A complaint can be filed in court as a civil action as well but a person cannot do both.

City: Buffalo, New York

Effective Date: January 1, 2014

Known As: **Fair Employment Screening Ordinance**

Located At: *City of Buffalo Code Chapter 154 § 25-28*

Applies to: "Employer" means the city or any person, partnership, corporation, labor organization, not-for-profit, or association having fifteen or more employees.

Prohibited Actions:

(1) It is an unlawful discriminatory practice for an employer to make any inquiry regarding, or to require any person to disclose or reveal, any criminal conviction during the application process. The application process shall begin when the applicant inquiries about the employment sought and shall end when an employer has accepted an employment application.

(2) It shall be an unlawful discriminatory practice for an employer to make any inquiry regarding, or to require any person to disclose or reveal, any criminal conviction against such person before a first interview. If an empoyer does not conduct an interview, the employer must inform the applicant whether a criminal background check will be consuted before employment is to begin.

Exception: There are four exceptions to the blanket prohibition against asking an applicant or Employee for criminal history information on a written application. An employer may ask about criminal convictions if: (1) The state or federal government have such bar against applicants with certain convictions or violations (2) hiring for licensed professions, including positions as interns and apprentices (3) An employer shall comply with Article 23-A of the NYS Correcton Law and nothing in the ordinance shall be construed to limit an employer's authority to withdraw conditional offers of employment for any lawful reason (4) shall not apply to positions with Department of Police and Department of Fire.

Enforcement

By: **Supreme Court, or complaint to Commission on Citizens' Rights and Community Relations**

Time Frame: Not Specified

Filing: Can be filed through the mail

Fines: Injunctive relief, damages and other appropriate relief in law or equity against an aggrieved person. A penalty of five hundred dollars for the first violation of this Article; a penalty of one thousand dollars for each subsequent violation of this article.

Jurisdiction: Applies to vendors. Employment is an occupation, vocation, job, work for pay, contracted work, contingent work, and employment agency or any form of vocational or education training with our without pay.

City:	Baltimore, Maryland
Effective Date:	August 13, 2014
Known As:	**Fair Criminal Record Screening Practicces**
Located At:	*Article 11 § 14-1 to 14-16*
Applies to:	"Covered Employer" or "Employer" means any person that employes 10 ore more full time equivalent mployees in the city of Baltimore.

Prohibited Actions:

Before a conditional offer is made, a covered private employer may not:

(1) Require any applicant to disclose or reveal whether he or she has a criminal record or otherwise has had criminal accusations brought against him or her;

(2) Conduct a criminal background check on the applicant; or

(3) Otherwise make any inquiry of the applicant or of others about whether the applicant has a criminal record or otherwise has had criminal accusations brought against him or her.

Although the Ordinance defines the term "conviction" as "any sentence arising from a verdict or pleas of guilty or nolo contendere," it does not restrict an employer's pre-conditional offer inquiries only to convictions. Rather, the Ordinance broadly prohibits an employer from obtaining *any information* in an applicant's criminal background until a condition offer of employment is made.

Exceptions:

(1) The Ordinance does not apply to any inquiry into an applicant's criminal history that is required or authorized by another applicable city, federal, or state law or regulation

(2) The Ordinance also specifically exempts facilities providing services to minors or vulnerable adults, defining the latter as "an adult who lacks the physical or mental capacity to provide for his or her own daily needs."

Enforcement

By: **Baltimore Community Relations Commission**

Time Frame: One Year

Filing: A person aggrieved by an alleged violation can file a complaint. The BCRC will investigate the complaint in the same manner as it investigates discrimination claims and, if a violation is found, may award an applicant or employee back pay, reinstatement, compensatory damages, and reasonable attorney's fees. A decision of the BCRC may be appealed to the Circuit Court for Baltimore City.

Fines: Any person who violates the Ordinance also may face criminal penalties of up to a $500 fine and 90 days in prison for each violation.

City: Rochester, New York

Effective Date: November 18, 2014

Known As: **Fair Employment Screening Standards Ordinance**

Located At: Municipal Code of City of Rochester *Chapter 63 § 13-16*

Applies to: "Employer" means an employer with no fewer than four persons in his or her employ that applies to the city, its vendors, or any entity that employs persons in a position for which the primary place of work is located within the City of Rochester including a person, partnership, company, business corporation, limited liability company, public corporation, labor organization, not-for-profit corporation, or association, including but not limited to temporary, job placement, referral, or other employment agencies.

Prohibited Actions:

(1) It is an unlawful discriminatory practice for an employer to make any inquiry regarding, or to require any person to disclose or reveal, any criminal conviction during the application process. The application process shall begin when the applicant inquiries about the employment sought and shall end when an employer has accepted an employment application.

(2) It shall be an unlawful discriminatory practice for an employer to make any inquiry regarding, or to require any person to disclose or reveal, any criminal conviction against such person before a first interview. If an empoyer does not conduct an interview, the employer must inform the applicant whether a criminal background check will be consuted before employment is to begin.

Exception: There are two exceptions to the blanket prohibition against asking an applicant or Employee for criminal history information on a written application. An employer may ask about criminal convictions if: (1) Authorized by other applicable law (2) shall not apply to positions with Department of Police and Department of Fire.

Enforcement

By: **Action in Civil Court**

Time Frame: One Year

Filing: Can be filed through the court. Costs and attorney fees available if relief granted.

Fines: Injunctive relief, damages and other appropriate relief in law or equity against an aggrieved person. A penalty of five hundred dollars for the first violation of this Article; a penalty of one thousand dollars for each subsequent violation of this article.

Jurisdiction: Applies to vendors that service the City of Rochester. Employment is any work for pay, contracted work, contigent work, work through temporary services, job placement, referral or other employment agency, for any work or position for which the primary place of work is located within the City of Rochester.

City:	Columbia, Missouri
Effective Date:	December 1, 2014
Known As:	**Employment Opportunities for Qualified Applicants Ordinance**
Located At:	*City Code Chapter 12 § 90-94*
Applies to:	"Employer" is not defined by any specified number, public or private.

Prohibited Actions:

(1) For an employer to inquire, question or otherwise seek information on an employment application as to whether an individual has ever been arrested for, charged with, or convicted of any crime.

(2) For an employer to inquire, question or otherwise seek information as to whether an applicant has ever been arrested for, charged with, or convicted of any crime until after the applicant has received a conditional offer of employment.

Exception: (1) Employers are required to exclude applicants with certain criminal convictions from employment due to local, state or federal law or regulation (2) A standard fidelity bond or an equivalent bond is required and an applicant's conviction of one or more specified criminal offenses would disqualify the applicant from obtaining such a bond; in which case, an employer may include a question or otherwise inquire whether the applicant has ever been convicted of any of those offenses; or (3) Employers employ individuals licensed under the Emergency Medical Services (EMS) Systems Act.

NOTE: This section does not prohibit an employer from notifying applicants in writing of the specific offenses that will disqualify an applicant from employment in a particular position. Employers are encouraged to not automatically ban jobseekers with a criminal history. Employers may make final employment-related decisions based on all of the information available to them, including consideration of the frequency, recentness and severity of a criminal record as well as rehabilitation efforts against the duties and responsibilities of the position.

Enforcement

By: **City of Columbia Human Rights Commission**

Time Frame: 180 days

Filing: Any individual who claims to be aggrieved by a violation of this article may file with the commission a complaint in writing stating the name and address of the person alleged to have committed such practice, the particulars thereof, and such other information as may be required by the commission. If the alleged violation is that an employer is seeking criminal history information on an employment application, then any individual may file a complaint and that individual need not necessarily be aggrieved before filing acomplaint. Form can be emailed to: can be emailed to HumanRights@GoColumbiaMo.com

Fines: Any person who shall violate any provision of this article shall be deemed guilty of a misdemeanor and shall, upon conviction, be punished by a fine of not more than one thousand dollars ($1,000.00), or imprisonment not exceeding thirty (30) days, or by both such fine and imprisonment.

Jurisdiction: Applies to all employers within city limits of Columbia, Missouri.

State:	Washington D.C.
Effective Date:	December 17, 2014
Known As:	**DC Fair Criminal Record Screening Act**
Located At:	*DC Act 20-422*
Applies to:	"Employer" means any person, company, corporation, firm, labor organization, or association, including the District government, but not including the Courts, that employs more than 11 or more employees in the District of Columbia.

Prohibited Actions:

(1) An employer may not make any inquiry about, or require an applicant to disclose or reveal, or require an applicant to disclose or reveal any arrest or criminal accusation made against the applicant, which is not then pending against the applicant and which did not result in a conviction. (b) An employer may not make any inquiry or require an applicant to disclose or reveal any criminal conviction until after making a conditional offer of employment.

(2) Even after making a conditional offer of employment, an employer only may take an adverse action against an applicant on the basis of his or her criminal record for a "legitimate business reason. Whether the business reason is legitimate is determined by 6 factors: A reasonable business purpose must be determined using six factors: (1) Specific duties and responsibilities necessarily related to the employment; (2) Fitness or ability to perform one or more job duties or responsibilities given the offense; (3) Time elapsed since the offense; (4) Age of the applicant when the offense occurred; (5) Frequency and seriousness of the offense; and (6) Any information about the applicant that indicates rehabilitation or good conduct since the offense occurred.

(3) Moreover, if an applicant "believes" that the employer took an adverse action on the basis of his or her criminal conviction, he or she may request, within 30 days of the adverse action, that the employer provide within 30 days of receipt of the request:

▪ a copy of any and all records procured by the employer in consideration of the applicant, including criminal records

▪ a notice that advises the applicant of his or her opportunity to file an administrative complaint with the D.C. Office of Human Rights

Exception: Does not apply (1) where a federal or D.C. law or regulation requires the consideration of an applicant's criminal history for purposes of employment; (2) to a position designated by the employer as part of a federal or D.C. program or obligation designed to encourage the employment of individuals with criminal histories; or (3) to any employer that provides programs, services, or direct care to minors or vulnerable adults.

Enforcement

By: **Office of Human Rights** (OHR)

Time Frame: One Year

Filing: "Aggrieved" persons may file an administrative complaint with the OHR through an intake form.

Fines: For violations of the Act, the OHR is to impose fines (half of which is to be awarded to the complainant) on employers with:

▪11 to 30 employees of no more than $1,000;

▪31 to 99 employees of no more than $2,500; or

▪100 or more employees of no more than $5,000

Jurisdiction: The Act expressly disavows a private cause of action in any court.

Forms can be downloaded from:

http://ohr.dc.gov/page/returningcitizens/applicants

The Act defines an "inquiry" to mean any direct or indirect conduct intended to gather criminal history information from or about an applicant using any method, including application forms, criminal history checks, and interviews (an "interview" being any direct contact by the employer with the applicant, whether in person or by telephone, to discuss the employment being sought or the applicant's qualifications).

For purposes of the law, "applicants" include applicants for paid employment, including work that is temporary or seasonal, contracted, contingent, or through an employment agency, as well as any form of vocational or educational training with or without pay, where the physical location of the employment is in whole or substantial part within D.C.

State: Illinois

Effective Date: January 1, 2015

Known As: **The Job Opportunities for Qualified Applicants Enforcement Act**

Located At: *820 Ill Comp Stat. §75*

Applies to: *"Employer"* means any person or private entity that has 15 or more employees in the current or proceeding calendar year, and any entity of such agent or person. *"Employment Agency"* means any person or entity regularly undertaking with or without compensation to procure employees for an employer or to procure for employees opportunities to work for an employer and includes an agent of such a person. Employment means any occupation or vocation.

Prohibited Actions:

(1) An employer or employment agency may not inquire about or into, consider, or require disclosure of the criminal record or criminal history of an applicant *(applicant being defined as any person pursuing employment with an employer or with or through an employment agency)* until the applicant has been determined qualified for the position and notified that the applicant has been selected for an interview by the employer or employment agency or, if there is not an interview, until after a conditional offer of employment is made to the applicant by the employer or employment agency. This Section does not prohibit an employer from notifying applicants in writing of the specific offenses that will disqualify an applicant from employment in a particular position due to federal or State law or the employer's policy.

Exception: There are two exceptions to the blanket prohibition against asking an applicant for criminal history information on a written application. An employer may ask about criminal convictions if: (1) employers are required to exclude applicants with certain criminal convictions from employment due to federal or State law; or (2) a standard fidelity bond or an equivalent bond is required and an applicant's conviction of one or more specified criminal offenses would disqualify the applicant from obtaining such a bond, in which case an employer may include a question or otherwise inquire whether the applicant has ever been convicted of any of those offenses.

Enforcement

By: **Illinois Department of Labor**

Time Frame: Not Specified

Filing: Written Notification to Department of Labor Director

Fines:

1. A written warning on the first offense with notice regarding penalties for subsequent violations. The employer has 30 days to remedy the violation.

2. A civil penalty of up to $500 on the second offense OR if the first offense is not corrected within 30 days of notice.

3. A civil penalty of up to $1,500 on the third offense OR if the first offense is not corrected within 60 days of notice.

4. Additional civil penalties of up to $1,500 for every subsequent violation OR if the first violation is not remedied within 90 days of notice, additional penalties of up to $1,500 for every 30 days that passes without correction.

Jurisdiction: The Department of Labor will file in circuit court for enforcement or in any administrative court and is at all times represented by the Attorney General. All moneys obtained go into the Job Opportunities for Qualified Applicants Enforcement Fund and can only be used to enforce violations of the Act. The Department has the ability to adopt rules and administrative procedures to adjudicated claims and issue final and binding decisions subject to the Adminstrative Review Law.

County :	Montgomery County, Maryland
Effective Date:	January 1, 2015
Known As:	**Fair Criminal Record Screening Standards**
Located At:	*Article XII, Chapter 27§ 71-75 Montgomery County Code*
Applies to:	"Employer" means any person, individual, proprietorship, partnership, joint venture, corporation, limited liability company, trust, association, or other entity operating and doing business in the County that employs 15 or more persons full time in the county including the county government.

Prohibited Actions:

(1) An employer must not require an applicant or potential applicant to disclose on an employment application the existence or details of the applicant's or potential applicant's arrest record or conviction record.

(2) In connection with the proposed employment of an applicant, an employer must not, at any time before [a conditional offer of employment is made] the conclusion of the first interview: (1) require the applicant to disclose whether the applicant has an arrest record or conviction record, or otherwise has been accused of a crime; (2) conduct a criminal record check on the applicant; or (3) inquire directly or indirectly using any mode of communication of the applicant or others about whether the applicant has an arrest record or conviction record or otherwise has been accused of a crime.

(3) An employer must not retaliate for lawfully opposing any violation of this article including for filing a complaint, testifying, assisting or participating in any manner in an investigation or obstruct orprevent compliance with this Article.

(4) In making an employment decision baed on an applicant' or employee's arrest record or conviction record, an employment must conduct an individualized assessment, considering only specific offenses that may demonstrate unfitness to perform the duties of the position sought by the applicant or held by the employee, the time elapsed since the specific offenses, and any evidence of inaccuracy in the record.

(5) If an offer is rescinded on the basis of arrest or conviction the employer must (1) provide the applicant with a copy of any criminal record report (2) notify the applicant of the intention to rescind the conditionl offer and (3) delay rescinding for 7 days to permit dispute by way oof inaccuracy of an item or items on which the intention to rescind the conditional offer is based.

(6) If given the information the demployer must delay the aderse action for a reasonable period and reconsider the prospective adverse action in light of the information. The final adverse action notice rescinding the offer must be in writing.

Exception: An interview does not include written correspondence or email or direct contact made for the purpose of scheduling a discussion. (1) if the inquiry is permitted by applicable federal, state or county law or regulation (2) do not apply to County Police Department, County Fire and Rescue Service or the County Department of Corrections and Rehabilitaton. (3) to any employer that provides programs, services or direct care to minors or vulnerable adults. (4) to an employer hiring for federal government security clearance.

Enforcement

By: **Montgomery County Human Rights Commission**

Time Frame: 300 Days

Filing: Can be sent in via mail on separate complaint form. Separate complaints for sex/race/national origin a must.

Fines: A penalty of up to $1,000 for each violation payable to Montgomery County.

Link: http://www.montgomerycountymd.gov/humanrights/Ban_the_Box.html

City: Prince George County, Maryland

Effective Date: January 20, 2015

Known As: **Fair Criminal Records Screening Standards**

Located At: *Subtitle 2 Division 12 Subdivision 10 § 2-231.02-231.08*

Applies to: "Employer" shall mean any person, individual, proprietorship, partnership, joint venture, corporation, limited liability company, trust, association, or other entity operating and doing business in the County that employs twenty-five (25) or more persons full-time in the County.

Prohibited Actions:

(1) Inquiry on application. An employer shall not require an applicant or potential applicant to disclose on an employment application the existence or details of the applicant's or potential applicant's arrest record or conviction record.

(2) Preliminary inquiry into criminal record. In connection with the proposed employment of an applicant, an employer shall not, at any time until the conclusion of a first interview: (1) require the applicant to disclose whether the applicant has an arrest record or conviction record, or otherwise has been accused of a crime; (2) conduct a criminal record check on the applicant; or (3) inquire of the applicant or others about whether the applicant has an arrest or conviction record or otherwise has been accused of a crime.

An employer shall not (1) retaliate against any person for: (A) lawfully opposing any violation of this Subdivision; (B) filing a complaint, testifying, assisting, or participating in any manner.

Exceptions:

(1) The prohibitions of this law do not apply if they are expressly authorized by an applicable federal, State, or County law or regulation.

(2) Prohibitions do not apply to any County public safety agencies or to positions that, in the judgment of the County, have access to confidential or proprietary business or personal information, money or items of value, or involve emergency management.

(3) They also do not apply to an employer that provides programs, services, or direct care to minors or vulnerable adults.

Withdrawal of Job Offer:

(a) In making an employment decision based on an applicant's arrest record or conviction record, an employer shall conduct an individualized assessment, considering only specific offenses that may demonstrate unfitness to perform the duties of the position sought by the applicant, the time elapsed since the specific offenses, and any evidence of inaccuracy in the record.
(b) If an employer intends to rescind an offer of employment based on an item or items in the applicant's arrest record or conviction record, before rescinding the offer of employment the employer shall:
(1) provide the applicant with a copy of any criminal record report;
(2) notify the applicant of the intention to rescind the offer of employment and the items that are the basis for the intention to rescind the offer of employment; and (3) delay rescinding the offer of employment for seven (7) days to permit the applicant to give the employer notice of inaccuracy of an item or items on which the intention to rescind the offer of employment is based.
(c) If an employer decides to rescind an offer of employment based on the arrest record or conviction record of an applicant, the employer shall notify the applicant of the rescission of the offer of employment in writing.

Enforcement

By: **Human Relations Commission**

Time Frame: Two Years

Filing: A person aggrieved by an alleged violation of this Subdivision may file a written complaint with the Director pursuant to Title 2, Division 12 of the County Code.

Fines: Not specified.

Data: The Human Relations Commission shall maintain data on the number of complaints filed pursuant to this Subdivision, demographic information on the complainants, the number of investigations it conducts, and the disposition of every complaint and investigation.

State: New Jersey

Effective Date: March 1, 2015

Known As: **The Opportunity To Compete Act**

Located At: *N.J. C.34:6B-11 to N.J. C. 34:6B-19*

Applies to: "Employer" means any person, company, corporation, firm, labor organization, or association which has 15 or more employees over 20 calendar weeks and does business, employs persons, or takes applications for employment within this State, including the State, any county or municipality, or any instrumentality thereof. The term shall include job placement and referral agencies and other employment agencies, but excludes the United States or any of its departments, agencies, boards, or commissions, or any employee or agent thereof.

Prohibited Actions:

(1) An employer shall not require an applicant for employment to complete any employment application that makes any inquiries regarding an applicant's criminal record during the initial employment application process. "Employment application" means a form, questionnaire or similar document or collection of documents that an applicant for employment is required by an employer to complete.

(2) An employer shall not make any oral or written inquiry regarding an applicant's criminal record during the initial employment application process. "Initial employment application process" means the period beginning when an applicant for employment first makes an inquiry to an employer about a prospective employment position or job vacancy or when an employer first makes any inquiry to an applicant for employment about a prospective employment position or job vacancy, and ending when an employer has conducted a first interview, whether in person or by any other means of an applicant for employment.

Exception: if an applicant discloses any information regarding the applicant's criminal record, by voluntary oral or written disclosure, during the initial employment application process, the employer may make inquiries regarding the applicant's criminal record during the initial employment application process.

(3) Unless otherwise permitted or required by law, an employer shall not knowingly or purposefully publish, or cause to be published, any advertisement that solicits applicants for employment where that advertisement explicitly provides that the employer will not consider any applicant who has been arrested or convicted of one or more crimes or offenses. "Advertisement" means any circulation, mailing, posting, or any other form of publication, utilizing any media, promoting an employer or intending to alert its audience, regardless of size, to the availability of any position of employment.

Exception: The provision shall not apply to any advertisement that solicits applicants for a position in law enforcement, corrections, the judiciary, homeland security, or emergency management, or any other employment position where a criminal history record background check is required by law, rule or regulation, or where an arrest or conviction by the person for one or more crimes or offenses would or may preclude the person from holding such employment as required by any law, rule or regulation, or where any law, rule, or regulation restricts an employer's ability to engage in specified business activities based on the criminal records of its employees.

The provision shall not apply if the employment sought or being considered is for a position designated by the employer to be part of a program or systematic effort designed predominantly or exclusively to encourage the employment of persons who have been arrested or convicted of one or more crimes or offenses.

Enforcement

By: **Commissioner of Labor and Workforce Development**

Fines: Any employer who violates this act shall be liable for a civil penalty in an amount not to exceed $1,000 for the first violation, $5,000 for the second violation, and $10,000 for each subsequent violation collectible by the Commissioner of Labor and Workforce Development in a summary proceeding pursuant to the "Penalty Enforcement Law of 1999," *P.L.1999, c.274 (C.2A:58-10 et seq.)*. An MC-31 Form is filed in order to inform the Commissioner of violations.

<u>Private Right Of Action</u>

Nothing set forth in this act shall be construed as creating or establishing a standard of care or duty for employers with respect to any law other than this act. Evidence that an employer has violated, or is alleged to have violated, the provisions of this act, shall not be admissible in any legal proceeding with respect to any law or claim other than a proceeding to enforce the provisions of this act. Nothing set forth in this act shall be construed as creating, establishing or authorizing a private cause of action by an aggrieved person against an employer who has violated, or is alleged to have violated, the provisions of this act.

City: New York City

Effective Date: October 27, 2015

Known As: **Fair Chance Act (Intro 318)**

Located At: *N.Y.C. Admin Code Section 8-107 (10a and 11a)*

Applies to: "Employer" means any person, agent or business with 4 or or more employees, including independent contractors.

Prohibited Actions:

(1) The Fair Chance Act prohibits employers from declaring, printing, or circulating solicitations, advertisements, or publications that state or imply that an applicant's chances of employment may be limited by an arrest or criminal conviction. (2) It prohibits employers from making any statements or inquiries into an applicant's conviction record or arrests before making a conditional offer of employment, whether in an employment application, a background check, a search of publicly available records, during an interview, or any other similar form of pre-offer screening. (3) The Fair Chance Act permits an employer to inquire into an applicant's arrest or conviction record after it makes a conditional offer of employment. But an employer must take certain steps before taking any adverse action based on information obtained through such an inquiry. First, an employer must provide the following to the applicant, in writing: (1) a copy of the inquiry that the employer had made into the applicant's background (e.g., the background check report) and (2) an analysis, with reasons for the action, under N.Y. Corrections L. §23-A (which requires employers to consider several factors and determine that hiring the applicant would pose an unreasonable risk to property or to public or individual safety, or that the offense bears a direct relationship to the job). The employer must then allow the applicant a "reasonable" time to respond (at least three business days) while holding the position open.

Exception: It makes limited exceptions for certain positions, such as police officers and peace officers, and where state, federal, or local law requires employers to perform criminal background checks for employment purposes or prohibits employment based on criminal history.

Enforcement

By: **New York City Commission on Human Rights**

Fines: Any person who fails to comply with paragraph (b) of this subdivision shall be liable to an aggrieved person for damages of at least $1,000 and shall be presumed, unless shown by clear and convincing evidence otherwise, to have engaged in an unlawful discriminatory practice as defined in paragraph (a) of this subdivision. An applicant's response to an inquiry or statement that violates paragraph (b) of this subdivision shall not disqualify him or her from the prospective employment, or any lawful activity, occupation, profession or calling, or make him or her guilty of perjury or offering a false statement.

Private Right Of Action

The law provides for a private right of action in state court and also allows the City Commission on Human Rights to bring a charge against the employer. The applicant has three years from the alleged violation to commence an action and may seek damages—including punitive damages—and injunctive relief.

Enforcement

By: **New York City Human Rights Commission**

Time Frame: 1 Year

Filing: Can be sent in via mail on separate complaint form.

Fines: Damages to be determined for violations.

State: Oregon

Effective Date: January 1, 2016

Known As: **Fair Chance Act (HB 3025B)**

Located At: ORS 659A.820 to 659A.865

Applies to: "Employer" is not defined by number.

Prohibited Actions:

(1) It is an unlawful practice for an employer to exclude an applicant from an initial interview solely because of a past criminal conviction. (2) An employer excludes an applicant from an initial interview if the employer: (a) Requires an applicant to disclose on an employment application a criminal conviction; (b) Requires an applicant to disclose, prior to an initial interview, a criminal conviction; or (c) If no interview is conducted, requires an applicant to disclose, prior to making a conditional offer of employment, a criminal conviction. (3) Subject to subsections (1) and (2) of this section, nothing in this section prevents an employer from considering an applicant's conviction history when making a hiring decision.

Exception: (4) Subsections (1) and (2) of this section do not apply: (a) If federal, state or local law, including corresponding rules and regulations, requires the consideration of an applicant's criminal history; (b) To an employer that is a law enforcement agency; (c) To an employer in the criminal justice system; or (d) To an employer seeking a nonemployee volunteer.

Enforcement

By: **Commissioner of the Bureau of Labor and Industries.**

No Fines Specified.

State:	Connecticut
Effective Date:	January 1, 2016
Known As:	**Fair Chance Act (HB 5327)**
Located At:	Conn. Gen. Stat. § 31-51i
Applies to:	"Employer" is one or more employees.

Prohibited Actions:

Sec. 31-51i. Employer inquiries about erased criminal records prohibited. Discrimination on the basis of erased criminal records prohibited. Erased and nonerased criminal records on employment application forms.

a. For the purposes of this section, "employer" means any person engaged in business who has one or more employees, including the state or any political subdivision of the state.

b. No employer or an employer's agent, representative or designee may require an employee or prospective employee to disclose the existence of any arrest, criminal charge or conviction, the records of which have been erased pursuant to section 46b-146, 54-76o or 54-142a.

c. An employment application form that contains any question concerning the criminal history of the applicant shall contain a notice, in clear and conspicuous language: (1) That the applicant is not required to disclose the existence of any arrest, criminal charge or conviction, the records of which have been erased pursuant to section 46b-146, 54-76o or 54-142a, (2) that criminal records subject to erasure pursuant to section 46b-146, 54-76o or 54-142a are records pertaining to a finding of delinquency or that a child was a member of a family with service needs, an adjudication as a youthful offender, a criminal charge that has been dismissed or nolled, a criminal charge for which the person has been found not guilty or a conviction for which the person received an absolute pardon, and (3) that any person whose criminal records have been erased pursuant to section 46b-146, 54-76o or 54-142a shall be deemed to have never been arrested within the meaning of the general statutes with respect to the proceedings so erased and may so swear under oath.

d. No employer or an employer's agent, representative or designee shall deny employment to a prospective employee solely on the basis that the prospective employee had a prior arrest, criminal charge or conviction, the records of which have been erased pursuant to section 46b-146, 54-76o or 54-142a.

e. No employer or an employer's agent, representative or designee shall discharge, or cause to be discharged, or in any manner discriminate against, any employee solely on the basis that the employee had, prior to being employed by such employer, an arrest, criminal charge or conviction, the records of which have been erased pursuant to section 46b-146, 54-76o or 54-142a.

f. The portion of an employment application form which contains information concerning the criminal history record of an applicant or employee shall only be available to the members of the personnel department of the company, firm or corporation or, if the company, firm or corporation does not have a personnel department, the person in charge of employment, and to any employee or member of the company, firm or corporation, or an agent of such employee or member, involved in the interviewing of the applicant.

g. Notwithstanding the provisions of subsection (f) of this section, the portion of an employment application form which contains information concerning the criminal history record of an applicant or employee may be made available as necessary to persons other than those specified in said subsection (f) by:

    1. A broker-dealer or investment adviser registered under chapter 672a in connection with (A) the possible or actual filing of, or the collection or retention of information contained in, a form U-4 Uniform Application for Securities Industry Registration or Transfer, (B)

the compliance responsibilities of such broker-dealer or investment adviser under state or federal law, or (C) the applicable rules of self-regulatory organizations promulgated in accordance with federal law;

2. An insured depository institution in connection with (A) the management of risks related to safety and soundness, security or privacy of such institution, (B) any waiver that may possibly or actually be sought by such institution pursuant to section 19 of the Federal Deposit Insurance Act, 12 USC 1829(a), (C) the possible or actual obtaining by such institution of any security or fidelity bond, or (D) the compliance responsibilities of such institution under state or federal law; and

3. An insurance producer licensed under chapter 701a in connection with (A) the management of risks related to security or privacy of such insurance producer, or (B) the compliance responsibilities of such insurance producer under state or federal law.

Enforcement

By: **Conneticut Department of Labor**

Time Frame: 300 Days

Filing: Can be sent in via mail on separate complaint form.

Private Right of Action: None

Fines: To be levied by Labor Dept

State	Vermont
Effective Date:	July 1, 2017
Known As:	**Vermont Fair Chance Act**
Located At:	21 V.S.A. § 495j
Applies to:	"Employer" either public or private with 5 or more employees

Prohibited Actions:

(a) Except as provided in subsection (b) of this section, an employer shall not request criminal history record information on its initial employee application form. An employer may inquire about a prospective employee's criminal history record during an interview or once the prospective employee has been deemed otherwise qualified for the position.

(b)(1) An employer may inquire about criminal convictions on an initial employee application form if the following conditions are met: (A)(i) the prospective employee is applying for a position for which any federal or State law or regulation creates a mandatory or presumptive disqualification based on a conviction for one or more types of criminal offenses; or

(ii) the employer or an affiliate of the employer is subject to an obligation imposed by any federal or State law or regulation not to employ an individual, in either one or more positions, who has been convicted of one or more types of criminal offenses; and (B) the questions on the application form are limited to the types of criminal offenses creating the disqualification or obligation. (2) An employer shall be permitted to inquire about criminal convictions on an initial employee application form pursuant to subdivision (1) of this subsection even if the federal or State law or regulation creating an obligation for the employer or its affiliate not to employ an individual who has been convicted of one or more types of criminal offenses also permits the employer or its affiliate to obtain a waiver that would allow the employer or its affiliate to employ such an individual. (c) If an employer inquires about a prospective employee's criminal history record information, the prospective employee, if still eligible for the position under applicable federal or State law, must be afforded an opportunity to explain the information and the circumstances regarding any convictions, including postconviction rehabilitation.

Time Frame: One year from the time of the act.

Filing: State Labor Commission

Fines: An employer who violates the provisions of this section shall be assessed a civil penalty of up to $100.00 for each violation.

Private Right of Action: None

State	California
Effective Date:	January 1, 2018
Known As:	**California Fair Chance Act**
Located At:	AB 1008, Section 12952 to the Government Code
Applies to:	"Employer" either public or private with 5 or more employees

Prohibited Actions:

(1) To include on any application for employment, before the employer makes a conditional offer of employment to the applicant, any question that seeks the disclosure of an applicant's conviction history.

(2) To inquire into or consider the conviction history of the applicant, including any inquiry about conviction history on any employment application, until after the employer has made a conditional offer of employment to the applicant.

(3) To consider, distribute, or disseminate information about any of the following while conducting a conviction history background check in connection with any application for employment:

(A) Arrest not followed by conviction, except in the circumstances as permitted in paragraph (1) of subdivision (a) and subdivision (f) of Section 432.7 of the Labor Code.

(B) Referral to or participation in a pretrial or posttrial diversion program.

(C) Convictions that have been sealed, dismissed, expunged, or statutorily eradicated pursuant to law.

(4) To interfere with, restrain, or deny the exercise of, or the attempt to exercise, any right provided under this section.

(b) This section shall not be construed to prevent an employer from conducting a conviction history background check not in conflict with the provisions of subdivision (a).

(c) (1) (A) An employer that intends to deny an applicant a position of employment solely or in part because of the applicant's conviction history shall make an individualized assessment of whether the applicant's conviction history has a direct and adverse relationship with the specific duties of the job that justify denying the applicant the position. In making the assessment described in this paragraph, the employer shall consider all of the following:

(i) The nature and gravity of the offense or conduct.

(ii) The time that has passed since the offense or conduct and completion of the sentence.

(iii) The nature of the job held or sought.

(B) An employer may, but is not required to, commit the results of this individualized assessment to writing.

(2) If the employer makes a preliminary decision that the applicant's conviction history disqualifies the applicant from employment, the employer shall notify the applicant of this preliminary decision in writing. That notification may, but is not required to, justify or explain the employer's reasoning for making the preliminary decision. The notification shall contain all of the following:

(A) Notice of the disqualifying conviction or convictions that are the basis for the preliminary decision to rescind the offer.

(B) A copy of the conviction history report, if any.

(C) An explanation of the applicant's right to respond to the notice of the employer's preliminary decision before that decision becomes final and the deadline by which to respond. The explanation shall inform the applicant that the response may include submission of evidence challenging the accuracy of the conviction history report that is the basis for rescinding the offer, evidence of rehabilitation or mitigating circumstances, or both.

(3) The applicant shall have at least five business days to respond to the notice provided to the applicant under paragraph (2) before the employer may make a final decision. If, within the five business days, the applicant notifies the employer in writing that the applicant disputes the accuracy of the conviction history report that was the basis for the preliminary decision to rescind the offer and that the applicant is taking specific steps to obtain evidence supporting that assertion, then the applicant shall have five additional business days to respond to the notice.

(4) The employer shall consider information submitted by the applicant pursuant to paragraph (3) before making a final decision.

(5) If an employer makes a final decision to deny an application solely or in part because of the applicant's conviction history, the employer shall notify the applicant in writing of all the following:

(A) The final denial or disqualification. The employer may, but is not required to, justify or explain the employer's reasoning for making the final denial or disqualification.

(B) Any existing procedure the employer has for the applicant to challenge the decision or request reconsideration.

(C) The right to file a complaint with the department.

(d) This section does not apply in any of the following circumstances:

(1) To a position for which a state or local agency is otherwise required by law to conduct a conviction history background check.

(2) To a position with a criminal justice agency, as defined in Section 13101 of the Penal Code.

(3) To a position as a Farm Labor Contractor, as described in Section 1685 of the Labor Code.

(4) To a position where an employer or agent thereof is required by any state, federal, or local law to conduct criminal background checks for employment purposes or to restrict employment based on criminal history. For purposes of this paragraph, federal law shall include rules or regulations promulgated by a self-regulatory organization as defined in Section 3(a)(26) of the Securities Exchange Act of 1934, as amended by 124 Stat. 1652 (Public Law 111-203), pursuant to the authority in Section 19(b) of the Securities Exchange Act of 1934, as amended by 124 Stat. 1652 (Public Law 111-203).

(e) The remedies under this section shall be in addition to and not in derogation of all other rights and remedies that an applicant may have under any other law, including any local ordinance.

(f) For purposes of this section:

(1) "Conviction" has the same meaning as defined in paragraphs (1) and (3) of subdivision (a) of Section 432.7 of the Labor Code.

(2) Notwithstanding paragraph (1), the term "conviction history" includes:

(A) An arrest not resulting in conviction only in the specific, limited circumstances described in subdivision (f) of Section 432.7 of the Labor Code, when an employer at a health facility, as defined in Section 1250 of the Health and Safety Code, may ask an applicant for certain positions about specified types of arrests.

(B) An arrest for which an individual is out on bail or his or her own recognizance pending trial.

Enforcement

By: California Department of Fair Employment and Housing

Time Frame: One year from the time of the act.

Filing: Use of a complaint form issued by the DFEH available on its website to be mailed in.

Fines: Injunctive relief, damages and other appropriate relief in law or equity against an aggrieved person.

Jurisdiction: Applies to any application or advertisement within California by an employer.

State   Washington

Effective Date: June 7, 2018

Known As: **Washington Fair Chance Act**

Located At: Title 49.94 RCW Sec 1-9

Applies to: "Employer" anyone with 1 or more employees

Prohibited Actions:

(1) An employer may not include any question on any application for employment, inquire either orally or in writing, receive information through a criminal history background check, or otherwise obtain information about an applicant's criminal record until after the employer initially determines that the applicant is otherwise qualified for the position. Once the employer has initially determined that the applicant is otherwise qualified, the employer may inquire into or obtain information about a criminal record.

(2) An employer may not advertise employment openings in a way that excludes people with criminal records from applying. Ads that state "no felons," "no criminal background," or otherwise convey similar messages are prohibited.

(3) An employer may not implement any policy or practice that automatically or categorically excludes individuals with a criminal record from consideration prior to an initial determination that the applicant is otherwise qualified for the position. Prohibited policies and practices include rejecting an applicant for failure to disclose a criminal record prior to initially determining the applicant is otherwise qualified for the position.

By: **Washington State Attorney General**

Time Frame: One year from the time of the act.

Filing: Use of an online interactive complaint form issued by the AG office

Fines: Monetary penalities to be assessed by AG

Jurisdiction: Applies to any application or advertisement within Washington by an employer.